D0745864

A Companion to
Metaphysics

*Blackwell
Companions to
Philosophy*

A Companion to Metaphysics

Edited by

JAEGWON KIM

and

ERNEST SOSA

Copyright © Basil Blackwell Ltd 1995
Editorial organization © Jaegwon Kim and Ernest Sosa 1995

First published 1995

Blackwell Publishers, the publishing imprint of
Basil Blackwell Ltd
108 Cowley Road, Oxford OX4 1JF, UK

Basil Blackwell Inc.
238 Main Street
Cambridge, Massachusetts 02142, USA

British Library Cataloguing in Publication Data

A CIP catalogue record for this book is available from the British Library.

Library of Congress Cataloging-in-Publication Data

A Companion to metaphysics / edited by Jaegwon Kim and Ernest Sosa.
     p.   cm.   — (Blackwell companions to philosophy)
   Includes bibliographical references and index.
   ISBN 0-631-17272-6 (alk. paper)
   1. Metaphysics—Dictionaries. I. Kim, Jaegwon. II. Sosa,
Ernest. III. Series.
BD111.C626   1994
110′.3—dc20   93-48296
                                                                              CIP

ISBN 0-631-17272-6

Typeset in 9½ on 11pt Photina by Acorn Bookwork, Salisbury, Wiltshire
Printed in Great Britain by Hartnolls Ltd, Bodmin, Cornwall

This book is printed on acid-free paper

Contents

Contributors

Felicia Ackerman
Brown University

Robert Ackermann
University of Massachusetts–Amherst

Marilyn McCord Adams
Yale University

Robert Merrihew Adams
Yale University

Jan A. Aertsen
*Thomas-Institut at the University of
Cologne, Germany*

C. Anthony Anderson
University of California, Santa Barbara

Richard E. Aquila
University of Tennessee

D.M. Armstrong
University of Sydney, Australia

Keith Arnold
University of Ottawa, Canada

Bruce Aune
University of Massachusetts–Amherst

Thomas Baldwin
Clare College, Cambridge

George Bealer
University of Colorado, Boulder

Frederick Beiser
Indiana University

John Bigelow
Monash University, Australia

Akeel Bilgrami
Columbia University

John Biro
University of Florida

Simon Blackburn
University of North Carolina at Chapel Hill

Ned Block
Massachusetts Institute of Technology

Paul A. Boghossian
New York University

M.B. Bolton
Rutgers University

Michael E. Bratman
Stanford University

Harold I. Brown
Northern Illinois University

Douglas Browning
University of Texas at Austin

Panayot Butchvarov
University of Iowa

Robert E. Butts
University of Western Ontario, Canada

Steven M. Cahn
*City University of New York, Graduate
School*

Keith Campbell
University of Sydney, Australia

Albert Casullo
University of Nebraska – Lincoln

Peter Caws
George Washington University

Arindam Chakrabarti
University of Delhi

John J. Compton
Vanderbilt University, Tennessee

John Corcoran
State University of New York at Buffalo

John Cottingham
University of Reading

Edwin M. Curley
University of Michigan

Harry Deutsch
Illinois State University

Cora Diamond
University of Virginia

Alan Donagan†

Rolf A. Eberle
University of Rochester, New York

Catherine Z. Elgin
Lexington, Massachusetts

Fred Feldman
University of Massachusetts–Amherst

Dagfinn Føllesdal
Stanford University and University of Oslo, Norway

Graeme Forbes
Tulane University, Louisiana

Richard Fumerton
University of Iowa

Richard M. Gale
University of Pittsburgh

Patrick Gardiner
Magdalen College, Oxford

Brian Garrett
Australian National University

Don Garrett
University of Utah

Rolf George
University of Waterloo, Canada

Roger F. Gibson
Washington University

Carl Ginet
Cornell University

Peter Godfrey-Smith
Stanford University

T.A. Goudge
University of Toronto

Jorge J.E. Gracia
State University of New York at Buffalo

Reinhardt Grossmann
Indiana University

Charles Guignon
University of Vermont

Michael Hallett
McGill University, Montreal

Chad D. Hansen
University of Hong Kong

Ross Harrison
King's College, Cambridge

W.D. Hart
University of Illinois, Chicago

John Heil
Davidson College, North Carolina

Mark Heller
Southern Methodist University, Texas

Eli Hirsch
Brandeis University, Massachusetts

Herbert Hochberg
University of Texas at Austin

Christopher Hookway
University of Birmingham

James Hopkins
King's College, London

Terence E. Horgan
University of Memphis, Tennessee

Paul Horwich
Massachusetts Institute of Technology

M.J. Inwood
Trinity College, Oxford

Frank Jackson
Australian National University

Lynn S. Joy
University of Notre Dame

Christopher Kirwan
Exeter College, Oxford

John Lachs
Vanderbilt University, Tennessee

Karel Lambert
University of California, Irvine

Keith Lehrer
University of Arizona

Ramon M. Lemos
University of Miami

Ernest LePore
Rutgers University

John Leslie
University of Guelph

Barry Loewer
Rutgers University

Lawrence Brian Lombard
Wayne State University, Michigan

Douglas C. Long
University of North Carolina at Chapel Hill

William Lyons
Trinity College, Dublin

Charles J. McCracken
Michigan State University

Brian P. McLaughlin
Rutgers University

Ernan McMullin
University of Notre Dame

Joseph Margolis
Temple University, Pennsylvania

Gareth B. Matthews
University of Massachusetts–Amherst

Alfred R. Mele
Davidson College, North Carolina

Joseph Mendola
University of Nebraska at Lincoln

Phillip Mitsis
Cornell University

CONTRIBUTORS

J.M. Moravcsik
Stanford University

Alexander P.D. Mourelatos
University of Texas at Austin

Kevin Mulligan
University of Geneva, Switzerland

Martha C. Nussbaum
Brown University

Anthony O'Hear
University of Bradford

Dominic J. O'Meara
University of Fribourg, Switzerland

George S. Pappas
Ohio State University

Terence Parsons
University of California, Irvine

David Pears
University of California, Los Angeles and Christ Church, Oxford

Terence Penelhum
University of Calgary, Canada

Alvin Plantinga
University of Notre Dame

Ruth Anna Putnam
Wellesley College, Massachusetts

Diana Raffman
Ohio State University

Peter Railton
University of Michigan

Andrew J. Reck
Tulane University, Louisiana

Nicholas Rescher
University of Pittsburgh

Thomas Ricketts
University of Pennsylvania

Richard Robin
Mount Holyoke College, Massachusetts

Gideon Rosen
Princeton University

Jay F. Rosenberg
University of North Carolina at Chapel Hill

Gary Rosenkrantz
University of North Carolina at Greensboro

David M. Rosenthal
City University of New York, Graduate School

David-Hillel Ruben
London School of Economics

Paul Rusnock
University of Waterloo, Canada

Nils-Eric Sahlin
Lund University, Sweden

R.M. Sainsbury
King's College, London

Wesley C. Salmon
University of Pittsburgh

David H. Sanford
Duke University

Geoffrey Sayre-McCord
University of North Carolina at Chapel Hill

Richard Schacht
University of Illinois at Urbana-Champaign

Frederick F. Schmitt
University of Illinois at Urbana-Champaign

Richard Schmitt
Brown University

George Schumm
Ohio State University

Charlene Haddock Seigfried
Purdue University

David Shatz
Yeshiva University, New York

Fadlou Shehadi
Rutgers University

Donald W. Sherburne
Vanderbilt University

Sydney Shoemaker
Cornell University

Peter Simons
University of Salzburg, Austria

Lawrence Sklar
University of Michigan

John Skorupski
University of St Andrews

Robert C. Sleigh, Jr
University of Massachusetts–Amherst

Barry Smith
*Internationale Academie für Philosophie,
Liechtenstein and State University of New
York at Buffalo*

Quentin Smith
Western Michigan University

Elliott Sober
University of Wisconsin–Madison

Roy A. Sorensen
New York University

Robert Stalnaker
Massachusetts Institute of Technology

Howard Stein
University of Chicago

Guy Stock
University of Dundee

Richard Swinburne
University of Oxford

Paul Teller
University of California, Davis

Neil Tennant
Ohio State University

James E. Tomberlin
California State University, Northridge

Martin M. Tweedale
University of Alberta, Canada

Michael Tye
*Temple University, Pennsylvania and
King's College, London*

James Van Cleve
Brown University

J. David Velleman
University of Michigan, Ann Arbor

Georgia Warnke
University of California, Riverside

Gary Watson
University of California, Irvine

Joan Weiner
University of Wisconsin–Milwaukee

CONTRIBUTORS

Nicholas White
University of Utah

S.G. Williams
Worcester College, Oxford

Kenneth P. Winkler
Wellesley College, Massachusetts

Kwasi Wiredu
University of South Florida

Allen W. Wood
Cornell University

John P. Wright
University of Windsor, Canada

Larry Wright
University of California, Riverside

Edward N. Zalta
Stanford University

Introduction

JAEGWON KIM AND ERNEST SOSA

Because it is the most central and general subdivision of philosophy, and because it is among the oldest and most persistently cultivated parts of the field, metaphysics raises special difficulties of selection for a companion such as this. The difficulties are compounded, moreover, by two further facts. First, metaphysics is not only particularly old among fields of philosophy; it is also particularly widespread among cultures and regions of the world. And, second, metaphysics has provoked levels of scepticism unmatched elsewhere in philosophy; including scepticism as to whether the whole subject is nothing but a welter of pseudo-questions and pseudo-problems.

In light of this a project such as ours needs to delimit its approach. In accomplishing this, we had to bear in mind the space limitations established by the series, and also the fact that other volumes in the series would be sure to cover some questions traditionally viewed as metaphysical. These considerations led to our including some such questions, which we thought would be covered more extensively in Samuel Guttenplan's *A Companion to the Philosophy of Mind*, for example, or in Peter Singer's *A Companion to Ethics*, but which should be treated in this *Companion*, if only briefly and for the sake of a more complete and self-contained *Companion to Metaphysics*. In addition, we tried to give a good sense of the sorts of sceptical objections that have been raised to our field as a whole. As for the spread of metaphysics across cultures, traditions, and regions of the world, we opted again to include some coverage of the non-western, while at the same time keeping our focus firmly on the western tradition from the Greeks to the present. What is more, even within the western tradition we needed to be selective, especially once we came to the present century. Philosophy in the present century has grown explosively, especially in the so-called analytic traditions common to North America and the British Commonwealth countries, along with Scandinavia and some enclaves in the rest of Europe and on other continents. Our focus has been for the most part on these traditions, although, again, as with non-western traditions, we have paid some attention to the schools and traditions that have flourished best in Continental Europe.

We had to be selective also in our treatment of contributors to metaphysics. The account of the work of a philosopher included in our *Companion* will most often reflect the contributions of that philosopher to metaphysics. A certain artificiality is therefore inevitable, and readers should bear this in mind. Other companions in our series will, therefore, provide, at least sometimes, a helpful supplement to the discussions of individual figures found in these pages.

Cross-references will be made by the use of small capitals, both in the text and at the end of each article.

Finally, we wish to acknowledge the help we have received from Rex Welshon, Michael DiRamio, Maura Geisser and John Gibbons. We thank them for their excellent and manifold work on our project.

Brown University

A

Abelard, Peter (1079–1142) French philosopher, logician and theologian. Born near Nantes in France in 1079 Abelard studied logic in his youth under Roscelin, notorious for his antirealist interpretation of logic, and went on to become the most sought-after teacher of logic in Europe. Beyond logic Abelard involved himself in theological debates, and his interpretation of the Holy Trinity, a topic which called forth his best work on the concept of sameness, was condemned twice by the church. Abelard's life was a stormy one including the much celebrated romance with and marriage to Héloïse, his subsequent castration by thugs hired by her uncle, and a bitter series of disputes with William of Champeaux over universals.

It was the topics of universals and identity that elicited Abelard's main efforts in metaphysics. While arguing that no universal, i.e. nothing common to many, is any 'real' thing, that is has an existence independent of the mental and linguistic activities that involve signification of things in the world, Abelard proposed that nevertheless there are *status* which serve as objective significates of predicates that are true of many distinct things. He gave the *status* much the same treatment as he proposed for *dicta*, which are the significates of sentences and the primary bearers of truth and falsity. They are not things in the world, not even psychological or linguistic things, but they can exist and be known objectively.

Taking off from remarks by Aristotle in the *Topics* Abelard distinguished different sorts of identity and distinctness. Most important is the contrast between sameness in 'essence' and sameness in property. The former means that the items in question have all their parts in common; the latter requires that the items be defined in the same way. He claimed that objects and the matter of which they were composed were the same in the former sense but not in the latter.

WRITINGS

Logica ingredientibus ('Logic for beginners'), in *Peter Abaelards Philosophische Schriften*, fascicules 1–3, ed. B. Geyer, in *Beiträge zur Geschichte der Philosophie des Mittelalters*, Vol. 21, fascicules 1–4 (Münster: Aschendorff, 1919–27).

Logica 'nostrorum petitioni sociorum' (Logic in response to the request of our friends'), in *Peter Abaelards Philosophische Schriften*, fascicule 4, ed. B. Geyer, in *Beiträge zur Geschichte der Philosophie des Mittelalters*, Vol. 21, fascicules 1–4 (Münster: Aschendorff, 1919–27). (A second edition by the same publisher appeared in 1973.)

Theologia Christiana ed. E.M. Buytaert in *Corpus Christianorum Continuatio Mediaevalis* 11–12 (Turnholt: Brepols, 1969).

Dialectica ('Dialectic') ed. L.M. de Rijk, 2nd edn (Assen: Van Gorcum, 1970).

MARTIN M. TWEEDALE

abstract *see* CONCRETE/ABSTRACT

accident *see* ESSENCE/ACCIDENT

acquaintance Acquaintance is a central notion in Russellian metaphysics, as well as Russellian epistemology and philosophy of language. RUSSELL distinguishes knowledge by acquaintance from knowledge by description, and characterizes the former as follows.

(1) 'We shall say we have *acquaintance* with anything of which we are directly aware, without the intermediary of any process of inference or any knowledge of truths' (Russell, 1959, p. 46, italics in original).

(2) 'it is possible, without absurdity, to doubt whether there is a table at all, whereas it is not possible to doubt the sense-data' (Russell, 1959, p. 47). The table is not an object of acquaintance, but the sense-data are, and this condition is supposed to provide a general contrast between objects of acquaintance and other things.

(3) 'All our knowledge, both knowledge of things and knowledge of truths, rests upon acquaintance as its foundation' (Russell, 1959, p. 48).

(4) Russell also specifies objects of acquaintance by extension.

'We have acquaintance in sensation with the data of the outer senses, and in introspection with the data of what may be called the inner sense – thoughts, feeling, desires, etc.; we have acquaintance in memory with things which have been data either of the outer senses or of the inner sense. Further, it is probable, though not certain, that we have acquaintance with Self, as that which is aware of things or has desires towards things.

In addition to our acquaintance with particular existing things, we also have acquaintance with . . . *universals*' (Russell, 1959, pp. 51–2, italics in original).

These four specifications cannot be assumed to coincide. What, if anything, is the foundation of our knowledge and what, if anything, is known 'directly' are, of course, themselves matters of philosophical controversy. And the second specification has its own special problem, since UNIVERSALS and sense data, far from being indubitable, are just the sorts of entities whose existence many philosophers doubt. Russell recognizes that many people doubt or deny the existence of universals, but he does not seem to recognize the problem this fact raises for the conjunction of his view that objects of acquaintance include universals and his view that objects of acquaintance, are such that their existence cannot be doubted (see Russell, 1959, chs 9 and 10). James Van Cleve has mentioned that any philosopher holding an indubitability thesis will need to formulate it so as to avoid the conclusion that we have indubitable knowledge of anything that is in fact philosophically controversial. But the way to do this in the present case seems to be, for example, to replace such claims as Russell's that 'it is not possible to doubt the sense-data' (Russell, 1959, p. 47) with claims to the effect that it is not possible to doubt that one seems to see something blue, or that one is in pain, etc. This no longer involves reference to any *object* of acquaintance whose existence cannot be doubted.

For Russell, only an object of acquaintance can be the referent of a logically proper name, i.e. a name that refers directly, without describing, and whose sole semantic function is to stand for it referent. By his principle of acquaintance, '*Every proposition which we can understand must be composed wholly of constituents with which we are acquainted*' (Russell, 1959, p. 58, italics in original). Donnellan offers a useful formalization of this notion of a constituent, when he says that if, and only if, Socrates is a constituent of the proposition expressed by the sentence 'Socrates is snub-nosed', this proposition 'might be represented as an ordered pair consisting of Socrates – the actual man, of course, not his name – and the predicate (or property, perhaps), being snub-nosed' (Donnellan, 1974, p. 225).

Russell grants that his principle of acquaintance entails that much of a person's language is private (in the sense that it is logically impossible for anyone else to apprehend the propositions expressed by the speaker) as well as ephemeral (in the sense that it is logically impossible for anyone to apprehend at time t_2 the proposition he expressed at t_1. (For Russell on ephemerality, see Russell, 1956, pp. 201–4.) But Russell overstates the extent of privacy his principle of acquaintance requires. He says

> When one person uses a word, he does not mean by it the same thing as another person means by it . . . It would be absolutely fatal if people meant the same things by their words . . . the meaning you attach to your words must depend on the nature of the objects you are acquainted with, and since different people are acquainted with different objects, they would not be able to talk to each other unless they attached quite different meanings to their words. We should have to talk only about logic. (Russell, 1956, p. 195)

By Russell's own lights, this claim is overstated, since he does not limit objects of acquaintance to sense data, oneself, and entities of logic, such as sets. He also includes universals. Thus, on the principle of acquaintance, we would not 'have to talk only about logic' in order to attach the same meanings to our words. We could also talk about blueness, roundness, etc., and we could discuss such propositions as the proposition that blue is more like purple than either is like orange. But this qualification is unlikely to assuage the doubt of opponents of the principle of acquaintance, especially since the argument Russell offers for the principle is drastically inadequate. He says

> it is scarcely conceivable that we can make a judgement or enter a supposition without knowing what it is that we are judging or supposing about. We must attach *some* meaning to the words we use, if we are to speak significantly and not utter mere noise; and the meaning we attach to our words must be something with which we are acquainted. (Russell, 1958, p. 58, italics in original)

Of course this is not really an argument. It begs the question (see Ackerman, 1987).

BIBLIOGRAPHY

Ackerman, F.: 'An argument for a modified Russellian Principle of Acquaintance', in *Philosophical Perspectives* Vol. 1, *Metaphysics* ed. J. Tomberlin (Atascadero, CA: Ridgeview, 1987), 501–12.

Donnellan, K.S.: 'Speaking of nothing', *Philosophical Review* 83 (1974), 3–31; repr. in *Naming, Necessity and Natural Kinds* ed. S.P. Schwartz (Ithaca, NY: Cornell University Press, 1977), 216–44.

Russell, B.: 'The philosophy of logical atomism', in his *Logic and Knowledge* ed. R.C. Marsh (London: George Allen and Unwin, 1956), 177–281.

Russell, B.: *The Problems of Philosophy* (New York: Oxford University Press, 1959).

FELICIA ACKERMAN

action theory Action theory deals with that concept of action that applies only to beings who have wills. The questions it addresses include: (1) what is the mark of action? (2) How should actions be individuated? (3) What makes an action intentional? (4) Is freedom of action compatible with determinism? (5) What makes true the sort of explanation peculiar to action, namely, that the agent did the action for certain reasons?

THE MARK OF ACTION

What distinguishes an action from other sorts of events of which a person may be the subject, such as sensations, perceptions, feelings, unbidden thoughts, tremblings, reflex actions? Two main sorts of answer have been offered. According to one, what marks an event (say, a movement of one's body) as an action is something extrinsic to the event, namely its having been caused in the right sort of way by the subject's desires (or intentions) and beliefs (see Goldman, 1970, ch. 3, and Davidson, 1980, essay 1). The right sort of causal connection is important, because, for example, the fact that a desire to have another drink results

3

in the subject's falling down does not make that event an action. This sort of view seems, however, not to cover spontaneous actions whose occurrence is not explained by any antecedent motives of the agent.

The other kind of account finds the mark of an action in the intrinsic nature of the event, rather than in something external to it. The idea is that an event is an action because it is, or begins with, a special sort of event. Some hold that the special event is an occurrence of a quite special sort of causation, where an event is caused, not by another event, but by the agent herself; an agent is the only sort of enduring thing that can be the subject of this special kind of causation (see Taylor, 1966; Chisholm, 1976). Others hold that the special event is mental; for some, what makes it special is its functional role (Davis, 1979, chs 1–2), and for others, it is its phenomenal character (Ginet, 1990, ch. 2). In actions that go on to become voluntary bodily exertions this event is a willing (or volition) to act. Some (for example, Hornsby, 1980) think that the content of this volition may be anything that the agent was trying to do in the action. Reflection on our experience of voluntary bodily exertion suggests, however, that there is in it something to be called volition that is quite distinct from intention and the content of which is limited to the immediately present exertion of the body (see Ginet, 1990, ch. 2).

THE INDIVIDUATION OF ACTION

Suppose that just now I moved my right index finger and thereby pressed a key and thereby put a character on the computer screen. Each of the following is a description of an action I performed: (1) 'I moved a finger'; (2) 'I moved my right index finger'; (3) 'I pressed a key'; and (4) 'I put a character on the screen.' How many different actions do these four descriptions pick out? One view holds that they pick out four different actions; because an action is an exemplifying of an action property by an agent at a time, and our four descriptions express four different action properties (see

Goldman, 1970). Another view holds that they all describe the same action in terms of different properties; my action was just the minimal thing *by* (or *in*) doing which I did the things attributed to me by all the descriptions (see Davidson, 1980, essay 3; Hornsby, 1980). (On some views this BASIC ACTION is the bodily movement, on others it is a volition.) Between these extreme views, one may take the position that, although an action is normally thought of as a more concrete entity than an exemplifying of a property (so that (1) and (2) describe the same concrete action in terms of different intrinsic properties), one action can be a proper part of a distinct action in which something that is not an action, namely, a consequence of the first action, is an additional part (so that (3) picks out a larger action of which (1)–(2) is merely the initial part, and (4) picks out a still larger action of which (4) is merely the initial part) (see Thomson, 1977; Ginet, 1990, ch. 3).

THE INTENTIONALITY OF ACTION

Smith swung the racket intentionally and in so doing inadvertently hit his opponent with it. Smith's hitting his opponent with the racket was not intentional, but it could have been. Whether an action is intentional or not often makes a big difference for the sort of evaluation it deserves. What determines whether an action is intentional or not (under a given description)? This can be divided into two questions, depending on whether or not the action description in question is basic. An action description, of the form 'S's *A*-ing', is basic just in case there is no other, non-equivalent action description, 'S's *B*-ing', such that it is true that S *A*-ed by *B*-ing. With respect to a basic description, it is plausible to hold that whatever makes an event it fits an action also makes it intentional under that description. (This is especially plausible if the basic descriptions attribute mental acts of volition.)

The question with respect to non-basic descriptions is more difficult. One might think that it would have been sufficient for Smith's hitting his opponent with the racket intentionally that he intended of his voluntary bodily movement that by it he would cause the racket to hit his opponent. But suppose he was too far from the opponent for the swing to hit as he intended; however, his grip loosened as he swung and the racket flew out of his hand and hit the opponent. We cannot then say that his hitting his opponent with the racket was intentional. Perhaps it is *sufficient* for his action's being intentional if he caused the racket to hit his opponent *in the way he intended*. But this appears not to be *necessary*. Suppose Smith stumbled slightly as he swung, causing him to hit the opponent slightly below the spot he intended to hit; in this case, though he did not hit him in just the way he intended, it seems that he still hit him intentionally. In light of such difficulties (there are others), it is clear that it will not be a simple matter to devise a satisfactory necessary and sufficient condition for an action's being intentional under a description. (For one complex proposal, see Ginet, 1990, ch. 4.)

FREE ACTION AND DETERMINISM

I have freedom of action at a given time just in case more than one alternative action is then *open to me* (*see* FREE WILL). We continually have the impression of having more than one alternative action open to us (indeed, a great many alternative actions normally seem open to us: consider all the different ways that, as it seems to me, I could next move my right hand). DETERMINISM is the thesis that, given the state of the world at any particular time, the laws of nature (*see* LAW OF NATURE) determine everything that happens thereafter down to the last detail. Some philosophers have argued that our impression of freedom is always an illusion if determinism is true *or* if, though false, it fails to be false in the right places (see van Inwagen, 1983, ch. 3; and Ginet, 1990, ch. 5). (This last disjunct is important because, although contemporary physics

may give us good reason to think that determinism is false, it does not give us good reason to think it is false in the right places: as yet we do not even know precisely what the right places are.)

The essential premises of the argument that determinism is incompatible with freedom of action are two: (1) No one ever has it open to him or her to make true a proposition that contradicts the laws of nature. (2) No one ever has it open to him or her to determine how the past was, i.e. to make true one rather than another of contrary propositions that are entirely about the past. From (2) it follows that (3) one can have it open to one at a given time to perform a certain action *a*, only if, for any truth entirely about the past, *p*, one has it open to one to make it the case that: *p* and one does *a*. From (1), (3), and determinism it follows that one never has it open to one to do anything other than what one actually does. Suppose that at 2 o'clock it seemed to me to be open to me to raise my hand then, but I did not do so. If determinism is true then there is a true proposition, *p*, which is entirely about the past relative to 2 o'clock and such that it follows from the laws of nature that: if *p* then I did not raise my hand at 2 o'clock. From (3) it follows that it was open to me to make it the case that I did raise my hand at 2 o'clock only if it was open to me to make it the case that: *p* and I raised my hand at 2 o'clock. But, given (1), it could not have been open to me to make that proposition true, for it contradicts the laws of nature. Therefore, if determinism is true (and so also are (1) and (3)), then (contrary to my impression) it was not open to me to do *a* at *t*.

This argument is obviously valid and so philosophers who resist the conclusion that determinism is incompatible with freedom of action (and many do) must reject either (1) or (2). Arguments against (2) are possible, but the more popular, and perhaps more promising, line is to attack (1) (see Fischer, 1988; Lewis, 1981). (1) could be put this way: if it follows from the laws of nature that if *p* then *q*, then it is never in anyone's power to make it the case that: p and not-q. This principle seems appealing because it seems that we ordinarily feel compelled to make inferences in accordance with it. For example, if I know that X's brain state at t is such as to nomically necessitate X's being unconscious for at least one minute after t, then that seems good enough to infer that it is not open to X at t to voluntarily raise his or her arm during the minute after t. To account for the apparent cogency of such an inference, while rejecting (1), one might suggest that what really underlies its validity is not (1) but a more complex principle, something like the following: if p nomically necessitates that X does not act in a certain way at t, *and the necessitation does not run through X's internal processes in the way that it does in normal seemingly free action*, then it is not open to X to act in that way at t. This more complex principle, says the critic of (1), will account for all the acceptable inferences that *seem* to invoke (1). But will it? Imagine a possible world where determinism is true and Martians control all of X's actions over a long period through controlling X's normal psychological processes of motivation and deliberation. If you are inclined to think this would mean that X has no more freedom of action than a puppet, then, it seems, you are inclined to operate with (1) and not just the more complex principle (for the latter would not justify that inference).

THE NATURE OF ACTION EXPLAINED BY REASONS

Typically when one acts one has motives or reasons for acting in the way one does *and* one acts in that way *for* those reasons. For example, my reason for opening the window was that I wanted to let out the smoke. I opened the window *in order* to let out the smoke, that is, *because I intended* thereby to let out the smoke.

The main metaphysical issue concerning explanations of this sort is whether they are essentially *nomic*, that is, whether the truth of one of them entails that the case be subsumable under causal laws which dictate that whenever motives of the same sort as those the explanation cites occur in sufficiently similar circumstances they (the motives and the relevant circumstances) causally necessitate an action of the same sort (see Ayer, 1946; and Davidson, 1980, essays 1, 11, for expressions of this view). The nomic view of reasons explanations would tend to be confirmed if we knew (or had good evidence for) the relevant laws in most cases of true reasons explanations. But we do not. Indeed, it may be that, as yet, there is no true reasons explanation of any action for which anyone knows causal laws that govern the explanation. Of course, this ignorance does not show that the nomic view is wrong or that, on it, we are not justified in believing any reasons explanations. Perhaps we need not know what the relevant causal laws are in order to be justified in giving a reasons explanation in a particular case. We must, however, be justified in believing that there are laws that govern the case (whether or not their contents are known to us); and it might well be doubted whether there is any case for which we are justified in believing even this.

The nomic view nevertheless has a strong appeal for many philosophers. This may be because they find it hard to see what else, if not a nomic connection, could make a genuine *explanatory* connection between motives and action. This is a fair question, which one must answer if one wants to make a good case against the nomic view. One must specify a condition that is clearly sufficient for the explanatory connection, does not imply a nomic connection, and is easy to know is present (especially for the subject). Here is a sketch of how one might try to do that (see Ginet, 1990, ch. 6 for a fuller exposition).

Suppose that concurrently with my action of opening the window I remembered my antecedent desire to rid the room of smoke and I intended of that action I was engaging in that I would thereby satisfy that desire. These conditions seem clearly sufficient to make the explanatory connection between the desire and the action, to make it true that I opened the window because I wanted to rid the room of smoke; and just as clearly they seem to be compatible with there being no true causal laws which dictate that always a desire of that same sort in sufficiently similar circumstances must produce the same sort of action. That is, they give a non-nomic sufficient condition for a reasons explanation of an action. (Of course the obtaining of a non-nomic sufficient condition does not rule out the possibility of a nomic sufficient condition, perhaps even for the same explanation of the same action.)

That reasons explanations need not be nomic is important for the view that freedom of action is incompatible with determinism. Otherwise, that view would be committed to the counterintuitive proposition that no free action (one for which there were alternatives open to the agent) could have a reasons explanation.

BIBLIOGRAPHY

Chisholm, R.M.: 'The agent as cause', in *Action Theory* ed. M. Brand and D. Walton (Dordrecht: Reidel, 1976), 199–211.

Davidson, D.: *Essays on Actions and Events* (Oxford: Clarendon Press, 1980).

Davis, L.: *Theory of Action* (Englewood Cliffs, NJ: Prentice-Hall, 1979).

Fischer, J.M.: 'Freedom and miracles', *Noûs* 22 (1988), 235–52.

Ginet, C.: *On Action* (New York: Cambridge University Press, 1990).

Goldman, A.I.: *A Theory of Human Action* (Englewood Cliffs, NJ: Prentice-Hall, 1970).

Hornsby, J.: *Actions* (London: Routledge and Kegan Paul, 1980).

Lewis, D.: 'Are we free to break the laws?', *Theoria* 47 (1981), 112–21.

Taylor, R.: *Action and Purpose* (Englewood Cliffs, NJ: Prentice-Hall, 1966).

Thomson, J.J.: *Acts and Other Events* (Ithaca, NY: Cornell University Press, 1977).

van Inwagen, P.: *An Essay on Free Will* (Oxford: Clarendon Press, 1983).

CARL GINET

actuality   *see* POTENTIALITY/ACTUALITY

adverbial theory   The adverbial theory is, at root, the view that to have a perceptual experience is to sense in a certain manner. Traditionally, the most popular analysis of perceptual experience has been the opposing sense-datum theory (*see* SENSA). According to this theory, having a perceptual experience amounts to standing in a relation of direct perceptual awareness to a special immaterial entity. In particular cases this entity is called an after-image or a mirage or an appearance, and, in the general case, a sense-impression or a sense-datum. The sense-datum is required, so it is normally argued, in order to explain the facts of hallucination and illusion: since a person can have a visual sensation of a red square, say, even when there is no *real* red, square object in his general vicinity, it is typically inferred that he is related, through his experience, to a red, square sense-datum.

The sense-datum theory leads to a number of perplexing questions. For example, can sense-data exist unsensed? Can two persons experience numerically identical sense-data? Do sense-data have surfaces which are not sensed? What are sense-data made of? Are they located? Historically, the desire to avoid questions like these was one reason for the development of the adverbial theory.

This position – that having a perceptual experience is a matter of sensing in a certain manner rather than sensing a peculiar immaterial object – is arrived at by reflecting on the fact that, on *standard* views, appearance, after-images, and so on, cannot exist when not sensed by some person. The explanation the adverbial theorist offers for this fact is that statements which purport to be about appearances, after-images, and so on, are in reality statements about the way or mode in which some person is sensing. Hence, a statement of the general form, 'Person, P, has an F sense-impression', or 'P has an F sensation', is reconstructed adverbially as, 'P senses F-ly', or as it is sometimes put, 'P senses in an

F manner.' This transformation has a number of grammatical parallels. 'Patrick has a noticeable stutter', for example, is equivalent to 'Patrick stutters noticeably', and 'Patrick stutters in a noticeable manner.' Similarly 'Jane does a charming waltz', may be transcribed as, 'Jane waltzes charmingly.' It should be obvious that the adverbial view can account for the facts of hallucination and illusion. If, for example, I am correctly described as having a visual sensation of something blue then 'blue' in this description is taken upon analysis to function as an adverb which expresses a mode of my sensing. Hence, my having the sensation does not require that there be a blue physical object (or anything else for that matter) in my general vicinity – it suffices that I sense bluely.

Although the adverbial theory began as, and is still most strongly associated with, the analysis of perceptual experience, it has also been applied elsewhere. For example, it is often held by adverbialists that our ordinary talk of bodily sensations is misleading, and that in reality there are no such items as pains and itches to which persons are related when they have a pain or feel an itch. Rather statements about bodily sensations have an underlying adverbial structure. 'Jones has an intense pain', for example, is analysed as 'Jones is pained intensely'; hence it is about the *way* in which Jones is pained. The motivation for this approach runs parallel to the one for perceptual experience: countenancing pains and other sensory objects in our ontology generates a host of philosophical puzzles. For example, are pains really located about the body as our ordinary pain talk suggests? If so, then presumably they are material objects. Why, then, are they never revealed by surgical examination of the appropriate limbs? Can pains exist in parts of the body without their being felt? Can two persons ever feel one and the same pain? All these puzzles dissolve once the adverbial view is adopted.

Some philosophers have argued that the adverbial theory can even be extended to the analysis of belief and desire discourse.

Thus, having the belief that snow is white, say, is not a matter of bearing the 'having' relation to a particular belief, but rather a matter of believing in a certain way. Whether this extension is defensible, and indeed whether the adverbial theory is viable anywhere, depends ultimately on how the theory is further spelled out. Recent work (see Tye, 1989) has supplied a clear semantics and metaphysics for the theory with the result that the adverbial approach is no longer open to the charge that it is just a rather trivial grammatical transformation without any real constraints. Indeed, once fully elucidated, the adverbial theory is seen to be a very powerful and well-founded approach which has the resources to answer all the more obvious objections.

BIBLIOGRAPHY

Ducasse, C.J.: 'Moore's refutation of idealism', in *Philosophy of G.E. Moore* ed. P.A. Schilpp (Chicago: Northwestern University Press, 1942), 225–51.
Chisholm, R.M.: *Perceiving* (Ithaca, NY: Cornell University Press, 1957).
Sellars, W.: *Science and Metaphysics* (London: Routledge and Kegan Paul, 1968), 9–28.
Tye, M.: 'The adverbial approach to visual experience', *Philosophical Review* 93 (1984), 195–225.
Tye, M.: *The Metaphysics of Mind* (Cambridge: Cambridge University Press, 1989).

MICHAEL TYE

Alfarabi [al-Fārābī] (*c.*870–950) Islamic logician, metaphysician, political philosopher, also wrote commentaries on ARISTOTLE's logical treatises and expositions of PLATO's and Aristotle's philosophies.

Alfarabi was the first to raise the question of how the philosopher writing in Arabic which has no copula, can do logic and supply precise vocabulary for the Greek concept of being. He proposes to use derivatives of *wjd* (to find) for all the functions of 'to be', in a stipulative fashion, including the most general sense of 'being' (Shehadi, 1982, pp. 45–51).

Existents are divided by Alfarabi into the possible and the necessary. In the case of possible beings, existence is not a property and cannot be part of their essence (*see* ESSENCE/ACCIDENT; ESSENTIALISM). Asked whether 'Man exists' has a predicate, Alfarabi replied that for the logician, 'exists' is a predicate in the proposition. But it is not a predicate to the investigator into the nature of things. However, in the case of the First, existence is Its essence, for It is the being necessary through itself.

In Islamic philosophy Neoplatonic (*see* NEOPLATONISM) emanationism gets its first full statement by Alfarabi. Islamic Neoplatonists were influenced by an Arabic translation of a pseudo *Theology of Aristotle* which was in fact a summary of sections of PLOTINUS' *Enneads*, as well as by a translation of the *Liber de causis*.

The First is one, uncomposed, and beyond human knowledge. From its activity of thinking itself emerges the First Intellect which thinks itself as well as its source. The emanations proceed until the Tenth Intellect, each intellect with its corresponding cosmic sphere.

Of special interest is Alfarabi's transformation of Aristotle's active intellect into a separate entity between humankind and the First, one of the separate substances above the terrestrial sphere. While it still makes the knowable known, its cosmological status prepares the way for the eschatological and mystical roles that it plays in Islamic philosophy.

BIBLIOGRAPHY

Fakhry, M.: *A History of Islamic Philosophy* (New York: Columbia University Press, 1970).
Hammond, R.: *The Philosophy of Alfarabi and its Influence on Medieval Thought* (New York: Hobson Book Press, 1947).
Rescher, N.: *Al-Farabi: An Annotated Bibliography* (Pittsburgh: University of Pittsburgh Press, 1962).
Rescher, N.: 'Al-Fārābī on the question: is existence a predicate?', in his *Studies in the History of Arabic Logic* (Pittsburgh: University of Pittsburgh Press, 1963) 39–42.
Shehadi, F.: *Metaphysics in Islamic Philosophy* (Delmar: Caravan Books, 1982).

FADLOU SHEHADI

analysis Consider the following proposition.

(1) To be an instance of knowledge is to be an instance of justified true belief not essentially grounded in any falsehood.

(1) exemplifies a central sort of philosophical analysis. Analyses of this sort can be characterized as follows:

(a) The *analysans* and *analysandum* are necessarily coexistensive, i.e. every instance of one is an instance of the other.
(b) The *analysans* and *analysandum* are knowable a priori to be coextensive.
(c) The *analysandum* is simpler than the *analysans* (a condition whose necessity is recognized in classical writings on analysis, such as Langford, 1942).
(d) The *analysans* does not have the *analysandum* as a constituent.
(e) A proposition that gives a correct analysis can be justified by the philosophical example-and-counterexample method, i.e. by generalizing from intuitions about the correct answers to questions about a varied and wide-ranging series of simple described hypothetical test cases, such as 'If such-and-such were the case, would you call this a case of knowledge?' Thus, such an analysis is a philosophical *discovery*, rather than something that must be obvious to ordinary users of the terms in question.

Condition (d) rules out circularity. But since many valuable quasi-analyses are partly circular (e.g. knowledge is justified true belief supported by *known* reasons not essentially involving any falsehood), it seems best to distinguish between full analysis, for which (d) is a necessary condition, and partial analysis, for which it is not.

This core notion of analysis fits the intuitive idea the term 'analysis' suggests, which is that something is analysed by breaking it down into its parts (see Moore, 1903, sects 8 and 10). But Moore also holds that analysis is a relation solely between concepts, rather than one involving entities of other sorts, such as linguistic expressions, and that in a true analysis, *analysans* and *analysandum* will be the same concept (see Moore, 1942). These views give rise to what is nowadays generally called 'the' paradox of analysis: how can analyses such as (1) be informative? Philosophers have proposed various solutions, such as relaxing the requirement that *analysans* and *analysandum* are the same concept (Langford, 1942), and denying that (1) is genuinely informative to someone who *fully* grasps the concepts involved (Sosa, 1983).

Regardless of how this paradox is to be handled, there are types of analysis other than that exemplified by (1). One such type of analysis involves an *analysans* and *analysandum* that are clearly epistemically equivalent and that hence do not raise the paradox discussed here, although they do raise a different paradox (see Ackerman, 1990). Other types of analyses include new-level analysis, which aims at providing metaphysical insight through metaphysical reduction (for example, the analysis of sentences about physical objects into sentences about sense data (see Urmson, 1956, ch. 3), and reformatory analysis, which seeks to reduce sloppiness and imprecision by replacing a concept considered in some way defective with one considered in the relevant way improved. Reformatory analysis makes no claim of conceptual identity between *analysans* and *analysandum* and hence gives rise to no paradox of analysis.

Aside from the possibility of paradox, philosophers have raised various objections to analysis as a philosophical method. It is a commonplace to object that analysis is not all of philosophy. But, of course, the claim that analysis is a viable method does not amount to saying that it is the only one. WITTGENSTEIN (see Wittgenstein, 1968, especially sects 39–67) has raised objections to the atomist metaphysics and epistemology underlying Russellian new-level analysis (*see* LOGICAL ATOMISM; RUSSELL). But most of these objections do not apply to other types of analysis. It can also be objected that it is virtually impossible to produce an example of an analysis that is both philosophically interesting and generally accepted as true. But virtually all propositions philosophers put forth suffer from this problem. (See Rescher, 1978; Ackerman, 1992a.) The hypothetical example-and-counterexample method the sort of analysis (1) exemplifies is fundamental in philosophical inquiry, even if philosophers cannot reach agreement on analyses and often even individually cannot give full analyses and have to settle for less, such as one-way conditionals, partially circular accounts, and accounts (like that of being a game) that are justified in the same general way as analyses but that are too open-ended even to purport to yield necessary and sufficient conditions.

BIBLIOGRAPHY

Ackerman, F.: 'Analysis, language, and concepts: the second paradox of analysis', in *Philosophical Perspectives* vol. 4, *Philosophy of Mind and Action* ed. J. Tomberlin (Atascadero, CA: Ridgeview, 1990), 535–43.

Ackerman, F.: 'Philosophical knowledge', in *A Companion to Epistemology* ed. J. Dancy and E. Sosa (Oxford: Blackwell, 1992a), 342–5.

Ackerman, F.: 'Analysis and its paradoxes', in *The Scientific Enterprise: The Israel Colloquium Studies in History, Philosophy, and Sociology of Science* vol. 4, ed. E. Ullman-Margalit (Norwell, MA: Kluwer, 1992b).

Langford, C.H.: 'The notion of analysis in Moore's philosophy', in *The Philosophy of*

G.E. Moore ed. P.A. Schilpp (Evanston, IL: Northwestern University Press, 1942), 319–43.

Moore, G.E.: *Principia Ethica* (New York–London: Cambridge University Press, 1903).

Moore, G.E.: 'A reply to my critics', in *The Philosophy of G.E. Moore* ed. P.A. Schilpp (Evanston, IL: Northwestern University Press, 1942), 660–7.

Rescher, N.: 'Philosophical disagreement', *Review of Metaphysics* 22 (1978), 217–51.

Sosa, E.: 'Classical analysis', *Journal of Philosophy* 53 (1983), 695–710.

Urmson, J.O.: *Philosophical Analysis* (Oxford: Oxford University Press, 1956).

Wittgenstein, L.: *Philosophical Investigations*, 3rd edn, ed. and trans. G.E.M. Anscombe (New York: Macmillan, 1968).

FELICIA ACKERMAN

Anscombe, G.E.M. (1919–) G.E.M. Anscombe is a philosopher of great range, many of whose important contributions to philosophy lie in metaphysics and in fields which substantially overlap metaphysics, especially philosophy of logic and philosophy of mind.

In 'Causality and determination' (1971) she questioned a central assumption made in virtually all philosophical writing about CAUSATION, namely, 'If an effect occurs in one case and a similar effect does not occur in an apparently similar case, there must be a further relevant difference.' The most disparate views of causation, from ARISTOTLE's and SPINOZA's to HOBBES's, HUME's and RUSSELL's, all accept that causation involves universality or necessity or both; but Anscombe argues that such views cannot stand up. She shows the core idea in causation to be that of *derivativeness*, exemplified by making a noise, pushing, wetting. Her view that these causal notions do not involve universality or necessity might be questioned, so she examines different sorts of examples, like Feynman's case of a bomb which may be caused to explode by some

radioactive emission. The absence of necessitation is irrelevant to the causing of the subsequent explosion. Anscombe also examines the relevance of non-necessitating causes to freedom of the will (*see* FREE WILL).

She has discussed the subject of causation in several other essays. An important theme is the different *kinds* of causal relation (see, for example, 1974a). In 'Times, beginnings and causes' (1974b), she examines Hume's claim that it is logically possible for something to begin to exist without a cause. She develops an argument of Hobbes's to show how judgements about beginnings of existence depend on the application of causal knowledge.

Among the other topics in metaphysics which she has discussed is that of the self. In 'The first person' (1975), she argues that DESCARTES's view of the self would be correct if 'I' were genuinely a referring expression, but that it is not a referring expression. Metaphysical problems concerning time and SUBSTANCE are the focus of some of her other essays.

WRITINGS

'Aristotle: the search for substance', in G.E.M. Anscombe and P.T. Geach *Three Philosophers* (Oxford: Blackwell, 1963), 5–63.

'Causality and determination' (inaugural lecture at Cambridge University, Cambridge, 1971); repr. in (1981), vol. II, 133–47.

'Memory, "experience" and causation', in *Contemporary British Philosophy* ed. H.D. Lewis (London: George Allen and Unwin, 1974[a]) 15–29; repr. in (1981), vol. II, 120–30.

'Times, beginnings and causes', *Proceedings of the British Academy* 60 (1974[b]) 253–70; repr. in (1981), vol. II, 148–62.

'The first person', in *Mind and Language: Wolfson College Lectures 1974* ed. S. Guttenplan (Oxford: Clarendon Press, 1975) 45–65; repr. in (1981), vol. II, 21–36.

Collected Papers 3 vols (Oxford: Blackwell, 1981; Minneapolis: University of Minnesota Press, 1981); papers bearing on metaphysics are in Vol. I *From Parmenides to Wittgenstein* and Vol. II *Metaphysics and the Philosophy of Mind*.

BIBLIOGRAPHY

Diamond, C. and Teichman, J. ed.: *Intention and Intentionality: Essays in Honour of G.E.M. Anscombe* (Brighton: Harvester Press, 1979).

CORA DIAMOND

Anselm of Canterbury, St (1033–1109) Scholastic philosopher and Archbishop of Canterbury, born at Aosta, Italy. Like AUGUSTINE before him, Anselm is a Christian Platonist in metaphysics (*see* PLATONISM). In the *Monologion*, he deploys a cosmological argument for the existence of the source of all goods, which is Good *per se* and thus supremely good, identical with what exists *per se* and is the Supreme Being. In *Proslogion* c.ii, Anselm advances his famous ontological proof: namely, that a being a greater than which cannot be conceived exists in the understanding, since even a fool understands the phrase when he hears it; but if it existed in the intellect alone, a greater could be conceived which existed in reality. A parallel *reductio* in c.iii concludes that a being a greater than which cannot be conceived exists necessarily. And in his *Reply to Gaunilo*, he offers a modal argument for God's necessary existence, based on the premise that whatever does not exist is such that if it did exist, its nonexistence would be possible. God is essentially whatever it is – other things being equal – better to be than not to be, and hence living, wise, powerful, true, just, blessed, immaterial, immutable and eternal *per se*; even the paradigm of sensory goods – Beauty, Harmony, Sweetness and Pleasant Texture, in its own ineffable manner. Nevertheless, God is supremely simple, *omne et unum, totum et solum bonum*, a being a more delectable than which cannot be conceived.

God is both the efficient cause of everything else and the paradigm of all created natures, the latter ranking as better in so far as they are less imperfect ways of resembling God. Such natures have a teleological structure, which is at once internal to them (a created *f* is a true (defective) *f* to the extent that it exemplifies (falls short of) that for which *f*'s were made) and established by God. From TELEOLOGY, Anselm infers a general obligation on all created natures (non-rational as well as personal): since they *owe* their being and well-being to God as their cause, so they *owe* their being and well-being to God in the sense of having an obligation to praise Him by fulfilling their *teloi*.

Anselm's distinctive ACTION THEORY reasons that if the *telos* of rational natures is unending beatific intimacy with God, their powers of reason and will have been given to promote that end. Thus, the will's freedom must be *telos*-promoting, and – since sin is deviation from the *telos* – should not be defined as a power for opposites (the power to sin and the power not to sin), but rather as the power to preserve justice for its own sake (*see* FREE WILL). Choices are imputable only if spontaneous (from the agent itself). Since creatures have their natures from God and not from themselves, they cannot act spontaneously by the necessity of their natures. To enable creatures to be just of themselves, God endowed them with two motivational drives towards the good – the *affectio commodi*, or tendency to will things for the sake of their benefit to the agent itself; and the *affectio justitiae*, or tendency to will things because of their own intrinsic value. It is up to the creature whether or not to align them (by letting the latter temper the former). Anselm's motivational theory contrasts sharply with AQUINAS's Aristotelian account, but was taken up and developed by DUNS SCOTUS.

WRITINGS

S. Anselmi. Opera Omnia. Ed. by F.S. Schmitt (Edinburgh: Thomas Nelson and Sons, 1946–61) Vols I–VI.
Anselm of Canterbury Vols. 1–3 (Toronto–New York: Edwin Mellor Press, 1974–76).

BIBLIOGRAPHY

Adams, R.M.: 'The logical structure of Anselm's arguments', *The Philosophical Review* 80 (1971), 28–54.

Henry, D.P.: *The Logic of Saint Anselm* (Oxford: Clarendon Press, 1967).

Hopkins, J.: *Anselm of Canterbury* Vol. 4 *Hermeneutical and Textual Problems in the Complete Treatises of St. Anselm* (Toronto–New York: Edwin Mellen Press, 1976).

Kane, G.S.: *Anselm's Doctrine of Freedom of the Will* (New York–Toronto: Edwin Mellen Press, 1981).

MARILYN McCORD ADAMS

antinomies An antinomy is a pair of apparently impeccable arguments for opposite conclusions. Obviously, the arguments cannot both be sound because a proposition and its contradictory must have opposite truth values. Thus the two appearances of cogency are not 'all things considered' judgements because conflicting appearances cancel out. The challenge posed by an antinomy is at the level of adjudication and diagnosis. We know that at least one arm of the antinomy is fallacious. But which? And exactly where does it go wrong?

'Antinomy' is most closely associated with Immanuel KANT's attack on metaphysics. In the *Critique of Pure Reason*, he lays out parallel arguments literally side by side to emphasize their utter deadlock. As long as we assume that things-in-themselves are objects of knowledge, we can mount a knock-down argument for the thesis that the world has beginning in time and a knock-down argument for the antithesis that the world has no beginning. Metaphysicians can prove that we are free by exposing the absurdity of an actual infinity of past events and metaphysicians can disprove our freedom by demonstrating the incoherency of a break in the causal order. This embarrassment of riches constitutes the data for Kant's meta-argument in favour of the critical point of view: instead of aiming at knowledge of a mind-independent reality, we

should abandon the classical metaphysical enterprise and restrict the objects of knowledge to appearances. We can then see that the antinomies are a product of transcendental illusion which arises from the temptation to apply the principles that constitute the framework for knowledge of phenomenal reality to noumenal reality (*see* NOUMENAL/PHENOMENAL).

Contemporary philosophers do not share Kant's awe at the cogency of the clashing arguments. Indeed, cosmologists and infinitistic mathematicians dismiss the pros and cons about the extent of SPACE AND TIME as amateurish fallacies. However, Kant's unconvincing choice of examples does not undermine the philosophical interest of the concept of an antinomy. After all, 'apparent' needs to be relativized to epistemic agents. An antinomy for an eighteenth-century figure need not be an antinomy for a twentieth-century thinker.

In any case, there certainly are argumentative deadlocks. Recently, a Japanese group of topologists announced a result that contradicted the result of an American group of topologists. Since both proofs involved complex calculations, they exchanged proofs to check for mistakes. Despite their high motivation and logical acumen, neither team has been able to find an error in the other's reasoning. The Japanese–American deadlock is not an antinomy if it is caused by a slight but subtle slip. The appearance of cogency must be due to a 'deep error' – not a mistake due to bad luck or ignorance surmountable by merely mechanical methods.

Metaphysicians have a particular interest in antinomies that turn on false existential presuppositions. The Barber paradox features a village in which a barber shaves all and only those people who do not shave themselves. Does the barber shave himself? First argument: if the barber shaves himself, then he is a self-shaver. But he only shaves those who do not shave themselves. Therefore, the barber does not shave himself. Second argument: if the barber does not shave himself, then he is among the non-self-shavers. But he shaves all those who do not shave themselves. Therefore, the barber does shave himself! The lesson to be learned from this modest antinomy is that the barber cannot exist.

More ambitious resolutions of antinomies aim at a more dramatic impact on our ontology or cosmology. The paradox of the stone (can God make a stone so large that He Himself could not lift it?) is used to disprove God's existence. The Buddhists use antinomies to disprove the existence of the self. The Eleatics (see PRESOCRATICS) and nineteenth-century idealists (see IDEALISM) deployed antinomies against the assumption that material things exist and that they are spatially related.

Other antinomies turn on false dichotomies. For example, the old arguments for and against infinite space tended to assume that 'finite' and 'unbounded' were mutually exclusive terms. Albert Einstein's application of Riemannian geometry makes sense of a 'spherical' universe that is finite but unbounded. So besides subtracting entities and relationships from metaphysical systems, antinomies enrich these systems by stimulating the discovery of new entities and possibilities.

An antinomy cannot prove anything on its own. Indeed, its internal conflict makes it a paradigm of dialectic impotence. However, the meta-arguments that grapple with antinomies are powerful tools of metaphysical inquiry.

See also APORIA; SORITES ARGUMENTS; TRANSCENDENTAL ARGUMENTS; ZENO.

BIBLIOGRAPHY

al-Asm, S.J.: *The Origins of Kant's Arguments in The Antinomies* (Oxford: Oxford University Press, 1972).
Kant, I.: *Critique of Pure Reason* (Riga, 1781); trans. N. Kemp Smith (London: Macmillan, 1933).
Quine, W.V.: *The Ways of Paradox* (Cambridge: Harvard University Press, 1976).
Sainsbury, R.M.: *Paradoxes* (Cambridge: Cambridge University Press, 1988).
Sorensen, R.: *Pseudo-Problems* (London: Routledge, 1993).

ROY A. SORENSEN

antirealism By 'antirealism' we mean here *semantic* antirealism, of the kind advanced by DUMMETT in numerous writings. The main thesis of semantic antirealism is that we do not have to regard every declarative statement of our language as determinately true or false independently of our means of coming to know what its truth value is. That is, the semantic antirealist refuses to accept the principle of bivalence.

ANTIREALISM IS NOT A FORM OF IDEALISM OR NOMINALISM

Semantic antirealism is to be distinguished from *ontological* antirealism. Ontological antirealism casts doubt on the existence of objects. It comes in varying degrees. The ontological antirealist may doubt the existence of *any* objects in the external world (IDEALISM); or, more modestly, doubt the existence of the unobservable entities posited by science (Bas van Fraassen's constructive empiricism (1980)); or, more traditionally, doubt the existence of abstract objects, such as numbers (see NUMBER), or of UNIVERSALS (NOMINALISM). Semantic antirealism is compatible with both Platonistic (see PLATONISM) and nominalistic views about numbers. In the case of mathematics, G. Kreisel's dictum is often stressed: what one is concerned with is not so much the existence of mathematical objects, as the OBJECTIVITY of mathematical statements.

ANTIREALISM IS COMPATIBLE WITH NATURALISM

Indeed, one might even maintain that it is a *consequence* of NATURALISM. By naturalism we mean the metaphysical view that all things, events, states and processes are material or physical. Naturalism asserts SUPERVENIENCE, but does not claim reductionism (*see* REDUCTION, REDUCTIONISM). It asserts that all mental, moral, semantic and social facts supervene on material or physical facts. The physical facts, that is, fix the mental, moral, semantic and social facts. But naturalism does not claim that psychology, moral theory, semantics or the social sciences can be reduced to physics. On the contrary, each of these special sciences is autonomous. Each presents important aspects of reality in its own terminology. Indeed, antirealism itself is a theory whose content would be lost were it not formulated in its own special terms, terms which defy reduction to physics.

ANTIREALISM STRESSES OBSERVABLE BEHAVIOUR AS THE SOURCE OF MEANING

The antirealist is centrally concerned with grasp of meanings, or contents (*see* CONTENT); and with the conditions under which speakers and thinkers can acquire such grasp and display it. It lays great stress on what have become known as the *acquisition* and *manifestation* arguments. These arguments are used to cast doubt on the claim, concerning sentences in any given area of discourse, that their meanings consist in verification-transcendent truth conditions. For, if they did, so these arguments conclude, speakers of the language would never be able fully to acquire or display grasp of meaning. The observable conditions surrounding their discourse, and their own observable behaviour, prevent such overly enriched contents from being grasped and assigned to sentences. The acquisition and manifestation arguments, as developed by Dummett, show most clearly the influence of the later WITTGENSTEIN on Dummett's thinking.

ANTIREALISM CONTRASTED WITH QUINEANISM

One way to understand antirealism is to consider how QUINE and the antirealist react to an argument on which they both agree. The argument has three premises

and a conclusion that they both reject:

(1) Meaning is given by truth conditions.
(2) Meaning is determinate.
(3) Truth is bivalent.

---

(4) Grasp of meaning cannot be manifested fully in observable behaviour.

Both Quine and the antirealist agree on the first premise. Quine holds that meaning (via translation) is indeterminate, but that truth is bivalent. The antirealist, by contrast, holds that meaning is determinate, but that truth is *not* bivalent.

ANTIREALISM ENJOINS A MOLECULAR, AS OPPOSED TO AN HOLISTIC, THEORY OF MEANING

The antirealist believes in determinate sentential contents. He or she adopts a compositional approach. One familiar ground for this comes from theoretical linguistics, which rightly stresses our recursive, generative or creative capacity to understand new sentences as we encounter them. Another ground is that the opposing holistic view (*see* HOLISM) simply cannot account for language learning. We do, it would appear, master language fragments progressively as learners, and are able to isolate or excise them for theoretical study later on. Meanings of words remain relatively stable under increase of vocabulary and during developments in our ability to produce and understand more complicated utterances. These considerations point to a compositional approach.

ANTIREALISM IS CONCERNED WITH NORMATIVITY

As we have just seen, the antirealist maintains determinacy of meaning. Precision about contents brings with it commitment to normative connections among them: their justification conditions and their entailments. One of the main aims of antirealism is to give an accurate picture of such contents as the speaker or thinker can genuinely grasp or entertain in thought, and convey in language. This means that

15

antirealism has to have some answer to sceptical problems about the objectivity of rule following. For it is only by conforming to, or keeping faith with, rules for the use of expressions that the speaker can claim to have mastered their meanings.

ANTIREALISM FAVOURS REFORMISM RATHER THAN QUIETISM

In particular, the antirealist critique of genuinely graspable meanings can be brought to bear on the meanings of the *logical* expressions of our language: the connectives and the quantifiers. The observable conditions of their use (especially in mathematics) concern the discovery, construction, presentation and appraisal of *proofs*. Central features of the use of logical expressions – in particular, their introduction rules – serve to fix their meanings. Other features need to be justified as flowing from the central features. We can justify the elimination rules, because these are in a certain sense in balance or harmony with the introduction rules. But on this model of meanings and how one comes to grasp them, there does not appear to be any justification for the strictly classical rules of reasoning, especially as they concern negation. There does not appear to be any justification for the Law of Excluded Middle (either *a* or not-*a*) or for the Law of Double Negation Elimination (from not-not-*a* infer *a*) or any of their equivalents. Thus the antirealist response has been to favour logical reform: crucially, to drop the strictly classical negation rules and opt for *intuitionistic* logic. Thus intuitionism is the main form of mathematical antirealism (*see* INTUITIONISM IN LOGIC AND MATHEMATICS). When the antirealist generalizes from the mathematical case, with its conditions of constructive proof, he or she looks for appropriate *conditions of warranted assertability*.

THE CHALLENGE OF AN ANTIREALIST ACCOUNT OF EMPIRICAL DISCOURSE

In moving to empirical discourse, and especially statements about other minds, one has to attend closely to the *criteria* in accordance with which one ventures any informative claim. Here the situation is very different from mathematics. For in mathematics, once a statement is proved it remains proved. In empirical discourse, however, statements are *defeasible*. That is, they can be justified on a certain amount of evidence; but may have to be retracted *or even denied* on the basis of new evidence accreting upon the old. (A modern way of putting this is to say that they are governed by a *non-monotonic* logic.) There is also the familiar problem from the philosophy of science, that no general claim about natural kinds (*see* NATURAL KIND) can ever conclusively be proved. At best, such claims can be conclusively *refuted*; but no amount of humanly accessible evidence can entail them. The combination of *defeasibility* with this familiar asymmetry between proof and refutation makes particularly problematic the provision of a satisfactory antirealist account of meaning for empirical discourse.

ANTIREALISM TENDS TO BE PIECEMEAL, RATHER THAN GLOBAL

Most writers on antirealism try to explore its strengths and weaknesses on particular *areas of discourse*: mathematics, statements about other minds, statements about the past, counterfactual statements (*see* COUNTERFACTUALS), and so on. In each area one looks critically at the observational basis on which one can acquire grasp of meaning. One examines the criterial structure governing how speakers venture, and are taken at, their words. One tries (if necessary) to deflate any overly realistic classical conception of how, in response to each such area of discourse, a mind-independent region of reality might inaccessibly yet determinately be. The realist sometimes complains that the antirealist is guilty of *epistemic* hubris in taking the human mind to be the measure of reality. The antirealist responds by charging the realist with *semantic* hubris in claiming to grasp such propositional contents as could be determinately truth-valued independently of our means of coming to know what those truth values are.

ANTIREALISM IS NOT A CRUDE FORM OF VERIFICATIONISM

There was an old principle of the logical positivists (*see* LOGICAL POSITIVISM) which, over the years, fell into deserved disrepute. This was the verificationist principle that every meaningful declarative sentence was, in principle, decidable. That is, in grasping its meaning a speaker would have recourse to a method which, if applied correctly, would within a finite time yield the correct verdict as to the truth or falsity of the sentence. Despite its emphasis on assertibility conditions, antirealism lays claim to no such principle.

ANTIREALISM STRESSES COMPOSITIONALLY

Antirealism stresses, instead of the positivists' naive decidability principle, various *canonical* ways of establishing statements with prominent occurrences of expressions whose antirealistically licit meaning is at issue. (An example of this would be dominant occurrences of logical operators, in the context of their introduction rules.) Various such expressions could then be combined into a sentence which is meaningful but which the antirealistic need not claim is decidable. The sentence will be meaningful by virtue of the way those expressions are combined within it, and by virtue of their central meanings *as conferred by those special contexts*. It is at this point that modern antirealism is crucially influenced by the contribution of FREGE to logical semantics.

SUMMARY OF MAIN FEATURES OF THE ANTIREALIST POSITION

(1) refusal to accept the principle of bivalence;
(2) behaviourist emphasis on the epistemology of linguistic understanding: acquisition and manifestation arguments;

(3) confidence in the determinacy of sentence meaning, leading to a molecular as opposed to an holistic theory of meaning;
(4) stress on the compositionality of meaning, thereby allowing meaningful though undecidable sentences;
(5) advocacy of some kind of logical reform, making one's logic more intuitionistic or constructive;
(6) a generally naturalistic metaphysical outlook, and a quietist demurral from extreme sceptical misgivings or theses in epistemology.

MAIN ALLEGED WEAKNESSES IN THE ANTIREALIST POSITION

(1) Alleged failure to do justice to the intuition that the world is robustly independent of human cognitive faculties;
(2) alleged failure to appreciate the strength of independent arguments to the effect that translation is indeterminate, that there can be no firm analytic/synthetic distinction, that meaning (such as it is) is graspable at best only holistically;
(3) alleged failure to appreciate that, in so far as meaning is determined (by the antirealist's own lights) by the *use* we make of our expressions, we should accordingly accept classical rules of inference (such as Double Negation Elimination) as justified by the very use we make of them;
(4) alleged instability in the antirealist's own argumentative strategy: why stop at intuitionism, for example? Why not go all the way to strict finitism? Why treat of decidability *in principle* rather than *feasible* decidability?
(5) alleged failure to understand the semantic contribution of the negation operator in embedded contexts;
(6) alleged failure to appreciate that there are, even within the constraints set by the antirealist, resources enough to secure the realist's grasp of verification-transcendent propositional contents;
(7) alleged failure to appreciate that the

semantic issue of logical reform is independent of the metaphysical and epistemological issues at the heart of antirealism.

WRITINGS IN THE MODERN REALISM VS ANTIREALISM DEBATE

Michael Dummett put forward his classic challenge to the principle of bivalence in his essay 'Truth'. His defence of intuitionistic logic as the correct logic on an antirealist construal of mathematics was given in his essay 'The philosophical basis of intuitionistic logic'. This treatment was amplified in the chapter on philosophical reflections in his book *The Elements of Intuitionism* (1977). He explored the implications of antirealism for statements about the past in his essay 'The reality of the past'. Dummett's essays are collected in his book *Truth and Other Enigmas* (1978).

Dag Prawitz has provided an excellent exposition and amplification of Dummett's line of argument in his paper 'Meaning and proofs: on the conflict between classical and intuitionistic logic' (1977). *Crispin Wright* has written widely on antirealism in mathematics, on statements about the past and on statements about other minds. He has also treated the problems of criteria, defeasibility and the objectivity of rule following. See his book *Wittgenstein on the Foundations of Mathematics* (1980), and his collection of essays *Realism, Meaning and Truth* (1986). *Neil Tennant*, in his book *Anti-Realism and Logic* (1987), has extended the antirealist critique and the logical reform it arguably entails in favour of the system of intuitionistic relevant logic. He also explores antirealism as a consequence of naturalized epistemology. *John McDowell* has pursued subtle variations on realistic and antirealistic themes in his essays 'Anti-realism and the epistemology of understanding' (1981), and 'Truth conditions, verificationism and bivalence (1970).

Opposition by the realists has been led most notably by *Peter STRAWSON* (1976), *Christopher Peacocke* (1986) and *J.J.C. Smart* (1986). *Saul Kripke* gave great impetus to the debate about the objectivity of rule following with the publication of his provocative monograph *Wittgenstein on Rules and Private Language* (1982). Kripke adopts an antirealistic construal of content-attribution statements in his 'sceptical solution'.

See also REALISM.

BIBLIOGRAPHY

Dummett, M.A.E. (with the assistance of R. Minio): *The Elements of Intuitionism* (Oxford: Clarendon Press, 1977).

Dummett, M.A.E.: *Truth and Other Enigmas* (London: Duckworth, 1978).

Kripke, S.: *Wittgenstein on Rules and Private Language* (Oxford: Blackwell, 1982).

McDowell, J.: 'Truth conditions, verificationism and bivalence', in *Truth and Meaning* ed. G. Evans and J. McDowell (Oxford: Clarendon Press, 1976), 42–6.

McDowell, J.: 'Anti-Realism and the epistemology of understanding', in *Meaning and Understanding* ed. H. Parret and J. Bouveresse (Berlin and New York: De Gruyter, 1981), 225.

Peacocke, C.: *Thoughts: An Essay on Content* (Oxford: Blackwell, 1986).

Prawitz, D.: 'Meaning and proofs: on the conflict between classical and intuitionistic logic', *Theoria* 43 (1977), 2–40.

Smart, J.J.C.: 'Realism v. idealism', *Philosophy* 61 (1986), 295–312.

Strawson, P.F.: 'Scruton and Wright on anti-realism, etc.', *Proceedings of the Aristotelian Society* 77 (1976), 15–22.

Tennant, N.: *Anti-Realism and Logic* (Oxford: Clarendon Press, 1987).

Wright, C.J.G.: *Wittgenstein on the Foundations of Mathematics* (London: Duckworth, 1980).

Wright, C.J.G.: *Realism, Meaning and Truth* (Oxford: Blackwell, 1986), 2nd edn.

Wright, C.J.G.: *Truth and Objectivity* (Cambridge, MA: Harvard University Press, 1992).

NEIL TENNANT

aporia   An apory is a small set of individually plausible but jointly inconsistent propositions. Aporia gained initial popularity from CHISHOLM's demonstration of how they help to motivate and structure philosophical issues. For instance, he regiments the problem of ethical knowledge with a set containing the following three members:

(1) We have knowledge of certain ethical facts.
(2) Experience and reason do not yield such knowledge.
(3) There is no source of knowledge other than experience and reason.

To avoid inconsistency, thinkers need to reject at least one member of the set. Thus the sceptic denies (1), the naturalist rejects (2), while the intuitionist argues against (3). The aporetic cluster provides each position with a ready-made argument. For the negation of any member of the set is the conclusion of an argument containing the remaining members as premises. Since members of the original set are jointly inconsistent, the argument will be valid. And since the members are individually plausible, the audience will also find each premise of the argument persuasive.

BIBLIOGRAPHY

Chisholm, R.M.: *Theory of Knowledge* 2nd edn (Englewood Cliffs, NJ: Prentice Hall, 1977).

ROY A. SORENSEN

appearance/reality   Nothing is more commonplace than the remark that things are not always what they seem. We all know that a thing can appear to be some way and yet be really quite otherwise. Unlike some other distinctions philosophers are enamoured of, the distinction between appearance and reality is firmly rooted in everyday experience and discourse. It is not surprising, then, that it has, since the dawn of philosophy, served to structure debates about what there is to know and how, if at all, it can be known.

When Socrates objected to the relativism of the Sophists, with its ugly moral consequences, it was their refusal to allow that there could be a gap between '*x* appears to be *F*' and '*x* is *F*' that he had to show to be untenable. When DESCARTES, and after him, most thinkers of the modern era, struggled with the sceptic's challenge, the threat posed by that challenge was the possibility that that same gap was too great, that no reliable evidence about reality was ever furnished by what appeared in experience. In part inspired by that challenge, one empiricist strain (*see* EMPIRICISM), strangely echoed in a late flowering of RATIONALISM, concludes that what appears to the well-functioning mind (in perception or in reasoning) is, and must be, the real, and it must be just as it appears. Found in both BERKELEY's and HEGEL's form of IDEALISM, this manoeuvre closes the gap the Sophists had ruled out, but does so from the opposite side. Where the Sophist insists that whatever appears must be real the idealist argues that only what is real can appear. For both, the real must be just as it appears to be; either way, the commonsense distinction is rendered philosophically moot (and needs to be explained, or explained away, in complicated and, to some, implausible, ways).

In both its everyday and its philosophical versions, the appearance/reality distinction must be seen as a completely general one. While its most obvious illustrations involve sense perception, it extends naturally to all dimensions of thought and experience. It may seem to someone that two and two add up to five. Arguably, it may just seem to one that one desires or fears something. Hence it is a mistake to draw the distinction by identifying one side with one metaphysical category and the other with another, for example, the real with the material and appearances with the mental.

What, then, is at the heart of the commonsense distinction, and what, if any-

19

thing, is philosophically interesting about it?

I mentioned the perennial sceptical worry about whether appearances can tell us whether there are things other than appearances and, if so, what they are like. Scepticism is an epistemological position. But the very idea that there *is* a way things are, whether or not one can know what that way is, expresses a metaphysical belief, usually labelled REALISM. Thus scepticism itself involves a metaphysical component. What account can we give of the appearance/reality distinction that does justice to both these components? Here is where the notion of evidence can provide the needed general framework.

An appearance is always an appearance *to* someone, just as a piece of evidence is always evidence *for* someone. The former notion, in fact, represents a special case of the latter. But the concept of evidence also involves the thought of something *for* which the evidence is evidence. Thought of in this way, so does the idea of an appearance, as the appearance *of* something. Even KANT, who insists on the 'empirical' reality of what he calls 'appearances', arguably sometimes treats them as representing, albeit in a special and highly problematical sense, a 'transcendent' reality (*see* NOUMENAL/ PHENOMENAL). It is a conceptual truth that even the best evidence must fall short of certainty (else it would not be evidence for something other than itself). In the same way, the very concept of an appearance requires it to be distinct from that of which it is an appearance. This is why the idealist attempt to identify reality with appearances, no matter how the latter are idealized, is a mistake. It involves a non-evidential, hence a non-epistemic, conception of appearances; in doing so, it loses contact with the point of the commonsense distinction out of which the philosophical one grows.

What makes the appearance/reality distinction both important and slippery is that it straddles the division between epistemology and metaphysics. Other well-worn philosophical distinctions are either internal to one or another of the traditional divisions of the subject (particular/universal, necessary/contingent, a priori/a posteriori, or CONCRETE/ABSTRACT) or indifferent to them (EXTRINSIC/INTRINSIC, specific/general, objective/subjective). Thinking of the appearance/reality distinction in the evidential way as suggested here can save us from mistaking it for a metaphysical one, one between two different kinds of entity. There may be good reasons for thinking that there are appearances, as opposed to just the various ways the things there are appear. But there are dangers in this reification of them (*see* HYPOSTASIS, REIFICATION). First, it can lead to intractable metaphysical problems that are in fact avoidable. Second, it misleads us as to the true nature of the distinction between appearance and reality. Only when understood as involving the relation between epistemological and ontological concepts can it both retain the intuitive content of the commonsense distinction and yield a general philosophical problem that is not the artefact of some special metaphysical doctrine.

BIBLIOGRAPHY

Austin, J.L.: *Sense and Sensibilia* (Oxford: Oxford University Press, 1962).
Ayer, A.J.: *The Foundations of Empirical Knowledge* (London: Macmillan, 1940).
Burnyeat, M.: *The Skeptical Tradition* (Berkeley: University of California Press, 1983).
Grayling, A.C.: *The Refutation of Scepticism* (La Salle, IL: Open Court, 1985).

JOHN BIRO

Aquinas, St Thomas (1224/5–74) The philosophy of St Thomas Aquinas was strongly influenced by ARISTOTLE and by the Islamic philosophers AVICENNA and AVERROES, whose works became available in Latin translations at the beginning of the thirteenth century. But Aquinas's metaphysical thought contains a number of elements that are not to be found in his leading sources.

THE SUBJECT MATTER OF METAPHYSICS

Aristotle's divergent statements on the nature of first philosophy led to an intensive discussion of the subject matter of metaphysics among medieval thinkers. In *Metaphysics* iv c.1 (1003a21–32), Aristotle speaks of a science which studies being as being and opposes it to other sciences which investigate beings from a particular point of view, for instance, in so far as they are mobile. The science of being as being, by contrast, is universal. But in Book vi c.1 (1026a23–32), Aristotle distinguishes three theoretical sciences – physics, mathematics and the 'divine science' – and calls theology the first science, because it is concerned with immobile and immaterial beings. The medieval discussion is focused on the question how Aristotle's theological conception of first philosophy is related to the conception of metaphysics as the universal science of being (see Zimmermann, 1965).

In the prologue to his *Commentary on the Metaphysics*, Aquinas argues that metaphysics is concerned with both being as being and the immaterial substances, although not in the same way. He develops his synthesis with the help of the logician Aristotle, for Aquinas's argument is based on the theory of science in the *Posterior Analytics*. The unity of a science consists in the unity of its subject (*subiectum*). What is sought in every science are the proper causes of its subject. Now the immaterial substances are the universal causes of being. Therefore, being in general (*ens commune*) and the properties belonging to it are the subject of metaphysics. God is studied in this science only in so far as he is the cause of the subject of metaphysics, that is, in so far as he is the cause of being as such. God is not the subject, but rather the end of metaphysical investigation. By this feature metaphysics is distinguished from Christian theology ('the theology of sacred scripture'), for the subject matter of this science is God himself (cf. *Summa theologiae* I.1.7).

From this account it appears that Aquinas does not adopt the theological conception of metaphysics that was prevalent among the Greek commentators on Aristotle. According to them first philosophy is the science of the most eminent being, the divine being. Aquinas's view is ontological: metaphysics is the *scientia communis*, for its subject matter is being in general.

THE DOCTRINE OF THE TRANSCENDENTALS

Against the background of Aquinas's ontological conception of metaphysics, the significance of a doctrine that was developed in the thirteenth century, the doctrine of the transcendentals, becomes understandable, for *transcendentia* are the universal properties of being as such (see Aertsen, 1988). The term 'transcendental' suggests a kind of surpassing or going beyond. What is transcended is the special modes of being which Aristotle called 'the CATEGORIES'. While for the latter the categories are the most general genera of being, Aquinas considers them as special modes of being, as contractions of that which is: not every being is a SUBSTANCE, or a quantity, or a quality, or a relation, etc. By contrast, the transcendentals express general modes of being. They transcend the categories, not because they refer to a reality beyond the categories but because they are not limited to one determinate category. Unlike the categories, the transcendentals do not exclude each other, but are interchangeable or convertible (*convertibilis*) with being and each other.

In *De veritate* 1.1, Aquinas presents his most complete account of the transcendentals, of which the most important are being, one, true and good. Being is the first transcendental. The other transcendentals, although convertible with being, add conceptually something to being, in the sense that they express a mode of it which is not yet made explicit by the term 'being' itself. The general mode of being expressed by 'one' pertains to every being in itself (*in se*); 'one' adds to being a negation, for it signifies that being is undivided. 'True' and 'good' are relational transcendentals: they express the conformity (*convenientia*) of every being to something else. The condition for this relation is something whose nature it is to accord with every being. Such is, Aquinas argues, the human SOUL, which according to Aristotle (*De anima* iii c.8, 431b21) 'is in a sense all things'. In the soul there is both a cognitive power and an appetitive power. The conformity to the appetite or will is expressed by the term 'good', the conformity to the intellect by the term 'true'. Truth as transcendental signifies the intelligibility of things.

Aquinas's innovation in the doctrine of the transcendentals is the correlation he introduces between the human soul and being. He understands the transcendentals true and good in relation to the faculties of a spiritual substance. This understanding means an acknowledgement of the special place human being has among other beings in the world. A human being is marked by a transcendental openness; its object is being in general. This openness is the condition of the possibility of metaphysics.

The doctrine of the transcendentals plays a central role in Aquinas's metaphysics. It integrates the theory of knowledge ('truth') into an ontology and it provides the foundation for the first principle of morality: 'good is to be done and pursued, and evil avoided' (*Summa theologiae* I–II.94.2). The doctrine is also fundamental for philosophical theology. Within the framework of a reflection on the divine names 'Being', 'Unity', 'Truth' and 'Good' Aquinas discusses the relation between the transcendentals and God. Because the transcendentals are self-evidently knowable, and because they do not express a limited, categorical mode of being, they are seen as providing the basis for the possibility of rational knowledge of God.

THE HISTORY OF THE QUESTION OF BEING

In *Summa theologiae* I.44.2, Aquinas sketches the history of philosophical reflection about the origin of being. This text can be regarded as the medieval origin of the question 'Why is there something and not rather nothing?' Three main phases can be distinguished in the progression of philosophy as Aquinas sees it.

The first step was taken by the PRESO-CRATICS. They held that MATTER is the 'substance' of things and that all forms are accidents. They posited one or more substrata (water, fire, etc.) which they regarded as the ungenerated and indestructible principle of all things. To the extent to which they acknowledged CHANGE in the SUBSTRATUM, it consisted only in 'alteration', a change of its accidental forms (*see* MATTER/FORM).

The second stage in the progress of philosophy was reached when philosophers made a distinction between 'matter' and 'substantial form'. They posited a prime matter that is purely potential and is brought into actuality through a form. Aquinas regards it as one of Aristotle's great merits that with his doctrine of the potentiality of matter he made it possible to acknowledge a substantial change, or 'generation'.

Aquinas emphasizes, however, that the final step had not yet been taken, for the generation, too, presupposes something, in keeping with a common supposition of Greek thought: 'nothing comes from nothing' (*ex nihilo nihil fit*). The philosophers of the first and second phases considered the origin of being under some particular aspect, namely, either as 'this' being or as 'such' being. As a result, the causes to which they attributed the becoming of things were particular. Their causality is restricted to one category of being: accident (as in the first place), or substance (as in the second).

The third phase began when 'some thinkers raised themselves to the consideration of being as being'. In this metaphysical analysis they assigned a cause to things not only in so far as they are 'such' (by accidental forms) and 'these' (by substantial forms), but also as considered according to all that belongs to their *being*. The origin considered by the metaphysician is transcendental, it concerns being as such, not merely being as analysed into natural categories. The procession of all being from the universal cause is not a generation, because it no longer presupposes anything in that which is caused. It is creation *ex nihilo*.

A striking feature of Aquinas's view of the progress of philosophy is that the idea of creation appears as the result of the internal development of human thought, independent of revelation. In the context of the idea of creation Aquinas elaborates two central ideas of his metaphysics: the composition of essence and existence in created things, and the doctrine of participation.

THE COMPOSITION OF ESSENCE AND EXISTENCE – PARTICIPATION

The distinction between essence and existence (*esse*) was introduced by Islamic thinkers in order to explain the contingent character of caused beings (*see* ESSENCE/ACCIDENT). Existence does not belong to the essence of what is caused, for it has received its being from something else. The relation between essence and existence was interpreted by Avicenna according to the model of substance and accident: *esse* is an accident superadded to essence.

Aquinas teaches the real composition of essence and existence in all creatures already in one of his earliest works, *De ente et essentia*. In chapter 4 he discusses the essence of the 'separated substances' or spiritual creatures. This issue engaged Aquinas a great deal – he even devoted a particular treatise to it, *De substantiis separatis* – for it concerns the ontological structure of finite substances. This structure cannot consist in the composition of form and matter, since spiritual substances are 'separated' from matter. Yet although such substances are pure forms, they do not have complete simplicity. All creatures are composed of essence and existence, because they have their *esse* not of themselves, but from God.

According to Aquinas, however, existence is not an accident superadded to essence. Existence and essence are related to each other as act to potency. He extends the notions of act and potency, which were correlative with the notions of form and matter in Aristotle, to being as such. In a famous text in his *De potentia* (7.2 ad. 9), Aquinas states: 'That which I call *esse* is the actuality (*actualitas*) of all acts, and for this reason it is the perfection of all perfections.' For Aquinas to be is not a bare fact, but the ultimate act through which a thing achieves its perfection. 'Every excellence of any thing belongs to it according to its *esse*. For man would have no excellence as a result of his wisdom unless through it he *were* wise' (*Summa contra Gentiles* I.28). It was Gilson (1949) in particular, who has emphasized the existential character of Aquinas's metaphysics against the dominant 'essentialist' tradition in modern philosophy.

Closely connected with the distinction of essence and existence in created things is Aquinas's doctrine of participation. No finite being is its *esse*, but has it. Only in God are essence and existence identical: he is essentially Being. All other things participate in being. One of the most significant innovations in Thomistic scholarship since the Second World War has been the discovery of the 'Platonist' Thomas (*see* PLATO, PLATONISM). Pioneering studies were the works of Fabro (1961) and Geiger (1942), which showed the central role of the Platonic notion of participation in Aquinas's metaphysics, a notion that was sharply criticized by Aristotle. Aquinas interprets the idea of creation philosophically in terms of participation. The relation of creatures to the first cause is the relation of participation in being.

WRITINGS

The critical edition of Aquinas's works, the Leonine edition, is still unfinished: *Opera omnia. Iussu impensaque Leonis XIII, P.M. edita* (Rome: Vatican Polyglot Press, 1882–). For a complete listing of the various editions, see J.A. Weisheipl, *Friar Thomas d'Aquino* (Washington, DC: The Catholic University of America Press, 1983), 355–404.

BIBLIOGRAPHY

Aertsen, J.A.: *Nature and Creature. Thomas Aquinas's Way of Thought* (Leiden: Brill, 1988).

Fabro, C.: *Participation et causalité selon S. Thomas d'Aquin* (Louvain and Paris: Nauwelaerts, 1961).

Geiger, L.-B.: *La Participation dans la philosophie de S. Thomas d'Aquin* (Paris: 1942); 2nd edn (Paris: Vrin, 1953).

Gilson, E.: *Being and Some Philosophers* (Toronto: 1949); 2nd edn (Toronto: Pontifical Institute of Mediaeval Studies, 1952).

Wippel, J.F.: *Metaphysical Themes in Thomas Aquinas* (Washington, DC: The Catholic University of America Press, 1984).

Zimmermann, A.: *Ontologie oder Metaphysik? Die Diskussion über den Gegenstand der Metaphysik im 13. und 14. Jahrhundert* (Leiden: Brill, 1965).

JAN A. AERTSEN

archetype From the Greek ἀρχέτυπον, a pattern or model. The word is applied to the reality – whether in the mind of God in nature itself, or in a third, abstract realm – to which a conception is referred. Archetypes sometimes play a causal role in originating those conceptions; their reference or truth is then assured (or at the very least argued for) by their causal ancestry. The Greek word was applied by Platonists (though not by PLATO himself, who spoke instead of παραδείγματα) to the forms (*see* PLATONISM). Later Platonists placed these forms or archetypes in the mind of God. Philosophers of the seventeenth and eighteenth centuries conceived of them more broadly. DESCARTES described the external cause of an idea as 'like an archetype'. LOCKE applied the word to the things the mind 'intends [its ideas] to stand for, and to which it refers them'. BERKELEY applied the word, with some reluctance, to ideas in the mind of God, which were, he argued, no less serviceable as archetypes than the corporeal substances of the materialists.

Berkeley, G.: 'Third dialogue' in *Three Dialogues between Hylas and Philonous* (London: 1713); repr. in *The Works of George Berkeley, Bishop of Cloyne* ed. A.A. Luce and T.E. Jessop (London: Thomas Nelson, 1948–57), vol. 2, 227–63.

Berkeley, G.: *Philosophical Correspondence between Berkeley and Samuel Johnson 1729–30* (New York: 1929); repr. in *The Works of George Berkeley* ed. A.A. Luce and T.E. Jessop (London: Thomas Nelson, 1948–57), vol. 2, 271–94.

Descartes, R.: 'Third meditation' in *Meditations on First Philosophy* (Paris: 1641); repr. in *The Philosophical Writings of Descartes* ed. and trans. J. Cottingham, R. Stoothoff and D. Murdoch (Cambridge: Cambridge University Press, 1984), vol. 2, 29.

Locke, J.: *An Essay concerning Human Understanding* (London: 1689); ed. P.H. Nidditch (Oxford: Clarendon Press, 1975), Book II, ch. xxxi, sects 1–3.

Plato: *Republic* V, VI (many versions).

KENNETH P. WINKLER

Aristotle (384–322 BC) Greek philosopher born in Stagira. Aristotle's writings can be said to have set the agenda for the western tradition in metaphysics. Indeed, 'metaphysics' is a term derived from a first century BC edition of Aristotle's work, in which a collection of his writings was put together under the title *Ta Meta ta Phusika*, which means simply 'What comes after the writings on nature' (*ta phusika*). Since the writings thus put together concerned topics that seemed in certain ways related – substance and being, change and explanation, unity and plurality, potentiality and actuality, non-contradiction, the nature of the eternal and unchanging – these topics were subsequently taken to be the subject matter of 'metaphysics', which increasingly became a separate department of philosophy. But Aristotle himself did not group these topics together. He does have a conception of 'the study of being *qua* being' – the study of what is true of all things that are, as such – that links some of the contents of the *Metaphysics*. But there is dispute about what that study is, and how much of the work it includes. Nor are Aristotle's inquiries into the topics we now call metaphysical confined to the work called *Metaphysics*. There is an especially close link between that work and his inquiries into natural change and explanation.

SUBSTANCE, CHANGE AND IDENTITY

Aristotle once remarked that the central concern of previous philosophers, when they asked questions about what 'being' is, was really, at bottom, a question about what substance is. (The term we translate 'substance' is *ousia*, a verbal noun formed from the participle of the verb 'to be'.) 'For it is this,' he continues, 'that some claim to be one in number, some more than one, and some limited, others unlimited.' He himself devotes much effort to the task of finding an adequate account of 'substance', and on defending the priority of substance to other items such as qualities and materials. It is not, however, intuitively obvious what Aristotle means by the question, 'What is substance?', all the more since the term *ousia* is primarily an Aristotelian term, with no clear history. We must search in his arguments and examples for an understanding of his motivation and goal: to what real puzzles does such a search respond?

As Aristotle characterizes earlier inquiries into substance, they focus on two questions, rather closely related: (1) a question about the explanation of change; and (2) a question about identity. We observe many changes in the world around us, such as the cycle of the seasons, the birth, growth and death of living creatures. Early Greek mythology explained these changes by invoking the capricious will of anthropomorphic beings; early philosophers, instead, looked for lawlike explanations. In the process, they had to ask themselves, first, what sorts of entities are relatively

stable and persisting, the things to which changes happen and in terms of whose underlying stability change could be coherently explained. (Plato had cogently argued that coherent talk about change presupposes at least some stability: for a change has to be the change *of* something, and that thing cannot at the same time be ceasing to be the thing it is, or we will not be able to say anything about it.) The search for substance is, in part, a search for these most basic persisting entities, which Aristotle calls 'substrata' or 'subjects' (two different translations of his Greek term *hupokeimenon*, literally 'that which underlies').

The second question is what Aristotle calls the 'What is it?' question. It may be illustrated by countless common examples. Suppose I am considering some particular thing in my experience, say, Socrates. I have a sense that, in order to pursue my curiosity about this thing further, I must have some answer to the question, 'What is this?' I want to know what it is about this thing that makes it the thing it is, what enables me to single it out as a distinct particular and mark it off from its surroundings, to reidentify it later as the same thing I encountered earlier. But to know this I need, it seems, to separate the attributes of the thing into two groups: properties (such as a sun-tan, or knowledge of history) that may come to be present, or depart, without affecting Socrates' persistence as the same entity, and properties (such as, perhaps, the ability to metabolize food, or the ability to think and choose) whose presence is constitutive of the individual's identity, whose departure would mean the end of an individual. The identity question has a special urgency where living creatures are concerned, since it is connected with complicated ethical and political issues, for example, the determination of death and the moral status of the foetus. Thus Aristotle holds that a creature dies whenever it loses one of the properties in the second group (the 'essential' properties); and he holds that the foetus at an early stage of life is not a human being, and does not exhibit identity with the human being that may in due course come to be, since it does not yet have all the essential properties of the human being.

In one way, these two questions seem to point in opposite directions, identifying different things as 'the substance' of a thing. For the question about persistence through change might lead us to hold that material stuffs are the basic substances of the things they compose, seeing that these stuffs (for example, the materials that make up the body of Socrates) pre-exist the birth of Socrates and post-date his death. On the other hand, for this very reason they do not give the answer to questions about necessary and sufficient conditions for Socrates' identity. We are inclined, there, to look in the direction of the structure characteristic of Socrates' species, his human make-up and functioning. For it seems that it is the disruption of those modes of organization that spells the end of his existence.

On the other hand, looked at in another way the two questions seem to be closely intertwined. An adequate theory of change must single out, as its substrates, things that are not only relatively enduring, but also definite and distinct. Unless we can individuate an item from its surroundings and say something about what it is, it will be difficult to make it the cornerstone of an explanatory enterprise. And a good answer to the 'What is it?' question, asked about a particular such as Socrates, must tell us, among other things, what changes Socrates can endure (as a substrate) and still remain one and the same.

As Aristotle sees it, his predecessors went wrong because they pursued one prong of the substance inquiry to the neglect or distortion of the other. Early natural scientists, seeing that material stuffs were the most persisting things around, surviving the deaths of humans and animals, held that these were the real substance of things and the best answer to the 'What is it?' question, when asked about particular substances. What Socrates really is, is the materials that compose him. This leads to paradoxical conclusions: no substance ever

perishes, and substances continue to exist although their parts are widely dispersed in space and time. Above all, this view fails to capture a distinction that is fundamental in our discourse and practices, namely the distinction between property change (*alloiosis*) and real coming-into-being and going-out-of-being (*genesis* and *phthora*), between Socrates getting a sun-tan and the death of Socrates.

Platonists (*see* PLATONISM), on the other hand, focus on the identity question, and on the UNIVERSALS that are, as they see it, the best answer to that question. Each aspect of Socrates is explained by his 'participation' in some universal 'form', such as the form of Justice, which is imagined as existing apart from particulars and as explaining the possession of that property in all the particulars that have it. Aristotle finds fault with this emphasis on the universal, because it fails to come to grips with the material changing character of the individual substance. Nor, in its Platonic form at least, does this approach even succeed in separating universals such as the Human, which must be true of Socrates as long as he exists, from universals such as the White, which he might lose (getting a sun-tan) while still remaining the same individual.

In his early work, the *Categories*, Aristotle focuses on two tasks: demarcating the role of particulars and universals in answering 'What is it?' questions about things, and defending the central role of natural-kind concepts in answering both change and identity questions. The famous enumeration of ten 'categories' or (literally) 'predications' is an attempt to enumerate different ways we might characterize a particular in our experience: we might speak about its substantial nature, its quantity, its qualit(ies), its relation(s), its place, time, position, state, activity, passivity. At the same time, Aristotle also introduces a fourfold distinction of 'things that are', separating (1) universals in the substance category, called Secondary Substance – e.g. human being, horse; (2) particulars in non-substance categories, such as this item of knowledge, this instance of pink colour; (3) universals in non-substance categories, such as knowledge, colour; (4) particulars in substance categories, called Primary Substance, e.g. this human being, this horse. The motivation for these distinctions emerges when Aristotle explains the fundamental classifying role of natural-kind universals. His point is that we do not pick things out and trace them through time as bare unclassified matter; fundamental to our practices of identifying and explaining is the ability to say to what kind the thing belongs. (His later writings give natural kinds a special place here, since artefacts have comparably unclear criteria of identity.) When we point at Socrates and say, 'What is it?' we are asking about a particular, and it is that particular thing that exists; classifying universals have no existence apart from particulars. But the universal is of fundamental importance in coming to grips with the particular's identity – and not just any universal, but the one, 'human being', that gives the kind to which he belongs from birth to death. To answer, 'Socrates is a sitting thing', or 'Socrates is a white thing', is a less revealing answer, parasitic on our ability already to pick out Socrates as a human being. In short: the category of substance, which includes the natural-kind universals and the particulars that fall under them, has priority over the other categories in both explaining and identifying. Within this category, particulars in a sense take priority, as the most basic substrates of change; but they get their identity from the universal under which they fall.

FORM AND MATTER

So far, Aristotle has said nothing about the coming-to-be and passing-away of substances. Nor has he spoken about the matter that composes them. To these tasks he turns in *Physics* i 7–9 and in *Metaphysics* vii. He acknowledges that living substances are essentially enmattered structures: they cannot continue as the things they are without suitable matter to make them up and perform their life-activities. On the other hand, he insists that matter all by itself cannot give us the identity of a particular: for it is a mere 'lump' or 'heap' without the form or structure that it constitutes. Nor, indeed, despite matter's purported claim to be the substrate *par excellence*, does matter even turn out to be as continuous as form, with respect to the individual species member: for the matter that composes Socrates is changing continually, as he eats and excretes, while he himself remains one and the same.

Looking more closely into the question of what does provide Socrates with his identity over time, Aristotle's answer is that this is his 'essence', and that this essence is a particular instance of characteristic species organization or 'form' (*see* HYLOMORPHISM), not different in kind from that of other species members, but a countably different instance, tracing a distinct career through time and space. (There are many different interpretations of Aristotle's final position on the contribution of the universal and the particular in identity, but this one has broad support.)

In later books of the *Metaphysics* Aristotle investigates the role of form in making a thing a unity, providing still further arguments against thinking of material stuffs as what a thing is. Introducing the important ideas of capability or potentiality (*dunamis*) and activity or actuality (*energeia*), he argues for the explanatory priority of a thing's actual nature to its potentialities. Aristotle here begins to think about matter as a set of potentialities for functioning, which can be explicated only when we have grasped the actual functional structure of the entity that matter composes.

The famous twelfth book of the *Metaphysics* then gives an account of god as an immortal immaterial substance whose entire form is thinking, and whose entire being is actuality rather than potentiality. God imparts movement to the universe by being an object of passionate love to the heavenly bodies, who are themselves imagined to be living thinking beings.

BEING *QUA* BEING AND THE BASIC PRINCIPLES OF THOUGHT

In Book iv of the *Metaphysics*, Aristotle defends the idea of a general study of the attributes of things that are as such, or of 'being *qua* being' – an idea that he seemed to attack in some earlier writings as insufficiently attentive to the multiplicity of types of being. Here, by contrast, he argues that the many ways in which we speak of 'being' have more than a verbal unity: for all are understood through an inquiry into substance, which is in some sense the basic type of being in our explanation and understanding of the world. Aristotle's project here has been understood in two very different ways. Some interpreters understand him to be calling for a general study of substances, focusing in particular on living creatures, and for an illumination of properties, of activity and passivity, and so forth, that would be based upon that understanding. Others have understood him to be referring to god as the primary and central substance, a study of which is the focal point for all study of substance. The fact that the relevant texts of the *Metaphysics* derive from different periods in Aristotle's life and are not edited into their present order by him makes resolution of this question very difficult. One can at least say, however, that in the central books in which Aristotle does in fact investigate the nature of substance (Books vii–ix), there is no discussion of god, and no sign that we need to understand the nature of god before answering questions about form's relation to matter. The same is true of the *De anima*, where bodiless substance is an anomaly, briefly mentioned, in the work's systematic study of the necessary interrelatedness of form and matter (*see* HYLOMORPHISM).

Aristotle then goes on to argue that in any inquiry whatever, a basic role is played by two logical principles: the principle of non-contradiction and the principle of the excluded middle. Formulating Non-Contradiction as the principle that contradictory predicates cannot apply to a single subject at the same time in the same respect, Aris-

totle argues that this is 'the most secure starting point of all', concerning which 'it is impossible to be in error'. Confronting an opponent who claims to doubt the principle (apparently a relativist who holds that if x seems F to observer O, x simply is F, and if x to observer P not to be F, x simply is not F), Aristotle argues that this opponent himself refutes himself, if he utters any coherent sentence, or even any definite word. For any meaningful utterance must, in putting something definite forward, at the same time implicitly rule out something – at the very least, the contradictory of what is put forward. He adds that if the opponent is silent and refuses to say anything definite, he loses this way too: for he is 'pretty much like a vegetable', and it is 'ridiculous to look for words to address to someone who doesn't use words'. Moreover, even definite action without words reveals a commitment to Non-Contradiction: for when one acts one must have some definite belief about what one is aiming to do, and such beliefs, propositional in form, presuppose a commitment to Non-Contradiction.

METHODOLOGY: APPEARANCES AND UNDERSTANDING

In passages such as the one from *Metaphysics* iv just discussed, Aristotle appears to derive support for what he calls 'the most basic principle of all' simply by showing its depth and ubiquity in our discourse and practices. And elsewhere he states that in all inquiries the aim should in fact be, first to 'set down the appearances' – by which he seems to mean the record of human experience on the issue – and then, working through the puzzles this record presents, to go on to 'save' as true 'the greatest number and the most basic' of those 'appearances'. This procedure can be seen at work in many of his inquiries, both in natural science and in ethics.

On the other hand, in the *Posterior Analytics* Aristotle presents an account of the structure of scientific understanding, and the goal of inquiry, that seem, at first, distinctly different. He argues that an inquirer can claim *episteme*, or scientific understanding, only when he has been able to arrange the results of inquiry into a deductive explanatory system, internally consistent and hierarchically ordered, depending on first principles that are true, necessary, basic and explanatory of the other truths of the science in question. By itself this need not conflict with Aristotle's emphasis elsewhere on sorting out the record of experience: for he is simply adding the point that this sorting-out must be one that yields a systematic grasp and the ability to give explanations. But in *Posterior Analytics* ii 19, Aristotle makes some remarks about the nature of his first principles that seem to go in a different direction: for he holds that, after experience provides us with the material of a science, its first principles must be grasped by a faculty which he calls *nous*. In traditional mediaeval interpretations of Aristotle, this has been understood to be a faculty of intellectual intuition that seizes on first principles a priori, and thus sets the science on an extra-experiential foundation.

Recent interpretations of the passage, however, have pointed out that this is not a plausible way of understanding what is meant by *nous* in Aristotle (or, indeed, in the ordinary vocabulary of cognition from which he derives the term). *Nous* is insight based upon experience; and what Aristotle is saying is that true understanding is not achieved until, in addition to the grasp and use of principles, we gain understanding of the fundamental explanatory role. This is exactly what the person who follows Aristotle's arguments about Non-Contradiction does derive: so there is no need to see the *Posterior Analytics* as in tension with that passage or others in which the method of philosophy is understood to involve a systematization of experience.

NATURE AND EXPLANATION

Aristotle's account of explanation, in the second book of his *Physics*, is closely linked to his arguments about substance. He iden-tifies four different types of explanation that are standardly given when we ask the question 'Why?' about some entity or event in our experience. (These are often called the 'four causes', but it would be better to think of them as the 'four becauses'.) First, we often enumerate the material constituents of a thing; but this, Aristotle argues, explains nothing about a thing unless we have already said what sort of thing it is. The second sort of explanation, which cites the thing's form or structure, is in that sense prior to the first. The third sort, which Aristotle calls 'the origin of change', and which is often called 'efficient cause', corresponds rather closely to our notion of causal explanation: asked why something happened, or why a thing is as it is, we cite some other event or agency that acted in such a way as to produce it.

Finally, Aristotle introduces the explanation 'that for the sake of which', often called 'teleological explanation' (*see* TELEOLOGY). Here we say that the reason x happened was for the sake of y, where y is in the future. It is not difficult to understand the relevance of this sort of explanation in the context of intentional human action ('He did this in order to get that'). What is harder to understand is the role Aristotle gives it in explaining the growth and development of living creatures of all sorts, including many (such as plants) that are not, in his view, capable of intentional action. He recommends that we should give accounts of the development of a seed, for example, or of various life processes in a mature plant, by saying that they happen 'for the sake of' the form or structure of the plant. Aristotle is at pains to insist that he is not invoking any causal factors external to the nature of the organism in each case. It seems wrong to see any implications of a grand teleology of nature or an argument from design such as was developed later by the Stoics. Instead, Aristotle's interest is in the plastic and self-maintaining, self-nourishing character of living systems: in a variety of circumstances, they will behave in the way best suited to realize and then maintain their forms and structures. And understanding this will enable us to grasp their doings in a unified way – predicting, for example, that a plant's roots will grow in the direction of the water supply, wherever that happens to be. Teleological explanations do not invoke mysterious notions; they grow from a biologist's observation that organic systems function in integrated and form-preserving ways.

Aristotle's passionate interest in biology animates much of his metaphysical writing. He spent about twenty years of his career doing first-hand biological research, much of it very fine. And his biological writings provide rich insight into metaphysical issues such as the relation of form and matter and the nature of functional explanation. To students who evidently preferred theology to the study of worms and shellfish, he makes a reply that might perhaps serve as an excellent introduction to Aristotle's temperament as metaphysician and philosopher of nature:

We must not enter upon the study of the lesser animals with childish disgust. For in every natural thing there is something wonderful. There is a story which tells how some foreigners once wanted to meet Heraclitus. When they entered, they saw him warming himself in front of the stove. They hesitated; but he told them, 'Come in; don't be afraid; there are gods here too.'

WRITINGS

Categories, On Interpretation, Physics, De anima (On the Soul), Parts of Animals, Generation of Animals, Metaphysics.
Translations: the best general collection is *The Collected Works of Aristotle* ed. J. Barnes, 2 vols (Princeton, NJ: Princeton University Press, 1984). See also the commentaries and translations in the Clarendon Aristotle Series, especially those of *Categories and On Interpretation* by J.L. Ackrill, of *Metaphysics* iv–vi by C. Kirwan (Oxford: Clarendon Press, 1963, 1971), of *Parts of Animals I* and *Generation of Animals I* by David Balme (1972).

A useful collection of good translations can be found in *A New Aristotle Reader* ed. J.L. Ackrill (Oxford: Clarendon Press, 1987).
Editions and commentaries: W.D. Ross, *Aristotle's Metaphysics* (Oxford: Clarendon Press, 1924); M. Frede and G. Patzig, *Aristoteles: Metaphysik Z*, 2 vols (Munich: C.H. Beck, 1988); G. Fine, *On Ideas* (Oxford: Clarendon Press, 1993) (on the fragments of Aristotle's lost *Peri Ideon*, a critique of Plato's theory of forms).

BIBLIOGRAPHY

Ackrill, J.L.: *Aristotle the Philosopher* (Oxford: Oxford University Press, 1981).
Barnes, J.: *Aristotle* (Oxford: Oxford University Press, 1982).
Burnyeat, M.: 'Aristotle on understanding knowledge', in *Aristotle on Science: The Posterior Analytics* ed. E. Berti (Padua: Antenori, 1981), 97–139.
Furth, M., *Substance, Form, and Psyche: An Aristotelian Metaphysics* (Cambridge: Cambridge University Press, 1988).
Gill, M.L.: *Aristotle on Substance: The Paradox of Unity* (Princeton, NJ: Princeton University Press, 1989).
Hartman, E.: *Substance, Body, and Soul* (Princeton, NJ: Princeton University Press, 1978).
Irwin, T.H.: *Aristotle's First Principles* (Oxford: Clarendon Press, 1988).
Kosman, A.: 'Substance, being, and *energeia*', *Oxford Studies in Ancient Philosophy* 2 (1984), 121–49.
Lesher, J.: 'The role of *nous* in Aristotle's *Posterior Analytics*', *Phronesis* 18 (1973), 44–68.
Nussbaum, M.: 'Aristotle', in *Ancient Writers: Greece and Rome* ed. T.J. Luce (New York: Charles Scribner's Sons, 1982) vol. 1, 377–416.
Owen, G.E.L.: *Logic, Science, and Dialectic: Collected Papers in Ancient Philosophy* (London and Ithaca, NY: Cornell University Press, 1986).
Owens, J.: *The Doctrine of Being in the Aristotelian Metaphysics* (Toronto: University of Toronto Press, 1978).

Ross, W.D.: *Aristotle* 5th edn (London: Methuen, 1949).

Witt, C.: *Substance and Essence in Aristotle: An Interpretation of Metaphysics VII–IX* (Ithaca, NY: Cornell University Press, 1989).

MARTHA C. NUSSBAUM

Armstrong, David Malet (1926–) Australian philosopher, born in Melbourne and educated at the University of Sydney and Exeter College, Oxford. After Oxford, he spent a brief period teaching at Birkbeck College in the University of London, then seven years at the University of Melbourne. He held John Anderson's chair as Challis Professor of Philosophy in Sydney from 1964 until his retirement at the end of 1991.

Armstrong's work in philosophy ranges over many of the main issues in epistemology and metaphysics, where he has helped to shape philosophy's agenda and terms of debate. Several themes run through it all: it is always concerned to elaborate and defend a philosophy which is ontically economical, synoptic, and compatibly continuous with established results in the natural sciences. Accordingly, he has argued for a NATURALISM which holds all reality to be spatio-temporal, for a materialism (*see* PHYSICALISM, MATERIALISM) which aims to account for all mental phenomena without appeal beyond the categories of physical being, and for an EMPIRICISM which both vindicates and draws strength from the methods and successes of the natural sciences.

In *Perception and the Physical World* (1961), he confronted then-fashionable phenomenalist tendencies (*see* PHENOMENALISM) with a direct realism which had no place for sense data or other mentalistic items (*see* SENSA). He urged the objections to sense data from their indeterminacy, their hidden features, and the identification problems they face. He began also to develop a realist account of secondary qualities (*see* QUALITY, PRIMARY/SECONDARY).

A Materialist Theory of the Mind (1968) was the first full-dress presentation of central-state materialism, which identifies states of mind with states of the central nervous system (*see* MIND/BODY PROBLEM). The theory is as naturalistic as the behaviourism it aspired to supplant, yet much more plausible and scientifically fruitful as a philosophy of mind. Armstrong presents an analysis of mental phenomena in terms of what they are apt to cause, or be caused by, then proceeds to claim that the most likely items to fit those places in the causal networks of human perception, feeling, memory and action are structures, states and processes in the central nervous system. The view is refined in further essays. With hindsight, Armstrong's philosophy of mind counts as a type–type identity theory, a precursor of contemporary FUNCTIONALISM.

During the 1970s, Armstrong turned his attention to the problem of universals. In *Universals and Scientific Realism* (1978) he built a case for an immanent REALISM in which UNIVERSALS, and particulars (*see* UNIVERSALS AND PARTICULARS) are equally abstractions from states of affairs. The work has three principal themes: first, all the widely accepted varieties of NOMINALISM are deeply implausible. Second, an empiricist naturalism need not, and should not, bear the nominalist burden. Third, to establish the actual existence of any universal calls for a substantive enquiry for which the fundamental sciences alone are equipped.

This scientific realism about universals was promptly put to work in developing a philosophy of the laws which apparently govern the cosmos. *What is a Law of Nature?* (1983) argues that the regularity theories of law, deriving from HUME, are all fatally flawed (*see* LAW OF NATURE). It goes on to urge that laws relating particular states of affairs rest on a relation of necessitation holding between the universals involved.

Armstrong's next major project was *A Combinatorial Theory of Possibility* (1989). Here he attempts to build, from a foundation in the thought of WITTGENSTEIN's

Tractatus, an account of modality in which a spatio-temporal naturalism is upheld. Non-actual possibilities do not exist, nor are they given *ersatz* treatment. The attempt makes use of the idea of fictive reorderings of strictly actual cosmic constituents. Here again, Armstrong's doctrine about universals, as abstractions from states of affairs on an equal footing with particulars, stands him in good stead.

See also LOGICAL ATOMISM; MODALITIES AND POSSIBLE WORLDS.

WRITINGS

Perception and the Physical World (London: Routledge and Kegan Paul, 1961).
A Materialist Theory of the Mind (London: Routledge and Kegan Paul, 1968).
Universals and Scientific Realism, 2 vols, Vol. 1 *Nominalism and Realism*; Vol. 2 *A Theory of Universals* (Cambridge: Cambridge University Press, 1978).
The Nature of Mind and Other Essays (Brisbane: Queensland University Press, 1980).
What is a Law of Nature? (Cambridge: Cambridge University Press, 1983).
A Combinatorial Theory of Possibility (Cambridge: Cambridge University Press, 1989).

BIBLIOGRAPHY

Bacon, J.B., Campbell, K. and Reinhardt, L. eds: *Ontology, Causality, and Mind; Essays in honour of D.M. Armstrong* (Cambridge: Cambridge University Press, 1993).

KEITH CAMPBELL

Arnauld, Antoine (1612–94) A French Roman Catholic theologian and philosopher. Arnauld was born in Paris into a family associated with Jansenism. Angelique Arnauld, his sister, was abbess of PORT-ROYAL, which became, under her direction, a centre of Jansenism. One aspect of Jansenism is adherence to whatever view of the relation of divine grace to human freedom is expressed in *Augustinus*, a work written by Cornelius Jansen and published posthumously in 1640. Numerous Roman Catholics, including various popes, believed that the Jansenist account of grace is incompatible with the Roman Catholic dogma that divine grace can always be resisted by a free agent. Much of Arnauld's theological writings is devoted to a defence of the Jansenist account of divine grace and the claim that it is consistent with Roman Catholic dogma. Another important segment of Arnauld's theological writings concerns the role of the sacraments in the process of absolution, where Arnauld emphasized the attitude that the penitent must bring to the process if the sacrament is to absolve.

In connection with a school associated with Port-Royal Arnauld wrote or co-wrote three important textbooks that influenced seventeenth-century thought: *Grammaire générale et raisonnée* (1660), *La Logique, ou l'art de penser* (1662) and *Nouveaux éléments de géométrie* (1667).

In his Jansenist phase Arnauld offered and argued in favour of an historical approach to theology on the ground that the essential theological truths could be extracted from the work of the Fathers of the Church and, in particular, at least with respect to matters of divine grace and freedom, from the work of AUGUSTINE. He, therefore, strongly opposed what he took to be the innovative, speculative philosophical theology of LEIBNIZ and MALEBRANCHE. Criticism of Malebranche generated the majority of Arnauld's positive contributions to philosophy.

While Arnauld was a conservative in theology, he believed that scholastic philosophy had been exposed as inadequate by the seventeenth-century scientific revolution and Cartesian mechanics (*see* DESCARTES). In philosophy, Arnauld regarded himself as a Cartesian, specifically associating himself with Descartes's theses concerning the nature and origin of ideas, the idea of God, the distinction between the soul and the body, and the nature of MATTER. This may seem odd, given Arnauld's famous criticisms of Descartes' *Meditations on First Philosophy*, including a brilliant critique of Descartes' arguments intended to prove that the SOUL and body are distinct substances (*see* MIND/BODY PROBLEM), a critique of one of Descartes' arguments for the existence of God, a query concerning the possibility of avoiding circularity, given Descartes' way of establishing the principle of clear and distinct perception, and a criticism of Descartes' thesis that nothing occurs in the soul of which it is not conscious. Except for this last thesis, which Arnauld regarded as inessential to Descartes' programme, his criticisms were aimed at Descartes' arguments, not the conclusions of those arguments.

Arnauld criticized some of Descartes' doctrines because of their theological implications. The majority of Arnauld's criticisms of Malebranche centre on what he viewed as Malebranche's speculative and innovative contributions to theology. But in the process, Arnauld formulated a theory of perception, which he presented as a mere recasting of Descartes' theory, but which, in fact, involves many ideas original to Arnauld. Arnauld's theory of perception is contained in two works aimed at Malebranche: *Des vraies et des fausses idées* (1683) and *Défense de M. Arnauld, contre la réponse au livre des vraies et des fausses idées* (1684). In these works, Arnauld articulated and defended a subtle form of a direct realist position, based on an act theory of ideas, in which ideas are identified with representative acts of the mind rather than objects of the mind that serve as intermediaries between an act of the mind and the external reality thereby represented.

WRITINGS

Oeuvres de Messire Antoine Arnauld, docteur de la maison et société de Sorbonne 43 vols (Paris: 1775–839); repr. Brussels: Culture et Civilisation, 1967).

La Logique, ou l'art de penser (Paris: 1662); ed. and trans. J. Dickoff and P. James (Indianapolis: 1964).

On True and False Ideas, New Objections to Descartes' Meditations and Descartes' Replies (Cologne: 1683); trans. E.J. Kremer (Lewiston–Queenston–Lampeter: Edwin Mellen Press, 1990).

BIBLIOGRAPHY

Nadler, S.M.: *Arnauld and the Cartesian Philosophy of Ideas* (Princeton, NJ: Princeton University Press, 1989).
Ndiaye, A.R.: *La Philosophie d'Antoine Arnauld* (Paris: J. Vrin, 1991).

ROBERT C. SLEIGH, JR

artefact Any object produced to design by skilled action. Artefacts are continuants, that is, objects persisting in time: an event such as a pianist's performance is itself an action and not the persisting product of one. Artefacts are not exclusively human: consider a beaver's dam, or the cosmos viewed by creationists. But the most elaborate artefacts we know, requiring conscious planning, training and sophisticated forms of representation, are human: levels of culture are even measured by the kinds of artefacts people produce, from stone axes to moon rockets. Artefacts contrast with natural objects: ARISTOTLE considered artefacts, defined by function rather than an autonomous principle of unity and persistence, not to be substances. Mechanistic world views tend to blur this distinction. The identity conditions (*see* INDIVIDUATION) of artefacts are however vaguer and more convention-bound than those of natural objects: the puzzle of the Ship of Theseus notably concerns an artefact.

BIBLIOGRAPHY

Aristotle: *Physics* ed. W.D. Ross (Oxford: Clarendon Press, 1950) Bk 2, 192.
Hobbes, T.: *De corpore* (London: 1655); in his *Opera philosophica* ed. W. Molesworth (London: 1839) vol. I, Part II, ch. 11.

Wiggins, D.: *Sameness and Substance* (Oxford: Blackwell, 1980), esp. ch. 3.

PETER SIMONS

associationism Associationism is the attempt to explain mental phenomena through relations among mental contents and representations – particularly relations such as contiguity or simultaneity, resemblance and constant conjunction – that cause them to become associated with one another. Although ARISTOTLE, HOBBES and SPINOZA, among others, described phenomena of association, associationism as a psychological programme achieved its greatest influence in eighteenth- and nineteenth-century Britain. LOCKE was the first to use the term 'association of ideas', but he used it only to describe a cause of error, in which accidental or logically irrelevant relations among ideas usurp the role of logical relations. BERKELEY put association to more positive and extensive use in *An Essay towards a New Theory of Visions* (1709), arguing that visual perception of distance is the result of an association between certain kinds of visual ideas and certain kinds of non-resembling tactile ideas, an association resulting from their repeated conjunction in past experience. David HUME's cognitive psychology gives a fundamental role to three 'principles of association': contiguity, resemblance and causation, the latter based on 'constant conjunction'. Hume uses these relations to explain both the formation of complex ideas from simpler ideas, and the succession of ideas in thought. For Berkeley and Hume, in particular, the association of ideas provided a way of explaining mental phenomena without presupposing intellectual insight into the metaphysical structure of the world. David Hartley (1705–57), a physician and Hume's contemporary, also sought to explain a variety of mental phenomena associationistically, proposing to explain the influence of associative relations through their relation to 'vibrations' in the brain. Later associationists included Thomas Brown (1778–1820), James Mill (1773– 1836), JOHN STUART MILL and Alexander Bain (1818–1903).

BIBLIOGRAPHY

Bain, A.: *Mental Science* (New York: 1868); (New York: Arno Press, 1973).
Bain, A.: *The Senses and the Intellect* 4th edn (New York: Appleton, 1894).
Berkeley, G.: *The Works of George Berkeley, Bishop of Cloyne* ed. A.A. Luce and T.E. Jessop, 9 vols (London and New York: Nelson, 1948–57).
Brown, T.: *Inquiry into the Relation of Cause and Effect* (Edinburgh: 1806); repr. as *The Doctrine of Mr. Hume: Concerning the Relation of Cause and Effect* (New York: Garland, 1983).
Hartley, D.: *Observations on Man, His Frame, His Duty, and His Expectations* (London: 1749); (New York: Garland, 1971).
Hume, D.: *An Enquiry concerning Human Understanding* (London: 1777); in *Enquiries concerning Human Understanding and concerning the Principles of Morals* ed. L.A. Selby-Bigge (Oxford: Clarendon Press, 1893); 3rd edn rev. P.H. Nidditch (Oxford: Clarendon Press, 1975).
Hume, D.: *A Treatise of Human Nature* (London: 1839–40); ed. L.A. Selby-Bigge (Oxford: Clarendon Press, 1888); 2nd edn rev. P.H. Nidditch (Oxford: Clarendon Press, 1978).
Locke, J.: *An Essay concerning Human Understanding* (London: 1690); ed. P.H. Nidditch (Oxford: Clarendon Press, 1975).
Mill, J.: *Analysis of the Phenomena of the Human Mind* (London: Longmans, 1829).
Mill, J.S.: *An Examination of Sir William Hamilton's Philosophy* (London and Boston: Spencer, 1865).

DON GARRETT

atomism Atomism takes the world to be made up of indivisible and imperceptibly small material units. (*Atomos* in Greek means indivisible.) The diverse qualities of perceptible bodies are to be explained by the simple quantitative properties of the atoms composing them. Perceptible changes are to be understood as rearrangements of the underlying atoms. In its origins, atomism was primarily a metaphysical doctrine; it was not, indeed, until the early nineteenth century that the atomic hypothesis was linked tightly enough to the explanation of specific empirical data to count as physical theory in the familiar modern sense.

EARLY ATOMISM

The first atomist doctrines are best understood as a response to the challenge of Parmenides' analysis of change. Parmenides argued that, despite the evidence of our senses, our reason compels us to conclude that change is illusory. Being obviously cannot just come to be from Non-Being or abruptly cease to be. And where one sort of Being appears to become another sort, the difference must itself count as Being, so that there is no real change. Being is thus ultimately immutable and one. For a 'physics', that is, an account of the regularities of perceived change, to be possible, this paradoxical conclusion had to be overcome.

The atomism of Leucippus and Democritus retained something of Parmenides' sharp dichotomy being Being and Non-Being, while modifying it in two fundamental respects. Instead of one Being, there is an infinite multitude of indistinguishable beings, each (like the Parmenidean original) one and immutable. And instead of Non-Being, there is the Void in which atoms can move. The Void is almost Non-Being; indeed, Democritus calls it Nothing. But it is just sufficient to make change possible, though only one kind of change, local motion. Thus all change must (despite appearances) reduce to local motion of entities that themselves must be imperceptibly small since no local motion is actually perceived when, for example, a leaf changes colour. Likewise, the manifold qualitative differences between perceptible things must reduce to differences of atomic configuration, size and shape. And since the analysis is a perfectly general one, it must extend to *all* things, to soul, for

example, whose atomic constituents presumably are small and round so that they can direct the vital functions of the living body. Atomism in this 'pure' form thus entails a strongly reductionist form of materialism. Its appeal is to the coherence of its very general account of change, though there are hints of a more specific sort of warrant also; evaporation and condensation are said to be explained by different degrees of 'packing' of atoms, for example.

Though atomism itself was not immediately influential, the atomic metaphor can be found everywhere in the philosophic thinking of Parmenides' successors. One finds hints of it in Empedocles' four elements, in Anaxagoras' seeds, and in PLATO's elemental geometrical shapes. ARISTOTLE proposed an alternative analysis of change in terms of matter, form and privation that countered Parmenides' doctrine without yielding to the reductionism and lack of teleology that he found so objectionable in the atomist proposal. Yet Aristotle also objected to Anaxagoras' assumption that physical things can be divided without limits. There are, he said, least natural parts. The limits of divisibility depend on the kind of thing being divided.

This suggestion was the occasion for a vast and ingenious elaboration among later Aristotelian commentators of the doctrine of the *minima naturalia*, that is, of the conceptual limits of physical divisibility. AVERROES and his later followers seem to have been the first to present these 'least parts' as separately existent, indeed as potentially capable by their intermixing of explaining the qualitative changes we today call chemical. Such Renaissance Aristotelians as Julius Caesar Scaliger (1484–1558) and Agostino Nifo (1473–1538) propounded a doctrine of *minima* which was close to atomism in significant ways, since the *minima* were regarded as real constituents whose manner of union explains the properties of sensible bodies. What separated these philosophers from Democritean atomism was their commitment to matter-form composition, and especially to the role of substantial form in making the product of the union of *minima* into a qualitatively new kind of thing.

TRANSITION

With the seventeenth century the transformation of a philosophic doctrine into a physical theory began. Most of the natural philosophers of the century subscribed to the 'corpuscular philosophy'. Though it had roots in classical atomism (here the role of GASSENDI in modifying and popularizing the ancient doctrine was important) and in *minima* theory (the main spokesman here being Daniel Sennert (1572–1657)), the more important motivation came from the 'new science' of mechanics. If mechanics were to be as all-explanatory as its exponents expected it to be, the primary properties of things had to be those which made things subject to mechanical law: size, shape, mobility, solidity and, perhaps eventually, mass. Other properties (the 'secondary' ones) would then have to be explicable in terms of the primary ones (*see* QUALITY, PRIMARY/SECONDARY).

This requires explanation in terms of something like atoms. Since, however, the atoms do not have to be strictly indivisible, the term 'corpuscle' was preferred. But how were these invisible corpuscles to be known? How, in practice, could their sizes, shapes, and motions explain such a property as yellowness? LOCKE was pessimistic about the prospects of linking the two sorts of properties in a demonstrative science, though he suggested that plausible analogies might yield at least a weak kind of probability.

Meanwhile, chemists were trying to understand chemical combination in corpuscular and quantitative terms. Robert Boyle (1627–91) proposed that the corpuscles constituting the chemical elements could combine to form complex corpuscles that yielded chemical compounds. He conceded that the former might themselves be 'primary concretions', composites made up of Democritean atoms. But in practice, these primary concretions could be regar-

ded as basic from the point of view of the chemist because they remained unaltered through chemical change. The problem was how to decide which concretions *were* primary, how to distinguish element from compound. Boyle could not discover a consistent way to carry this all-important distinction through.

By the end of the century the separation between philosophers and scientists (as the latter would come to be called) was widening. Scientists were convinced of the underlying corpuscular character of the world, but they had no real evidence (as evidence in natural science was coming to be understood) in support of their hypothesis. There was as yet no satisfactory atomic theory.

ATOMIC THEORY

Atomic theory took shape only very gradually, and in two different parts of natural science, in chemistry first and later in the physics of gases. The Newtonian project of organizing chemical research around short-range laws of force operating between corpuscles proved fruitless (*see* NEWTON). Careful weighing of the products of chemical combination ultimately, in the hands of Antoine Lavoisier (1743–94), yielded the first victory. Aided by the assumption that weight is conserved through chemical change, Lavoisier provided for the first time a reliable way of distinguishing element from compound, enabling him to identify many of the commonest elements. Joseph Louis Proust (1754–1826) proposed that each compound is made up of elements combined in a constant way. But it was John Dalton (1766–1844) in *A New System of Chemical Philosophy* (1808) who drew from the ancient notion of atom the crucial clue. He proposed that the simplest underlying structure that would explain the empirically established laws of definite proportions (a compound contains fixed proportions by weight of its constituents) and of equivalent proportions (the ratio of the weights of *a* and *b* that react with a given amount of *c* is independent of *c*), was an atomic one. Each atom of an element is like any other atom of that element; each element is constituted by a different kind of atom. Compounds are formed by a simple and uniform juxtaposition of elemental atoms in compound particles (molecules). The key to chemical analysis is thus the determination of relative atomic weights.

This turned out to be a more difficult matter than Dalton had anticipated, and the contributions of many other researchers (notable among them Joseph Louis Gay-Lussac (1788–1850), Amedeo Avogadro (1776–1856) and Stanislao Cannizzaro (1826–1910)) were needed before the atomic model of chemical change was established to the satisfaction of chemists generally. The kinetic theory of gases followed in physics; many of the physical properties of gases were shown to be derivable from the hypothesis that gases are made up of vast numbers of molecules in rapid motion. Despite this convergence of chemistry and physics, empiricists like MACH argued that the notable successes of the atomic hypothesis did not warrant belief in the actual existence of atoms and molecules. Atomic theory was acceptable as a calculational device but no more. The debate was once more philosophical, though numerous scientific issues were also involved. Only after Einstein made use of the molecular hypothesis in 1905–6 to derive in a strikingly detailed way the main parameters of Brownian motion did the critics concede. Not that scientific realism would from henceforward be immune to challenge!

From Democritus to Einstein is a long road, and the atom of modern quantum theory bears little resemblance to the immutable qualityless particle of the first atomists. But the claim that the world around us consists of a swarm of imperceptible entities whose properties can causally explain the properties of that larger world evokes echoes all along that road. The transition from metaphysical doctrine to physical theory has no clearer illustrative example.

BIBLIOGRAPHY

Furley, D.J.: *Two Studies in the Greek Atomists* (Princeton, NJ: Princeton University Press, 1967).

Kirk, G.S., Raven, J.E. and Schofield, M.: *The Presocratic Philosophers* 2nd edn (Cambridge: Cambridge University Press, 1983), 402–33.

Lasswitz, K.: *Geschichte der Atomistik vom Mittelalter bis Newton* 2 vols (Hamburg: Voss, 1890).

Nash, L.: *The Atomic-Molecular Theory* (Cambridge, MA: Harvard University Press, 1950).

Nye, M.J.: *Molecular Reality* (London: Macdonald, 1972).

van Melsen, A.G.: *From Atomos to Atom* (Pittsburgh: Duquesne University Press, 1952).

ERNAN McMULLIN

Augustine of Hippo, St (354–430) Theologian, born in North Africa. Augustine drew his metaphysics from 'the Platonic philosophers, who said that the true God is at once the author of things, the illuminator of truth, and the giver of happiness' (*City of God* 8.5). He knew Latin versions of PLOTINUS and of his disciple and editor Porphyry (AD *c*.232–*c*.303). These pagan Platonists – 'Neoplatonists' (*see* NEOPLATONISM) to us – were the chief instrument of his rescue from Manichean dualism and from Ciceronian scepticism at the time when, as a 31-year-old teacher in Milan, he resumed the Christianity of his childhood and planned the little African philosophical community whose life was to be cut short by his ordination (AD 391) four years later. His philosophical education was Latin, and narrow, enriched during his career as a Christian controversialist only by the Bible.

According to Augustine there are three 'natures', i.e. kinds of SUBSTANCE: corporeal, which are mutable in time and place; spiritual, mutable in time only; and God, immutable (*De Genesi ad litteram* 8.20.39).

37

Souls are not corporeal since they see and judge 'similitudes' which are not corporeal; therefore God is not corporeal either (*City of God* 8.5). Among non-corporeal beings are angels and demons, but at most one God since only what is supreme is divine (*De vera religione* 25.46). Everything is from God, since all good things are from God and everything is good (*De natura boni* 3); miracles differ from natural events only in not proceeding 'by an ordinary route' (*De Trinitate* 3.6.11). The 'perfectly ordinary course of nature' is the regular (and planned) unfolding of causal or seminal reasons (*De Genesi ad litteram* 9.17.32), which date from the creation when God 'completed' his work (ibid. 6.11.18–19). These reasons do not all necessitate (ibid. 6.15.26). At some places Augustine's conception of God seems to combine the two roles, cause of truth and cause of knowledge, assigned by PLATO to the form of the good: the latter role makes God the only teacher (*De magistro*), illuminator of truths as the sun illuminates visible things (*De libero arbitrio* 2.13.36); the former makes him 'truth itself' (ibid.).

Following Varro (116–27 BC), Augustine proposed that 'the question what a man is is the question whether he is both [a body and a soul], or only a body, or only a soul' (*De moribus ecclesiae catholicae* 4.6). He chose the first answer, but felt forced to conclude that 'the *way* in which spirits adhere to bodies and become animals is altogether mysterious' (*City of God* 21.10.1).

His celebrated investigation of time in *Confessions* 11 and *City of God* 11–12 meets the pagan challenge against creationism, 'Why *then?*', with a response developed from Philo Judaeus (*c.*20 BC–AD *c.*50) that God made time too; follows Plotinus and anticipates BOETHIUS in a perplexing account of eternity; and wrestles with ARISTOTLE's puzzle how times can exist, since they are all past, future or durationless (Augustine's speculative solution, arising from his insight that we measure times by memorizing their length, is that they are affections of the mind).

His various writings on FREE WILL provided materials for both parties in the Reformation debates, for example between Erasmus and Luther, which set the scene for modern treatments of the subject. He failed to find a consistent response to the contrary pressures on him, arguing (e.g. in *De correptione et gratia* against the Pelagians) that God's prevenient grace cannot be resisted, but refusing to repudiate his earlier argument (e.g. in *De libero arbitrio* against the Manichees) that some evils are, and others punish, sins freely committed.

WRITINGS

Augustine's works are in *Patrologiae cursus completus, series latina* ed. J.P. Migne, vols 32–47 (Paris: 1844–55) (*PL*); many are also in *Corpus scriptorum ecclesiasticorum latinorum* (Vienna: Tempsky, 1866–) (*CSEL*), and in *Corpus christianorum, series latina* (Turnhout: Brepols, 1953–) (*CCL*). Various of his works are translated into English in: *A Select Library of the Nicene and Post-Nicene Fathers of the Christian Church* ed. P. Schaff (New York: The Christian Literature Co., first series 1886–8; repr. Grand Rapids, MI: Wm B. Eerdmans, 1971–80) (*NPNF*); *Library of Christian Classics* ed. J. Baillie, J.T. McNeill and H.P. van Dusen (Philadelphia: Westminster Press, 1953–) (*LCC*); *Fathers of the Church* ed. R.J. Deferrari *et al.* (Washington, DC: Catholic University of America Press, 1947–) (*FC*); *Ancient Christian Writers* ed. J. Quasten and J.C. Plumpe (Westminster, MD: Newman Press, 1946–) (*ACW*); *Basic Writings of Saint Augustine* (New York: Random House, 1948) (*BW*). A useful compendium of excerpts in translation is: *The Essential Augustine* ed. V.J. Bourke, 2nd edn (Indianapolis: Hackett, 1974). The list below is of works cited; numbers denote volumes.

De moribus ecclesiae catholicae (AD 387–9): *PL* 32; trans. *NPNF* 4, *FC* 56, *BW* 1.

De libero arbitrio (AD 388, 391–5): *PL* 32, *CSEL* 74, *CCL* 29; trans. *LCC* 6, *ACW* 22, *FC* 59, and elsewhere.

De magistro (AD 389): *PL* 32, *CSEL* 77, *CCL*

29; *trans. LCC* 6, *ACW* 9, *FC* 59, *BW* 1, and elsewhere.

De vera religione (AD 391): *PL* 34, *CSEL* 77, *CCL* 32; trans. *LCC* 6, and elsewhere.

Confessions (*Confessiones*, AD 397–401): *PL* 32, *CSEL* 33, and elsewhere; trans. *NPNF* 1, *LCC* 7, *FC* 21, *BW*, and elsewhere; text and (old) translation also in Loeb Classical Library (London: Heinemann; Cambridge, MA: Harvard University Press, 1912).

De natura boni (AD 399): *PL* 42, *CSEL* 25.2; trans. *NPNF* 4, *LCC* 6, *BW* 1.

De trinitate (AD 399–419): *PL* 42, *CCL* 50, 50A; trans. *NPNF* 3, *FC* 45.

De genesi ad litteram (AD 401–14); *PL* 34, *CSEL* 28.1; trans. *ACW* 41–2.

City of God (*De civitate Dei contra paganos*, AD 413–26): *PL* 41, *CSEL* 40, *CCL* 47–8, and elsewhere; trans. *NPNF* 2, *FC* 8, 14, 24; text and translation also in Loeb Classical Library (London: Heinemann and Cambridge, MA: Harvard University Press, 1966–72).

De correptione et gratia (AD 426): *PL* 44; trans. *NPNF* 5, *FC* 2.

BIBLIOGRAPHY

Kirwan, C.A.: *Augustine* (London and New York: Routledge, 1989).

Kirwan, C.A.: 'Augustine on souls and bodies', in *Logica, mente e persona* ed. A. Alberti (Florence: Olschki, 1990), 207–41.

Markus, R.A.: *Later Greek and Early Medieval Philosophy* ed. A.H. Armstrong (Cambridge: Cambridge University Press, 1967), chs 21–7.

Sorabji, R.R.K.: *Time, Creation and the Continuum* (London: Duckworth, 1983).

CHRISTOPHER KIRWAN

Averroes, [Ibn Rushd] (1126–98) Spanish-Islamic philosopher who lived in Cordoba and Seville, a thoroughgoing Aristotelian, wrote commentaries on most of ARISTOTLE's works, but is better known in Islam as the defender of philosophy against the attacks by al-Ghazali (1058–1111), in *The Incoherence of the Philosophers* and as a reconciler of philosophy and religion.

The Aristotelian commentaries were based on excellent translations that gave reliable access to Aristotle without Neoplatonic eyes (*see* ALFARABI; NEOPLATONISM), and thus played an important role in the Latin and Jewish Aristotelian tradition.

In his *Incoherence of the Incoherence* Averroes takes up Ghazali's attacks on Alfarabi and AVICENNA. To safeguard God's omnipotence Ghazali had rejected their claim of a necessary connection between cause and effect. According to Ghazali, such necessity is not given in observation. All we see is a temporal sequence between, say, fire and cotton burning. God, the only agent, causes the occurrence of fire, the burning of cotton and the coincidence which it becomes our habit to expect.

Against this Averroes argued that to deny cause is to deny knowledge. It is also to deny human agency and the distinction between the voluntary and the involuntary. Further, it violates the view that things have a real nature. Finally, if there is no regularity nor design in creation, we cannot infer a wise Agent.

Resting on Aristotelian grounds, Averroes criticized Avicenna for confusing the logical and metaphysical features of being by making the definitional separation of essence and existence characteristic also of existing things, thus espousing an un-Aristotelian ESSENTIALISM. A similar confusion is said to occur with respect of the numerical and the metaphysical one. (See Shehadi 1982, pp. 93–111 for a fairer view of Avicenna.)

On the doctrine of creation Averroes argues that creation *ex nihilo* of both world and time does not have Qur'ānic support. On the contrary, some verses (11:6, 41:10) suggest that matter and time pre-existed with God, making Aristotle's God consistent with Scripture.

WRITINGS

Tahāfut al-Tahāfut ed. M. Bouyges (Beyrouth: 1930); trans. S. van den Bergh *The Inco-*

herence of the Incoherence 2 vols (London: Luzac, 1954).

BIBLIOGRAPHY

Fakhry, M.: *A History of Islamic Philosophy* (New York: Columbia University Press, 1970).
Fakhry, M.: *Islamic Occasionalism and its Critique by Averroes and Aquinas* (London: Allen and Unwin, 1958).
Kogan, B.S.: *Averroes and the Metaphysics of Causation* (Albany, NY: SUNY Press, 1985).
Mehren, I.: 'Etudes sur la philosophie d'Averroes concernant ses rapports avec celle d'Avicenna et de Ghazzali', *Muséon* VII (1888–9).
Shehadi, F.: *Metaphysics in Islamic Philosophy* (Delmar: Caravan Books, 1982).

FADLOU SHEHADI

Avicenna [Ibn Sīnā] (980–1037) Islamic philosopher. Avicenna was the most systematic and sophisticated, as well as the most influential of Islamic philosophers, although much of his thought is already in ALFARABI.

Being is a primary intuition of the soul. It can be known without the mediation of any other concept, and it cannot be defined without circularity. Even 'thing', its co-equal in extension, presupposes being and cannot be used in explaining it without circularity. Being is the most general concept; its opposite is the absolute nothing.

On the relation between essence and existence in Avicenna one must distinguish three contexts in which these could be related (*see* ESSENCE/ACCIDENT; ESSENTIALISM). First, the logical, where in any definition, say, of a horse, existence must be excluded from the essence of a horse. Excluded also is any property that is not part of what a horse is, even 'universal'. For although a horse *qua* essence is universal, i.e. applies to many, being universal is not part of what makes a horse a *horse*.

Second, the metaphysical context: essence and existence are inseparable in individual things. While 'existence' and 'one' are distinct from the *meaning* of 'horse', they are metaphysically part of what makes a horse *this* horse, and are not accidental to it *qua* substance.

Third is the theological context. Following Alfarabi, Avicenna divides beings into the possible in itself, though necessary through another, and the necessary in itself. The existence of the former is contingent and its non-existence possible, while the non-existence of the Necessary Being is impossible. God gives existence to all contingent beings. And while existence is a necessary feature of a thing *qua* substance, it is accidental to it *qua* contingent.

Avicenna reproduces the emanationist scheme of Alfarabi. The soul being an emanation of the Active Intellect turns to this intermediary between humans and God for knowledge and mystical illumination.

BIBLIOGRAPHY

Fakhry, M.: *A History of Islamic Philosophy* (New York: Columbia University Press, 1970).
Goichon, A.M.: *La Distinction de l'essence et de l'existence d'après Ibn Sīnā* (Paris: Desclée, 1937).
Goodman, L.: *Avicenna* (London: Routledge, 1992).
Gutas, D.: *Avicenna and the Aristotelian Tradition: Introduction to Reading Avicenna's Philosophical Works* (Leiden: E.J. Brill, 1988).
Shehadi, F.: *Metaphysics in Islamic Philosophy* (Delmar: Caravan Books, 1982).

FADLOU SHEHADI

avowals The verb 'to avow' has been adopted by many philosophers of mind as the translation of the German verb *äussern*. The usual alternative translations are 'to express' or 'to utter'.

In WITTGENSTEIN's later work avowals are the keystone of a new philosophy of mind, founded on the rejection of the Cartesian idea that a person discloses the contents of his mind by identifying inner objects and describing them (*see* DESCARTES). According to Wittgenstein, an avowal of an intention is not based on a self-examination which parallels the investigation of the world around us: it is only marginally liable to error, and in certain cases is an artificial expression of the intention replacing a natural one (e.g. a raised fist). Each of these three points makes its contribution to the new philosophy of mind, which some of Wittgenstein's followers have accepted in its entirety and which, perhaps, nobody can totally reject. But the third point may be the most important one, because it shows how language can develop directly out of behaviour which antedates it. This makes it possible to explain how we can learn, and communicate with, mentalistic language, which were things that remained mysterious when intentions, feelings, and so on, were treated as private objects. So it prepares the way for a naturalistic, rather than an intellectualist answer to scepticism about other minds.

BIBLIOGRAPHY

Malcolm, N.: *Nothing is Hidden* (Oxford: Blackwell, 1986), esp. ch. 8.
Wittgenstein, L.: *Philosophical Investigations* trans. G.E.M. Anscombe, 3rd edn (London: Macmillan, 1969).

DAVID PEARS

Ayer, Alfred Jules (1910–89) British philosopher. Ayer was famous for the attack on metaphysics in his *Language, Truth and Logic* (1936). According to the verification criterion of meaning (*see* LOGICAL POSITIVISM; PRINCIPLE OF VERIFIABILITY), only analytic or synthetic statements were meaningful, and synthetic statements were understood to be ultimately verifiable in sense experience. One intention of the verification criterion was to rule out as meaningless the wordy, but empirically uncheckable claims of metaphysicians in the Hegelian tradition. But while the criter-

ion did allow those who held it to dismiss much of HEGEL's *Science of Logic* (1812–16), say, without the trouble of reading it, it had the not so welcome effect of rendering meaningless such unverifiable statements as 'Every event has a cause' or even 'For every action, there is an equal and opposite reaction.' Even the proposal Ayer made to treat these statements as heuristic aids to living and to scientific enquiry implicitly admitted their meaningfulness. For reasons outlined in later editions of *Language, Truth and Logic* the verification criterion was dropped by Ayer, and metaphysics, at least in a certain sense, re-admitted to the canon of meaningful discourse.

Ayer remained sceptical to the end of his life concerning the pretensions of some metaphysicians to inform us of any suprasensible reality, or to delineate the most general characteristics of being as such. Nevertheless, in another sense, in much of his philosophy subsequent to *Language, Truth and Logic* he was engaged in metaphysical enquiry. Although the motivation of his philosophy was largely epistemological, concerning the status of our claims to knowledge, many of its conclusions were metaphysical, concerning what there actually is. Indeed, throughout the whole of his philosophical career, Ayer was concerned about the nature of physical objects in particular. There is, in fact, an interesting transition in Ayer's work from the phenomenalistic stance (*see* PHENOMENALISM) of *Language, Truth and Logic* to the sophisticated REALISM of *The Central Questions of Philosophy* (1976).

Ayer always rejected what he called naive realism. That is to say, he denied that objects are just as they appear. He was further convinced that there was an inference involved in any transition from appearance to object, on the grounds that there is always more involved in assertions about objects than is available to us in our perceptions. What, then, is the relation between the objects and the perceptions?

Ayer came to reject phenomenalism on the grounds that the percepts that are presented even to the totality of observers are

41

too scanty to answer to our conception of the physical world. He also rejected the causal theory of perception, largely because that theory would render the causes of our perceptions unobservable occupants of an unobservable space. Instead he proposed what he called a construction, in which the subject of experience is initially presented with a mass of sensory data; he then begins to perceive patterns within this data, which tend to cluster in predictable ways. At a certain stage in the process, the clusters or 'visuo-tactual continuants' as Ayer calls them are 'cut loose from their moorings' and regarded as having an existence quite independent of their being perceived.

Our common-sense view of the world is thus seen as a theory relative to our perceptions; but it is a theory, which once accepted, ontologically downgrades the perceptions on which it was originally based.

It cannot be said that everything about this construction is clear. Ayer denies that he is telling a psychological story about how children actually learn about the physical world, but he insists that 'an exercise of the imagination' is required in the passage from percepts to objects. He also insists that under the dominion of the theory our imagination has led us to, the existence of physical objects becomes a matter of objective fact, and he denies the possibility of any straightforward phenomenalist reduction. At the same time, the suspicion remains that there is a sense in Ayer's story in which sense qualia (*see* SENSA), rather than objects, are the basic stuff of the world. On this point Ayer himself would probably have said – as he did on related issues – that the matter is ultimately undecidable. It is just a matter of decision, based on experiential coherence of any story we tell. If this was indeed his attitude, it would certainly be in a direct line of descent from his earlier repudiation of metaphysics as meaningless.

WRITINGS

Language, Truth and Logic (1936) 2nd edn (London: Victor Gollancz, 1946).
The Problem of Knowledge (Harmondsworth: Pelican, 1956).
The Central Questions of Philosophy (Harmondsworth: Pelican, 1976).

BIBLIOGRAPHY

Foster, J.: *Ayer* (London: Routledge and Kegan Paul, 1985).

ANTHONY O'HEAR

B

---

bare particular Bare particulars are the individuators of concrete objects. The basis for this contention can be articulated only if the problem of INDIVIDUATION is placed in the broader context of the issues raised by the relationship between a concrete object and its properties. For it is an antecedent commitment to property realism (*see* UNIVERSALS) and anti-essentialism (*see* ESSENCE/ACCIDENT; ESSENTIALISM) that provide key premises in the argument for bare particulars.

An account of the relationship must explain two features: (1) some objects have properties in common with other objects; yet (2) no object is identical with any other object. According to REALISM, the properties of objects are universals. Hence, if two objects have a property in common, say redness, the redness of one object is *identical* with the redness of the other. The realist has three basic options available for explaining (2): (a) non-identical objects differ in the universals they instantiate; (b) non-identical objects differ in some feature *other than* the universals they instantiate; and (c) the noni-dentity of objects is primitive.

Option (a) is associated with the view, often called the BUNDLE THEORY, that concrete objects are complex entities whose sole constituents are universals. Proponents of bare particulars, such as BERGMANN, reject this view on the grounds that (i) it is committed to the necessary truth of the principle of the IDENTITY OF INDISCERNIBLES; but (ii) the principle is not a necessary truth. Option (c) is rejected on the grounds that the non-identity of objects is insufficiently fundamental to be taken as primitive.

Theories exercising option (b) fall into two broad categories depending on their explanation of identity through time. Concrete objects typically change their properties over time while remaining the same object. One explanation is that there is a constituent of every object which endures through time and remains unchanged despite the changes in the object itself. Furthermore, this enduring constituent, often called a SUBSTANCE, has some of its properties essentially. Since proponents of bare particulars are anti-essentialists, they reject this explanation. Instead, they maintain that a concrete object is a temporal series of momentary objects which stand in some complex contingent lawlike relations (*see* TEMPORAL PARTS/STAGES). The endurance of an object through time is explained in terms of the obtaining of these contingent relations among the momentary objects. Change is explained by differences in the properties of successive momentary objects.

Bare particulars are the individuators of momentary concrete objects. Such particulars differ from substances in two significant ways: (1) they are momentary entities rather than continuants; and (2) they have no essential properties. The particularity of bare particulars consists in the fact that it is impossible for the same bare particular to be a constituent of two different momentary concrete objects. Since difference in bare particulars is sufficient to insure difference in any two momentary objects, even two with all properties in common, the theory is not committed to the necessary truth of the identity of indiscernibles. There are two important features of the relationship between a bare parti-

43

cular and the universals it instantiates. Universals exist only if instantiated by some bare particular and bare particulars exist only if they instantiate some universal. Neither is capable of independent existence. Furthermore, the instantiation of a universal by a bare particular requires a nexus. A nexus, unlike a relation, can unite two distinct entities into a complex without some further relation. Hence, a momentary object is a complex entity, often called a fact, whose constituents must include a bare particular, a nexus, and a universal.

There are two familiar objections to bare particulars. The first alleges that theories invoking them are incompatible with an empiricist epistemology (*see* EMPIRICISM). This objection rests on the claim, articulated in Allaire (1963), that, according to empiricism, the basic entities of an ontological theory must be entities with which we are directly acquainted. This claim, however, ties empiricism to PHENOMENALISM in a manner few contemporary empiricists would accept. The second alleges that the theory is incoherent since its central thesis, 'Bare particulars instantiate properties', is equivalent to 'Entities which have no properties have properties' which is self-contradictory. But, as Loux (1978) points out, a bare particular is *not* an entity which has no properties but one none of whose properties is *essential*. Loux, however, maintains that the latter thesis is itself problematic since bare particulars have essentially the property of having no properties essentially. This contention rests on the assumption that the predicate 'has no properties essentially' designates a property, and this is denied by Bergmann (1967) and Armstrong (1978).

Critics also allege that bare particulars are unnecessary and have little explanatory value. Proponents of the theory maintain that an adequate account of the non-identity of two concrete objects must 'ground' it in some difference in the constituents of the objects. Yet, they also maintain that the non-identity of two bare particulars is a primitive fact. It is not evident, as Hochberg (1965) contends, that explaining the non-identity of objects in terms of constituents whose non-identity is primitive is more illuminating than maintaining that the non-identity of the objects themselves is primitive. Proponents of the bundle theory, such as Russell (1948) and Casullo (1988), argue that it is a *contingent* truth that concrete particulars are complexes of universals and that this view does *not* commit them to the *necessary* truth of the identity of indiscernibles. They also maintain that the purported counterexamples to the necessary truth of the principle are questionable.

BIBLIOGRAPHY

Allaire, E.B.: 'Bare particulars', *Philosophical Studies* 14 (1963), 1–8.

Armstrong, D.M.: *Universals and Scientific Realism* 2 vols, Vol. 1, *Nominalism and Realism* (Cambridge: Cambridge University Press, 1978).

Bergmann, G.: *Realism: A Critique of Brentano and Meinong* (Madison, WI: University of Wisconsin Press, 1967).

Casullo, A.: 'A fourth version of the bundle theory', *Philosophical Studies* 54 (1988), 125–39.

Hochberg, H.: 'Universals, particulars, and predication', *Review of Metaphysics* 19 (1965), 87–102.

Loux, M.: *Substance and Attribute* (Dordrecht: Reidel Publishing Company, 1978).

Russell, B.: *Human Knowledge: Its Scope and Limits* (New York: Simon and Schuster, 1948).

ALBERT CASULLO

basic action Basic actions, broadly characterized, differ from non-basic actions in not being performed by way of the agent's performing another action.

The term was introduced in Danto (1963), where the following analysis is offered: '*B* is a *basic action* of *a* if and only if (i) *B* is an action and (ii) whenever *a* performs *B*, there is no other action *A* performed by *a* such that *B* is caused by *A*.' This analysis fails for a variety of reasons (see Goldman, 1970; Hornsby, 1980). The fundamental problem (or a symptom thereof) is that the difference between basic and non-basic actions does not hinge on causal transactions of the kind specified in (ii). Typically, when an agent does one thing *by* doing another, the latter is more basic than the former. If by moving her right index finger upward Jane flips a switch, and by flipping the switch illuminates the room, Jane's moving her finger upward is more basic than her flipping the switch, and both are more basic than her illuminating the room. However, Jane's moving her finger does not *cause* her flipping the switch. (It does cause the switch's moving upward, but the latter event must be distinguished from Jane's flipping the switch.) Nor does her flipping the switch cause her illuminating the room. Indeed, Jane's flipping the switch and her illuminating the room might not be caused by any action of hers. Still, they are not basic actions. Just how Jane's actions are related is controversial. Some philosophers say that they are the same action under different descriptions; others that they are distinct actions related by 'causal generation', as opposed to causation; yet others that the more basic actions are components of the less basic (*see* ACTION THEORY).

In the same vein, an action caused by another action of the agent's might nevertheless be a basic action. Suppose that Jane's turning on her computer caused a power surge that cut off the electricity in her study, with the effect that, moments later, she illuminated her utility room so that she could see the fuse box. Presumably, Jane illuminated the room by performing some basic action or other; and this basic action has Jane's turning on her computer as a causal antecedent.

Influential analyses of basic 'act-types' and 'act-tokens' that avoid these difficulties are offered in Goldman (1970, pp. 67, 72). Goldman's proposals are framed in terms of his own theory of act-individuation. Neutral approximations are:

An act-type, *b*, is a *basic act-type* for an agent, S, at a time if, and only if, (a) given normal conditions, if S wanted on balance to do a *b*, S would do so; and (b) the truth of (a) does not depend upon S's 'cause-and-effect knowledge' nor upon any knowledge of S's of the form '*x*-ing may be done by *y*-ing'.

An action, *b*, done by S is a *basic act-token* if, and only if, (a) *b* instantiates an act-type that is basic for S; (b) S's *b*-ing 'is caused, in the characteristic way, by an action-plan of S'; (c) S does not *b* by doing anything, *a*, that satisfies clauses (a) and (b).

Some philosophers have denied that there are basic actions. Suppose that Jane's illuminating the room – which is not a basic action – is the same action (under another description) as her moving her finger. Given this identity, one might argue, Jane's moving her finger is not a basic action either. However, assuming the theory of action presupposed by this argument, the notion of basic action may be relativized to action-*descriptions*. Jane's *a*-ing, under the description 'illuminating the room', is not a basic action; but her *a*-ing might be basic under another description – perhaps 'moving her finger'.

An important distinction between *causally* and *teleologically* basic action, framed in terms of action-descriptions, is developed in Hornsby (1980). Hornsby contends, concerning any pair of descriptions, *d* and *d'*, of an action *a*, that *d* is causally more basic, 'if the effect that is introduced by [*a* under description *d*] causes the effect that is introduced by [*a* under description *d'*]' (1980, p. 71). By comparison, *d* is teleologically more basic than *d'* if, and only if, 'in virtue of' *a*'s occurrence, a statement to the effect that S intentionally *a*-ed-under-*d'* by *a*-ing-under-*d* is true (ibid., p. 78). The aptness of causally basic descriptions blocks a vicious causal regress, while the appropriateness of teleological counterparts prevents an epistemic regress. If, to *a* under any description at all, we always had to *a* under a causally more basic description, we would never act;

similarly, if intentionally *a*-ing-under-*d*, for any *d*, required the possession of means–end knowledge identifying *a* under a teleologically more basic description, we would be lost in thought.

BIBLIOGRAPHY

Danto, A.C.: 'What we can do', *Journal of Philosophy* 60 (1963), 435–45.
Danto, A.C.: 'Basic actions', *American Philosophical Quarterly* 2 (1965), 141–8.
Goldman, A.I.: *A Theory of Human Action* (Englewood Cliffs, NJ: Prentice-Hall, 1970).
Hornsby, J.: *Actions* (London: Routledge and Kegan Paul, 1980).

ALFRED R. MELE

being and becoming The idea of *being* functions primarily in three contrast-contexts: (1) *being/non-being*, with the contrast of the non-existent or unreal; (2) *being/seeming*, with the contrast of that which is merely suppositional, imaginary or visionary; and (3) *being/becoming* with a view to the origination of that which is not or not heretofore. Becoming in this third context (Greek: *einai/genesis*) is a matter of a shift from non-being to being, which can be either *absolute* via a transition from non-being to being (an origination) or its reverse (an annihilation) or *relative* via a change from one state or condition of being to another.

With respect to being/becoming, the ancient Greeks puzzled over the aporetically inconsistent triad (*see* APORIA): (1) absolute becoming involves a transition from non-being to being; (2) absolute becoming occurs: there are some things that exist (now or sometime) that did not do so at an earlier time; (3) becoming presupposes being: only something that is *already* in being can undergo any sort of alteration or transition. These propositions are incompatible as they stand. For, by (2), there is something, say *x*, that instantiates absolute

becoming – something that exists but yet did not do so at an earlier juncture and only came into being at some particular time. But then, by (3), *x* must have had some pre-existent state prior to that time, contrary to (1)'s stipulation of the nature of absolute becoming. The dialectic of this perplexity is encapsulated in the paradoxes of ZENO.

Different theorists resolved the problem differently. Heraclitus (*c.*535–*c.*475 BC) rejected (3), maintaining that becoming is all-predominant and exhaustive: only becoming occurs and nothing is (has being) but everything is perpetually becoming. The Eleatics, by contrast, rejected (2), denying all becoming and insisting that everything just unchangingly is, with change relegated to the condition of an illusion of sorts. The atomists (*see* ATOMISM) Leucippus (fifth century BC) and Democritus (*c.*460–*c.*370 BC) made yet another resolution by rejecting (1): for them absolute becoming is simply the rearrangement of pre-existing (and totally unchanging) units, the atoms. PLATO struck a compromise position: with the Eleatics he saw the real as unchanging (namely, the realm of ideas), while with Heraclitus he accepted the world of sensory experience as ever changing but also as pervaded by illusion. Because genuine knowledge is confined to what really is, only mere opinion about the changeable world of sense is possible, so that any authentic knowledge of the material world is impossible. (*See* PRESOCRATICS.)

The Eleatic idea that being excludes all becoming has an ever-renewed appeal. In modern times its main exponent has been MCTAGGART ('The universe is eternally the same and eternally perfect. The movement is only in our minds' (McTaggart, 1896, p. 71), and by BRADLEY, whose *Appearance and Reality* (1897) maintains the self-contradictory and consequently unreal character of change and time. The problem of how an unchanging reality can accommodate the mental changes that occur in the domain of appearance is left obscure by these neo-Eleatics.

The philosopher of becoming par excellence is LEIBNIZ, who saw the calculus as providing a mathematics of change, thereby overthrowing the static mathematics of the Greeks as reflected in Zeno's paradoxes. Leibniz envisioned the prospect of bringing the domain of becoming into the range of a rigorous science. His *monads* (*see* MONAD, MONADOLOGY) are centres of activity, preserving their programmatic identity of lawful development through an ever dynamic course of perpetual becoming.

Harking back to the preoccupation of early Greek philosophers with being/becoming, the German philosopher HEIDEGGER reproached the post-Platonic philosophical tradition with a neglect (forgetfulness) of being (*Dasein*). According to Heidegger, philosophers have been so concerned with *explanation* – with pursuing a theoretical account of how things have become what they are – that they neglect the *immediate experience* of our human presence in the world. This charge comes down to complaining that, after Plato, philosophy turned away from feeling to thinking, from the path of art (of experience and *aisthesis*) to the path of science (of understanding and *episteme*). Whether through disapproval or failed understanding, such a doctrine that theorizing is a betrayal of authenticity abandons the Leibnizian vision of an integration of sensibility and intellect.

A cognate position is that of the pessimistic philosophical tradition of Spain which is captivated by the paradoxical-seeming idea that all being is caught up in a process of becoming that leads inexorably to non-being – to death or annihilation. Unable in actual fact to escape this all-pervasive destruction, humanity seeks escape in thought, be it by way of art (poems, after all, can be more durable than mausoleums), or by way of science or religion. The preordained ultimate failure of these efforts at evasion makes them at once futile and noble, a paradox which lies at the core of UNAMUNO's classic, *The Tragic Sense of Life* (1913).

See also CHANGE.

BIBLIOGRAPHY

Bradley, F.H.: *Appearance and Reality* 2nd edn (New York: Macmillan, 1897).

McTaggart, J.M.E.: *Studies in Hegelian Dialectic* (1896); 2nd edn (Cambridge: Cambridge University Press, 1922).

Unamuno, M. de: *The Tragic Sense of Life* (1913); (London: Macmillan, 1921).

NICHOLAS RESCHER

Bentham, Jeremy (1748–1832) British philosopher who studied law. As a thinker whose 'fundamental axiom' was the principle of utility, Bentham was a practical thinker. Hence traditional metaphysical questions, such as the existence of material objects, did not particularly interest him. He thought that we should suppose that they existed because 'no bad consequences' could possibly arise from the supposition. The centre of Bentham's interest was not such abstract questions but the practical topic of law. However, his deep investigations into the nature of law led him, in spite of himself, into original metaphysical analysis. For he had to account for such legal entities as property, rights, duties and laws.

Bentham said that metaphysics was 'to know and to be able to make others know what it is we mean'. Doing metaphysics was making things comprehensible; metaphysical theories were theories of meaning. So, faced with explaining rights or duties, Bentham's task was to explain how such terms as 'right' or 'duty' can have meaning.

The traditional approach to an analysis of *obligation* or *duty*, as in LOCKE, would be to say that it was a complex idea, composed of simple ideas. Part of this Bentham adopts, in that he thinks analysis should terminate with simple ideas which are, or refer to, objects of direct perception, and which can be immediately understood. Prominent amongst such simple ideas for Bentham are *pleasure* and *pain*. These ideas he takes to be immediately comprehensible and universally understood.

However Bentham saw that the method of directly analysing a term like 'obligation'

47

into simple ideas does not work. So instead he invented the method he called *paraphrasis*. In this the term to be analysed is placed in a sentence (for example 'John is under an obligation to . . .'). This whole sentence is then taken to be equivalent to another sentence, which does not contain the term being analysed but, rather, terms referring to more directly perceptible entities. So, for obligation, the analysis is by sentences mentioning sanctions (for example, 'John is threatened with pain if he . . .'). We have now reached pain, a directly perceptible entity.

Entities which need such an analysis, Bentham called *fictitious*; entities which can be perceived, or inferred from perception, Bentham called *real*. Examples of fictitious entities are right, obligation, privilege, legal possession, property; and (away from the law) motion, quality, necessity, certainty. Examples of real entities are not just tables and chairs but also pains.

Fictitious entities, whose meaning can be unfolded by analysis in terms of real entities, and which, Bentham says, are essential for the purposes of language and communication, are importantly different from what he calls *fabulous entities*. Fabulous entities, such as the Devil, or the golden mountain, are quite simply non-existent. They can be imagined, but there is nothing in reality corresponding to them. By contrast, if someone is said to be under a duty, although there is literally no duty there, this may still express something true, a truth which can only be properly unfolded when it is analysed in terms of the sanctions threatened to the person who is said to be under the duty.

WRITINGS

Essay on Language, in *Works* ed. J. Bowring (Edinburgh: Tait, 1843) vol. VIII.
Essay on Logic, in *Works* ed. J. Bowring (Edinburgh: Tait, 1843) vol. VIII.
Fragment on Ontology, in *Works* ed. J. Bowring (Edinburgh: Tait, 1843) vol. VIII.

Bentham's Theory of Fictions ed. C.K. Ogden (London: Kegan Paul, 1932).
Of Laws in General ed. H.L.A. Hart (London: Athlone, 1970), Appendices B, C.
Chrestomathia (1817); ed. M.J. Smith and W.H. Burston (Oxford: Oxford University Press, 1983) appendix IV.
Fragment on Government (1776); ed. J.H. Burns and H.L.A. Hart (Cambridge: Cambridge University Press, 1988), ch. V.

ROSS HARRISON

Bergmann, Gustav (1906–87) Austrian-American philosopher. Bergmann was one of the younger members of the Vienna Circle (*see* LOGICAL POSITIVISM). In 1938 he had to leave Austria and, with the help of Otto Neurath (1882–1945), emigrated to the United States. In the United States, Herbert Feigl, another member of the Vienna Circle, secured a position for Bergmann at the University of Iowa initially as an assistant to Kurt Lewin in his endeavour to use topological methods in theoretical psychology. Bergmann taught at the University of Iowa until his retirement.

At the beginning, like most members of the Vienna Circle, Bergmann was interested in the philosophy of science and, particularly, in the foundations of psychology. He eventually published a short book on philosophy of science (Bergmann, 1957). But around 1945 his interest turned more and more to metaphysics and to what he called 'the heart of metaphysics', namely, ONTOLOGY. He used to tell an anecdote about how the title of his article 'A positivistic metaphysics of consciousness' (1945) upset CARNAP when he was visiting Iowa City.

Much of Bergmann's work in metaphysics is contained in two collections of articles (Bergmann, 1959, 1964). Unlike most members of the Vienna Circle and their students, Bergmann defended realism (*see* PLATONISM) against NOMINALISM and mind/body dualism against materialism (*see* PHYSICALISM, MATERIALISM; MIND/BODY PROBLEM). His philosophy, as a consequence, revolved around two main topics:

The proper ontological analysis of ordinary perceptual objects and the intentional relationship between a mind and its objects (*see* INTENTIONALITY).

Bergmann held that the dialectic of numerical difference and qualitative sameness among perceptual objects requires an ontology of bare particulars (*see* BARE PARTICULAR) and UNIVERSALS. An ordinary object, a white billiard ball, is a complex entity, containing a bare particular and the universal whiteness. According to this analysis, an ordinary object turns out to be a FACT. Bergmann's ontology, therefore, embraces facts as well as particulars and universals. Particulars are called 'bare' because they do not have natures. They resemble the haecceitates (*see* HAECCEITY) of DUNS SCOTUS. Universals can be subdivided into properties and relations. Among relations, a special place is occupied by the nexus of exemplification, which holds between particulars and their universals, and the nexus of intentionality, which holds between minds and what they are about.

A mind, according to Bergmann, consists essentially of mental acts. He follows in this regard in the footsteps of another school of Austrian philosophers, namely, BRENTANO and his students. Every mental act has two characteristic properties: a property that determines the kind of act it is, say, a remembering, or a desiring, and a property that determines which particular object an act intends. It is this latter property, the 'content' of the act, which stands in a unique and unanalysable relation, the intentional nexus, to the object of the act. But a mind may intend an object that does not exist, and this creates one of the most intractable problems of the philosophy of mind, a problem that Bergmann discussed for many years: How can the intentional nexus hold between a mental act ('content') and something that does not exist, that is not there at all? Bergmann discusses this problem and other problems of the philosophy of mind in his main work (Bergmann, 1967). His solution to the 'problem of NON-EXISTENT OBJECTS' is that states of affairs,

the 'objects' of mental acts, may exist in either of two modes: the mode of actuality or the mode of potentiality. A non-existent state of affairs, therefore, does exist, but exists in the mode of potentiality (*see* POTENTIALITY/ACTUALITY).

Bergmann's ontology culminates in the investigation of the ontological ground of logic. He finds this foundation in the world's form. In particular, he attributes ontological status, subsistence, to the so-called 'quantifiers' (generality and existence) and 'connectives' (conjunction, disjunction, etc.) (see Bergmann, 1962).

During the last years of his philosophical work, Bergmann developed a completely new ontology, an ontology explained in a posthumously published book (see Bergmann, 1991).

WRITINGS

'A positivistic metaphysics of consciousness', *Mind* 45 (1945), 193–226.
Philosophy of Science (Madison, WI: University of Wisconsin Press, 1957).
Meaning and Existence (Madison, WI: University of Wisconsin Press, 1959).
'Generality and existence', *Theoria* 28 (1962), 1–26.
Logic and Reality (Madison, WI: University of Wisconsin Press, 1964).
Realism: A Critique of Brentano and Meinong (Madison, WI: University of Wisconsin Press, 1967).
New Foundations of Ontology ed. William Heald (Madison, WI: University of Wisconsin Press, 1991).

REINHARDT GROSSMANN

Bergson, Henri (1859–1941) French philosopher. Bergson formulated a new and impressive conception of metaphysics early in the twentieth century. It attracted wide attention not only for its content but also because of its opposition to the prevailing classical view that metaphysics is the inquiry into the universe as a whole. This inquiry was taken to be a purely intellectual one, aimed at embodying its results in a coherent system of ideas or basic truths about reality.

Bergson rejected this view of metaphysics, because it mistakenly assumed that the human intellect is a truth-finding capacity, whereas it is in fact a capacity which has evolved to promote man's practical action in the world. Because of its role the intellect treats what it deals with as individual entities in space, and seeks to understand them in mathematical terms. Hence the entities are regarded as static and immobile. But this is not the way the world is presented to us in immediate experience. Here we are aware of a continuous flowing of things and events in time. This time, however, is not the mathematical time of the physical sciences, but is what Bergson calls 'duration' or real time. Scientific time is a fiction, albeit a useful one. Metaphysical time can only be obtained by having recourse to 'intuition' or introspection of our immediate experience, not by the employment of the intellect in using abstract concepts. Hence the scientific picture of the universe as a mechanistic and deterministic system in imaginary. It leads to a misconception of both freedom and creativity. Such phenomena are intimately related to the claim that evolution results from a vital impulse (*élan vital*) or current of consciousness that has penetrated matter and has given rise to a multiplicity of interwoven potentialities which constitute the evolutionary process.

The above metaphysical doctrines are persuasively presented by Bergson in his writings, often with the aid of striking metaphors and analogies. But these may not satisfy many contemporary readers who are perplexed by the scarcity of logical arguments and supporting reasons for the doctrines being advanced.

WRITINGS

Time and Free Will (London and New York: Macmillan and Co., 1910).
Creative Evolution (London and New York: Macmillan, 1911).

Mind Energy (London and New York: 1914, 1920).
The Creative Mind (New York: The Wisdom Library, 1946).
Introduction to Metaphysics (New York: Liberal Arts Press, 1949).

THOMAS A. GOUDGE

Berkeley, George (1685–1753) Irish philosopher. Berkeley argued forcefully against the existence of MATTER or material substance. His arguments, HUME later wrote, '*admit of no answer and produce no conviction*', but Berkeley himself was convinced that the denial of matter (or *immaterialism*) was closer to common sense, more remote from scepticism, and friendlier to recent developments in science than the MATERIALISM (*see* PHYSICALISM) he found in DESCARTES, MALEBRANCHE, LOCKE and NEWTON. Berkeley did not deny the existence of bodies; instead, he construed statements about bodies as claims about perceptions or ideas. 'The table I write on, I say, exists,' he wrote, 'that is, I see and feel it; and if I were out of my study I should say it existed, meaning thereby that if I was in my study I might perceive it, or that some other spirit actually does perceive it.' (*Works*, vol. 2, p. 42).

In 1707–8, as a student and fellow at Trinity College, Dublin, Berkeley completed two notebooks now known as the *Philosophical Commentaries*. They announce and argue for what Berkeley then called 'the Principle': to be is to be perceived, or to perceive (or will, or act). The houses, mountains and rivers whose *esse* is *percipi* (whose *being* is *being perceived*) have no existence apart from the minds or spirits who perceive or act upon them.

THEORY OF VISION

Berkeley's first important book, *An Essay towards a New Theory of Vision* (1709), is an attempt to explain how we see the distance, size and orientation of objects, on the assumption (carried over from earlier writers) that they are not seen directly. Berkeley assumes that distance, size and orientation *are* directly perceived by touch. We see distance, for example, only because experience invests visual appearances with tangible meaning. We come to associate tangible ideas (including ideas of our own body and its movements) with ideas attending vision – the sensation arising from the 'turn' of the eyes, the 'confusedness' of the visual appearance, and the strain of holding these appearances in focus. Correlations between the two kinds of ideas are contingent or 'arbitrary'; Berkeley argues against the view, attributed (perhaps unfairly) to Descartes, that we compute an object's distance by a kind of 'innate geometry', inferring it from the size of the angle formed by the two 'optic axes' as they meet at the eye.

Berkeley assumes in the *Essay* that the objects of touch do not depend for their existence on the mind. 'Not that to suppose that vulgar error', he later wrote, 'was necessary for establishing the notion therein laid down, but because it was beside my purpose to examine and refute it in a discourse concerning *vision*.' (*Works*, vol. 2, p. 59). Berkeley also speaks of the objects of touch as *ideas*, but he warns that the *Essay* does not assume that ideas are mind-dependent. 'When I speak of tangible ideas,' he explains, 'I take the word idea for any immediate object of sense or understanding, in which large signification it is commonly used by the moderns.' (*Works*, vol. 1, p. 188)

Because the ideas attending vision are arbitrary signs of the objects of touch, Berkeley views them as a language – a visual language in which God speaks to us of tangible objects to come. Thus the *Essay* affords the first glimpse of Berkeley's substitute for the image of nature as machine, blindly obeying laws laid down, long ago, by a now-indifferent God. For Berkeley, nature is a text or speech, renewed at every moment, and bespeaking a continuing providence. Like a text or speech, its signs have no power over what they signify. They are useful to us not because of what they bring about, but because of the divine intentions they communicate.

ABSTRACT IDEAS

Berkeley's main work, *A Treatise Concerning the Principles of Human Knowledge* (1710), begins with an attempt to untangle what its author calls 'the fine and subtle net of *abstract ideas*'. 'It is agreed on all hands,' Berkeley reports, 'that the qualities or modes of things do never really exist each of them apart by itself, and separated from all others, but are mixed, as it were, and blended together, several in the same object' (*Works*, vol. 2, p. 27). Yet according to the doctrine of abstraction (as contained, according to Berkeley, in Locke's *Essay Concerning Human Understanding* (1689), the mind can, for example, form an idea of an object's colour apart from its other modes or qualities. When the mind later observes that different colours are alike, it can form 'an idea of colour in abstract which is neither red, nor blue, nor white, nor any other determinate colour'. And 'by the same precision or mental separation', Berkeley reports, it is alleged to form abstract ideas of composite things, such as the idea of a human being, or of a triangle in general (*Works*, vol. 2, p. 28).

Berkeley's main argument against abstract ideas rests on the premise that we cannot conceive of the impossible. Because the object of an abstract idea cannot exist in isolation, it cannot be conceived in isolation. Locke himself had insisted that every existing thing, whether SUBSTANCE or MODE, is particular. He inferred from this that every idea is particular. Berkeley urges the further conclusion that every idea is *of* a particular. Yet he does not deny the possibility of abstract or general thinking. When we think of human nature in general, he suggests, we *consider* or *attend to* a single aspect of a fully determinate idea. And when we prove theorems in geometry, we take a single triangle as the impartial representative of them all.

Berkeley traces the doctrine of abstraction to the assumption that every significant word stands for an idea – an assumption he denies. He observes that a word need not excite an idea on every occasion of its use, and he argues that some words, used to express emotion or incite action, do not stand for ideas at all. In *Alciphron* (1732), Berkeley argues that words such as *force* and *grace* owe their meaning not to ideas we can conceive in isolation, but to their place in a system of signs with a bearing on practice or experience.

IMMATERIALISM

The medium of Berkeley's philosophy is argument: he uses it not only to persuade, but to expound and clarify. Of the many arguments he offers against the existence of matter, the following five are central:

(1) It is a dictate of common sense that we immediately perceive such things as houses, mountains, and rivers. But philosophy teaches that we immediately perceive only our own ideas. (In the *Principles*, Berkeley tends to assume, without argument, that ideas are mind-dependent.) It follows that houses, mountains and rivers are ideas, and that they do not exist 'without' (i.e. independently of) the mind.
(2) If we inquire into the meaning of the word *exist* when it is applied to sensible things, we discover that it means only that they are perceived or perceivable. Hence the existence of unthinking things 'without ... relation to their being perceived' is 'perfectly unintelligible' (*Works*, vol. 2, p. 42)..
(3) The notion of *matter* is either self-contradictory or empty. It is self-contradictory if sensible qualities are said to exist in it (so that they require nothing else for their existence), because sensible qualities are ideas, and ideas cannot exist without the mind. If we try to escape the contradiction by saying, vaguely, that matter is a SUBSTRATUM or 'support' of qualities unknown, we deplete the notion of content.
(4) It is impossible even to conceive of bodies 'unthought of or without the mind'. 'The mind, taking no notice of itself, is deluded to think' it can do so,

but the attempt is self-defeating, because the bodies the mind brings forward as examples 'are apprehended by or exist in it' (*Works*, vol. 2, pp. 50–1).
(5) Even if matter exists we cannot know that it does. We cannot know it by sense, because we immediately perceive only our own ideas. Nor can we know it by reason – that is, by demonstrative or probable argument. We cannot know it by demonstrative argument because there is no necessary connection between matter and ideas. And we cannot know it by probable argument (that is, by explanatory inference) because we cannot comprehend the action of matter on the mind.

Berkeley develops these arguments in both the *Principles* and the *Three Dialogues between Hylas and Philonous* (1713). In the *Principles*, the conflict between immaterialism and common sense is, at least at times, openly acknowledged. Berkeley writes at one point, for example, that belief in things without the mind is 'strangely [i.e. greatly] prevailing amongst men'. In the *Dialogues* he is more concerned to emphasize the harmony between the two. The *Dialogues* also fills a gap in arguments (1) and (3), by arguing for the assumption that the immediate objects of perception are mind-dependent ideas. Philonous (Berkeley's spokesman) seeks to establish this by an appeal to perceptual relativity: because the immediate objects of perception vary with changes in us, he argues, they must exist only in the mind. But neither Philonous nor Berkeley infers from this that qualities themselves exist there. They reach this further conclusion by arguing that mind-dependent ideas cannot represent mind-independent qualities. This is because one thing can represent another only if they are alike, and 'an idea can be like nothing but an idea' (*Works*, vol. 2, p. 44).

Berkeley repudiates a version of the distinction between primary and secondary qualities, according to which the primary qualities (such as extension and figure) are independent of the mind although the secondary qualities (colour and taste, for example) are not (*see* QUALITY, PRIMARY/SECONDARY). He argues that we cannot conceive of an object bereft of all secondary qualities; it follows that the primary qualities exist where the secondary do – 'in the mind and nowhere else'. A purely geometrical conception of body is, he maintains, an illegitimate abstraction; our conception of body is forever marked or stained by its origin in sense. In *De motu* (1721) and *Siris* (1744), however, Berkeley shows that he is willing, for scientific purposes, to consider body as including only primary qualities. This distinction between primary and secondary qualities is pragmatic rather than metaphysical: the primary qualities, more useful in prediction and control, become objects of selective attention.

Berkeley regards bodies or real things as sensations or 'ideas of sense'. Although they are more regular, vivid, and constant than ideas of imagination, they are, he cautions, 'nevertheless *ideas*' (*Works*, vol. 2, p. 54). Their reality – their greater strength, order and coherence – is no argument that they exist without the mind.

Berkeley often suggests that bodies are clusters or collections of simpler ideas, but he provides little guidance as to how these clusters should be understood. Perhaps they are literal collections; if so, they seem to include ideas of several senses, existing in different minds at different times. But other passages suggest that Berkeley is a phenomenalist, holding that statements about bodies are equivalent in meaning (or at the very least in truth conditions) to statements about what we perceive, or would perceive, under certain circumstances (*see* PHENOMENALISM).

SUBSTANCE AND SPIRIT

Phenomenalism is sometimes described as 'Berkeley without God'. But Berkeley's phenomenalism is theocentric: statements about what we *would* perceive are true, he thinks, only because of the standing volitions of the deity. Berkeley recognizes that divine agency cannot be 'blind'. Hence God's sustaining activity has two aspects: he wills that we have certain ideas under certain circumstances, and he perceives the ideas he wills.

Ideas of sense, Berkeley observes, are independent of our will. This fact, coupled with the wisdom and power they exhibit, constitutes Berkeley's main argument for God's existence. In *Alciphron*, Berkeley's presentation of the argument emphasizes the languagelike character of our experience. The inference to God's existence is akin to the inference from speech or writing to the existence of other finite minds.

Berkeley argues that the only substance is spirit. He does not abandon the traditional view that perceived qualities or modes need a substratum. But the substratum in which they exist is a mind or spirit. Yet even though colour and shape, for example, exist in the mind, they cannot be predicated of the mind. They are in the mind 'not by way of mode or attribute, but by way of idea' (*Works*, vol. 2, p. 61).

How does Berkeley know there are substances? He thinks our own substance-hood is known immediately and reflexively. But he insists that we have no idea of substance, because spirits are active beings, and ideas, being passive and inert, cannot resemble them. In the second edition of the *Principles* (1734), Berkeley explains that we have *notions* of mind or spirit. This is not a theory of representation, but a way of saying that we understand words such as *mind* or *soul*. The basis seems to be our understanding of the word *I* – our reflexive awareness of our own selves. We are also said to have notions of relations, because according to Berkeley they involve an act of the comparing mind.

SCIENCE

Berkeley argues that the only true causes are spirits; corporeal 'causes' are marks or signs. We say, of course, that fire heats, and water cools, but 'in such things we ought to *think with the learned, and speak with the vulgar*' (*Works*, vol. 2, p. 62). The only true cause at work in nature is God, 'the author of nature', and a scientific law is a rule of the language in which he speaks.

THE METAPHYSICS OF *SIRIS*

Passages in *Siris* have convinced some readers that late in life, Berkeley turned to PLATONISM – to a belief in the existence of objects of pure intellect more real than sensible things, of which they are the patterns or archetypes. But *Siris* is often a tentative book, one whose 'hoary maxims' are proposed not 'as principles, but barely as hints' (*Works*, vol. 2, p. 157), and its objects of pure intellect are not, in any case, archetypes of *sensible* objects, but spirits, or aspects of spirit.

WRITINGS

The Works of George Berkeley, Bishop of Cloyne ed. A.A. Luce and T.E. Jessop (London: Thomas Nelson, 1948–57).

BIBLIOGRAPHY

Atherton, M.: *Berkeley's Revolution in Vision* (Ithaca, NY: Cornell University Press, 1990).
Dancy. J.: *Berkeley: An Introduction* (Oxford: Blackwell, 1987).
Grayling, A.C.: *Berkeley: The Central Arguments* (La Salle, IL: Open Court, 1985).
Luce, A.A.: *Berkeley and Malebranche* (London: Oxford University Press, 1934).
Pitcher, G.: *Berkeley* (London: Routledge and Kegan Paul, 1977).
Tipton, I.C.: *Berkeley: The Philosophy of Immaterialism* (London: Methuen, 1974).
Urmson, J.O.: *Berkeley* (Oxford: Oxford University Press, 1982).
Warnock, G.J.: *Berkeley*, 3rd edn (Oxford: Blackwell, 1982).
Winkler, K.P.: *Berkeley: An Interpretation* (Oxford: Clarendon Press, 1989).

KENNETH P. WINKLER

Blanshard, Brand (1892–1987) Blanshard integrated metaphysics with epistemology and the other branches of philosophy in a systematic whole. His *The Nature of Thought* (1939) moves from psychological and epistemological investigations to the more abstruse topics of metaphysics. Metaphysically, he advocated the theory of the concrete universal, the doctrine that all relations are internal, and the thesis of cosmic necessity.

For Blanshard, the things which are the objects of perception are not the ultimately real things. When analysed into their properties and relations, they are found to be interconnected with all other things, their very natures being affected by their relations. Based on the doctrine of INTERNAL RELATIONS, Blanshard's theory envisages a network of relatedness among things tantamount to the entire universe.

Moreover, on Blanshard's account, UNIVERSALS, the objects of ideas, are more real than things. The kinds of universals are abstract, generic, qualitative and specific. Rejecting abstract universals, he favoured instead the theory of the concrete universal. The generic universal he viewed as a being in thought requiring further determination, while he considered the qualitative universal, such as whiteness or sweetness, to be subsumable under the generic universal. Specific universals, such as a specific colour or odour or taste, he admitted into nature, contending that individual things are congeries of such universals. Because every thing is composed of specific universals and is internally related to all other things, its particularity as spatio-temporal is exposed as unreal, and must be reconceived as its being part of a whole. Hence 'the only true particular is the absolute' (Blanshard, 1939, vol. I, p. 639).

Blanshard's theory of the world as a system of necessarily related parts is, in sum, his conception of cosmic necessity, a necessity both causal and logical. Since the aim of thinking is to express this cosmic necessity, reason is the human faculty which seeks the relations that bind all things together in a necessary whole. In mid-career Blanshard undertook to prepare a trilogy in defence of reason, construed as sovereign, against what he despised as its detractors in contemporary thought. At this juncture Blanshard preferred that his philosophy be called 'rationalist' rather than 'idealist' (*see* IDEALISM; RATIONALISM). The volumes of Blanshard's trilogy are *Reason and Goodness* (1961), *Reason and Analysis* (1962) and *Reason and Belief* (1974).

The absolute for Blanshard is the only true individual. In principle intelligible throughout, it embraces all things in the network of necessary relations. Yet Blanshard could find no reason for, and many reasons against, the attributions of rightness and goodness, mind or consciousness, to the absolute. Ultimate reality, the universe, the absolute (he used these terms interchangeably), is to be found 'in no part of it, however great, but only in the whole. It is the universe itself, not indeed as a scattered litter of items but as the one comprehensive and necessary order that a full understanding would find in it' (Blanshard, 1974, 523).

WRITINGS

The Nature of Thought (1939); (New York: Macmillan, 1940).
Reason and Goodness (New York: Macmillan, 1961).
Reason and Analysis (New York: Macmillan, 1962).
Reason and Belief (New York: Macmillan, 1974).

ANDREW J. RECK

body John LOCKE (Locke, 1690) distinguishes between two kinds of bodies: mere masses of matter and living bodies. These kinds are distinguished from each other and from persons by way of their persistence conditions. What it takes for a person to survive, for a person at one time to be identical to some person that exists at a later time, is for there to be a continuity of consciousness between the earlier person and the later one. In contrast, a living body can survive a change of parts without any consciousness being present, so long as that change is in accordance with the kind of diachronic organization that would be considered a single life. Masses, on the other hand, cannot survive any gain or loss of parts. What it is to be a given mass is just to be that collection of that stuff. A collection of different stuff is, therefore, a different mass. So says Locke.

The intuition behind Locke's identity conditions for masses is that they are *mere* masses; all there is to such an object is the matter that composes it. If we are to respect this 'mereness', there seems no principled reason for placing any restrictions on which collections of matter should count as objects. Any collection of matter, no matter how arbitrarily grouped, has just as much claim to being a mass as any other collection. If we view the world four-dimensionally, as I prefer, the grouping of matter along the temporal dimension is equally arbitrary. Any collection of matter at one time and any collection of matter at a later time compose, along the temporal dimension, a single persisting mass. If the earlier collection and the latter one contain different parts, the persisting mass that is composed of them has survived a change of parts. Whereas the mereness of masses led Locke to hold very strict conditions for their continued existence, so strict as to prohibit change of parts, the mereness leads me in just the opposite direction. I call four-dimensional collections of matter 'hunks' and hold that any filled region of space-time, no matter how arbitrarily delineated, contains such a body.

Many philosophers would insist that a body must at least be spatio-temporally continuous. Even a mere collection of matter must be *collected*, must have some internal unity. However, spatio-temporal continuity itself seems an inadequate condition for unity. Along the spatial dimension, contact alone does not seem a significant enough connection to make two objects compose one. And along the temporal dimension, it seems possible for one object to be replaced by an extremely similar object in a way that makes for spatio-temporal continuity without the two objects either being or composing a single object. Thus many philosophers are led to require causal connectedness between the temporal stages of an object and between the parts of any one stage. It is not easy to specify which kinds of causal connections are the right kinds to generate a single body. Perhaps one plausible candidate is provided by Locke: the various interactions between objects are of the right sort to make those objects compose a single object if the interactions together constitute a life. But this is no clearer than the term 'life'. Furthermore, like Locke's persistence conditions for masses, his conditions for living bodies will exclude many ordinary objects. So, if we want to count ordinary objects as bodies we need some criteria in addition to, or instead of, Locke's.

How are we to choose the right persistence conditions for bodies from among all these alternatives? Perhaps we should simply accept many different kinds of bodies, a different kind for each persistence condition that has been mentioned. Locke himself accepted both masses and living bodies. This suggestion becomes less plausible once we realize that a great multitude of persistence conditions might be recommended and that many of these different kinds of bodies would be existing simultaneously in a single location. To avoid this problem, we should select one persistence condition. I accept the non-restrictive condition: any collection of matter, no matter how arbitrarily delineated, is a body. What there are are mere hunks of matter. Some of these hunks are counted as mountains, some as dogs and some as people. A single hunk might count as a living thing, a person, an athlete, an adult and a woman, but this does not require that there be several different things in one place simultaneously. It is one body that plays different roles. In spite of the many arguments in the literature defending more restrictive conditions the selection of any of those conditions, I believe, would be fundamentally arbitrary. Positing mere hunks recognizes the arbitrariness involved in any distinction between bodies and non-bodies and respects that arbitrariness by rejecting the distinction.

See also ARISTOTLE; BUNDLE THEORY; CHANGE; CHISHOLM; CONTINUANT; IDENTITY; MATTER; MODALITIES AND POSSIBLE WORLDS; ONTOLOGY; PART/WHOLE; PERSONS AND PERSONAL IDENTITY; SUBSTANCE; TEMPORAL PARTS.

BIBLIOGRAPHY

Cartwright, R.: 'Scattered objects', in *Analysis and Metaphysics*, ed. K. Lehrer (Dordrecht: Reidel, 1975), 153–71.
Chisholm, R.M.: 'Parts as essential to their wholes', *Review of Metaphysics* 26 (1973), 581–603.
Heller, M.: *The Ontology of Physical Objects* (Cambridge: Cambridge University Press, 1990).
Locke, J.: *An Essay Concerning Human Understanding* (London: 1690); ed. P.H. Nidditch (Oxford: Oxford University Press, 1975), 328–48.
van Inwagen, P.: *Material Beings* (Ithaca, NY: Cornell University Press, 1990).

MARK HELLER

Boethius (*c.*480–524)   Roman philosopher. Boethius's work that had the greatest influence on the history of metaphysics in the Latin world was not his famous *De consolatione philosophiae*, but a treatise that was referred to in the Middle Ages as *De hebdomadibus*. Its real title is a question submitted to Boethius by a friend: 'How can substances be good in virtue of the fact that they have being when they are not substantial goods?' (*Quomodo substantiae in eo quod sint bonae sint cum non sint substantialia bona*). The most striking thing about this work is the way in which Boethius approaches the problem. He will solve this question according to the method 'that is usual in mathematics'. His exposition starts therefore with eight propositions from which the remainder of the argument can be deduced. Boethius presents the model of an axiomatic metaphysics that proceeds *more geometrico*.

The second axiom reads: 'Being (*esse*) and

that which is (*quod est*) are different.' For being itself does not exist, but that which actually exists is 'that which is'. The precise meaning of this difference is controversial. It is usually interpreted as the distinction between a concrete thing and its substantial form, that by which a thing is (*quo est*). Boethius uses this distinction for the explanation of the ontological difference between created being and the highest being. The mark of created being is that it is composed: its being and *quod est* are not identical. Through this composition it is distinguished from the highest being, which is simple. 'Every simple has its being and that which is as one' (Axiom VIII).

De hebdomadibus was intensively commented upon from the Carolingian times. One of the most important commentaries was that of AQUINAS in the thirteenth century. In that century Boethius's axioms were frequently cited in the debates about the distinction between essence and being (existence) in things.

WRITINGS

The Latin text of *De hebdomadibus* with an English translation in H.F. Steward, E.K. Rand and S.J. Tester, ed. and trans.: *Boethius, The Theological Tractates and the Consolation of Philosophy* (Cambridge, MA: Harvard University Press, 1978).

BIBLIOGRAPHY

McInerny, R.: *Boethius and Aquinas* (Washington, DC: The Catholic University of America Press, 1990).
Schrimpf, G.: *Die Axiomenschrift des Boethius (De hebdomadibus) als philosophisches Lehrbuch des Mittelalters* (Leiden: Brill, 1966).

JAN A. AERTSEN

Bolzano, Bernard (1781–1848) Mathematician, logician and metaphysician, Bolzano was professor of theology in Prague 1805–19, when he was dismissed because of his liberal views.

Bolzano's main work, the *Wissenschaftslehre* (1837) (*Theory of Science*), postulates propositions 'in themselves', defined as 'assertions . . . [which] may or may not have been put in words or even formulated in thought' (1837, sect. 19) (*see* PROPOSITION, STATE OF AFFAIRS). Propositions are the 'matter' of human judgements; they, not the acts of thinking are the concern of logic. Properties and relations of these Platonic (*see* PLATO; PLATONISM) entities, like analyticity, implication and probability, are defined for the first time with the aid of variables. When a truth implies *and explains* a second, it is its *ground*. This relation orders truths in themselves so that 'from the smallest number of simple premisses [follows] the largest possible number of the remaining truths' (1837, sect. 221).

In opposition to KANT he took mathematics to be grounded not in intuition, but in pure concepts. He strove to provide adequate arithmetic definitions of real NUMBER, function, continuity, limit, point, etc., recast the foundations of geometry in terms of structured point sets, and showed that infinite sets have no paradoxical properties (1851). Bolzano took MATTER to be a continuous array of monads (*see* MONAD, MONADOLOGY), and argued that the SOUL is simple and indestructible (1827). He offered a new cosmological argument for the existence of God, claiming that mutable substances require a 'constant and unchangeable source of force' (1827, p. 296). In agreement with BENTHAM he measured all actions by the standard of public utility; even religion is 'the sum of doctrines or opinions that have a beneficial or detrimental effect upon the virtue or happiness of a person'.

Bolzano, a lone forerunner of analytic philosophy, endeavoured to clarify basic philosophical and mathematical concepts which 'everyone knows and does not know'. He advanced no claim without circumspect argument; his exposition is a model of clarity and precision. Regrettably, his attempt to rescue philosophy from the epigones of IDEALISM failed because of the growing rift between philosophy and the exact sciences, and because of his persecution. Interest was revived through HUSSERL's *Logical Investigations* (1900–1), and is now reflected in numerous articles and monographs (see the bibliographies in the *Gesamtausgabe* (1969ff.)).

WRITINGS

Athanasia (Sulzbach: 1827); (Frankfurt: Minerva, 1970).
Wissenschaftslehre (Sulzbach: 1837); ed. W. Schultz (Leipzig: Meiner, 1929); (Aachen: Scientia, 1970); trans. R. George *Theory of Science* (Oxford: Blackwell, and Berkeley: University of California Press, 1972). Another edition ed. J. Berg, trans. B. Terrell (Dordrecht: Reidel, 1973).
Paradoxien des Unendlichen (Leipzig: 1851); trans. D.A. Steele, *Paradoxes of the Infinite* (London: Routledge, 1950).
Gesamtausgabe; founded by E. Winter, ed. J. Berg, with B. van Rootselaar, A. van der Lugt, J. Loužil *et al.* (Stuttgart: Fromann, 1969ff.), 36 vols in 1994. With introductions, comprehensive bibliographies, and a biography by E. Winter.

BIBLIOGRAPHY

Berg, J.: *Bolzano's Logik* (Stockholm: Almqvist and Wiksell, 1962).
Coffa, J.A.: *The Semantic Tradition from Kant to Carnap* (Cambridge: Cambridge University Press, 1991).
Morscher, E.: *Das logische An-Sich bei Bernard Bolzano* (Salzburg and Munich: Anton Pustet, 1973).

ROLF GEORGE
PAUL RUSNOCK

boundary The boundaries of extended objects may be thought of in two ways: as limits or as thin parts. Limits of the object have fewer dimensions than it has itself: a three-dimensional brick has surfaces without thickness; the edge where two faces meet is a one-dimensional line; the corner where three faces meet is a point. An enduring event like a kiss has a beginning and an end without duration. There are also inner boundaries, like the half-way point in the flight of an arrow. Boundaries in this sense raise many ontological questions. Do they really exist or are they mathematical fictions? Are they parts of their objects, or of the surroundings, or neither? Alternatively, boundaries are simply 'thin' parts of the same dimensionality as their wholes. At stake is whether the highly successful mathematics of continuous structures, like the real numbers, which treat extents as composed of extensionless points, truly depict reality.

BIBLIOGRAPHY

Aristotle: *Metaphysics* ed. W. Jaeger (Oxford: Clarendon Press, 1957) Bk 5, ch. 17, 1022; Bk 11, ch. 3, 1061.
Stroll, A.: *Surfaces* (Minneapolis: University of Minnesota Press, 1988).
Whitehead, A.N.: *An Enquiry Concerning the Principles of Natural Knowledge* (Cambridge: 1919); 2nd edn (Cambridge: Cambridge University Press, 1925), esp. Part III, 'The method of extensive abstraction'.

PETER SIMONS

Bradley, Francis Herbert (1846–1924) British philosopher. A convenient way of placing Bradley's monism (*see* MONISM/PLURALISM) and IDEALISM in context is to see him as finding logical and epistemological grounds for rejecting (1) an ultimate ontology of externally related facts (*see* LOGICAL ATOMISM); and (2) a physicalism (*see* PHYSICALISM, MATERIALISM) of the influential physics-based kind (cf. QUINE).

THE REJECTION OF ULTIMATE FACTS

This rejection rests on Bradley's often misunderstood argument to the effect that unconditional predication is incoherent. The argument is here stated for *monadic* predications in respect of a single individual as ultimate subject but it applies equally to *relational* predications with respect to pairs, etc. (*Essays on Truth and Reality* (1914) pp. 225–33; *Appearance and Reality* (1893) chs II, III; *Principles of Logic* (1883) vol. I, pp. 99–100).

Assume 'R' is the proper name of an individual. If '*Ra*', '*Rb*', '*Rc*', etc. express genuinely unconditional predications then the only condition under which, for example, '*Ra*' could be true would be *R*'s being *a*, and the only condition under which '*Ra*' could be false would be *R*'s not being *a*. The truth value of '*Ra*' could not depend on the truth values of any other of the propositions '*Rb*', '*Rc*', etc. Hence such propositions would all have to be logically independent of one another and any one of them could, as a matter of logical possibility, be the only one true, i.e. be a complete description of and give 'perfect' knowledge of reality. But if, for example, '*Ra*' alone could be a complete description of reality then '*Ra*' must be construed as asserting not merely that *R* is *a* but in effect as asserting that *R* is merely *a*; and likewise for '*Rb*', '*Rc*', etc. However, if this is so, as Bradley argues, a contradiction arises, since if '*Ra*' were true then '*Rb*' and '*Rc*' etc. would have to be false (given that *a* is neither *b* nor *c*, etc.).

Bradley concludes that the unconditional *verbal form* which we must in fact employ to express the predications involved in our thinking must be seen as misleading with respect to the form of the judgements we make. Any judgement must always be *radically* conditional in form and might more properly be expressed by, for example, the formula '*R(x)a*'. This formula must be read not as indicating that the truth value of any conceivable predication will be conditioned, at the ultimate limit of analysis, by conditions that will in fact be unknown. It must be read as indicating that there cannot conceivably be an absolute, unconditional, determination of the truth value of *any* predication. Hence our knowledge cannot be a *superstructure* underpinned by an ultimate ontology of externally related,

or atomistic, perceptible facts (*Essays*, pp. 209–10).

TRUTHS, DEGREES OF TRUTH AND 'IDEAL CONSTRUCTIONS'

Bradley therefore concludes that with respect to any linguistically communicable truth whatsoever it can only make sense to describe it as true, or false, relative to a specified *ideal construction*. Any such a construction will be a more or less comprehensive logically interrelated system of ideal contents predicated as a connected whole of reality (i.e. of the genuinely individual, ultimate subject of predication). Thus for Bradley the primary repository of truth comes to be, not the proposition construed as a content capable of possessing in isolation a determinate *eternal* truth value, but the ideal construction viewed *diachronically*.

Hence an ideal construction is not (except for special purposes) to be construed as a determinate system of contents subject to the operations of a Fregean propositional or predicate calculus (*see* FREGE). In its primary sense it will be a system of ostensibly coherent ideal contents which is continuously confrontable in practice with a *given* and which is prone to modification and supplantation by extended, and sometimes logically incompatible, versions of itself (e.g. *Essays*, pp. 75–9). Such extended versions will, so far as they are internally coherent, allow a person to have knowledge which will be nearer – but on a path which of necessity is only asymptotic – to absolute truth with respect to the given reality.

THE IDEAL CONSTRUCTIONS OF PHYSICISTS AS NOT PRIVILEGED METAPHYSICALLY

If the argument against absolute truth and falsehood is valid it follows that no system of objects knowable through any ideal construction (e.g. the physical world as identified through the ideal contents internal to ultimate particle theories) can be taken *as such*, for the purpose of *metaphysics*, to be identical with reality. In Bradley's alternative terminology, no such system can constitute anything other than a more or less partial and inadequate appearance of reality. However, equally, it follows that reality will be present, albeit as a partial and inadequate appearance, in the contents of even the most fragmentary ideal constructions (*Essays*, pp. 28–42; *Appearance and Reality*, pp. 323–7; *Principles*, vol. I, pp. 110–11, fn. 40). Hence for Bradley there can be no question but that the theories of physics, at any time in their history, will contain truth and allow us to have more or less extensive knowledge of reality. But this knowledge will have no special significance for the metaphysician, despite its enormous practical significance in *our real world* (*Essays*, p. 123; *Appearance and Reality*, pp. 231–6, 434–5).

EPISTEMOLOGICAL PRIORITY OF THE IDEAL CONSTRUCTION OF OUR REAL WORLD

The system of objects, according to Bradley, that we ordinarily call 'our real world' will be the object of our knowledge when, at any waking moment, we think of the unlimited totality of particulars of humanly perceptible kinds and sentient subjects that presently exist, or have existed, or will exist, at some time, somewhere in space, relative to the egocentrically demonstrable objects of our present perceptions (i.e. relative to our bodies) (*Essays*, pp. 28–49, ch. XVI; *Appearance and Reality*, pp. 187–8). It is by contrast with *this* world alone that we can give *primary* application to distinctions like those between the genuinely historical and the fictional, the real and the merely imagined, the existent and the non-existent, what is true and what is false, what is actual and what is merely possible, etc. And it is within terms of the more or less fragmentary constructions from which the ideal construction of our real world will have developed in the course of our lives that we initially come to have knowledge of ourselves as

opposed to others, of the inner as opposed to the outer and so on (*Essays*, pp. 356–7). Hence, it is from within the ideal construction of our real world, the material for which is fundamentally given in our waking sense perceptions, that any of the indefinitely various, more or less discrete, ideal constructions that we frame will be predicated of reality (e.g. *Essays*, p. 210).

TIME AND SPACE NOT 'PRINCIPLES OF INDIVIDUATION'

At this juncture it is essential to appreciate the significance of Bradley's contention that time and space are not 'principles of individuation' (*Principles*, vol. I, pp. 63–4; see also *Appearance and Reality*, Appendix C, pp. 527–33). Any ideal content that we can exercise in thinking will be *universal* (e.g. *Appearance and Reality*, p. 34) hence, Bradley maintains, there can be nothing in the idea of a temporal and/or spatial series that logically guarantees that there is not an indefinite multiplicity of spatio-temporally unrelated spatio-temporal series.

We can have no reason, therefore, to hold that the spatio-temporal series of our real world is uniquely real. In fact Bradley maintains that there is an indefinite multiplicity of such series that can be objects of our knowledge (e.g. *Appearance and Reality*, pp. 186–7). For example, the spatio-temporal series of our real world is distinguishable in our thinking from those spatio-temporally unrelated series which are the intentional objects of dream experiences, of works of fiction, of the ideal constructions of ultimate particle physicists and so on. The reality of such series, Bradley maintains, cannot be reduced to the datable psychological acts occurring in the spatio-temporal series of our real world but on the other hand they clearly cannot be thought of as identical with any part of that series.

We can distinguish our so-called *real* spatio-temporal series from indefinitely many less real series by reference to the idea that it is the one that contains the intentional objects of *these* perceptions we are having *now*. However, given that time and space are not principles of individuation, it follows that the uniqueness of *these* perceptions that we are having (e.g. in reading *this now*) cannot, according to Bradley's metaphysics, be consistently thought to derive their uniqueness from being datable states attributable to particulars of spatio-temporally locatable kinds existing in a given *uniquely real* spatio-temporal series.

BRADLEY'S FINITE CENTRES OF IMMEDIATE EXPERIENCE

Such experiences are, Bradley maintains, to be construed ultimately (i.e. within metaphysics) as experiences in a plurality of *finite centres of immediate experience*. It is only within and via the representative activities of such centres that systems of intentional objects of any discernible kinds whatsoever (mental as opposed to physical, human as opposed to non-human, self as opposed to not-self, temporal as opposed to eternal, etc.) can be distinguished and known. However, these centres are not construed as LEIBNIZ's monads are (*see* MONAD, MONADOLOGY): they are not contingently existing *individuals*. Their mode of being, Bradley holds, must be taken to be *adjectival* on that which is truly individual or real. Nevertheless Bradley maintains that in the experiences and activities of the plurality of finite centres that which is truly individual (the *Absolute*) can be coherently taken (1) to have its whole being and self-realization; (2) to be *immediately* but non-relationally present; and (3) to be knowable propositionally with increasing – but of necessity never complete – adequacy through increasingly coherent and comprehensive ideal constructions (*Appearance and Reality*, chs XIII, XIV, XXVI; *Essays*, chs XIV and XI, p. 350, fn. 1; *Principles*, vol. II, Bk III, pp. 590–1, p. 595, fn. 25).

WRITINGS

Principles of Logic (London: 1883); 2nd revised edn with commentary and terminal essays, corrected, 2 vols (Oxford: Oxford University Press, 1967).

Appearance and Reality. A Metaphysical Essay (London: 1893); (Oxford: Clarendon Press, 1968).

Essays on Truth and Reality (Oxford: 1914); (Oxford: Clarendon Press, 1962).

BIBLIOGRAPHY

Ingardia, Richard; Bradley: *A Research Bibliography* (Bowling Green: The Philosophy Documentation Center, 1991).

Manser, A.R. and Stock, G. eds: *The Philosophy of F.H. Bradley* (Oxford: Clarendon Press, 1984).

Wollheim, R.: *F.H. Bradley* (Harmondsworth: Penguin Books, 1959).

GUY STOCK

Brentano, Franz (1838–1917) German philosopher-psychologist. Brentano taught for much of his life in the University of Vienna, where his students included HUSSERL, Christian von Ehrenfels (1859–1932), Carl Stumpf (1848–1936), Kasimir Twardowski (1866–1938) and MEINONG. Of these Husserl, notoriously, was the founder of PHENOMENOLOGY, Ehrenfels and Stumpf were instrumental in the formation of the Gestalt-psychological movement in Berlin, Twardowski was almost single-handedly responsible for the founding of modern Polish philosophy, and Meinong established what has come to be known as the 'theory of objects'. Common to all of these thinkers is the use of psychology, following the example of Brentano himself, as the basis for the development of new and original ideas in ONTOLOGY. Brentano's rigorous and analytic style of teaching and his doctrine of the unity of scientific method (*see* UNITY OF SCIENCE) formed part of the background also of the LOGICAL POSITIVISM of the Vienna circle.

Brentano's early works concern the metaphysics and psychology of ARISTOTLE. For Aristotle, as seen through Brentano's eyes, the two realms of thinking and of corporeal substance are, as it were, attuned to each other. Perceiving and thinking amount to something like a *taking in of form* from the one into the other. Forms or UNIVERSALS exist, accordingly, in two different ways: within corporeal substance and (as 'inexistent') within the soul. They exist only as immanent to individual substances in one or other of these two different ways. When I see a red object, then I see something that is composed of matter and form. What I take in is the form alone, but this form is in fact still connected to (and thus individuated by) its matter. What I know intellectually is this form itself, for example the redness. And this is not a transcendent redness subsisting in some Platonic realm, but rather a redness here on earth (*see* PLATO; PLATONISM).

Only one sort of essence is, as far as Aristotle is concerned, free of materiality in this sense: the essence *mind* or *intellect*. Of this essence, and of the concepts abstracted therefrom, we can have knowledge other than via sensory images. Mind or intellect is, as Brentano puts it, 'with the highest intelligibility completely intelligible' (1867, p. 136, trans. p. 90). Psychology, accordingly, enjoys a peculiarly noble status within the system of the sciences, and our knowledge of psychological phenomena (for example of mental causality, of the relations of part, whole and dependence among mental phenomena) can provide a firm foundation for our knowledge of corresponding concepts as these are applied also to entities of other sorts.

It will be clear from the above how one has properly to interpret Brentano's thesis in Psychology from an Empirical Standpoint (1924) to the effect that 'Every mental phenomenon is characterized by what the Scholastics of the Middle Ages called the intentional (or mental) inexistence of an object' (1924, p. 124, trans. p. 88). As Brentano himself puts it in the very next sentence: 'Every mental phenomenon includes something as object within itself.' This thesis is to be taken literally – against the grain of a seemingly unshakeable tendency to twist Brentano's words at this point. Only in the writings of Husserl, Meinong and other students of Brentano do we find a systematic treatment of INTENTIONALITY as a matter of the mind's directedness to transcendent objects in the world.

By the time of his lectures on descriptive psychology given in Vienna University in 1889–90, Brentano has developed a rich ontological theory of parts and of unity. As Brentano himself puts it, he seeks to construct a psychological *characteristica universalis*, whose letters and words would reflect the different mental constituents or elements of the mind, and whose syntax would reflect the relations between these constituents in different sorts of mental wholes. His ideas here can be seen to stand at the beginning of a tradition which results *inter alia* in Husserl's development of the formal ontology of parts and wholes in the *Logical Investigations*, as also in Leśniewskian mereology and categorial grammar (*see* LEŚNIEWSKI).

In the theory of substance and accident put forward toward the end of his life (see his *Theory of Categories* (1933)), Brentano adopts a new sort of mono-categorial ontology, seeking once more to develop and refine an original Aristotelian theory.

Where Brentano had earlier held that mental acts have an inferior being in relation to their subjects, he gradually came to believe that all entities exist in the same way, that 'existence' has only a strict and proper sense (that all uses of this term which depart therefrom are illegitimate). Everything that exists, he now says, is a concretum, a 'real thing'. Hence he has to find some way of coping with what Aristotle wants to say about the relation between accident and substance – and with what he himself wants to say about mental acts and their subjects – without appealing to special, inferior, 'dependent' entities. Brentano solves this problem by turning Aristotle's theory on its head: it is not, for Brentano, that the accident is an inferior entity existing *in* or *on* its substance. Rather, the substance itself is included within the accident as its proper part. That is, Brentano conceives the accident as the substance itself *augmented* in a certain way.

Thus when one has a mental act, then the subject of this act (one's self) is present as a part of the act. The act, according to Brentano, is not some extra entity attached to the self; it is the self momentarily augmenting itself, mentally, in a certain way. This gives Brentano a means of explaining how it is, when one is seeing and hearing, that it is the same self that is subject in both acts. That is, it gives him a means of accounting for the unity of consciousness, which is to say, for the fact that experience does not resolve itself into a bundle or multiplicity of scattered bits.

It is crucial to the Brentanian theory that there be no extra entity which would make up the difference between substance and accident. For this third entity would be precisely an 'inferior existent' of the sort he is now determined to get rid of. An accident is a thing, no less than its substance. There are no jumps and runs, on this new dispensation, but only jumpers and runners; no thinkings and perceivings, but only thinkers and perceivers. In this way, as CHISHOLM has noted, Brentano anticipated contemporary developments in the direction of an ADVERBIAL THEORY of perception.

What, then, are the ultimate substances of Brentano's ontology? One group of ultimate substances we have met already: they are the mental substances or souls which become augmented to form those half-way familiar things we call hearers, thinkers, and so on. It is natural, now, to suppose that the remaining ultimate substances in the Brentanian ontology are just material or concrete things, and Brentano's philosophy has indeed often been interpreted along these lines, particularly by those who would see him as having anticipated a reist or concretist doctrine of the sort propounded by Leśniewski or Kotarbiński (1886–1981). In fact, however, Brentano takes as non-mental substances – as ultimate individuators – the *places* which material things occupy. Things in the normal sense are accidents of such places. The totality of places is itself a substance, a certain spatial continuum (*see* SPACE AND TIME). Movement within this continuum is not, as we normally suppose, a matter of the perseveration of one thing through a continuum

of places which it successively occupies. Rather, it is a matter of neighbouring parts of the unitary substance experiencing in succession a chain or ripple of similar accidental determinations. Here, therefore, Brentano anticipates later substantival interpretations of the space–time continuum which were formulated in the wake of the Special Theory of Relativity.

WRITINGS

Psychologie des Aristoteles (Mainz: 1867); trans. R. George, *The Psychology of Aristotle* (Berkeley: University of California Press, 1977).
Deskriptive Psychologie; ed. R.M. Chisholm and W. Baumgartner (Hamburg: Meiner, 1982).
Psychologie vom empirischen Standpunkt vol. I (Leipzig: 1874) 2nd edn (Leipzig: 1924); trans. A.C. Rancurello, D.B. Terrell and L.L. McAlister, *Psychology from an Empirical Standpoint*.
Kategorienlehre (Hamburg: 1933); trans. R.M. Chisholm and N. Guterman, *The Theory of Categories* (The Hague, Boston and London: Martinus Nijhoff, 1981).

BIBLIOGRAPHY

Chisholm, R.M.: *Brentano and Meinong Studies* (Amsterdam: Rodopi, 1982).
Smith, B.: *Austrian Philosophy: The Legacy of Franz Brentano* (La Salle, IL: Open Court, 1994), ch. 3.

BARRY SMITH

Broad, Charlie Dunbar (1887–1971) British philosopher. Broad wrote extensively about a wide variety of traditional metaphysical topics, including existence, substance, qualities, relations, things, processes, events, change, time, space, causation, objects, mind, self and consciousness. His views were formed before the impact of 'linguistic method' made philosophers more cautious about regarding metaphysics as a search for general truths about reality. He did not engage in speculative system building, but in 'critical philosophy', analysing and clarifying fundamental concepts, drawing distinctions overlooked by common sense and science alike, and examining dispassionately the evidence for our basic beliefs. Few could match his ability to distinguish subtly different theses or his patience in marshalling arguments for and against each. Often he conceded that he was not sure which thesis won out, and, as one might expect of someone originally trained in the sciences, he hoped that empirical evidence would eventually provide answers.

Scientific Thought (1923) is notable for his discussion of the analogies and disanalogies between SPACE AND TIME, as well as for a critique of the argument against the reality of time by his teacher and predecessor at Cambridge, MCTAGGART (1923, ch. 2). Broad offered final views on this subject in volume 2, part 1, of *Examination of McTaggart's Philosophy* (1933–8). Discussing CAUSATION, he expressed doubts about the orthodox analysis of singular causal propositions in terms of general laws (1933, pp. 241–5).

In *Scientific Thought* (ch. 8) and *The Mind and Its Place in Nature* (1925, ch. 4), he followed LOCKE in arguing that physical objects have shape, size, position and mass, the 'primary qualities' recognized by physics, but no 'secondary qualities', such as colour or temperature (*see* QUALITY, PRIMARY/SECONDARY). Public, persistent, physical objects act causally on our perceptual systems to produce private, short-lived, non-physical, and mind-dependent existents he called 'sensa'. These SENSA have the familiar visual, auditory, and tactual qualities that constitute perceptual experience, which is the basis for our judgements about reality. Broad was unmoved by the objection that introducing sensa makes the existence of physical objects a speculative hypothesis.

The ontology of human beings presented in *The Mind and Its Place in Nature* is akin to but not identical with classical dualism. Substantial VITALISM and the more modern view that organisms are biological mechanisms are rejected in favour of 'emergent vitalism', the belief that their behaviour is due to properties of matter which first appear at the organic level (1925, ch. 2). Reductive materialism (*see* PHYSICALISM, MATERIALISM), which identifies mental processes with molecular movements in the brain, he judged to be false because the two types of events have different properties (1925, p. 622). To analytic behaviourism he objected that, however completely a body answers to behaviouristic tests for intelligence, it makes sense to ask 'Has it a mind or is it an automaton?' (1925, p. 614). His own suggestion was that a mind is a 'compound' comprising a living brain and nervous system together with a 'psychic factor', which interacts with appropriate living organisms to produce mental activity and which might even survive the death of the body (1925, p. 651). He favoured this theory because it accommodated evidence for paranormal psychical phenomena that he thought should be taken seriously.

WRITINGS

Perception, Physics, and Reality; An Enquiry into the Information that Physical Science Can Supply about the Real (Cambridge: Cambridge University Press, 1914).

Scientific Thought (London: Kegan Paul, Trench, Trubner and Co., 1923).

The Mind and Its Place in Nature (London: 1925); (London: Routledge and Kegan Paul, 1951; New York: The Humanities Press, 1951).

Examination of McTaggart's Philosophy, 2 vols, Vol. 1 (Cambridge: Cambridge University Press, 1933), Vol. 2 in 2 parts (Cambridge: Cambridge University Press, 1938).

Religion, Philosophy and Psychical Research (London: Routledge and Kegan Paul, 1953; New York: Harcourt, Brace and Company, 1953).

Kant: An Introduction ed. C. Lewy (Cambridge: Cambridge University Press, 1978). This contains Broad's Cambridge lectures (1950–1, 1951–2) on the philosophy of Kant, especially as found in the *Critique of Pure Reason*.

BIBLIOGRAPHY

Schilpp, P.A. ed.: *The Philosophy of C.D. Broad* (New York: Tudor Publishing Company, 1959). This volume includes Broad's reply to critics and a complete bibliography of his writings through July 1959.

DOUGLAS C. LONG

bundle theory The view that an individual thing is nothing more than a bundle of properties. It is opposed to the view that an individual thing is a SUBSTANCE or SUBSTRATUM. BERKELEY voices preference for a bundle theory over a substance theory (at least in the case of unthinking things) in the following passage:

In this proposition 'a die is hard, extended, and square,' [some] will have it that the word 'die' denotes a subject or substance distinct from the hardness, extension, and figure which are predicated of it, and in which they exist. This I cannot comprehend; to me a die seems to be nothing distinct from those things which are termed its modes or accidents. (*Principles of Human Knowledge*, para. 49)

Bundle theories are often motivated by the fear that a substance would be (in LOCKE's phrase) 'something I know not what', or worse yet, a *bare* something, devoid of features (see BARE PARTICULAR). The fear is misplaced, however, since from the fact that a substance is something distinct from its properties, it does not follow that it does not *have* any properties; nor does it follow that its nature cannot be known.

In the discussion that follows, it will be assumed that a bundle of properties is a *set* of properties, but what is said should hold equally well if a bundle is any other sort of complex entity (e.g. a whole) of which properties are the sole constituents.

If a thing were really nothing more than a set of properties, then any set of properties would constitute a thing. That is absurd – there is no individual constituted by the set of properties (being an alligator, being purple). To avoid this objection, sophisticated bundle theorists (such as RUSSELL and GOODMAN) typically say that a thing is not just any set of properties, but a set of properties united by the relation of *co-instantiation*. Intuitively speaking, co-instantiation is the relation that holds among a number of properties just in case they are all possessed by the same individual. For purposes of the bundle theory, however, it must be assumed that co-instantiation is a relation relating properties alone, not a relation relating properties to an already constituted individual. We are to explain individuals in terms of co-instantiation rather than vice versa.

The version of the bundle theory that identifies things with bundles of co-instantiated properties is open to two notable objections. First, if a thing were a set of properties, how could anything ever CHANGE its properties? For a thing to have a property, according to the bundle theory, is for that property to be a member of it. So a thing could change its properties only if the set identical with it could change its members. But that is impossible; a set is *defined* by its members.

Bundle theorists might seek to avoid this objection by identifying a thing with a *sequence* of sets of properties – for example, the sequence containing *FGH* on Monday, *FGK* on Tuesday, and so on. They could then say that a thing changes its properties by having different properties as members of successive elements in the sequence. Whether this is an adequate account of change or not, it invites the objection that a thing's entire career is now made essential to it. The individual identical with the sequence above changes from having *H* to having *K*; but since sequences are defined by their elements just as much as sets by their members, the individual could have had no other history than *FGH* followed by *FGK*.

The second objection to the bundle theory is that it implies a dubious version of LEIBNIZ's principle of the IDENTITY OF INDISCERNIBLES. By the standard principle of individuation for sets, a set x and a set y are distinct if, and only if, one has a member that the other lacks. If individuals are sets of properties, it follows that two individuals are distinct only if one has a property that the other lacks. But is it not conceivable that there could be two individuals that were perfectly alike in all their properties – the same in colour, shape, mass, and so on – yet distinct for all that? There is no guarantee that individuals can always be differentiated by their properties unless we have recourse to *impure* properties – properties such as being identical with Socrates or being six feet to the north of Plymouth Rock. Such properties presuppose already constituted individuals and so could not be the ultimate materials from which individuals are assembled.

One can imagine a third version of the bundle theory that escapes the objections so far mentioned. This version would be analogous to linguistic versions of PHENOMEN-ALISM, which decline to identify material objects with systems of sense data, but maintain none the less that material-object discourse is translatable into sense-datum discourse (*see* SENSA). Similarly, the third version of the bundle theory would refuse to identify an individual with any set of properties, but would offer instead to translate any statement about individuals into a statement exclusively about properties. For example, it might translate 'There is a red, round thing here' as 'Redness and round-ness are here co-instantiated'; but it would not identify the red, round thing with the complex of properties at the place in question, or indeed with anything at all. The sentence 'There is a red, round thing here' would get counted true as a whole sentence, even though the phrase 'red, round thing' lacks a referent.

Note how the third version of the bundle theory avoids our two objections. By refusing to identify things with items (such as sets) that are defined by their constituents,

it avoids the objection about change. It also accommodates the possibility of a world in which (intuitively speaking) two things are exactly alike, since it admits the possibility of a world in which the same total set of properties is co-instantiated twice over. Since the co-instantiated sets are not allowed to crystallize into things, there is no question about what makes the two things two.

The third version of the bundle theory is not without its costs. It avoids the objections to previous versions by refusing to find within one's ontology any elements or complexes of elements with which individuals may be identified. But if individuals are not identical with anything, then strictly speaking, they do not exist. Any individual who wishes to believe in his or her own existence must therefore reject the third form of the bundle theory.

Another philosophical position that goes by the name 'bundle theory' is the view, most famously espoused by HUME, that a self is nothing but a bundle of thoughts and experiences. This view bears obvious analogies to the more general bundle theory discussed above, and it must deal with similar objections – for example, how to allow for the logical possibility that two selves might have exactly the same thoughts and experiences. It, too, is more plausibly developed in a translational than in an identificational direction, and it may take in its stride (or, as in Buddhist philoso-phy, gladly embrace) the consequence that there are no selves. But it faces stiff chal-lenges. For example, how are we to trans-late *negative* judgements, such as 'I am not now feeling pain', into an idiom free of reference to the I? The passive construction 'Pain is not now felt' is too sweeping – perhaps pain is felt by someone, even if not by the speaker. 'Pain is not now felt *here*' similarly oversteps what is known to be the case – however small *here* is, perhaps some tiny creature shares that space with the speaker and feels pain. '*This sensation* is now occurring and is not co-instantiated with pain' is a good try, but still fails to be equivalent with the original; it implies, as 'I am not in pain' does not, that a particular sensation is occurring.

Perhaps the best strategy for bundle theorists would be to try to steer a course between the second two versions of the theory considered here. This would involve holding that individuals are entities in their own right that come into being when certain sets of properties are co-instantiated. They are not identical with sets of properties (as in version 2), nor is talk of them merely a way of speaking about the patterns of co-instantiation among properties (as in version 3). Instead, individuals are ontological emergents; they emerge from bundles of properties, but are not identical with them.

BIBLIOGRAPHY

Castañeda, H.-N.: 'Thinking and the structure of the world', *Critica* 6 (1972), 43–81.
Chisholm, R.M.: 'On the observability of the self', *Philosophy and Phenomenological Research* 30 (1969), 7–21.
Goodman, N.: *The Structure of Appearance* 2nd edn (Indianapolis: Bobbs-Merrill, 1966), 200–11.
Loux, M.: *Substance and Attribute* (Dordrecht: Reidel, 1978), 115–39.
Russell, B.: *An Inquiry into Meaning and Truth* (London: 1940); (Baltimore: Penguin Books, 1967), 89–101, 121–3.
Van Cleve, J.: 'Three versions of the bundle theory', *Philosophical Studies* 47 (1985), 95–107.

JAMES VAN CLEVE

Buridan, Jean (*c.*1295–1358) Philosopher and scientist, born at Béthune, France. Buridan studied at the University of Paris under OCKHAM and also taught there, serving as rector in 1328 and 1340. He also served as ambassador for the university at the papal court in 1345. Buridan's main philosophical works are the *Summulae de dialectica* (1487) and various commentaries on works of ARISTOTLE.

Buridan's overall philosophical tendency was nominalistic (*see* NOMINALISM) and sceptical. He is best known for his work in logic and his doctrine of FREE WILL. In logic he developed theories of the modality of propositions (*see* PROPOSITION, STATE OF AFFAIRS) and the syllogism, and he appears to have been the first to provide a deductive derivation of the laws of deduction. The means he developed to find the middle term of a syllogism came to be known as 'the bridge of asses' (*pons asinorum*), because it allowed dull students to pass from the premises to the conclusion of a syllogism.

Buridan's doctrine of free will may be characterized as a form of intellectual determinism. The will chooses what reason represents to it as best, although there is no particular time frame within which the will must choose. This view has the extraordinary consequence that if reason presents two alternative choices as equally good, the will cannot make a choice. This difficulty is usually illustrated by what has come to be called 'Buridan's ass'. According to this example, a hungry donkey given equal bales of hay would starve to death; since its intellect could not represent one as better than the other, its will could not make a choice. It is not known who used this example first, but there are some antecedents in Ghazali (1058–1111) and Aristotle. Buridan himself speaks of a dog starving when confronted with equal portions of food.

WRITINGS

Summulae de dialectica (Paris: 1487).
Perutile compendium totius logicae Joannis Buridani cum praeclarissima solertissimi viri Joannis Dorp expositione (Venice: 1499); (Frankfurt/Main: Minerva, 1965).
Quaestiones on Aristotle's *Ethics* (Paris: 1498), *Physics* (Paris: 1509), *De anima* and *Parva naturalia* (Paris: 1516), and *Politics* (Paris: 1530).
In Metaphysicam Aristotelis quaestiones (Paris: 1518); (Frankfurt/Main: Minerva, 1964).
Consequentiae, in *Iohannis Buridani Tractatus*

de consequentiis ed. H. Hubien (Louvain: Publications Universitaires de Louvain, 1976).

Sophismata, in T.K. Scott, *Johannes Buridanus: Sophismata* (Stuttgart-Bad Cannstatt: Frommann-Holzboog, 1977).

BIBLIOGRAPHY

Hughes, G.E.: *John Buridan on Self-Reference: Chapter Eight of Buridan's 'Sophismata'* (Cambridge and New York: Cambridge University Press, 1982).

Pinborg, J. ed.: *The Logic of John Buridan* (Copenhagen: Museum Tusculanum, 1976).

JORGE J.E. GRACIA

Butler, Joseph (1692–1752) British moral philosopher and natural theologian, best known today for the ethical theories in his *Sermons* (1726), but is also noteworthy for the substantial metaphysical treatise, *The Analogy of Religion* (1736). This is the most influential work in the tradition of empirical, or experimental, theism.

Butler's metaphysical arguments, like his ethical ones, have a deeply practical motive. He seeks to persuade his readers to turn to a Christian way of life. To do this he combats the most fashionable anti-Christian arguments of his day. These were offered not by atheists, but by deists, who accepted philosophical demonstrations of the existence and governance of God (particularly the argument from design) but rejected belief in divine intervention and the claims of revelation, holding that a rational deity could sustain and guide us without such special devices.

Butler assumes at the outset that God exists and governs the world, since his opponents also did. In the first part of the *Analogy* he argues that someone who accepts divine governance can find evidence in nature that we live in what he calls a 'state of probation': that is, that we inhabit a world in which we are given the opportunity (and obligation) to choose a path toward moral maturity that will fit us for entry into another life. In the second part he argues that if this is accepted, there is no good reason to turn aside from the signs of revelation that such a providential scheme would give us reason to expect.

Butler's arguments are inductive, or, in his language, analogical, not demonstrative. He begins by making a case for the reality of an afterlife (one that does not require prior agreement on the existence of God). He stresses the frequency of radical transformation in nature (e.g. from caterpillars to butterflies), and argues that death may consist, not in the destruction of persons and the powers they have, but the mere destruction of those means the body provides for the exercise of those powers. Hence death may, for all we know, entail transformation rather than destruction.

He then invokes the theistic TELEOLOGY that he shares with his opponents, and argues that just as we are able, within this life, to learn lessons from both the good and the bad experiences of youth, that fit us for adult life, so the experiences of earthly life as a whole may be intended by God to prepare us for another. He therefore draws an analogy between the earlier and later stages of this life on the one hand, and the pre-mortem and post-mortem lives of human agents on the other. He insists at length that the order we discern in this life is a moral one, in which our creator 'declares for virtue'; the moral structure of human nature, described in the *Sermons*, is part of the evidence for this.

Once the probationary character of human life is accepted, Butler maintains, it is foolish to ignore the likelihood that God will have made revelatory signs available to us. Given his prior commitment to divine governance, the deist has no good reason to hold he would not have done so. Butler's case is throughout prudential as well as inductive: that even if the probability of life's being probationary is not as high as he holds, as long as there is *some* reasonable degree of likelihood of this, it is foolish to ignore the demands of virtue, or reject the claims of revelation without careful examination.

While many of Butler's detailed arguments are shrewd and ingenious, his metaphysical claims depend in large measure on assuming the prior proof of God's existence. The *Analogy* is still of great value, but more as a mine of apologetic defences than as a body of metaphysical argument. In an era where most apologists, wisely or not, seek to defend Christianity without NATURAL THEOLOGY, the probability of life being a state of probation, and the probability of the Christian revelation being true, have to be judged together rather than in sequence. Butler remains the finest classical advocate of the view that, given the depth of our ignorance of divine purposes, probabilities are all most of us have available, and that our religious decisions should therefore be taken with prudence.

WRITINGS

The Analogy of Religion, Natural and Revealed, to the Constitution and Course of Nature (1736); Vol. II of *The Works of Bishop Butler* ed. J.H. Bernard (London: Macmillan, 1900).

BIBLIOGRAPHY

Broad, C.D.: 'Bishop Butler as theologian', in his *Religion, Philosophy and Psychical Research* (London: Routledge and Kegan Paul, 1953), 202–19.

Jeffner, A.: *Butler and Hume on Religion* (Stockholm: Diakonistyrelsens Bokforlag, 1966).

Mossner, E.C.: *Bishop Butler and the Age of Reason* (New York: B. Blom, 1971).

Penelhum, T.: *Butler* (London: Routledge and Kegan Paul, 1985).

TERENCE PENELHUM

C

<hr>

Cantor, Georg (1845–1918) One of a group of late nineteenth-century mathematicians and philosophers (with FREGE, Dedekind (1831–1916), Peano (1858–1932), Hilbert (1862–1943) and RUSSELL) who, in their different ways, transformed both mathematics and the study of its philosophical foundations. The philosophical import of Cantor's work is threefold. First, it was primarily Cantor who turned arbitrary collections into objects of mathematical study, *sets* (*see* CLASS, COLLECTION, SET), thereby reshaping the conceptual structure of basic mathematics. Second, and in connection with this, he created a coherent *mathematical* theory of the infinite, in particular a theory of *transfinite numbers*. Third, he was the first to indicate that it might be possible to present mathematics as nothing but the theory of sets, or at least to push in this direction, among other things making set theory (thus, in fact, the theory of the *infinite*) the study of the basis on which mathematics is founded. This has had a profound effect on the philosophy of mathematics, not least because it contributes substantially to the view that the foundations of mathematics should itself become an object of mathematical study, and because it emphasizes that classical mathematics involves infinity in an essential and variegated way. Indeed, Cantor's work renders study of such philosophically important matters as continua and the infinite vacuous without some knowledge of the mathematical developments he wrought (*see* FINITE/INFINITE).

Cantor's main, direct achievement is his theory of transfinite numbers and infinity during 1880–95. This necessitates extensive revision of traditional doctrines going back, via the scholastics, to ARISTOTLE, which reject the actual-infinite as a subject of rational treatment. Cantor introduced a division of the actual-infinite into the *transfinite* (or *increasable*) infinite, and the *absolute* infinite. According to Cantor, only the latter is beyond rational (thus mathematical) treatment. He argued convincingly that the transfinite is in fact implicitly present in ordinary mathematics, which should therefore take the infinite seriously. Like Frege, Cantor characterized sameness of size (*cardinal equivalence*) in terms of one-to-one onto correspondence, thus accepted the various paradoxical results known to Galileo and others (e.g. that the collection of *all* natural numbers has the same cardinality as that of all *even* numbers). He added to the stock of these surprising results by showing in 1874 that there are only as many algebraic (and thus rational) numbers as there are natural numbers, and in 1878 that there are *more* points on a line than there are natural (or rational or algebraic) numbers, thus showing for the first time that there are at least two different kinds of infinity present in ordinary mathematics, so exposing the need for a coherent theory of these infinities. *Cantor's theorem* of 1892 (that the set of all subsets, the *power set*, of a given set must be cardinally greater than that set) goes further, for it shows that ordinary mathematics must accept indefinitely many different kinds of infinity. Cantor's work in mathematical analysis in the period 1878–82 also showed a pressing need for an extension into the infinite of the indexing (counting) function of the natural numbers. Cantor identified the fundamental property of the natural numbers as counting numbers (their discreteness) in their being *well-ordered*, thus that, in addition to being linearly ordered, there is a first element, and every element with a successor has a *unique* successor (*see* CONTINUOUS/DISCRETE). There being nothing to restrict well-ordering to finite collections, Cantor introduced a scale of general ordinal or counting numbers (the first infinite number was eventually called ω by Cantor) to reflect well-orderings in general.

Cantor's radical idea for a theory of infinite size was to base the notion of cardinality on that of ordinality. Although cardinal and ordinal number coincide in the finite case, this is false of infinite collections. Cantor shows how to circumvent this obstacle by dividing the ordinal numbers into the *number classes*, each consisting of those ordinals representing sets of the same size. Cantor then introduced a scale of cardinal numbers of well-ordered sets (the $\aleph$-numbers) standing for these classes. If one assumes, not only that all sets have a size, but that all sets can be well-ordered (as Cantor did, and as has later been accepted by modern set theory, not without controversy), then all infinite sizes are represented in the scale of alephs. The *continuum problem*, of enormous importance in the development of Cantor's work, is the problem of which aleph represents the cardinality of the continuum. Cantor's famous *continuum hypothesis* (CH) is the conjecture that this cardinality is $\aleph_1$, the second infinite aleph, represented by Cantor's second number-class. The continuum problem was the first in Hilbert's list of 24 central mathematical problems in a celebrated address in 1900, and is now widely thought to be insoluble. CH was shown to be independent of the standard axioms of modern set theory in two steps, the first due to GÖDEL (the consistency, 1938) and the second Paul Cohen (1934–) (the consistency of the negation, 1964). Moreover, work stemming from that of Cohen shows that it is consistent to assume that the cardinality of the continuum can be represented by almost any of the vast sequence of $\aleph$-numbers.

Cantor's conception of set has given rise to some dispute. It is often thought that it is wide enough to admit the universe of sets itself as a set, thus giving rise to what has become known as *Cantor's paradox*. If the universe were a set, Cantor's theorem would say that its power set must be larger than it; but since this latter is a set of sets, it must be *contained* in the universal set, and thus be smaller. Cantor's statements about the nature of sets are too vague to allow of decisive judgement, but it seems to follow from his earlier considerations of the absolute infinite that the collections involved in the paradoxes cannot be proper sets. Other indications also point in this direction (see Hallett, 1984). Moreover, correspondence with Hilbert in the late 1890s and Dedekind in 1899 (see Cantor, 1991) shows clearly that Cantor was well aware that contradictions will arise if such collections *are* treated as ordinary sets. Indeed, in this correspondence Cantor suggested explicitly that consistency be taken as a criterion of set existence, thus presaging a doctrine central to Hilbert's work.

WRITINGS

Gesammelte Abhandlungen mathematischen und philosophischen Inhalts (Berlin: 1932; Berlin, Heidelberg and New York: Springer-Verlag, 1980).
Briefe, ed. H. Meschkowski and W. Nilson (Berlin, Heidelberg and New York: Springer-Verlag, 1991).

BIBLIOGRAPHY

Hallett, M.: *Cantorian Set Theory and Limitation of Size* (Oxford: Clarendon Press, 1984).
Purkert, W. and Ilgauds, H.J.: *Georg Cantor* (Basel: Birkhäuser, 1987).

MICHAEL HALLETT

Carnap, Rudolf (1891–1970) A leading German logical positivist (*see* LOGICAL POSITIVISM). At university, Carnap studied both physics and philosophy. From 1925–36, he was an important participant in the

Vienna Circle. In 1936 Carnap emigrated to the United States, where his work in philosophy of science, philosophy of language, modal logic and inductive logic shaped and promoted the absorption of logical positivist ideas into the American philosophical mainstream. In his autobiography (in Schilpp, 1963, p. 45), Carnap laments the vague, inconclusive character of traditional metaphysics: 'most of the controversies in traditional metaphysics appeared to me sterile and useless . . . I was depressed by disputations in which the opponents talked at cross purposes; there seemed hardly any change of mutual understanding, let alone of agreement, because there was not even a common criterion for deciding the controversy.' This anti-metaphysical animus informs Carnap's two most important books, *Der logische Aufbau der Welt* (1928) and *Logische Syntax der Sprache* (1934). In both these works Carnap proposes to replace philosophy with a successor discipline devoted to the application of modern logic to the clarification of the concepts of science.

In *Der logische Aufbau der Welt* Carnap advocates the development of constitution systems as the successor to philosophy. A constitution system is an ordered system of definitions of scientific concepts. Constitution systems are to be comprehensive, embracing all the concepts of all the formal and empirical sciences. By 'definition', Carnap means explicit definition. Carnap assumes, in effect, a version of the simple theory of types as the background language and logic for constitution systems; and he takes WHITEHEAD and RUSSELL to have demonstrated that mathematics can be unproblematically developed in this framework. Each constitution system has a basis: a domain of individuals and primitive relations over the domain. Carnap believes that there are alternative bases for constitution systems, and hence distinct, though equivalent, systems; he holds forth the prospect of systems with a physical basis of fundamental particles and fundamental magnitudes. However, to illustrate constitution systems, Carnap sketches the development of an epistemologically oriented system with an autopsychological basis: the individuals are the total momentary experiences of a person; the single undefined relation is that of recollected similarity. The order of definition in this system is to reflect epistemological priority in the application of concepts.

A constitution system contains definitions for the concepts employed by the existing formal and empirical sciences. Carnap relies on this feature of these systems to motivate his claim that any rational statement can be formulated within a constructional system. Statements drawing on concepts not so definable are non-rational. Carnap believes his autopsychological constitution system expresses the core common to various epistemological positions, capturing the insights each emphasizes. This achievement makes evident that these epistemological positions differ only in their non-rational, metaphysical assertions. So, Carnap holds that his sample system captures the Kantian insight that objective knowledge requires the synthesis of something given to the form of the unity of the object (*see* KANT). However, for Carnap, synthesis is not understood in terms of an ordering that a transcendental subject imposes on a given manifold in accordance with the immutably valid forms of thought, as neo-Kantians held (*see* TRANSCENDENTAL EGO). Instead, type theory replaces transcendental logic; formal definitions replace synthesis. Talk of transcendental subjects as well as unconceptualizable things-in-themselves disappears (*see* NOUMENAL/PHENOMENAL). Similarly, in defining scientific concepts from an autopsychological basis, this constitution system captures the Machian empiricist insight that all empirical knowledge arises from experience, that every scientific statement is reducible to an equivalent one concerning elementary experiences (*see* EMPIRICISM; MACH). But this reducibility does not in any way ontologically privilege the elementary experiences over objects defined at later stages of the system.

In *Logische Syntax der Sprache* Carnap urges that philosophy be replaced by the logic of science, by the logical syntax of languages for science. Central to Carnap's view of logical syntax is his notion of a language or linguistic framework, a notion that, with modifications, Carnap held for the rest of his career. Languages are to be described in purely formal terms via formation rules defining sentencehood and transformation rules defining a consequence relation for the language. The logical pluralism voiced in Carnap's Principle of Tolerance gives logical syntax its significance: *'In logic, there are no morals.* Everyone is at liberty to build up his own logic . . . All that is required of him is that . . . he must state his methods clearly, and give syntactical rules instead of philosophical arguments' (Carnap, 1934, p. 52). In denying that there is a right or wrong in logic, Carnap rejects any framework transcendent notion of fact or truth. He accordingly comes to distinguish sharply between the decision to adopt a linguistic framework and the epistemic evaluation of sentences of a particular framework. The former is a matter of practical decision, ultimately of preference. The latter evaluations are constrained by the defining rules of a particular language.

Carnap adopts the Principle of Tolerance in response to disputes in the foundations of mathematics, disputes that struck him as sterile as traditional philosophical debates. In *Logische Syntax der Sprache* Carnap explicates analyticity in terms of consequence. He exhibits specifications of languages of differing logical strengths all of whose mathematical truths are analytic. Carnap thus seeks to persuade us that mathematics flows from the defining rules of a language. He maintains that foundational debates arise from the adoption of different languages. Tolerance counsels that these quarrels should be replaced by the metamathematical investigation of languages formalizing various foundational approaches. It should be noted, however, that the mathematics required in Carnap's metalanguage for the crucial definition of consequence makes his understanding of the analyticity of mathematics vulnerable to the charge of vicious circularity.

Carnap applies logical syntax to the problem of explicating empirical testability (Carnap, 1936, 1937). For Carnap, empiricism is not a thesis; it is rather a recommendation that investigators restrict themselves to certain languages as the frameworks for formalizing scientific theories. Here again we see Carnap's distinctive approach to philosophy: the explication (that is, the replacement) of a hitherto philosophical notion by a precise, formal notion and the corresponding construal of a philosophical thesis as the recommendation of a linguistic framework.

WRITINGS

Der logische Aufbau der Welt (Berlin: Weltkreis-Verlag, 1928); trans. R. George, *The Logical Structure of the World* (Berkeley: University of California Press, 1969).
Logische Syntax der Sprache (Vienna: 1934); trans. A. Smeaton, *The Logical Syntax of Language* (London: Routledge and Kegan Paul, 1937).
'Testability and meaning', *Philosophy of Science* 3 (1936), 419–71; 4 (1937), 1–40.
Foundations of Logic and Mathematics, in *Foundations of the Unity of Science* vol. 1, ed. O. Neurath *et al.* (Chicago: University of Chicago Press, 1939), 139–213.
Meaning and Necessity (Chicago: University of Chicago Press, 1947).

BIBLIOGRAPHY

Schilpp, P.: *The Philosophy of Rudolf Carnap* (La Salle, IL: Open Court, 1963).

THOMAS RICKETTS

Castañeda, Hector-Neri (1924–91) One of America's leading analytical metaphysicians. His principal contribution in this area is *guise theory*, first expounded in Castañeda (1974) and subsequently developed and refined in numerous essays leading to his (1989) volume. Guise theory is at once a complex and global view of language, mind, ontology and predication.

To launch guise theory, Castañeda directs us to triads such as the following:

(1)
> Before the pestilence Oedipus believed the previous King of Thebes was dead.

(2)
> It is false that before the pestilence Oedipus believed that Antigone's paternal grandfather was dead.

(3)
> Antigone's paternal grandfather was the same as the previous King of Thebes.

Evidently (1)–(3) are all true (and hence mutually consistent). But, Castañeda queries, how can this be so, given that tenets (T1)–(T3) are each theoretically plausible?

(T1)   For any individuals x and y, if x is (genuinely or strictly) identical with y, then, for any property P, x has P if, and only if, y has P.

(T2)   The sameness relation expressed by statement (3) is genuine identity.

(T3)   In so far as a statement like (1) says something of or about the previous King of Thebes, the sentential matrix 'Before the pestilence Oedipus believed ____ was dead' predicates a property of the denotation (if any) of the singular term filling the blank.

As a closer inspection reveals, however, it is quite impossible that all of (1)–(3) and (T1)–(T3) are true. For (1) and (3), taken in conjunction with the trio (T1)–(T3), entail:

(4)
> Before the pestilence Oedipus believed that Antigone's paternal grandfather was dead.

And (4) flatly contradicts (2).

In guise theory the above puzzle is resolved as follows. Holding fast to the truth of (1)–(3), Castañeda also accepts (T1) and (T3), dictating thereby a rejection of (T2). Theorizing that the sameness relation expressed by statement (3) is weaker than strict identity – he dubs the relation in question *consubstantiation* – guise theory finds that the previous King of Thebes and Antigone's paternal grandfather are genuinely different individuals: Castañeda's *guises*. As he puts it, the network of triads such as (1)–(3) 'is like a huge prism: it breaks down ordinary objects into a system of (infinitely) many guises' (1978, p. 195). Owing to this theoretical stance toward (1)–(3), notice, Castañeda's ontological prism proves unrelenting: since there are perfectly analogous triads as regards, say properties and propositions, each of these join ordinary concrete individuals in separating into their component guises, where the latter are one and all genuinely *different* items in the ontological inventory.

According to Castañeda, guises are complex entities generated as follows. Given any number of properties, say $F_1, \ldots, F_n$, the *set forming operator* $\{\ldots\}$ generates the set $\{F_1, \ldots, F_n\}$. Next, for any such set, the *concretizer operator*, c, generates the guise $c \{F_1, \ldots, F_n\}$. Guises are adjudged identical exactly on the condition that their cores have exactly the same members, where the *core* of $c \{F_1, \ldots, F_n\}$ is the set $\{F_1, \ldots, F_n\}$. For every set of properties, observe, there is a corresponding guise, and each guise enjoys a bona fide ontological status. Because some of these individuals actually exist, e.g. the current president of the United States, whereas others do not, e.g. the round square, the ontology and semantics of guise theory is *Meinongian* (*see* MEINONG). In addition to strict identity and consubstantiation, guise theory includes at least these additional sameness relations: conflation, consociation, transsubstantiation and transconsociation. Properties are predicated of guises either *internally* or *externally*, where P is had internally by a guise g just in case P belongs to g's core, and P is had externally by g if, and only if, there is a sameness relation R and a guise g' having P in its core, and g bears R to g'. So fortified, Castañeda documents that guise theory provides a unified account of a wide range of problems concerning reference to non-existents, negative existentials, referential opacity, names and rigid designation, index-icals, and other matters (Castañeda, 1989, pp. 235–61).

WRITINGS

'Thinking and the structure of the world', *Philosophia* 4 (1974), 3–40.
'Philosophic method and the theory of pre-dication and identity', *Nous* 12 (1978), 189–210.
'Reference, reality, and perceptual fields', *Proceedings and Addresses of the American Philosophical Association* 53 (1980), 763–823.
'Direct reference, the semantics of thinking, and guise theory', in *Themes From Kaplan* ed. J. Almog, J. Perry and H. Wettstein (New York and Oxford: Oxford University Press, 1989).
Thinking, Language, and Experience (Minnea-polis: University of Minnesota Press, 1989).

BIBLIOGRAPHY

Tomberlin, J.E. ed.: *Agent, Language, and the Structure of the World* (Indianapolis, IN: Hackett, 1983).
Tomberlin, J.E.: *Hector-Neri Castañeda* (Dor-drecht: Reidel, 1986).

JAMES E. TOMBERLIN

categories The philosophically most useful and reasonably precise notion of categories was introduced by ARISTOTLE, whose *Cate-gories* is the *locus classicus* for discussions of the topic. Categories are the most general kinds of things ('thing' being used here as applicable to anything whatever), the highest, summa, genera. The ideal theory of categories must satisfy at least two condi-tions: (1) it must be exhaustive, i.e. every thing must fall under one of the theory's categories; and (2) its categories must be mutually exclusive, i.e. no thing may fall under more than one category. To know what categories of things there are would thus be to know the most general constitu-tion of reality, which is a defining goal of metaphysics. The summa genera are ordi-narily the highest ends of complex hier-archies of subordinate genera, reaching at their other ends the so-called infimae species, i.e. kinds no longer divisible into subordinate kinds.

The genus/species relationship (approxi-mated in twentieth century philosophy, with respect to qualities, by the determin-able/determinate distinction, e.g. between colour and red) must not be confused with any kind of composition (*see* DETERMI-NATE/DETERMINABLE). For example, human being is a species of animal, but its being an animal is not a characteristic simply added to, say, being two-footed; rather, the latter is a way in which the former is determinate. A real definition states the genus (e.g. animal) under which the species defined (e.g. human being) falls, and the latter's differentia (e.g. two-footed) distinguishes it from other species falling under that genus. Therefore, a category, being a summum genus, i.e. a genus that falls under no other genus, cannot be given a real definition. Of course, it can be given a nominal definition (an explanation of the usual meaning of the name of what is defined), but a nominal definition, unlike a real definition, may tell us little if anything about the nature of what is defined.

The above is the classical, Aristotelian theory of categories. In his *Categories* Aris-totle lists ten categories: SUBSTANCE (e.g. a horse), quantity (e.g. two yards long), quality (e.g. white), relation (e.g. double), place (e.g. in the Lyceum), time (e.g. yester-day), position (e.g. sitting), possession (e.g. armed), action (e.g. cutting) and being acted upon (e.g. being cut). The Aristotelian theory dominated classical and medieval philosophy. It has been generally rejected in modern philosophy, largely because the Aristotelian theory of substance has been rejected. According to Aristotle, a substance is an individual, particular thing that endures through change. The items in the other categories, called accidents, owe their being solely to their presence in substances. If, as modern philosophers generally have done, one thinks of the items Aristotle regarded as substances as mere bundles of qualities, or volumes of extension, or aggregates of corpuscles, the distinction between substance and accident appears to lose its significance (*see* ARISTOTLE; BUNDLE THEORY). Hence, there has been little use of the notion of a category in modern philosophy, except in the vague sense of any fundamental or basic class or concept or even word.

A major exception to this was KANT, who applied it to what he regarded as the twelve fundamental pure (non-empirical) concepts of the understanding, which correspond to what he took to be the twelve most general forms of judgement and hence make possible our knowledge of objects; for this reason they are called by him transcendental concepts. All judgements are (1) universal or particular or singular; (2) affirmative or negative or 'infinite' (e.g. 'The soul is non-mortal'); (3) categorical or hypothetical or disjunctive; and (4) problematic or assertoric or apodeictic. The respective pure concepts are (1) unity, plurality, totality; (2) reality, negation, limitation; (3) inherence (of a predicate in a subject), causality, reciprocity (interaction); and (4) possibility, existence, necessity. Kant's categories are better thought of as epistemological in nature, and thus quite different from Aristotle's, although the distinction between metaphysics and epistemology does not have a straightforward application to Kant's philosophy.

In the philosophy of language, the notion of a category has been used rather loosely for types of words or uses of words, and the phrase 'category mistake' was introduced by RYLE (1949) for statements or views that involve confusion of such types. A non-philosophical example he gave was that of someone's asking 'But where is the University?' after having been shown the various buildings, offices and departments constituting the University. Ryle's well-known chief philosophical example was the view that certain psychological words, such as 'thinks', signify the occurrence of non-physical, mental events, since *ex hypothesi* they do not signify the occurrence of physical events; while the truth is, according to Ryle, that they do not signify the occurrence of events at all. We shall limit ourselves here to a discussion of the metaphysical topic of categories. Such a discussion may be helped by considerations about knowledge or about language, but must not be confused with them.

It is fairly clear that Aristotle's list of categories is not exhaustive, and that some of them overlap, or are reducible to others, or are not sufficiently basic to qualify as categories. For example, it can be argued that place and time should be understood as reducible to spatial and temporal relations, and then they would belong to the category of relations. The rest of Aristotle's categories, except that of substance, seem to be subordinate genera of the more general kind that today is called a property and arguably is more properly classified as a category. As a result of this line of reasoning, we reach the most common contemporary list of categories, namely, that of individual things (which may include Aristotelian substances but also momentary particulars such as sense data (*see* SENSA)), properties and relations. But in order to avoid paradoxes (which seem to arise if we speak of *all* properties, thus implying that all properties have a common property, the property of being a property) we may need to accept RUSSELL's theory of types, according to which a sharp distinction must be made between properties of individual things, properties of such properties, properties of these properties, and so on, each level constituting a distinct category for the precise reason that the items on it can have no common property with the items on any of the others and thus cannot belong with any of them to the same genus and so to the same category.

But many contemporary philosophers believe that further categories, not rooted in Aristotle's list, should be acknowledged. The most familiar example is states of affairs, which if actual are called facts (*see* FACT; PROPOSITION, STATE OF AFFAIRS). These would be the entities that supposedly correspond to (usually indicative) sentences, somewhat as individual things correspond to (some) proper names and properties correspond to (some) predicates. Another example is sets, e.g. the set containing as its members this article, the Parthenon, and Alpha Centauri. Many believe that sets are needed for understanding the nature of mathematics.

Even if we revise the theory of categories in these ways, it faces severe difficulties. First, there is the challenging and often discouraging task of determining with respect to each alleged category whether it is not reducible to some of the other categories. What causes the difficulty is the vagueness of the notion of reduction (*see* REDUCTION, REDUCTIONISM). The mere fact that something involves, or even consists of, certain things, does not mean that it is reducible to them in the philosophically interesting sense of no longer needing to be taken into account as a distinct entity. An example is the category of states of affairs. The state of affairs *Jones being white* seems to consist of nothing more than Jones, the colour white, and perhaps the so-called 'nexus' of exemplification. But knowing this provides us with no adequate account of what it is for these constituents of the state of affairs to 'hang together' and make up a single entity. A related problem is whether an alleged category is in fact not subsumable under another category, presumably as a subordinate genus, even though one of a very high order. Often, attempts at such a subsumption do not cast much light on any metaphysical issue. An example is the category of events. Is it subsumable under the category of individual (particular) things? Indeed, like the latter, events have spatiotemporal location, but the fact remains that they are too fundamentally different from paradigmatic individual things (e.g. a horse) to make illuminating the claim that they belong to the same genus, and thus to the same category.

A second difficulty is the possibility of cross-classification. A familiar view is that there are only two categories: the mental and the material. If so, mental properties and mental individuals would be sub-ordinate genera of the mental, and material properties and material individuals would be subordinate genera of the material. But it seems obvious that mental and material properties have something in common, namely, being properties, and therefore cannot belong to different categories, and *mutatis mutandis* for mental and material individuals. Yet is it not just as obvious that mental properties and mental individuals have something in common, namely, being mental, and therefore cannot be assigned to different categories, and *mutatis mutandis* for material properties and individuals?

A third difficulty is presented by the existence of concepts, and thus possibly of corresponding entities, that do not seem to fit in any of the usual categories. The following would be examples.

(1) Existence and identity (whether of individuals or of properties, the latter being either specific, 'exact similarity', or generic, 'inexact similarity', and thus admitting of degree); it is surely at least hasty to classify existence as a property and identity as a relation.

(2) Actuality and possibility, understood as characteristics of states of affairs; to classify them as properties would be to ignore the categorial status of states of affairs by allowing that they have something in common with individual things, namely, properties.

(3) Simplicity and complexity; these cannot be properties of individual things if an individual thing consists at least in part of its properties, i.e. is not a BARE PARTICULAR.

(4) The logical connectives (negation, disjunction, etc.), exemplification (what is expressed by 'is' in its sense of predication, as in sentences of the form 'x is F'), and the quantifiers (all, some), the ontological status of all of which has been vigorously defended by BERGMANN (1992) and Grossmann (1983).

Some of the concepts occasioning this third difficulty may be definable in terms of others, but it is certain that some must be taken as undefined, as primitive.

A fourth difficulty, related to the third, was recognized by Aristotle himself and was accorded much attention by the mediaeval philosophers. That is the existence of concepts even more general than those represented by Aristotle's list of categories and ranging over the things subsumed under the latter; they cannot be Aristotelian categories precisely because they range across Aristotle's categories. The concepts in question are what the mediaeval philosophers called transcendentals, the most common examples being Being, One, True and Good. Could it be that they are themselves the categories, i.e., the summa genera, Aristotle's categories being subordinate genera? This might seem plausible especially in the case of Being, which may be thought of as the genus under which all things must fall. But in the *Metaphysics* (998b15–28) Aristotle argued that being is not a genus, on the (questionable) grounds that if it were the differentiae dividing it into subordinate genera and species would not *be*, since it is impossible for a genus to be a predicate of the differentiae of its subordinate genera or its species. This argument was in effect the basis of the doctrine of the transcendentals. Aristotle and the mediaeval philosophers who were influenced by him held that such transcendental concepts apply to everything, but at most by analogy, not by representing common properties, whether generic or specific.

Is there a way out of these difficulties for a traditional theory of categories, whether Aristotelian or modern, a way to allow metaphysics the goal of giving the most general account of the constitution of reality? We may attempt to do so by regarding the concepts that do not fit in the hierarchy of the categories, and are not reducible to any that do, as principles or concepts that allow us to think and speak of reality, which does have a categorial structure, but do not themselves correspond to parts of reality, and thus can be properly called syncategorematic. In this way we could resolve, for example, the difficulties concerning subsumption and cross-classification, since they (indeed, the theory of categories as a whole) have to do with classification and therefore arise out of our relying on the concept of identity (especially generic identity of properties, or similarity.) They concern ultimately questions about what is more like what, and if nothing in reality corresponds to the concept of identity, then its applications cannot be judged as true or false, but at most as normal or idiosyncratic, and may be expected sometimes to be in conflict yet remain equally legitimate.

To reach such a conclusion is, of course, to take what has been called a transcendental turn, though one less extreme than Kant's or that (quite different from Kant's) taken by some recent linguistic philosophers, and perhaps closer to the mediaeval doctrine of the transcendentals. To take such a turn is to recognize that our conception of reality necessarily involves elements that do not themselves correspond to items in reality. But how exactly it does so requires detailed examination of the role of each of the relevant concepts, which, following the tradition, we can now call transcendental. It is quite insufficient and indeed misleading just to speak vaguely of 'our making the world'. The categorial structure of the world is fixed, it is in no way subject to personal whim or cultural or linguistic custom or convention, and the adequacy of our statements, thoughts, and theories can be judged by comparing them with the world, once the primary (paradigmatic) applications of the transcendental concepts, especially that of generic identity (inexact similarity of properties), are themselves fixed. And even though these applications are not fixed by corresponding to something in reality, to suppose that they are fixed by personal whim or cultural or linguistic custom or convention would be to ignore their fundamental status as the determinants of our whole conception of reality, and therefore as presupposed by any attempted explanation or justification of them.

BIBLIOGRAPHY

Aristotle: *Categories* (many versions).

Aristotle: *Metaphysics* (many versions).

Bergmann, G.: *New Foundations of Ontology* (Minneapolis: University of Minnesota Press, 1992).

Brentano, F.: *The Theory of Categories* (Hamburg: 1933); trans. R.M. Chisholm and N. Guterman (The Hague: Martinus Nijhoff, 1981).

Butchvarov, P.: *Being Qua Being: A Theory of Identity, Existence, and Predication* (Bloomington, IN and London: Indiana University Press, 1979).

Chisholm, R.M.: *On Metaphysics* (Minneapolis: University of Minnesota Press, 1989).

Grossmann, R.: *The Categorial Structure of the World* (Bloomington, IN: Indiana University Press, 1983).

Kant, I.: *Critique of Pure Reason* (many versions).

Ryle, G.: *The Concept of Mind* (London: Hutchinson's University Library, 1949).

Whitehead, A.N. and Russell, B.: *Principia Mathematica* (Cambridge: Cambridge University Press, 1910–13).

PANAYOT BUTCHVAROV

causation Making something happen, allowing or enabling something to happen, or preventing something from happening. Mental and extra-mental occurrences, of all spatial and temporal dimensions, great and small, have causes and are causes. Our awareness of the world and our action within the world depends at every stage on causal processes. Although not all explanations are causal, anything that can be explained in any way, can be explained causally. Like other metaphysical concepts, the concept of causation applies very broadly. Yet this fundamental concept continues to elude metaphysical understanding. While there is some general philosophic agreement about causation, there is also considerable disagreement. Causal theories of knowledge, perception, memory, the mind, action, inference, meaning, reference, time and identity through time, take a notion as fundamental that philosophers understand only incompletely.

HUME is the dominant philosopher of cause and effect. A running commentary on Hume's views and arguments, pro and con, could cover most contemporary philosophical concerns with causation (Hume, 1739, esp. Bk I, Pt III; Hume, 1748, esp. Sects IV, V, VII). Limitations of space preclude extensive quotation and discussion of primary texts. In what follows, a number of paragraphs begin with the statement of a view about causation. The next sentence then classifies the view as *prevailing, majority,* or *controversial*. (These classifications serve the purpose of this article. They do not reflect a consensus among philosophers.) Discussions of majority views include treatments of minority positions. Discussions of controversial views outline the controversies. There will be no discussion of cogent objections to prevailing views.

Causes and effects are events. This is a majority view (*see* DAVIDSON; and Davidson, 1980). Idiomatic speech often mentions something other than a change, or non-change, or occurrence, as a cause or effect, as in 'Richard makes me furious.' The question is whether an available paraphrase such as 'Reading what Richard writes makes me become furious' brings events back into the picture as causes and effects. If both causes and effects are always of the same kind, then causal paths can continue indefinitely both from the past and into the future. On the other hand, the strategy of reducing all causal statements by paraphrase to statements about events does not convince philosophers who hold that facts, properties, aspects of events, or substances are irreducible relata of the causal relation. The view of *agent causation* holds that in human action a person is an irreducible cause (*see* ACTION THEORY). Although Lucy's putting on her shoes involves event causation throughout, the ultimate cause of Lucy's shoes being put on is Lucy herself.

We cannot directly perceive causal rela-

79

tions. This is a majority view that Hume influences greatly with his example of the impact of billiard balls. We can see motions and changes in motion in the balls. We can see that one ball touches the other immediately before the second begins to move. We cannot see that there is a causal relation between the two motions. Nor can we tell, just by observing the sensible qualities of a thing, what are its causal capacities and dispositions. A minority view here appeals to other sense modalities. Not by seeing, but by our sense of touch and our perception of the positions and movements of our own limbs, we can perceive a causal relation between arm movement and cue movement. Associated with this view is the minority position that the concept of human action, a person's making something happen, is the foundation of our concept of physical causation in general (see von Wright, 1971, pp. 66–74, and for further references, pp. 189–90, fn.). This theory must deal, by appeal to analogy or imagination, with causal instances in which humans do not and sometimes cannot actually participate, such as those that involve clusters of galaxies.

Continuous causal paths connect causes with their effects. This is a prevailing view. Causes and effects are often not contiguous. A switch on the wall is some distance from the electric light overhead that it controls. Pulling a button on an alarm clock makes it ring six hours later. The New York performance of three musicians in 1937 contributes causally to what one hears on the Perth radio in 1997. Although intervals of space, time, or space-time separate the causes and effects in these examples, spatio-temporally continuous causal paths connect them. The path has no spatial or temporal gaps or breaks. (A rigorous definition of CONTINUITY requires the notion of a *limit* found in calculus textbooks.) The path is causal because for any two positions, a and c, on the path, there is an intermediate position b on the path such that either something at a causes something at b that causes something at c, or the causation runs in the other direction, *cba*. An explanation of what

constitutes a causal path that does not use the notion of causation would serve as a reductive definition of causation. The explanation above, which blatantly uses the notion of causation, serves only to state a spatio-temporal necessary condition of causation.

By the very nature of causation, a cause is earlier than its effect. This is a controversial view. Other requirements of causal connection are symmetric in form; they do not distinguish effects from causes. Drawing this distinction by temporal priority thus has theoretical appeal. But there is also a theoretical drawback: the equally appealing account of temporal priority by reference to causation will be circular if the explanation of causal priority is to be temporal. There are, in addition, doubts whether all causes are prior to their effects. Mackie (1974, ch. 7) discusses the conceptual possibility of 'backward causation' and provides further references. Simultaneous causation appears to be not merely possible, but actual. Physics assures us that much of this appearance is illusion. Since nothing transmits motion faster than the speed of light, the motion of one's fingers, that grip the handle of a teaspoon, does not, strictly speaking, cause the simultaneous motion of the bowl of the spoon. Other cases of apparent simultaneous causation, however, do not involve bridging a spatial gap, as when a moving belt turns a pulley with which it is in direct contact.

There is no element of genuine a priori reasoning in causal inference. This is a majority view. Most philosophers believe that Hume refuted the rationalists (*see* RATIONALISM) before him (such as SPINOZA, DESCARTES and, on this issue, HOBBES) and the idealists after him (such as MCTAGGART and BLANSHARD) who hold that causation is intrinsically intelligible. Given a determinate event, according to Hume, anything might happen next, so far as reason and logic are concerned. 'The contrary of every matter of fact is still possible; because it can never imply a contradiction' (Hume, 1748, p. 25). Cause and effect are distinct existences, and 'the mind never perceives any real connexion among distinct existences' (Hume, 1739, p. 636). Reason by itself cannot predict what will happen next after one billiard ball bumps into another. But from what are such predictions to be attempted? From descriptions of the events in question? If so, which logical relations do or do not obtain will depend on the nature of the description. Any event has logically independent descriptions, and any two events have descriptions that are not logically independent (see Davidson, 1980, essay 1). The view that there is at least sometimes an intelligible connection between cause and effect, does not rely on logical tricks. Rather, it concedes a lot to Hume without conceding everything. Just from observing its sensible qualities, we cannot figure out a thing's causal capacities. And when we do come to believe, from a much broader experience, what they are, our evidence does not entail our conclusion. It is still logically possible that anything will happen next. Our beliefs about the physical properties of belts and pulleys are fallible and based on more than an initial visual impression. Still, given the physical properties of the belt and pulley, the spatial relations between them, and the assumption that the belt moves in a certain direction, one can figure out which way the pulley rotates. Although one can draw on experience of similar set-ups that involve belts and pulleys when closing the final gap of causal inference, it is unnecessary to do so. Reason can bridge the gap unaided by additional experience.

Every cause/effect pair instantiates a physical law (see LAW OF NATURE). This is a majority view. According to Hume, it is not the experience of an individual causal transaction, but experience of other transactions, relevantly similar, that provides what causation involves in addition to priority and contiguity. Experience of regularities or constant conjunctions condition our expectations. We project our conditioned feelings of inevitability on external objects as a kind of necessity that resides in the objects themselves (see Hume, 1748, sect. VII). Hume's discussion of regularity calls for a distinction between lawlike and accidental generalizations. Many true statements of the form 'All As are Bs' have nothing to do with causation. Providing an account of the difference between laws and accidental generalizations is a major theoretical undertaking. Events related as cause and effect, according to the majority view, when appropriately described, fall under a covering law. These descriptions typically do not use the same concepts as we ordinarily would in describing the causal transaction. Causation in the everyday world supervenes on causal relations that the fundamental laws of nature directly cover. If such SUPERVENIENCE is universal, there are no causal differences without differences of fundamental properties and spatio-temporal arrangements. A singular causal statement need not entail a law, but it does entail that there is a law that covers, probably as described differently, the events mentioned (see Davidson, 1980, essay 7). A minority view rejects this contention and holds that references to regularities, uniformities, constant conjunctions, and so forth, are extraneous to the individual relation between a particular cause and effect.

Causal relations obtain because the associated counterfactual conditional statements are true. This is a controversial view. Hume connects causation with conditionals in this famous passage:

Similar objects are always conjoined with similar. Of this we have experience. Suitable to this experience, therefore, we may define a cause to be *an object, followed by another, and where all the objects similar to the first are followed by objects similar to the second. Or in other words, if the first object had not been, the second never had existed.* (Hume, 1748, p. 76)

What Hume puts 'in other words' is scarcely a restatement of what goes before. It nevertheless expresses an important and influential claim, that a cause is necessary for its effect.

Kate turned the key, and the engine

started. But if the engine would have started at that very moment anyway, without Kate's key turn, then Kate's turning the key did not start the engine.

If-then statements about what would have happened if something else had occurred are called COUNTERFACTUALS, *contrary-to-fact* or *subjunctive* conditionals. A conditional of the form 'If *a* had not happened, then *b* would not have occurred' says that *a* is necessary for *b*: it is impossible for *b* to occur without *a*. If it is impossible for *a* to occur without *b*, then *a* is *sufficient* for *b*. For example, the downward movement of a lever of the first kind is sufficient for the upward movement of its other end. The necessity of *a* for *b* is often separate from the sufficiency for *a* for *b*; the thesis that a cause is both necessary and sufficient for its effect is quite strong. Events or conditions we single out as causes often are neither necessary nor sufficient for their effects. Adding Bob's Super-Grow fertilizer speeded up the growth of the lawn, but it was not really necessary. Other brands would have had the same effect. Just by itself, moreover, it also was not sufficient; for other factors, independent of adding the fertilizer, such as light, water and the absence of large amounts of concentrated sulphuric acid, were also necessary for the quick growth of the lawn. We can still use the notions of *necessity* and *sufficiency* to spell out the causal relevance of adding Bob's Super-Grow to the lawn's rapid growth. It is presumably an *inus condition* of the growth; that is, it is an *insufficient* but *non-redundant* part of an *unnecessary* but *sufficient* condition of rapid growth (Mackie, 1974, p. 62). Inus conditions involve somewhat complicated counterfactual conditionals. The pair of simpler conditionals that express necessity and sufficiency, 'If *a* had not happened, neither would *b*' and 'If *a* had happened, then so would *b*' together express *counterfactual dependence*. Some philosophers define causal dependence in terms of counterfactual dependence (Lewis, 1986, essays 17 and 21). Others maintain that a better explanation runs in the opposite direction:

causal relations do not obtain because certain conditional statements are true. On the contrary, certain conditional statements are true because of causal relations that obtain (see Sanford, 1989, chs 11–14).

a is necessary for *b* if, and only if, *b* is sufficient for *a*. This is a prevailing view that follows from the standard explanations of the terms involved. It does not entail the stronger view that *a* is a necessary condition of *b* if, and only if, *b* is a sufficient condition of *a*. Causal examples, among others, show that 'condition of' is not a symmetric relation. The presence of light, for example, is a causally necessary condition of the growth of grass, which is not in turn a causally sufficient condition for the presence of light. No one attempts to produce light by growing grass. A theory of the direction of conditionship can help account for the direction of causation (Sanford, 1975).

A totality of conditions necessary for an occurrence is jointly sufficient for it. This is a controversial view, and not a logical truth, in the technical sense of *sufficient* spelt out above. In an ordinary sense of *sufficient*, however, namely 'enough, lacks nothing', if everything necessary for *b* obtains, the aggregate is collectively sufficient for *b*'s occurrence, because jointly the members of the aggregate are enough – nothing necessary for *b* is missing (see Anscombe, 1981, p. 135). The following controversial view is related to this one.

Something necessitates every effect. This is a controversial view. Although what we call a 'cause' often falls far short of being sufficient for its effect, it is common to assume that every effect has some, usually more complicated, sufficient cause. If every effect has a sufficient cause, and every event is an effect, then a classic version of DETERMINISM is true. Modern physics discourages belief in determinism. Indeterminism requires the possibility of events that lack sufficient causes, but it does not require the possibility of uncaused events. The controversial issue in question is precisely whether every event that is caused has a sufficient cause. Definitions that resemble Mackie's definition of an inus condition provide for the possibility of causation without sufficiency: *a* is a *suni condition* of *b*, for example, if there is something *x* such that the disjunction *a* or *x* is a necessary condition of *b*, and *x* is not a necessary condition of *b* (Sanford, 1984, p. 58).

Questions of causation, inductive support, laws of nature, and counterfactual conditionals are bound closely together. This is a prevailing view. The following distinctions are closely associated, and any one can explain the others: acceptable vs unacceptable counterfactual conditionals; laws of nature vs accidental generalizations; a particular observation's inductively confirming vs not confirming a hypothesis. Acceptable counterfactual conditionals, but not unacceptable ones, fall under laws (as CHISHOLM and GOODMAN have argued). On the other hand, laws, but not accidental generalizations, support acceptable counterfactuals. Laws, unlike accidental generalizations, are hypotheses that their instances confirm. These interconnections, although mutually explanatory, are arranged in a tight circle and thus evoke a sense of theoretical uneasiness. Philosophers who aspire to develop a theory of causation attempt to break out of the circle by explaining one distinction in the family without appeal to additional distinctions in the same family. Different theories attempt to break out in different places and also differ in their assignments of explanatory priority. For example, one theory holds that a relation between particulars is causal when it falls under a law, while another holds that a generalization is a law when particular causal relations fall under it. No views prevail about the best way to achieve equilibrium in these theoretical matters concerning causation.

In Book II of the *Physics*, ARISTOTLE discuss four kinds of *aitia* or causes. The present article deals only with *efficient* causes. In the 'Second Analogy' of the *Critique of Pure Reason* (1781), KANT argues that all changes conform to the law of cause and effect. In 'Of Induction', Book III of *A System of Logic* (1843), J.S. MILL pre-

sents experimental methods for establishing causal relevance. In his 1912 lecture, 'On the notion of cause', RUSSELL claims that the law of causation 'is a relic of a bygone age'; but Russell's own theoretical constructions in some later writings depend heavily on causal notions.

BIBLIOGRAPHY

Anscombe, G.E.M.: *Metaphysics and the Philosophy of Mind, Collected Philosophical Papers* vol. 2 (Minneapolis: University of Minnesota Press, 1981).

Davidson, D.: *Essays on Actions and Events* (Oxford: Oxford University Press, 1980).

Hume, D.: *A Treatise of Human Nature* Book I (London: 1739); ed. L.A. Selby-Bigge (Oxford: Oxford University Press, 1888); rev. P.H. Nidditch, 2nd edn (Oxford: Oxford University Press, 1978).

Hume, D.: *Enquiry concerning Human Understanding* (London: 1748); ed. L.A. Selby-Bigge (Oxford: Oxford University Press, 1894); rev. P.H. Nidditch, 3rd edn (Oxford: Oxford University Press, 1975).

Lewis, D.K.: *Philosophical Papers* vol. II (Oxford: Oxford University Press, 1986).

Mackie, J.L.: *The Cement of the Universe* (1974); 2nd edn (Oxford: Oxford University Press, 1980).

Sanford, D.H.: 'The direction of causation and the direction of conditionship', *Journal of Philosophy* 73 (1975), 193–207.

Sanford, D.H.: 'The direction of causation and the direction of time', *Midwest Studies in Philosophy* 9 (1984), 53–75.

Sanford, D.H.: *If P, then Q: Conditionals and the Foundations of Reasoning* (London: Routledge, 1989).

von Wright, G.H.: *Explanation and Understanding* (Ithaca, NY: Cornell University Press, 1971).

DAVID H. SANFORD

change An object undergoes a change if, and only if, it possesses a property at one time and does not possess this property at an earlier or later time. The explication of this definition depends on one's theory of objects, one's theory of time and one's theory of properties.

Objects can be conceived in one of two ways, as substances or as wholes of temporal parts (see SUBSTANCE; TEMPORAL PARTS, STAGES). If an object x is a substance, then x is a particular that exists at each time x is said to exist and that exemplifies each property that x is said to have. If an object x is a whole of temporal parts, then x is composed of distinct particulars, each of which exists at one instant only, such that whatever property x is said to have at a certain time is exemplified by the particular (temporal part) that exists at that time. If x is a substance, then 'x possesses a property at one time and does not possess this property at an earlier or later time' implies that the particular that possesses the property at one time is identical with the particular that does not possess this property at another time. If x is a whole of temporal parts, then this definition implies that one temporal part of x possesses a certain property F at one time and that another temporal part of x does not possess F at another time.

A further explication of our original definition of change is possible if we introduce two different theories of time, the tenseless theory and the tensed theory. According to the tenseless theory, temporal determinations consist only of the relations of earlier, later and simultaneity. On this theory, changes are described by permanently true tenseless sentences of such forms as 'The object x possesses (tenseless) F at the time t and does not possess (tenseless) F at the later time t''. The tensed theory has several versions, but one of them holds that in addition to the temporal relations there are temporal properties of pastness, presentness and futurity (even though these are not properties of the ordinary sort, such as redness). The tensed theorist would describe changes by using transiently true tensed sentences of the form 'The object x now possesses F-ness but will soon not possess F-ness'. A central difference is that the tensed theorist supplements our original definition of change (which explained change solely in terms of temporal relations) by an account in terms of temporal properties. An object changes from being F to not being F if, and only if, the F-ness of x first possesses presentness and later possesses pastness. On this account, change may be viewed as the acquiring and losing of temporal properties by the states of an object.

A second version of the tensed theory of time holds that only what is present possesses properties and that there are no properties of futurity or pastness. Change would be described by such sentences of the form 'It is (now) the case that the object x possesses F-ness and it will be the case that x does not possess F-ness'. But proponents of this view have not yet succeeded in offering an adequate semantic and metaphysical analysis of such sentences. For example, what is the semantic content of 'it will be the case that'? If this phrase does not ascribe the property of futurity to the obtaining (truth) of a certain state of affairs (proposition), what is its semantic content?

A third way to explicate our original definition is in terms of the theory of properties. There are at least two theories of properties, the causal theory and the consistency theory.

According to the causal theory, something is a property if, and only if, it bestows upon its possessor a causal power, i.e. the capacity to affect something else or be affected by something else. For example, a ball satisfies the grammatical predicate 'is moving' and since the ball's motion bestows upon the ball the power to impinge upon and move some other thing, this predicate expresses a property of the ball. By contrast, the ball satisfies the grammatical predicate 'is being remembered by John' but since being remembered by John does not bestow upon the ball any causal power, this is not a property of the ball. Thus, if the ball is moving at time t_1 and is resting at time t_2, it undergoes a change, but if it is being remembered by John at t_1 but not at t_2, it does not (in this respect) undergo a change.

According to the consistency theory, something F is a property if, and only if, it is possible to predicate 'F' of something consistently. Since it is consistent to predicate 'being remembered by John' of the ball, this predicate expresses a property of the ball. But it is not consistent to predicate of the ball or of anything else the predicate 'has no properties', since if something satisfied this predicate it would have at least one property, namely, the property of satisfying this predicate. According to this view, the ball does change from t_1 to t_2 by virtue of the fact that it is being remembered by John at the first time but not at the second time.

BIBLIOGRAPHY

Armstrong, D.M.: *Universals and Scientific Realism* (Cambridge: Cambridge University Press, 1978).
Mellor, D.H.: *Real Time* (Cambridge: Cambridge University Press, 1981).
Oaklander, L.N.: 'Delmas Lewis on persons and responsibility: a critique', *Philosophy Research Archives* 13 (1987–8), 181–7.
Smith, Q.: 'Problems with the new tenseless theory of time', *Philosophical Studies* 52 (1987), 77–98.
Smith, Q.: 'A new typology of temporal and atemporal permanence', *Nous* 23 (1989), 307–30.

QUENTIN SMITH

Chisholm, Roderick Milton (1916–) American epistemologist and metaphysician who has been a seminal figure in contemporary philosophy, Chisholm has helped renew interest in metaphysics during the last third of the twentieth century. Raising the art of philosophical analysis to new heights, his Socratic searches for analyses are legendary (*see* ANALYSIS).

Chisholm challenged influential anti-metaphysical analytical movements such as LOGICAL POSITIVISM and linguistic philosophy. His brand of analytical metaphysics incorporates the Aristotelian notion that metaphysics is a 'first science' which studies fundamental ontological categories, and utilizes techniques and theories of modern logic to construct philosophical analyses

and metaphysical theories (*see* ARISTOTLE; CATEGORIES; ONTOLOGY).

Chisholm defends an ontology of *concreta* and *abstracta* which includes as fundamental entities substances (material objects and persons) and attributes (which have necessary existence) (*see* CONCRETE/ ABSTRACT; SUBSTANCE; UNIVERSALS). Thus, he combines two traditional forms of REALISM: Aristotelianism about substances and PLATONISM about attributes.

Chisholm strives for a parsimonious account of the intuitive data (*see* SIMPLICITY, PARSIMONY): (1) sense data are eliminated in favour of persons and ways of appearing, for example, 'I see a blue sense datum' is paraphrased as 'I am appeared to bluely' (*see* ADVERBIAL THEORY; SENSA); (2) any material thing which can persist through mereological change is eliminated in favour of a sequence of material objects such that none of them can survive the loss of a part and each of them differs in some part from its predecessor and successor in the sequence (*see* PART/WHOLE); (3) Chisholm intimates that persons are persisting physical substances which do not undergo mereological change (*see* PERSONS AND PERSONAL IDENTITY); (4) eliminating places and times, he finds a need for boundaries (*see* BOUNDARY; SPACE AND TIME).

In two other cases, Chisholm has changed his ontology. In these cases, difficulties appear to arise due to a need for entities which seem to be a hybrid of *concreta* and *abstracta*. (a) Typically, events are changes in spatio-temporally located things, yet some such events *recur* (*see* EVENT THEORY). Chisholm held that concrete events are eliminable in favour of repeatable states of affairs, *abstracta* such as *A person's walking* or *Jones's talking* (*see* PROPOSITION, STATE OF AFFAIRS). He then switched to the view that an event is a state of an individual, where such a state, x's *being F*, is a repeatable *concretum* that exists if, and only if, x is F. (b) Consider a belief, b, a person, S, has about himself and which is expressible in first-person language. Chisholm shifted from the view that *b* is directed upon an abstract state of affairs entailing S's non-qualitative HAECCEITY to the view that an *abstractum* cannot be non-qualitative and *b* is S's self-attribution of a qualitative attribute. Accordingly, Chisholm holds that individuals do not exist *in* possible worlds: all such worlds are qualitative *abstracta* (*see* MODALITIES, AND POSSIBLE WORLDS).

Chisholm maintains that *abstracta* are individuated by their cognitive content, that a self-presenting psychological state is not identical to a physical state (*see* MENTAL/PHYSICAL; MIND/BODY PROBLEM) and that there are synthetic a priori propositions. The latter two points relate to Chisholm's important foundationalist epistemological theories.

Chisholm also holds that INTENTIONALITY uniquely characterizes the psychological, and that REFERENCE is a function of the psychological (not of linguistic or causal phenomena).

Lastly, Chisholm argues that an adequate account of human freedom and power entails causal indeterminism (*see* FREE WILL). Here (and elsewhere) Chisholm makes important contributions to ethical theory.

WRITINGS

Theory of Knowledge (Englewood Cliffs, NJ: Prentice Hall, 1966).
Person and Object: A Metaphysical Study (La Salle, IL: Open Court, 1976).
'Objects and persons: revisions and replies', *Grazer Philosophische Studien* 7/8 (1979), 317–88.
The First Person (Minneapolis: University of Minnesota Press, 1981).
On Metaphysics (Minneapolis: University of Minnesota Press,1989).

GARY ROSENKRANTZ

class, collection, set These three distinct notions are usually taken to represent totalities made up of *elements*, which are said to *belong to* them. There are intuitively clear differences between the three, which however are less clear than is apparent at first sight.

A *class* is often thought of as the extension of a property (or concept), the collection of all those things (of whatever realm one is talking about) which have that property or fall under that concept (*see* EXTENSION/INTENSION). The elements in the class are thus 'unified' by the property whose extension they make up. A *collection* is intuitively thought of simply as an agglomeration or aggregate of objects not necessarily united by any specific property. In practice, though, it is hard to conceive of any collections that do *not* have a unifying property, for the very description of apparently amorphous collections *specifies* a unifying property, even if this only amounts to a simple enumeration. Still, one might say that such properties are *accidental*, perhaps due more to artefacts of our language than anything else. (We will come back to this.) The notion of *set* is different again, for the central difference between sets on the one hand and classes and collections on the other is that sets are assumed to be themselves *single* objects of the same (logical) type as the elements that compose them, this is meant in the sense that they are themselves available for being taken as elements of further sets (or collections or classes). The relation of sets to properties is again often taken to be accidental, and it is assumed that there is a primitive notion of collection prior to any sophisticated consideration of classes. But note that the description of collections, thus the specification of an underlying property, is indispensable once we start considering infinite collections, as mathematics has to. With both classes and sets, the correct identity principle is that of *extensionality*. This says that any two classes (sets) with the same elements are identical, even if they have been described on the basis of two different properties.

The philosophical interest of the theory of sets (founded by CANTOR and others) stems from both its mathematical and its logical importance. There are three reasons for this. First, concentration on sets allowed the collection of numbers or points without there being any obvious form, geometric or otherwise, to hold the elements together, and then, despite this, stressed that such a collection be treated as a self-subsistent mathematical object, i.e. as an object as legitimate and justified as numbers or well-known, even intuitable, functions or forms. Second, this reinforced the claim that mathematics is necessarily based on some kind of privileged intuition, particularly spatio-temporal intuition. In particular, it was allowed that the sets so produced might be infinite as well as finite, and that the mathematical properties they can possess will include those of being ordinally and cardinally numerable. In accordance with this, Cantor developed a widely accepted and precise theory of infinity, including a theory of infinite number. Third, the theory of sets (and classes) was intimately connected with the development of logic through the work first of FREGE and then of RUSSELL, since it was what they intended as the basic of logicism, the thesis that mathematics ultimately reduces to pure logic.

Can sets be completely arbitrary? Or, more precisely, can every class (i.e. the extension of every property) be treated as a set? Both Frege and Russell assumed at first that the answer is yes, as is implicit in Frege's *Basic Law V* (Frege, 1893) and Russell's *Principle of Comprehension* (CP) (Russell, 1903). This gives some credence to logicism, if one assumes (1) that mathematics operates with the extensions of concepts; and (2) that logic should (among other things) give the basic laws governing the behaviour of concepts and their extensions. However, the set-theoretic antinomies show that Basic Law V or CP, when taken as principles about sets, cannot be right; the extensions of some properties cannot be 'simple' objects (thus sets) on pain of contradiction. This is shown clearly by *Russell's paradox*, discovered independently by Russell (in 1900) and by Zermelo (before 1902). Other more complicated antinomies were discovered before this (e.g. that of the greatest cardinal, Cantor's paradox), but all

involved other assumptions which could be, and were, challenged. Russell's paradox has the merit of isolating CP as the principle at fault, thus destroying the assumption of a neat connection between classes and sets, and (despite Russell's later efforts) between logic and sets.

The twentieth century has seen the development of a very important axiomatic theory of sets based on a more complicated connection between extensions of properties (classes) and sets, regulated by Zermelo's *axiom of separation* or the stronger *axiom of replacement*. This axiomatization began with Zermelo (1871–1953) in 1908, and was followed by the contributions of Fraenkel (1891–1965), Skolem (1887–1963), von Neumann (1903–1957), GÖDEL and Bernays (1888–1977) through the 1920s and 1930s. Together with the development of precise logical frameworks, this led to formal systems such as that known as the Zermelo–Fraenkel system (ZF). This is loosely based either on the so-called 'iterative' conception or on some idea of limiting size, the idea that classes can be sets provided they are not 'too big' (see Hallett, 1984). Such frameworks preserve the spirit of Cantorian set theory, and (providing one maintains Zermelo's Axiom of Choice to provide a proof of the well-ordering theorem) enables in particular a faithful representation of the theories of infinite number that Cantor had developed. A general consequence of this development is the *discretization* of mathematics (see CONTINUOUS/DISCRETE). More particularly, the axiomatized theory (together with the recognition of the importance of meta-mathematical problems) enables a precise formulation to be given to the question of whether set theory can solve certain of its central problems, in particular the *continuum problem*.

Zermelo style set theory is a theory of pure sets, with the more general notion of class left out altogether. But there are theories which introduce classes in something like the original sense alongside sets, thus as a second sort of object in the sense that they are quantified over, but not in the sense that they can be members (of sets or classes) in the way that sets themselves can. (Some classes are sets, but clearly not all can be.) Which predicates of the language give rise to classes? There is a conservative view, expressed in the system known as Gödel-Bernays set/class theory, which says that any predicate which does not contain quantifiers over classes determines a class. This system is essentially no stronger than ZF set theory, and is in effect a convenient way of allowing reference to the properties of ZF sets *in the theory*. A more liberal view is that *any* predicate determines a class, and this system is indeed stronger. (There are others. See Fraenkel, Bar-Hillel and Levy, 1973, ch. 2, sect. 7.) In both systems, full complementation (denied for sets) is restored; the complement of the class determined by the property ψ is the class determined by ψ (the 'opposite' of ψ), and the two classes always exhaust the whole domain. The two simplest complementary classes are the *empty class* (set), the extension of the property 'not identical with itself' (or any other contradictory property), and the *universal class*, the extension of the property 'identical with itself'. The restriction of membership, however, is enough to block the derivation of the known paradoxes.

Set theories in the tradition of Zermelo allow the extension of as many properties as possible to be sets while staying free of the known contradictions. But there is a more restrictive view going back to Russell (the *vicious circle principle*, and the Ramified Theory of Types), Poincaré (1854–1912) and Weyl (1885–1955). According to this view, the paradoxes are not due to the assumption that 'overly large' classes are sets, but rather to use of *impredicative specifications* to pick out sets. (As a first approximation, the specification of a set is *impredicative* if it contains quantifiers whose range includes the object being specified.) This position faces difficulties. It has to explain why it is wrong to accept as sets collections which, when so taken, do not give rise to paradoxes like Russell's, collections such as the classical continuum. Second, if important sets such as these are to be exclu-

ded, then a replacement for the classical theory of real numbers and real functions has to be developed. However, the difficulty is to arrive at a natural predicative system which achieves this (see Beeson, 1985).

BIBLIOGRAPHY

Beeson, M.J.: *Foundations of Constructive Mathematics* (Berlin: Springer-Verlag, 1985).

Fraenkel, A., Bar-Hillel, Y. and Levy, A.: *Foundations of Set Theory* (Amsterdam: North-Holland, 1973).

Frege, G.: *Grundgesetze der Arithmetik* vol. I (Jena: 1893); (Hildesheim: Olms, 1966).

Hallett, M.: *Cantorian Set Theory and Limitation of Size* (Oxford: Clarendon Press, 1984).

Russell, B.A.W.: *The Principles of Mathematics* (Cambridge, 1903); 2nd edn (London: George Allen and Unwin, 1937).

MICHAEL HALLETT

clear and distinct A central concept in Cartesian epistemology, where it provides a criterion of truth ('whatever we perceive very clearly and distinctly is true' – cf. *Œuvres de Descartes*, vol. VI, p. 33, vol. VII, p. 35) and a rule for making judgements ('include nothing more in your judgements than what presents itself to your mind so clearly and distinctly that you have no occasion to doubt it' – cf. ibid., vol. VI, p. 18, vol. VII, p. 59). DESCARTES concedes that it is difficult (particularly in metaphysics) to distinguish clear and distinct perceptions or ideas from those which are not clear and distinct (ibid. vol. VII, p. 157, vol. VIIIB, p. 352). He offers no formal definition of these notions until the *Principles of Philosophy* (1644) (vol. I, p. 45), where his account, though widely cited, is unhelpful.

Descartes believes the distinction is best explained by examples (*Œuvres*, vol. VII, p. 164), and uses the wax example (ibid., vol. VII, pp. 30–1) for this purpose. Our perception of this body becomes clear and distinct when we eliminate from it whatever we are not compelled to ascribe to the body, namely, everything except extension, flexibility and changeability. Similarly, our conception of the mind becomes clearer and more distinct when we recognize that we cannot but ascribe thought to it, but can deny it sensation (when sensation is conceived as involving the body). Systematic doubt provides a technique for achieving clarity and distinctness.

These concepts do not, for Descartes, imply adequacy. We can form a concept of God which is clearer and more distinct than any other idea we have. When we conceive him as supremely perfect, this enables us to identify many properties we must, and many properties we must not, ascribe to him; but though we do have that much knowledge of his essence, he has countless attributes we cannot grasp (ibid., vol. VII, p. 46). Clarity and distinctness does imply conceptual possibility, and hence (since the existence of God guarantees that there is a power capable of creating whatever we conceive clearly and distinctly), real possibility (cf. ibid., vol. VII, pp. 71, 78).

BIBLIOGRAPHY

Descartes, R.: Œuvres de Descartes 12 vols, ed. C. Adams and P. Tannery (Paris: Leopold Cerf, 1897–1913).

EDWIN CURLEY

concept In the history of philosophy the term 'concept' and kindred expressions have been used in a variety of technical senses (e.g. by AQUINAS, KANT, FREGE). The majority of contemporary philosophers, however, use the term in its central non-technical sense, which is exhibited in complex gerundive phrases of the form 'the concept of being F'. In what follows 'concept' will be used in this way.

Concepts are intensional entities in the sense that two concepts can apply to exactly the same objects and nevertheless be distinct. For example, the concept of being a triangle is not identical with the concept of being a trilateral. This example shows that

concepts are indeed hyperintensional in the sense that they can be distinct even if they necessarily apply to the same objects. Because concepts are hyperintensional, they are ideally suited to serve as the senses (meanings) of predicates. For example, 'is a triangle' expresses the concept of being a triangle; 'is a trilateral' expresses the concept of being a trilateral. Since these concepts are not identical, we have a neat explanation of why the indicated predicates are not exact synonyms.

Concepts are a kind of universal, so each of the standard views on the ontological status of UNIVERSALS has been applied to concepts as a special case. NOMINALISM: only particulars (and perhaps collections of particulars) exist; therefore, either concepts do not exist or they are reducible (in the spirit of CARNAP) to collections of particulars (including perhaps particulars that are not actual but only possible). CONCEPTUALISM: concepts exist but are dependent on the mind. REALISM: concepts exist independently of the mind. Realism has two main versions: *in rebus* realism – a concept exists only if it has instances; *ante rem* realism – a concept can exist even if it has no instances. For example, the concept of being a man weighing over a ton has no instances; however, it is plausible to hold that this concept does exist. After all, this concept would seem to be what is expressed by the predicate 'is a man weighing over a ton'.

Perhaps the most perplexing question about concepts is how they succeed in being about objects. On one view, there is a primitive, unanalysable relation of representation that holds between concepts and objects. This view has the disadvantage of making representation an unexplained mystery. A second view is that the relation of representation is analysable in terms of resemblance, causation, or some other naturalistic notion. While not mysterious, none of these analyses has, thus far, succeeded in avoiding clear-cut counterexamples. A third view is that what is needed is a certain sort of logical theory, specifically, an intensional logic. An intensional logic promises to provide a systematic account of the logical behaviour of intensional entities – properties, RELATIONS, states of affairs, propositions and concepts (*see* PROPOSITION, STATE OF AFFAIRS). The idea is that concepts are logical constructs whose ultimate 'constituents' are the real properties and relations of things in the world. A concept is about those objects that have the properties and relations required by the correct logical analysis of the concept. On this approach, the need for a primitive relation of representation thus disappears; at the same time, the easy counterexamples that beset naturalistic analyses (*see* NATURALISM) can evidently be avoided.

BIBLIOGRAPHY

Bealer, G.: *Quality and Concept* (Oxford: Clarendon Press, 1982).

Carnap, R.: *Meaning and Necessity* (Chicago: University of Chicago Press, 1947).

Frege, G.: 'On Sense and Reference', *Translations of the Philosophical Writings of Gottlob Frege*, P. Geach and M Black, eds. (Oxford: Basil Blackwell, 1952).

Peacock, C.: *A Study of Concepts* (Cambridge, MA: MIT Press, 1992).

GEORGE BEALER

concrete/abstract Realists and antirealists presuppose an intuitive distinction between *abstracta* and *concreta* in their debates about the problem of UNIVERSALS (*see* NOMINALISM; PLATONISM). Examples of *abstracta* are squareness (a property); betweenness (a relation); there being horses (a proposition); the null set; and the number 7 (*see* CLASS, COLLECTION, SET; PROPOSITION, STATE OF AFFAIRS). Examples of *concreta* are a stone (a material SUBSTANCE); God (a disembodied spiritual substance); Hurricane Carol (an event); instants and seconds (times); points and expanses of space (places); the particular wisdom of Socrates (a TROPE); the sum of Earth and Mars (a collection); the Earth's surface (a limit); and shadows and holes (privations). It is desirable that a philosophical analysis of the concrete/abstract distinction allow for the possibility of entities of any intelligible sort, given some plausible view about the nature, existence conditions and interrelationships of entities of those sorts. This desideratum seems to require allowing for the possibility of entities of the aforementioned kinds. Six attempts have been made to analyse the concrete/abstract distinction.

(1) Unlike *abstracta*, *concreta* are spatially located or spatially related to something.
(2) Unlike *abstracta*, *concreta* are capable of moving or undergoing intrinsic CHANGE.
(3) *Concreta* have contingent existence, whereas *abstracta* have necessary existence.
(4) Unlike *concreta*, *abstracta* are exemplifiable.
(5) Unlike *concreta*, *abstracta* are (intellectually) graspable.
(6) Unlike *abstracta*, *concreta* can be causes or effects.

(1) is inadequate because a disembodied spirit is concrete but neither spatially located nor spatially related to something. (2) is inadequate because points and instants are concrete but incapable of either moving or undergoing intrinsic change. (3) faces two difficulties. First, a being such as God is concrete yet has necessary existence. Second, according to Aristotelian realism (*see* ARISTOTLE), a property cannot exist unexemplified. Aristotelian realism implies that some properties are abstract yet have contingent existence. (4) is objectionable because sets, propositions and properties such as being a spherical cube are abstract but could not be exemplified. (5) is unsatisfactory because it would seem that *abstracta* of certain kinds could not be grasped, e.g. sets of *concreta* or haecceities which can be exemplified by necessarily non-conscious material substances (*see* HAECCEITY). (6) is unsatisfactory for the following

reasons. According to one camp, causes and effects are concrete events (*see* CAUSATION). On this view, (6) has the absurd implication that substances are non-concrete. One reply is that substances (but not *abstracta*) can be *involved* in causal relations. But, if causes and effects are concrete events, then it is hard to fathom the sense of 'involvement' intended. For according to an event ontology, an event's occurring does *not* entail that a substance exists, and an event is *not* a substance's exemplifying a property at a time or the like (*see* EVENT THEORY). Moreover, since causal relations hold in virtue of *laws* correlating *properties* of things, in a sense *abstracta* are *involved* in causal relations (*see* LAW OF NATURE). Finally, there is evidence that facts or the like can be causes or effects (*see* FACT), but facts are *abstracta* (cf. Kim, 1981).

Below is an attempt to devise an adequate analysis of the concrete/abstract distinction.

Step 1 A category, C_1, and a category, C_2, are *equivalent* if, and only if, C_1 and C_2 are necessarily co-instantiated; C_1 is *instantiable* if, and only if, C_1 is possibly instantiated; and C_1 *subsumes* C_2 if, and only if, C_1 and C_2 are such that necessarily, any instance of C_2 is an instance of C_1, and possibly, some instance of C_1 is not an instance of C_2. The modalities employed here and elsewhere in this article are metaphysical (*see* MODALITIES AND POSSIBLE WORLDS).

Step 2 There is an intuitive notion of a hierarchy of levels of generality among ontological categories (Rosenkrantz and Hoffman, 1991). At the highest level (level A) is the category of being an entity which everything instantiates and which is therefore a kind of limiting case. At a lower level (level B) are the categories of concreteness and abstractness. At a yet lower level (level C) are the categories which are the various types of *concreta* and *abstracta*, just provided that these categories are instantiable. Below, I list typical or core categories that are at level C on the foregoing proviso.

List L

Property, Relation, Proposition, Event, Time, Place, Trope, Collection, Limit and Privation.

Seemingly, some categories at C level are not on L, e.g. Substance and Set.

Presumably,

(A1) There are at least two (non-equivalent) instantiable categories of *concreta* at level C (at least one of which is on L), and there are at least two (non-equivalent) instantiable categories of *abstracta* at level C (at least one of which is on L).

This presupposes that not every instance (actual or possible) of a category on L is identifiable with an instance of another level C ontological category. (The *irreducibility* of a category on L that this implies is consistent with the *eliminability* of an entity of such a category in favour of an entity of another ontological category.) If the foregoing presupposition is mistaken, then the categories that make it so should be removed from L. The only limitation to be placed on this process of removal is that (A1) is true, and that whatever categories satisfy (A1) are compatible with the above presupposition.

Step 3

(D1) A category C_1 is at level C $=_{df}$ either (a) C_1 is on L, and C_1 is instantiable; or (b) (i) C_1 is not on L, and C_1 does not subsume an instantiable category on L, and no category on L subsumes C_1; and (ii) there is no category C_2 which satisfies the conditions in (b) (i) and which subsumes C_1.

Note that by a 'category' what is meant is an ontological category in an intuitive sense (*see* CATEGORIES). Although all categories are properties, some properties are not categories, e.g. redness, squareness, bachelorhood and (the disjunctive property of) being a substance or a surface. A property which is not a category *ipso facto* fails to satisfy (D1).

Step 4

(D2) x is concrete $=_{df}$: x instantiates a

level C category which possibly has an instance having spatial or temporal parts.

(D3) x is abstract $=_{df}$ x is non-concrete.

BIBLIOGRAPHY

Aristotle: *Categoriae* trans. J.L. Ackrill, *Aristotle's Categories and De Interpretatione* (Oxford: Oxford University Press, 1963).
Campbell, K.: *Metaphysics: An Introduction* (Encino, CA: Dickenson, 1976).
Kim, J.: 'The role of perception in *a priori* knowledge: some remarks', *Philosophical Studies* 40 (1981), 339–54.
Loux, M.L. ed.: *Universals and Particulars: Readings in Ontology* (Garden City, NY: Doubleday, 1970).
Rosenkrantz, G.: *Haecceity: An Ontological Essay* (Dordrecht: Kluwer, 1993), 56–68.
Rosenkrantz, G. and Hoffman, J.: 'The independence criterion of substance', *Philosophy and Phenomenological Research* 51 (1991), 835–53.

GARY ROSENKRANTZ

consciousness The terms 'conscious' and 'consciousness' cover a number of phenomena, all of them central to our mental lives. Though closely related, these phenomena are distinct, and it's important to distinguish them.

One phenomenon has to do roughly with being awake. A person or other animal is conscious when it is awake and mentally responsive to its environment; otherwise it is unconscious. It is this phenomenon we talk about most often in everyday contexts.

A second phenomenon we call consciousness is equivalent to being aware of something. We are conscious of something when we perceive it or think about it.

We also use the term 'consciousness' to refer to a property of mental states. We describe mental states as being conscious when we are aware of them in a way that is intuitively immediate. Thus LOCKE wrote that '[c]onsciousness is the perception of what passes in a Man's own Mind' (Locke, 1700, II, i, 19).

Usually we do not focus attention on our conscious states; they just occur within the scope of our awareness. Those we do deliberately attend to we describe as being introspectively conscious. It is through such introspective consciousness that we are conscious of ourselves as distinctively mental beings (*see* SELF-CONSCIOUSNESS).

Locke, like DESCARTES, held that mental functioning is always conscious; as Descartes put it, 'we cannot have any thought of which we are not aware at the very moment when it is in us' (Descartes, 1641, vol. II, p. 171). This thesis in effect identifies mind with consciousness; mental states are all conscious because being conscious is essential to being mental.

Not everybody accepts this claim. FREUD maintained that many mental states occur without being conscious; most contemporary cognitive and social psychologists agree, though for somewhat different reasons. Even common sense seems to countenance mental states that are not conscious; we sometimes know that somebody wants or feels something even though that person is wholly unaware of wanting or feeling it.

Mental states fall into two broad categories: intentional states, such as thoughts and desires (*see* INTENTIONALITY), and sensory states, such as pains and sensations of red (*see* SENSA). So it might be that all the states in one category are conscious, but not all those in the other. Descartes, who believed that all mental states are intentional states, held that intentional states are always conscious. By contrast, many today who believe that intentional states are not always conscious would still insist that all sensory states are. How, they ask, could a sensory quality such as redness or painfulness occur without our being immediately conscious of it? What would such a quality be like?

The idea that all sensory states are conscious is inviting; even Freud denied that feelings can, strictly speaking, be unconscious. Indeed, those who hold that sensory states are always conscious sometimes use 'consciousness' just to mean conscious sensory quality; this is a sense of 'consciousness' distinct from those described above.

A conscious creature apprehends things in a characteristic way and from a particular point of view. And an individual's point of view brings a certain unity to its conscious states. This apparent unity is yet another phenomenon called consciousness (*see* PERSONS AND PERSONAL IDENTITY).

Each of these distinct kinds of consciousness helps to capture the various ways in which people differ from everything else. However, some theorists have gone further and held that consciousness marks an unbridgeable gulf separating us from the rest of reality. Many find this idea tempting; we have all experienced that odd cognitive disorientation which results from reflecting on how we, as conscious beings, could possibly fit into the natural order (*see* MENTAL/PHYSICAL; MIND/BODY PROBLEM).

Our sense of mystery about consciousness is reinforced if being mental implies being conscious. We cannot, of course, explain consciousness without appeal to mental phenomena. But if being mental presupposes consciousness, explaining consciousness in mental terms will be circular. And if no satisfactory explanation of consciousness is possible, we cannot hope to bridge the gap between mind and non-mental reality.

Nagel (1974) has raised a related challenge about whether any objective account of consciousness is possible. Having conscious experiences, he urges, means that there is something that it is like to be a creature with those experiences. And this can be understood only from the point of view of the relevant kind of creature. But an objective account of something, Nagel holds, must be independent of any particular point of view. Since consciousness is tied essentially to particular points of view, he concludes that no objective account of it is possible.

But dependence on viewpoints need not preclude objectivity. Points of view are essential to consciousness because the qualitative properties of experiences depend on a creature's perceptual apparatus. This dependence is wholly objective. It does not matter that we cannot always extrapolate from a particular perceptual mechanism to the resulting kind of experience. Without help from a suitable scientific theory, we cannot always extrapolate from microprocesses to their macroscopic effects, even when those effects are uncontroversially objective. Nor, it seems, is objectivity undermined by points of view understood in any other way – for example, one's vantage point in place and time.

The notion of what it is like to have a conscious experience seems to cover the various phenomena we call consciousness. But because of that, this notion very likely runs together phenomena that require independent treatment. What it is like to have a conscious experience involves both sensory quality and our immediate awareness of these qualities. These are distinct phenomena. Even if sensory states were always conscious, they would differ, as MOORE (1922) emphasized, in virtue of having distinct sensory qualities, even though they all share the very same property of being conscious. So the two kinds of property very likely demand different explanations.

A mental state's being conscious consists in our being immediately conscious of it. So this sense of consciousness is a matter of how we know about our mental states. Since Descartes, many have held that our access to our own mental states is strongly privileged. These theorists also tend to conceive of consciousness ontologically, as part of the nature of mental states. In effect they infer from the way we know about our mental states to their nature – from our having infallible or exhaustive or incorrigible access to our mental states to something in their nature that might explain this access. But how we know about things is often an unreliable guide to their nature; so it is questionable whether the way we know about our own mental states tells us anything significant about their intrinsic nature.

Moreover, a straightforward explanation is possible of what it is for mental states to be conscious. A state's being conscious consists in one's being conscious of it. As in other cases of being conscious of something, being conscious of a mental state is just perceiving it or having a thought about it. The way we are conscious of our conscious states does seem to be immediate, but that may well be simply because our perceptions or thoughts of these states seem not to rely on inference.

Mental states that we do not perceive or think about will not be conscious. So even when we do perceive or think about a mental state, our thought or perception of it may itself not be conscious. Indeed, it usually will not be; we are normally unaware of any such thoughts or perceptions. Introspection is the special case in which our thought or perception of a mental state is actually conscious. So the fact that we do not seem to be aware of any such thoughts or perceptions is no objection to this account. Explaining consciousness this way, in terms of states that are mental but not conscious, helps diminish the gulf that seems to separate consciousness from nonmental reality.

BIBLIOGRAPHY

Dennett, D.C.: *Consciousness Explained* (New York: Little Brown, 1991).
Descartes, R.: *The Philosophical Writings of Descartes* (1641); ed. and trans. J. Cottingham, R. Stoothoff and D. Murdoch, 3 vols (Cambridge: Cambridge University Press, 1984–91), vol. II.
Freud, S.: 'The unconscious', in *The Complete Psychological Works of Sigmund Freud* ed. and trans. J. Strachey, 24 vols (London: Hogarth Press, 1966–74) vol. 1, 166–215.
Locke, J.: *An Essay Concerning Human Understanding* 4th edn (London: 1700); ed. P.H. Nidditch (Oxford: Clarendon Press, 1975).
McGinn, C.: *The Problem of Consciousness* (Oxford: Blackwell, 1991).
Moore, G.E.: 'A refutation of idealism', in his *Philosophical Studies* (London: Routledge and Kegan Paul, 1922), 1–30.
Nagel, T.: 'What is it like to be a bat?', *Philosophical Review* 83 (1974), 435–50.
Nisbett, R.E. and Wilson, T.D.: 'Telling more than we can know: verbal reports on mental processes', *Psychological Review* 84 (1977), 231–59.
Rosenthal, D.M.: 'Thinking that one thinks', in *Consciousness* ed. M. Davies and G.W. Humphreys (Oxford: Blackwell, 1993), 197–223.
Searle, J.R.: *The Rediscovery of the Mind* (Cambridge, MA: The MIT Press/Bradford, 1992).

DAVID M. ROSENTHAL

content Mental states appear to come in two distinct kinds. On the one hand, there are states, like pains or tickles, whose nature is exhausted by what it *feels* like to have them, by their individuative phenomenologies. Such states appear not to be 'about' anything or to 'mean' anything. On the other hand, there are states, like believing that snow is white, or desiring that the cat not scratch the furniture, which appear to have no interesting phenomenologies whatever, but which do seem to be about things, to mean something.

For these latter sorts of state – states which RUSSELL dubbed 'propositional attitudes' – what they mean is referred to as their *propositional content*, or content for short. (The other part, the part designated by such psychological verbs as 'believe' and 'desire', is the *attitude* adopted towards the propositional content.) The content of a propositional attitude is typically specified, in language, through the use of a 'that-clause' – Jane desires *that the cat not scratch the furniture*, John believes *that snow is white*.

The notion of propositional content raises a number of vexed questions in metaphysics, about which there is nothing but controversy. On the face of it, a belief attribution like the one mentioned in the preceding paragraph (*mutatis mutandis* for the other psychological states) appears to relate John by way of belief to some *thing* – the proposition that snow is white (*see* PROPOSITION, STATE OF AFFAIRS). Thus, it seems correct to infer from

John believes that snow is white

to

There is something that John believes.

This seems to show that propositional contents are objects of some sort, to which persons can bear various psychological relations. But what sorts of objects are propositional contents, what sorts of thing are things believed? They seem to be *abstract*: that snow is white is not in Manhattan or in my car. They seem to be *language-independent*: that snow is white looks as if it might have been true even if no one had devised a language in which to express it. They seem to be independent of the existence of any particular mind: two people can share the thought that snow is white. They seem even to be independent of the existence of any mind whatever: that snow is white looks as if it might have been true even if no one had, or even if no one could have, thought about it. Furthermore, and as the examples illustrate, propositional contents have conditions of truth (and falsity) and appear, indeed, to have their truth conditions essentially: no proposition could be the proposition that snow is white unless it were true if and only if snow is white.

All of the preceding points are accommodated by the view that a propositional content is a set of POSSIBLE WORLDS, namely, the set of all the worlds at which the proposition is true. Such a view has been quite popular in recent philosophy. But there are problems with it. Consider the belief *that either snow is white or it is not white* and the belief *that 2 + 2 = 4*. These appear to be distinct beliefs: it seems possible to believe the one without *thereby* believing the other. Yet since they are both necessarily true, they are both true in all possible worlds. A possible worlds conception of propositional content would appear, therefore, not to be able to discriminate

between them. It would appear to have to conclude that anyone who believes one necessary truth believes them all. And that does not seem right. (For further discussion see Stalnaker, 1984.)

These considerations give one reason to hold that propositional contents are not merely sets, but more like structured complexes of objects and properties. The content of the belief that snow is white is the structured complex made up out of the substance snow and the property of being white (along with the property of exemplification or instantiation). This gets around the problem of believing necessary truths: the difference between the belief that $2 + 2 = 4$ and the belief that *either snow is white or it isn't* consists, in part, in the fact that the former involves the property of addition, whereas the latter does not.

Unfortunately, a famous set of considerations due to FREGE (1892) seems to indicate that it cannot be right either. Consider the belief that water is potable and the belief that H_2O is potable. These appear not to be the same belief, for it seems as if someone may have the one without thereby having the other. Indeed, it seems as if a person may believe that water is potable and not only fail to believe that H_2O is potable, but in fact actively believe, without contradiction, that H_2O is not potable. The *property* of being water, however, just is the property of being H_2O – or so science appears to teach us. So it seems as if belief contents must be made up out of constituents that are even more fine-grained than objects and properties. Such more fine-grained constituents are normally referred to as *modes of presentations* of objects and properties. One of the large unresolved questions in the metaphysics of content concerns the nature of modes of presentation. (For further discussion see Salmon, 1986; Schiffer, 1990.)

Another important class of metaphysical problems raised by the topic of propositional content concerns the *content relation*. By virtue of what sort of fact is some token neural state the belief that *p*? (*See* MIND/BODY PROBLEM.) This question may be broken up into two others: By virtue of what sort of fact is a token state a *belief* (as opposed to, say, a desire)? And, by virtue of what sort of fact does it express that proposition that *p*?

Concentrating on the second question, many philosophers are inclined to believe that the fact in question must be naturalistic (*see* NATURALISM), probably causal. There are many reasons for this conviction. Some are purely ontological: philosophers are loath to countenance properties that are not either identical with, or supervenient upon, the properties described by physics (*see* PHYSICALISM, MATERIALISM; REDUCTION, REDUCTIONISM; SUPERVENIENCE). Others are of a more explanatory character: it is hard to see how to give the content properties of beliefs a causal role in the explanation of behaviour, on the assumption that they are not fundamentally naturalistic in nature. A non-reductive naturalism about content properties seems committed, implausibly, either to a peculiar sort of double causation or to the essential incompleteness of physics (see Kim, 1979).

It seems, then, that there is much to be said for a reductive naturalism about the content properties of beliefs. Unfortunately, however, attempts to articulate a reductive naturalism of the required kind have met with very little success. Indeed, important arguments are available to the effect that content properties cannot be naturalized. Many of these highlight the allegedly *normative* character of the notion of content (see Davidson, 1980; Kripke, 1982).

The current impasse over the metaphysics of content has had a predictable effect – it has encouraged a growing scepticism about content. A significant number of contemporary philosophers are inclined to think that perhaps there are no mental states with content at all, that the idea of a contentful mental state is simply part of a bad and false ordinary psychological theory (see Churchland, 1981). It is unclear whether their scepticism is justified; indeed, it is unclear whether it is even coherent (see Boghossian, 1990).

BIBLIOGRAPHY

Boghossian, P.A.: 'The status of content', *Philosophical Review* 99 (1990), 157–84.
Churchland, P.M.: 'Eliminative materialism and the propositional attitudes', *Journal of Philosophy*, 78 (1981), 67–90.
Davidson, D.: 'Mental events', in his *Essays on Actions and Events* (Oxford: Clarendon Press, 1980).
Frege, G.: 'On sense and meaning' (1892), in *Translations from the Philosophical Writings of Gottlob Frege* ed. P. Geach and M. Black (Totowa: Rowman and Littlefield, 1980) 56–78.
Kim, J.: 'Causality identity and supervenience in the mind–body problem', *Midwest Studies in Philosophy* 4 (1979), 31–49.
Kripke, S.: *Wittgenstein on Rules and Private Language* (Cambridge, MA: Harvard University Press, 1982).
Salmon, N.: *Frege's Puzzle* (Cambridge, MA: MIT Press, 1986).
Schiffer, S.: 'The mode-of-presentation problem', in *Propositional Attitudes* ed. C.A. Anderson and J. Owens (Stanford: CSLI, 1990), 56–78.
Stalnaker, R.: *Inquiry* (Cambridge, MA: MIT Press, 1984).

PAUL A. BOGHOSSIAN

contingent identity   *see* IDENTITY

continuant   Continuants continue through time. They persist. In contrast, occurrents occur. Paradigm continuants are people, tables and rocks. Paradigm occurrents are events, such as an avalanche or a birth. Continuants change. The changes themselves are occurrents.

A continuant persists if its temporal parts are connected in the right way. The right connection might be mere mereological summation, spatio-temporal continuity, causal dependence or, for people, continuity of consciousness.

Many philosophers would object to this appeal to temporal parts. First, some hold that in order for a continuant to persist it must be one and the same thing that exists at different times and that the account here has two different things, two distinct temporal parts, existing at the different times. Second, some hold that, by definition, continuants cannot have temporal parts. The occurrent/continuant distinction, they say, just *is* the distinction between having temporal parts and not having them.

See also BODY; BROAD; CHANGE; EVENT THEORY; TEMPORAL PARTS/STAGES.

BIBLIOGRAPHY

Broad, C.D.: *An Examination of McTaggart's Philosophy* (London: 1933); (Cambridge: Cambridge University Press, 1976), 138 ff.

Hirsch, E.: *The Concept of Identity* (Oxford: Oxford University Press, 1982).

Shoemaker, S.: *Identity, Cause, and Mind* (Cambridge: Cambridge University Press, 1984).

Swoyer, C.: 'Causation and identity', *Midwest Studies in Philosophy* 9 (1984), 593–622.

Wiggins, D.: *Sameness and Substance* (Cambridge, MA: Harvard University Press, 1980).

MARK HELLER

continuity A concept which now, strictly speaking, applies to a mathematical function, and not primarily to a domain. Initially, continuity was thought of as a notion that applies to the whole function (as in, for instance, a continuous line), with exceptional points specified where a 'break' is. However, in the early nineteenth century, the property of *continuity at a point* was defined (by Cauchy (1789–1857) and BOLZANO), which means intuitively that the correlates under the function of points which are 'close' to the given point are also 'close'. One is then free to say that a func-

tion is continuous at no points or at one point, or over a range of points, and there is then no need to assume the intuitive 'unity' of this range. This frees the notion of the continuity of a function from any assumption that the underlying domain must be continuous (*see* CLASS, COLLECTION, SET). What it depends on instead is the underlying neighbourhood structure which is used to make the notion of 'close' precise. (For instance, in the modern conception, which generalizes Bolzano's definition to the context of topological spaces, the continuity of a function does *not* depend on either the domain or range themselves being continua.)

The continuity of things other than functions is either derivative on this latter, as with motion (the assumption that there is a continuous function from time to position), or is a loose way of saying that one is actually dealing with a CONTINUUM, as in the 'continuity of space'.

See also CONTINUOUS/DISCRETE.

MICHAEL HALLETT

continuous/discrete The notions discrete and continuous apply to two different kinds of quantity corresponding to the two different kinds of question 'How many?' and 'How much?' For instance, one can ask '*How many* apples are there on the tree?' and '*How much* water is there in the lake?', whereas the questions '*How much* apples are there?' and '*How many* water is there?' make no sense. The first kind of quantity (*numerical quantity*) applies to concepts under which fall differentiated *individual* objects (the concept itself specifies some unit), and the second (*continuous quantity*) to concepts under which fall undifferentiated material (*see* MASS TERMS) and where it can be sensibly asked in what *measure* or *magnitude* the substance is present, for instance, about its volume, area, length or weight. (Of course, it makes sense to ask quite different questions like

'What is the weight of the apple?', or 'How many *cups* of water are there?', since individual objects are often composed of continuous material, and undifferentiated material can be separated into units.) The distinction in this form goes back at least to ARISTOTLE, and the two different kinds of quantity in later mathematical guise become the two notions *whole number* and *real number*. In modern physics, the distinction is alive in the two notions of *quantum* and *field*. Note that it is the paradigmatically continuous quantities that are taken as basic in classical physics, thus mass, position, time, velocity, momentum and acceleration.

Connections between the two notions have been of deep philosophical and mathematical interest since the Pythagoreans' claim that 'All is like number', a claim complicated by the discovery of irrational quantities (*see* PRESOCRATICS). For instance, a descendant of this view is the position (the subject of ZENO's celebrated paradoxes of motion) that SPACE AND TIME, while both continua, are actually composed of *discrete* elements, points and instants. The most profound ancient attempt to bridge the gap between discrete and continuous was that of Eudoxus (as given in Book V of Euclid's *Elements*: see Heath, 1925), which attempts reduction of irrational measured quantity ultimately to ratios between numbered quantities, an attempt in which one can recognize Dedekind's nineteenth-century theory of real number (see Stein, 1990).

Why should one think that numerical and continuous quantity are connected? First, there is clearly an arithmetical component to continuous quantity (when divided into units) which is closely related to the algebra of whole numbers, for we *combine* the two types of quantity, for instance in saying that we have a total weight of $9 \times w$. This intermixing increases when one extends the algebra of whole numbers to that of the positive and negative integers and then to the rational numbers. Moreover, it is exploited and underlined in achievements like the Archimedean *method of exhaustion*, for this shows that one can get arbitrarily good approximations to measured quantities such as area, by using discrete sums. Here the order structure of the rationals, particularly their *denseness* (i.e. the fact that between any two rationals there is a third, in effect the assumption of *infinite divisibility*) plays an important role, as does the so-called 'Archimedean axiom', which says that whenever we have two quantities x and y with $x < y$, then there will always be an n such that $y < nx$ (see Stein, 1990). Consequently, the structure of the discrete quantities, the whole numbers, and that of the rational numbers, ought to be embedded in the continuous quantities. A further question is then whether it is possible to generate the structure of the continuous out of the discrete. It was often mistakenly thought (e.g. by KANT) that infinite divisibility is actually what characterizes continuity and therefore continuous magnitude. In fact, this is not enough. The situation was only finally clarified by the development of the theories of real number and sets through the combined work of BOLZANO, Dedekind (1831–1916), CANTOR and Hilbert (1862–1943) in the nineteenth century.

Bolzano's work was important in two respects. First, Bolzano saw that what is important in real quantity is the combination of the algebraic and the order structures. Indeed, he isolated one fundamental property, namely that every bounded increasing sequence has a least upper bound (the *l.u.b. property*). Second, Bolzano thought it a mistake to try to base the general notion of real magnitude in the particular types of continuous magnitude referred to in the theories of space, time or motion, thus in effect eschewing any intuitions thought central to these. What Bolzano lacked was any precise account of how the algebraic and order structures of real number (what we would now call the system of *complete, ordered fields*) can be constructed from that of natural number. This was provided independently by Dedekind and Cantor. Dedekind gave a profound analysis of the notion of continuity, for which the l.u.b. property holds, and a demonstration of how the ordered field of real numbers (continuous quantity) can be defined in terms of the field of rational numbers, thus in effect in terms of the whole numbers (numerical quantities). Cantor and Dedekind were even clearer than Bolzano in rejecting the idea that direct intuition of space and time is what underlies the theoretical concept of the continuum. (This position is consciously anti-Kant, since Kant argued that mathematics must be based on 'pure intuition' of space and time.) They argued, on the contrary, that the theoretical notion of continuity is itself needed in order to give a precise account of the nature of space and time. Indeed, it then becomes an hypothesis (or an 'axiom') that space is actually continuous.

The reduction effected by Cantor and Dedekind only works when one appeals to the concept of infinity and the modern theory of sets (*see* CLASS, COLLECTION, SET). The set-theoretic continuum has a very rich structure, and as a result, particularly with Cantor's distinction between countable and uncountable infinities, the modern theory of Lebesgue measure shows that some of the paradoxes presented by several of the Zeno arguments can be overcome. It is consistent to assume both that the continuum is made up of points, and that, while the points themselves have no size, and while no 'small' (countably infinite) sub-collection of points has a positive size either, the whole continuum *does* have a size (see Grünbaum, 1968).

The Cantor and Dedekind definitions take as their basis the notion of whole number, the measure of discrete quantity. It was Aristotle's conception that what distinguishes discrete collections from a continuous mass is that the collection itself can be divided into elements 'with no common boundary'. In the modern analysis, due to FREGE, Cantor and Dedekind, this requirement on the *objects* being counted is replaced by a requirement on the *ordering* in the counting numbers, namely that there is a first element, and that each element in the order has a

unique successor. The smallest infinite such collection is, in effect, the natural number sequence. (Part of Frege's and Dedekind's achievement was to show how to characterize this sequence. Frege also argued further that, properly speaking, number specifies a property of the concept itself, thus something necessarily abstract, and does not reflect a property of the objects that fall under it.) Cantor generalized this requirement to the notion of well-ordering, thus extending the notion of counting number, and thus of discreteness, to the infinite. The acceptance by modern set theory that all sets (infinite as well as finite) can be well-ordered is therefore tantamount to the claim that *all* mathematics can be based on discrete collections. On the other hand, the continuum problem (see CANTOR) perhaps shows that indeed there are still mysteries in the assumption that the continuum is made up of discrete points.

BIBLIOGRAPHY

Frege, G.: *Grundlagen der Arithmetik* (Breslau: 1884); trans. J.L. Austin, *The Foundations of Arithmetic* (Oxford: Blackwell, 1953).
Grünbaum, A.: *Modern Science and Zeno's Paradoxes* (London: Allen and Unwin, 1968).
Heath, T.H.: *The Thirteen Books of Euclid's Elements*, 3 vols, 2nd edn (Cambridge: Cambridge University Press, 1925; New York: Dover Publications, 1956).
Stein, H.: 'Eudoxus and Dedekind: on the ancient Greek theory of ratios and its relation to modern mathematics', *Synthese* 84 (1990), 163–211.

MICHAEL HALLETT

continuum Any mathematical domain that possesses the property of being continuous. Since ancient times, continua have been of perennial concern to philosophers, e.g. through the questions of whether space, time, matter and motion, etc., are continuous, and what this might mean. The question reached genuine precision in the nineteenth century with the clarifications wrought by BOLZANO, Dedekind (1831–1916), CANTOR and Hilbert (1862–1943), leading to a categorical characterization of the continuum of real numbers (e.g. through Dedekind cuts) as a *complete, ordered field*. This is generally taken to be the paradigm of a continuum, although it is possible to give definitions of continuity, and therefore of continua, in frameworks which do not presuppose classical set theory.

See also CLASS, COLLECTION, SET; CONTINUITY; CONTINUOUS/DISCRETE.

MICHAEL HALLETT

convergence If the methods of science were applied to ever widening data sets over a hypothetical infinite long run, would they have to converge on the truth? The pragmatic theory of truth says 'Yes' (*see* PRAGMATISM; THEORIES OF TRUTH). Pragmatists define truth as that upon which inquiry converges. Realists disagree; they hold that it is a priori possible that evidence might be misleading, even in the limit.

Even if truth cannot be defined in terms of convergence, the question remains of whether successive theories in fact take us closer to the truth. This is one gloss of the idea that science is 'progressive'. The difficulty is to define the idea of closeness to the truth. When two theories are both false, what makes one more truth-like? If Jane is 6 feet tall, the hypothesis that she is 5 feet 10 inches is clearly closer to the truth than the hypothesis that she is 5 feet 7 inches. The problem is to extend this idea to other sorts of hypotheses.

BIBLIOGRAPHY

Laudan, L.: 'A confutation of convergent realism', in *Scientific Realism* ed. J. Leplin (Berkeley: University of California Press, 1984), 218–49.
Peirce, C.S.: 'How to make our ideas clear', in *Essays in Philosophy of Science* ed. V. Thomas (Indianapolis, IN: Bobbs Merrill, 1957), 31–56.
Russell, B.: 'Pragmatism', in his *Philosophical Essays* (New York: Simon and Schuster, 1966), 79–111.
Russell, B.: 'William James' conception of truth', in his *Philosophical Essays* (New York: Simon and Schuster, 1966), 112–30.
Sober, E.: 'Likelihood and convergence', *Philosophy of Science* 55 (1988), 228–37.

ELLIOTT SOBER

copula In traditional formal logic the statement 'Socrates is wise' is analysed into subject, predicate and copula ('is'). In metaphysics, however, the term 'copula' is understood to refer to that fundamental connection that some philosophers suppose to hold between UNIVERSALS AND PARTICULARS, and which may also be spoken of as 'instantiation' or 'exemplification'. The latter two terms are, indeed, more usual. More generally, the term refers to the supposed fundamental connection between substance and attribute, whether or not the attribute is taken as a universal. Johnson (1964) and STRAWSON (1959, ch. 5, ss 8–9) spoke instead of a 'non-relational tie', BERGMANN (1967, Bk 1, Pt 1) of a 'tie' or 'nexus'. The idea is always that here is a connection that is deeper, and stands behind, mere relation. FREGE's idea that functions (very roughly, attributes) are 'unsaturated', that they call for completion by objects (1891), may reflect the same idea. Alternatively, it may reflect the opposite idea, that a copula is redundant in metaphysics and may be dispensed with!

BIBLIOGRAPHY

Bergmann, G.: *Realism* Milwaukee and London: University of Milwaukee Press, 1967).
Frege, G.: 'Function and concept' (1891); in *Translations from the Writings of Gottlob Frege* ed. and trans. P. Geach and M. Black (Oxford: Blackwell, 1960), 21–41.

Johnson, W.E.: *Logic* 3 vols (New York: Dover, 1964).

Strawson, P.F.: *Individuals* (London: Methuen, 1959).

D. M. ARMSTRONG

cosmology In a wide sense, *cosmology* equals *metaphysics*: reality studied philosophically. This entry will instead discuss the study of the COSMOS at large scales, using data from astronomy and physics.

Cosmology involves severe verificational difficulties. Since light takes time to travel, far distant objects are seen as they were billions of years ago; how, then, shall we distinguish *spatial* from *temporal* variations in our universe's properties? Again, if current cosmological models are even roughly correct then very much is so distant that light from it cannot yet have reached us, while on many models most of it will never be visible. Cosmologists must observe things very indirectly – i.e. with the aid of much theory – and must grant that much will never be knowable. Their science makes nonsense of neo-verificationism's equation of the true with what would, in the long run, have warranted assertability (*see* PRINCIPLE OF VERIFIABILITY). How could a cosmologist ever be warranted in saying, for instance, exactly which path a particular particle followed after falling into a region from which light could not escape?

Trust in simplicity has carried cosmology far, however. Present-day observations are all consistent with NEWTON's principle that the same basic laws operate everywhere. General relativity's elegant equations, which associate gravity with spatial curvature, have likewise withstood all tests – and gravity rules supreme at large scales. True, the beautifully simple *Perfect Cosmological Principle*, that our universe is much the same in all big spatio-temporal regions, now seems erroneous: the associated Steady State models have given way to Big Bang ones which more straightforwardly explain why galaxies, like ink spots on an inflating balloon, rush apart at speeds proportional to the distances between them. Evidence for a Bang, a universe-wide explosion in which space itself began expanding, includes cosmic background radiation greatly uniform over the sky, and the observed amounts of hydrogen, helium, lithium and deuterium. All this would be explicable by immense early pressures and temperatures; and telescopes, as they probe further back in time, do indeed reveal more and more density and violence. Still, the almost equally beautiful *Cosmological Principle*, that our universe is much the same in all big *spatial* regions *at any one time*, has proved more successful than anyone dared hope. Starting life as a mere simplifying hypothesis, it is now a seldom-questioned dogma.

It might nevertheless turn out that the Bang started off cold, which could help explain how galaxies managed to form in a highly uniform universe. (The cosmic background radiation which suggests a very hot Bang could come instead from early, massive stars.) Or the picture of near-total uniformity might need to be replaced by one of a space split into topologically ill-integrated domains. Cosmic strings, walls and other defects at domain boundaries could influence the matter distribution importantly: strings might be seeds for galaxies, for instance. There is actually a problem of why our universe is not crammed with knot-like defects, 'monopoles' so massive and so numerous that their gravity would re-collapse it at once. And there is the more general Horizon or Smoothness Problem: the problem of how it could be in the least uniform, granted that at early times it could seem to have been split into vastly many parts which had never interacted. (How could ships over one another's horizons behave in coordinated fashion without benefit of signalling?) A currently popular solution is Inflation, the theory that everything exploded extremely rapidly before switching to much more leisurely expansion. A tiny, well coordinated region would in this case have come to include much more than is now visible to us; monopoles would be pushed far apart; and space's resultant flatness – think of the surface of a gigantically inflated balloon – would yield the leisurely expansion in question, an expansion just fast enough to prevent or defer gravitational re-collapse and just slow enough to encourage galaxies to form. In Inflation's absence, the early expansion speed would need enormously accurate tuning to permit their formation.

If Inflation occurred then we can see only a minuscule fragment of the cosmos: perhaps as little as one part in one-followed-by-a-million-zeros. Everything else lost any causal tie with us during the inflationary process, and has not since had time to link up with us. Now, the cosmos is by definition Absolutely Everything; there cannot be two 'cosmoses'; but contemporary cosmologists often speak of multiple *universes*, meaning *gigantic domains having few or no causal ties with one another*. Belief in several universes is clearly 'metaphysical' in that only one of them could be directly known. Yet an 'anti-metaphysical' opponent of them will have to reject Inflation, and Inflation is the dominant cosmological hypothesis nowadays because it solves so many puzzles so straightforwardly. It can even say how all parts of our huge universe managed to spring into existence and begin expanding nearly or completely simultaneously. Starting from a tiny seed, perhaps a mere quantum fluctuation, inflationary expansion would be driven by gravitational processes which could create more and more at no cost in energy because gravitational binding energy, like all binding energies in physics, is negative energy. It could precisely cancel the mass-energy of newly created matter.

Multiple universes can be obtained in other ways as well. Instead of being 'closed', curved round upon itself (thanks to gravity) like the surface of a sphere, space may be 'open' – as it must be unless the gravitating matter visible to us is supplemented by much 'dark matter' (massive neutrinos, perhaps). It then extends infinitely far, so we get infinitely many universes in the sense explained above: infinitely many regions causally distinct from one another because of light's finite speed. Or, if closed, space might oscillate, Bangs and Squeezes succeeding one another for ever; now, each new oscillation might be called a new universe. Or again, if one universe could spring into existence through a quantum fluctuation then would it not be simpler to believe that greatly many had done so? Or might there not be an eternally inflating situation in which universes appear as bubbles inside which Inflation has ended? These various scenarios are all defensible (and attackable, even refutable) by physical arguments.

There is little reason to suppose that all universes would seem to possess the same properties. Simplicity may demand that their most basic laws and properties be the same, yet contemporary physics suggests how *derived* laws and *overt* properties could be different. Gravity, electromagnetism, and the nuclear strong and weak forces, were probably unified into a single force at early-Big-Bang temperatures, all particles perhaps then being massless. As things cooled, forces and particles could well have become differentiated in ways varying from place to place. Rather as a freezing pond becomes covered by ice-crystal domains with random orientations, the cooling products of a Hot Big Bang could split into regions differently oriented in an abstract 'space': the space in which overt properties become fixed during the 'symmetry breaking' of which today's physicists talk. Force strengths and particle masses could be determined by scalar fields which differed from region to region in a largely random way. It might thus be that in some regions – 'other universes' pushed by Inflation far beyond the reach of our telescopes – the gravitational force between two protons was about as strong as the electromagnetic instead of being many trillion times weaker, while protons and electrons were about equally massive. As HUME and KANT suspected, the situation visible to us may be very untypical of the cosmos as a whole. It could actually be that in many regions the overt geometry of space-time was, say, five- or six-dimensional. 'Super-strings theory' suggests that the large scale four-dimensionality of the space-time familiar to us results from 'compactification' in which further dimensions become tightly curled up. We cannot be confident that in absolutely all regions the same number of dimensions would compactify.

Another ground for accepting greatly many universes with very varied (overt) properties is that this could help us understand the fact that there is a universe – ours – with life-permitting properties. Recent findings suggest that our universe is 'fine-tuned for life' in the sense that slight changes in force strengths and particle masses would have ruled out organisms of any plausible kind. This could be an illusion, no doubt. Very odd life forms might be possible. Life in the sun might be based on plasma fields. Organisms inside neutron stars might use the nuclear strong force much as our bodies use the electromagnetism which underlies chemistry. However, such oddities can seem implausible. It can further be argued that much fine tuning is needed for there to be neutron stars, or suns, or atoms, or a universe lasting more than a microsecond and containing more than light rays and black holes. Considerable interest therefore attaches to the *Anthropic Principle* that the cosmic region which we observe must (self-evidently) possess properties compatible with the existence of observers. It is altogether plausible that most regions *do not*.

Note (1) that the Anthropic Principle – as stated above, on the basis of a careful reading of B. Carter who enunciated it – is as tautologous as that villains are knaves; (2) that it can none the less give us an important reminder that the life-permitting situation which we see may very well not be typical of the cosmos, since even if life-permitting situations were rare we should still (self-evidently) find ourselves inside one; (3) that use of the Principle to help make our cosmic placement unmysterious *is not* a suggestion that the cosmos was planned for intelligent observers, let alone for humankind; or that we caused our cosmic region to have life-permitting properties; or that the existence of many other regions had somehow made it *more probable* that our particular region *would develop* life-permitting properties when the dice of random

symmetry-breaking were tossed. Users of the Anthropic Principle need say nothing more controversial than (a) that in a cosmos large enough and varied enough it would be likely that life would appear *somewhere or other* even if it demanded very precise tuning of such things as force strengths and particle masses; and (b) that any region which living beings observed would be (believe it or not) one in which life was possible.

Much confusion has been caused by distinguishing a 'weak' from a 'strong' Anthropic Principle. As intended by Carter, the weak Principle says that our spatio-temporal surroundings are (self-evidently) life-permitting; the strong, that (equally evidently) our universe is so. Alas, what one cosmologist calls a universe, another may describe as spatio-temporal surroundings. Again, Carter's remark that our universe *must be* life-permitting has been widely misunderstood. It does not say that it *was deterministically fated to become* life-permitting, let alone that it had to become life-*containing* or that God fine-tuned it. If our universe is just one region of a very varied cosmos, a region perhaps very unusual in the fact that living beings can observe it, then it might easily look exactly as if it had been fine-tuned by God without having been so in fact.

Theologians, however, could comment that the existence of multiple universes is no less conjectural than God's. The reasons for believing in multiple universes are ultimately reasons of simplicity, and it is by no means clear that God would be non-simple. An infinite person, a divine Fine Tuner, might be in important respects simpler than any finite being. Or God might not be a person at all. Conceived Neoplatonically, God is the unconditionally real ethical requirement that there be a cosmos, a requirement which is itself creatively effective. Its cosmos-producing power would not, of course, follow from its sheer definition, yet linguistic analysis can seem to show that it would be the sort of reality which might have such power – and that the having of it would be exactly as simple as the lack of it.

Theologians might also claim that God provides the best or the only answer to why there is any cosmos: any realities beyond mere possibilities and truths about them, such as the truth that two apples and two apples would be four apples or that good possibilities ought to be actualized. Yet is the sheer presence of a cosmos, a world of existing things, a genuine puzzle? Cosmologists have differed widely over this. G. Gamow (1904–68) thought it would indeed be one if the cosmos had a temporal starting point. He therefore proposed that the Bang was preceded by an infinitely prolonged contraction. F. Hoyle's fight for a Steady State was largely motivated by a wish to avoid a beginning of things. W.B. Bonnor and J.A. Wheeler much preferred an infinity of cosmic oscillations to any infinitely dense state in which everything originated. S.W. Hawking prided himself on removing all need for a creator by making time progressively more space-like at ever earlier moments in the Bang. Others have seen similar advantages in C.W. Misner's idea that earlier and earlier processes ran progressively faster so that by the 'clocks' of those processes themselves our universe could stretch backwards infinitely, or in A.D. Linde's eternal Inflation (with bubble universes), or in the notions of E.P. Tryon and A. Vilenkin, that universes appear as quantum fluctuations in an eternally existing superspace or in a 'foam' lacking clear distinctions of space and time. On the other hand, philosophers such as Hume and A. Grünbaum have said there would be nothing problematic in a beginning of things even if one granted (which Grünbaum would not) that time could exist before things did. And while some theologians – most notably Pius XII – have treated the Bang as proving God's existence, others have insisted that God's creative action is in no way specially associated with a first cosmic instant.

See also FINITE/INFINITE; WHY THERE IS SOMETHING; WORLD.

BIBLIOGRAPHY

Barrow, J.D. and Tipler, F.J.: *The Anthropic Cosmological Principle* (Oxford: Clarendon Press, 1986).

Davies, P.C.W.: *The Accidental Universe* (Cambridge: Cambridge University Press, 1982).

Feinberg, G. and Shapiro, R.: *Life Beyond Earth* (New York: William Morrow, 1980).

Harrison, E.R.: *Cosmology* (Cambridge: Cambridge University Press, 1981).

Hawking, S.W. and Israel, W. eds: *Three Hundred Years of Gravitation* (Cambridge: Cambridge University Press, 1987).

Leslie, J.: *Universes* (London and New York: Routledge, 1989).

Leslie, J. ed.: *Physical Cosmology and Philosophy* (New York: Macmillan, 1990).

Munitz, M. ed.: *Theories of the Universe* (New York: Macmillan, 1957).

Rozental, I.L.: *Big Bang, Big Bounce* (Berlin: Springer-Verlag, 1988).

Weinberg, S.: *The First Three Minutes* 2nd and rev. edn (London: Fontana, 1983).

JOHN LESLIE

cosmos On one widely accepted definition, the cosmos is the totality of existing things and events: it thus contrasts with any timeless realm of mere possibilities or Platonic truths. On this definition, God might be held to be part of the cosmos. Often, however, as in theistic 'cosmological arguments', God is viewed as its creator and orderer, existing outside it. Again, the cosmos may be contrasted with chaos, for to the Greeks *kosmos* meant 'order' as well as 'world'. In this case it might exist side by side with chaos, or it might have replaced chaos as in Hesiod and Milton (*Paradise Lost*, Bk III: 'at His Word, the formless mass . . . came to a heap . . . and wild Uproar stood ruled, stood vast Infinitude confined').

Such points all provoke philosophical disputes. Some urge that existents and their causal orderliness are brute facts, not God-produced. Others think, with SPINOZA, that the cosmos has properties such that it can itself be called 'God'. Among Neoplatonists (*see* NEOPLATONISM), a first might describe God as the creatively powerful ethical requirement that there exist a good cosmos; a second, as the ethical requiredness of such a cosmos, a requiredness which acts creatively; a third, as the cosmos, considered as having this requiredness. The first would then say God was distinct from the cosmos; the second, that God was an aspect of the cosmos; the third, that God and the cosmos were identical. These would be merely verbal disagreements.

Other philosophers, again, have argued that an absence of all existents would be logical nonsense, or that events cannot fail to have orderliness. And still others have doubted the meaningfulness of talk about existence as a whole, or about any order beyond what minds impose on their experiences.

It would seem, however, that an absence of all existents involves no actual contradiction, and that events have a causal orderliness which is neither logically inevitable nor created by our minds. Modal realism, the view that logical possibilities must all exist somewhere, is treated with suspicion by most logicians and may even render induction untrustworthy (since logically possible worlds which were orderly only in part could seem to form a wider range than ones orderly throughout; *see* MODALITIES AND POSSIBLE WORLDS). And the view, often attributed to KANT, that events have no causal order in themselves, would appear to make our unconscious minds into super-geniuses able to impose patterns whose complexity modern science only just begins to grasp. FICHTE and F.W.J. Schelling (1775–1854), indeed, described the structure of the cosmos as a product of imagination, but it is a structure too complicated for this to be plausible. It also survives attempts to trivialize it by saying that absolutely any objects or events, like any dots scattered on graph paper, must obey some formula or other. It survives them because the vast majority of such formulas would be too messy for scientists to grasp at all. The cosmos, though indeed complicated, is not a chaos and can be understood.

Let us reject, too, the idea that it is meaningless to talk of existence in its totality. It is one thing to insist with HUME and Kant that we cannot know the entire cosmos, and quite another to deny meaning to *all existing things*, a phrase a child might understand. Intelligibility outruns verifiability. Modern cosmologists recognize that vastly much material lies beyond the horizon set by how far light can have travelled towards us since the start of the Big Bang, and that most of it may well never be visible from our cosmic region. The same applies to material nearer by but inside black holes. Things surely do not drop out of existence as soon as they fall through black-hole horizons!

The sum of all existents must be singular, obviously – and 'cosmos' has no plural so one cannot so much as speak of 'many possible cosmoses'. However, modern cosmologists often talk of many possible *universes* and even propose their actual existence side by side or in succession. To them, 'a universe' may mean only a huge cosmic domain, perhaps entirely separate from all other such domains or perhaps linked to them spatially or temporally. One ground for believing in multiple universes is that this may be simplest: any mechanism able to generate one universe might be expected to generate many. A second is that various physical theories suggest that a cosmos would soon split into huge domains with different properties. (It would thus cease to be 'a cosmos' if this had to mean a unity in which such matters as the relative strengths of gravity and electromagnetism, or the relative masses of the electron, the proton and the neutron, were the same everywhere.) A third is that the existence of greatly many such domains might help explain why at least one domain is life permitting.

Nowadays a popular theory is that our universe was born from the chaos of a 'space-time foam', then quickly inflated enormously before settling down to more leisurely expansion. Another possibility is that chaotic cosmic inflation continues eternally: our universe is just one of countless bubbles inside which it has ended.

See also COSMOLOGY; FINITE/INFINITE; PANTHEISM; WHY THERE IS SOMETHING; WORLD.

BIBLIOGRAPHY

Diamandopoulos, P.: 'Chaos and cosmos', in *The Encyclopedia of Philosophy* ed. P. Edwards, 8 vols (New York: Macmillan, 1967) vol. 2, 80–1.
Laird, J.: *Theism and Cosmology* (London: Allen and Unwin, 1940).
Leslie, J.: 'Demons, vats and the cosmos', *Philosophical Papers* 18 (1989), 169–88.
Linde, A.D.: *Inflation and Quantum Cosmology* (San Diego: Academic Press, 1990).
Munitz, M.K.: 'One universe or many?', *Journal of the History of Ideas* 12 (1951), 231–55.

JOHN LESLIE

counterfactuals We distinguish how things actually were, are or will be from how things would have been or would be in this, that or the next eventuality. Nixon was re-elected, but had the American public known the truth about Watergate during the campaign he would not have been re-elected. My lawn is green, but had it not been watered during the week it would be brown. I will be alive tomorrow, but were I to jump from the Empire State building today I would not be alive tomorrow. Conditionals like: 'If the American public had known the truth about Watergate, then Nixon would not have been re-elected', 'If my lawn had not been watered during the week, then it would (now) be brown', and 'If I were to jump from the Empire State building today, I would not be alive tomorrow' are called 'counterfactual conditionals', or simply 'counterfactuals'. They are often symbolized as '$p \;\square\!\!\rightarrow q$' (read 'If p had been the case, q would have been the

case' or 'If p were the case, q would be the case'). p is the antecedent and q is the consequent of the conditional, and '$\square\!\!\rightarrow$' is used to distinguish counterfactual conditionals from indicative conditionals like 'If my lawn was not watered last week, it is now brown' and 'If I jump from the Empire State building today, I will not be alive tomorrow' (sometimes symbolized as '$p \rightarrow q$'), and the material conditional (usually symbolized as '$p \supset q$') which is true if, and only if, either p is false or q is true (or both). It has sometimes been argued that '$p \rightarrow q$' and '$p \supset q$' are logically equivalent. It is obvious though that '$p \;\square\!\!\rightarrow q$' and '$p \supset q$' are not logically equivalent: 'If I were to jump from the Empire State building today, I would be alive tomorrow' is false, and yet it has a false antecedent and a true consequent.

The term 'counterfactual conditional' comes from the fact that use of the constructions 'If p had been the case, q would have been the case', and 'If p were the case, q would be the case' typically indicates that the speaker, or writer, takes p to be false; but there are exceptions, witness: 'I realized that Smith was the murderer when I realized that had the 6:40 a.m. train been late, his alibi would have been worthless.' Also, although counterfactuals typically have consequents the speaker or writer takes to be at least doubtful, they can be used in contexts where it is known that the consequent is true, witness: 'Smith failed, and he still would have failed had he worked.'

Counterfactuals are central to the discussion of at least three major topics in metaphysics: dispositional properties, laws, and CAUSATION (*see* DISPOSITION; LAW OF NATURE). What makes solubility in water a dispositional property is the fact that for x to be soluble in water is, roughly, for x to be of a nature such that were it put in water, it would dissolve. What makes 'Metals expand on heating' a law (approximately speaking) is the fact that not only is it the case that heated metals expand, it is in addition true that those not in fact heated would have expanded had they been heated. It is this latter fact which reflects the fact that it is no accident that heated metals expand. Finally, the sense in which a cause c brings about its effect e is connected to the fact that typically had c not occurred, e either would not have occurred or would have occurred in some significantly different way. Had CFCs not been released into the atmosphere, there would either be no hole in the ozone layer or a much less serious one. In all three cases there is dispute about how exactly to tease out the connection with counter-factuals, but not whether there is a conceptual connection to be teased out.

It is natural to think of a counterfactual conditional '$p \,\Box\!\rightarrow q$' as about a possible (but typically non-actual) state of affairs where p obtains but which is otherwise much as things actually are (see MOD-ALITIES AND POSSIBLE WORLDS; POSSI-BLE WORLDS). When we say that had the American public known the truth about Watergate, Nixon would not have been re-elected, we are saying that in the possible but non-actual state of affairs where the American public knew the truth about Watergate but where things otherwise were much as they actually were – the truth about Watergate was as it actually was, the voting system was as it actually was, the values of the public were much as they actually were, and so on – Nixon was not re-elected. Thus the appeal of accounts (e.g. Stalnaker (1984) or Lewis (1973)) of the truth conditions of counterfactuals in terms of possible worlds of the following general shape: '$p \,\Box\!\rightarrow q$' is true (that is, is true at the actual world) if, and only if, the possible worlds most similar to the actual world where p is true are worlds where q is true.

BIBLIOGRAPHY

Lewis, D.: *Counterfactuals* (Oxford: Blackwell, 1973).
Jackson, F. ed.: *Conditionals* (Oxford: Oxford University Press, 1991).
Stalnaker, R.: *Inquiry* (Cambridge, MA: MIT Press, 1984).
Sosa, E. ed.: *Causation and Conditionals* (Oxford: Oxford University Press, 1975).

FRANK JACKSON

D

Davidson, Donald (1917–) Davidson's general approach to metaphysics follows a long-standing tradition in trying to derive the basic features of reality from the structure of language. The particular angle he introduces comes from his suggestion that the structure of language and its revelations about the large features of reality are refracted in the effort to formulate a comprehensive, formal theory of truth for a canonically regimented version of natural language (see Davidson, 1984, essay 13; for some criticisms of this approach to metaphysics, see Rovane, 1986).

The most original specific application of this method to metaphysics is to be found in Davidson's claim that such a theory for that fragment of language which contains sentences such as 'The boiler exploded', yields an ontology of events. That is to say, it yields the idea that events such as explosions exist as particulars, in the way that boilers do. There is something very natural and appealing about the suggestion because, among other things, it allows for our re-description of the same event in different ways. Thus one can say of the same event that it was an explosion and that it was a domestic disaster (see Davidson, 1980, essay 9; for a different, more universalist view of events, see Chisholm, 1970. For a different view of events as particulars, see Kim, 1976. Davidson discusses the criterion for individuation of events in 1980, essay 8, and in Davidson, 1985.)

Davidson extends the point to sentences such as 'Jones buttered the bread', arguing that these sentences about human agency too are to be treated as quantifying over events which get intentional descriptions. He points out that this affords a satisfying theoretical treatment of sentences with adverbial modifiers. In the standard predicate calculus, adverbially modified predicates are usually represented as distinct predicates, but that representation fails to capture the seeming validity of the argument which goes from, say, 'Jones buttered the toast with a knife' to 'Jones buttered the toast.' There is simply no sanction for Ga from Fa. But the intuitive validity of the argument is preserved if we take events to exist as particulars, and treat the canonical representation or 'logical form' of such sentences as quantifying over them. Thus we may go from $\exists x$ (x was a buttering of the toast by Jones, and x was with a knife) to $\exists x$ (x was a buttering of the toast by Jones) (see Davidson, 1980, essay 6. There are, of course other suggestions in the literature for handling adverbial modification, such as, for instance, that one should introduce not quantification but modifiers of predicates.)

He further exploits the point to give an analysis of sentences citing causes, such as, 'His pressing the button caused the explosion.' The ontology of events allows him to make a distinction between two different aspects of what these sentences convey: causal relations which hold between events and which are purely extensional, and causal explanations which are intensional in the sense that they, unlike causal relations, depend upon how the events are described (Davidson, 1980, essay 7).

Davidson, then, develops this distinction to provide a solution to the traditional MIND/BODY PROBLEM. Mental events are identical with physical events, but when we gather these mental events into types, there is a principled objection to their being identical with the types we gather physical events into. This is because unlike the particulars (the tokens of mental events), the types are essentially dependent on the concepts we employ in describing the events; and there are no lawlike correlations between these mental concepts and the concepts we employ in physical descriptions of events. So, at the level of concepts there is no reduction of the mental to the physical, but, as far as ONTOLOGY goes this does not imply a dualism since any mental event is identical with some physical event or other. He calls this hybrid position, 'anomalous monism', and the view of identity it proposes, 'token-identity' (Davidson, 1980, essay 11).

In addition to token-identity, Davidson's metaphysics of mind posits a dependency relation between the mental and the physical, which he calls SUPERVENIENCE. This is the idea that a psychological predicate will not distinguish anything that is not also distinguished by some physical predicate(s). The underlying motivation for such a dependency was to make a claim in the philosophy of mind parallel to a position in the study of values which both denied a reduction of values to facts of nature at the same time as it did not make values mysteriously autonomous. In positing supervenience, Davidson was able to claim that a denial of a definitional as well as a nomological reduction of mental properties to physical properties was compatible with a dependency relation between them which disallowed one from saying that two things were indistinguishable physically but were different in some mental respect. This allowed the scientific study of physical nature maximum comprehensiveness in its dominion without any concession to mind/body reductionism. More recently he has also invoked supervenience to quell a worry which has loomed at least since DESCARTES – that the mental is epiphenomenal. In contemporary discussions this worry has sometimes been expressed as the worry that mentality makes no difference to causal relations. (See Kim, 1984 and Sosa, 1984 who raise this worry for Davidson's anomalous monism, in particular. For a response

on behalf of Davidson, see LePore and Loewer, 1987.) So expressed, supervenience is not needed to deal with it. The worry is handled in Davidson's metaphysical framework by simply appealing to the extensional nature of causal relations. Since events which enter causal relations are often described in mental terms, mental events (uncontroversially) enter causal relations. But for him it makes no sense to go on to ask whether mental events make a difference to causal relations in the sense that they cause other events *in virtue of being mental*. Causal relations being purely extensional do not hold or occur in virtue of anything, mental or physical. However the worry about epiphenomenalism is sometimes expressed as not being about causal relations in particular, but more generally as, say, the idea that we may alter (in the limit, even strip all) mental properties without at all affecting the physical properties of things. It is to this worry that Davidson responds by pointing out that if it were true it would contradict the weak dependency relation of supervenience as characterized above. However this subject throws up many questions issuing from modal intuitions about identity, intuitions whose relevance Davidson has always been suspicious of; these questions are at present the subject of much controversy in metaphysics and the philosophy of mind.

There are other aspects of Davidson's philosophy – such as his views on REALISM, OBJECTIVITY and the nature of truth – which may be treated as being part of metaphysics, but because of their integral relation with epistemological themes, are best discussed within epistemology.

See also EVENT THEORY; REDUCTION, REDUCTIONISM; THEORIES OF TRUTH.

WRITINGS

Essays on Actions and Events (Oxford: Oxford University Press, 1980).
Inquiries into Truth and Interpretation (Oxford: Oxford University Press, 1984).
'Reply to Quine on events' (1985), in

Actions and Events: Perspectives on the Philosophy of Donald Davidson ed. E. LePore and B. McLaughlin (Oxford: Blackwell, 1986).

BIBLIOGRAPHY

Chisholm, R.M.: 'Events and propositions', *Noûs* 4 (1970).
Kim, J.: 'Events as property exemplifications', in *Action Theory* ed. M. Brand and D. Walton (Dordrecht: Reidel, 1976).
Kim, J.: 'Epiphenomenal and supervenient causation', *Midwest Studies in Philosophy* 9 (1984).
LePore, E. ed.: *Truth and Interpretation: Perspectives on the Philosophy of Donald Davidson* (Oxford: Blackwell, 1986).
LePore, E. and Loewer, B.: 'Making mind matter more', *Journal of Philosophy* 93 (1987).
LePore, E. and McLaughlin, B. eds: *Actions and Events: Perspectives on the Philosophy of Donald Davidson* (Oxford: Blackwell, 1986).
Rovane, C.: 'The metaphysics of interpretation', in *Truth and Interpretation: Perspectives on the Philosophy of Donald Davidson* ed. E. LePore (Oxford: Blackwell, 1986).
Sosa, E.: 'Mind–body interaction and supervenient causation', *Midwest Studies in Philosophy* 9 (1984).

AKEEL BILGRAMI

death Death provokes a wide variety of philosophical questions. There is the fundamental conceptual question about the nature of death itself. There is the metaphysical question about whether we continue to exist after death. There is the epistemic question whether death is in some distinctive way unknowable. Finally, there are ethical and value-theoretic questions about death: is death an evil for the one who dies? Is it irrational to fear death? Why is it wrong to kill people? Specialists in medical ethics have written extensively on the problem of formulating an acceptable *criterion* of death for human beings. While this is an important public-policy issue to which philosophers may make useful contributions, it seems not to be as fundamentally metaphysical in nature as the question about the *analysis* of the concept of death.

Some of the philosophical literature on death seems to presuppose that there is a concept of death uniquely applicable to people. However, it seems more natural to suppose that the central concept of death applies uniformly to things of every biological sort and that the word 'dies' expresses this 'biological concept of death' whenever we say (using the word literally) that some organism dies.

THE STANDARD ANALYSIS

According to the most popular analyses, 'x dies at t' means roughly the same as 'x ceases to live at t'. Reflection on facts about suspended animation suggest that this analysis fails to capture precisely what we mean when we say that something dies. When an organism enters suspended animation (as for example a microscopic laboratory specimen does when placed in liquid nitrogen), it ceases to be alive. Yet it does not die – this is especially clear if the organism is going to be revived later.

Further reason to doubt that death can be defined as the cessation of life is provided by organisms that reproduce by division. When such an organism divides, it apparently ceases to exist. Hence, it ceases to be alive. Yet, once again, it is inappropriate to say that it has died.

THE SURVIVAL OF DEATH

In the *Phaedo*, PLATO presents a dualistic conception of persons according to which each person is composed of two main parts, a body and a SOUL. Death occurs when body and soul are separated. The body is purely physical and begins to deteriorate at death. Unless mummified, it will soon disintegrate and go out of existence. On the other hand, since the soul is that in virtue of which the organism lives, it must be immortal and imperishable. It existed prior to birth and will continue to exist after death. Thus, on this view, though the *person* does not survive death, the *body* may survive for a short time, and the *soul* survives eternally. This view has obvious affinities to traditional Christian doctrines.

Materialists hold that a person is a living human body. Some hold that life is essential to persons, so that at the moment of death the person ceases to exist, and is replaced by a corpse. Other materialists deny that life is essential to the things that are persons. They claim that death marks a change in state of a continuing entity – the body. On this view, most people continue to exist as corpses for a few months or years after death. They cease to exist when they disintegrate. Continued existence of this sort would almost certainly be devoid of experience, and if so would be of no value to the dead (former) person.

THE MYSTERY OF DEATH

A number of philosophers have maintained that death is a mysterious or unknowable phenomenon. Some who maintain this view apparently do so because they believe that in order to understand death, one must understand how the experience of being dead presents itself to those who are dead. If one also believes that the dead have no psychological experiences, one will face this paradox: in order to understand death, one must understand how it feels to feel nothing at all.

It seems, however, that the underlying epistemic requirement is unreasonable. Being dead is not an experience; it does not 'feel like' anything at all to those who are dead; hence, the understanding of death cannot call for an understanding of what death feels like to those who are dead. Perhaps we understand death well enough when we take note of its occurrence in other organisms. Assuming that one is also a biological organism, one can conclude that one's own death will be relevantly like those other deaths.

THE EVIL OF DEATH

It is natural to fear death, and to think that death is ordinarily a great evil for the one who dies. EPICURUS argued that the fear of death is irrational since death is never evil for the one who dies. His argument was based on two main premises: (1) the notion (derived from his dualistic conception of persons) that each person ceases to exist at death; and (2) the claim that nothing bad can happen to a person at a time when he or she does not exist.

Defenders of the Deprivation Approach acknowledge that people cannot undergo painful experiences once they are dead. Nevertheless, they insist, death may be bad for the deceased inasmuch as it deprives them of the good things they would have experienced if they had not died.

Murder is generally taken to be the paradigm of morally impermissible action, yet it is not easy to explain precisely why murder is wrong. If the Epicurean view were true, then (provided it were done painlessly) murder would never harm its victim. The Deprivation Approach seems to imply that whenever continued life would be of overall negative value to the victim, he or she is not harmed by painless murder. This also seems wrong. Traditional forms of utilitarianism imply that murder is morally required whenever the intended victim is 'dragging down' the worldwide utility total. This seems to imply (absurdly) that we ought to kill everyone who would lead a life that is, on the whole, unhappy.

See also LIFE; MIND/BODY PROBLEM; PERSONS AND PERSONAL IDENTITY; PHYSICALISM/MATERIALISM; VITALISM.

BIBLIOGRAPHY

Donnelly, J. ed.: *Language, Metaphysics, and Death* (New York: Fordham University Press, 1978).

Epicurus: 'Letter to Menoeceus', trans. C. Bailey, in *The Stoic and Epicurean Philosophers* ed. with an introduction by W.J.

Oates (New York: The Modern Library, 1940), 30–4.

Feldman, F.: *Confrontations with the Reaper: A Philosophical Study of the Nature and Value of Death* (New York: Oxford University Press, 1991).

Fischer, J.M.: *Essays on Death* (Stanford: Stanford University Press, 1993).

Nagel, T.: 'Death', *Noûs* IV (1970), 73–80; repr. in his *Mortal Questions* (Cambridge: Cambridge University Press, 1979), 1–10.

Plato: *Phaedo*, in *The Dialogues of Plato* trans. B. Jowett (New York: Random House, 1937), vol. 1, 441–501.

FRED FELDMAN

Descartes, René (1596–1650) French philosopher and mathematician. It would be hard to overestimate the philosophical influence of Descartes. Often called the 'father of modern philosophy', his arguments on doubt, the foundations of knowledge, and the nature of the human mind, are familiar to countless students. But while Cartesian ideas almost inevitably form the point of departure for our understanding of how epistemology and philosophy of mind developed from the early modern period to the present day, the situation with respect to metaphysics is not so simple. There is some evidence that Descartes's own motivating interests in philosophy were not primarily metaphysical. *Non adeo incumbendum esse meditationibus* ('You should not give such obsessive attention to metaphysical meditations') he told the young student Frans Burman (*Œuvres de Descartes* vol. V, p. 165; *The Correspondence*, p. 346); he gave similar advice to that keen amateur metaphysician Princess Elizabeth of Bohemia (*Œuvres de Descartes* vol. III, pp. 692ff.; *The Correspondence*, pp. 227ff.). Most of Descartes' time as a young man was occupied with mathematical and scientific concerns, including detailed work in specific areas such as geometry and optics (on both of which subjects he published essays in 1637) as well as grand theorizing about COSMOLOGY and the nature of MATTER (developed in his unpublished treatise *Le Monde* (1633)). Even when he came to publish the *Discourse on the Method* (1637), he devoted only one short section (Part IV) to metaphysics; the rest of the work is concerned with his early education and intellectual development, current scientific interests, and plans for future research. In general, there is a considerable amount of evidence to support the thesis of Charles Adam that metaphysics was of merely subsidiary interest to the historical Descartes, and that he embarked on metaphysical inquiries for one reason alone – to provide solid foundations for his scientific system (*Œuvres de Descartes* vol. XII, p. 143).

But whatever Descartes' own personal priorities may have been, metaphysics none the less forms an integral part of his conception of philosophy. In the celebrated simile which he deploys in the 1647 Preface to the French Edition of the *Principles of Philosophy*, philosophy is compared to a tree of which 'the roots are metaphysics, the trunk is physics, and the branches emerging from the trunk are the other sciences' (ibid. vol. IXB, p. 14; *The Philosophical Writings of Descartes* vol. I, p. 186). Even here, it is the fruit to be collected from the extremities of the branches which Descartes goes on to stress: the value of the system lies in the practical benefits it can bring to mankind (cf. *Œuvres de Descartes* vol. VI, p. 62; *Philosophical Writings* vol. I, p. 142). But it is also made clear that only a soundly rooted tree can bear such fruit. One of Descartes's frequent criticisms of the scholastic philosophy in which he had been trained as a young man is that it often started from principles which were either obscure or doubtful or both: 'nothing solid could have been built on such shaky foundations' (*Œuvres de Descartes* vol. VI, p. 8; *Philosophical Writings* vol. I, p. 115).

We know from Descartes's correspondence with his friend Marin Mersenne that as early as 1629 he had begun to compose a 'little treatise' on metaphysics which aimed to prove 'the existence of God and of our souls when they are separated from the body' (*Œuvres de Descartes* vol. I, p. 182; *The Correspondence*, p. 29). The treatise was, however, laid aside, and by the time he came to write his metaphysical masterpiece, the *Meditations* (1641), Descartes had broadened his conception of metaphysical inquiry; he wrote to Mersenne that he had chosen the title 'Meditations on First Philosophy' to show that 'the discussion is not confined to God and the soul, but treats in general of all the first things to be discovered by philosophizing' (*Œuvres de Descartes* vol. III, p. 235; *The Correspondence*, p. 157). In the order of discovery unfolded in the *Meditations*, what the meditator reaches first of all is the indubitable knowledge of his own existence (Second Meditation). This result suggests (at the start of the Third Meditation) a general rule for the development of further knowledge, namely that 'whatever I perceive very clearly and distinctly is true' (*Œuvres de Descartes* vol. VII, p. 35; *Philosophical Writings* vol. II, p. 24); however, since the doubts of the First Meditation have still left open the possibility that we might go astray even in our clearest and simplest perceptions, the meditator rapidly realizes that no further progress can be made 'until I examine whether there is a God, and if there is, whether he can be a deceiver' (*Œuvres de Descartes* vol. VII, p. 36; *Philosophical Writings* vol. II, p. 25). The remainder of the Third Meditation is spent establishing the existence of a perfect, non-deceiving God: the idea of such a being, which I find in my mind, could not have been generated from my own resources, but must have as its cause an actually existing God. 'By the word "God" I understand a substance that is infinite, eternal, immutable, independent, supremely intelligent, supremely powerful ... All these attributes are such that the more carefully I examine them, the less possible it seems that they could have originated from me alone. So it must be concluded that God necessarily exists' (*Œuvres de Descartes* vol. VII, p. 45; *Philosophical Writings* vol. II, p. 31).

The existence of God, once established, is used to set up a sound method for humans to seek the truth, namely restraining their will so as to assent only to what is clearly perceived: God, though he has given man a limited intellect, guarantees none the less that it is, in principle, a reliable instrument for the pursuit of truth, and that, when carefully used, it will not lead us fundamentally astray (Fourth Meditation). Once this principle is established, the meditator can proceed to lay down the metaphysical foundations for a secure philosophical system: these are, on the one hand, my perception of matter as an 'extended thing' – whatever can be quantitatively defined, and is the 'subject matter of pure mathematics' (Fifth Meditation), and, on the other hand, my perception of myself as a 'thinking, non-extended thing' which is entirely distinct from the body (Sixth Meditation). This last result is of course the famous thesis of so-called 'Cartesian dualism' – the conception of mind and body as separate and incompatible substances. It is significant that when Descartes presents the thesis, he provides direct metaphysical underpinning for it, in the shape of an appeal to the deity: 'the fact that I can clearly and distinctly understand one thing [mind] apart from another [body] is enough to make me certain that the two things are really distinct, since they are capable of being separated, at least by God' (*Œuvres de Descartes* vol. VII, p. 78; *Philosophical Writings* vol. II, p. 54).

It may be seen from this brief summary that the role of God in Cartesian metaphysics is absolutely central. But Descartes's reliance on the deity in developing the foundations of his philosophy is problematic in at least two ways. The first is the famous puzzle of the 'Cartesian circle': if God is to be invoked to underwrite the reliability of the human mind, how can we be sure of the reliability of those perceptions we need to establish the existence of God in the first place? (cf. *Œuvres de Descartes* vol. VII, p. 246; *Philosophical Writings*, vol. II, p. 171). The second problem concerns the details of Descartes's proof of God's existence. Despite his professed aim of sweeping away all preconceived opinions and basing his 'first philosophy' on completely clear and transparent premises, the proof of God in the Third Meditation relies on what are (to the modern ear at least) highly questionable assumptions about CAUSATION. According to Descartes, the cause of my idea of God must actually contain all the perfection represented in the idea. It is 'manifest by the natural light', claims Descartes, that 'there must be at least as much reality in the cause as in the effect', and hence 'that what is more perfect cannot arise from what is less perfect' (*Œuvres de Descartes* vol. VII, p. 40; *Philosophical Writings* vol. II, p. 28). What Descartes is in effect presupposing here is a theory of causation that is deeply indebted to the scholastic philosophical apparatus which it is his official aim to supplant. According to the scholastic conception, causality is generally understood in terms of some kind of property-transmission: causes pass on or transmit properties to effects, which are then said to derive their features from the causes. This traditional conception of causality is largely bypassed in Descartes's mathematically based physical science; but here in his metaphysics he appears to accept it all on trust. This type of problem, indeed, is not confined to presuppositions about causation. Throughout the argument for God's existence, the reader is faced with a positive barrage of traditional technical terms ('substance' and 'mode', and terms denoting various grades of reality – 'formal', 'objective', 'eminent' and the like), whose application the reader is asked to take as self-evident. In short, when endeavouring to establish the metaphysical foundations for his new science, Descartes seems unable to free himself from the explanatory framework of his scholastic predecessors. (Similar strictures are applicable to Descartes's other strategy for proving God's existence, the so-called 'ontological argument' which Descartes puts forward in the Fifth Meditation: *Œuvres de Descartes* vol. VII, p. 66; *Philosophical Writings* vol. II, p. 46).

The structure of Cartesian metaphysics is often described as 'rationalist' in character. The term is an awkward and often ambiguous one. Sometimes it is used to denote a purely a prioristic conception of knowledge; but Descartes's conception is certainly not of this kind. It is true that his version of the ontological argument does try to prove God's existence simply from the definition or essence of God, but many other elements of his metaphysical system (the *Cogito*, the causal proof of God's existence, and the proof of the external world in the Sixth Meditation) proceed a posteriori, and rely on existential premises of various kinds. What makes the term 'rationalist', in a broader sense, seem appropriate, is Descartes's belief that the human mind is innately endowed with a God-given 'light of reason' or 'natural light', on the basis of which it has the power to discern the nature of reality. In Descartes's early work, the *Rules for the Direction of our Native Intelligence* (circa 1628), it is the light of reason that enables us to intuit the 'simple natures' – the fundamental building blocks for systematic knowledge of God, mind and matter (see Rule Four and Rule Twelve).

This broadly 'rationalistic' aspect of Descartes's metaphysics is complicated by one of his most perplexing doctrines – that of the divine creation of the eternal truths. This doctrine is not found in the *Meditations*, but it is explicitly asserted in Descartes's correspondence, as early as 1630, and it surfaces again in the *Replies* to the *Objections*: 'God did not will that the three angles of a triangle should be equal to two right angles because he recognized that it could not be otherwise; . . . it is because he wills that the three angles of a triangle should necessarily equal two right angles that this is true and cannot be otherwise' (*Œuvres de Descartes* vol. VII, p. 432; *Philosophical Writings* vol. II, p. 291; cf. Letter to Mersenne of 15 April 1630, *Œuvres de Descartes* vol. I, p. 145; *The Correspondence*, p. 23). Descartes thus departs from the traditional theological notion that God's omnipotence extends only to what is logically possible. For Descartes, God is not only the creator of all actually existing things, but he is the author of necessity and possibility; he was 'just as free to make it not true that the radii of a circle were equal as he was free not to create the world' (*Œuvres de Descartes* vol. I, p. 152; *The Correspondence*, p. 25). Some of Descartes's critics objected that this was incoherent, but Descartes replied that just because we humans cannot grasp something, this is no reason to conclude that it is beyond the power of God. God thus turns out, on Descartes's conception, to be in a real sense *incomprehensible*: our soul, being finite, cannot fully grasp (Fr. *comprendre*, Latin *comprehendere*) or conceive him (ibid.).

The doctrines of the divine creation of the eternal truths and the incomprehensibility of God make the character of Descartes's metaphysics very much less 'transparent' than the rationalist label implies. If the structure of the fundamental principles of logic is not ultimately accessible to human reason, but depends on the inscrutable will of God, then the human mind is not, after all, able to uncover their fundamental rationale. Indeed, if the principles of logic are arbitrary fiats of the divine will, which could be otherwise (though in a sense not accessible to our intellect), then there appear to be elements of opacity and contingency at the very heart of Cartesian metaphysics. If this is right, then the contrast between Descartes's metaphysical 'rationalism', with its alleged optimism about the powers of human reason, and HUME's later scepticism about our ability to discern the ultimate basis for the way things are, turns out not to be as stark as is often supposed.

See also CLEAR AND DISTINCT; LIGHT OF NATURE; MIND/BODY PROBLEM; RATIONALISM.

WRITINGS

Descartes's main metaphysical works are the *Meditations on First Philosophy* (1641) and Part I of the *Principles of Philosophy* (1644). See also Part IV of the *Discourse on the Method* (1637). Descartes's correspondence is also a valuable source for his views on metaphysics. All these materials are contained in the following editions.

Œuvres de Descartes ed. C. Adam and P. Tannery revd edn, 12 vols (Paris: Vrin/CNRS, 1964–76).

The Philosophical Writings of Descartes ed. and trans. J. Cottingham, R. Stoothoff and D. Murdoch, 2 vols (Cambridge: Cambridge University Press, 1985).

The Correspondence ed. and trans. J. Cottingham, R. Stoothoff, D. Murdoch and A. Kenny, *The Philosophical Writings of Descartes* vol. 3 (Cambridge University Press, 1991).

BIBLIOGRAPHY

Beyssade, J.-M.: *La philosophie première de Descartes* (Paris: Flammarion, 1979).

Cottingham, J.: *Descartes* (Oxford: Blackwell, 1986).

Cottingham, J. ed.: *The Cambridge Companion to Descartes* (Cambridge and New York: Cambridge University Press, 1992).

Gaukroger, S.: *Cartesian Logic* (Oxford: Clarendon Press, 1989).

Kenny, A.: *Descartes* (New York: Random House, 1968).

Marion, J.-L.: *Sur la théologie blanche de Descartes* (Paris: Presses Universitaires de France, 1981, rev. 1991).

Wilson, M.D.: *Descartes* (London: Routledge, 1978).

JOHN COTTINGHAM

determinable *see* DETERMINATE/DETERMINABLE

determinate/determinable In 1921, the Cambridge logician W.E. Johnson introduced the contemporary use of the terms 'determinate' and 'determinable' into the philosophical lexicon by citing a pair of exemplars:

> I propose to call such terms as colour and shape *determinables* in relation to such terms as red and circular which will be called *determinates*. (1921; p. 174)

The determinable–determinate relation thus holds between pairs of *predicables* or *properties*, and Johnson proceeded to characterize it by citing four of its characteristic marks or features.

First, determinate properties come in *families*, and to each such family of determinates corresponds one and only one determinable from which it 'emanates'.

> [Any] one determinable such as colour is distinctly other than such a determinable as shape or tone: i.e. colour is not adequately described as indeterminate, since it is, metaphorically speaking, that from which the specific determinates, red, yellow, green, etc., emanate; while from shape emanates another completely different series of determinates. (1921, pp. 174–5)

Second, determinables and determinates plainly differ in *scope*. Determinable properties are broader or more general than their corresponding determinates; determinate properties, narrower or more specific than their superordinate determinables. Determinables and determinates of a given family thus form a hierarchy of scope-inclusions, after the manner of *coloured* and *red*, *red* and *crimson*, and *crimson* and *Harvard crimson*. In Johnson's terminology, pairs of predicables belonging to such an hierarchy are related as (narrower) *sub*-determinates to (broader) *super*-determinates.

Third, such determinables as shape, pitch, and colour are

> ultimately *different*, in the important sense that they cannot be subsumed under some one higher determinable, with the result that they are incomparable with one another. (1921, p. 175)

Highest-level determinables in consequence mark out ultimate dimensions of comparison. They are qualitative *respects* in which objects are deemed to resemble and differ.

The fourth and final mark of the determinable–determinate relation, however, is decisive. The relation is *non-conjunctive*.

That is, the subset relationship obtaining between the extension of a pair of predicables related as super- to sub-determinate does not admit of explanation or analysis in terms of a third, differentiating property's being *conjoined* with the super-determinate to restrict the resultant extension to that of the sub-determinate, as *equal-sided* may be conjoined with *parallelogram* to single out the narrower extension of *rhombus* or, classically, the differentium *rational* is conjoined with the genus *animal* to pick out the species *man*. In contrast, the only property that could be conjoined with, e.g., *coloured* to yield a predicable having the extension of *red* is *red* itself. An item is not red by virtue of being *both* coloured *and* F, for some property F distinct from *red*. Being red is not being something *in addition* to being coloured; being red is rather a *way* of being coloured.

Essentially these features are singled out in the discussion of the determinable–determinate relation offered by Searle as well. Searle's focus is on *specificity*. His chief concern is to distinguish the specificity relationship obtaining between super- and sub-determinate properties from those obtaining between genus and species, between a conjunction of diverse determinates and the determinable of one its members, between an arbitrary disjunction and one of its disjuncts, and between a disjunction that includes a determinable and one of that determinable's determinates. He concludes that a is a determinate of b just in case a is both *non-conjunctively* more specific than b and *logically related* to every c which is non-conjunctively more specific than b, where two terms are logically related if either entails the other or the negation of the other. Formally a is more specific than b provided that a entails b, but not conversely, and a is non-conjunctively more specific than b provided that, in addition, there are no properties c and d such that a is equivalent to $(c \& d)$ and c, but neither d nor its negation, entails b.

Historically, the notion of a family of determinate qualities falling under a common single determinable forms the framework of the eighteenth-century dispute between LOCKE and BERKELEY on the topic of 'general ideas'. Locke was interpreted as holding that one could form ideas of determinables that were not at the same time ideas of lowest-level (narrowest) determinates of those determinables – for example, the (determinable) idea of a triangle that was not the idea of any determinate sort of triangle (equilateral, isosceles, right, scalene, etc.). Berkeley, in contrast, argued that even the most 'general' ideas resembled particular images in necessarily *being* completely determinate, their 'generality' deriving entirely from the manner in which they were considered and applied in comparative judgements of similarity and difference.

On the contemporary scene, the general decline of interest in traditional questions of Platonistic metaphysics has led to a correlative scarcity of work specifically addressed to the relationships of inclusion, exclusion, subordination, and incompatibility obtaining among determinable and determinate qualities. Recognition of the special characteristics of those relationships, however, potentially carries with it interesting consequences for a variety of metaphysical concerns.

The non-conjunctivity of the relationship of sub- to super-determinate qualities (at every level of generality), for example, is *prima facie* difficult to reconcile with the thesis of *elementarism*, that descriptive predicates of the second and higher types are in principle eliminable in favour of predicates of the first type, a traditional stop on the road toward some forms of NOMINALISM. Such higher-order determinable predicates as 'is a colour' and 'is a shade of red' (true of, e.g. scarlet, crimson, carmine and maroon) at least do not readily lend themselves to any obvious reductive analysis in terms of first-order predicates.

The 'ultimate difference' of such highest-level determinables as colour and shape, on the other hand, suggests that they may play the role of descriptive (as opposed to pure or metaphysical) CATEGORIES, thereby functioning to limit negative predications as much as positive ones. In particular, one can hold that both the positive and the negative predication of a determinate quality *presuppose* the correct ascription of its corresponding highest-level determinable, so that *neither* 'red' *nor* 'not-red', for example, can be truly predicated of any item – e.g. an electron, the number seventeen – of which 'coloured' is not also correctly predicable.

Finally, we may note the fact that the family of determinates under a common determinable at each level of specificity appears to consist of pairwise *incompatible* qualities. No spatially extended particular, for example, can co-instantiate both red and green or (more determinately) both crimson and scarlet at every point of its surface. Same-level determinates under a single determinable, that is, evidently (necessarily) *exclude* one another. If this is correct, however, it may ultimately prove illuminating to treat such a higher-order relationship of 'quality exclusion' as the fundamental form of 'negative fact', underlying both predicate and propositional negation and supplying a basis in terms of which they can be analysed and understood.

See also PLATONISM.

BIBLIOGRAPHY

Johnson, W.E.: *Logic* vol. 1 (Cambridge: Cambridge University Press, 1921: repr. New York: Dover Publications, 1964).
Searle, J.: 'On determinables and resemblance', with S. Körner, *Proceedings of the Aristotelian Society* suppl. vol. 33 (1959), 141–58.

JAY F. ROSENBERG

determinism The thesis that the world is deterministic is the thesis that the state of the world at one time 'fixes' or 'determines' the state of the world at any future time (or at both future and past times in some stronger versions of the claim). As such the thesis must not be confused either with the thesis of FATALISM (that what will happen at a time is 'destined' to happen, irrespective of what happens at some earlier time, in particular irrespective of an agent's choices at that earlier time), nor with the claim sometimes made against those who deny 'determinate reality' to the future (or to the past and the future) that reality is 'timeless' in the sense that even what is not present in time and even what is future still has full reality.

The notion of 'fixation' or 'determination' that is usually had in mind is this: from a total description of the state of the world at one time, and a specification of all of the laws of nature, a total description of the world at any other time can be derived by a purely logical, deductive, inference. Naturally, given the richness of magnitudes in the world, no claim that such descriptions could be given in any reasonably finitistic language is intended. This general idea of determinism is quite problematic, however, as many issues concerning what is to count as a state of the world, and of its full specification, and many issues concerning what is to count as a LAW OF NATURE, arise.

As RUSSELL pointed out, a too liberal reading of what counts as a law of nature, one that lets any true general correlation between states at different times have lawlike status, would make the deterministic nature of the world trivially true, for there would, then, always be a law connecting the state at one time to the states at all other times so that the latter were fully fixed by the former, no matter what the world was like. Similarly, a too generous stance with what can count as a state at a time can trivialize the notion of determinism. If we let states at one time include reference to features of some other time (by, for example, letting 'is such that five minutes later the following magnitude holds of the following object' count as a state feature) then one would be able to infer the later state from the earlier even without references to laws of nature, no matter what the world was like. The necessity, familiar from other problem areas of philosophy, of restricting the notion of lawlike generalization to a proper subset of all true

generalizations and of delimiting the appropriate features to be considered genuine occurrent physical properties of the world appears here as a necessary condition to avoid trivializing the notion of determinism.

The idea that the world is deterministic if, and only if, it is 'predictable in principle' has been common since the time of Laplace (1749–1827). But it is far from clear that such a tight association of determinism with predictability, even in principle, should be drawn. One can, for example, imagine worlds that are, intuitively, deterministic, but where some in-principle limitation on the ability of any cognizer to know the state of the world at one time is posited. Under these circumstances while future states would be fully determined by present states, the in-principle block on complete knowledge of the present state would make in-principle prediction impossible. On the other hand when the attempt is made to delimit the class of generalizations that are to be counted as laws of nature, various suggestions for necessary conditions for lawlikeness do have an epistemic tinge to them (that, for example, the functional connections of states to states be computable, for example).

The questions involved when one asks if an idealized world described by some specified fundamental physical theory is one in which determinism holds or does not hold are fraught with great complexity. Even for such 'simple' cases as Newtonian particle mechanics, issues involved in projecting motion through multiple particle collisions and in the possibility of particles entering an interaction by 'coming in from infinity' in a finite time serve to make naive claims that a Newtonian particle world is deterministic less than straightforwardly acceptable. Much attention has been directed recently to 'chaotic systems'. Here while the future behaviour of a system is, in some idealized sense, fully fixed by its initial state, there exist, arbitrarily close to that initial state, states that would lead to a radically different future evolution for the system. One could argue that such systems are deterministic, but not predictable, as noted above, or one could, as some theorists have, argue that the existence of such systems casts doubt on the reality of 'exact' initial states as genuine features of the world as opposed to idealizations of theory that go beyond reality. Here, again, we see how important issues of what counts as legitimate physical state intertwine with issues of determinism.

The variety of space-times allowed by General Relativity make issues of determinism even more complex (*see* SPACE AND TIME). Singularities in the space-time, space-times in which the global partitioning of the space-time into spaces at a time is impossible, and space-times that have closed causal loops, are all new possibilities that complicate the issue of whether or not a specified world ought to be characterized as deterministic.

Finally there is the current quantum-theoretic picture of the world. The state attributed to systems by the theory, the system's quantum state, is generally taken to observe an equation of evolution that is deterministic in nature. But, it is argued, the real states of the world, values observed upon measurement, are determined from the quantum state only probabilistically. The correlations between observed values at one time and those at some other time are then, apparently, non-deterministic. Further, there are a number of important theorems, so-called 'proofs of the non-existence of hidden variable', that are designed to show that the non-deterministic relation among observed values at different times cannot be generated out of a deterministic relation between the values of some 'deeper' 'hidden' parameter values at those times. Since that status of measurement in quantum mechanics is itself very problematic, as is the physical interpretation of the quantum states, it is impossible to argue without controversy that quantum theory, if true, shows, once and for all, the world to be non-deterministic. But the theory clearly describes a world in which determinism, if it does hold, will be a subtler matter than previously imagined.

Traditionally philosophy has often contended with the issue of the alleged incompatibility of determinism and 'FREE WILL'. It is, however, far from clear that any understanding of the place of the notions of free agency, choice and will in human action will really hinge upon a showing that the world is non-deterministic in the sense intended above. At least it seems clear that indeterminacy in the world will not, by itself, provide a 'place' for free will. An act generated by a spontaneous or non-determined physical happening seems as remote from our idea of an act generated out of free will as does one generated out of a determined physical happening.

See also NEWTON; SPACE AND TIME.

BIBLIOGRAPHY

Earman, J.: *A Primer of Determinism* (Dordrecht: Reidel, 1986).

LAWRENCE SKLAR

Dewey, John (1859–1952) American pragmatist. In *Experience and Nature* (1925). Dewey applies the empirical method to a rich notion of EXPERIENCE in order to develop an ONTOLOGY that undercuts the many dualisms that plague philosophy and are his targets in his numerous other writings. Dewey objects to the dichotomies of classical and modern philosophy – of BEING AND BECOMING, mind and matter, theory and practice, facts and values – not only because they give rise to sterile philosophical puzzles but because they reflect and perpetuate class distinctions between those who enjoy the life of the mind and those who must engage in physical labour. He speaks of the 'hateful irony' (1925, p. 99) of a philosophy that exalts the life of reason while paying no attention to the conditions that make such a life possible.

Experience is, for example, setting a watch, being pushed by the wind, listening to the fourth Brandenburg Concerto, understanding how watches work. Only in reflection do we distinguish experiencing and that which is experienced, noting that experiencing is not restricted to knowing and that what is experienced is the rich world of our everyday lives.

Metaphysics, which deals with the most general traits of existence, finds that existence is both stable and precarious, that it shows both recurrent features and individuality. There is for Dewey only one realm of Being, every existent is an event. Events have immediate, final qualities that are not known, though they stimulate the inquiry that leads to knowledge and the deliberate production of values. Events have beginnings and endings, they have and are causes and effects. Just as it is a mistake to regard (as did the Greeks) our world of becomings as inferior to a realm of Being (or of finalities), so it is a mistake to regard (as do the moderns) causes or the earlier parts of a history as more real than effects or the later parts of that history.

Thus life, self-sustaining interactions between a thing and its environment, appeared later than inanimate matter (stable, recurrent orders of events), and minded behaviour (interactions of an organism with others of its kind through speech) occurred even later; but ontologically they are on the same level. Though Dewey regards the life of the mind as the most conspicuous of nature's ends, and as one of our highest goods, he warns against identifying ends (endings) with goods; *qua* endings they may be good, bad, or indifferent.

Consciousness presupposes communication. A baby's cry, an organic response, becomes a signal when it elicits a useful response from an adult but it is not yet language; language is present when one language user counts on another's understanding and cooperation. Thus speech with others precedes speech with ourselves (thought), meanings are not psychic existences but primarily properties of cooperative behaviour and secondarily of objects. Objects (in the first instance the things of our ordinary lives, but also the objects of the various sciences) are events with meanings. 'Meaning' is, however, in Dewey's use multivocal. Things have meanings or even 'essences' when we take them as signalling consequences that are important for us; things have meaning when they make sense. The existence of error shows that meanings are objective, they indicate possible interactions, hence mistakes are possible. Meanings are values; literature, ceremony, etc., provide the meanings in terms of which life is judged. What all these meanings share is that they are deliberately constructed means to our various ends, including that greatest human good, shared experience (1925, p. 159). Communication is thus both instrumental and final.

There is no mind/body problem in the traditional sense, there is instead the distinction between routine behaviour and intelligent behaviour, i.e. ultimately a social problem. Thinking occurs when a situation is indeterminate, when the outcome depends on what we do. In a closed deterministic world, there would be no consciousness. It follows from the priority of communication to thought that human individuals are products of their society who bring to the simplest experience the habits and meanings they have been taught. Yet, when a situation is indeterminate, when it provokes thought, the result will be reconstruction. Though Dewey is not an idealist (*see* IDEALISM) – there is an existence antecedent to knowledge – the object of knowledge is not that antecedent existence, it is what the knower makes of it, how it is taken, what meaning it is given. The same event may be known as a piece of paper, as a valuable historical document, or as something which will aid in making a fire.

All individuals are products of their society, yet 'every thinker puts some portion of an apparently stable world in peril and no one can wholly predict what will emerge in its place' (1925, p. 172). Dewey is profoundly aware of the fact that all change in social relations, for better or for worse, is due to individuals who question and challenge the existing order. In nature as a whole, in the arts, and in the life of the community, there is a tension between stability and spontaneity, between that which is predictable and that which is original. Without either there would be no human flourishing.

120

Experiences are either useful labour or consummatory, and in the best cases, the former are also the latter. One of Dewey's great contributions to modern thought is the notion of a consummatory experience. Unless some enjoyments had come to us fortuitously, we would never inquire into their conditions, we would never attempt to secure or reproduce them. Values are the result of the critical evaluation and deliberate production of enjoyments that come to us naturally, i.e. values are natural events. Philosophical criticism heightens our appreciation of the goods of art, science and social companionship and makes us aware of their arbitrary distribution which prevents most human being from having 'the richest and fullest experience possible' (1925, p. 308). Although Dewey distinguishes between metaphysics and morality, the motivation for his unitary ontology is his moral commitment to a humane and liberal society.

See also IDENTITY; PRAGMATISM.

WRITINGS

The collected works of Dewey have been published in three series (The Early Works, The Middle Works, The Later Works) ed. J.A. Boydston (Carbondale, IL: Southern Illinois University Press). *Experience and Nature* (1925) is Vol. I of The Later Works (1981).

BIBLIOGRAPHY

Rorty, R.: 'Dewey's metaphysics', in his *Consequences of Pragmatism* (Minneapolis: University of Minnesota Press, 1982), 72–89.
Santayana, G.: 'Dewey's naturalistic metaphysics', in *Dewey and His Critics* ed. S. Morgenbesser (New York: The Journal of Philosophy, 1977), 343–58.
Sleeper, R.W.: *The Necessity of Pragmatism* (New Haven and London: Yale University Press, 1980).

RUTH ANNA PUTNAM

discrete *see* CONTINUOUS/DISCRETE

disposition A tendency to be or to do something. Fragility, solubility, elasticity, ductibility and combustibility are all dispositions. Fragile things tend to break when struck; water-soluble things tend to dissolve when immersed in water. A type of thing a disposition is a tendency to be or to do is a *manifestation* of the disposition. Thus, breaking is a manifestation of the disposition of fragility; dissolving is a manifestation of the disposition of solubility. Dispositions have *activating conditions*. Striking a fragile object can activate the disposition of fragility; immersing a water-soluble object in water can activate the disposition of water-solubility. A disposition can have many types of manifestations and many types of activating conditions. Both cracking and shattering, for example, can manifest the disposition of fragility, and both being struck and being dropped can activate it.

To activate a disposition, an activating occurrence must cause a manifestation of the disposition in 'the right sort of way', where that way varies from disposition to disposition (Prior, 1985, pp. 9–10; Smith, 1985). For example, for a striking to activate the disposition of fragility in an object, it must break the object. To do that, it must cause the object to break. But not just any way of causing an object to break counts as breaking the object. If one person's striking an object causes another person to become angry and kick the object in such a way as to break it, then the first striking of the object did not break the object, even though it was a cause of the object's breaking; the kick, not the first strike, broke the object. The question arises as to how a striking must cause something to break to make it the case that the striking broke the thing. This is a problem of 'deviant' or 'wayward' causal chains, a problem that remains unresolved.

It is fairly widely held that dispositional properties are *counterfactual* properties (Prior, 1985, pp. 5–10; Ryle, 1949, p. 43). Possession of a disposition is satisfaction of a (perhaps complex) counterfactual condition. The view is typically formulated as a thesis about dispositional terms: dispositional terms can be defined by counterfactual sentences. On this view, the property of water-solubility is (roughly) expressed by the counterfactual 'were x immersed in water, x's immersion would (at least begin to) dissolve x'. Thus, something is water-soluble if, and only if (roughly) it is such that were it immersed in water, its immersion in water would (at least begin to) dissolve it. Those who hold this view divide into the *phenomenalist* camp and the *realist* camp (Mackie, 1973, p. 142).

The phenomenalist camp denies that to possess a disposition an object or substance must possess some other property in virtue of which it has the disposition, that is, in virtue of which it satisfies the counterfactual condition (Ryle, 1949, p. 43). The phenomenalist denies that water-soluble things must have some property in virtue of which they are such that were they immersed in water, their immersion would (at least begin to) dissolve them. On the phenomenalist view, it is possible for two things be exactly alike except that one does and the other does not satisfy this counterfactual condition. There need not be any other difference between the two things in virtue of which the one does and the other does not satisfy the condition.

The realist view of dispositions claims that things have dispositions in virtue of having other properties. The properties in virtue of which things possess dispositions are *bases* or *grounds* for the disposition. Labelling it the 'realist' view is, however, somewhat misleading. For proponents of phenomenalism hold that there really are dispositions. Moreover, proponents can allow that a disposition has a basis; they need deny only that dispositions logically or *metaphysically* require bases (Prior, 1985, p. 29).

According to the realist view, dispositions must have bases (Armstrong, 1986, pp. 87–8). But realists divide over whether dispositions must have bases which are *intrinsic* properties of the things that possess the

disposition (Prior, 1985, ch. 4). It has been claimed that it is at least logically possible for the only basis for a disposition to be an historical property, such as, for example, the property of having been produced by a certain process (Mackie, 1973, p. 131; Tooley, 1972, p. 287). This claim implies that it is logically possible for two things to have exactly the same intrinsic properties yet for the one to possess a certain dispositional property and the other to lack that property, solely in virtue of differences in their causal histories. At best, however, this would show only that it is logically possible for a disposition to fail to have an intrinsic basis. But a reason that might be given for the thesis that dispositions typically do not have intrinsic bases is this: whether an object or substance will manifest a disposition typically depends not only on the thing's intrinsic properties and whether an activating event occurs, but also on surrounding circumstances. Glass, for example, would not shatter were it struck when encased in protective covering; steel would shatter were it struck under extremely cold temperatures (Smith, 1977, pp. 441–3). Activating occurrences for dispositions will activate the dispositions only under certain circumstances, circumstances that are *standing conditions* for the manifestations of the disposition. Thus, it might be held that the bases for dispositions typically include *extrinsic* properties. This reason for holding that dispositions typically lack purely intrinsic bases can, however, be rejected. Nothing is, for example, fragile *period*; things are only fragile under certain circumstances. For example, steel is fragile under extremely cold temperatures, though it is not fragile under ordinary room temperatures (Prior, 1985, pp. 46–9). We ordinarily say simply that glass is fragile and that steel is not because it is understood that we are talking about fragility under certain ordinary conditions. On this view, dispositional predicates such as 'is fragile' are incomplete predicates. The complete predicates for 'is fragile' will be ones of the form 'is fragile under conditions C' (Prior, 1985, pp. 8–9). An intrinsic property of a certain kind of object may be a basis for fragility under C but not a basis for fragility under C^*, a distinct standing condition from C.

Realists also divide over whether dispositions must ultimately have *categorical bases* (Armstrong, 1986, pp. 87–8; Prior, 1985, ch. 5). Categorical bases are properties (or states) that are *not* themselves dispositional properties (or states). The view that dispositions must have categorical bases implies that dispositional properties are not fundamental properties: they are invariably possessed in virtue of the possession of non-dispositional, non-counterfactual properties. Dispositions, as noted above, are often taken to be counterfactual properties. The counterfactual properties in question are, some realists claim, 'potentialities' that must be ultimately grounded in 'actualities', namely categorical bases. Categorical properties are often understood to be intrinsic properties. Thus, the strongest version of the thesis that dispositions must have categorical bases is that it is metaphysically necessary that if something has a disposition, then it has some non-dispositional, non-counterfactual, intrinsic basis for the disposition. This strongest version of the thesis is, however, controversial.

Finally, realists also divide over the relationship dispositions bear to their bases (Prior, 1985, ch. 6). One view has it that when something possesses a disposition, the disposition *is* the basis for it in the thing in question. One problem for this view is that a disposition can have multiple bases. The basis of fragility can vary with the kind of thing in question; the basis may be a certain crystalline structure in one kind of object and a different crystalline structure in another. Indeed, a given disposition may have more than one basis within the same substance. A certain piece of cloth may have two bases for being water-absorbent: its threads may be made of water-absorbent material, and the cloth may be weaved in such a way that it absorbs water between its inner threads (Mackie, 1973, p. 148). Since the bases in question are not identical, they cannot both be identical with the property of water-absorbency. Moreover, concerns about multiple bases aside, a property will be a basis for a disposition only relative to the laws of a world. But sameness of *extension* in every *possible world* is at least a necessary condition for property identity. Thus, a property may be a basis for a disposition in our world and yet fail to be a basis for the disposition in a logically possible world in which different laws are operative. The disjunction of the bases (in our world) for a disposition will not be coextensive with the disposition in every possible world.

The leading theory of dispositions today is the *functionalist* theory, a realist theory according to which a disposition is a second-order state, a state of having a state with a certain causal role (Lewis, 1986a, pp. 223–4; Prior, 1985, ch. 7; Prior, Pargetter and Jackson, 1982). The causal role will consist of the first-order state's (appropriately) causing the manifestation(s) of the disposition in response to appropriate activating conditions under certain standing conditions. The bases are *realizations* of the dispositions: they are the first-order states with the relevant causal roles. On this view, a state can be dispositional relative to certain states and non-dispositional relative to others since it can be second-order relative to certain states and first-order relative to others. Dispositions will ultimately have non-dispositional bases only if some states are not second-order relative to any others.

The basis of a disposition is a cause of the manifestation(s) of the disposition. But some functionalists deny that types of disposition states are causally relevant to the causation of manifestation(s) of the dispositions (Lewis, 1986a, pp. 223–4; Lewis, 1986b, p. 268; Prior, 1985; Prior, Pargetter and Jackson, 1982). However, be this as it may, it seems that we can at least causally explain a manifestation of a disposition by citing the disposition itself. We say that the substance dissolved because it is soluble, or that it shattered because it is fragile. The explanation in the case of solubility, for example, seems to amount to this: the thing dissolved because it is in a state that makes it dissolve when immersed in water. This explanation excludes other hypotheses about why the thing in question dissolved (Block, 1990, pp. 162–3).

See also COUNTERFACTUALS; LAW OF NATURE; POSSIBLE WORLDS.

BIBLIOGRAPHY

Armstrong, D.M.: *A Materialist Theory of Mind* (London: Routledge, 1968).

Block, N.: 'Can the mind change the world?', in *Meaning and Method: Essays In Honor of Hilary Putnam* ed. G. Boolos (Cambridge: Cambridge University Press, 1990), 137–70.

Lewis, D.: 'Causal explanation', in his *Philosophical Papers* vol. II (Oxford: Oxford University Press, 1986[a]), 214–40.

Lewis, D.: 'Events', in his *Philosophical Papers* vol. II (Oxford: Oxford University Press, 1986[b]), 241–69.

Mackie, J.L.: *Truth, Probability and Paradox* (Oxford: Oxford University Press, 1973).

Prior, E.: *Dispositions* Scots Philosophical Monographs (Aberdeen: Aberdeen University Press, 1985).

Prior, E., Pargetter, R. and Jackson, F.: 'Three theses about dispositions', *American Philosophical Quarterly* 19 (1982), 251–7.

Ryle, G.: *The Concept of Mind* (London: Hutchinson, 1949).

Smith, A.D.: 'Dispositional properties', *Mind* 86 (1977), 439–45.

Tooley, M.: 'Armstrong's proof of the realist account of dispositional properties', *Australasian Journal of Philosophy* 50 (1972), 283–7.

BRIAN P. McLAUGHLIN

Dummett, Michael (1925–) Michael Dummett has been influential in recent Anglo-American analytical philosophy by putting the philosophy of language at centre stage, and advocating a revisionist philosophy of logic. He has established himself as perhaps the foremost commentator and interpreter of FREGE and the later WITTGENSTEIN. His most important contribution is the *thesis of semantic antirealism*. On Dummett's formulation, this thesis, for any given region of discourse, is that we do not have to regard every declarative statement of that region as determinately true or false independently of our means of coming to know what its truth value is. That is, the semantic antirealist refuses to accept the principle of bivalence for the region of discourse in question; and accordingly has to revise classical logic, which embodies that principle. Dummett emphasizes the *manifestation requirement*, to the effect that one's grasp of any aspect of meaning should in principle be capable of being manifested in one's observable behaviour. This behaviourist principle, which he draws from the work of the later Wittgenstein, is then used to argue for the legitimacy of intuitionistic, as opposed to classical, meanings of the logical operators.

The thesis of semantic antirealism had its origins in his classic paper 'Truth' (1959). There it concerned the determinacy of truth value of claims about other minds. The thesis has been extended to affect statements about the past, the future, counterfactual conditionals and, most importantly, mathematical statements.

In the case of mathematics, Dummett's major contribution has been a new meaning-theoretic foundation for intuitionistic logic and mathematics, based on considerations of reducibility and harmony drawn from modern proof theory. The *loci classici* here are his papers 'The philosophical basis of intuitionistic logic' (1973c) and 'The justification of deduction' (1973b), and his monograph *Elements of Intuitionism* (especially the section 'Concluding Philosophical Remarks').

Other important ideas in contemporary theory of meaning derive from Dummett's work, which represents a synthesis of the lasting insights of Frege and Wittgenstein. In his monumental studies on Frege and his highly influential two-part essay 'What is a theory of meaning?' (1975, 1976) he argued for molecular, as opposed to atomistic or holistic, theories of meaning; and for full-blooded, as opposed to modest, theories.

A molecular theory takes the meanings of sentences as primary. A full-blooded theory aims at an explanatory reduction of semantic notions. In a theory of meaning, a theory of *force* will form a shell around a theory of *sense*. The aim of the theory of sense is to characterize the *assertability conditions* of sentences, which are the primary bearers of meaning. Although sentences express thoughts, and thought would be impossible without language, thoughts do not, according to Dummett, subsist in a Fregean third realm. The characterization of the senses of sentences will nevertheless proceed in a compositional manner, as first articulated by Frege. From Wittgenstein we draw the lesson that meaning is public; language is essentially social. This is what grounds the norms of reasoning and logic. Dummett has made an enduring contribution in pursuing these lines of thought to revisionist conclusions in metaphysics and the philosophy of logic and mathematics.

See also INTUITIONISM IN LOGIC AND MATHEMATICS.

WRITINGS

'Truth' (1959); repr. in *Truth and Other Enigmas* (London: Duckworth, 1978), 1–24.

Frege: Philosophy of Language (London: Duckworth, 1973[a]).

'The justification of deduction' (1973[b]); repr. in *Truth and Other Enigmas* (London: Duckworth, 1978), 290–318.

'The philosophical basis of intuitionistic logic' (1973[c]); repr. in *Truth and Other Enigmas* (London: Duckworth, 1978), 215–47.

'What is a theory of meaning (I)?', in *Mind and Language* ed. S. Guttenplan (Oxford: Oxford University Press, 1975), 97–138.

'What is a theory of meaning (II)?', in *Truth and Meaning* ed. G. Evans and J. McDowell (Oxford: Clarendon Press, 1976), 67–137.

The Interpretation of Frege's Philosophy (London: Duckworth, 1981).

Truth and Other Enigmas (London: Duckworth, 1978).

Elements of Intuitionism with the assistance of R. Minio (Oxford: Oxford University Press, 1977).

The Logical Basis of Metaphysics (Cambridge, MA: Harvard University Press, 1991).

Frege: Philosophy of Mathematics (Cambridge, MA: Harvard University Press, 1991).

NEIL TENNANT

Duns Scotus, John (*c.*1265–1308) One of the most influential and respected of the medieval scholastic theologian/philosophers (known to subsequent generations of scholastics as the 'Subtle Doctor'), was born probably in the town of Duns in Scotland. He is known to have studied at Oxford before going to Paris, the chief centre of learning in Europe at the time, where he encountered the radical Augustinian Henry of Ghent (d. 1293), Godfrey of Fontaines (thirteenth century), and others. Around 1300 he was back lecturing in Oxford for a spell, and on his return to Paris he became involved on the side of Pope Boniface (1235–1303) in his quarrel with Philip the Fair. Political troubles eventually forced him to desert Paris for Cologne, where he died.

Given the shortness of his life the amount of written work he produced is remarkable. There is the usual commentary on the *Sentences* of Peter Lombard in several versions, *Questions on Logic*, *Questions on Aristotle's De Anima*, *On the First Principle* (perhaps the most elaborate of the many scholastic attempts to prove the existence of God), *Most Subtle Questions on Aristotle's Metaphysics*, and a set of *Quodlibetal Questions*, as well as some less significant treatises.

Scotus was in the Franciscan Order from an early age and participated in the late scholastic effort to reinterpret the then dominant Aristotelian–Arab philosophical tradition in a way that made room for the truth of the basic dogmas of orthodox Christian theology. The Franciscans, influenced as they were by the Augustinian tradition, were more willing than most to deviate from the philosophic norms of the day in order to save theology, and Scotus's work is perhaps best viewed as a reworking of the Aristotelian and Avicennian materials he inherited to produce a philosophic framework within which the difficult doctrines of Christian dogma, such as the Trinity, the Incarnation, divine foreknowledge and providence, etc., could be understood. Although Scotus always thought of himself as preserving the basics of Aristotelian philosophy, in metaphysics the result of his work was a radical revision of the Aristotelian programme.

Where ARISTOTLE had argued that being was not univocally predicated of things in different CATEGORIES (e.g. SUBSTANCE, quantity, quality, etc.), Scotus, after some hesitations, claimed in his later works that there is a univocal concept of being applicable across the Aristotelian categories and applicable both to God and creatures. This doctrine allowed Scotus to treat metaphysics as a science of 'being *qua* being' in a much stricter sense than Aristotle had. He developed a theory of 'transcendental' terms, i.e. concepts which like 'being' applied cross-categorically and treated metaphysics as the study of these.

Scotus also took Aristotle's notions of distinctness in number and distinctness in being or form and developed out of them several notions of IDENTITY and distinctness. Entities that are at least by divine power separable, i.e. at least one of them can exist even if the other does not, are 'absolutely really' distinct, and those that cannot be so separated are 'absolutely really' the same. But within the class of entities that are 'absolutely really' the same we find pairs of entities which are 'qualifiedly' distinct. For example, where *a* and *b* are absolutely really the same but each is definable independently of the other, *a* and *b* are 'formally' distinct. This distinction is, as Scotus says, 'on the side of the thing'; it is not a mere conceptual distinction. Since formal distinction is compatible with 'real' sameness, formal sameness turns out to be

more restrictive than 'real' sameness. Even among entities that are formally the same Scotus allows for certain kinds of distinction, including 'mental' distinctions which cannot occur prior to the entities' being thought of. The principle that whatever is true of some subject is true of anything the same as that subject, holds, in Scotus's view, unrestrictedly only of items which are in no way distinct, a kind of logical sameness which Scotus does not think of as a real relation. Certainly items which are only absolutely really the same can differ in respect of what is true of them.

On the vexed topic of UNIVERSALS Scotus improved on the solution offered by AVICENNA. He believed that there were entities that did not of themselves have numerical unity but only a unity less than that, i.e. either specific unity or generic unity. These entities, sometimes called common natures, could be considered in three ways: (1) in themselves where each of them was neither existent nor non-existent, neither one nor many; (2) as they exist in particular realities and where each of them is numerically many; and (3) as objects of cognitive acts and states where they have 'objective' existence and numerical unity (*see* OBJECTIVITY). It is only in the last way that these natures are subjects for logical predicates such as universality. Scotus is particularly emphatic in his belief that whatever actually exists is in fact either one or many *individual* things, although this oneness or manyness belongs to common natures only accidentally (*see* UNIVERSALS AND PARTICULARS).

The individuation of a common nature is accomplished not by its enmatterment, as had been the view of many Aristotelians, but by an ultimately unknowable entity which determines a specific common nature to a particular individual in the way a specific difference determines a genus to one of its species. This individuating difference is in the individual in question really the same as the common nature it determines but nevertheless formally distinct from it. His theory of individuators enabled Scotus to treat Aristotelian natural forms as individuated prior to their belonging to matter and thus as much better candidates for human souls in Christian theology.

Finally, Scotus made a fundamental break with the classical tradition in claiming that free, contingent causes, i.e. those that were not determined to bring about what they in fact do, could be superior in ontological perfection to the necessary causes with which Greek philosophy had populated the divine and eternal realm. The result was an acceptance of the basic contingency of the world and of the indeterminacy of causal chains in it which was quite foreign to Aristotelians.

WRITINGS

Opera omnia ed. P.C. Balic (Vatican, 1950–); far from complete but includes most of the commentary on the sentences in two versions known as the *Ordinatio* and the *Lectura* respectively.

Opera omnia 26 vols (Paris: Vives, 1891–5); reproduces most of the Lyons edition (ed. Wadding) of 1639; most of Scotus's known works are included but also some spurious ones.

A Treatise on God as First Principle trans. and ed. A. Wolter OFM (Chicago: Franciscan Herald Press, 1966).

Duns Scotus, Philosophical Writings trans. and ed. A. Wolter OFM (New York: Nelson, 1962).

God and Creatures: The Quodlibetal Questions trans. F. Alluntis OFM and A. Wolter OFM (Princeton, NJ: Princeton University Press, 1975).

BIBLIOGRAPHY

Balic, P.C., OFM: 'The life and works of John Duns Scotus', in *John Duns Scotus, 1265–1965* ed. J.K. Ryan and B.M. Bonansea (Washington DC: The Catholic University of America Press, 1965), 1–27.

Bettoni, E., OFM: *Duns Scotus: The Basic Principles of his Philosophy* trans. B. Bonansea OFM (Washington DC: The Catholic University of America Press, 1961).

Clatterbaugh, K.C.: 'Individuation in the ontology of Duns Scotus', *Franciscan Studies* 32 (1972), 65–73.

Jordan, M.J.: *Duns Scotus on the Formal Distinction* (Ann Arbor, MI: University Microfilms International, 1984).

Wolter, A., OFM: *The Transcendentals and their Function in the Metaphysics of Duns Scotus* (Washington DC: The Catholic University of America Press, 1946).

MARTIN M. TWEEDALE

E

element One constant throughout the early history of philosophy and the later history of natural science has been a simple procedural one: when faced with a complex whole, resolve it into its constituent parts, its 'elements'. The natural philosophers of Ionia sought to determine the 'elements' (*stoicheia*) of which all bodies are composed or from which these bodies originally derived. Empedocles (*c.*495–*c.*435 BC) suggested that the elements are fire, air, earth and water, each with its own natural place and characteristic set of qualities; this fourfold division was widely accepted by later philosophers. Euclid (fl. *c.*300 BC) titled his pioneering work on geometry, *The Elements*; he had shown how all of the multiplicity of propositions regarding plane figures could be derived from a small set of simple definitions and axioms. Medieval theories of method spoke of analysis and synthesis, or of resolution and composition, and recommended the breaking down into elements and subsequent reconstituting of the original complexes as the primary mode of understanding.

Boyle built his new chemistry in the 1660s around the distinction between elements and compounds, each having distinctive chemical properties. Chemical elements are simple and unmixed, incapable of resolution into other bodies. It proved much more difficult than Boyle had expected to determine which was element and which was compound. Only a century later did the analytical methods of Lavoisier (1743–94), based on precise weight measurement, yield the first table of chemical elements. Dalton's (1766–1844) atomic theory linked elements with atoms possessing distinctive chemical properties; Avoga-dro (1776–1856) explained compounds in terms of molecules; Berzelius (1779–1848) successfully distinguished elements on the grounds of relative atomic weight. A chemical element is defined today in terms of the number of protons in the nucleus of its atom; its chemical properties depend on the normal number of electrons in its outer shell. Since the number of neutrons in the nucleus of an element may vary, the element may have different 'isotopes' depending on the number of such neutrons, or (which amounts to the same thing) on the total atomic weight.

See also PRESOCRATICS.

BIBLIOGRAPHY

Hintikka, J. and Remes, U.: *The Method of Analysis: Its Geometrical Origin and Its General Significance* (Dordrecht: Reidel, 1974).
Kirk, G.S., Raven, J.E. and Schofield, M.: *The Presocratic Philosophers* 2nd edn (Cambridge: Cambridge University Press, 1983).
Knight, D.: *Ideas in Chemistry: A History of the Science* (New Brunswick, NJ: Rutgers University, 1992).

ERNAN McMULLIN

empiricism Empiricism is a broad tendency in the theory of knowledge. Each of its many forms lays stress on experience (typically sensory experience) as a source of knowledge or belief. The Greek equivalent of 'empiricism' was first used nearly two thousand years ago by Galen (AD 129–199), who argued that medical knowledge was solely a matter of experience. Empiricism has played an important role in philosophy ever since, but the influence of the 'British empiricists' of the seventeenth and eighteenth centuries has been especially enduring. Empiricism, on their account, makes two complementary claims, one concerning the content of thought (here called *content-empiricism*), and another concerning the justification of belief (*justification-empiricism*). According to the claim concerning content, experience is the ultimate source of all of our conceptions. As LOCKE, for example, put it, all of our ideas – the only 'immediate object[s] of Perception, Thought, or Understanding', according to him (*Essay* II viii 8) – spring from experience. 'Our Observation employ'd either about *external, sensible Objects; or about the internal Operations of our Minds*', Locke held, '*is that, which supplies our Understandings with all the materials of thinking*' (*Essay* II i 2). According to the claim concerning justification, experience is the only source of evidence for our beliefs, or the only source for those beliefs that are non-analytic, 'factual' or informative. As HUME for example, wrote, 'it is only experience, which . . . enables us to infer the existence of one object from that of another' (*Enquiries*, p. 164) and the existence of the other, if it is not inferred, can be known only by sensation or reflection.

Neither content-empiricism nor justification-empiricism is, on its face, a metaphysical claim, but each has metaphysical bearing. Content-empiricism tends to limit the extent of legitimate metaphysical thinking. We can genuinely think of x, it tells us, only if we can derive a conception of x from experience. If a conception of SUBSTANCE, for example, cannot be so derived, then we cannot really think of it. On the assumption that an expression is meaningful only if a conception lies behind it (an assumption endorsed by some empiricists but denied by others), it follows that we cannot meaningfully speak of substance. Justification-empiricism tends to limit the extent of justified (or justifiable) metaphysical belief. Even if we can conceive (and meaningfully speak) of substance, we can justifiably believe in it only if experience warrants.

Empiricist constraints have been applied not only to the conceptions of professed metaphysicians (SUBSTANCE, UNIVERSALS, *the external world*), but to the conceptions of religion (*God*, the SOUL, *freedom of the will*), science (*atoms or corpuscles, physical forces, absolute space and time*), and everyday life. Empiricist metaphysicians have responded to these constraints in three broad ways: by refusing to endorse certain metaphysical claims, at times disavowing the very possibility of 'metaphysics'; by positively denying certain claims, and banning (from their systems of the world) the entities those claims presuppose; and by reconstructing suspect conceptions or beliefs, so as to protect them from empiricist criticism. The third response calls not only for a clear sense of what is 'given' in experience (as do the first two), but for an identification of those constructions or routines that add to the stock of available conceptions without violating content-empiricism. Locke and Hume spoke, for example, of combining ideas into larger wholes; combination and recombination were, they thought, acceptable routines. Empiricists in the early twentieth century spoke not of combination but of logical construction, claiming that in certain cases, sentences expressing initially suspect conceptions could be derived, by deductive means (logical principles together with definitions), from more basic sentences free of suspicion. Their successors were more liberal, allowing a conception to be genuine (or an expression to be meaningful) if claims in which it figured could be confirmed, inductively, by observation-reports. There is a fourth and perhaps more elusive response to empiricist constraints, in which a suspect claim or conception is not reconstructed but reclassified. An apparent claim of fact becomes a tool for coping with experience; a word appearing to designate a property becomes (part of) an expression of emotion or allegiance (*see* OBJECTIVISM AND PROJECTIVISM). As BERKELEY wrote, 'the communicating of ideas marked by words is not the chief and only end of language, as is commonly supposed. There are other ends, as the raising of some passion, the exciting to, or deterring from an action, the putting the mind in some particular disposition' (*Works*, vol. 2, p. 37). The history of empiricism illustrates all four of the responses sketched here: sceptical unbelief, outright denial, reconstruction and reclassification.

LOCKE

According to Locke's influential statement of content-empiricism, all ideas are derived from sensation (the mind's perception of external objects) or reflection (the mind's perception of its own operations). The mind is originally 'void of all Characters' (*Essay* II i 1); hence no idea or notion is innate. But the mind can transform what experience supplies: it can break ideas down into their simple parts; it can arrange the parts in new ways; it can arrive at ideas of infinite space and duration by enlarging ideas of finite intervals (and by seeing, in a manner Locke does not elaborate, that the process of enlargement needn't end); and it can frame ideas of UNIVERSALS by abstracting traits from resembling particulars. We have, Locke argued, no clear idea of substance, because no such idea can be derived by any of these means. Our only idea of substance is obscure and relative: a supposition of 'we know not what' supporting qualities. Locke, as Berkeley later observed, 'banter'd' – mocked or ridiculed – the idea of substance. 'Here,' Locke wrote, 'as in all other cases, where we use Words without having clear and distinct *Ideas*, we talk like Children' (*Essay* II xxiii 2). But Locke held none the less that there are both corporeal and incorporeal substances, leaving his successors to wonder whether a consistent empiricist can do so.

The obscurity of the idea of substance convinced Locke that some metaphysical topics could not be usefully investigated. He therefore tried to detach certain practical questions from their metaphysical underpinnings, proposing, for example, that personal identity depends not on identity of substance, but on continuity of consciousness (*see* PERSONS AND PERSONAL IDENTITY). LEIBNIZ objected that 'for all its apparent thinness', the idea of substance is 'less empty and sterile' than Locke supposed. Leibniz's objection was encouraged by his belief that the idea of substance is innate. This belief admits of many interpretations, but on one rather modest reading (suggested by Leibniz himself), it means merely that reflection enables us to find, within ourselves, a metaphysically fertile idea of substance. Locke denied even this, because reflection, he thought, reveals no more about substance than sensation does.

Leibniz sometimes portrayed Locke as believing that justification always rests on experience (on 'induction and instances', as Leibniz put it), but Locke's views are more complex. Locke believed that mathematical knowledge is a priori, even though it is not uninformative or 'trifling'. 'We may be *certain* in Propositions, which affirm something of another', Locke wrote, 'which is a necessary consequence of its precise complex *Idea*, but not contained in it' (*Essay* IV viii 8). But our beliefs about nature rest entirely on experience. This renders them uncertain, and because knowledge (for Locke as for DESCARTES) requires certainty, our knowledge of nature is very slight. We can, however, have more or less well-supported beliefs about a wide range of things. It is likely, for example, that bodies are systems of tiny corpuscles, too small to be seen or felt. The 'corpuscular hypothesis' provides the best explanation of the changing world and our perception of it. There is, Locke believed, a necessary connection between a body's 'real essence' (its corpuscular constitution) and its observed or manifest qualities. If we had insight into that essence – if we had, for example, microscopical eyes – we could predict those qualities without trial. But in our present state such insight is beyond us.

BERKELEY

Berkeley used content-empiricism to argue against the very possibility of MATTER or material substance. Talk of matter (or of existence 'without the mind') is, he argued, either contradictory or empty. 'As to what is said of the absolute existence of unthinking things without any relation to their being perceived,' he wrote, 'that seems perfectly unintelligible' (*Works*, vol. 2, p. 42). Berkeley retained belief in spiritual substance; we have, he insisted, a 'notion' of it, derived from reflection on our own selves.

Bodies undoubtedly exist, Berkeley argued, because they are nothing more than collections of ideas of sense. These ideas are 'more strong, orderly, and coherent than the creatures of the mind' (ibid. p. 54). The distinction between reality and illusion is not merely preserved, but rendered empirical.

Early modern empiricists, like their rationalist contemporaries, denied the existence of abstract universals. 'All things that exist', as Locke proclaimed, 'are only particulars' (*Essay* III iii 6). How then do we think in universal terms? According to Locke we form abstract ideas. We make ideas general, he explained, 'by separating from them the circumstances of Time, and Place, and any other *Ideas*, that may determine them to this or that particular Existence' (ibid.). Berkeley, followed by Hume, denied that abstraction is possible. It is a received axiom, Berkeley wrote, 'that an impossibility cannot be conceiv'd'. Because 'nothing abstract or general' can exist in the world, 'it should seem to follow, that it cannot have so much as an ideal existence in the understanding' (*Works*, vol. 2, p. 125). We think in universal terms not by forming abstract or indeterminate ideas, but by attending to selected parts or aspects of determinate ones.

HUME

The mind's perceptions, Hume held, are either impressions or ideas. Impressions are the forceful perceptions we have when we sense and feel; ideas the more feeble perceptions we have when we think and reason. According to Hume's statement of content-empiricism, all ideas are copies of impressions. 'When we entertain . . . any suspicion that a philosophical term is employed without a meaning or idea', Hume wrote, 'we need but enquire, *from what impression is that supposed idea derived?*' 'If it be impossible to assign any,' he concluded, 'this will serve to confirm our suspicion' (*Enquiries*, 8, 22).

Substance as the support of qualities is an 'unintelligible chimera'. We have no impression of substance, and it is difficult to see how we could come to have one. 'Philosophers begin to be reconcil'd', Hume wrote, 'to the principle, *that we have no idea of external substance, distinct from the ideas of particular qualities*. This must pave the way for a like principle with regard to the mind, *that we have no notion of it, distinct from particular perceptions*' (*Treatise*, p. 635). Hume denied the suggestion (made among others by Locke and Berkeley) that an active mind presides over the ideas that pass within it. Ideas succeed one another according to impersonal associative principles (*see* ASSOCIATIONISM). This is an aspect of Hume's NATURALISM, his conviction that human nature is continuous with nature as a whole. And like the rest of nature it should, he urged, be studied empirically. According to Hume's justification-empiricism, the objects of human reason or inquiry are either *relations of ideas* or *matters of fact*. Relations of ideas are discoverable a priori, 'without dependence on what is anywhere existent in the universe' (*Enquiries*, p. 25), because it is a contradiction to deny them. Matters of fact, including all existence claims, can be known only by experience. God's existence, therefore, cannot be established a priori. Empirical arguments for God's existence cannot be dismissed so readily, but they too are unsuccessful.

KANT AND HIS INFLUENCE

KANT rejected the content-empiricism of his predecessors: 'though all knowledge begins with experience', he wrote, 'it does not follow that it all arises out of experience' (Critique, p. 41). Certain concepts or

CATEGORIES, among them *substance* and *cause and effect*, are necessary conditions for the possibility of experience. It follows that experience cannot be their source.

Kant also rejected justification-empiricism. The categories enter into truths which are, be held, both synthetic and a priori. ('Every event has a cause' is one example.) But these truths apply, he insisted, only to the objects of possible experience.

Kant was largely responsible for an important shift in the way content-empiricism was understood. Locke, Berkeley and Hume were concerned with what might be called the *genesis* of content. The human mind, they suggested, is at first content-free; it is later stocked with conceptions by experience. In the basic case the mind is passive, a receptacle waiting for whatever experience deposits. Kant questioned whether *any* idea or concept could be acquired in this way. Post-Kantian empiricists, persuaded by his arguments, turned their attention from genesis to *analysis*. They worried less about the coming-to-be of conceptions, and more about their empirical import. At about the same time, and for related reasons, philosophers came to believe that whole thoughts or propositions are more revealing, as objects of analysis, than isolated concepts or expressions. MILL is one nineteenth-century empiricist who shows the influence of these developments. When he defined 'matter' as 'a permanent possibility of sensation', he did not describe how to generate the concept from sensations. He tried instead to show that for every statement or thought about material objects, there is 'an equivalent meaning in terms of Sensations and Possibilities of Sensation alone'. The analytic emphasis of empiricism grew more pronounced in the twentieth century.

JAMES

JAMES, who dedicated *Pragmatism* to Mill's memory, described his *pragmatic method* as 'a method of settling metaphysical disputes that otherwise might be interminable'

(Pragmatism, p. 28). 'To attain perfect clearness in our thoughts of an object', he claimed, 'we need only consider what conceivable effects of a practical kind the object may involve – what sensations we are to expect from it, and what reactions we must prepare' (ibid, p. 29). The pragmatic method helped to support *radical empiricism*, the view that relations, like things themselves, are matters of direct experience. Relations, James believed, are all that is required to hold experience together; 'the directly apprehended universe needs no extraneous trans-empirical connective support'. From this James inferred that the dualism of mental and physical (*see* MENTAL/PHYSICAL; MIND/BODY PROBLEM) is not fundamental; one experience can be mental or physical – subject or object – depending on its relations to other experiences. (See PRAGMATISM.)

RUSSELL

According to RUSSELL's *principle of* ACQUAINTANCE, *'every proposition which we can understand must be composed wholly of constituents with which we are acquainted'* (*Problems*, p. 58). This criterion of content is not itself empiricist, because acquaintance, defined by Russell as direct awareness, may take non-empirical forms. But Russell went on to exclude this possibility. The objects of acquaintance are either particulars we experience (sense data or objects of introspection), or universals abstracted from them (*see* SENSA).

Physical objects, Russell held, are not among the objects of acquaintance. In *The Problems of Philosophy* (1912) he viewed them as the causes of sense data. He defended the instinctive belief in their existence as a hypothesis accounting for 'the facts of our own life'. Elsewhere, obeying the maxim that *'wherever possible, logical constructions are to be substituted for inferred entities'*, Russell tried, like Mill, to reduce propositions about physical objects to propositions about actual and possible sense data.

LOGICAL POSITIVISM

According to the logical positivists (or 'logical empiricists'), traditional metaphysics lacks cognitive meaning or significance (*see* LOGICAL POSITIVISM). A metaphysical utterance about God or the absolute may express an emotion or attitude, but it is incapable of being true or false, and it can make no contribution to knowledge. Cognitively meaningful propositions are either *analytic*, true or false as a matter of logic and definition, or *empirical*, confirmable or disconfirmable by observation. Hence no truths are synthetic and a priori; metaphysics, dogmatic or Kantian, is impossible. If philosophy is more than a purely analytical enterprise (a 'department of logic', as AYER called it), it is an attempt to achieve 'a synthesis and generalization of the results of the various sciences' (as CARNAP suggested in Ayer, 1959, p. 80). This attempt can (as Carnap allowed) be called metaphysics, but in depending on science it differs strikingly from both the 'completely isolated speculative science of reason' whose 'groping' Kant had lamented (*Critique*, p. 21), and the metaphysics of experience he had sought to put in its place.

In 'Empiricism, semantics, and ontology' (1950), Carnap introduced the notion of a *linguistic framework*, a system of linguistic forms governed by fixed rules. He suggested that questions of existence are either *internal* to a framework, in which case they can be answered by empirical or analytic means, or *external*, in which case they are practical questions about the value of adopting a framework. This suggests that traditional metaphysics is more than emotive: it is a response to questions we cannot avoid *if we hope to theorize*, even though it misconstrues those questions as theoretical.

QUINE

QUINE's repudiation of analytic truth led to an extreme justification-empiricism: 'no statement', he argued, 'is immune to revision' – to *reasonable* revision, he seemed to say – in response to 'recalcitrant experience' (1980, p. 43). Quine remained a content-empiricist, quoting with approval the empiricist slogan *nihil in mente quod non prius in sensu* ('[there is] nothing in the mind which [is] not first in sense') (1992, p. 19), but he argued against the assumption that single sentences, or even whole theories, are independent vehicles of empirical meaning. (According to Quine's HOLISM, single sentences or theories are generally too small to bear meaning in isolation. Reductionist projects such as Russell's are therefore bound to fail (*see* REDUCTION, REDUCTIONISM).) 'Ontological questions', Quine wrote, 'are on a par with questions of natural science.' (ibid, p. 45). Physical objects, for example, are 'irreducible posits', justified because they 'expedite our dealings' with experience (ibid, pp. 44, 45).

EMPIRICISM AND METAPHYSICS

Empiricism continues to influence the practice of metaphysics. Recent metaphysical writing is, for example, deeply informed by the *results* of science. Writers on the metaphysics of colour pay careful attention to work in colour science; writers on space, time and causality look closely at theories in physics. No one suggests that science can dictate metaphysical conclusions, if only because 'science' does not speak with a single voice. Modest metaphysicians may want to clarify and systematize what scientists have to tell us. Bolder metaphysicians may want to argue (for example) that the success of one theory tells against the existence claims of another, or that existence claims in one domain can be reduced to those in a second.

Recent metaphysical writing is also informed by the *method* of science. Metaphysical theories are often tested by their conformity to 'data'; if the theory and the data can be brought into reflective equilibrium, the theory has a claim on our allegiance. Even when the data are not themselves 'empirical' – when they include, for example, the pre-analytically plausible judgements sometimes known as 'intuitions' – both the method and the theory have some right to be called 'empiricist'. (STRAWSON's *descriptive metaphysics* is empiricist in this broad sense.) Whether data qualify as 'empirical' is, in any case, a contested question. For many metaphysicians, the 'facts of experience' include far more than they did for Locke or Hume.

Recent metaphysics has also been shaped by changes in empiricism. Some recent philosophers of mind, for example, have denied the existence of qualia or conscious states (*see* CONSCIOUSNESS). Their case is broadly empirical: we can best account for the 'facts of experience', they argue, without invoking conscious states. For empiricists such as Hume and Russell, the facts of experience *are* those conscious states. They are more certain than anything else, providing the material for our conceptions and the evidence for our beliefs. For the critics of qualia, empirical facts must be intersubjectively available. They may include one's saying that one is in a conscious state, or even one's believing that one is, but if we can best account for such facts without invoking the state itself, then metaphysics can simply do without it.

See also RATIONALISM.

BIBLIOGRAPHY

Ayer, A.J. ed.: *Logical Positivism* (New York: Free Press, 1959).
Berkeley, G.: *The Works of George Berkeley* ed. A.A. Luce and T.E. Jessop (London: Nelson, 1949), vol. 2.
Carnap, R.: 'Empiricism, semantics, and ontology' (1950); repr. in *Meaning and Necessity* enlarged edn (Chicago: University of Chicago Press, 1956).
Carnap, R.: *Meaning and Necessity*, enlarged edn (Chicago: University of Chicago Press, 1956).
Hume, D.: *Enquiries concerning Human Understanding and concerning the Principles of Morals* (London: 1748); ed. L.A. Selby-Bigge and P.H. Nidditch (Oxford: Clarendon Press, 1975).
Hume, D.: *A Treatise of Human Nature* (London: 1739–40); ed. L.A. Selby-Bigge and P.H. Nidditch (Oxford: Clarendon Press, 1978).
James, W.: *Pragmatism* (New York: 1907); (Cambridge, MA: Harvard University Press, 1975).
Kant, I.: *Critique of Pure Reason* (Riga: 1781, 1787); trans. N. Kemp Smith (New York: St Martin's, 1965).
Locke, J.: *An Essay concerning Human Understanding* (London: 1690); ed. P.H. Nidditch (Oxford: Clarendon Press, 1975).
Quine, W.V.: *From a Logical Point of View*, 2nd edn, rev. (Cambridge: Harvard University Press, 1980).
Quine, W. V.: *Pursuit of Truth*, revised edn. (Cambridge: Harvard University Press, 1992).
Russell, B.: *The Problems of Philosophy* (London: 1912); (Oxford: Oxford University Press, 1959).

KENNETH P. WINKLER

Epicurus (341–271 BC) Greek philosopher and founder of the Epicurean school. Epicurus adopts many key metaphysical doctrines from the atomic theory of Democritus (mid to late fifth century BC), but he attempts to eliminate from ATOMISM its tendencies toward reductionism (*see* REDUCTION, REDUCTIONISM), scepticism and DETERMINISM. Like Democritus, he holds that reflection on the nature of being and not being shows that the universe consists of unchanging, indivisible material bodies and void. Beginning with the Parmenidean principle that nothing comes into being out of non-being or perishes into non-being. Epicurus argues that the totality of what exists can never vary, since something existent can neither perish into the non-existent nor be generated from it. If, moreover, only things that are spatially extended can exist, and only tangible things are spatially extended, what exists must be tangible – hence a material body. That motion and change exist, he believes, is a self-evident empirical fact that demonstrates the existence of void: bodies can move only if there is something intangible or void which allows them passage by giving way and offering no resistance. Epicureans sometimes speak of void as either place or unoccupied space, which some have thought to be a confusion. But the confusion is only apparent. ARISTOTLE had argued that Democritean atomism treats void as a place that is either empty or filled; thus when an object moves into a void, body and void will be coextensive in the same place (*Physics* 216a26ff.). But, whereas the existence of occupied place is hardly controversial, atomism also needs a stronger conception of void that treats bodies and void as mutually exclusive; void, that is, must serve as the interval between bodies. In attempting to meet such challenges to Democritean atomism, Epicurus arguably develops the first conception of space in antiquity broad enough to encompass both the location of bodies and the intervals between them. That tensions in his theory remain is not surprising, given the long history of debates between proponents of absolute and relational theories of space.

The dualism of body and void explains the continual change we see in the world and also the permanence and conservation of being. It also shows, he believes, that there must be atoms. At the macroscopic level, we see material bodies changing, breaking or wearing away. Such bodies are divisible, hence penetrated by void. But the divisibility of matter, he argues, must be finite, since infinite physical divisibility would lead to bodies being destroyed into non-being. When processes of physical division arrive at bodies with no admixture of void, what remains are 'atomic' (meaning 'uncuttable') bodies. Because they are eternal and indestructible, they account for the conservation of being while underwriting the processes of loss and repair visible in macroscopic bodies. To meet the objection that physical atoms might be theoretically or conceptually divisible to infinity, Epicurus offers a theory of minimal parts. He argues that a finite magnitude

cannot contain an infinite number of smaller magnitudes (as ZENO had claimed); rather, atoms contain but a finite number of theoretical minima.

Size, weight, shape and tangibility are the basic properties of atoms. Accidental properties, which occur at the phenomenal level, include such secondary properties as colour, and time, which Epicurus takes to be an accident associated with the motions of bodies (*see* QUALITY, PRIMARY/SECONDARY). However, unlike Democritus, he takes phenomenal properties to be real and he nowhere suggests that they enjoy a diminished epistemological or ontological status. Nor does he believe that the right kind of bridging laws would enable us to reduce macroscopic properties to more primary ontological components. To be sure, he thinks that all states and events are rooted in the movements of atoms. But he rejects the eliminative materialism of Democritus along with his scepticism about macroscopic properties.

These general aspects of Epicurus' metaphysics are most readily seen in his philosophy of mind, where he is at great pains to make room for the data of folk psychology. He thinks that both reductionism and determinism eliminate the concepts of belief, desire, and rationality needed to describe and understand mental life. For example, he claims that reductionism and determinism are self-refuting since they abolish all grounds for distinguishing rational from non-rational argument. Reductionism, in effect, requires us to view ourselves in a way that we cannot; it demands that we ultimately adopt a view of the world that eliminates from it our own point of view as rational agents. Similarly, when one tries to argue for determinism, one must engage in a rational action (i.e. arguing) that presupposes exactly what one is attempting to deny – that one's action is not predetermined by antecedent causes. These objections to reductionism and determinism have no doubt received more sophisticated formulations since, but Epicurus is the first to have given these issues their particular shape. So too, he is the first philosopher in antiquity to hold an explicitly incompatibilist theory of action. Unfortunately, almost all the details of his positive account have been lost. It is reasonably certain that he postulates unpredictable, random motions in atoms – 'swerves' – which are supposed to prevent our actions from being wholly determined by our genetic make-up and environment. However, the precise connections he sees between microscopic indeterminacy and our macroscopic intentions, settled habits, and character remain largely a matter of speculation.

For the Epicurean, the study of metaphysics has instrumental value at best. Its chief goal is to alleviate human suffering by freeing individuals from fears about the gods and death. Only atomism, he believes, provides the requisite metaphysical solace. It shows that the present configuration of the cosmos is merely one of innumerable rearrangements of the infinite store of atoms. Our world has taken its form by purely natural, non-teleological mechanisms, and it will be destroyed by those same mechanisms. Atomism therefore frees us from the fear of the gods, since they play no role in nature. It also eliminates our fear of DEATH. When we die, our atoms merely disperse; we are therefore annihilated and no longer vulnerable to harm. Nor can death harm us when we are alive, since 'when we exist death is not present, and when it is present, we do not exist'. For the Epicurean, demonstrating that death is nothing to us is the highest achievement of metaphysics and its greatest consolation.

WRITINGS

The Hellenistic Philosophers 2 vols, ed. A.A. Long and D. Sedley (Cambridge: Cambridge University Press, 1987); contains extensive bibliography.
Epicurea ed. H. Usener (Leipzig: 1887); (Rome: L'Erma di Bretschneider, 1963).

BIBLIOGRAPHY

Annas, J.: *Hellenistic Philosophy of Mind* (Berkeley: University of California Press, 1992).

Furley, D.: *Two Studies in the Greek Atomists* (Princeton, NJ: Princeton University Press, 1967).
Nussbaum, M.C.: *The Therapy of Desire: Theory and Practice in Hellenistic Ethics* (Princeton, NJ: Princeton University Press, 1994).

PHILLIP MITSIS

essence/accident The *essential* properties of a thing, collectively called its *essence*, are those of its properties that it must have so long as it exists at all; they are the properties that the thing would have in any possible world. The *accidental* properties of a thing, by contrast, are those of its properties that it could exist without. If you heat a piece of wax (to use a famous example from DESCARTES's *Meditations*), it loses its hardness and its previous shape, but continues to exist, thereby showing that those properties were accidental to it. But the property of being extended or spread out in space is, according to Descartes, essential to the wax: to think of the wax as no longer being extended is to think of it as no longer existing at all.

The notion of essence as just introduced must not be confused with another that sometimes misleadingly goes by the same name. When it is a necessary truth that all Ks are Ls, people sometimes speak of Ks as being essentially Ls, or of L-hood as being an essential property of Ks. This is only to say that any K must be an L if it is to remain a K; it is not necessarily to say that any K must be an L if it is to continue to exist at all. For example, it is a necessary truth that all sprinters are two-legged; but this does not imply that a given sprinter could not lose a leg. Unfortunately, he could – in which event he would no longer be a sprinter, but would still exist and be the same individual as before. So being two-legged is not part of the essence of any individual sprinter, even if it is part of the essence of the *kind* sprinter (in the sense that it is a necessary condition for belonging to the kind). Confusion on this score would be avoided if the term 'essential property' were always reserved for those properties that are necessary to a thing's very existence and not merely to its membership in some kind.

In logical symbols, the notion of an essential property may be defined as follows: for any individual x and property P, P is an essential property of x if, and only if, Nec(x exists $\rightarrow$ x has P). Note that this is a formula involving what logicians call necessity *de re*: a free variable occurs within the scope of a modal operator. By contrast, statements saying what is necessary for membership in a kind involve only necessity *de dicto*: in 'Nec $\forall x(Kx \rightarrow Lx)$' the only variables occurring within the scope of modal operators are bound variables.

Which properties of a thing are essential to it and which merely accidental? There are two extreme answers to this question: pan-essentialism, or the view that everything has all of its properties essentially, and anti-essentialism, or the view that nothing has any of its properties essentially (except perhaps for 'universal' properties, such as existing and being such that $1 + 1 = 2$). The first answer is often thought to be implied by LEIBNIZ's doctrine that all the properties of an individual are contained in its 'complete concept'; it was also advocated by some of the Absolute Idealists under the slogan 'All relations are internal' (i.e. essential to their relata) (*see* IDEALISM). For criticisms of some of the arguments of the pan-essentialists, see MOORE (1919–20). The other extreme answer has been advocated by many empiricists, including LOCKE, MILL, AYER and QUINE (*see* EMPIRICISM). Their view is that the necessity of a thing's having one property is always conditional upon its having some other property; in the terminology above, there are no properties essential to individuals, but only properties essential to kinds.

There are also many views that fall between the extremes. A famous in-between view is that of Descartes, who held that there are two kinds of things in the universe, each with its own essence: material things, whose essence is extension, and thinking things, whose essence is thought. (Here it is important to note that 'All thinking things are essentially thinking things' is not the triviality it may appear to be. Its proper logical symbolism is not the *de dicto* 'Nec $\forall x(Tx \rightarrow Tx)$', but the *de re* '$\forall x(Tx \rightarrow$ Nec(x exists $\rightarrow$ Tx)'. Another in-between position, one that recognizes more essential properties than Descartes's famous two, is that of ARISTOTLE, who held that the species to which any individual belongs (e.g. *man* or *horse*) is essential to the individual. For Aristotelians, one cites the essence of a thing whenever one correctly answers the question 'What is it?'

Anti-essentialists (e.g. Quine, 1963, and Putnam, 1983) have sometimes argued that essentialism breeds contradictions. Consider the following three statements about a statue of a swan made out of a lump of clay:

(1) The statue (s) is identical with the clay (c).
(2) Being swan-shaped is essential to the statue.
(3) Being swan-shaped is not essential to the clay.

By Leibniz's Law, if s and c are identical, whatever is true of s must be true of c; hence (1)–(3) form an inconsistent set. Foes of essence have claimed that believers in essential properties would have to accept all three.

In fact, however, there is no reason why believers in essence should accept all three statements. Those who recognize relatively few essential properties would reject (2), perhaps voicing the suspicion that some who accept it have confused the uncontroversial *de dicto* statement 'Necessarily, all statues of swans are swan-shaped' with the disputable *de re* statement 'All statues of swans are necessarily swan-shaped.' Those who are more liberal in the number of properties they count as essential might accept (2), but would in that case no doubt deny (1). The statue is one thing and the lump of clay another, they might say, even if both occupy the same place and contain exactly the same molecules. The two differ precisely in that being swan-shaped is essential to the statue, but not to the clay.

Multiplication of essences thus leads to a corresponding multiplication of entities.

See also MODALITIES AND POSSIBLE WORLDS; POSSIBLE WORLDS.

BIBLIOGRAPHY

Cohen, S.M.: 'Essentialism in Aristotle', *Review of Metaphysics* 31 (1977–8), 387–405.

Hughes, G. and Cresswell, M.: *An Introduction to Modal Logic* (London: Methuen, 1968).

Moore, G.E.: 'External and internal relations', *Proceedings of the Aristotelian Society* XX (1919–20), 40–62; repr. in his *Philosophical Studies* (Totowa, NJ: Littlefield, Adams and Co., 1968), 276–309.

Plantinga, A.: *The Nature of Necessity* (Oxford: Clarendon Press, 1974).

Putnam, H.: 'Why there is no ready-made world', in his *Realism and Reason* (Cambridge: Cambridge University Press, 1983), 205–28.

Quine, W.V.: 'Reference and modality', in his *From a Logical Point of View* (New York: Harper and Row, 1963), 139–59.

Wiggins, D.: *Sameness and Substance* (Cambridge, MA: Harvard University Press, 1980).

JAMES VAN CLEVE

essence and essentialism Essentialism is fundamentally an idea about property possession: an object has a property *essentially* if it has it in such a way that it is not even possible that it exist but *fail* to have it. The clearest examples seem to involve abstract objects: the number two has the property of being even, for example, and it is certainly hard to see how it could exist but lack that property. The null set (if indeed there is such a thing) has the property of having no members; it seems clear that it could not have had, say, four or five members, or, indeed, any members at all. But it is not only abstract objects that can plausibly be thought to have essential properties. According to traditional theology, God has his most important properties (wisdom, knowledge, power, benevolence, being the creator of everything distinct from himself) essentially. It is also plausible to think that human persons have essentially such properties as *possibly being conscious*, *possibly knowing that 7 + 5 = 12*, *possibly being able to act*, *possibly having goals*, and the like. Somewhat stronger essential properties of human beings would be such conditional properties as *being conscious if functioning properly* (if not subject to dysfunction); *being able to act if functioning properly*, and the like. And all things have trivially essential properties essentially: such properties as *being self identical*, and *not being a married bachelor*.

The idea of essential properties is connected with a mediaeval distinction between modality *de dicto* and modality *de re*. Roughly speaking, a statement of modality *de dicto* predicates possibility or necessity of a proposition: for example, *possibly, the number of planets is greater than 9*. A statement of modality *de re*, on the other hand, predicates of some object the property of having some property essentially or accidentally: for example, *the number of planets (i.e. nine) is essentially greater than 7*, or *Socrates was accidentally snubnosed*. A *de dicto* proposition may be true when the corresponding *de re* proposition is false: *possibly, the number of planets is greater than 9* is true, but *the number of planets is possibly greater than 9* is false. (It is also possible that the *de dicto* proposition be false when the corresponding *de re* proposition is true.) Although the distinction between *modality de re* and *modality de dicto* was the stock in trade of every mediaeval graduate student in philosophy, it was disastrously lost in the modern repudiation of all things mediaeval; it was painfully re-won during the present century.

An object has a property essentially if and only if it has it and could not possibly have lacked it. Another way to put the same thing is to say that an object *x* has the property *P* essentially if and only if *x* has it in every possible world in which *x* exists. It would be incorrect (although not uncommon) to say that an object has a property essentially if and only if it has it in *every* possible world; the problem with this is that if it were correct, then either contingent objects such as you and I and the rest of us have no essential properties (because we do not exist in every possible world) or we have properties in worlds in which we do not exist. (That is, there are possible worlds in which we do not exist but nevertheless have properties.) Neither of these alternatives is at all palatable. A consequence of this account of essential property possession is that the property *existence* is essential to whatever has it: for clearly whatever exists is such that it could not have existed but lacked existence. If actualism (the view that there neither are nor could be things that do not exist) is true, then everything has existence and furthermore has it essentially.

A special case of a property essential to an object is its *essence* (or essences): an essence *E* of an object *x* is a property it has essentially which is furthermore such that it is not possible that there be something distinct from *x* that has *E*. Some think the idea that there are individual essences goes back to ARISTOTLE; it is clearly present in BOETHIUS, and was discussed in some detail by DUNS SCOTUS. Haecceities are a special kind of individual essence; the HAECCEITY of an object is the property of being that very object. (Clearly an object *x* has essentially the property of being that very object; and clearly nothing else could have had the property of being *x*.)

Essentialism has had something of a checkered career in twentieth-century philosophy. At the beginning of the century, those who were at all willing to think about essentialism and essences were inclined to think these notions belonged to a period of philosophy which was long past. The second third of the century saw the rise and *floruit* of LOGICAL POSITIVISM; the positivists were inclined to think not just that essences and essentialism belong to an outmoded past, but that the very idea of an essential property is incoherent. (Indeed, on this way of thinking, there really *is not* any such idea; such terms as 'essence' and

'essentialism', while they *look* as if they mean something sensible, are in fact cognitively meaningless.) The middle third of the century also saw determined attacks on the notion of essential properties by QUINE (1953). Calling the idea that there are such things 'Aristotelian Essentialism', he mounted a tenacious attack on the coherence of the notion of a thing's having an essential property. It is widely conceded at present, however, that this attack is question begging in that it takes for granted (contrary to what the essentialist thinks) that alleged examples of modality *de re* are really disguised examples of modality *de dicto*.

Through a delicious historical irony, however, essences and essentialism received a new lease on life partly through the efforts of the logical positivists. The positivists very commendably emphasized the importance of logic for philosophy, or at least for certain areas of philosophy; by virtue of this emphasis there arose a renewed interest in modal logic and the semantics of modal logic; and it is but a short step from the semantics of modal logic to an appreciation of the notions of essential properties and essences.

See also ESSENCE/ACCIDENT; MODALITIES AND POSSIBLE WORLDS; POSSIBLE WORLDS.

BIBLIOGRAPHY

Adams, R.: 'Actualism and thisness', *Synthese* 57 (1981), 3–42.
Kripke, S.: *Naming and Necessity*, in *Semantics of Natural Language* (Dordrecht: 1972); published separately by Harvard University Press, 1980.
Menzel, C.: 'The true modal logic', *Journal of Philosophical Logic* 20 (1991).
Plantinga, A.: *The Nature of Necessity* (Oxford: Clarendon Press, 1974).
Quine, W.V.: 'Three grades of modal involvement' (1953), in his *The Ways of Paradox, and Other Essays* (Cambridge, MA: Harvard University Press, 1976).

Salmon, N.: *Reference and Essence* (Princeton, NJ: Princeton University Press, 1981).

ALVIN PLANTINGA

event theory An event is anything that happens, an occurrence; something that occurs in a certain place during a particular interval of time.

Though the concept of CHANGE has a philosophical history that is coeval with western philosophy itself, and though the concept of an event seems inextricably tied to that of change, the concept of an event seems not to have been the focus of sustained philosophical treatment until fairly recently. Due no doubt to a re-emergence of interest in the concept of change and to the growing use of the concept of an event in scientific writing and in theorizing about science, the idea of an event began, in modern times, to take on a philosophical life of its own in the work of McTAGGART, WHITEHEAD, and BROAD. Perhaps the most recent interest in the nature of events has been sparked by versions of the Mind/Body Identity Thesis (*see* MIND/BODY PROBLEM) formulated explicitly in terms of events (e.g. every mental event is a physical event) and by the idea that getting a clear picture of the nature of events would facilitate discussion of other philosophical issues (e.g. CAUSATION).

Current discussion of events had focused on two fundamental questions: (1) 'Are there events?'; and (2) 'If so, what is the nature of these entities?' Philosophers have usually treated the two questions together, since whether or not there are events depends at least in part of what events would be like if there were any.

Some philosophers simply assume that there are events; others argue explicitly for that assumption. Such arguments have typically been concerned with the finding of semantic theories for certain ordinary claims that apparently have to do with the fact that some agent has done something or that some thing has changed; and this semantic focus is correct. A metaphysically appropriate reason for thinking that there are entities belonging to some kind or other consists of (1) a deductive argument, whose premise is a commonsensical claim (e.g. 'Vesuvius erupted') and whose conclusion is that there are entities belonging to the kind in question (there are eruptions, which are events); and (2) an inference to the best explanation of the fact that the commonsensical premise means what it does, where what it means is at least in part revealed by the logical relations it bears to other claims. And that best explanation, if the deductive argument is valid, will show that the premise entails that there are entities belonging to the kind in question.

It is in this way that DAVIDSON has argued that there are events, by arguing that, to explain the entailment of 'Jones killed Smith' by 'Jones killed Smith in the kitchen' (and other claims involving adverbial modifiers) and the entailment of 'There was a short circuit' and 'There was a fire' by the singular causal claim, 'The short circuit caused the fire', we should suppose that such claims implicitly quantify over killings, short circuits, and fires, which are events. Thus, for example, the best analysis of 'Jones killed Smith in the kitchen' is said to be 'There was a killing of Smith by Jones and it was performed in the kitchen', in symbols, $\exists x(\text{Killing}(\text{Smith}, \text{Jones}, x)$ & $\text{In}(\text{the kitchen}, x))$, which entails '$\exists x(\text{Killing}(\text{Smith}, \text{Jones}, x))$', the analysis of 'Jones killed Smith'. But '$\exists x(\text{Killing}(\text{Smith}, \text{Jones}, x))$' says that there are killings, which are actions (which Davidson takes to be a species of event). (See Davidson, 1980, essays 6, 7, 8.)

Opponents of Davidson's analyses (e.g. Horgan (1978)) have argued that an alternative semantic theory is able to explain the semantic features of Davidson's target sentences without its being the case that they entail that there are events (or actions). More recently, Parsons (1990) has shown how to extend (with modifications) Davidson's semantic theory to a much broader class of sentences.

While the idea that the meaning of certain sentences appears to require supposing that those sentences speak of events has been an idea particularly associated with Davidson (and lately, Parsons), the semantics of singular terms for events has been extensively studied by Vendler (1967), Bennett (1988), and others. Of particular interest is the distinction between perfect nominals, like 'Jones's killing of Smith', which behave semantically as if they refer to events (or actions, or sometimes, states), and imperfect nominals, like 'Jones's killing Smith', which behave semantically as if they refer to fact-like entities. Bennett has argued that much of what is wrong in some theories of event (e.g. Kim, 1973) can be traced to confusions involving these two sorts of nominals and to expressions, e.g. 'the killing', that are ambiguous between an event- and a fact-interpretation.

Most philosophers presume that the events whose existence is proved by such arguments are abstract particulars, 'particulars' (*see* UNIVERSALS AND PARTICULARS) in the sense that they are non-repeatable and spatially locatable, 'abstract' (*see* CONCRETE/ABSTRACT) in the sense that more than one event can occur simultaneously in the same place.

Some philosophers who think this way associate (however inexplicitly) the concept of an event with the concept of *change*; an event is a change in some object or other. (Some philosophers, like Bennett, have doubts about this; others, like Kim and Lewis (1986), deny it outright.) Thus, the time at which an event occurs can be associated with the (shortest) time at which the object, which is the subject of that event, changes from the having of one to the having of another, contrary property. Since no object can have both a property and one of its contraries at the same time, there can be no instantaneous events, and every event occurs at some interval of time.

Some philosophers (e.g. CHISHOLM) take events to be UNIVERSALS and thus to be capable of recurrence. For an event to recur is for there to be distinct times, t and t', such that it occurs at t and also occurs at t'.

But, while an event can be occurring at a moment that is only part of the whole time during which it occurs (e.g. the movement of the planet during July was occurring at noon on 4 July), no event occurs at any time that does not include *all* the times at which it is occurring. Thus, for an event to recur, it must occur at a time, e.g. t, that does not include a time, namely t', during which it is occurring. Therefore, events cannot recur.

Events inherit whatever spatial locations they have from the spatial locations, if any, of the things that those events are changes in. Thus, an event that is a change in an object, x, from being F to being G, is located wherever x is at the time it changes from being F to being G. Thus, events do not get their spatial locations by occupying them; if they did, the way physical objects apparently do, then distinct events could not occur in the same place simultaneously (just as distinct physical objects cannot occupy the same place at the same time). But it does seem that more than one event can occur at the same time and place. However, some philosophers (e.g. QUINE) hold that events, like physical objects, are concrete, and hold that events and physical objects are not to be thought of as belonging to distinct metaphysical kinds.

It seems clear that some events are those of which another event is composed (e.g. the sinking of a ship seems composed of the sinkings of its parts), in much the way that at least some physical objects are composed of parts. However, it also seems clear, though some have denied this (e.g. Thomson (1977)), that not every group of events are those of which another is composed; there just is no event composed of a certain explosion on Venus and my birth in 1944. What is not clear is what the principles are that determine when events compose more complex events.

Some views of events seem compatible with there being subjectless events, events that are not the changes in anything whatsoever. Perhaps Whitehead's is such a view of events. Whether such a view is possible is an unsettled issue. What seems clear, however, is that subjectless events could not be changes, for it seems absurd to suppose that there could be change that was not a change in or of anything whatsoever. And it is not clear what to make of a concept of an event that was detached from that of change.

Any serious theory about the nature of entities belonging to some metaphysically interesting kind must address the issue of what properties, if any, such entities have essentially (*see* ESSENCE/ACCIDENT; ESSENTIALISM). In the case of events, the issue is made more pressing, for example, by the fact that certain current theories concerning event causation (e.g. Lewis's) require that reasoned judgements be made with regard to whether certain events would occur under certain, counterfactual circumstances (*see* COUNTERFACTUAL). To deal with such issues, the essential features of events must be determined. In the recent literature on events, attention has been given to four essentialist issues.

The first is whether the causes (or effects) of events are essential to the events that have them; van Inwagen (1978) has suggested that an event's causes (but not its effects) are essential to the events that has them, while Lombard (1986) has argued that neither the causes nor the effects of events are essential to them. The second is whether it is essential to each event that it be a change in the entity it is in fact a change in. Bennett and Lewis appear to have suggested that the subjects of events are not essential, while Lombard and Kim have argued that they are. The third is whether it is essential to each event that it occur at the time at which it in fact occurs. Lombard has argued in favour of this proposal, while Bennett and Lewis have argued against it. And the fourth is whether it is essential that each event be a change with respect to the properties it is in fact a change with respect to. Though the first three essentialist issues have received some attention, the issue attracting by far the most has been the last. This is due to the prominence given to debates between the defenders of Kim's views and the defenders of Davidson's views on the identity of events.

Once the question of the existence of events is settled (either by argument or assumption) in the affirmative, philosophers then turn to the construction of theories about events. Often, the theory has, as a chief component, a 'criterion of identity' for events, a principle giving conditions necessary and sufficient for an event e and an event e' to be one and the same event. Though there is no general agreement on this, such a principle, it appears, is sought because, when it satisfies certain constraints, it is a vehicle for articulating a view about what it is to be an event and how events are related to objects belonging to other kinds. Current in the literature are several general types of theory about events, all of which have their supporters and their opponents.

Quine holds that physical objects, like events, have temporal parts, and that events may be identified with the temporal parts of physical objects, and are thus concrete particulars (*see* TEMPORAL PARTS/STAGES). Events and physical objects would thus share the same condition of identity: sameness of spatio-temporal location. (Whitehead at one time expressed the view that events are the most fundamental particulars and that they are more basic than physical objects in that the latter are constructions out of events. Variations on this idea seem to be found in more contemporary writers, such as Quine.) It would appear that such a view could not be correct, however, if it were the case that the very idea of an event is the idea of a change in some physical object.

Kim's interest in events centres, in part, on the fact that they seem to figure as the objects of empirical explanations. Since what is typically explained is an object's having of a property at a certain time, Kim takes an event to be the exemplification of a property (or relation) by an object (or objects) at a time. This idea, combined with some other views that Kim holds, has lead him to the view that an event e is the same as an event e' if, and only if, e and e' are the exemplifications of the same property by the same object(s) at the same time. Kim's view has been criticized, principally by Lombard and Bennett, on the grounds that what it says about events is more plausibly seen as truths about facts. In addition, the view has been subjected to criticism from those whose intuitions concerning the identity of events more closely match those of Davidson.

Davidson was interested in finding a 'coordinate system' in which to 'locate' events, in the way that spatio-temporal coordinates specify the locations of physical objects; as a result, Davidson proposed that the network of causes and effects provides such a framework and that events, being essentially the things that cause and are caused, are identical just in case they occupy the same place in that framework, that is, just in case they have the same causes and effects. Brand (1977) has objected to Davidson's view on the grounds that (a) there are counterexamples, involving the fission of particles followed by a fusion of their parts, to the proposed criterion of identity, and (b) it implies that it is impossible for there to be more than one event which lacks both causes and effects. Recently, Davidson has abandoned this position in favour of Quine's.

Another view that places the concept of causation at the heart of the idea of an event is Lewis's (see Lewis, 1986). Lewis apparently thinks that events are of philosophical interest only in so far as they bear on other philosophical topics, and that what one should say about events should be driven by the demands of these other issues. Lewis holds that only events are causes and effects and has tried to construct a theory of events whose features would make events fit neatly into Lewis's counterfactual analysis of causation. In some respects, Lewis's view is like Brand's, in that both are moved by the idea that more than one event can occur simultaneously in the same place. Lewis takes an event to be a property-in-intension (a function from POSSIBLE WORLDS to sets of things that have that property) of a spatio-temporal region, so

that while two distinct events can occur in the same place at the same time, they are such that one could have had a spatio-temporal location different from that of the other.

Bennett, like Lewis, thinks that not much of a theory about events is forthcoming if one thinks about events on their own; their nature should be supposed to be whatever (and only whatever) it needs to be in order to make constructive use of them in the discussion of other philosophical issues. Also, like Lewis, Bennett takes an event to be a property. But, for Bennett, such a property seems to be a property-in-extension (one related to the set of things that actually have that property) and is a particular. That is, Bennett thinks that events are TROPES.

Lombard's view (1986) is, like Kim's, a variation on a property exemplification account. According to Lombard, this idea is derived from the idea of events as the (non-relational, 'non-Cambridge') changes that physical objects undergo when they change. Such changes are construed as 'movements' by objects from the having of one to the having of another property through densely populated quality spaces, where each quality space is a class of contrary properties the mere having of any member of which by an object does not imply change. Events can then be divided into atomic events and events composed of atomic events, where an event is atomic just in case (roughly) it is a continuous change in a single partless thing with respect to certain (atomic) quality spaces. Non-atomic events are identical just in case they are composed of the same atomic events; and atomic events are identical just in case they are simultaneous movements by the same atomic object through the same portion of the same atomic quality space.

BIBLIOGRAPHY

Bennett, J.: *Events and Their Names* (Indianapolis: Hackett Publishing Company, 1988).
Brand, M.: 'Particulars, events, and actions', in *Action Theory* ed. M. Brand and D.

Walton (Dordrecht: Reidel, 1976), 133–57.

Brand, M.: 'Identity conditions for events', *American Philosophical Quarterly* 14 (1977), 329–37.

Broad, C.D.: *An Examination of McTaggart's Philosophy* (Cambridge: Cambridge University Press, 1933).

Chisholm, R.M.: 'Events and propositions', *Noûs* 4 (1970), 15–24.

Chisholm, R.M.: 'States of affairs again', *Noûs* 5 (1971), 179–89.

Davidson, D.: *Essays on Actions and Events* (New York: Oxford University Press, 1980).

Davidson, D.: 'Reply to Quine on events', in *Actions and Events: Perspectives on the Philosophy of Donald Davidson* ed. E. LePore and B. McLaughlin (Oxford: Blackwell, 1985), 172–6.

Horgan, T.: 'The case against events', *Philosophical Review* LXXXVII (1978), 28–37.

Kim, J.: 'Events and their descriptions: some considerations', in *Essays of Honor of Carl G. Hempel* ed. N. Rescher *et al.* (Dordrecht: Reidel, 1969), 198–215.

Kim, J.: 'Causation, nomic subsumption, and the concept of event', *Journal of Philosophy* 70 (1973), 217–36.

Kim, J.: 'Events as property exemplifications', in *Action Theory* ed. M. Brand and D. Walton (Dordrecht: Reidel, 1976), 159–77.

Lewis, D.: 'Events', in his *Philosophical Papers* Vol. II (New York: Oxford University Press, 1986), 241–69.

Lombard, L.B.: *Events: A Metaphysical Study* (London: Routledge and Kegan Paul, 1986).

Lombard, L.M.: 'Causes, enablers, and the counterfactual analysis', *Philosophical Studies* 59 (1990), 195–211.

McTaggart, J.M.E.: *The Nature of Existence* Vol. II (Cambridge: Cambridge University Press, 1927).

Parsons, T.: *Events in the Semantics of English: A Study in Subatomic Semantics* (Cambridge, MA.: The MIT Press, 1990).

Quine, W.V.: 'Things and their place in theories', in his *Theories and Things* (Cambridge, MA: Harvard University Press, 1981), 1–23.

Quine, W.V.: 'Events and reification', in *Actions and Events: Perspectives on the Philosophy of Donald Davidson* ed. E. LePore and B. McLaughlin (Oxford: Blackwell, 1985), 162–71.

Thomson, J.J.: *Acts and Other Events* (Ithaca, NY: Cornell University Press, 1977).

van Inwagen, P.: 'Ability and responsibility', *Philosophical Review* 87 (1978), 201–24, esp. 207–9.

Vendler, Z.: 'Facts and events', in his *Linguistics and Philosophy* (Ithaca, NY: Cornell University Press, 1967), 122–46.

Whitehead, A.N.: *The Principles of Natural Knowledge* (Cambridge: Cambridge University Press, 1919).

Whitehead, A.N.: *Process and Reality* (Cambridge: Cambridge University Press, 1929).

LAWRENCE BRIAN LOMBARD

evolution In ordinary language, evolution means CHANGE. In biology, the term has a narrower sense, according to which only a population of organisms can evolve; this happens precisely when there is change in the population's genetic composition.

Biological use of the term emphasizes the idea of *common descent*. Current theory says that all terrestrial life is genealogically related. Evolutionary biology also seeks to explain patterns of similarity and difference. Natural selection is widely taken to be important; the extent of its importance is a matter of continuing debate.

Despite the gap between biological and vernacular usage of the term 'evolution', the idea of extending the biological concept has exercised a continuing allure. Herbert Spencer (1820–1903) thought that Darwin's theory could be generalized into an all-encompassing theory of change; more recently, theories of cultural evolution have attempted a more modest extrapolation from biological ideas. It remains to be seen whether the biological metaphor is a fruitful one.

BIBLIOGRAPHY

Bowler, P.: *Evolution: The History of an Idea* (Berkeley: University of California Press, 1984).

Futuyma, D.: *Evolutionary Biology* (Sunderland, MA: Sinauer Publishers, 1986).

Sober, E.: *Philosophy of Biology* (Boulder, CO: Westview Press, 1993).

ELLIOTT SOBER

existence Perhaps the most fundamental questions about the concept of existence are what sort of concept it is, whether it can be analysed or elucidated, and what falls under it. We shall here concentrate on the first two of these questions, with primary emphasis being placed on the first. In so doing, we shall inevitably pay some attention to the third question; but it will only be considered in detail elsewhere in the volume (for detailed discussion *see* FICTIONAL TRUTH, OBJECTS AND CHARACTERS; HYPOSTASIS, REIFICATION).

WHAT SORT OF CONCEPT IS EXISTENCE?

Here attention has been focused chiefly on the question whether existence is a property. Since KANT many philosophers have thought this question crucial to a proper assessment of the so-called Ontological Argument for the existence of God. But in order to avoid the question whether properties themselves exist, and to help clarify the logical grammar of existence claims, it is often held to be convenient to concentrate instead on the linguistic analogue of this question. This is whether the *word* 'exists' is a *predicate*, i.e. whether it is an expression which is *true or false* of things.

Examples of predicates are expressions like 'is an author' or 'is triangular' as they occur in such sentences as 'Goethe is an author' and 'France is not triangular'. So why should 'exists', as it occurs in such sentences as 'Kangaroos exist', 'Dodos don't exist', 'Goethe exists' and 'Holmes doesn't exist', not be similar? One thought – trace-able to HUME and Kant – is that predicating 'exists' of an individual, unlike 'is an author' (say), appears to be redundant. 'Goethe exists and is German' does not tell us anything more than does 'Goethe is German'. But predicating 'is an author' of an individual certainly can add something. 'Goethe is an author and is German' is considerably more informative than 'Goethe is German'. In itself, however, this does not show that 'exists' is not a predicate. At best, it shows that 'exists' is a predicate true of everything. Admittedly, this would make 'exists' an odd kind of predicate, a limiting case like 'is either triangular or not triangular'; but it would remain a predicate none the less.

However, the apparent fact that, if 'exists' is a predicate, it must be true of everything, does indicate a difficulty. For it seems hard to reconcile its being a predicate true of everything with the truth of *present-tense, singular negative existential claims* such as 'Holmes doesn't exist'. To see this, consider the true sentence 'France is not triangular' which contains the complex predicate 'is not triangular'. This is true since the predicate is true of the referent of 'France', i.e. France. But nothing similar can be said of the expression 'doesn't exist'. For if 'exists' is true of everything, 'doesn't exist' is true of nothing. And so the equally true sentence 'Holmes doesn't exist' cannot be true by virtue of the phrase 'doesn't exist' being true of anything. Thus (the argument goes) the expression 'doesn't exist' cannot be a predicate, and so neither can 'exists' itself.

One response – associated in the first instance with FREGE – is to treat 'exists' not as what is called a *first*-level predicate, a predicate true of *individuals*, but as a *second*-level (or more generally an *n* + *1th*-level) predicate, a predicate of first-level (or *nth*-level) concepts. This seems to sit well with such claims as that kangaroos exist and that dodos do not. For these claims can easily be construed as saying that the concept *kangaroo* is instantiated or that the concept *dodo* is not. *Exists*, then, becomes like the concept *numerous*. To say, for example, that cockroaches are numerous is

145

to say that the concept *cockroach* has numerous instantiations.

But how is this to go over to *singular* claims? Here advocates of the view that 'exists' expresses a second- or higher-level concept are apt to claim at least initially that names like 'Goethe' and 'Holmes' really do express concepts in some way. The most familiar way of elaborating this suggestion is via a treatment of definite descriptions – expressions paradigmatically of the form 'the *F*' in English – suggested by RUSSELL (1905). Russell argued that the best way to understand apparent subject-predicate sentences containing them – sentences of the form 'The *F* is *G*' – is to treat them as a conjunction, something equivalent to: the concept *F* is uniquely instantiated and the thing that instantiates it is *G*. But then 'The *F* exists' amounts to the claim that the concept *F* is uniquely instantiated and the thing that instantiates it exists, or more simply, since the last conjunct is redundant, that the concept *F* is uniquely instantiated. So sentences of the form 'The *F* exists' can be seen to involve 'exists' functioning as a second-level predicate, the predicate 'is instantiated'. The trick now is to interpret names in some way as definite descriptions. Thus if 'Goethe' is interpreted as meaning the same as 'the author of *Faust*', then 'Goethe exists' will amount to the claim that the author of *Faust* exists, i.e. the concept *author of* Faust is uniquely instantiated. And if 'Holmes' is interpreted as 'the greatest detective', then 'Holmes doesn't exist' will mean that the greatest detective does not exist, i.e. that the concept *greatest detective* is not uniquely instantiated.

However, even leaving aside problems with Russell's particular theory of definite descriptions, the idea that all apparent singular referring expressions should be thought of as covert definite descriptions is not very plausible. It is possible of course to define a particular name (say) so that it is synonymous with some definite description; such names are often called 'descriptive names'. But to model all singular referring expressions on descriptive names is to disregard two facts. First, it is possible to understand sentences involving demonstratives – words such as 'this' and 'that' used, for example, to refer to objects manifestly occurring within one's perceptual field – without that understanding's being mediated by descriptive information. And second, the understanding of a definite description does not in itself presuppose knowledge of who or what satisfies the description. (There may be no such satisfier, for example.) Whereas no one could understand referring demonstratives, and probably most names, without knowing which objects or people they referred to. Or so it is claimed.

If this is right, then the view that 'exists' is invariably a second- or higher-level predicate looks difficult to defend. It is perhaps conceivable that for the most part genuine referring expressions do not function as covert descriptions, but that in existential claims they do. But names do not seem to vary in function in this way. 'Goethe' surely means the same thing in 'Goethe is an author' as in 'Goethe exists.' And in any case there is much direct evidence that 'exists' does sometimes function as a first-level predicate.

One piece of evidence is that 'exists' does not function in exactly the same way as 'numerous' does. For 'numerous', which is undoubtedly a predicate of concepts, does not sensibly form singular claims: 'Goethe is numerous' does not make sense. But 'Goethe exists' certainly does. Second, tensed and modal expressions of existence seem much less problematically to involve predications of individuals. Thus 'France did not exist' is true by virtue of the predicate 'did not exist' being true of the referent of 'France'. Similarly with 'France might not have existed'. But if these forms of words use complex predicates of individuals, it seems implausible, without further explanation, to suppose that ordinary present tense, singular negative existentials do not.

To be sure, something has to be said about those existence claims in which 'exists' is most naturally treated as a predicate of concepts ('Kangaroos exist', 'Dodos do not exist', and so on). But it is arguable that 'exists' can function as both a first- and a higher-level predicate without being ambiguous. Compare the case of 'disappears'. In 'Dodos have disappeared' it is plainly functioning as a second-level predicate, while in 'Lord Lucan has disappeared' it is plainly functioning as a first-level predicate. Of course, both 'exists' and 'disappears' would be being used in slightly different ways in the different types of sentence, but this is a far cry from saying that they are ambiguous. The ordinary conception of ambiguity is not that fine-grained.

This still leaves the problem of present tense, singular negative existentials, which appear to show that 'exists' cannot be a first-level predicate. If it were (so the argument goes), then 'Holmes doesn't exist' would be true by virtue of 'doesn't exist''s being true of the referent of 'Holmes'; and this is surely false, since Holmes does not exist. But now contrast the ontologically expansionist suggestion of MEINONG. According to this suggestion, we should take such claims as 'Holmes doesn't exist' at face value. We should take them to be saying of some individual – in this case, the fictional detective Holmes – that he does not exist. So the claim 'Holmes doesn't exist' is true precisely because the complex predicate 'doesn't exist' is true of the referent of 'Holmes', i.e. Holmes himself. And 'exists' can happily function as a first-level predicate in these claims. On the face of it, of course, this seems to entail a contradiction: that Holmes exists and that he does not. But (says the Meinongian) this would be a mistake. All it entails is that there are individuals who do not exist and that one of them is Holmes. Being a non-existent object is not the same as being a non-existent existent.

According to the Meinongian, therefore, there are non-existent objects; indeed the world is full of them. Not only are there all the characters of fiction, but there are also objects corresponding to any combination of ordinary properties: the golden mountain, the eightieth President of the USA, even the round square. But then one might think with Russell that if the account is so liberal

as to allow such things as round squares, it cannot escape contradiction. What could be more contradictory than a round square? As Parsons (1980) has shown, however, this need not follow. Everything depends upon whether one thinks that being round excludes being square. According to Parsons, it will for objects which exist; but otherwise not. So it is not contradictory to suppose that there is a round square.

Nevertheless there are problems. First, it is clear that the theory as it stands cannot without contradiction allow every description to have an object corresponding to it. For example, 'the object which has the properties of being round, square and existent' would indeed generate a contradiction if anything satisfied it. How then should we understand the sentence 'The object which has the properties of being round, square and existent doesn't exist'? In the present context, the reason for introducing non-existent objects was to explain negative existentials. But if some descriptions do not have objects corresponding to them, then the explanation must fail for the corresponding negative existentials. Of course the Meinongian could try to deal with these negative existentials in another way – perhaps in some such manner as Russell's. But this seems *ad hoc* at best. Second, the account threatens to draw a distinction without a genuine difference. Is there really a difference between there being something and there existing something? If not, then the claim that there are non-existent objects becomes incoherent. And third, the account has an air of ontological profligacy. Even if the idea of non-existent objects is coherent, the supposition that there are any seems to violate the maxim that theories which imply an unnecessary or implausible ontology should be avoided.

A third response to the argument, embodying a more robust sense of reality than the Meinongian, but still allowing 'exists' to be a first-level predicate, would be to deny, by appealing to considerations of scope, that if 'exists' is a predicate, then 'Holmes doesn't exist' is true if, and only if, 'doesn't exist' is true of Holmes. The truth of this claim (according to the response) presupposes that 'not' is functioning as an internal adverb rather than a sentential operator. But if it is construed in the latter way, the sentence 'Holmes doesn't exist' will have the form 'It is not the case that Holmes exists.' And on the face of it, no problem need then arise. For in general sentences of the form 'not a is F' can be true in two ways – one if 'a' has a referent and 'F' is not true of it, the other if 'a' has no referent. Applying this to 'It is not the case that Holmes exists', we find that this is true if, and only if, either 'Holmes' has a referent but 'exists' is not true of the referent or it has no referent at all, i.e. if, and only if, 'Holmes' has no referent. But this is true if, and only if, Holmes does not exist, precisely the correct truth condition.

In response, it will be said that we have not yet explained how 'Holmes' could both be a name and not have a referent. But formally at least there is no real difficulty. For although the sense of a name is standardly given by specifying its referent – one knows the meaning of 'Goethe' once one knows it refers to Goethe – there is no compulsion to proceed in this way. One could, for example, specify the sense of a name by means of a conditional reference clause which does not entail it has a referent. Thus one could specify the sense of 'Holmes' by means of the clause: 'Holmes' refers to something if, and only if, that thing is Holmes. Provided the biconditional 'iff' is so construed that 'Fa iff Gb' means that a exists and is F if, and only if, b exists and is G, this clause will not entail that Holmes exists.

There is still, however, a problem. For this account does not seem to contain an accurate representation of our understanding of singular terms in general. Descriptive names would fit the bill; but as noted earlier, an understanding of perceptual demonstratives, and probably most names, requires a knowledge of who or what their referents are. It might be claimed that this only applies to referring singular terms and that the others can be dealt with in the 'existence-free' way just elaborated. But many empty singular terms are arguably used on the assumption that they have a referent and that in their being so used, nothing literally gets said. When someone unknowingly hallucinates a little green man and says, 'That little green man is wrinkled', he or she will fail, literally, to say anything.

Such a view is controversial and seems particularly difficult to sustain precisely in respect of present tense, negative existentials. The problem is that in the circumstances just described the sentence 'That little green man does not exist' ought on this view to be senseless, when in fact it is obviously true. However, by exploiting the way in which we connive with the (sometimes unwitting) authors of make-believe, Evans (1982) has proposed a framework in which the difficulty might begin to be tackled.

Evans claims that when we talk about a film or a novel (say), we can either speak about the piece of make-believe as such or we can connive with the author in speaking within the pretence that he or she has created. In ordinary use, if I say that one of the greatest detectives of all time lived in Baker Street, this will be assessed as true just in case one of the greatest detectives of all time did in fact live in Baker Street. And this is presumably false. But if I use it in such a way that I connive with Conan Doyle, it is true. For in the conniving use it is true just in case it is make-believedly true; and in the Holmes stories, this is so. Now in these kinds of cases, although the sentences when used non-connivingly are only make-believedly true, the propositions they express are real enough: the sentences have real meaning. The problem with ordinary sentences involving apparent referring expressions which fail to refer – 'That little green man is wrinkled', say – is that when used in a non-conniving way they do not actually say anything, they do not have real meaning. Evans points out, however, that when we use such expressions in a conniving way to talk of make-believe characters, although we do not really mean anything by our words, we nevertheless pretend to do so: we pretend to refer to someone by 'that little green man'. Hence such sentences have a pretend or make-believe meaning; they make-believedly express a proposition. His idea then is to exploit this make-believe meaning to explain the real meaning of negative existentials. He suggests that when a sentence like 'That little green man does not exist' is uttered meaningfully it is elliptical for 'That little green man does not *really* exist.' Here the word 'really' acts as a way of moving from the world of make-believe to the real world. (More precisely: 'Really *A*' is true if, and only if, there is a proposition *p* such that *A* make-believedly means that *p*, and *p*.) But this implies that 'That little green man does not really exist' will be true just in case there is no proposition *p* such that 'That little green man exists' make-believedly means that *p*, and *p*. And this is true since there is no such proposition as that that little green man exists, even though there is *make-believedly* such a proposition. We thus (it seems) get a correct truth condition for the negative existential without being committed to fictional or hallucinatory objects. And of course 'exists' remains a first-level predicate.

CAN EXISTENCE BE ANALYSED?

Aside from a few unhelpful aphorisms, this question has not received a great deal of attention. Perhaps existence has been felt to be too basic a notion to permit of analysis. There are of course many *theories* of existence, theories about *what exists*. But since they generally deny existence to whole ranges of objects which, given our ordinary practice, it is doubtful should be excluded merely by what is involved in the idea of existence, they cannot be treated as serious attempts to analyse the concept. For instance, materialists maintain that to exist is at least to be located in space and time, and so purely abstract objects are excluded. But this cannot be a consequence merely of what is involved in the concept of existence.

At this point it is helpful to return to the idea of Hume and Kant that predicating 'exists' of an individual does not add any-

thing. Thus according to Hume, the idea of existence, 'when conjoined with the idea of any other object, makes no addition to it'. Now this may seem a difficult doctrine to uphold. It seems to entail that existence claims are analytic and hence that they are necessary; and Hume even goes so far as to conclude that conceiving of an object is the same as conceiving of it as existent. With some care, however, these conclusions can either be regarded as perfectly acceptable or shown not to follow. Thus although it is arguable that at least such existential claims as 'I exist' and 'Goethe exists' are analytic – it is impossible to understand them without appreciating what 'I' and 'Goethe' refer to and hence that I and Goethe exist – we can resist both the conclusion that they are necessary and the conclusion that it is impossible to conceive their being false. For (*post*-Kripke) there is no compulsion to see all analytic truths either as necessary or as having inconceivable negations. And this is fortunate, since it is patently not necessary that I or Goethe should exist, and certainly possible to conceive of us not existing.

But how can this idea help? In essence Hume's claim may be taken to express the thought that there is nothing more to understanding the predicate 'exists' (or the concept of existence) than is given by, for instance, the schema: *a* is *F* if, and only if, *a* exists and is *F*, where '*F*' is a place-holder for any genuine predicate (and '*a*' a place-holder for any name occurring outside the scope of any structure in '*F*'). Thus, in order to understand the concept of existence, one need appreciate no more about it than that Goethe is German if, and only if, he exists and is German, that France is not triangular if, and only if, it exists and is not triangular, and so on. To be sure, there may be many other things that one might subsequently discover about existence: that everything that exists is in some sense spatio-temporal, for example. But (according to this minimalist account) all that is required to *understand* the concept of existence is given by the schema. (Notice that the issues here are similar to those involved in what is sometimes called the redundancy or minimalist theory of truth (*see* THE-ORIES OF TRUTH).)

Now in the light of our discussion of the first question, it may be objected that since 'exists can function as more than a predicate of individuals – it can double up as a second-level predicate – the above schema cannot explain its use in 'Kangaroos exist'. However, since 'exists''s duality of role does not entail that it is ambiguous, the answer is simply to extend the schema so that it embraces both concept words (used as noun phrases) and singular terms. It is true that this would have the consequence that 'Unicorns are white' is false. But this may be acceptable, provided it is realized that it is false only in the non-conniving use of the term 'unicorn'; if it is used in a conniving way then it will be true. A second objection is that the schema will not work for all instances of *F*; compare, for example, 'is fictional'. However, this objection will be successful only if such expressions are best construed in logical grammar as predicates, and this is not at all obvious. Thus 'Holmes is fictional' might be construed in terms of a sentential operator as 'It's a matter of fiction that Holmes exists', say. (By parity with Evans's account of 'really', this would be true if, and only if, there is (only) fictionally a proposition *p* such that 'Holmes exists' means that *p*.) Indeed, the schema itself may then be thought to provide a partial elucidation of what it is to be a genuine predicate, and hence a *mutual* elucidation of both this and existence.

BIBLIOGRAPHY

Chisholm, R.M.: *Realism and The Background of Phenomenology* (New York: Free Press, 1960).

Evans, G.: *The Varieties of Reference* (Oxford: Oxford University Press, 1982).

Quine, W.V.: 'On what there is', in his *From a Logical Point of View* (New York and Evanston: Harper and Row, 1963), 1–19.

Parsons, T.: *Nonexistent Objects* (New Haven and London: Yale University Press, 1980).

Russell, B.: 'On denoting', *Mind* 14 (1905), 479–93; repr. in *Logic and Knowledge* ed. R.C. Marsh (London: George Allen and Unwin, 1956), 41–56.

Williams, C.J.F.: *What is Existence?* (Oxford: Oxford University Press, 1981).

S.G. WILLIAMS

existentialism In the narrower and more popular of its several senses, 'existentialism' designates the worldview and depiction of the human condition advanced by SARTRE and others (notably Camus (1913–60)) in the shadow of the Second World War. More broadly and significantly conceived, it refers to the radicalized 'subjective turn' initiated by the mid-nineteenth-century reaction of Kierkegaard (1813–55) against HEGEL's IDEALISM, and developed during the second quarter of the twentieth century in opposition to objectivity-oriented (naturalistic and positivistic as well as idealistic and rationalistic) treatments of human reality (*see* LOGICAL POSITIVISM; NATURALISM). This movement attained prominence first in Germany, in the late 1920s, and then in France a generation later, as various German and French philosophers directed their attention to the purportedly fundamental 'subjectivity' of 'what it means to exist as a human being' (as Kierkegaard had framed the issue). The twentieth-century figures most closely and influentially associated with it prior to Sartre and Camus were HEIDEGGER and Jaspers, whose *Being and Time* (1927) and three-volume *Philosophy* (1932) (respectively) launched it anew, and remain its most important texts. Both Heidegger and Jaspers repudiated the term 'existentialism', owing to its association with the views of Sartre from whom they wished to dissociate themselves. Their common concern with the distinctive character of human 'existence' (*Existenz* in German), however, has given rise to the more neutral and accurate designation of this movement as 'existential philosophy' (*Existenzphilosophie*).

EXISTENTIALISM

'Existentialism' construed along the former lines found its most extensive elaborations in Sartre's *Being and Nothingness* (1943) and Camus's *The Myth of Sisyphus* (1942), and its most influential popular expressions in their associated literary efforts (e.g. Sartre's *Nausea* and plays, and Camus's *The Stranger*), through which it first became known and inspired widespread interest in the English-speaking world. The worldview it represents is radically different from Kierkegaard's, whose impassioned religious faith led him to very different conclusions – except that it is rather like the outlook he suggests would be the bleak and desperate outcome of *abandoning* that faith. It is strikingly similar, on the other hand, to that advanced by his atheistic and pessimistic contemporary SCHOPENHAUER. For Sartrean existentialists, as for Schopenhauer, there is no God of any sort, and there further are no absolutes in the realms of value and morality. Human beings are condemned to a meaningless fleeting existence (their illusions to the contrary notwithstanding), thrown into a godless and irrational world in which the only certainties are futile striving, pointless suffering, and final oblivion. Schopenhauer's radically negative stance with respect to living in such a world is rejected, however, in favour of a determination to affirm our existence in it nonetheless (somewhat in the spirit of NIETZSCHE's like response to Schopenhauer).

For these existentialists (as for Kierkegaard, and in contrast to both Schopenhauer and Nietzsche), human beings differ fundamentally from all mere 'things' in this world. We are *free* in a radical sense – inexplicably, but none the less actually – notwithstanding the limitations and 'facticity' associated with our human biology, individual heredity and historical, social and biographical circumstances (*see* FREE WILL). Confronted with a range of alternatives, we can and must make choices among them entirely on our own (even though we may deceive ourselves about

this in various ways). We *are* this very freedom, together with what we come to be through the choices we make in the situations in which we find ourselves – our 'existence' is held to 'precede' the only sort of concrete 'essence' we thereby come to have – and so we are completely responsible for all that we do.

We thus are 'condemned' to freedom and to responsibility. Despite the absurdity and futility of it all, however, the recognition and exercise of our freedom and our responsibility for the choices we make and lives we lead are of the greatest importance. For there is nothing else that matters more (or indeed at all); and it is only in this way that we may attain the possible 'authenticity' or integrity that is the source of the only non-illusory sort of human dignity and worth available to us in this barren and inhospitable world.

It is no accident that this 'existentialism' was developed in the land of DESCARTES and the Enlightenment. Its radical distinction between conscious, self-determining human subjects and the world of mere objects is strongly reminiscent of Cartesian dualism; but in the spirit of Voltaire and his fellow *philosophes*, God is emphatically rejected, leaving these subjects to their own devices in a world of objects alien to them. The void left by the absence of God is reflected in the dismay with which the human condition is depicted. The existentialism of Sartre, Camus and their followers may thus be regarded as a disillusioned Cartesianism, conceding the world to positivism but making the most of the *cogito*.

EXISTENTIAL PHILOSOPHY

'Existential philosophy', more broadly conceived, is not to be identified with this or any other worldview and assessment of the human condition. It is neutral, for example, with respect to any such question as whether, beyond ourselves and the things of this world, it makes sense to suppose that there is either a God or some other transcending and encompassing higher reality. It is to be understood, rather, in terms of its focus upon 'human existence', its assignment of priority to the account of 'what it means to exist as a human being' over all merely objective descriptions of the kind of creature human beings may be observed to be, and its adoption of a mode of elucidating the character of such 'existing' that is attuned above all to our 'lived experience'. More specifically, its point of departure is Kierkegaard's contention that the 'truth' of human existence is to be conceived in terms of our irreducible and inescapable 'subjectivity'.

Another of its nineteenth-century sources was Nietzsche's critique of metaphysics, and in particular of the notion of the self as a quasi-substantial entity with an unchanging essential nature. It most emphatically did not follow Nietzsche, however, in his naturalistic reinterpretation of human life, on which all human capacities – consciousness and volition included – are conceived as the outcome of an interplay of biological, social and cultural processes and circumstances. (This renders his common inclusion among them highly problematical.)

Post-Kierkegaardian existential philosophy was more directly influenced by the anti-naturalistic PHENOMENOLOGY of HUSSERL. Fidelity to the forms and contents of the varieties of our experience precisely as these phenomena present themselves to us, at the expense of all theorizing about them, was the first principle of Husserlian phenomenology. This approach seemed to Heidegger and others to lend itself to the project of exploring the subjectivity of human existing while fending off all challenges to its reality. Husserl's own project, however, was more akin to those of Descartes and KANT; for his concern was with the character and attainment of genuine knowledge and with the associated essential structures of the TRANSCENDENTAL EGO. The appropriation of his 'phenomenological method' by existential philosophy, therefore, was accompanied by a fundamental reorientation of philosophical purpose.

Kierkegaard posed and undertook to answer the question of 'what it means to exist as a human being' in the context of his religiously motivated concern to salvage the idea that each of us has (and fundamentally is) a unique SOUL that is not reducible to or derivative of anything and everything pertaining to merely natural and social processes and relations; and for him the essential task associated with it is a matter of our responsibility before God for the manner in which we make our choices and lead our lives. In his more philosophical writings he employed the terminology of the 'self' and 'subjectivity'; but it was his Christian notion of the soul, bestowed by and answerable to a personal and transcendent God, that he drew upon in his discussions of them. Eschewing all attempts to provide reasoned arguments for the Christian interpretation he embraced (recognizing that nothing but a 'leap of faith' could sustain it), he adopted an indirect mode of discourse intended to draw one toward it by prompting one to think about 'what it means to exist as a human being' in personal rather than impersonal terms, and to see the kinds of fundamental choices that human existing involves.

Existential philosophy after Kierkegaard may be conceived as a variety of attempts to salvage something like his conception of 'existing as a human being' and his notions of the 'self' and its irreducible 'subjectivity' in the aftermath of the abandonment of his religious faith. Most existential philosophers have sought to recast their enterprise in entirely non-religious terms, supposing that Kierkegaard was on to something important about human existence, but that it required to be given a different interpretation and expression. Some, such as Sartre, broke radically with him; while others, such as Jaspers, retained the notion of our relation to a higher reality transcending ourselves and the things of our world which he fittingly but obscurely designated as 'Transcendence'.

Existential philosophy undertakes to comprehend human existence from the standpoint of one involved in living it. It thus gives what might be termed a 'first-person' rather than a 'third-person' account of existing as a human being. It does not presuppose that everyone exists in the very same way; on the contrary, it is attentive to the various humanly actual and possible kinds of ways in which we do and may lead our lives (certain of which are usually suggested to be preferable to others). But it does proceed on the assumption that there are general features of the character of human existing that may be discerned. While making much of our subjective selves, existential philosophy follows Nietzsche in rejecting the hypostatization of the self, and construes human reality instead in terms of our general manner and various possible ways of carrying on our existence, which are inseparable from the ways in which we relate ourselves to things and others, our circumstances and our possibilities. Its concern is with human existence in the sense of human *existing*; with our identity in the sense of our possible ways of *identifying*; with our subjectivity in the sense of our *experiencing*, *reflecting* and *choosing*; and with our selves or selfhood in the sense of our *constituting* ourselves in various ways in the course of leading our lives.

Existential philosophy thus differs fundamentally from other forms of inquiry into our nature focusing upon any or all of the elements of the classical definition of a human being as a rational and social animal. In contrast to all such approaches, it accords priority to the exploration of the subjectivity missed by any such analysis, in an attempt to be more faithful to the 'lived reality' and possibilities of our manner of existing as we each lead our lives. While existential philosophers do attempt to give an account of human reality, they take it to be axiomatic that the human reality to be understood is, in each instance, something lived out by a particular person responding to particular situations in ways affected by that person's thinking and choosing. Hence, one characteristic theme of existential philosophy is that human existing is inadequately understood if conceived *either* on the model of some other type of entity (thing, animal, mechanism) *or* primarily in terms of objectively conceived (biological, psychological, social or rational) processes,

practices and operations. All such ways of conceiving of our manner of existence leave out the peculiar character of human selfhood and subjectivity.

For some, like Kierkegaard, Marcel and Jaspers, the matter is complicated by the supposition of a further relationship in which we stand to a higher reality transcending ourselves and the things and institutions of this world, apart from which our subjectivity purportedly degenerates. For others, like Heidegger and Sartre, nothing of the kind is envisioned, and the attempt is made to show that our subjectivity can be sustained and developed in the absence of any such relationship (although for Heidegger it and the meaning of our manner of existing are bound up with what he calls 'the meaning of Being' and our rarely exercised ability to attend to it). Yet another complication arises from the fact that for some (e.g. Jaspers and Marcel) the possibility of genuine subjectivity is inseparable from a certain sort of *intersubjectivity* or interaction and communication with other subjects; while for others (including Kierkegaard as well as Heidegger and Sartre) this is not the case, and relations with other human beings are generally taken to have the opposite effect.

A second general theme is that our subjective selves *come to be* what they are in a manner that is not determined in advance, and that is at least in part *their own doing*. Our subjectivity thus is taken to transcend both the causal order of nature and all 'ensembles of social relations', even if it exists only in relation to them – and further to transcend the confines and structures of the 'laws' of logic and reason, and of the rules of language and the norms of culture as well, in the sense that none of them (or any other such objective state of affairs) inescapably governs it. The spectre of DETERMINISM, which Kierkegaard felt no need even to take seriously, is therefore of little concern to subsequent existential philosophers, for whom its claims are subverted by attention to actual human experience.

This leads to a third theme of existential philosophy: the assignment of priority to the results of explorations of the kinds of experiences human beings have as they live their lives – both in commonplace situations and when they confront crises – over more abstract theoretical considerations that might be brought forward with respect to human nature. Kierkegaard's employment of quasi-literary devices in this connection has been continued by some; others have seized upon the phenomenological method of Husserl as lending itself even better to the discernment of what human existing involves.

Like Husserlian phenomenology, post-Kierkegaardian existential philosophy is not content merely to describe various notable kinds of 'lived experience'. It involves the further attempt to achieve an understanding of the basic character of the existing human subject who 'lives' these experiences and comes to be a self of one sort or another in doing so – not merely in this or that particular case, but in any and all such cases. So Heidegger undertook to work out an 'existential analysis' of the distinctive 'ontological' structure of our *Dasein* – our way of 'being', which for him is 'being-there', or 'being in the world', and involves such features as practical involvement with things, being with others, being towards death, and the threefold temporal modalities of being in the present out of the past into the future. Sartre elaborates an alternative 'phenomenological ontology' of 'human reality'; and Jaspers offers yet another analysis of the various dimensions of human existence, though not under the same rubric.

As the case of Heidegger shows, our manner of existing is characterized by existential philosophers in ways which often seem surprisingly and disappointingly obvious – at least once one sees what they have in mind, which frequently is obscured by the highly artificial terminology they tend to favour. To this complaint, however, their reply is that philosophers all too often have been forgetful of these things or have failed to take sufficient account of them; and that (as Hegel observed) what is familiar is not necessarily well understood, and indeed may require special effort if it is to be adequately comprehended. On the other hand, the obviousness of the features identified serves to provide the account of human existence given with the plausibility and force needed to make it convincing, by enabling us to recognize it as indeed applying to ourselves.

The analysis of these evident features of human existence is often supplemented by drawing attention to various kinds of experiences the occurrence of which is similarly undeniable. And the usual next and crucial move is to go on to reflect upon what they presuppose or otherwise show about the basic character or structures of our subjectivity and human reality. The method typically employed in doing so (following Husserl) is modelled upon Kant's tactic of 'transcendental argument' (*see* TRANSCENDENTAL ARGUMENTS). It proceeds, after first identifying and describing certain sorts of experience, by inquiring into what they presuppose – the 'conditions of their possibility' – in and about ourselves.

It is in connection with the preliminary stage of this endeavour that some existential philosophers find literature or quasi-literary devices to be quite useful, in virtue of their power to highlight and explore the human possibility of the kinds of experiences in question. The real work of existential philosophy, however, only *begins* with the selection and exploration of these more or less obvious features and salient kinds of experience. It further involves attempting to provide a more comprehensive and fundamental interpretation of human existence that takes account of them and makes integrating sense of them.

Existential philosophy is thus a contest of interpretations, relating to something that is by its very nature beyond the reach of both logical and linguistic considerations and all forms of empirical-theoretical inquiry. But it is not a contest in which all claims to soundness and comprehension give way to mere exhortation or self-expression; for it proceeds by case-making and a recognizable form of argument, in which considerations are brought forward both in support of and in opposition to various accounts of our existence. The contest may be a very untidy and inconclusive affair, in which one is always left having to make up one's own mind; but as the past century and a half has shown, it is a very lively one – and the stakes could hardly be higher.

Post-structuralists (see STRUCTURAL-ISM), like existential philosophy's earlier analytical critics, have sought to put an end to it, supposing it to be mere sound and fury signifying nothing. But the last word may well belong to neither of them. It may be – as Sartre himself ultimately concluded – that existential philosophy does not and cannot by itself provide an adequate account of human existence; and that therefore if it is to have a future, it will be as a part of a more comprehensive philosophical anthropology, in which its role will be that of a corrective to other approaches focusing upon the biological, social, cultural and other such objectively accessible dimensions of human life. This more modest role, however, could prove to be an important and even indispensable one, in the philosophical attempt to do justice to what it means to exist as a human being.

Existentialism so construed, *along with* positivism, may perhaps best be understood not as a *revolt against* the mainstream of classical modern philosophy from Descartes to HUME, Kant and Hegel, but rather as a *radicalization* of an element of it. In both, 'experience' was taken to be the point of departure and only reliable guide. The element seized upon by positivism, however, was the ideal of a reconstruction of knowledge, in which the passion for certainty overrode all other considerations; while in the case of existential philosophy, the preoccupation was with a reinterpretation of the status of the subject of all (human) experience, in which the overriding concern was with the activity of the experiencing subject.

While positivism thus made a fetish of OBJECTIVITY, existential philosophy did likewise with subjectivity. From Descartes to Hume, Kant and Hegel (and subsequently Husserl), classical modern philosophy may be regarded as a series of attempts to interpret both the nature of the subject and the outcome of its activity in the light of an analysis of certain sorts of experiences that were taken to be basic or otherwise salient. Kant and Hegel remained wedded to the idea that they ultimately have to do with rationality; but they both made much of sorts of experience that went beyond the limits of reasoning as it had been understood by these predecessors.

While positivism drew back into narrower confines in the experiences it privileged, existential philosophy went further, and took as paradigmatic for the understanding of the human subject aspects and kinds of experience in which even these attenuated notions of rationality could no longer be retained and employed to interpret what is going on. It radicalized the 'subjective turn' with which Descartes inaugurated early modern philosophy, as he sought to demythologize but preserve the idea of the soul as something essentially inward and distinct from the body (and indeed from everything merely worldly).

For Descartes, the true nature of the subject-self is revealed most clearly and fundamentally through experiences of *thinking*, among which those associated with reasoning and willing were considered paradigmatic, with priority being assigned to the former. Kant accorded special importance to the moral experiences of the sense of duty and respect for the moral law; but they too were assimilated to the model of rationality. Hegel's broadened notion of rationality took in a great deal more than those of Descartes and Kant had; but for him too, the self was conceived essentially as spirit (*Geist*) that is ultimately at once 'subject' and 'substance', with the latter being construed as rational structure.

Along with Schopenhauer, MARX and Nietzsche, Kierkegaard rejected the interpretation of the subject as essentially rational; but unlike them, he held on to the notion of the subject-self as distinct from our bodily natural and social existence, bound up with it but transcending it, and at least capable of determining itself in accordance with demands of a sort differing from all mundane imperatives. For Descartes, Kant and Hegel, these higher-order demands had been the claims of reason; but for Kierkegaard, they were in the first instance the claim of God's will upon us, and secondarily the requirement that we assume responsibility for the commitments on the basis of which we lead our lives.

Existential philosophy after Kierkegaard may be conceived as the further exploration of what might be termed the logic and dynamics of this notion of human subjectivity. Here too, as for earlier and less radical modern philosophers who followed Descartes in taking the 'subjective turn', the key to the understanding of the subject-self was taken to be various sorts of *experience*. In keeping with the abandonment of the idea of its essential rationality, however, the sorts of experience selected for attention were typically those in which the individual subject is confronted with situations requiring decisions, of the kind that existing human beings must make in the course of leading their lives.

The fundamental premises of existential philosophy are thus that it makes good and important sense to interpret human existence in terms of the irreducible subjectivity of such subject-selves playing itself out in various possible ways under the circumstances associated with the human condition – and further, that there are certain general features or structures characterizing it, beyond the particular details of each of our lives and experiences, that may be grasped and articulated (or at least meaningfully indicated) if the proper approach to them is taken. If one rejects either the idea that human subjectivity amounts to anything more than the reflection in consciousness of objective realities of various sorts, or the idea that anything general remains to be discerned about it beyond the particular contents that it happens to have, one will conclude – as the many critics of existential philosophy in both the Anglo-American and European traditions have concluded – that it is much ado about nothing. (This pre-

sumably would have been the verdict of Hegel, Marx and Nietzsche as well, along with Hume and Kant.) The fact that even Heidegger and Sartre subsequently backed away from their earlier adherence to these premises raises further doubts about them. Like other extreme positions taken in the history of philosophy, however, this radicalized version of the 'subjective turn' with which modern philosophy began remains a philosophical possibility deserving to be reckoned with; and it may well be that no other attempt to hold on to something like the notion of the soul has any better prospects.

BIBLIOGRAPHY

Camus, A.: *The Myth of Sisyphus* (1942); trans. J. O'Brien (New York: Knopf, 1955).

Grossmann, R.: *Phenomenology and Existentialism* (London: Routledge and Kegan Paul, 1984).

Heidegger, M.: *Being and Time* (1927); trans. J. Macquarrie and E. Robinson (New York: Harper, 1962).

Jaspers, K.: *Philosophy* (1932); trans. E.B. Ashton, 3 vols (Chicago: University of Chicago Press, 1969–71).

Kierkegaard, S.: *Concluding Unscientific Postscript* (1846); trans. D.F. Swenson and W. Lowrie (Princeton, NJ: Princeton University Press, 1965).

Marcel, G.: *The Mystery of Being* (1950); 2 vols, trans. G.S. Fraser and R. Hague (Chicago: Regnery, 1950–1).

Reinhardt, K.F.: *The Existentialist Revolt*, 2nd edn (New York: Ungar, 1960).

Sartre, J.-P.: *Being and Nothingness* (1943); trans. H. Barnes (New York: Philosophical Library, 1956).

Schraeder, G.-A., Jr. ed.: *Existential Philosophers: Kierkegaard to Merleau-Ponty* (New York: McGraw-Hill, 1967).

Solomon, R.: *From Rationalism to Existentialism* (New York: Harper and Row, 1972).

Wahl, J.: *Philosophies of Existence* trans. F.M. Lorry (London: Routledge and Kegan Paul, 1969).

Warnock, M.: *Existentialism* (Oxford: Oxford University Press, 1970).

Wild, J.: *The Challenge of Existentialism* (Bloomington, IN: Indiana University Press, 1959).

RICHARD SCHACHT

experience Few would deny that we experience tables, trees and headaches. In the hands of philosophers, this commonplace has tended to be transformed into a theory depicting experiences as dynamic mental occurrences through which we endeavour to apprehend our circumstances. The conception has epistemological and metaphysical dimensions. For classical empiricists like LOCKE and HUME, experience was epistemically fundamental: empirical beliefs are warranted only if they are based on experience. Others take experience to be causally but not epistemically relevant to the justification of empirical belief. In either case, experiences are regarded as occupying a central position on the metaphysical landscape.

Theorists differ as to whether experiences exhibit intentional or propositional content (*see* INTENTIONALITY). Some, echoing JAMES, imagine experience to be a 'blooming buzzing confusion', an inchoate sensory presentation requiring conceptualization or interpretation. What we experience is 'given'. In interpreting the given, we make of it what we will. Others follow KANT in supposing that the 'given' is a myth (Sellars, 1956). Experience, they hold, is always *as of* something definite, and this depends, not merely on the character of the experience itself, but on the conceptual repertoire of the experiencer as well. Suppose you and I view a supernova. Our experiences on this occasion might be indiscernible qualitatively. If I have and you lack the CONCEPT of a supernova, however, then my experience, but not yours, may be *as of a supernova*.

In recent years, much has been made of the notion that when one has an experience, there is 'something it is like' to have it (see Nagel, 1974). This something cannot be known, cannot even be comprehended, except by one who has the sort of experience in question. This approach suggests that experience is largely a private affair, thus leaving open the possibility that beings otherwise similar could differ dramatically with respect to the qualitative character of their experiences. What it is like when your finger is pricked or when you view a tomato in bright sunlight might or might not be what it is like when my finger is pricked or when I spy a tomato.

Suppose I have a visual experience of the sort I have when viewing a ripe tomato in bright sunlight. Does this mean that there must *be* something reddish and round that is the immediate object of my experience? Many philosophers have thought so (see Price, 1932). It is widely recognized, however, that properties experienced can differ markedly from those we are inclined to attribute to material objects. This, together with the apparent possibility that, in hallucinating or dreaming, I may undergo experiences indistinguishable from those I should have in viewing a tomato, might seem to imply that objects of experience are not material bodies, but 'sense data', 'qualia', SENSA. My encounter with a material body like the tomato is mediated by an experience of a phenomenal object. In an hallucination or dream, the experience and its object, though perhaps not its cause, remain intact. A view of this sort poses obstacles to materialist attempts to resolve the MIND/BODY PROBLEM. Once we detach experienced colours, or tastes, or sounds from material bodies, it is not easy to see where in the material world we might locate them. (*See* PHYSICALISM/MATERIALISM.)

A distaste for the multiplication of entities has led some philosophers to engage in deflationary manoeuvres *vis-à-vis* objects of experience. One suggestion is that reports of experiences are 'topic neutral' (see Smart, 1959). When I claim to experience something reddish and round, I am merely reporting an occurrence that is like what occurs when my eyes are open and I am looking at a ripe tomato in broad daylight. This occurrence need be neither reddish nor round, indeed *it* need have no phenomenal qualities at all. Other opponents of the act–object model of experience have suggested that experiences are analysable adverbially (see Chisholm, 1966, ch. 6). In experiencing something reddish and round, I am not encountering a private reddish round object, I am experiencing 'reddishly and roundly'. I may do this, it is contended, even if nothing at all in me or in my vicinity is reddish and round.

Although such conceptions of experience dispense with a special class of sensory object, it is not clear that they thereby avoid the mind–body puzzles associated with traditional act–object theories. It appears, for instance, that there remains an ineffable 'something it is like' to experience a tomato visually. This 'something', whether a feature of an object or of an 'experiencing', seems invariably to be left out of objective 'third-person' accounts of the material world however exhaustive. In response, materialists argue that there is good reason to suppose that these subjective qualities are, at bottom, identifiable with or reducible to unmysterious physical properties of sentient creatures. The debate thus far has been a stand-off.

See also EMPIRICISM.

BIBLIOGRAPHY

Chisholm, R.M.: *Theory of Knowledge* 1st edn (Englewood Cliffs, NJ: Prentice Hall, 1966).

Nagel, T.: 'What is it like to be a bat?', *Philosophical Review* 83 (1974), 435–50.

Price, H.H.: *Perception* (London: Methuen, 1932).

Sellars, W.: 'Empiricism and the philosophy of mind', *Minnesota Studies in the Philosophy of Science*, Vol. 1, ed. H. Feigl and M. Scriven (Minneapolis: University of Minnesota Press, 1956), 253–329.

Smart, J.J.C.: 'Sensations and brain-processes', *Philosophical Review* 68 (1959), 141–56.

JOHN HEIL

extension/intension The *extension* of an expression is the object or objects to which the expression applies. For example, the extension of the noun 'rose' is the collection of all roses, and the extension of the definite description 'the number of planets' is the number 9. Some hold that the extension of a (declarative) sentence is its truth value. The *intension* of an expression is its meaning.

The semantic analysis of natural language calls for a sharp distinction between extension and intension. Many different definite descriptions may describe the same object – and hence have the same extension. For example, 'the number of planets', 'the successor of 8', 'the number of a cat's lives' (according to myth), all have as their extension the number 9; and they all differ, not only in vocabulary, but in meaning, in *intension*. Furthermore, many meaningful expressions lack extension. For example, the predicate 'cat with nine lives' (literally speaking) and the definite description 'the largest number' have this property. Moreover, the extension of an expression can vary over time (and with respect to other parameters) without the expression changing in meaning. The extension of the predicate 'rose' changes as old roses fade and new ones bloom, but the word does not change in meaning.

These examples show that there is such a thing as the extension/intension distinction. What to make of it is another matter. The cases of 'same extension, different intension' are compatible with the principle that expressions with the same intension must have the same extension; but this principle may seem to conflict with the examples of univocal expressions with varying extensions. The disparity is resolved if the principle is revised to assert that expressions with the same intension have the same *range* of extensions with respect to extension-determining factors such as the passage of time. Call this version of the principle 'IDE' ('intension determines extension').

Coextensive expressions with different intensions cannot in general be substituted for one another within an expression *e* while preserving the extension of e (assuming that the extension of a declarative sentence is its truth value). For example, Jones might believe that 9 is divisible by 3 and yet not believe that the number of planets is divisible by 3. Hence, substituting 'the number of planets' for '9' in the true sentence

(1) Jones believes that 9 is divisible by 3.

results in the false sentence

(2) Jones believes that the number of planets is divisible by 3.

It is often thought that such failures of substitutivity constitute a positive test or argument that the exchanged expressions do not have the same intension. This amounts to an appeal to the principle that cointensive expressions may be freely substituted for one another in any syntactic context. The principle is plausible because it follows from a principle of *composition* for intensions:

Composition
The intension of a syntactically complex expression is a function solely of the intensions of its syntactic parts.

From IDE it follows that (1) and (2) have different intensions; and from this and *composition* it follows that the two terms have different intensions. The trouble with *composition*, however, is that a strong case can be made that no two distinct expressions are freely interchangeable within belief contexts. (See Mates, 1950, for the argument.) If so, *composition* entails that no two expressions can have the same intension. In fact, *composition* has some quite paradoxical consequences. From *composition* it follows that if expressions u and v of the same syntactic type are such that $\varphi(u)$ but not $\varphi(v)$, then u and v do not have the same intension. (Here, φ is any sentential context not involving quotation.) But it seems likely that for no predicate F did George IV believe that

not all F's are F. (Church (1988) credits George IV with a healthy respect for the first law of identity (that $x = x$, for all objects x); and we may assume the same of the principle that all F's are F, for every F.) It now follows that if George IV believed that not all F's are G's, then 'F' and 'G' have different intensions. Thus, merely by having certain beliefs, George IV could control the semantical facts about a public language. (This argument is an ironic analogue of one developed in Church (1992)). It appears that *composition* is too strong (*see* Putnam, 1954).

If we postulate the converse of IDE – that expressions with the same range of extensions have the same intension – then we have the point of view of possible worlds semantics, or more generally of 'index semantics'. The intension of, say, a common noun such as 'rose' is identified with the function which associates with each sequence of extension-determining factors $<p, t, w \ldots>$ (place p, time t, possible world $w \ldots$) the extension of 'rose' with respect to such parameters. This 'functional' analysis of intension can be extended to expressions of complex and higher type. For example, the relative adjective 'small' cannot be treated as a predicate of individuals. The sentence 'Dumbo is a small elephant' does not mean that Dumbo is an elephant and Dumbo is small; for if so, we could deduce that Dumbo is a small animal from the fact that Dumbo is a small elephant: 'small' combines with a noun phrase ('elephant') to produce another noun phrase ('small elephant'). Accordingly, the intension of 'small' is a function from common noun intensions (functions from indices to sets) to common noun intensions. This theory has had a considerable impact on research in theoretical linguistics (see Chierchia and McConnell-Genet, 1990). But it is open to many objections, not least of which is that it makes logical equivalence the criterion of sameness of intension, though perhaps the most important of which is that it has failed to date to accommodate certain counterexamples to IDE (see Putnam, 1975).

BIBLIOGRAPHY

Carnap, R.: *Meaning and Necessity* (Chicago and London: University of Chicago Press, 1947).

Chierchia, G. and McConnell-Genet, S.: *Meaning and Grammar. An Introduction to Semantics* (Cambridge, MA: MIT Press, 1990).

Church, A.: 'A remark concerning Quine's paradox about modality', in *Propositions and Attitudes* ed. N. Salmon and S. Soames (Oxford: Oxford University Press, 1988), 58–66.

Frege, G.: 'On sense and reference', in *Translations from the Philosophical Writings of Gottlob Frege* ed. and trans. P. Geach and M. Black (Oxford: Blackwell, 1952), 56–78.

Mates, B.: 'Synonymity', *University of California Publications in Philosophy* 25 (1950), 201–26; repr. in *Semantics and the Philosophy of Language* ed. L. Linsky (Urbana, IL: University of Illinois Press, 1952), 111–36.

Putnam, H.: 'Synonymity and the analysis of belief sentences', *Analysis* 14 (1954), 114–22; repr. in *Propositions and Attitudes* ed. N. Salmon and S. Soames (Oxford: Oxford University Press, 1988), 149–58.

Putnam, H.: 'The meaning of meaning', in his *Philosophical Papers ii: Mind, Language, and Reality* (Cambridge: Cambridge University Press, 1975), 215–71.

HARRY DEUTSCH

extensionalism A theory is said to be extensional if coextensive expressions of the theory are interchangeable in any syntactic context C while preserving the extension of C. Extensionalism is the doctrine that only (though certainly not all) extensional theories are legitimate in the sense of constituting 'serious science'. Extensionalism is most closely associated with the views of QUINE who goes so far as to claim that formulability within the framework of extensional predicate calculus is 'pretty nearly' a necessary condition of intelligibility (Quine, 1990).

Quine attacks the very notion of meaning (intension), arguing that on close examination this commonplace concept is of no scientific explanatory value; it is a myth, a will o' the wisp. Quine argues first (but my ordering here of Quine's doctrines is largely arbitrary) that the concept of meaning as the intensional correlate of individual words and sentences is an obscure notion, subject to no extensional criterion of individuation and definable only in terms of other, equally obscure, intensional notions (Quine, 1970). Second, he argues that the traditional analytic/synthetic distinction cannot be maintained. There is no principled distinction between statements true by definition or linguistic convention and those true in virtue of extralinguistic fact (Quine, 1951). Third, he observes that incompatible empirical hypotheses may each be fully compatible with the data, and hence insofar as individual hypotheses have 'empirical meaning', incompatible hypotheses may have the same empirical meaning. Quine infers from this that empirical significance is diffused over the entirety of theory. Only 'observation sentences' have, individually, in isolation from theory, any empirical significance (Quine, 1970). Fourth, he argues that quantified modal logic does not possess an adequate interpretation; at best it entails the onerous doctrine of 'Aristotelian ESSENTIALISM' (Quine, 1966 and elsewhere). Finally, he argues that REFERENCE is 'inscrutable' and translation 'indeterminate' (Quine 1960 and elsewhere).

The first point is based on a fact of elementary model theory: an isomorphism of one domain onto another leaves the truth values of sentences undisturbed; and it seems to follow that it simply does not matter, up to isomorphism, what our terms refer to. The thesis about translation is the claim that a theory of translation, that is, a theory about what expressions of the home language translate what expressions of the foreign language, may be underdetermined by all relevant linguistic data. But, unlike cases of underdetermination generally, in this case there is, Quine claims, no ultimate 'fact of the matter' to serve as arbiter. Quine's doubts about modal logic have been answered both by direct replies (see Kaplan, 1986; Marcus, 1991) and by the fruitful and now widespread application of intensional logic in philosophy and theoretical linguistics. Further, it is best to view the thesis of the inscrutability of reference as an undesirable consequence of Quine's brand of extensionalism – rather than as a reason in support of it. Reference is mediated by meaning and meaning-related factors, such as causal or historical connection. The reason the initials 'H.D.' denote the author of this entry and not some isomorphic image of him is that causal and historical conditions have intervened to establish the right connection. Reference is not mere unmediated correlation. And the implication of Quine's persuasive examples of revisable statements traditionally held to be analytic (e.g. that momentum is proportional to velocity) should be reassessed in light of the Kripke–Putnam insights concerning NATURAL KIND terms. The claim that translation is indeterminate seems to depend on a rather narrow, behaviourist criterion of what is to count as evidence for or against a given system of analytical hypotheses (a translation manual). (See Gibson, Jr (1986) for a clear exposition of Quine's views on translation.) Lately, Quine seems to take a more tolerant attitude toward the intensional, declaring that 'there is no dismissing it' for it 'implements vital communication' (Quine, 1990, p. 71).

In another vein, POSSIBLE WORLDS semantics is, technically, an extensional theory. (It is not extensional enough for Quine, of course, since it takes the notion of a possible world as primitive.) But following Saul Kripke and A.N. Prior intensional constructions are usually first regimented within an intensional object language which then in turn is fitted with an extensional semantics involving quantification over possible worlds, moments or intervals of time, and other relevant 'indices'. Thus, the question arises: why not skip the first step and go directly to the extensional language? From the point of view of logic alone – as opposed, say, to the analysis of natural language – the answer would seem to be: no reason. And this answer is supported by the interesting observation, due to van Bentham (1977), that as the expressive power of the intensional object language is increased by the addition of devices required to handle complex tense and modal discourse, it is transformed into a mere notational variant of a (many-sorted) extensional quantificational language (see also Cresswell, 1990).

See also EXTENSION/INTENSION.

BIBLIOGRAPHY

van Bentham, J.F.A.K.: 'Tense logic and standard logic', *Logique et Analyse* 80 (1977), 395–437.

Cresswell, M.J.: *Entities and Indices* (Dordrecht: Kluwer Academic Publishers, 1990).

Gibson, R.F. Jr: 'Translation, physics, and facts of the matter', in Hahn and Schilpp (1986), 139–54.

Hahn, L.E. and Schilpp, P.A. eds: *The Philosophy of W.V. Quine* (La Salle, IL: Open Court, 1986).

Kaplan, D.: 'Opacity', in Hahn and Schilpp (1986), 229–89.

Marcus, R.: 'A backward look at Quine's animadversions on modalities', in *Perspectives on Quine* ed. R. Barrett and R. Gibson (Oxford: Blackwell, 1990), 230–43.

Quine, W.V.: 'Two dogmas of empiricism', *Philosophical Review* 60 (1951); rept. in Quine (1981), 156–74.

Quine, W.V.: 'Three grades of modal involvement', *Proc. XI International Congress of Philosophy* 14, 65–81; repr. in Quine (1966), 156–74.

Quine, W.V.: *Word and Object* (Cambridge, MA: MIT Press, 1960).

Quine, W.V.: *From a Logical Point of View* (Cambridge, MA: Harvard University Press, 1961).

Quine, W.V.: *Ways of Paradox and Other Essays* (New York: Random House, 1966).

Quine, W.V.: *Philosophy of Logic* (Englewood Cliffs, NJ: Prentice Hall, 1970).
Quine, W.V.: *Pursuit of Truth* (Cambridge, MA: Harvard University Press, 1990).

HARRY DEUTSCH

extrinsic/intrinsic What are 'extrinsic' properties and how do they differ from 'intrinsic' properties? On one standard interpretation, F is an extrinsic property (of an object, state, event, process, etc.) just if to possess F is to stand in some relation to other, wholly distinct or non-overlapping, contingent things. Any property which is not extrinsic is intrinsic. The following are clear examples of extrinsic properties: being an uncle of Joe, being 100 km west of Sydney, being a war widow, once having met Barry Humphries, being Fred's favourite number. Examples of intrinsic properties are: being triangular, weighing 90 kg, being 6 ft tall, being identical to Nixon, being self-identical (note that the latter two properties, though intrinsic, are relational).

The fact that we generally and non-collusively agree on how to classify new cases confirms the genuineness of the extrinsic/intrinsic distinction. Can we characterize the distinction in other terms?

It might be thought that the distinction between intrinsic and extrinsic properties corresponds to that between causal and non-causal properties: perhaps all intrinsic properties are causal, and all extrinsic properties are non-causal (where a property is causal if its possession by an object contributes to the object's causal powers, or features in causal explanations). It is true that many intrinsic properties are causal, and that many extrinsic properties are non-causal. But some intrinsic properties are non-causal: for example, the property of being self-identical, or of being Nixon. Conversely, some extrinsic properties are causal: for example, the property of being more massive than other bodies nearby. An object's possession of this property causally explains why bodies move towards it, yet it is an extrinsic property. Further, my possession of the extrinsic property of once having met Barry Humphries implies the existence of various causal links between Humphries and myself. For these reasons, we cannot embed the intrinsic/extrinsic distinction within the causal/non-causal distinction.

It has sometimes been thought that we can understand the intrinsic/extrinsic distinction in terms of the types of changes which objects can undergo. In particular, a property is intrinsic if, and only if, its loss or acquisition by an object constitutes a 'real change' in the object. This definition fits some of our examples. When a woman becomes a war widow, she undergoes no 'real change'. (Of course, when she finds out that she is a widow, she will doubtless undergo many 'real changes', but those changes are linked to her acquisition of the property of believing that she is a widow, not to her acquisition of the property of being a widow.) In contrast, when I acquire the property of weighing 90 kg, I do indeed undergo 'real change', so this property is intrinsic.

Does the 'real change' account cover all cases? It does not apply to the property of being self-identical. This property is intrinsic, yet it cannot be 'lost' or 'acquired' by an object, in the normal sense of those words. Moreover, the point of the 'real change' criterion might be questioned: is it supposed to be easier to detect 'real change' than to detect 'intrinsicness'?

A sharper criterion is provided by the exact physical duplication test. According to this test, F is an intrinsic property of x if, and only if, necessarily, F is also a property of a molecule-for-molecule duplicate of x. The appeal of this test is evident. It explains why the property of being triangular is intrinsic, and why the property of once having met Barry Humphries is extrinsic.

However, since numbers are abstract objects and have no physical duplicates, the duplication test cannot explain why the property of being Fred's favourite number should be counted an extrinsic property of the number 9. Worse still, the test is extensionally incorrect. It classifies some extrinsic properties as intrinsic: for example, the property of existing in a world containing a duplication machine. It also classifies some intrinsic properties as extrinsic: for example, the property of being identical to Nixon. (More sophisticated versions of the duplication test may avoid some of these objections. For a useful discussion, see Humberstone (forthcoming).)

Each of the above elaborations of the extrinsic/intrinsic distinction (the causal criterion, the 'real change' test, and the duplication test) is open to objection. The extrinsic/intrinsic distinction cannot be characterized exclusively in terms of any one of them. But this is not objectionable. We can regard the various accounts as specifying features that typically accompany the property of extrinsicness, or as offering alternative sharpenings of the words 'extrinsic' and 'intrinsic' that may be useful in different contexts.

It is worth ending by mentioning one further worry. The property of being 6 ft tall is intrinsic. My being 6 ft tall does not consist in my standing in some relation to other objects. Yet I am 6 ft tall in virtue of the condition of many other objects: for example, the genes of my father and the condition of many other objects: for mother, various laws of nature, etc. What is the 'cash value' of the distinction between identity ('x's being F is x's standing in relation R to some wholly distinct y') and non-contingent dependency ('necessarily: x's being F depends upon x's standing in R to some wholly distinct y')? This question is hard to answer. Until we can answer it, the point of calling only certain properties 'extrinsic' will be unclear.

BIBLIOGRAPHY

Chisholm, R.M.: *Person and Object* (La Salle, IL: Open Court, 1976).
Humberstone, I.L.: 'Intrinsic/extrinsic', *Synthese* (forthcoming).
Kim, J.: 'Psychophysical supervenience', *Philosophical Studies* 41 (1982), 51–70.
Lewis, D.: 'Extrinsic properties', *Philosophical Studies* 44 (1983), 197–200.
Moore, G.E.: 'The conception of intrinsic value', in his *Philosophical Studies* (London: Routledge and Kegan Paul, 1922), 253–76.

BRIAN GARRETT

163

F

---

fact Correspondence THEORIES OF TRUTH have appealed to facts as truth grounds for true sentences. As sentences are complex linguistic patterns, facts have been construed as complex entities, for example, consisting of particulars in an arrangement, of entities exemplifying properties or standing in relations. Philosophers who appeal to facts face three fundamental questions. (1) Are there distinct kinds of facts corresponding to logically complex truths, such as negations, conjunctions, generalities? That is, are there negative facts, conjunctive facts, general facts? (2) Since some false sentences indicate possible situations, are there *possibilities* in addition to existent facts? (3) Do facts, taken as relations or arrangements of entities, involve a regress in that the relation or arrangement is then recognized as a further constituent that must be connected in turn?

To deal with the first question some argue that a *conjunctive* fact need not be taken as a truth ground for a sentence like 'This is red and that is yellow.' Since the conjunction is entailed by the conjuncts (the Rule of Conjunction), the facts that are the truth grounds for the conjuncts ground the conjunction. But *negative* facts cannot be avoided by such an argument, since there is no correlate of the Rule of Conjunction whereby the fact that the object is yellow can ground the truth of 'That is not red.' To argue that it can introduces an additional fact: the incompatibility of red and yellow (*see* NEGATION).

RUSSELL (1918–19) argued that one must also recognize *general* facts, since, given any set of facts of the form '*x* is f', it would not follow that everything is f. Russell argued that it must also be the case

that *every* fact of the form '*x* is f' is in the set or that the objects occurring in such facts are *all* the objects. In either case we introduce a general fact.

Proponents of facts who acknowledge logically complex facts, such as negative facts and general facts, face the problem of specifying the constituents of such facts. Some philosophers have acknowledged *logical forms*, such as *generality*. The purported general fact that everything is f would contain such a form and the property f. Others, like WITTGENSTEIN (1922), have claimed that general facts are unnecessary, since claims about the totality of objects being all the objects cannot be sensibly stated.

The second problem stems from a correspondence theory taking a sentence like 'This is red' to represent a situation or possible state of affairs and to be true when the fact *exists*, when the situation *obtains*. Since the situation is represented whether the sentence is true or false, the theory appears to acknowledge non-obtaining situations or possible facts, as well as existent or actual facts. Such possible facts may then provide an ontological ground for speaking of POSSIBLE WORLDS, construed as sets of facts with at least one member being a possible fact, as the actual world can be taken to be the totality of actual facts. (*See* PROPOSITION/STATE OF AFFAIRS.)

The third problem is a variant of BRADLEY's purported demonstration that all relations are unintelligible. While it does not show that, it does show that facts are complex entities that are no more reducible to their constituents than a pointillist painting is reducible to a set of colour dots. The fact that something is yellow is not a mere collection of the object and the colour, or of the object, the colour, and the exemplification relation. It must be construed as the object's *having* or *exemplifying* the colour. Bradley's argument reveals, first, that facts involve a connection between terms and properties; second, that facts are not mere sets of terms, properties, and such a connection; and, third, that such a connection is logically different from standard relations.

Facts have been attacked by proponents of the so-called 'redundancy' theory of truth, advocated early in the twentieth century by RAMSEY. Ramsey argued that (1) 'It is true that this is yellow' and (2) 'It is a fact that this is yellow' are equivalent to (3) 'This is yellow.' Some think this shows that to say that a fact is a ground of truth is to say nothing. Others, like MOORE (1953), hold that the equivalences support a correspondence theory of truth. Moore argued that the equivalences did not mean that (1), (2) and (3) 'say the same thing', and that only a correspondence theory of truth could account for the equivalence of (1) and (3).

The redundancy theory lies behind a recent and widely accepted but fallacious argument rejecting facts. The argument employs Russell's theory of definite descriptions and two principles: (a) logically equivalent sentences may be interchanged; (b) substitutions based on true identity statements may be made. It seeks to show that a theory appealing to facts is forced to take any two true sentences to denote the same fact. By assuming, as premises, (1) '*s*' denotes the fact that *s*, (2) *s*, and (3) *t*, it purports to derive (c) '*s*' denotes the fact that *t*. The 'derivation' employs the threefold identity '(the *x* such that *x* = *b* & *s*) = (the *x* such that *x* = *b*) = (the *x* such that *x* = *b* & *t*)' and the *logical equivalence* of '*s*' with '(the *x* such that *x* = *b* & *s*) = (the *x* such that *x* = *b*)' and of '*t*' with '(the *x* such that *x* = *b* & *t*) = (the *x*, such that *x* = *b*)', where '*b*' is a proper name. Such equivalences depend on the assumption that '*b* = *b*' and '(the *x* such that *x* = *b*) = *b*' are logical truths. (c) is then purportedly derived by appropriate substitutions in accordance with (a) and (b). But the argu-

ment is easily seen to be fallacious when one expands the definite descriptive phrases.

FREGE's attack on the correspondence theory is not so easily dismissed. The theory claims that it *is true* that a true statement denotes a fact. To Frege this involves two vicious regresses: (1) a further fact must ground that truth; and (2) the analysis employs the concept being analysed.

See also EVENT THEORY.

BIBLIOGRAPHY

Davidson, D.: 'True to the facts', *Journal of Philosophy* 66 (1969), 748–64.

Hochberg, H.: 'Facts and truth', in his *Logic, Ontology, and Language* (Munich: Philosophia Verlag, 1984).

Moore, G.E.: *Some Main Problems of Philosophy* (London: George Allen and Unwin Ltd, 1953).

Mulligan, K. ed.: *Logic, Truth and Ontology* (Amsterdam: 1992).

Russell, B.: 'The philosophy of logical atomism', *The Monist* 28 (1918), 495–527, 29 (1919), 32–63, 190–222, 345–80.

Wittgenstein, L.: *Tractatus Logico-Philosophicus* (1922); trans. D.F. Pears and B.F. McGuinness (London: Routledge and Kegan Paul, 1961).

HERBERT HOCHBERG

fact/values There is obviously a difference between how things are and how they should be, between how people act, feel or think, and how they ought to act, feel or think. It is not that things are always other than they should be or that people always act in ways they should not; it is that noticing that things are a certain way or that people act in certain ways is different from thinking things are as they should be or people act as they ought.

The sense that evaluative claims are distinctive has a long history. It goes back at least to PLATO's celebration of the form of the Good and the contrast he drew between it and everything else, including all other forms. It shows up as well in ARISTOTLE's distinction between *sophia* and *phronesis*, in HUME's between reason and taste, and in KANT's between theoretical and practical reason. And it is often expressed by saying that there is a fundamental distinction between fact and value.

Yet expressing matters in this way faces an immediate problem. Evaluative claims – for instance, that things *ought* to be thus and so, or that someone *should* act in a certain way, or that the world would be *better* if only . . . – look as if they purport to report *facts*, as if, were they true, it would be because the facts are as they report. This puts pressure on the thought that the relevant difference is between facts on the one hand and something altogether distinct, values, on the other.

Defenders of the fact/value distinction face this pressure in either of two ways. Some (non-naturalists) grant that evaluative claims do report facts and then argue that the facts are, or would have to be, *sui generis* and so markedly different from all other facts. According to them, the point of the fact/value distinction is to mark not a difference between all facts and something else but a metaphysically significant difference in kind among (possible) facts. Others (non-cognitivists) resist as misguided the suggestion that evaluative claims, in so far as they are evaluative, report facts at all, arguing that they are essentially non-descriptive in character. According to them, the point of the fact/value distinction really is to mark a difference between facts (which non-evaluative claims do report) and values (which evaluative claims might express, endorse, prescribe, or recommend but which they do not report). Either way, the defenders of the fact/value distinction maintain that evaluative claims are so distinctive that they should not be seen as reporting the kinds of facts captured by non-evaluative claims.

Not surprisingly, given the intuitive appeal of the fact/value distinction, evaluative claims exhibit a number of distinctive features that recommend setting them apart. Two stand out. First, evaluative claims are so intimately tied to action that accepting an evaluative claim apparently involves, *ipso facto*, seeing oneself as having a reason to act in certain ways, under appropriate conditions. Second, evaluative claims are so resistant to empirical methods of rational inquiry, so insulated from EXPERIENCE, that evaluative claims are disturbingly difficult to justify.

As it happens, virtually no one denies that evaluative claims, at least in standard cases, have these distinctive features. Any plausible theory of value needs to account for them. Still, controversy abounds as to whether what makes them distinctive provides grounds for thinking of them either (1) as reporting *sui generis* facts; or (2) as not reporting facts at all. Many have thought that evaluative claims can be understood in a way that explains their distinctive features even as it treats them as reporting metaphysically quite ordinary, though significant, facts. If they are right, then whatever the difference is between evaluative and non-evaluative claims, it is not a reflection of a fundamental distinction between fact and value.

Against such proposals, defenders of the fact/value distinction have found support, first, in Hume's observation that no 'ought' can be derived from an 'is' and, second, in MOORE's charge that any attempt to equate evaluative claims with non-evaluative ones will involve committing the 'Naturalistic Fallacy'.

What HUME noted is that non-evaluative premises appear never to *entail* evaluative conclusions. While something might be good because it is pleasant, or right because God commanded it, the fact that it is pleasant, or commanded by God, does not entail that it is either good or right; one can, with perfect consistency, accept the non-evaluative claims and deny the evaluative conclusions. Take whichever non-evaluative premises you please concerning how things are, were, or will be, and it seems (Hume observed) that no conclusion concerning how they ought to be can be derived from them alone – an evaluative premise will always have to be in play.

The most influential threat to Hume's view is found in the suggestion that evaluative claims are definable in terms of non-evaluative claims. If, for instance, 'good' simply means 'pleasant', so that to say of something that it is good is simply to report that it is pleasant, then a premise capturing this fact would legitimize inferences from premises concerning what is pleasant to conclusions concerning what is good. Or if 'right' simply means 'commanded by God', so that to say of something that it is right is simply to report that it is commanded by God, then a premise capturing this fact would legitimize inferences from premises concerning what is commanded by God to conclusions concerning what is right. Such definitions might, of course, themselves count as evaluative premises. Even if they do, however, it looks as if the truth of such definitions would be enough to undermine the fact/value distinction. For, if evaluative and non-evaluative claims can be inter-defined, one would be hard pressed to justify treating the first as fundamentally different from the second, when it comes to whether and what they might report.

In any case, no such definition looks to be even remotely plausible. To make this point, Moore deployed what has come to be called 'the Open Question Argument'. Consider, he suggested, the proposal that 'good' means 'pleasant', and then notice that one can intelligibly ask 'Is what is pleasant after all good?' That this is 'an open question' and asks something recognizably different from 'Is what is pleasant after all pleasant?' shows that 'good' and 'pleasant' do not have the same meaning. Substitute in any definition whatsoever that proposes to define an evaluative term with a non-evaluative one and the open question, Moore maintained, will remain. Because Moore saw the meaning of terms as being a function of the properties they 'denote', he thought two terms that have different meanings must denote different properties. Thus he diagnosed all mistaken definitions as reflecting a failure to recognize the differ-ence between distinct properties. When one exhibits this failure, by mistakenly defining an evaluative term using non-evaluative terms, one commits the Naturalistic Fallacy. Since the Open Question Argument could be deployed against any attempt to define evaluative terms using non-evaluative terms, Moore came to think of the properties denoted by the evaluative terms as *sui generis* and characterized them as non-natural.

Convinced by Moore's argument that evaluative terms do not denote non-evaluative properties, but troubled by a metaphysics of non-natural properties, non-cognitivists reject his assumption that evaluative terms have what meaning they do in virtue of denoting properties. According to them, the primary role of evaluative claims is not to report anything, but to express, endorse, prescribe or recommend values. Thus, like Moore, the non-cognitivists embrace a fundamental distinction between evaluative and non-evaluative claims. Yet, they do so while insisting that no metaphysical room need be found for evaluative facts or properties.

Significantly, when it comes to the fact/value distinction, one can easily make too much of the Open Question Argument and the Naturalistic Fallacy it is supposed to reveal. The Open Question Argument, after all, applies not just to attempts to define evaluative terms, but also (as Moore emphasized) to attempts to define certain non-evaluative terms – 'yellow' is Moore's example. None the less, claims using these terms report perfectly ordinary facts, so indefinability, by itself, does not have metaphysical implications. Moreover, it seems that two terms that have different meanings (on Moore's test) can denote the same thing. 'Is the morning star after all the evening star?' and 'Is H_2O after all water?' are both open questions, although the relevant terms in each case denote the same things. This suggests that non-evaluative and evaluative terms might denote the same metaphysically unpresupposing properties even if every proposed definition fell victim to Moore's argument.

Similarly, Hume's view that no evaluative claims are entailed by non-evaluative claims provides no direct support for the fact/value distinction. A parallel failure of entailment seems to hold between, for instance, biological and non-biological claims; non-biological premises appear never to entail biological conclusions. None the less, this presumably goes no way towards showing that biological claims do anything other than report metaphysically ordinary biological facts. The existence of a logical gap between 'is' and 'ought' should not, taken alone, count in favour of thinking evaluative claims do anything other than report metaphysically ordinary evaluative facts.

The real argument for the fact/value distinction needs to be found not in failures of entailment or definition but in how the admittedly distinctive features of evaluative claims are best explained. What underwrites the fact/value distinction is the conviction that their features can be accounted for only by enriching our metaphysics or by deflating their pretentions to report evaluative facts. What would undermine the distinction is an account of their distinctive features that avoided resorting to these extremes.

BIBLIOGRAPHY

Brink, D.: *Moral Realism and the Foundations of Ethics* (Cambridge: Cambridge University Press, 1989).
Frankena, W.: 'The Naturalistic Fallacy', *Mind* 48 (1939), 459–73.
Hare, R.M.: *The Language of Morals* (Oxford: Oxford University Press, 1952).
Hudson, W.D. ed.: *The Is–Ought Question* (London: Macmillan, 1969).
Hume, D.: *A Treatise of Human Nature* (London: 1739); 2nd edn (Oxford: Oxford University Press, 1978).
Moore, G.E.: *Principia Ethica* (Cambridge: Cambridge University Press, 1903).
Prior, A.N.: *Logic and the Basis of Ethics* (Oxford: Oxford University Press, 1949).
Sayre-McCord, G. ed.: *Essays on Moral Realism* (Ithaca, NY: Cornell University Press, 1988).
Stevenson, C.L.: *Facts and Values* (New Haven and London: Yale University Press, 1963).

GEOFFREY SAYRE-McCORD

fatalism The thesis that the laws of logic alone suffice to prove that no person ever acts freely. According to this view, the future is no more within our power than the past. Just as we cannot now undo the occurrence of any event that already occurred or bring about the occurrence of any event that did not occur, so we cannot now prevent the occurrence of any event that will occur or bring about the occurrence of any event that will not occur.

The fatalist does not deny that actions have consequences. For example, learning to swim may prevent my drowning. But if so, according to the fatalist, I was fated to learn to swim and fated to be saved by what I had learned.

ARISTOTLE

The most influential arguments in support of fatalism have their source in ARIS-TOTLE's *De interpretatione* (ch. IX). There he considers the case of a sea-fight that will or will not occur tomorrow. It is not a fact that the sea-fight will occur and not a fact that it will not occur. A genuine alternative exists. So how can it be true to say the sea-battle will occur or true to say it will not? What is true is that the sea-fight will or will not occur, the outcome depending on human choices yet to be made.

Aristotle's own view concerning the soundness of this line of reasoning has been a matter of much dispute. The central issue, however, is whether fatalistic conclusions can be avoided if statements about future contingencies are assumed to be true or, if not true, then false.

DIODORUS CRONUS

The Megarian logician Diodorus Cronus, a predecessor of the Stoics, formulated the so-called 'Master Argument', designed to prove the truth of fatalism. While not all the steps of this argument have been preserved, what is extant are two of his premises and his conclusion.

His first premise is that what is past is necessary. The second premise is that the impossible does not follow from the possible. He concluded that only the actual is possible.

In recent years various philosophers, including A.N. Prior, Jaakko Hintikka and Nicholas Rescher, have attempted to supply the missing steps. The challenge is that Diodorus' most illustrious contemporaries accepted the validity of his reasoning; they focused their attention exclusively on the truth of his premises and the plausibility of his conclusion.

THEOLOGICAL FATALISM

Many thinkers, especially during the Middle Ages, discussed the problem of fatalism within the context of a theological issue: is God's omniscience incompatible with human freedom?

If it is true I will perform a particular action, then God, who knows all truths, knows I will perform that action. But if I could refrain from that action, presumably I could confute God's knowledge, which is impossible. But if I cannot refrain from the action, it is not free.

Augustine replied that while God foreknows all things He causes, He is not the cause of all He foreknows. Jonathan Edwards (1703–58) responded to Augustine's position by observing that divine foreknowledge may not cause an event yet nevertheless prove its necessity.

But suppose, as Aristotle may have, that it is not true that I will perform a particular action tomorrow and not true that I will not. Then God does not know I will perform it and does not know I will not. This view was adopted by the mediaeval Jewish philosopher Levi ben Gersom (known as Gersonides) (1288–1344), who maintained that God is nevertheless omniscient, since He knows all truths, and the truth is that the

future is to some extent within our power. Thus did Gersonides reconcile God's omniscience and human freedom.

TAYLOR'S ARGUMENT

Recently, a new argument leading to the fatalistic conclusion was proposed by Richard Taylor. His strategy is to offer a proof demonstrating the non-controversial claim that it is not within our power to make genuine choices regarding the occurrence of past events, and then to present an analogous proof demonstrating that it is not within our power to make genuine choices regarding the occurrence of future events.

The first proof begins by assuming that my reading a headline today confirming the occurrence of a naval battle yesterday is sufficient for the occurrence of the battle. Therefore the occurrence of the battle is necessary for my reading the headline. Similarly, my not reading the headline is sufficient for the battle's not having occurred. Therefore the battle's not having occurred is necessary for my not reading the headline. If the battle did not occur, it is not within my power to read the headline, while if the battle did occur, it is not within my power not to read the headline. But either the battle did or did not occur. So either it is not within my power to read the headline or not within my power not to read it. Thus I am not free with regard to reading the headline.

The second proof assumes that my issuing an order today is sufficient for the occurrence of a naval battle tomorrow. Therefore the occurrence of the battle is necessary for my issuing the order. Similarly, my not issuing the order is sufficient for the battle's not occurring. Therefore the battle's not occurring is necessary for my not issuing the order. If the battle will not occur, it is not within my power to issue the order, while if the battle will occur, it is not within my power not to issue the order. But either the battle will or will not occur. So either it is not within my power to issue the order or not within my power not to issue it. Thus I am not free with regard to issuing the order.

THREE-VALUED LOGIC AND THE REALITY OF TIME

While Taylor's argument has been vigorously debated, its fatalistic conclusion can surely be avoided if statements about future contingencies are considered not as true or as false but as possessing a third truth value, namely, indeterminate. The best-known system of three-valued logic was created by Jan Lukasiewicz (1878–1956), who formulated it specifically for the purpose of defusing the threat of the fatalistic argument. The system was further developed in the work of A.N. Prior.

In such a three-valued logic propositions may change truth value from one time to another. For example, the statement 'A naval battle will occur tomorrow' may be indeterminate today and true tomorrow.

It would follow that time is real, since it can affect a proposition's truth value. And it would also follow that the mere passage of time can eliminate future possibilities and thereby restrict a person's powers to act in alternative ways.

Is it necessary to accept these views in order to affirm human freedom? That is the issue at the heart of the philosophical problem of fatalism.

See also FREE WILL.

BIBLIOGRAPHY

Albritton, R.: 'Present truth and future contingency', *Philosophical Review* 66 (1957), 29–46.
Cahn, S.M.: *Fate, Logic, and Time* (New Haven, CT and London: Yale University Press, 1967; repr. Atascadero, CA: Ridgeview Publishing Company, 1982).
Pike, N.: 'Divine omniscience and voluntary action', *Philosophical Review* 74 (1965), 27–46.
Prior, A.N.: *Formal Logic* (Oxford: Oxford University Press, 1962).

Rescher, N.: 'A version of the "master argument" of Diodorus', *Journal of Philosophy* 63 (1966), 438–45.
Ryle, G.: *Dilemmas* (Cambridge: Cambridge University Press, 1954).
Taylor, R.: 'The problem of future contingencies', *Philosophical Review* 66 (1957), 1–28.
Taylor, R.: 'Fatalism', *Philosophical Review* 71 (1962), 56–66.

STEVEN M. CAHN

Fichte, Johann Gottlieb (1762–1814), Although he is generally regarded as the first major metaphysician of the German idealist tradition. The main aim of Fichte's early (1794) *Wissenschaftslehre* ('Doctrine of Science') was to eliminate the last remnants of metaphysics in KANT's transcendental philosophy. Fichte's starting point was Kant's limitation of knowledge to possible experience. He argued that Kant had violated his own limitation upon knowledge by postulating the existence of the thing-in-itself, the noumenal self and the highest good, for these entities could not be verified in any possible experience (*see* NOUMENAL/PHENOMENAL). Fichte attempted to eliminate such entities by extending to them Kant's doctrine of regulative ideas: the thing-in-itself, the noumenal self and the highest good are not statements about what exists, but prescriptions for enquiry and moral conduct.

Fichte is often interpreted as an Absolute Idealist, that is, as someone who holds that all reality is created by a universal ego which is within the consciousness of everyone alike. But Fichte insisted, true to his regulative reading of metaphysical principles, that the absolute ego is only a moral ideal. It is more accurate to describe Fichte's idealism as 'ethical idealism' since he held that all reality *ought* to be ideal, that we *ought* to strive to make all of nature submit to our rational demands.

Fichte's *Wissenschaftslehre* was the final grand attempt in the classical tradition to sustain the claim of epistemology to be *phi-*

losophia prima, the presuppositionless starting point of philosophy. Like DESCARTES, LOCKE and Kant, Fichte regarded self-knowledge as the most plausible starting point of philosophy; he insisted, however, that epistemology could become a *philosophia prima* only if it possessed an adequate theory of self-knowledge. The abiding concern of Fichte's *Wissenschaftslehre* in all its many versions from 1794 to 1813, and its continuing interest to us today, consists in its reflections on the problem of self-knowledge. Fichte argued that previous attempts to explain the possibility of self-knowledge fail, because the self is hypostasized, distinguished from its knowledge of itself. If we make the self distinct as from the knowledge of itself, then we lapse into an infinite regress in the attempt at self-knowledge. To avoid such problems Fichte sketched a theory of self-knowledge according to which the self is 'posited' or constituted by its acts of knowing itself. Self-knowledge is essential to the very nature of subjectivity, so that the subject is only what it knows itself to be.

See also HYPOSTASIS, REIFICATION; IDEALISM; KANTIANISM.

WRITINGS

Werke (Berlin: 1845–6); ed. I. Fichte (Berlin: de Gruyter, 1971).
Gesammtausgabe der bayerischen Akademie der Wissenschaften ed. R. Lauth and H. Jakob (Stuttgart: Frommann, 1970).
The Science of Knowledge ed. P. Heath and J. Lachs (Cambridge: Cambridge University Press, 1982).

BIBLIOGRAPHY

Breazeale, D.: 'Fichte's Aenesidemus review and the transformation of German Idealism', *Review of Metaphysics* 34 (1981), 545–68.
Breazeale, D.: 'How to make an idealist: Fichte's "refutation of dogmatism" and the problem of the starting point of the *Wissenschaftslehre*', *The Philosophical Forum* 19 (1987–8), 97–123.
Cassirer, E.: *Das Erkenntnisproblem in der Philosophie und Wissenschaft der neueren Zeit* 3 vols, Vol. 3, *Die nachkantische Systeme* (Darmstadt: Wissenschaftliche Buchgesellschaft, 1974), 126–216.
Copleston, F.: *The History of Philosophy* Vol. VII (New York: Doubleday, 1965).
Gardiner, P.: 'Fichte and German idealism', in *Idealism Past and Present* ed. G. Vesey (Cambridge: Cambridge University Press, 1982), 111–26.
Guéroult, M.: *L'Evolution et la structure de la doctrine de la science chez Fichte* (Paris: Société d'Edition, 1930).
Henrich, D.: *Fichtes ursprüngliche Einsicht* (Frankfurt: Klostermann, 1967).
Kelly, G.: *Idealism, Politics and History* (Cambridge: Cambridge University Press, 1969).
Lachs, J.: 'Fichte's idealism', *American Philosophical Quarterly* 9 (1972), 311–18.
Leon, X.: *Fichte et son temps* 3 vols (Paris: Armand Colin, 1954).
Mandt, A.J.: 'Fichte's idealism in theory and practice', *Idealistic Studies* 14 (1984), 127–47.
Neohauser, F.: *Fichte's Theory of Subjectivity* (Cambridge: Cambridge University Press, 1990).

FREDERICK BEISER

fictional truth, objects and characters The problem of fiction concerns the correct analyses of the facts expressed by the following kinds of sentences:

(1) Augustus worshipped (the god) Jupiter.
(2) Jupiter doesn't exist.
(3) According to Roman myth, Jupiter exists.
(4) In Shakespeare's play, Hamlet is a prince.

A simple analysis suggests, for example, that (1) is true if, and only if, the object named 'Augustus' stands in the relation of worshipping to the object named 'Jupiter'. But then what kind of object does 'Jupiter' name, and how should one reconcile the appeal to such an object with (2)?

MEINONG was one of the first philosophers to take these questions seriously, though his naive view of fictional objects was undermined by objections raised by RUSSELL. Russell preferred to analyse away reference to fictions by first treating (1) as shorthand for the sentence 'Augustus worshipped the most powerful god in the Roman pantheon', and then analysing this latter as: there is an x such that x is a god more powerful than any other in the Roman pantheon and such that Augustus worshipped x. But this analysis fails to preserve the truth of (1), for on Russell's own view, there is (i.e. there exists) no such object.

The 'free logicians' and others have adopted Russell's view that names like 'Jupiter' and descriptions like 'the monster I dreamed about last night' do not denote objects. Free logicians, unlike Russell, treat such expressions as genuine terms (free logic is the study of non-denoting terms). But they have trouble distinguishing the truth of (1) from the falsehood 'Augustus worshipped Odin', for if neither 'Jupiter' nor 'Odin' are denoting terms, there is no principled way to distinguish the truth conditions of the two sentences. Free logic also fails to distinguish names and descriptions which clearly denote fictional objects from those such as 'the King of France in 1991' and 'the Earth's second moon' which denote nothing whatsoever. By contrast, there is a group of neo-Russellians who think that names like 'Jupiter' signify concepts (or properties) rather than objects. For them, (1) expresses a relationship between an object (Augustus) and a concept (the concept expressed by 'Jupiter'); and (2) expresses the fact that the concept Jupiter has no instances. However, this analysis of (1), if generalized, abandons the simple idea that, for example, 'x worships Bhagwan Rajneesh' expresses a two-place relation between x and an existing object. Moreover, the analysis of (4) becomes problematic,

since concepts do not exemplify the property of being a prince, not even in the context of a play. So these philosophers must alter our understanding of ordinary sentences like 'Hamlet is a prince.'

Consider, then, the philosophers who, following Meinong, agree that there are fictional objects and try to offer a metaphysical account of them. Such philosophers claim only to logically quantify over fictions (the same way they quantify over numbers or other abstract objects), not that such objects physically exist. To straighten out the inconsistencies in Meinong's naive theory, these authors focus on the relationships that fictional objects bear both to the properties attributed to them in their respective stories and to their other properties. For example, Hamlet's identity as an object seems to be bound up with the properties of being a prince, wanting to avenge his father's murder, being moody and indecisive, etc., all of which are attributed to him in the play. But these properties specify Hamlet's identity only incompletely, for there are many properties F such that neither F nor not-F is attributed to Hamlet in the play. Moreover, (2) and (3) demonstrate that a fictional object does not straightforwardly *exemplify* the properties attributed to it in the relevant story. Meinong's naive theory of fictional objects did not properly sort out these problems.

However, Terence Parsons, and others, have recently solved them by following Meinong's student Ernst Mally's idea of distinguishing *nuclear* (ordinary) and *extranuclear* (extraordinary) properties of objects. Objects are identified in terms of their nuclear properties, and Parsons's theory allows for objects that are incomplete with respect to their nuclear properties (though objects must be complete with respect to their extranuclear properties). Hamlet is treated as an object exemplifying just those *nuclear* properties attributed to him in the play, and so by (4), he exemplifies being a prince. Intentional properties and the property of existence are taken to be extranuclear, and so one cannot infer that Jupiter exists from (3). (1) and (2) are simply analysed as extranuclear properties of Jupiter.

A second group of neo-Meinongians uses an alternative idea of Mally's for solving these problems (see Zalta, 1988). These philosophers distinguish two modes of predication (i.e., two ways of having a property): *exemplifying* a property and *encoding* a property. Physically existing objects only exemplify properties, but fictional and other abstract objects both exemplify and encode properties. Every object must be complete with respect to its exemplified properties, but a fictional or other abstract object may be incomplete with respect to its encoded properties. Thus, Hamlet is treated as an abstract object that encodes just the properties he exemplifies in the play. The copula 'is' in (4) therefore expresses exemplification, and it follows from (4) that Hamlet encodes the property of being a prince (this encoding predication provides the sense in which the simple, unprefixed sentence 'Hamlet is a prince' is true). Analogously, (3) implies only that Jupiter encodes existence. However, (1) and (2) express properties that Jupiter exemplifies.

One last group of philosophers that should be mentioned are those who approach the problem of fiction by examining the nature of make-believe and pretence. These 'pretence theorists' investigate both the intentional activity in which we engage when constructing or apprehending fictions and the psychological and epistemological attitudes that underlie such judgements as (1)–(4). Many of these pretence theorists ultimately agree that we have to quantify over fictional objects in order to make sense of pretence, but while some have offered analyses of (1)–(4), none as yet have offered a complete account of what fictional characters are.

See also EXISTENCE.

BIBLIOGRAPHY

Meinong, A.: 'Über Gegenstandstheorie', *Untersuchungen zur Gegenstandstheorie und Psychologie* ed. A. Meinong (Leipzig: 1904); trans. R. Chisholm, I. Levi and D. Terrell, 'On the theory of objects', in *Realism and the Background of Phenomenology* ed. R.M. Chisholm (Glencoe: The Free Press, 1960), 76–117.

Parsons, T.: *Nonexistent Objects* (New Haven, CT: Yale University Press, 1980).

Russell, B.: 'On denoting', *Mind* 14 (1905), 479–93.

Zalta, E.: *Intensional Logic and the Metaphysics of Intentionality* (Cambridge, MA: Bradford/MIT Press, 1988).

EDWARD N. ZALTA

finite/infinite Crudely speaking, the finite is the limited; the infinite is the endless. As history shows, however, such crudeness can be unfortunate. ZENO's puzzle of how anyone could run a mile if having first to traverse a half-mile, then a quarter-mile, etc., is today often dismissed by saying that infinite sequences can have finite limits. Again, an argument in KANT's First Antinomy (*Critique of Pure Reason*, 1781), that infinite past time could not terminate today, forgets that an infinite line could have *one* end. On the other hand, space would be finite but unending if it were 'closed', curving round and joining up with itself. This ruins another argument of the Antinomy, that any world of finite size would have to be surrounded by infinite emptiness.

Other difficulties have likewise succumbed to mathematical advances. For instance al-Ghazali's (1058–1111) stumbling-block, that if time had been flowing for ever then Saturn would have orbited exactly as often as Jupiter instead of only half as often, merely illustrates CANTOR's claim that the numbers in the infinite sequence starting '2, 4, 6 . . .' can be placed in one-to-one correspondence with (and are in that way 'just as many as') those in the sequence starting '1, 2, 3, 4, 5, 6 . . . .' Mathematicians readily accept this – together with such oddities as that an infinite hotel with all rooms filled can welcome infinitely many further guests, and that there are endlessly many infinities each larger than the last, only the smallest being countable in infinite time.

We do not know whether the COSMOS is finite or infinite, in time and in space. Indeed, if time and space are infinitely divisible then what is finite by one measure may be infinite by another. Processes perhaps ran faster and faster, without limit, the earlier they were in the Big Bang. In a gravitationally produced Big Crunch, too, they might speed up limitlessly. By the 'clocks' of these processes themselves, time would then be infinite during what would be, by clocks like ours, infinitely hectic initial and final milliseconds. And similarly with tiny stretches of present-day space and time if they are infinitely finely structured – which can seem plausible to students of fractals. An infinitely wriggling fractal curve can fill part or all of a square or even a cube, yet have a structure 'simple' in that it looks the same at all magnifications. The structure might be tape-measure-like.

Many physicists believe that at Planck dimensions (10^{-33} cm and 10^{-43} secs approximately) space and time become 'foamy', ill-structured, which rules out infinity of the kind just now considered, infinity of detail within endlessly divisible milliseconds or millilitres. It could still be, though, that space is 'open', not curving round upon itself, in which case our expanding universe extended – says General Relativity – for infinitely many kilometres even in its first seconds, and will do so for endless future years. (Yes, infinite space can expand.) On the simplest models it then contains infinitely many galaxies and, presumably, infinitely many Earthlike planets. Intelligent life might last in it for ever, less and less energy being needed for information processing as temperatures fell.

If our universe were instead gravitationally 'closed', spatially finite, then it might oscillate indefinitely (Bang, Crunch, Bang, Crunch, Bang . . .) so it could still be infinite temporally. Further, it might be only one of endlessly many 'universes'. These could occur as bubbles in a perpetually inflating space, or their spaces and times might be fully separate.

Such scenarios yield problems for probability theory. Someone seemingly walking the waves had much preferably be viewed as treading a sandbar rather than as benefiting from how unusually many water molecules chance to push upwards at appropriate moments; yet how can this be preferable in an infinite cosmos in which both kinds of event happen endlessly often? An answer is that infinitely numerous events can – like points in and outside bull's-eyes – have *ranges* differing in extent.

Physicists often treat infinities (e.g. infinite densities) as signs of error, while philosophers tend to dislike any unending chain of explanations. As LEIBNIZ remarked, one could well keep asking why a book was *about geometry* even if it were explained to be the last of infinitely many, each copied from its predecessor. For AQUINAS as for many others, an endless past sequence of causes would need God as its timeless ground. God's infinitude, which includes unlimited power, presents us with a severe Problem of Evil. The suggestion, however, is that it is an explanatory terminus so very tidy that we must accept it despite how it makes murders and earthquakes puzzling. Is it genuinely tidy, though? May it not be boundlessly complex, hence infinitely messy? A reply is that God's unlimited complexity (of thought, for instance) is simpler than anything limited would be. The infinite fits a description so wondrously brief: namely, *it leaves nothing out!* There is then some pressure to say that the cosmos is God, or part of God. SPINOZA held that anything outside God would 'limit' him, destroying his infinitude.

Others, however, find nothing self-contradictory in the existence of many entities each having the infinitude Spinoza described – possession of infinitely many attributes from which infinitely many things follow. (There could be infinitely many such entities unless indiscernibles (*see* IDENTITY OF INDISCERNIBLES) must be *one and the same*. How many beings lacking spatial extension, and identical in all but spatial position, could be brought to the point of an infinitely sharp pin?) And still others urge that God's infinitude is Pure Being, Being not 'limited' by attributes. *That God knows everything* is then treated as an anthropomorphism scarcely more adequate than *that he is ignorant.* If Pure Being is next described as Pure Activity, this may express the Neoplatonic doctrine (*see* NEOPLATONISM) that God is a timeless requirement that a good cosmos exist, a requirement not only ethical but also able to create innumerable complex situations without guidance from any thought process. The ethical need for the infinite was nicely captured by Bruno when he argued for innumerable worlds. One cannot have too much of a good thing, said he. If our world were but one among infinitely many, would it be morally permissible to annihilate it? No!

Infinite situations can alternatively be argued for without appeal either to physical cosmology or to God. A principle of plenitude may be portrayed as stating democratically (or at any rate *simply* – another denial that only the finite is simple) that all possible things exist somewhere. Again, modal realism holds that they all exist with logical inevitability: 'being possible but not actual' just means existing elsewhere than in the speaker's own world.

See also CONTINUUM; COSMOLOGY; MODALITIES AND POSSIBLE WORLDS; PANTHEISM; POSSIBLE WORLDS; WHY THERE IS SOMETHING; WORLD.

BIBLIOGRAPHY

Dyson, F.J.: 'Time without end: physics and biology in an open universe', *Reviews of Modern Physics* 51 (1979), 447–60.
Farrer, A.M.: *Finite and Infinite* (London: Dacre Press, 1943).
Linde, A.D.: 'Eternally existing, self-reproducing, chaotic inflationary universe', *Physics Letters B* 175 (1986), 395–400.
Nozick, R.: *Philosophical Explanations* (Oxford: Clarendon Press, 1981), 121–37.
Thomson, J.: 'Infinity in mathematics and logic', in *The Encyclopedia of Philosophy* ed. P. Edwards, 8 vols (New York: Macmillan, 1967) Vol. 4, 183–90.

JOHN LESLIE

form *see* MATTER/FORM

free will The topic of free will brings together a number of independently important metaphysical notions: necessity and contingency, CAUSATION and chance, action and event, mind and MECHANISM. These make the topic an especially complex and challenging one. What gives the problem of free will its poignancy, however, is its connection with several central human values. In this way, morality has often been the mother of metaphysics.

In western philosophy, two related values have been prominent in discussions of free will. One is a concern with *moral responsibility* – the conditions of justified praise, blame, punishment, and similar aspects of moral practice. A second value concerns what might be called *autonomy* or self-determination: one's sense that one is not merely a passive bystander but indeed shapes one's own life from the world as one finds it and to that extent is the author of one's biography. The value of autonomy goes beyond an interpersonal concern for accountability. Threats to our autonomy are threats to our personal dignity; they demean our lives. Both of these values presuppose or involve a kind of freedom that turns out to be philosophically obscure.

THE CLASSICAL ISSUE

These two concerns animated the discussion of free will from the start. They were clearly at stake in the debate provoked by HOBBES three centuries ago. Hobbes's revolutionary project was to extend the new natural scientific theories to the understanding of human affairs. This meant to reduce human behaviour to 'matter in motion'. What we call 'voluntary behaviour' is no exception: it is behaviour that originates in the 'will', where the will is conceived as a desire or 'appetite' that leads to bodily motion in the 'direction' of the desired object. These motivational 'forces' are in turn understood to be incipient motions which are causally necessitated by other material processes extending beyond the body in space and time.

In the modern period, the history of the topic of free will largely consists of reflections on the implications of Hobbes's project. While Hobbes's science seems quaint by now, his reductionist vision is still very much alive. The seventeenth-century debate is therefore a good place to begin.

Hobbes himself insisted that this new understanding of human beings is consistent with the ordinary belief in freedom. For freedom, properly speaking, is the possession of an unimpeded will: 'A free agent is he that can do if he will, and forbear if he will' (Hobbes, 1654, p. 68). But 'Liberty and Necessity are consistent . . . the actions which men voluntarily do . . . (because they proceed from their will) proceed from liberty, and because every act of man's will . . . proceed from some cause, and that from another cause, in a continual chain, [voluntary actions] proceed from necessity.' Freedom, in short, is the power to do as one wills (Hobbes, 1651, p. 56).

Hobbes's contemporaries tended to find this doctrine morally shocking and metaphysically inadequate. What is needed, they insisted, is not just the power to do as one wills but the power to determine the disposition of one's will. As Hobbes's critics complained, without free will in this sense, human beings are degraded to the level of 'brute beasts', and the distinctively human practices of deliberation, consultation, and retribution would make no sense.

But Hobbes had no use for such a notion, nor did he think any important practices depended on this alleged power. Free agency is the power to do as one wills; free will would have to be the power to will as one wills, which is nonsense. No appeal to this nonsensical endowment is necessary to understand our common practices. Deliberation is simply the consideration of alter-

native courses of action; as Hobbes puts it, we deliberate only about what we think is possible. This is a causal process; which actions we perform depends upon what we will, and what we will depends upon our conception of the possible outcomes. So deliberation is not in vain. Similarly, punishment is the public provision of penalties for socially undesirable conduct. Punishment is thus a system for influencing deliberation and hence action. It is perfectly intelligible even if DETERMINISM is true. Indeed, its efficacy depends upon its location in a causal network.

But there is a difficulty in Hobbes's characterization of deliberation. On Hobbes's view everything is necessitated by what goes before. Nothing that does not occur *could* occur. If deliberation is about what one takes to be possible alternatives, then deliberation in a deterministic world involves false beliefs. It is not possible consistently to accept Hobbes's doctrines and to engage in deliberation.

To meet this point, Hobbes must modify his characterization of deliberation to say that it is a review of different actions that one takes to be *in one's power* in his sense. This just means that one supposes the outcome to depend on one's will. The point of deliberation is to assess the desirability of those outcomes that are in one's power. To put the point in terms of 'possibility', deliberation is the consideration of those actions or outcomes that one takes to be *conditionally possible*, relative to one's will. Things in one's power are possible in precisely this sense.

To make sense of deliberation, then, all that is needed are judgements of conditional possibilities. To deliberate whether to take path *a* or path *b*, one presupposes only that one is a free agent in Hobbes's sense: that one can take path *a* if one will to do so, and one can take path *b* if one wills to do so. Determinism does not imply that none of one's actions depends on one's will.

This attempt to define freedom without free will was sharply challenged about a hundred years later by REID. Reid's challenge is of great contemporary interest because it anticipates a number of important current positions. In effect, Reid argued that if we have no power over the will, we have no power whatever. His argument was this: 'to say that what depends upon the will is in a man's power, but the will is not in a man's power, is to say that the end is in his power, but the means necessary to that end are not in his power, which is a contradiction' (Reid, 1788, p. 329). The underlying principle here is, 'The effect cannot be in his power unless all the means necessary to its production be in its power' (ibid., p. 331). Since the will is a 'necessary means' to voluntary action, Hobbes's doctrine that we have no freedom of the will entails that we are totally powerless.

This principle permits of two interpretations, depending on whether 'means' is construed as 'necessary condition' or as 'means' in a stricter sense: that is, as conduct aimed at realizing some further end. On the first construal, the principle is this: 'If c is a necessary condition of e, and c is not in one's power, then e is not in one's power'. So construed, the principle is not true. The presence of oxygen is a necessary condition of one's lighting a match. But the fact that the presence of oxygen is not in one's power does not show that lighting the match is not in one's power. One's power and its exercise are contingent on all kinds of thing that are not necessarily in one's power. All that is required for one's power to light the match is that *some* necessary condition be in one's power and that the others *obtain* (whether by one's will or not).

Notice that a corresponding principle in terms of 'possibility' *is* valid: if c is a necessary condition of e, then if c is not possible, e is not possible. If it is not possible for oxygen to be present, then it is not possible for one to light the match. The difference between 'power' and 'possibility' is that some of the things not in one's power may be possible and thus obtain willy-nilly. It is open to Hobbes to maintain that the will to light the match is, like the presence of oxygen, a necessary condition that need not be in one's power.

On the second construal, where 'means' is taken in a strict sense, the principle seems to be true. If the only way one can light the match is to press the match head against the striker, and one cannot do that, then one cannot light the match. The reason why the principle holds for means in the strict sense is that, unlike other necessary conditions, if these are not in one's power (if one cannot take them), then they will not obtain.

But it seems clear that Hobbes would deny that the will to light the match *is* a means in the strict sense, precisely because it is not a voluntary action. 'The will' is a name for that desire that finally moves one to action. A voluntary action is something that proceeds from the will. The operation of the will is not an exercise of agency, but a function of the strength of appetite as determined by the agent's estimation of the relative harms and benefits of alternative courses of action, none of which is in one's 'own disposing'.

We come here to a fundamental divergence of outlook between Hobbes and Reid, as between compatibilists and 'libertarians' more generally. (Libertarians are those who insist that human beings are free in a way that precludes determinism.) Their dispute is not just about freedom but about what a human being is. For Reid, the will is not like an appetite, the object and strength of which are given by physiological and psychological conditions. As free agents, we determine what appetites, interests or motives we will act on: 'By the liberty of a moral agent, I understand a power over the determination of his own will' (Reid, 1788, p. 323). When a person is free in acting, the person determines the will that is expressed in the conduct. This determination is the most basic exercise of agency, and without it, none of our movements would exemplify active power. In contrast, Hobbes's reductionist programme, on Reid's view, implies that 'an intelligent being is an inert, inactive substance, which does not act but is acted upon' (ibid., p. 336). Hobbes can allow for only passive powers: the power to be moved by external forces.

Of course, Hobbes would protest this characterization, since he means to *analyse* activity and active power in terms of what depends upon and proceeds from the will. To speak of the person as a cause is either empty words or a shorthand way of referring to causal processes within the human body. For Hobbes, we are complicated causal systems and any intelligible account of freedom must be compatible with this truth. Libertarians rescue liberty from the net of necessity only by placing human beings beyond comprehension.

THE CONTEMPORARY CONTROVERSY

The classical debate established the framework of the contemporary controversy. Nevertheless, there are important differences in doctrine and emphasis. One difference derives from the shifting status of the doctrine of determinism. For generations, that doctrine seemed to bear the imprimatur of modern science. Therefore, as with Hobbes, much of the attraction of compatibilism came from the concern to make freedom and responsibility scientifically respectable. However, developments in twentieth-century physical theory have made determinism seem more of a dogma than a presupposition of rationality or scientific understanding. Consequently, in this respect, recent libertarians have had to be less defensive; to oppose determinism is not automatically to be anti-scientific.

But it is crucial to see that the burden of libertarianism is not only to oppose determinism. For the libertarian requirements for freedom would not be met merely by introducing indeterminacy into an otherwise Hobbesian picture – for example, by viewing a human being as a causal system whose output was highly probable, but not certain, given the antecedents. Suppose, for example, that such a being willed to take path *a* rather than *b*, and might have willed otherwise, given the totality of antecedent and concurrent conditions, including all the facts about the individual's desires, interests, values, preferences, beliefs, and so on. This 'liberty of indifference', as it used to be

called, would not suffice for moral liberty in Reid's sense. What is wanted is not just the absence of causal necessitation but causation by the agents themselves. Otherwise, we would have no more control over our conduct than we would if determinism were true.

Significantly, Reid's notion of necessity does not even imply causal determinism; he defines it as 'want of moral liberty' (Reid, 1788, p. 325), which could obtain in both a deterministic and indeterministic world. What destroys freedom (namely, necessity) is the lack of self-determination, and that results both when the will is determined by other events or states of affairs and when it is not determined at all. The negative requirement that the will not be causally necessitated by antecedent events is dictated by the positive requirement that the will be determined by the self.

The meaning and intelligibility of this requirement is as much an issue today as it was for Hobbes. (For an attempt to show how libertarianism can meet this requirement while avoiding the obscurities of agent-causation, see Kane, 1985.) It is this issue that makes compatibilism an important question even for those who do not believe in determinism, as many contemporary compatibilists do not. For if causal determinism seems threatening to freedom only because it is threatening to the libertarian conception of self-determination, then to abandon or reinterpret this requirement for freedom is to abandon the rationale for incompatibilism.

It should not be supposed that compatibilists must do without *any* notion of self-determination or autonomy; rather, they must do without any that requires causal indeterminacy. In this respect, contemporary compatibilists have improved upon Hobbes's treatment of freedom, which neglected important questions about the individual's will. On Hobbes's account, mice and men are equally free agents to the extent to which their wills are unimpeded. But a serious notion of autonomy has application only to reflexive beings who are capable of evaluational attitudes toward their own behaviour. Moreover, Hobbes's view ignores the relevance of various cognitive and volitional impairments to which human beings are susceptible; it is irrelevant on his view whether or not a person was severely addicted, phobic, hypnotized or brainwashed. But this neglect is not endemic to compatibilism. Recent compatibilists have had a lot more to say about the ways in which human beings can suffer from heteronomy, can be alienated from their own wills (see, for example, Frankfurt, 1971). (The point about mice is of course different from the point about the hypnotized or phobic. Mice lack autonomy not because their behaviour does not express their true selves, but because they do not have selves in the requisite sense.)

What compatibilists oppose, then, is not self-determination but the libertarian interpretation of that notion. They insist that any defensible and satisfiable requirement of self-determination will be compatible with determinism.

Nowadays, the most familiar incompatibilist argument proceeds independently of the condition of self-determination. The basic idea is that freedom requires the ability to do otherwise, whereas determinism rules this out:

(1) If determinism is true, then every action is causally necessitated.
(2) If every action is causally necessitated, we can never do otherwise than we do.
(3) If we can never do otherwise, then we are not free agents.
(4) Hence, if determinism is true, we are not free agents.
(5) If we are not free agents, then we are not responsible for our actions.

As we have been using the term 'determinism', (1) is true by definition (but see below). Therefore, the compatibilist must reject (2) or (3).

Hobbes would have accepted (2) and rejected (3). Only the actual is possible, and hence we cannot (unconditionally) do otherwise. Since free agency requires only that we can do otherwise *if* we will, free agency is compatible with determinism.

By and large, however, later compatibilists depart from Hobbes on this point; rather, they tend to identify free agency with being able to do otherwise, rejecting (2) and accepting (3). Neither choice is a fully happy one. The Hobbesian choice conflicts with the compelling thought that free agency requires *actual* ability to do otherwise. But to reject (2) instead, as subsequent compatibilists have tended to do, is to maintain that one can perform a causally impossible action.

The sense of paradox here, compatibilists maintain, is due to a systematic ambiguity in the word 'can': the 'can' of human ability is a different concept from the 'can' of causal possibility, and great philosophical mischief has resulted from their conflation. To support this, many have adopted a conditional analysis of 'can' (in the sense of 'is able to'); to say one is able to do otherwise is to say that one would do otherwise, if one chose (or willed, or tried . . .). Thus, there is no paradox in asserting that one might be able to do what is causally impossible.

Note that while ability is analysed conditionally, on this view, the ability itself is not conditional. Even when you do not will to do otherwise, you are (actually) able to do otherwise, so long as what you do depends on your will. Whereas Hobbes identifies free agency with conditional ability, this view identifies free agency with ability, conditionally defined. In both cases, it is the conditionalization that, at different points, blocks the foregoing argument.

But suppose the agent is unable to choose (or will or try . . .). Critics of the conditional analysis claim that whereas this supposition is perfectly consistent with the truth of the relevant conditional, it is obviously inconsistent with the belief that the agent was able to do otherwise. Therefore, the analysis fails. (On this debate, see Aune, 1967; Chisholm, 1967.) But the success of this criticism depends upon the relation between 'power' and 'possibility' that we discussed earlier. Here the critics are implicitly invoking Reid's principle: if you cannot will to do otherwise, then you cannot do otherwise.

As we have seen, this principle is problematic.

Another variation on compatibilism merits discussion here. Around the middle of the present century, a number of philosophers (under the influence of WITTGENSTEIN) rejected a presupposition of the classical debate, namely the idea that human action can coherently be subsumed under causal law. The language of action is conceptually and logically distinct from the language of causation. It is one thing to seek to explain bodily motion and quite another to explain human action. Human action is explained by *reasons* and *intentions* rather than causes; such explanations are therefore governed by the goal of making the individual's behaviour intelligible in terms of norms of rationality and social contexts. The explanation of bodily motion, however, is quite another matter, and is guided by a different set of interests entirely. Physiology might in principle be deterministic, these critics say. But to suppose that there might be deterministic explanations of human *action* is a conceptual mistake. (Representatives of this view include Ryle, 1949, and Melden, 1961.)

It would be misleading to classify these philosophers in the terms we have been employing. On the one hand, they reject the Hobbesian mechanist project completely; and they deny with libertarians that the social 'sciences' can and should become nomological. They are equally opposed, on the other hand, to the 'panicky metaphysics' of agent-causation. Human beings are neither Hobbesian machines nor the Cartesian ghosts that drive them. Still, they are compatibilists in the sense that they think that physical determinism is consistent with a belief in freedom and responsibility.

But the traditional problems are not avoided in this way. For even if the scope of deterministic explanation is in principle restricted to physical phenomena (or to phenomena physically described), compatibilism seems problematic. For if physical determinism is true, it is impossible for your body to move in any way other than its actual motion. This means that it is not possible that you will *move* your body in any different way, and hence that you will act in any way that requires a different bodily motion. If it is physically determined that your arm does not go up during a certain period, then it is not possible that you will signal the waiter, say, by raising your arm. Thus this version of compatibilism must explain how it can be the case that you are able to raise your arm during a time when it is causally impossible for your arm to go up. Therefore, the issues raised by the basic argument must still be confronted.

It is worth noting one further compatibilist response, this one inspired by HUME and MILL. Some compatibilists have tried to defuse determinism by dissociating it from 'necessity'. To say that determinism is true is simply to say that every event and state of affairs is capable of a (non-probabilistic) causal explanation. But causal explanations imply regularity, not necessity. They imply that whenever certain conditions obtain, certain other conditions obtain. They do not imply that any of these conditions *must* obtain. The idea is that the definition in the first premise of the basic argument involves an appeal to a philosophically suspect modality and should be rejected. (For this idea, see Ayer, 1954.)

Incompatibilism does indeed require a richer notion of determinism than a Humean can provide. But recent refinements of the basic argument have shown how to defend incompatibilism with comparatively modest modal assumptions. What is central to this refinement and to the definition of determinism it employs is the idea of a LAW OF NATURE. Determinism is the thesis that the set of laws of nature, conjoined with the set of true descriptions of the world at a particular time, entail every true description of the world at every time. Incompatibilism is the claim that determinism entails that we can never do otherwise than we do. The argument is this. If determinism is true, then the laws of nature and a complete description of the world before you were born imply your present behaviour. Therefore, you can do otherwise only if you can change the laws of nature or change the description of the world before you were born. Neither of these things is in your power. Therefore, it is not in your power to behave otherwise. Since this is true for all times and people, it follows that if determinism is true, then no one can ever do otherwise. (This argument is developed in van Inwagen, 1983.)

A merit of this argument is that it does not require a particular view of causal necessity or a full analysis of 'law': it requires only the assumptions that no human being is able to alter the past (or falsify a law of nature about the past), and that, whatever else they are, laws of nature identify natural correlations that no human being is able to falsify. While the latter assumption might be challenged by a few Humeans, it seems extremely plausible. Much of the current literature is devoted to an examination of this argument. (A useful discussion can be found in Fischer, 1986.)

CONCLUSION

While subsequent developments have sharpened and focused the issues, the basic questions remain what they were in the seventeenth century. For the compatibilist, the question is how a series of natural processes and events over which you have no control (for which you are not accountable) can result in processes and events over which you do have control (for which you are accountable). The fundamental challenge for libertarians is to show how an indeterministic power to do otherwise can be harmonized with self-determination.

Clearly these questions are not in the end 'purely metaphysical'. For what is needed is a theory that best respects both our scientific understanding and our values of accountability and autonomy. Our sense of the appropriate articulation of the concepts of freedom and power cannot proceed independently of the values with which those concepts are linked; and our understanding of those values must be informed by a sense of what is metaphysically coherent. Some are sceptical about the possibility of harmo-

nizing these things. The problem of free will has proven so intractable, that a pessimistic conclusion cannot be dismissed out of hand. And one important philosophical task is to trace out the ways in which we might live with this conclusion. But in view of the manifold complexity of this topic, pessimism would be somewhat hasty. All that can fairly be said is that it is too soon to say. (Some have thought that we would fare rather better without the 'illusion' of free will; so the acceptance of a 'pessimistic' conclusion about the philosophical problem might be taken as a hopeful step in human affairs. For one sceptical view, see Honderich, 1988. For a diagnosis of the sources of scepticism, see Nagel, 1986.)

See also ACTION THEORY; CAUSATION; DETERMINISM.

BIBLIOGRAPHY

Aune, B.: 'Hypotheticals and "can"', *Analysis* 27 (1967), 191–5.

Ayer, A.J.: 'Freedom and necessity', in his *Philosophical Essays* (New York: St Martin's Press, 1954), 271–84.

Chisholm, R.M.: 'He could have done otherwise', *Journal of Philosophy* 64 (1967), 409–17.

Fischer, J.M.: 'Van Inwagen on free will', *The Philosophical Quarterly* 36 (1986), 252–60.

Frankfurt, H.: 'Freedom of the will and the concept of the person', *Journal of Philosophy* 68 (1971), 5–20.

Hobbes, T.: *Leviathan* (1651); repr. in *British Moralists: 1650–1800* Vol. I, ed. D.D. Raphael (Oxford: Oxford University Press, 1969), 18–60.

Hobbes, T.: *Of Liberty and Necessity* (1654); repr. in *British Moralists: 1650–1800*, Vol. I, ed. D.D. Raphael (Oxford: Oxford University Press, 1969), 61–70.

Honderich, T.: *The Consequences of Determinism* (New York: Oxford University Press, 1988).

Kane, R.: *Free Will and Value* (Albany, NY: State University of New York Press, 1985).

Melden, A.I.: *Free Action* (London: Routledge and Kegan Paul, 1961).

Nagel, T.: *The View from Nowhere* (New York: Oxford University Press, 1986).

Reid, T.: 'The liberty of the moral agent', in his *Essays on the Active Powers* (1788); in *Inquiry and Essays*, ed. R.E. Beanblossom and K. Lehrer (Indianapolis, IN: Hackett Publishing Company, 1983), 297–368.

Ryle, G.: *The Concept of Mind* (New York: Barnes and Noble, 1949).

van Inwagen, P.: *An Essay on Free Will* (New York: Oxford University Press, 1983).

GARY WATSON

Frege, Gottlob (1848–1925) German mathematician, logician and philosopher. One of the earliest writings of Frege that is of interest to contemporary philosophers is the 1879 monograph, *Begriffsschrift* or *Concept-script*. The work introduced second-order logic and new notation, a fragment of which was the first notation adequate to express first-order logic as we know it. Frege envisioned *Begriffsschrift* as the first part of a project designed to define the real numbers from purely logical concepts and to show, by proving basic truths of arithmetic from definitions and logical laws, that all mathematics, with the exception of Euclidean geometry, was ultimately a branch of logic. This project was initially described in a philosophical monograph, *Foundations of Arithmetic* published in 1884 and its details were to have been carried out in a later, mathematical work, *Basic Laws of Arithmetic*. *Basic Laws* was to be published in three parts: a part which sets out the basic laws of logic, a part in which the positive integers are defined and the basic laws of arithmetic are proved, and a part in which the real numbers are defined and the foundations laid for assimilating analysis to logic. Volume I of *Basic Laws*, which contained Part I of the project and the beginning of Part II, was published in 1893. But when the second volume, published in 1903, was in press, Frege received a now-famous letter

in which RUSSELL showed that the logical system set up in Volume I was inconsistent. The source of this inconsistency was the addition, to the original *Begriffsschrift* laws, of Basic Law V – an addition which was essential to Frege's formulation of the definitions of the positive integers. Ultimately, Frege realized that the project he had conceived could not be carried out.

Although Frege's writings are primarily concerned with mathematics and logic, they are also read as addressing a traditional metaphysical question: what sorts of entities are there? Frege's apparent answer is that there are functions of various levels, concepts and objects. Not all objects are in physical space. In addition to the external world of physical objects and the internal world of ideas there is, Frege says (1984, p. 363), a third realm. The objects belonging to this realm include thoughts (what sentences express or, using Frege's term, their senses) as well as numbers, extensions of concepts and senses of other sorts of expressions. Truths about these objects are eternal and independent of us and our thought. Although Frege himself never uses the term *abstrakt* to describe these objects, most contemporary scholars attribute to him the view that these objects are abstract, a latter-day version of PLATONISM (see Resnik, 1980, 26–7, 161–71; Dummett, 1981, 481–98; for an opposing view see Weiner, 1990, 177–84). The failure of Frege's attempt to show that the truths of arithmetic can be proved from logical laws and definitions has been widely, although not universally (see Wright, 1983) taken to show the untenability of Frege's view that numbers are objects that are objective.

Frege's notion of concept is less widely discussed today but, for Frege, was probably more important. In a jotted note dated 5 August 1906 and headed 'What may I regard as the result of my work' Frege wrote, 'It is almost all tied up with the concept-script, a concept construed as a function' (1979, p. 184). The notion of concept, he says (1984, p. 133), belongs to logic, rather than psychology. Concepts are what can be predicated or said of objects

(1984, p. 182). Existence is a property of concepts (1984, p. 188) and a concept is that which has number (1984, p. 114). Although Fregean concepts seem similar to the more familiar UNIVERSALS or properties, there are important differences. Fregean concepts must have sharp boundaries; that is, they must be either true or false of each object (1984, pp. 133, 148; 1980a, p. 87). There can be no VAGUENESS nor can there be range limitations. Since our understanding of what it is to be bald is irrevocably vague, we have no concept of baldness. Indeed, even our apparently precise mathematical concepts are not, on Frege's view, concepts at all. For instance, if primeness is to be a legitimate concept it must be determinately true or false, not only of each integer, but of each real number, person or house. Thus, on Frege's view, because our conceptions of baldness and primeness do not meet his requirements, baldness cannot be predicated of a person nor primeness of an integer – such defective apparent concepts are 'inadmissible sham concepts' (1980b, p. 145). Moreover, this is the only requirement for the legitimacy of a concept. Concepts (such as 'square circle') under which no objects fall, are legitimate (1984, pp. 134, 226–8, 1980a, pp. 87–8, 105–6; 1964, pp. 11–12).

Frege's sharp boundary requirement and its consequences may seem absurd to someone with traditional metaphysical interests. And his discussions of the predicative, unsaturated (1984, pp. 187, 281–2) or incomplete (1984, p. 193) nature of concepts may seem even more absurd. According to Frege, what can be said about objects cannot be said about concepts (1984, p. 189). Consequently there is no identity relation between concepts (1984, p. 200). More mysteriously, virtually every attempt to say something about concepts will result in failure or nonsense. Because concepts are predicative, on Frege's view, nothing can be predicated of them. The expression 'the concept horse' cannot stand for a concept because it is not a predicative expression. If the expression does stand for anything, it stands for an object. Thus the claim, 'The concept horse is a concept', is false (1984, pp. 182–94, 81–283; 1980a, pp. 63, 77). Indeed, the predicate 'is a concept' is itself defective, since it can only signify something that is true or false of objects.

All of these exotic views are straightforward consequences of Frege's understanding of logic and of concept as a logical notion. Another consequence is that Frege cannot say, as part of an answer to the question 'What sort of entities are there?', 'There are concepts.' To understand why this is so, it is important to see what Frege means when he says that he construes a concept as a function.

The function/object distinction is first drawn in his Begriffsschrift and discussed throughout his writings. He says that, when an expression such as '$2.x^3 + x$' is used to designate a function, the function is actually designated by what is present over and above the letter 'x' (1984, p. 140). Frege suggests that this might be indicated by writing '$2.(\ )^3 + (\ )$'. He calls functions, and signs for functions, incomplete or 'unsaturated' (1984, pp. 141, 290). An object, on the other hand, is anything that is not a function and an object-expression has no empty place (1984, p. 147). The result of completing a function with an object (or argument) gives us the value of the function for the argument. For example, the value of the function designated by '$2.(\ )^3 + (\ )$' for the object designated by '1' can be designated by '$2.(1)^3 + 1$', i.e. 3. This is an example of a one-place first-level function, that is, a function that must be completed by one object. There are also functions of higher levels, functions with many places and unequal-level functions (1964, pp. 72–8).

This explanation of Frege's function/object distinction may seem to be nothing more than an awkward way of describing the mathematical notion of function. But, while the origin of his notion is in analysis, there are important differences between the mathematical understanding of function and Frege's understanding of function. Frege not only admits objects without restriction as arguments and values of functions, he also *requires* that a function have a value for each object. There can be no functions, for example, which take only numbers for arguments. Further, Frege includes, among his function-expressions, any incomplete expression. Such non-mathematical expressions as 'the mother of ( )' or '( ) is bald' are incomplete and, thus, function-expressions. It is not difficult to think of the former expression as yielding a value for an argument, since the result of completing it with an object-expression appears to be an expression that picks out some person (i.e. some object). On the other hand, it is more difficult to regard '( ) is bald' as a function expression. The result of completing this expression appears to be, not an expression that picks out an object, but a sentence.

In Frege's early writings, this seems less odd. One reason is that he frequently refers to the argument or value of a function as the content (*Inhalt*) of an expression. And it does not sound unreasonable to say that the content of a sentence is a function of the contents of its constituents. From 1891 on, however, Frege splits the content of an expression in two parts: its sense (*Sinn*) and its meaning (*Bedeutung*). The interpretation of Frege's sense/meaning distinction is both difficult and controversial. Frege says that the sense of an expression is its mode of presentation or value for knowledge (*Erkenntniswert*) (1984, p. 157) and that it is objective. But he provides little sustained discussion of what senses are, and the comments about sense that are scattered throughout his writings sometimes contradict one another.

The issues surrounding the correct interpretation (and translation) of *Bedeutung* are even more controversial. Language is typically used to talk about an extra-linguistic reality. One would expect an account of this use of language to include an account of the relation that holds between an expression and the piece of reality that the expression can be used to talk about. The relation between a name and its bearer looks like a paradigm. If Frege means to be providing an analysis of the workings of language, the relation between an expression and its meaning or *Bedeutung* is surely meant to play this role. Unfortunately, on this sort of interpretation there is a difficulty with the application of Frege's function/object analysis to sentences.

Sentences have no empty places thus, Frege says (1984, p. 147), a sentence must mean (or stand for) an object. On his view, sentences pick out, not everyday objects, but truth values. There are two truth values: the True and the False. And Frege writes, 'These two objects are recognized, if only implicitly, by everybody who judges something to be true – and so even by a sceptic' (1984, p. 163). This assimilation of sentences to object names has been vehemently criticized by DUMMETT, who argues that an analysis of the workings of language requires sentences and object names to have different logical roles (Dummett, 1981, pp. 182–4).

Many commentators today, however, do not hold that Frege was engaged in providing the sort of analysis of the workings of language that Dummett describes (see Sluga, 1980; Weiner, 1990). And if one abandons the assumption that Frege means to be providing such an analysis, it is not clear that there is a problem with Frege's treatment of sentences. For instance, it is possible that Frege understands the meaning of an expression simply as the contribution the expression makes to the truth value of sentences in which it appears. On this characterization, it is not particularly odd to view sentences themselves as having a meaning and of the meaning of a sentence as being its truth value.

What may still seem odd is Frege's introduction of the two truth values as objects. However, this apparent oddness is a result of the unwarranted assumption that the Fregean notion of objecthood is a familiar one. After introducing the True and the False as objects, Frege does not attempt to make his claim plausible by showing that the True and False are, in some respects, similar to everyday objects. Rather, he says,

'What I am calling an object can be more exactly discussed only in connection with concept and relation' (1984, pp. 163–4). The reasonableness of Frege's claim that truth values are objects depends on what it is to be an object in Frege's logical sense.

What, then, are Fregean objects? He says, 'An object is something that is not a function so that an expression for it does not contain any empty place' (1984, p. 147). But Frege never attempts to define the terms 'function' and 'object'. And, he writes (1984, pp. 147, 292), it is not possible to define these terms. One of the reasons is that the term 'function' is defective in much the way the term 'concept' is. The expression 'the function $F(x)$' cannot stand for a function and the expression 'is a function' designates something that can only be true (or false) of objects.

The defects of the terms 'function', 'concept' and 'object' prevent them from having a use in the expression of any theory that Frege would regard as correct. He recognizes that his attempts to use them in the expression of thoughts necessarily miss their mark. But given this situation, to what end can Frege possibly mean to be using them? These terms have a role to play in an important scientific enterprise that does not involve the statement of theories and laws. Frege argues that the primitive terms of a systematic science cannot be defined but can be introduced only by elucidatory propositions which involve ordinary, defective terms (1979, p. 207; 1984, p. 300). The purpose of elucidations is to achieve mutual understanding among investigators. Frege's own project requires the introduction of a systematic science of logic – a science whose laws are those in accord with which we must think if we 'are not to miss the truth' (1979, p. 149). Central to this aim is the introduction of a logical notation that permits the expression of all conceptual content of a statement – that is, of all content significant for inference. Frege uses the terms 'function', 'concept' and 'object' in elucidations designed to communicate the content of his primitive logical terms.

But this is not to say that the role of these defective terms is, or need be, limited to the initial introduction of the logical symbols in the opening sections of his *Begriffsschrift*. Frege uses, and discusses his understanding of, these terms throughout his writings. This is entirely appropriate. For, Frege says, the properties belonging to what is understood by the primitive terms of a science 'contain, as it were in a nutshell, its whole contents' (1984, p. 113). His discussions of the notions of function, concept and object are important and enlightening attempts to communicate the content of logic.

So the terms 'function', 'concept' and 'object', as Frege understands them, can play no role in the expression of any theory, metaphysical or otherwise. Further, the question 'What sort of entities are there?' makes sense only if it can be rephrased as 'What sort of objects are there?' Although Frege introduces some objects (e.g. the True), he attempts no systematic survey of the sorts of objects there are. His contribution to metaphysics is not a list of what sorts of objects there are. Rather, his contribution is to the assessment of the metaphysical enterprise. If Fregean functions and concepts play an important role in logic and science then, given the traditional aims of metaphysics, their nature must be a part of its subject matter. Yet, on Frege's conception of logic, nothing can be said about the nature of functions and concepts. His contribution is to show us how much of import metaphysical theories must leave out.

See also EXTENSION/INTENSION; PROPOSITION, STATE OF AFFAIRS; REFERENCE.

WRITINGS

Begriffsschrift, eine der arithmetischen nachgebildete Formelsprache des reinen Denkens (Halle: 1879); in *Frege and Gödel* ed. J. van Heijenoort, trans. Stefan Bauer Mengelberg (Cambridge MA: Harvard University Press, 1970), 5–82.

Die Grundlagen der Arithmetik (Breslau: 1884); trans. J.L. Austin, *The Foundations of Arithmetic* 2nd edn (Evanston, IL: Northwestern University Press, 1980[a]).

Grundgesetze der Arithmetik vol. I (Jena: 1893); trans. M. Furth, *The Basic Laws of Arithmetic* (Berkeley and Los Angeles: University of California Press, 1964).

Translations from the Philosophical Writings of Gottlob Frege ed. and trans. P.T. Geach and M. Black (Totowa, NJ: 1952); 3rd edn (Totowa, NJ: Rowman and Littlefield, 1980[b]).

Kleine Schriften ed. I. Angelelli (Hildesheim: 1967); ed. B. McGuinness, trans. M. Black *et al.*, *Collected Papers* (Oxford: Blackwell, 1984).

Nachgelassene Schriften ed. H. Hermes, F. Kambartel and F. Kaulbach (Hamburg, 1969); trans. P. Long and R. White, *Posthumous Writings* (Chicago: University of Chicago Press, 1979).

BIBLIOGRAPHY

Dummett, M.A.E.: *Frege Philosophy of Language* (London: 1973); 2nd edn (Cambridge, MA: Harvard University Press, 1981).

Resnik, M.D.: *Frege and the Philosophy of Mathematics* (Ithaca, NY: Cornell University Press, 1980).

Sluga, H.: *Gottlob Frege* (London: Routledge and Kegan Paul, 1980).

Weiner, J.: *Frege in Perspective* (Ithaca, NY: Cornell University Press, 1990).

Wright, C.: *Frege's Conception of Numbers as Objects* (Aberdeen: Aberdeen University Press, 1983).

JOAN WEINER

Freud, Sigmund (1856–1940) Austrian psychiatrist and founder of psychoanalysis. Freud was dedicated to science and the worldview which he took to go with it, and accordingly sought to provide a framework of concepts for understanding the mind as part of physical nature. In this he developed a range of views bearing on metaphysical questions about the mind.

In his 'Project for a scientific psychology' Freud advanced the idea that the brain stored and processed information by facilitating and inhibiting neural connections ('contact barriers'). In consequence, he held, mental processes could ultimately be understood as patterns of activation ('cathexis') in networks of differentially connected neurons. These he took to store neural representations of situations in which biologically significant drives, such as that of the infant to suck, were satisfied through appropriate behaviour, such as moving the body in such a way as successfully to nurse. Such representations linked need, perception (both internal and distal) and successful action; and they were automatically reactivated with the drives they served, so as to be overlain by further registrations of success and failure in doing so.

This model was framed to accord with clinical findings. These indicated that adult mental life was underlain by a series of unconscious prototypes, each based upon, and shaped by, those laid down in previous experience; and that these early paradigms could be reactivated in situations resembling or associated with those in which they had been laid down. (Thus the parents served as early paradigm objects of love and hate, as shown in the Oedipus complex; the relation to the breast served as a prototype of later satisfactions, early feeding as that of later acceptances and rejections, and so forth.)

Freud described the process of forming new prototypes of this kind as 'biological learning'. He took this to extend from such basic bodily activities as taking nourishment and eliminating waste through more complex behaviour, and also to encompass the learning of language, thus giving rise to the common-sense rational psychology of conscious mental life. Hence he saw daily human thought and action as directed by a densely overlain set of drive-through-action prototypes, rooted in early mastery of the body, but serving also as a constantly accumulating register of experience of all kinds.

The philosophical interest of this picture is just beginning to emerge, with the examination of connectionism, of which it is a detailed precursor. One aspect can be indicated by saying that the well-known connectionist exemplar, NETtalk, seems comparable to a 'reading machine' of the kind WITTGENSTEIN discussed at *Philosophical Investigations* sects 157ff.

See also MIND/BODY PROBLEM; PHYSICALISM, MATERIALISM.

WRITINGS

'Project for a scientific psychology', in *The Standard Edition of the Collected Psychological Works of Sigmund Freud* Vol. 1 (London: Hogarth, 1956), 283–388.

BIBLIOGRAPHY

Glymour, C.: 'Freud's androids', in *The Cambridge Companion to Freud* ed. J. Neu (Cambridge: Cambridge University Press, 1992), 44–85.
Pribram, K. and Gill, M.: *Freud's 'Project' Reassessed* (London: Hutchinson and Co., 1976).
Rosenberg, C.R. and Sejnowski, T.J.: 'Parallel networks that learn to pronounce English text', *Complex Systems* (1987), 145–68.
Wittgenstein, L.: *Philosophical Investigations* (Oxford: Blackwell, 1956).

JIM HOPKINS

function A function, traditionally, is what something is *for*. It is a special kind of effect or power, an effect something is 'supposed' to have. Although the human heart has a multitude of effects and dispositions, its ability to pump blood around the body has a special status that its other effects, such as making a thumping noise, do not have. Pumping blood is the heart's function.

Functions are related to goals and purposes. There has long been a suspicion that this family of 'teleological' concepts has no place in a modern scientific worldview, especially as ascriptions of function have a normative component; where there is function there can be *mal*function. In recent decades however, philosophers of science have argued convincingly that at least some functions can be made respectable. Functions are effects or powers which play a distinctive role in certain forms of explanation.

From the 1950s philosophers were concerned that an apparently common explanatory appeal to functions did not conform to prevailing standards for genuine explanation. Biologists appear to cite functions to explain why the functionally characterized entity exists within some larger system; to cite the function of the heart is apparently to say why our bodies contain them. But if explanations are inferences (Hempel, 1965), then we should be able to *infer* the existence of hearts within bodies from the fact that hearts can pump blood and from the role circulation plays in keeping us alive. Such an inference is not valid, as other devices could pump blood in people.

This debate was decisively reoriented by Larry Wright (1973, 1976). Wright argued that if a less demanding attitude to explanation is adopted, it becomes clear that in a variety of scientific and everyday contexts, it is possible to explain why something is there in terms of what it does. Wright argued that any effect which supports an explanation of this kind is a function: 'The function of X is that particular consequence of its being where it is which explains why it is there' (1976, p. 78). Paradigm cases are found in products of evolution by natural selection, and products of conscious design.

Functions, for Wright, are picked out from mere effects by their having a certain explanatory salience; they are effects which explain why something is there. But perhaps functions can be explanatorily salient effects with respect to different sorts of explanations as well. Cummins (1975) argued that philosophers had long been mistaken about the explanations functions are relevant to. In Cummins's analysis, functions are dispositions of components of larger systems, which contribute to the explanation of more complex dispositions and capacities displayed by this larger system. They explain how something is done, not why something is there.

Cummins's analysis was presented in opposition to Wright's, but there are good reasons for recognizing both conceptions of function. There is a point of agreement between the approaches: functions are effects distinguished by their explanatory salience. Wright and Cummins differ about the explanatory project involved, but there is no need to choose one project to the exclusion of the other. The functions of much evolutionary biology might be Wright's functions, while the functions of orthodox 'functionalist' philosophy of mind, when they are more than mere dispositions, can be understood as Cummins's functions.

Another tradition analyses functions as effects which contribute to goals, where the idea of a goal is independently analysed (Wimsatt, 1972; Boorse, 1976). As Wright argued, however, this view appears unable to distinguish between functions and fortuitous benefits; something can make a useful contribution, even a contribution integrated into the actions of a containing system, without being there *to* make this contribution.

Recent years have seen the development of more sophisticated analyses based upon the action of forces of selection, natural and conscious. This work is best understood as further elucidating Wright's sense of function. Though these theories tend to focus on biological functions, they can often be extended to other domains as well. Within this programme, some favour a historical view, locating functions in effects which explain the present existence of a structure in terms of past episodes of selection (Millikan, 1984; Neander, 1991). Others have proposed a 'forward-looking' approach, on which a function is an effect which bestows a propensity to succeed under selection (Bigelow and Pargetter, 1987). The explanatory significance of functions is clearer on a historical view; only the past can causally explain the present. However, propensity views respect the fact that many biologists explicitly distinguish between functional and historical questions about a trait (Tinbergen, 1963). One way of taking a middle road is to view functions as effects salient in *recent* episodes of selection maintaining a trait, where these selective forces may be different from those operating when the trait originated.

See also FUNCTIONALISM; TELEOLOGY.

BIBLIOGRAPHY

Bigelow, R. and Pargetter, R.: 'Functions', *Journal of Philosophy* 84 (1987), 181–97.

Boorse, C.: 'Wright on functions', *Philosophical Review* 85 (1976), 70–86.

Cummins, R.: 'Functional analysis', *Journal of Philosophy* 72 (1975), 741–65.

Hempel, C.G.: *Aspects of Scientific Explanation* (New York: Free Press, 1965).

Millikan, R.G.: *Language, Thought, and Other Biological Categories* (Cambridge, MA.: MIT Press, 1984).

Neander, K.: 'The teleological notion of "function" ', *Australasian Journal of Philosophy* 69 (1991), 454–68.

Tinbergen, N.: 'On the aims and methods of ethology', *Zeitschrift für Tierpsychologie* 20 (1963), 410–33.

Wimsatt, W.C.: 'Teleology and the logical structure of function statements', *Studies in the History and Philosophy of Science* 3 (1972), 1–80.

Wright, L.: 'Functions', *Philosophical Review* 82 (1973), 139–68.

Wright, L.: *Teleological Explanations* (Berkeley: University of California Press, 1976).

PETER GODFREY-SMITH

functionalism Functionalism is one of the great 'isms' that have been offered as solutions to the MIND/BODY PROBLEM. The question that all of these 'isms' promise to answer is: what is the ultimate nature of the mental? For example, what do thoughts have in common in virtue of which they are thoughts? Cartesian dualism said the ultimate nature of the mental was to be found in a special mental substance (*see* DESCARTES). Behaviourism identified mental states with behavioural dispositions; physicalism in its most influential version identifies mental states with brain states (*see* PHYSICALISM/MATERIALISM). Functionalism says that mental states are constituted by their causal relations to one another and to sensory inputs and behavioural outputs. Functionalism is one of the major theoretical developments of twentieth-century analytic philosophy, and provides the conceptual underpinnings of much work in cognitive science.

This idea can be introduced via the parity detecting automaton illustrated in figure 1, which tells us whether it has seen an odd or even number of '1's (though it counts zero as even). This automaton has two states, S_1 and S_2, two inputs, '1' and blank (—); and two outputs, it utters either the word 'odd' or 'even'. The matrix describes two functions, one from input and state to output, and another from input and state to next state. Each square encodes two conditionals specifying the output and next state given both the current state and input. For example, the top left box yields the following two conditionals: (1) if the machine starts in S_1 and sees a '1', it says 'Odd' (indicating that it has seen an odd number of '1's); and (2) if the machine starts in S_1 and sees a '1', it goes to S_2. The entire machine is specified by 8 such conditionals.

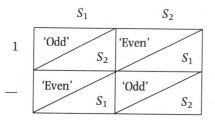

Now suppose we ask the question: 'What is S_1?' The answer is that the nature of S_1 is entirely relational, and entirely captured by the matrix. The nature of S_1 is given by the 8 conditionals, including that when in S_1 and having seen a '1' the machine goes into another state which is characterizable along the same lines as S_1.

Suppose we wanted to give an explicit characterization of 'S_1'. We could do it as

follows:

> x is in S_1 iff $\exists P \, \exists Q$ (If x is in P and gets a '1' input, then it goes into Q and emits 'Odd'; if x is in Q and gets a '1' input it goes into P and emits 'Even'; and so on for the remaining half of the table; & x is in P) (Note: read '$\exists P$' as *There is a property P*.)

A variant on this characterization that makes the functional identity thesis more explicit is that being in S_1 = being in the first of two states that are related to one another and to inputs and outputs as follows: being in one of the states and getting a '1' input results in going into the second state and emitting 'Odd'; being in the second of the two states and getting a '1' input results in going into the first and emitting 'Even'; and so on, for the remaining half of the matrix.

This illustration can be used to make a number of points. (1) According to functionalism, the nature of a mental state is just like the nature of an automaton state: exhausted by relations to other states and to inputs and outputs. (2) Because mental states are like automaton states in this regard, the illustrated method for defining automaton states is supposed to work for mental states as well. (3) S_1 is a second-order state in that it consists in the having of other properties, say mechanical or hydraulic or electronic properties that have certain relations to one another. These other properties, the ones quantified over in the definitions just given, are said to be the realizations of the functional properties. (4) One functional state can be realized in different ways. For example, an actual concrete automaton satisfying the machine matrix might be made of gears, wheels, pulleys and the like, in which case S_1 would be realized by a mechanical state; or S_1 might be realized by an electronic state, and so forth. (5) Since S_1 can be realized in many ways, a claim that S_1 *is* a mechanical state would be false, as would a claim that S_1 is an electronic state. For this reason, there is a strong case that functionalism

189

shows physicalism is false: if a creature without a brain can think, thinking cannot be a brain state. (6) Just as one functional state can be realized in different ways, one physical state can realize different functional states in different machines.

Suppose we have a theory of mental states that specifies all the causal relations among the states, sensory inputs and behavioural outputs. Focusing on pain as a sample mental state, it might say, among other things, that sitting on a tack causes pain and that pain causes anxiety and saying 'Ouch.' If this were all of the theory, functionalism would then say that we could define 'pain' as follows:

> x is in pain iff $\exists P \, \exists Q$ (sitting on a tack causes P & P causes both Q and emitting 'Ouch' & x is in P)

The identity variant is: being in pain = being in the first of two states, the first of which is caused by sitting on tacks, and which in turn causes another state and emitting 'Ouch.'

More generally, if T is a psychological theory with n mental terms of which the 17th is 'pain', we can define 'pain' relative to T as follows (the $F_1 \ldots F_n$ are variables that replace the n mental terms):

> x is in pain iff $\exists F_1 \ldots \exists F_n (T(F_1 \ldots F_n)$ & x is in F_{17})

In this way, functionalism characterizes the mental in non-mental terms, in terms that involve quantification over realizations of mental states but no explicit mention of them; thus functionalism characterizes the mental in terms of structures that are tacked down to reality only at the inputs and outputs.

There are four strands in the development of functionalism. First, Hilary Putnam and Jerry Fodor saw mental states in terms of an empirical computational theory of the mind, originating the functionalist argument against physicalism ((5) above). Second, J.J.C. Smart's 'topic-neutral' analyses led ARMSTRONG and Lewis to a functionalist

analysis of the meanings of mental terms. Such a view profits from the idea that if someone does not realize that, other things being equal, one would rather do without intense pain, then that person doesn't share all of our mental concepts. Third, WITTGENSTEIN's idea of meaning as use led to a version of functionalism as a theory of meaning, further developed by SELLARS and later Gilbert Harman. Finally, procedural semantics in cognitive science has led to a form of functionalism as a theory of meaning. See the introduction to the functionalism section in Block (1980) for references.

If T is an empirical theory, let us call the resulting functionalism psychofunctionalism. If T is intended to capture the meaning of mental terms, let us call the resulting functionalism conceptual functionalism. White (1986) has developed in an interesting way Smart's famous argument for topic-neutral analyses (see Smart, 1959), the upshot of which is that anyone who accepts any empirical identity thesis, be it functionalist or physicalist, should also be a conceptual functionalist. Here is the argument: suppose that we accept an empirical identity thesis, say, that pain = state S_{17}, where S_{17} can be either a psychofunctional state or a brain state. Since this is held not to be an a priori truth, the terms flanking the '=' sign must pick out this common referent via different routes involving different modes of presentation of the referent, in the manner of 'the evening star = the morning star.' After all, if the identity theorist believes both that he is in pain and that he is in S_{17}, these are distinct beliefs, as is shown by the fact that he could have believed that he was in pain but not S_{17}. So there must be different properties on the 'object' side in virtue of which the two terms pick out the same entity. There is no mystery about how 'S_{17}' picks out the referent, but what is the mode of presentation associated with 'pain'? Presumably, this will be some mental property, say the phenomenal aspect of pain. But the identity theorist will have to see this phenomenal aspect as itself something functional or physical, so if he resists conceptual functionalism, he will suppose that there is another empirical identity, e.g. the phenomenal aspect $= S_{134}$. But now we are back where we started, for we can ask the same question about the two modes of presentation exhibited by this identity. The only plausible way to escape an infinite regress, the argument concludes, is to accept an a priori identity between some mental property and a functional property, for only in the case of an a priori identity can the modes of presentation of terms flanking the identity sign be the same, and no physicalist or psychofunctionalist (or dualist) identities are plausibly a priori.

One way of resisting this conclusion would be to adopt a holistic picture of how words get their reference (*see* HOLISM). The holistic psychofunctionalist can suggest that we arrive at psychofunctional identities in choosing among theoretical perspectives on the basis of evidence. If we want to know what the meanings of mental terms are, they should be given in terms of the entire theory, and those 'definitions' will not be happily classifiable as a priori or empirical. Another way out (Loar, 1990) is to take the different modes of presentation to consist in the different functional roles of 'pain' and 'S_{17}' (thereby committing to a different sort of a priori functionalism), regarding the word–referent relation as unmediated by any other sort of mode of presentation.

FUNCTIONALISM AND PROPOSITIONAL ATTITUDES

The discussion of functional characterization given above assumes a psychological theory with a finite number of mental state terms. But if there is no upper bound on the number of beliefs, desires, etc., we will need a more sophisticated theory, one that involves some sort of combinatorial apparatus. It is generally agreed that belief must be treated as a relation, rather than having a primitive 'belief-that-2 + 2 = 4' predicate, a 'belief-that-grass-is-green' predicate, and so on in one's functionalized theory. Beyond this, however, there is little agreement. Field (1978) offered a solution to this problem,

taking belief to involve a relation between a person and a syntactically structured object in the brain. (See also Fodor's paper in Block, 1980; Loar, 1981; Schiffer, 1987. See Stalnaker, 1984, chs 1–3 for a critique of Field's approach.)

FUNCTIONALISM AND PHYSICALISM

Other theories of the mind have been concerned both with *what there is* (ONTOLOGY) and with what (say) pains have in common in virtue of which they are pains, a metaphysical issue, in one way of using the term.

Ontology: Dualism told us that there are both mental and physical substances, whereas behaviourism and physicalism are monistic, claiming that there are only physical substances.

Metaphysics: Behaviourism tells us that what pains (for example) have in common in virtue of which they are pains is something behavioural; dualism gave a non-physical answer to this question, and physicalism gives a physical answer to this question.

By contrast, functionalism answers the metaphysical question without answering the ontological question. Functionalism tells us that what pains have in common in virtue of which they are pains is their function; but functionalism does not tell us whether the beings that have pains have any non-physical parts. This point can be seen in terms of the automaton described above. In order to be an automaton of the type described, an actual concrete machine need only have states related to one another and to inputs and outputs in the way described. The machine description does not tell us how the machine works or what it is made of, and in particular it does not rule out a machine which is operated by an immaterial soul, so long as the soul is willing to operate in the deterministic manner specified in the table (see Putnam, 1967 and the paper by Fodor in Block, 1980).

191

Famously, there are two categories of physicalist theses. One version of physicalism competes with functionalism, making a metaphysical claim about the physical nature of mental-state types (and is thus often called 'type' physicalism). As mentioned above, there is a strong case that functionalism shows that type physicalism is false.

However, there are more modest physicalisms whose thrusts are ontological rather than metaphysical. Such physicalistic claims are not at all incompatible with functionalism. Consider, for example, a physicalism that says that every actual thing is made up entirely of particles of the sort that compose inorganic matter. In this sense of physicalism, most functionalists have been physicalists. Further, functionalism can be modified in a physicalistic direction, for example, by requiring that all properties quantified over in a functional definition be physical properties.

The claim that functionalism shows type-physicalism is false has been challenged repeatedly over the years, most effectively by Kim (1992). Kim notes that psychofunctionalists have taken the functional level to provide an autonomous level of description that is the right level for characterizing and explaining the mental because it lumps together all the different instantiations of the same mental structure, those made of silicon with those made of protoplasm. Kim argues that if functionalism is true, then mental terms are like 'jade' in not denoting natural kinds. A NATURAL KIND is nomic (suitable for framing laws) and projectible (see LAW OF NATURE). Jadeite and nephrite are natural kinds, but jade is not. If functionalism is true, then the natural kinds in the realm of the mental are physical rather than psychological – and thus as far as the scientific nature of the mental is concerned, physicalism is true, functionalism being demoted to a theory of mental *concepts* rather than mental kinds, and so conceptual functionalism displaces psychofunctionalism. The psychofunctionalist reply is that things that can have a mental life are physically disparate entities that resemble one another functionally because they have been subjected to forces like evolution and conscious design. These forces have *created* a level of description – characterized by common properties – genuine natural kinds.

FUNCTIONALISM AND MEANING

Functionalism says that understanding the meaning of the word 'momentum' is a functional state. On one version of the view, the functional state can be seen in terms of the role of the word 'momentum' itself in thinking, problem solving, planning, etc. But if understanding the meaning of 'momentum' is this word's having a certain function, then it is natural to suppose that the meaning of the word just *is* that function. Thus functionalism leads to a theory of meaning, a theory that purports to tell us the metaphysical nature of meaning. This theory is popular in cognitive science – where in one version it is often known as conceptual-role semantics. The theory has been criticized (along with other versions of functionalism) in Putnam (1988) and Fodor and LePore (1991).

OBJECTIONS TO FUNCTIONALISM

The automaton described above could be instantiated by four people, each one of whom is in charge of the functions specified by a single box. Similarly, the much more complex functional organization of a human mind could 'in principle' be instantiated by a vast army of people, but would such an army really have a mind? Conversely, it seems easy to imagine a very simple pain-feeling organism that shares little (perhaps even nothing) in the way of functional organization with us. How could pain be characterized functionally so as to be common to us and the simple organism? Part of the problem is that it is hard to see how we can give a functional characterization without chauvinistically excluding creatures with very different sensory apparatus from ours. The obvious alternative of characterizing the inputs and outputs functionally too would appear to yield an abstract structure which might be satisfied by, say, the economy of Bolivia, and thus falling to the opposite problem from chauvinism, namely, liberalism. One proposal for dealing with these sorts of problems is by thinking of functional roles as teleological (see the articles by Sober and Lycan in Lycan, 1990). (*See* TELEOLOGY.)

These two types of objections to functionalism get some of their force from attention to phenomenal states like the look of red. Such states seem to have their phenomenal properties intrinsically, and thus independently of relations to other states, inputs and outputs. Consider, for example, the fact that lobotomy patients often say that they continue to have pains but that the pains do not bother them. The same line of thought that makes us think pains are intrinsic makes what these patients say intelligible and believable, and thus we have reason to think that the phenomenal aspect of pain is non-functional (see the papers by Block, Dennett and Levin, in Lycan, 1990, sec. VII; Lycan, 1987; Shoemaker, 1984, chs 8, 9, 14, 15; Hill, 1991).

Functionalism dictates that mental properties are second-order properties, properties that consist in having other properties that have certain relations to one another. But there is at least a prima facie problem about how such second-order properties could be causal and explanatory in a way appropriate to the mental. Consider, for example, provocativeness, the second-order property that consists in having some first-order property (say redness) that causes bulls to be angry. The cape's redness provokes the bull, but does the cape's provocativeness provoke the bull? The cape's provocativeness might provoke the American Society for the Prevention of Cruelty to Animals, but is the bull not too stupid to be provoked by it? (See Block, 1990.)

Another problem is that functionalism appears to lead to holism. In general, transitions among mental states and between mental states and behaviour depend on the contents of the mental states themselves. My beliefs about the habits and capacities of sharks influence what I think and do if I come to believe that sharks are in the vicinity. Perhaps this is most easily seen with regard to the version of functionalism that provides a theory of meaning. If I accept a sentence and then reject it, the meaning of the sentence that I accept can't (it would seem) be the same as the meaning of the sentence that I later reject, since the transition relations that characterize the contents will be different at the two times. See Fodor and LePore (op. cit.). One functionalist reply is that some transitions are relevant to content individuation, whereas others are not. Other functionalists accept holism for 'narrow content' (see next paragraph), attempting to accommodate intuitions about the stability of content by appealing to wide content.

A further issue: the upshot of the famous 'twin earth' arguments has been that meaning and content are in part in the world and in the language community. But some functionalists propose to characterize these notions purely internally, and thus require a notion of 'narrow content' that, it is argued, may not be coherent. (This point was developed in the paper by Burge in Rosenthal, 1991.)

Functionalism continues to be a lively and fluid point of view. Positive developments include enhanced prospects for conceptual functionalism and the articulation of the teleological point of view. Critical developments involve problems with causality and holism, and continuing controversy over chauvinism and liberalism.

BIBLIOGRAPHY

A range of papers about functionalism are to be found in three anthologies, Block (1980), Lycan (1990) and Rosenthal (1991). Expositions of one or another version of functionalism are to be found in the Introduction and the papers by Block, Lewis and Putnam in Part III of Block (1980) and in Section IIIB of Rosenthal (1991). See also chapter 12 of Shoemaker (1984) and Schiffer (1987).

193

Block, N. ed.: *Readings in Philosophy of Psychology* Vol. 1 (Cambridge, MA: Harvard University Press, 1980).

Block, N.: 'Can the mind change the world?', in *Meaning and Method: Essays in Honor of Hilary Putnam* ed. G. Boolos (Cambridge: Cambridge University Press, 1990), 137–70.

Field, H.: 'Mental representation', *Erkenntnis* 13 (1978), 9–61.

Fodor, J. and LePore, E.: *Holism* (Oxford: Blackwell, 1992).

Kim, J.: 'Multiple realization and the metaphysics of reduction', *Philosophy and Phenomenological Research* LII (1992), 1–26.

Hill, C.S.: *Sensations* (Cambridge: Cambridge University Press, 1991).

Loar, B.: *Mind and Meaning* (Cambridge: Cambridge University Press, 1981).

Loar, B.: 'Phenomenal states', *Philosophical perspectives* Vol. 4, *Action Theory and Philosophy of Mind* ed. J. Tomberlin (Atascadero: Ridgeview, 1990), 81–108.

Lycan, W.G.: *Consciousness* (Cambridge, MA: MIT Press, 1987).

Lycan, W.G. ed.: *Mind and Cognition* (Oxford: Blackwell, 1990).

Putnam, H.: 'The nature of mental states' (1967); repr. in Block (1980), 223–31.

Putnam, H.: *Representation and Reality* (Cambridge, MA: MIT Press, 1988).

Rosenthal, D. ed.: *The Nature of Mind* (Oxford: Oxford University Press, 1991).

Schiffer, S.: *Remnants of Meaning* (Cambridge, MA: MIT Press, 1987).

Shoemaker, S.: *Identity, Cause and Mind* (Ithaca, NY: Cornell University Press, 1984).

Smart, J.J.C.: 'Sensations and brain processes', *Philosophical Review* 68 (1959), 141–56.

Stalnaker, R.C.: *Inquiry* (Cambridge, MA: MIT Press, 1984).

White, S.L.: 'Curse of the qualia', *Synthese* 68 (1986), 333–68.

NED BLOCK

G

Gassendi, Pierre (1592–1655) French Catholic priest, humanist scholar, and astronomer as well as philosopher, Gassendi is best known for his revival of Epicurean ATOMISM and his formulation of a Christian Epicurean metaphysics. He wrote the first full-scale Latin commentary on the Greek texts of EPICURUS (1649) and developed it into his *Syntagma philosophicum* (1658), a work analysing the merits of nearly all the ancient, mediaeval, and modern philosophical schools in Europe.

His metaphysics was defined in terms of his rejection of ARISTOTLE's theory of substance and DESCARTES's theory of mind, and by his espousal of an Epicurean account of bodies together with a generally Christian account of human nature. He held that all bodies are composed of material atoms and are not substances originating with the instantiation of a form in matter. Atoms are indestructible physical entities which underlie all changes in nature; they are not mathematical indivisibles, or extensionless points. In creating the world, God created these atoms, individuating them with reference to space and time but also giving them equal motions through the void and indefinitely many sizes and shapes. Gassendi's material principle thus differed from Epicurus' teachings that atoms were eternal entities and the world had no beginning.

His affirmation of the existence of incorporeal beings – including God, angels, and human rational souls – further departed from his Epicurean sources. Each human being, he maintained, is a union of a unique, immortal rational soul and a body individuated by its constituent atoms. He sharply distinguished this conception of human nature from that of his contemporary, Descartes, whose dualism of mind and body did not go far enough in acknowledging the dependence of the mind on bodily functions such as sensation. Gassendi's insistence that the Cartesian meditator is an embodied mind who, as such, cannot rid himself of his sense knowledge and his view that the meditator can only affirm or deny the content of an idea after the idea has been caused by sensation or by the intellect operating on a sense idea, resulted in his widespread reputation as Descartes's chief philosophical rival. His *Disquisitio metaphysica* (1644) contains several sophisticated rebuttals of Descartes's *Cogito* argument.

WRITINGS

Animadversiones in decimum librum Diogenis Laertii (Lyons: 1649); (New York and London: Garland Publishing, 1987).
Disquisitio metaphysica (Amsterdam: 1644); trans. Bernard Rochot, *Recherches métaphysiques* (Paris: J. Vrin, 1962).
Opera omnia 6 vols, Vols 1–2 *Syntagma philosophicum* (Lyons: 1658); (Stuttgart–Bad Cannstatt: F. Frommann, 1964).

BIBLIOGRAPHY

Bloch, O.R.: *La philosophie de Gassendi. Nominalisme, matérialisme, et métaphysique* (The Hague: Martinus Nijhoff, 1971).

Joy, L.S.: *Gassendi the Atomist, Advocate of History in an Age of Science* (Cambridge: Cambridge University Press, 1987).

Gödel, Kurt (1906–78) Gödel is perhaps best known among philosophers for his incompleteness theorems (1931). The first, as strengthened by Rosser (1936), says that for any consistent, axiomatic theory in which the recursive functions are representable, there is a sentence in the language of the theory such that neither it nor its negation is a theorem of the theory. This has been taken to mean that mathematical truth cannot be completely axiomatized in a single consistent formal theory, or yet more briefly, that truth outstrips provability. This in turn has been taken to count against formalism (NOMINALISM) in the philosophy of mathematics, and to cohere best with PLATONISM, the thesis that there are abstract, non-mental, non-physical objects (such as numbers or sets) to which the theorems of pure mathematics answer for their truth (*see* NUMBER; CLASS, COLLECTION, SET). Gödel's second incompleteness theorem says that for any theory of the sort described above, a sentence in the language of the theory that 'formalizes' the claim that the theory is consistent is not provable in the theory. It is well known among philosophers that Gödel was a Platonist, but he once suggested that since we can refute contradictions, since what is intuitively provable is true, and since what is actually proved is intuitively provable, perhaps the message of the second incompleteness theorem is that intuitive provability cannot be fully formalized. If so, that might undercut taking the first to show that mathematical truth outstrips intuitive provability.

On the epistemology of Platonism with regard to sets, Gödel argued famously that, 'despite their remoteness from sense experience, we do have something like a perception also of the objects of set theory, as is seen from the fact that the axioms force themselves upon us as being true'. This faculty he called mathematical intuition,

and he remarked that it need no more be conceived as giving immediate knowledge of mathematical objects than must sensation be taken by a Kantian to give immediate knowledge of physical objects (*see* KANT). But it has been argued persuasively that perception is by nature causal. Suppose we think of CAUSATION as the flow of energy, of information as structured parcels of energy, and of perception as the absorption of information from objects in structure preserving ways. Then we can begin to get a glimmer of how perception might justify beliefs about objects. But Gödel gives us not even a hint of how mathematical intuition might put us in touch with sets or numbers (which, being abstract and, unlike geometrical objects, unlocated, are utterly inert). So if we are to take mathematical intuition seriously, perhaps we must abandon our NATURALISM, our conviction that CAUSATION is, in HUME's words, *the* cement of the universe. But there is no consensus among us on what might go in its place.

Gödel also argued for a mathematical sort of inference to the best explanation. For example, the arithmetization of the consistency of number theory cannot, by his second incompleteness theorem, be proved in number theory; but anyone with mathematical commitments believes it, and it is easy to derive it in, say, set theory. So the more obvious arithmetical claim confirms the less immediate set theory. In this way Gödel contributed to epistemological holisms that have flourished since his time.

Collected Works ed. S. Feferman, J.W. Dawson, S.C. Kleene, G.H. Moore, R.M. Solovay and J. van Heijenoort (Oxford: Oxford University Press) vol. I (1986), vol. II (1990).

Rosser, J.B.: 'Extensions of some theorems of Gödel and Church', *Journal of Symbolic Logic* 1 (1936), 87–91.

W.D. HART

Goodman, Nelson (1906–) American philosopher. The solution to the problem of the one and the many (*see* UNIVERSALS AND PARTICULARS), Nelson Goodman maintains, is not to be found. Rather, it is made.

The members of any collection are alike in some respects, different in others. So examination alone cannot disclose whether two presentations are of the same thing or two things of the same kind. To determine that requires demarcating individuals and kinds. Category systems supply the demarcation. Such systems are human contrivances; we decide where to draw the lines.

Lines can be drawn in a variety of places, yielding divergent but equally effective systems. One might consider *The Boston Herald* (a later stage of) the same newspaper as *The Herald American*, another might count it a successor. One might consider isotopes with the same nuclide one element; another, two. Each is right relative to its own system or world version, wrong relative to its rival's. Neither is absolutely right or wrong.

If all overlapping world-versions are reducible to a single base, differences are ontologically insignificant. But such, Goodman contends, is not the case. We can construct a variety of individually adequate but irreconcilable world-versions. And we have no basis for choosing among them. A version that has the Earth at rest clashes with one in which the Earth moves. One is appropriate to astronomy, the other to geography. But a world that contains the Earth of one has no room for a planet like the other. There are, Goodman concludes, many worlds if any – one answering to each equivalence class of right world versions (Goodman, 1978).

Realists contend that at most one is right (*see* REALISM). If antithetical world-versions satisfy our criteria of acceptability, those criteria are not stringent enough. The difficulty is that we do not know how to take up the slack. We have no applicable standard of rightness.

Truth will not do. Since individuation and classification are version-dependent, truth is too. Each right verbal version generates its own truths. 'The Earth moves' is true in the world answering to one, false in the world of another.

Nor does it help to augment truth with the other desiderata of science. Those desiderata are multiply satisfiable, yielding many scientific worlds if any. Moreover, Goodman contends, science has no monopoly on rightness. The arts are equally important worldmakers (Goodman, 1968).

A world's constitution is relative to the version that defines it. And that version is a human construct. Still, we cannot make whatever we please. Worldmaking, Goodman insists, is subject to rigorous restraints – consistency, coherence, sensitivity to practice and precedent, and so on. Goodman's relativism is not one in which anything goes.

A controversial constraint Goodman imposes on his own constructions is NOMINALISM. The worlds he countenances consist entirely of individuals. This does not mean he eschews 'abstract entities'. For qualia and other such entities may be construed as individuals (see SENSA). The issue, Goodman believes, turns not on what the basic constituents are, but on what can be made of them. A world-version is nominalistic in Goodman's sense if, and only if, no two things can be composed of exactly the same basic elements. In (1951) and elsewhere, he demonstrates the power and beauty of such a stance.

See also NOMINALISM.

WRITINGS

The Structure of Appearance (Cambridge, MA: 1951); 3rd edn (Dordrecht: Reidel, 1977).

Fact, Fiction, and Forecast (London: 1954); 4th edn (Cambridge, MA: Harvard University Press, 1983).

Languages of Art (Indianapolis, IN: 1968); 2nd edn (Indianapolis, IN: Hackett, 1976).

Problems and Projects (Indianapolis, IN: Hackett, 1972).

GOODMAN, NELSON

Ways of Worldmaking (Indianapolis, IN: Hackett, 1978).

Of Mind and Other Matters (Cambridge, MA: Harvard University Press, 1984).

Reconceptions with C.Z. Elgin (Indianapolis, IN: Hackett, 1988).

BIBLIOGRAPHY

Elgin, C.Z.: *With Reference to Reference* (Indianapolis, IN: Hackett, 1983).

CATHERINE Z. ELGIN

H

haecceity Etymologically speaking, an haecceity is a *thisness* (from the Latin *haec*). The idea is that among the properties of an object, there is the property of being that very object. This notion arguably goes back to ARISTOTLE, but clearly goes back to BOETHIUS, and was developed in considerable detail by DUNS SCOTUS. An haecceity is one kind of *individual essence*: a property that is *essential* to its owner, and essentially *unique* to its owner, in the sense that it is impossible that there be something else that has it. Perhaps the chief question about haecceities is whether they are constructed out of qualitative properties – properties, unlike *being wiser than Plato*, or *being two feet to the left of Socrates*, or *being older than Sam*, that do not involve a reference to a specific person.

See also ESSENCE/ACCIDENT; ESSENTIALISM; INDIVIDUATION.

ALVIN PLANTINGA

Hegel, Georg Wilhelm Friedrich (1770–1831) German idealist philosopher. Hegel constructed his philosophical system in the wake of KANT's critique of metaphysics. He is often seen as a supremely metaphysical thinker who attempted to defend metaphysics against Kant's assault. But his relationship to traditional metaphysics is complex. He does not straightforwardly accept or straightforwardly reject it; he 'sublates' (*aufhebt*) it, that is at once destroys, preserves and elevates it.

Hegel associates 'metaphysics' and the 'metaphysical' with thinking and with thoughts or categories, in contrast to sense experience. Thus in one sense 'every cultivated consciousness has its metaphysics, its instinctive thinking', for 'metaphysics is nothing but the range of thought-determinations, as it were the adamantine net into which we bring all material and thereby make it intelligible' (Hegel, 1970, § 246, Addition). Such 'thought-determinations' as being, causality or force are used to structure and organize sensory material both in ordinary thought or discourse (for example, 'Our butter has melted in the sun' involves such thoughts as causality) and in disciplines such as physics. These thoughts are not necessarily the same in all periods; 'All revolutions, in the sciences as well as in world history, occur only because spirit has altered its categories' (ibid.).

Philosophers, however, have not simply used categories in the context of sense experience. They have also attempted to use CATEGORIES independently of sense experience in order to discern the true nature of things underlying their sensory exterior. In 'general metaphysics' they have explored the universal features of all beings as such, and in 'special metaphysics' the fundamental features of particular regions of the world or of particular entities such as God and the soul. These enterprises are metaphysical in a narrower sense: the essential features of entities or of the world as a whole are regarded as accessible to thinking alone and as describable in categories with a minimal sensory content. 'Metaphysics' and 'metaphysical' in this sense contrast with 'EMPIRICISM' and 'empirical'. Thus there may be two parallel sciences of a given subject matter, for example, the mind: a metaphysical science, 'rational psychology', which studies those features of the mind (or 'soul') that are accessible to thinking alone, and empirical psychology, which studies the 'appearance' of the mind, its empirical manifestations. However, Hegel often refers to empiricism and the empirical sciences as 'metaphysical', not only in the sense that they, like any other human enterprise, involve categories, but that they reify or hypostatize thoughts or the properties of things, speaking, for example, of 'forces' or, in the eighteenth century, regarding the heat of a body as a stuff that enters the pores of a body (*see* HYPOSTASIS, REIFICATION). In so far as scientists do this, their procedures are, on Hegel's view, metaphysical rather than wholly empirical.

The metaphysicians of the eighteenth century and earlier were, Hegel argued, correct in supposing that thinking reveals the true nature of things (the 'absolute'): we ordinarily assume that thinking and being are 'identical', and metaphysics brings this assumption to explicit consciousness. But pre-Kantian metaphysicians misconceived thoughts and thinking in several ways.

They tended to regard thoughts or categories, for example, being and causality, as sharply distinct from each other. In particular they assumed that 'opposites' are distinct and mutually exclusive, such that if something, for example, is infinite, then it is not finite, and if something is finite it is not infinite. It was this assumption, on Hegel's view, that enabled Kant to produce antinomies, maintaining that there are equally good arguments for the views that, for example, the world is finite in time and that it is infinite in time. The solution to such antinomies is to reject the assumption that opposites are incompatible, and to see that for example what is truly infinite must also be finite (since if the infinite is *distinct* from the finite, it is *bounded* by the finite and thus not *unbounded* or infinite). Hegel attempts to show, in his *Science of Logic* (1812–16), how categories, and in particular opposites, flow into each other and are not sharply distinct. To treat categories in this way is the function of 'reason' (*Vernunft*). In treating categories as discrete, pre-Kantian metaphysics was rather a metaphysics of the 'understanding' (*Verstand*) and was 'one-sided' or 'dogmatic' in its procedures and doctrines. (When Hegel charges empirical scientists with metaphysics, he often means that they separate what should not be separated, for example, heat, and thus employ understanding rather than reason.) Hegel, by contrast, attempts to ensure that his own philosophy is not a dogmatic or one-sided system coordinate and incompatible with other systems, but the 'universal' philosophy that embraces and 'sublates' all other philosophies.

The empirical manifestations of the world, or of an entity in the world, in contrast to its intelligible nature or essence, are themselves describable not only in such sensory terms as 'red', 'tree', etc., but also in terms of such relatively non-sensory thoughts as 'appearance', 'inessential', etc. (As Hegel says, thought 'overreaches' (*übergreift*) what is other than thought.) Thus the tendency of metaphysicians to regard the essential nature of things and their empirical manifestations as two parallel realms, the one accessible to thinking alone, the other accessible to sense experience, is itself an instance of their tendency to separate opposed thoughts and to apply them to distinct entities or realms, in this case the realm of essence or of the absolute and the realm of appearance or of the inessential. The separation of these thoughts is, Hegel argues, a mistake, since an essence that does not appear is not an essence (any more than something can be an acorn if it has no tendency to grow into an oak). Hence it is a mistake to postulate two realms, that of metaphysics and that of the empirical sciences. There is only one world involving both thoughts and sensory experience.

Metaphysicians usually express their doctrines in the form of a proposition with a subject (e.g. 'God', 'the soul') and a predicate (e.g. '(is) eternal, being, etc.', '(is) immortal, simple, etc.'). The predicate expresses a thought, while the subject refers to an entity to which the thought applies or in which it inheres. This is mistaken for at least two reasons. (a) The subject is either empty and has no content independently of the predicates applied to it (we do not know what 'God' refers to until we are told, for example, that God is being) or the subject is surreptitiously adopted from pictorial, non-philosophical discourse, such as traditional religion, and metaphysics is no longer pure thinking. (b) It suggests that, for example, God or the soul is a 'thing', a substratum in which properties inhere. Thus Hegel believes that metaphysics should abandon the propositional form, the predication of thoughts of a substratum, and focus exclusively on thoughts and their interrelations. Since this is what he attempted to do in his *Science of Logic* (and in the first part of his *Encyclopaedia*), he regards logic, which was traditionally distinguished from metaphysics, as coinciding with genuine metaphysics. (The concepts most characteristic of metaphysics, such as essence and substance, are considered mainly in the second book of the *Logic*, the 'Doctrine of essence'.)

In logic thoughts or categories are considered in the abstract. But thoughts do not inhere in a substratum that is accessible only to thinking. They are embedded in the world, initially in the world of nature. A magnet, for example, involves the thought of polarity. (That thoughts appear in nature is a requirement of logic itself, not only because it dissolves such sharp contrasts as that between essence and appearance, but also because it concludes with the 'absolute idea', in which the contrast between thought and what is other than thought is overcome.) Thoughts are not, on Hegel's view, imposed on nature (or on our raw sensory intuitions) by us, but nor are they immediately accessible to naive sensory observation. The thoughts involved in the various strata of nature are discerned by physics and other empirical sciences. The philosophy of nature (Hegel's own enterprise in the second part of his *Encyclopaedia*) then uses the results of these sciences to display the logical structure of nature as a whole. The thoughts embedded in nature are, as it were, its metaphysical essence. But philosophy of nature differs from metaphysics in the traditional sense, both because (unlike special metaphysics) it is heavily and avowedly dependent on prior empirical inquiry, and because (unlike general metaphysics) it presents not the common features of all beings as such, but regards nature as a hierarchy of levels, each of which embodies higher and more complex thoughts than its predecessor. Animals, for example, embody the concept of purpose or TELEOLOGY, in a way that space and pebbles do not. It is a serious error to attempt to account for higher types of entity in terms of categories suitable only for the conceptualization of lower types, to regard, for example, life as a mechanistic system.

The culmination of the world is, on Hegel's view, not nature but spirit (*Geist*), which includes not only the individual psychological features of human beings, but also, and more importantly, the interpersonal structures (such as the state and philosophy itself) which are created by human beings but in turn mould human beings. Spirit, unlike (on Hegel's view) nature, develops over time. It does so, at bottom, because spirit 'has altered its categories in order to understand and examine itself, to gain possession of itself, grasping itself more truly, deeply, in greater intimacy and unity with itself' (1970, § 246, Addition). Spirit thinks, both about other things and above all about itself. But in thinking about itself spirit changes itself and has to develop new thoughts in order to conceptualize its new reality. Spirit is not, on Hegel's view, merely the surface appearance of an underlying absolute or God. It is the highest phase of the absolute (as the fully grown oak is the highest phase of the acorn). Thus traditional metaphysicians were mistaken in supposing that they could give once and for all a definitive account of the fundamental nature of things. They tended to disregard their *own* thinking *about* the nature of things. The nature of things includes as its highest phase our attempts to think about it (especially in philosophy, but also in religion and art), and since we need to think in turn about our own thinking, spirit's account of the nature of things is never complete. Thus in opposition to the traditional view that God is essentially complete and self-contained independently of the nature he creates and of what human beings think about him, Hegel holds that human thought and worship is an essential phase of God: it constitutes his self-consciousness, a self-consciousness which will, however, never be complete. (Religion, on his view, presents philosophical truth in the form of pictorial representation, *Vorstellung*, rather than in that of conceptual thought.)

This suggests that metaphysics has an infinite task, a task that it can never complete. Infinity was central to Kant's account of metaphysics. In large part, metaphysics is, on Kant's view, an attempt (inevitable, if fruitless) to supply a completion to undigestible infinities: the infinity of the world in time and in space, the apparently endless divisibility of matter or the endless series of causes and effects. Hegel undercuts this diagnosis by reforming the concept of infinity: not only does the true infinite embrace the finite (as, e.g., the finite world is an essential phase of the infinite God), it is less like an endless line than a self-enclosed circle (as, e.g., space might be regarded as spherical, as finite but unbounded). Thus Hegel's system is a circle: he presents it in the order logic–nature–spirit, but the final phase of spirit is philosophy, more especially Hegel's own philosophy, and this returns to logic again. The world too, Hegel implies, is circular: the logical structure of things (the counterpart, on his view, of God the father) is alienated in nature (God the son) and returns to itself in spirit (the holy spirit), which unravels the logical structure of things. This undercuts both traditional metaphysics and Kant's diagnosis of it: the absolute is no longer distinct from its empirical manifestations, and its infinity no longer terminates, or underlies, an infinite series. But it leaves it unclear whether Hegel believes that the future, of philosophy and of history in general, is open-ended (but unpredictable, since future developments will involve new thoughts which we do not yet possess), or that history and philosophy

have ended, finally rounded out by his own system and by the political developments of his age.

Hegel's relation to pre-Kantian metaphysics may be schematically represented thus: initially we do not distinguish between a world of thought and a world of perception, but naively, though thoughtfully, experience the world about us. The metaphysician opens up a rift or opposition between the true world of thought and the merely apparent world of sense perception. By thinking through the concepts and procedures of metaphysics, the concepts of infinity, of essence and appearance, of opposition, for example, Hegel seeks to close the rift and thus arrives at a view that is considerably different from traditional metaphysics and yet an intelligible development out of it.

WRITINGS

Schellings und Hegels erste absolute Metaphysik (1801–1802): Zusammenfassende Vorlesungsnachschriften von I.P.V. Troxler ed. K. Düsing (Cologne: Dinter, 1988).

Differenz des Fichte'schen und Schelling'schen Systems der Philosophie (Jena: 1801); trans. H.S. Harris and W. Cerf, *The Difference Between Fichte's and Schelling's System of Philosophy* (Albany, NY: State University of New York Press, 1977).

Glauben und Wissen (Jena: 1802); trans. W. Cerf and H.S. Harris, *Faith and Knowledge* (Albany, NY: State University of New York Press, 1977).

Jenenser Logik, Metaphysik und Naturphilosophie ed. G. Lasson (Hamburg: 1923); trans. J. Burbidge and G. di Giovanni, *The Jena System, 1804–5: Logic and Metaphysics* (Montreal and Kingston: McGill–Queen's University Press, 1986).

Wissenschaft der Logik (Nuremberg: 1812–16); trans. A.V. Miller, *Science of Logic* (London: Allen and Unwin, 1969).

Enzyklopädie der philosophischen Wissenschaften im Grundrisse (Heidelberg: 1817, 1827, 1830; Berlin: 1840–5); 'Encyclopaedia of the Philosophical Sciences in Outline', Part I trans. T.F. Geraets, W.A.

Suchting and H.S. Harris, *The Encyclopaedia Logic* (Indianapolis, IN: Hackett, 1991); Part II trans. M.J. Petry, *Philosophy of Nature* (London: Allen and Unwin, 1970).

BIBLIOGRAPHY

Inwood, M.J.: *Hegel* (London: Routledge and Kegan Paul, 1983).
Inwood, M.J.: *A Hegel Dictionary* (Oxford: Blackwell, 1992).
Pätzold, D. and Vanderjagt, A. eds: *Hegels Transformation der Metaphysik* (Cologne: Dinter, 1991).
Soll, I.: *An Introduction to Hegel's Metaphysics* (Chicago: University of Chicago Press, 1969).
Taylor, C.: *Hegel* (Cambridge: Cambridge University Press, 1975).

M.J. INWOOD

Heidegger, Martin (1889–1976) Heidegger defined his life project as asking the 'question of being' – the question, 'What makes entities of various sorts (rocks, tools, thoughts, numbers, etc.) the entities they are?' In *Being and Time* (1927), he argues that the question of being must be prior to all other philosophical questions. 'Regional' or 'ontic' inquiries of various sorts (e.g. psychology, physics, epistemology, poetics) always operate with a set of tacit assumptions about the nature of the entities they study. These uncritical ontological assumptions pre-shape the inquiry, determining the kinds of questions one can ask and the answers that will make sense. In order to reflect critically on ontic inquiries, then, we need to work out an 'ontology in general' – an account of being as such (*see* ONTOLOGY). But since what entities *are* (their being) is accessible only in so far as things become intelligible to us (in so far as they show up as counting or mattering to us in some determinate way), any ontology must be preceded by a 'fundamental ontology' that clarifies the meaning (i.e. conditions of intelligibility) of being in general. Moreover,

since *our* existence is the arena in which entities become accessible in their being, fundamental ontology begins with an 'existential analytic' or account of human being (or *Dasein*, literally 'being-there') as the entity capable of understanding anything. The core of *Being and Time* therefore consists of an inquiry into the being of *Dasein*, an inquiry that starts out by examining our own concrete 'existentiell' ways of being at the current moment.

This project is made difficult by the fact that western metaphysics from its inception has been dominated by the 'substance ontology', the view that what is ultimately real is what remains continuously present through all CHANGE (*see* SUBSTANCE). When reality is regarded as static enduring presence, it is natural to think of everything as merely an object on hand for our use and inspection (the subject/object model of our relation to the world). To avoid falling into the uncritical assumptions of this 'metaphysics of presence', fundamental ontology calls for a twofold procedure. First, because the idea of substance arises when we focus on how things appear when we are engaged in theoretical reflection, we must start out with a description of how the world shows up in the midst of our everyday practical agency – our 'average everydayness', prior to reflection or theorizing. This phenomenology of everydayness is then accompanied by an interpretation or 'hermeneutic' aimed at revealing the background of intelligibility that makes possible our ways of encountering entities in the world. Second, in order to free ourselves from the presuppositions passed down to us by the history of western metaphysics, we must undertake a 'de-struction' of the history of ontology which aims at peeling off the layers of calcified tradition in order to retrieve those basic, though now 'forgotten', sources of understanding lying at the core of western thought.

The description of our pre-reflective practical affairs focuses on our concrete, 'existentiell' ways of being absorbed in a familiar practical 'world' (in the sense in which we speak of 'the world of theatre' or 'the business world'). Heidegger considers the example of hammering in a workshop when everything is running smoothly. What generally shows up for us in such activities is not a hammer-thing with properties, but rather hammering, which is 'in order to' nail boards together, which is 'for' building a bookcase, which is 'for the sake of' being a home craftsman. In our ordinary dealings with equipment, the work-world shows up as a totality of INTERNAL RELATIONS in which the *being* of any entity is defined by its uses – its 'readiness-to-hand' – within the wider context of functional relationships organized around our concerns. This web of means/ends relations Heidegger calls 'the worldhood of the world', and his claim is that what is most 'primordial' is the world as a holistic field of 'significance' relations in which the *being* of anything is defined by its place in an equipmental totality. Here there is no way to drive in a wedge between facts (what an entity *is*) and values (what it is *good* for) (*see* FACT/VALUE).

It follows that entities encountered as discrete objects with properties – the 'present-at-hand' – are derived from, and parasitic on, our prior involvement with the ready-to-hand. The present-at-hand emerges only when there is a 'breakdown' in the normally smooth functioning of a practical world. Such a breakdown leads to a 'change-over' in our ways of dealing with things: instead of 'dwelling' within a familiar context of significance, we stand back and make observations about objects on hand for analysis and manipulation. This account of the priority of practical involvements over theoretical reflection lets us diagnose the priority accorded to brute objects in the history of metaphysics as resulting from a tendency to overlook practical dealings and to concentrate on how things show up when we engage in theorizing.

The description of everydayness shows that the worldhood of the world is inseparably bound up with *Dasein*'s ways of being engaged in practical affairs. For Heidegger, as for existentialists generally, there is no human essence – no form of humanity or

proper way to be human that determines in advance what we are and should be (*see* ESSENCE/ACCIDENT). Instead, *Dasein* is a self-interpreting entity. We *are* what we *do* in the sense that our identity or being is something that comes to be defined and realized only through the course of our active lives in a concrete world. Understood in this way, *Dasein* is not an object or thing, but a 'happening' or a 'becoming' characterized by temporality and 'historicity'.

Regarded as an unfolding life story, Dasein has three essential structures or 'existentialia'. First, we find ourselves always already thrown into a specific cultural and historical world, already 'stuck' with obligations based on what has come before. This element of 'facility', disclosed in moods, makes up *Dasein*'s past or 'been-ness'. Second, we are always already engaged in concrete projects of various sorts. To be human is to *care* about what happens in one's life, and hence to take some stand on what one's life is adding up to. This taking a stand – getting involved in specific 'possibilities' (roles, occupations, forms of life) – Heidegger calls 'understanding'. In taking a stand, we exist as a 'projection' in the sense that, in all that we do, we are directed toward realizing something for the future. This future-directedness implies that our being or identity as humans is something that is still 'impending' so long as we are alive: we are 'being-toward-death'. Our future-directedness also lays out a 'fore-structure' of understanding on the basis of which we interpret what shows up in the world into a determinate 'as-structure'. Whereas the first and second existentialia make up *Dasein*'s past and future, the third determines *Dasein*'s way of being in the present. As 'discursive', we are always at home in a world, caught up in the midst of things, articulating entities in relation to our shared sense of how things can count for us.

The tripartite structure of *Dasein*'s temporal being is defined, then, as 'ahead-of-itself-being-already-in-(the world) as being-among (entities within the world'. Given

Heidegger's description of *Dasein*, there is a reciprocal interdependence between self and world. On the one hand, *Dasein's* temporality opens the 'clearing' or 'lighting' through which entities come to show up in familiar ways. On the other hand, the world provides the setting in which *we* can first become humans of specific sorts. This account of human existence has no use for the traditional distinctions between mind and matter (*see* MENTAL/PHYSICAL). These notions turn out to be constructs of some high-level theorizing rather remote from concrete existence. By undercutting the mind/matter distinction, Heidegger felt he had overcome both KANTIANISM and IDEALISM. Since the mental is one item among others in the shared world, there is no way to think that reality is constructed by, or exists only in, our minds. What is 'given', on Heidegger's view, is *Dasein* as the 'disclosedness' or 'truth' (in the original Greek sense of *a-letheia* or 'un-hiddenness') by virtue of which entities can be discovered *as* entities of such-and-such types.

Heidegger claims that human existence is not a matter of being an isolated 'I' or a subject set over against the world. Instead, we start out as 'being-with', that is, as participants and place-holders within the wider context of a historical culture. To be human is to be initiated into the practices and conventions of the community into which we are thrown – what Heidegger calls the 'they'. Thus, SELF-CONSCIOUSNESS is not a given, but is instead a fairly high-level achievement.

From the 1930s onward Heidegger focused less on analysing human existence and more on tracing the epochs of the history (or 'destining') of being. According to these more historicist later writings, western thought was inaugurated by a 'first beginning' in which the ancient Greeks understood being as *physis*, an emerging into presence that abides. Though the earliest Greeks saw that humans play a crucial role in the 'gathering' that articulates things into a coherent world, later Greek thinkers tended to overlook what lets entities appear (presencing) and instead focused

solely on what shows up in that presencing (the present as such). The first beginning formulated the 'guiding question' – 'What are entities?' – but failed to ask the 'basic question' – 'What is (the truth of) being?' As a result, the history of metaphysics has been a story of forgetfulness or concealment. As 'onto-theology', metaphysics thinks the 'beingness' (*Seiendheit*) of entities, understood as a grounding entity or as an essential property definitive of the presentness of entities, without thinking about the 'being' (*Sein* or *Seyn*) of entities. Heidegger anticipates a 'new beginning', heralded by the poet Hölderlin, in which we will overcome metaphysics and 'recollect' being as 'the event of appropriation into intelligibility' (*Er-eignis*).

In the later writings, being is not something humans do, but something that happens to humans. This 'anti-Humanism' treats concealment as resulting not just from human forgetfulness, but from the fact that things can come to appearance only by concealing their own conditions of appearing. There is a 'mystery' or 'abyss' beyond human understanding, something that only gets covered up by the calcified outlook of the dominant way of understanding being today, technology. Technology breeds the modern sense of being as framing (*Gestell*), according to which everything is an energy resource at our disposal for more and more efficient 'machinations'. Technology is not, however, something we can overcome by our will alone. Since technology is a dispensation of being and not a human creation, the most we can do is to prepare ourselves for a new disclosure of being by adopting a stance of acceptant 'letting be' (*Gelassenheit*) in which we are open to encountering things in their being. Heidegger's later reflections on such familiar things as a jug or a bridge suggest that there was a time when things were experienced as embodying the wider play of a Fourfold of earth and sky, humans and immortals. Humans, on this view, are preservers and receivers of the 'gift' of being, charged with safeguarding the nearness and belongingness within things.

205

See also EXISTENTIALISM; HERMENEUTICS; PHENOMENOLOGY.

WRITINGS

Sein und Zeit (Tübingen, 1927); trans. J. Macquarrie and E. Robinson, *Being and Time* (New York: Harper and Row, 1962).

Einführung in die Metaphysik (Tübingen, 1935); trans. Ralph Manheim, *Introduction to Metaphysics* (New Haven: Yale University Press, 1959).

Beiträge zur Philosophie (Vom Ereignis) (1936–8) ed. F.W. von Hermann, *Gesamtausgabe* vol. 65 (Frankfurt am Main: Klostermann, 1989).

Nietzsche (1936–46) 2 vols (Pfullingen: 1961); trans. D.F. Krell, F.A. Capuzzi and J. Stambaugh, *Nietzsche*, 4 vols (New York: Harper and Row, 1979–87).

BIBLIOGRAPHY

Dreyfus, H.L.: *Being-in-the-World: A Commentary on Heidegger's 'Being and Time' Division I* (Cambridge, MA: MIT Press, 1991).

Guignon, C.B.: *Heidegger and the Problem of Knowledge* (Indianapolis, IN: Hackett, 1983).

Okrent, M.: *Heidegger's Pragmatism: Understanding, Being, and the Critique of Metaphysics* (Ithaca, NY: Cornell University Press, 1988).

Zimmerman, M.: *Heidegger's Confrontation with Modernity: Technology, Politics, and Art* (Bloomington, IN: Indiana University Press, 1990).

CHARLES GUIGNON

hermeneutics A tradition of thought that deals with the understanding and interpretation of meaning. Originally it was that part of philology concerned with the questions regarding the authenticity of various versions of classical texts. In the sixteenth century it gained new prominence in the context of debates between Catholicism and Protestantism over the authentic meaning of the Bible and in the nineteenth-century thinkers such as F.D.E. Schleiermacher (1768–1834) extended the discipline to include questions of the meaning, not only of texts, but of expressions generally. Schleiermacher's specific contribution was to extend the idea of the hermeneutic circle of whole and part to include the place of a work or expression within its originator's psychological life. Thus, understanding required both understanding in terms of the text, part of the text, or conversation of which an expression was a part and understanding in terms of the whole of the life to which it belonged.

In the work of Wilhelm Dilthey (1833–1911) hermeneutics became the basis for distinguishing the methods of the human sciences or *Geisteswissenschaften* as a whole from those of the natural sciences. The human sciences differed from the natural sciences, he claimed, not because their objects differed, as the neo-Kantians had declared, but because they involved a different relation to human experience (*see* KANT; KANTIANISM). OBJECTIVITY in the natural sciences requires abstracting from the subjective characteristics of experience and quantifying its objects. In contrast, objectivity in the human sciences requires re-experiencing and understanding subjective experience in terms of its own original life. For Dilthey, the hermeneutic circle serves to facilitate this re-experience by constraining understanding within proper bounds and making possible the recreation of an original process of creation.

Although the concern with an objective understanding of an author's intentions marks the hermeneutics of Emilio Betti (1890–) and E.D. Hirsch (1928–), the impact that hermeneutics has had on philosophy stems mainly from the work of Hans-Georg Gadamer (1900–), whose *Truth and Method* was published in Germany in 1960 and translated into English in 1975. Drawing on the work of HEIDEGGER, Gadamer argues that if there is an affinity between hermeneutics and the human sciences, it is not because hermeneutics offers the latter a method for attaining objective knowledge. Rather, it is because for these forms of study, the concept of objectivity is irrelevant. The objects of the human sciences are part of our heritage, part of what Gadamer calls the 'effective history' (*Wirkungsgeschichte*) to which we already belong. Hence they are not alien objects that have to be brought within the compass of our understanding by techniques or methods of understanding. Instead, they are part of the history of influences that have constituted the nexus of assumptions, experiences and expectations that always already orients our understanding. In this way the hermeneutic circle becomes a historical circle and an element of our existence. In trying to understand past texts or such past text-analogues as historical actions, social practices and the like, we are bringing our understanding to bear on the very history that has helped to engender it.

In Gadamer's terminology, this circumstance means that understanding is always prejudiced. We can never re-experience a past expression along the lines of its original creation because we are always moved along by the particular effective history of which we are a part. We cannot experience *The Merchant of Venice*, for example, as Shakespeare or his original audience might have, without what we understand from our historical vantage point to be the consequences of anti-semitism. But to bring such prejudices to bear on what we are trying to understand is not to taint a more objective understanding. Rather, we must acknowledge that we are finite and historical beings and that, as long as we are, our understanding will be partial and interpretive. It will issue from a particular historical 'horizon' and will be conditioned by its particular concerns and purposes. By a 'fusion of horizons' Gadamer means that the horizon of concerns and purposes that the interpreter inhabits must be brought into relation with the horizon of the text, expression or action to be understood. Still, such a fusion is made possible by the circumstance that these horizons are not separate ones at all, but horizons connected by a wealth of effective historical connections and consequences.

The influence of *Truth and Method* can be found in the legal theory of Ronald Dworkin, in the recent political philosophy of such theorists as Charles Taylor and Alasdair MacIntyre and in Richard Rorty's attack on foundational epistemology in general. Whereas epistemology is concerned with a neutral adjudication of different beliefs and systems of belief, hermeneutics, according to Rorty, recognizes the contextual and pragmatic character of all claims to knowledge. Hence, it is concerned with edification, with a conversation in which we can enrich our various conceptions of ourselves and the world by trying to understand those of others. Hermeneutics here reaches its fullest extent thus far. If it began as a method for understanding literary texts and was expanded to account for the difference between the natural and the human sciences, in Gadamer's work it characterizes our finite existence as a whole and in Rorty's work, such finitude becomes the starting point for any science and for any claim to understand.

Hermeneutic thought has been attacked from two opposite sides: on the one side, by philosophers who think that in its emphasis on historical finitude it too quickly gives up on the Enlightenment's conception of reason (e.g. Jürgen Habermas) and, on the other side, by philosophers who think that in its presumption of textual unity and historical continuity it still accepts too much of the Enlightenment (e.g. Jacques Derrida). The first of these criticisms accepts the replacement of epistemological foundations with some sort of conversation. None the less, it insists that unless this conversation can allow for the free and equal participation of all, we must allow for the possibility that the understanding that results from it may be less the product of edification than that of power. The second form of criticism insists that all hermeneutic conversation is tied to power. In so far as it smooths out discontinuities and ruptures in texts and history, it performs the ideological function of suppressing 'difference' or that which cannot be made to fit within its metaphysics of unity and coherence.

To this second sort of criticism, hermeneutics might reply that a metaphysics of unity and coherence is basic even to attempts to find ruptures in either texts or history. For, if these ruptures are to count as ruptures they must already be ruptures of some meaning conceived in unitary terms to which they present a difference or disruption. To the first form of criticism, hermeneuticists have claimed that relations of power must themselves be accessible to hermeneutic understanding and interpretation. There is no standpoint independent of history from which power is power, only variously situated attempts to understand. Still, perhaps a more satisfying response to both sorts of criticism is to be found in the hermeneutics of Paul Ricoeur. 'Nothing', he writes, 'is more deceptive than the alleged antinomy between an ontology of prior understanding and an eschatology of freedom ... as if it were necessary to choose between reminiscence and hope' (Ricouer, 1981, p. 100).

BIBLIOGRAPHY

Dilthey, W.: *Der Aufbau der Geschichtlichen Welt in den Geisteswissenschaften* (Frankfurt: Suhrkamp, 1970).
Gadamer, H.-G.: *Truth and Method* (1965); 2nd rev. from 5th German edn *Gesammelte Werke* vol. 1 (New York: Crossroad Publishing Corporation, 1992).
Habermas, J.: 'The hermeneutic claim to universality', in *Contemporary Hermeneutics: Method, Philosophy and Critique* ed. Josef Bleicher (London: Routledge and Kegan Paul, 1980), 181–211.
Michellfelder, **D.P.** and Palmer, R.E. eds: *Dialogue and Deconstruction: The Gadamer–Derrida Encounter* (Albany, NY: State University of New York Press, 1992).
Ricoeur, P.: *From Text to Action/Paul Ricoeur* trans. K. Blamey and J.P. Thompson (Evanston, IL: Northwestern University Press).
Schleiermacher, F.D.E.: *Hermeneutik und Kritik* ed. Manfred Frank (Frankfurt: Suhrkamp, 1970).

GEORGIA WARNKE

historicism The term 'historicism' has been used to designate methodological positions of widely divergent, even opposed, sorts. It may not be unreasonable, however, to regard the accounts of history favoured by Leopold von Ranke (1795–1886) and Hans-Georg Gadamer (1900–) as fair examples of the most extreme positions of its range of use. POPPER (1961) has employed the term in a restricted sense to designate any theory that maintains that there are *sui generis* laws of historical change that are not reducible or expressible in terms of the nomic regularities of physical or social or psychological events (*see* LAW OF NATURE; REDUCTION, REDUCTIONISM). Popper's repudiation of such possibilities is premised on the conviction that there are invariant, exceptionless laws in physical nature and human affairs. The idea that would-be laws of nature may be idealized artefacts made to order for explanatory theories, which in the Anglo-American philosophy of science is associated with the work of Kuhn (1970), could be made to yield a corollary of historicism: namely, that the historied nature of science precludes the discovery, or the existence, of actual nomic invariances. The implied theory of history – that the world is a flux, as much in physical nature as in human affairs – is indeed the nerve of the historicism favoured by Gadamer and, in a more extreme form, by Michel Foucault (1926–1989). But it is noteworthy that recent historicists of Gadamer's and Foucault's sort usually neglect to generalize their claims to physical nature. One must invoke a figure like NIETZSCHE to find a sustained expression of a generalized historicism.

The essential contrast between nineteenth-century historicism (for example Ranke, 1973) and late twentieth-century historicism (Gadamer's, say) rests jointly with these considerations: (1) the advocacy of IDEALISM or, at the very least, neutrality with regard to idealism; (2) objectivism (*see* OBJECTIVITY) with regard to historical truth or, at the very least, the relativization of truth-claims (*not* truth itself) to the contingent histories of inquiring societies; and (3) the threat of self-referential paradox or, at the very least, puzzles that result from diachronizing serious inquiry under the conditions of the historical preformation of conceptual resources. The usual discussions tend to be focused on the limited standing of discursive history; but the implications of historicism, if coherent, are not likely to be confined to social or psychological phenomena, for the obvious reason that to construe inquiry in a strongly historied way would be tantamount to disallowing any principled conceptual disjunction between the natural and the human sciences. 'Objectivity', on that view, could not fail to be a posit of some kind made from within the limits of the encompassing symbiosis of language and world: hence, projected from within the horizontal limits of an inevitably tacit, incompletely fathomed history by which our rational resources are themselves first formed.

Seen thus, historicism is simply a radical version of the general attack on any form of REALISMS that is committed to some version of the correspondence theory of truth (in accord with which human inquiry addresses an independent reality, whose properties are, in principle, unaffected by any putatively 'constituting' function of language – in the Kantian or Husserlian sense (*see* HUSSERL; KANT; THEORIES OF TRUTH). The radicalization that recent versions of historicism bring to this picture concerns the history of thought itself: it involves the alleged fact that thinking has a history and that history cannot be endogenously grasped by the reflexive powers of human intelligence (itself variously and changeably formed by the processes of social existence). Objectivity is not rendered impossible on the historicist's view, but it becomes distinctly problematic: it becomes an artefact of history. In Gadamer's hands (1975), the issue of objectivity is weakly

presupposed (in the work of a responsible HERMENEUTICS) but it is almost never discussed. In Foucault (1977), truth is a salient concern but it is never pursued in a way that resolves the paradoxes of reference, those resulting from 'truth' being both an artefact of some 'discursive regime' and an 'objective' specification of how it functions under that condition.

Ranke's formula is more straightforward, but it is also self-defeating. Ranke opposes HEGEL's vision of an encompassing world-history. Every age is said to have its own distinctive *Geist* or unifying intentional genius, which the historian, working 'objectively' with its recorded archives, is able to recover. The pronouncements of the trained historian report how things objectively were in past history (*wie es eigentlich gewesen*), that is, what the true historical significance of these or those events is. The meaning of the events of the human world is said to be informed (and formed) by the pertinent age's *Geist*; and the historian is apparently able to escape the encumbrances of the *Geist* of his own age. The advocacy of these two themes is at the heart of nineteenth-century historicism – it is at once objectivist (committed to an appropriate correspondence thesis) and idealist (committed to historical truth's being concerned with the soul of an age, as God apprehends it). Ranke fails, however, to explore the grounds for cross-cultural objectivity, both synchronically and diachronically. Gadamer explicitly repudiates such paradoxical accounts, embracing instead the hermeneutic complexity of the historicist circumstances, namely: (1) that the meanings of human events have their own changing history; and (2) that they are grasped by an intelligence that must first posit such events and then interpret them in accord with its own historically changing nature.

Contemporary historicism is the result rather of combining a Kantian-like symbiosis and an insistence on the cognitive intransparency of the world together with the general theme that thinking is intrinsically historical. It need not be sceptical about the possibility of science, but it must reinterpret whatever science is said to accomplish – as the provisional achievement of a historical practice that cannot be assigned any progressive or teleological or objectivist standing. For on the argument, all such claims are posits internal to the horizonally skewed history in which they are themselves uttered. In this sense, historicism is strongly opposed to the inductivism, falsificationism, progressivism, objectivism characteristic of twentieth-century philosophies of science; but it need not be opposed to scientific objectivity or progress. What is decisive about its philosophical role is that, in its most temperate forms, historicism never functions criterially; for, of course, to propose a privileged form of historical interpretation would be to subvert the doctrine altogether. It is, therefore, more of a holistic constraint on distributed truth-claims than a particular claim itself, or a criterion governing the validity of particular claims.

BIBLIOGRAPHY

Foucault, M.: 'Nietzsche, genealogy, history', *Language, Counter-memory, Practice; Selected Essays and Interviews*, ed. D.F. Bouchard, trans. D.F. Bouchard and S. Simon (Ithaca, NY: Cornell University Press, 1977).

Gadamer, H.-G.: *Truth and Method* (1965); trans. G. Barden and J. Cumming (New York: Seabury Press, 1975).

Hempel, C.G.: 'The function of general laws in history', in *Aspects of Scientific Explanation and Other Essays in the Philosophy of Science* (New York: Free Press, 1965), 231–43.

Kuhn, T.S.: *The Structure of Scientific Revolutions* 2nd edn (Chicago: University of Chicago Press, 1970).

Ranke, L. von: *The Theory and Practice of History* ed. G.G. Iggers and K. von Moltke, trans. W.A. Iggers and K. von Moltke (Indianapolis: Bobbs-Merrill, 1973).

JOSEPH MARGOLIS

Hobbes, Thomas (1588–1679) Born in Malmesbury, England. He is justly famous for his writings in political philosophy, most notably *Leviathan* (1651) which propounded a social contract theory in defence of political absolutism.

Hobbes accepted the general thesis of materialism, that every existing entity is a physical being or object (*see* PHYSICALISM, MATERIALISM). Bodies are objects which do not depend on thought and so subsist by themselves (Hobbes, 1930, p. 77), and 'every object is either a part of the whole world, or an aggregate of parts. The greatest of all bodies . . . is the world itself' (Hobbes, 1930, p. 125). He saw that this implies that either there are no supernatural beings or that such beings are themselves corporeal in nature. Hobbes opted for the latter thesis, saying of God 'I answer, I leave him to be a most pure, simple, invisible, spirit corporeal' (Peters, 1956, p. 95). Hobbes also seems to have noticed that his materialist thesis is inconsistent with the existence of abstract entities. To this end, he developed a version of NOMINALISM according to which general terms do not stand for or signify UNIVERSALS. Rather, on Hobbes's view, 'names are signs, not of things, but of our cogitations' (Hobbes, 1839, vol. I, p. 17). In this respect, Hobbes seems to have anticipated the views of later empiricists such as LOCKE and BERKELEY.

Coupled with Hobbes's materialism was his acceptance of MECHANISM. During one of his trips to Continental Europe, beginning in 1629, Hobbes became persuaded that all events can be fully explained by the motions of physical bodies. Probably under the influence of Galileo (1564–1642), whom he visited in 1636, Hobbes tried to work out a general theory of physics in which mechanical explanations of all change was paramount.

A test case for such a theory occurs in sensation. Hobbes felt that in perception, certain phantasms or ideas are generated in the sentient, and so it seems initially that his view would be dualistic. Phantasms exist when and only when they are experienced, and so seem not to be physical entities. And such entities would be contrary to mechanism because, for Hobbes, genuine causal relations require contact between the causally related bodies. However, Hobbes points out that 'sense . . . in the sentient, can be nothing else but motion in some of the internal parts of the sentient; and the parts so moved are parts of the organs of sense' (Hobbes, 1930, p. 106). These motions, as they appear to a person, Hobbes calls 'fancy', so his view is that an internal motion as it appears to a percipient is a phantasm.

Hobbes tries to give a deeper account of sense with his doctrine of endeavour. Given that there is no action at a distance (Hobbes, 1930, p. 97), the causal process in perception must occur when something transmitted from the perceived object comes into contact with a sense organ: 'when the uttermost part of the organ is pressed, it no sooner yields but the part next within is pressed also; and in this manner, the pressure is propagated through all the parts of the organ to the innermost' (Hobbes, 1930, p. 107). This inward pressure, going first to the brain and then to the heart, Hobbes calls an inward endeavour. A terminal point of this inward pressure is reached at the heart where a reaction is generated, and fluids in the nerves then tend outwards. This reaction is an outward endeavour, about which Hobbes says, 'however little soever the duration of it be, a phantasm or idea hath its being; which, by reason that the endeavor is now outwards, doth always appear as something situate without the organ' (Hobbes, 1930, pp. 107–8). Hobbes's point seems to be that this outward endeavour, itself just bodily parts in motion, *is* the phantasm, so that the apparent conflict with materialism and mechanism is removed. Whether Hobbes is successful on this point is another matter, for something has to be said about the relation of *appearing*; phantasms are these internal motions as they appear to a percipient. However, on the status of appearing Hobbes is silent.

Hobbes also followed Galileo in holding that secondary qualities are not at all in external bodies (*see* QUALITY, PRIMARY/ SECONDARY). Instead, such qualities 'are in the object . . . but so many motions of the matter; . . . neither in us are they any thing else, but divers motions; for motion produceth nothing but motion. But their appearance to us is fancy, the same waking, that dreaming' (Hobbes, 1930, pp. 139–40). Primary qualities, on the other hand, are real qualities of bodies. Hobbes writes that 'the definition . . . of *body* may be this, a *body* is that, which having no dependence upon our thought, is coincident or coextended with some part of space' (Hobbes, 1930, p. 77). Later writers, especially BER-KELEY and HUME, argued that the primary quality/secondary quality distinction was suspect, and that the arguments from perceptual relativity that Hobbes offered in its defence can be extended to the primary qualities as well. Hobbes paid no attention to considerations of this sort. Nor did he comment on the possible threat of scepticism inherent in the account of perception which required that external bodies be perceived by means of intermediary phantasms.

Mechanism implies that all events, including human actions, are physically explicable. This, in turn, apparently implies that no actions are free, a criticism made of Hobbes's views by Bishop Bramhall (*see* FREE WILL). The core of Hobbes's reply is, perhaps, the first statement of a compatiblist position. He notes that we apply the term 'free' most properly to persons, and 'a free agent is he that can do if he will, and forbear if he will' (Hobbes, 1930, p. 208). Liberty is just the absence of restraint; as Hobbes says, 'Liberty is the absence of all the impediments to action that are not contained in the nature and intrinsical quality of the agent' (Hobbes, 1930, p. 206). But the willing cannot be said to be free, for 'when first a man hath an *appetite* or *will* to something, . . . the cause of his *will*, is not the *will* itself, but *something* else not in his own disposing' (Hobbes, 1930, p. 207). Voluntary actions are thus necessitated, just as events in nature are. But a person may still be said to be free, or to be at liberty to do or forbear, given the proper definitions of these terms. (*See* DETERMINISM.)

WRITINGS

English Works of Thomas Hobbes 11 vols, ed. W. Molesworth (London: John Bohn, 1839).
Opera Philosophica 5 vols, ed. W. Molesworth (London: John Bohn, 1845).
The Elements of Law, Natural and Political ed. F. Tonnies (London: Cambridge University Press, 1928).
Hobbes Selections ed. F. Woodbridge (New York: Scribner's, 1930).

BIBLIOGRAPHY

Brandt, F.: *Thomas Hobbes' Mechanical Conception of Nature*, trans. V. Maxwell and A. Fausboll (London: Hachette, 1928).
Peters, R.: *Hobbes* (London: Penguin Books, 1956).
Sorell, T.: *Hobbes* (London: Routledge, 1986).
Watkins, J.W.N.: *Hobbes' System of Ideas* (London: Hutchinson and Co., 1965).

GEORGE S. PAPPAS

Holbach, Paul Heinrich Dietrich d' (1723–89) German-born nobleman who spent most of his life in Paris where he was acquainted with many of the leading thinkers of the French Enlightenment period. Holbach's home in Paris was for many years a *salon* in which the Encyclopedists often met, and Holbach was himself a major contributor to the *Encyclopedia*. His own voluminous writings were likely to have been regarded as dangerous by the *ancien régime*, and so they were published abroad either anonymously or under a pseudonym and then secretly brought into France.

Holbach wrote extensively on religious and ethical matters. He attacked Christianity and deism alike, maintaining their sundry tenets were both false and pernicious, the latter because established religions have always supported repressive governments and also because religious beliefs and practices stand in the way of moral progress and human happiness. Atheism, Holbach felt, is necessary for correct moral teaching and practice.

Holbach's atheism is coupled with his thoroughgoing materialism and MECHANISM (*see* PHYSICALISM, MATERIALISM). In his very influential *Système de la nature* (1770; published in Amsterdam under the pseudonym 'Mirabaud'), he elaborates the view that everything that exists is material. There are no transcendent beings such as God; rather, the physical universe and its parts make up the sum total of existing entities, and everything in the physical universe is wholly material, consisting of arrangements of matter in various states of motion. The same applies to persons who, lacking souls or other non-material parts or attributes, are themselves merely very complex composites of material particles (*see* MIND/BODY PROBLEM).

Holbach also held that all events in the material world take place in accordance with strictly deterministic scientific laws (*see* DETERMINISM). There is thus no real human freedom (*see* FREE WILL). Rather than accept a kind of compatiblism, according to which a free action is just an uncoerced action, Holbach felt that putatively free actions are illusory. They are caused ultimately by a brain event that itself was not chosen and so was not freely chosen. Nevertheless, moral praise and blame retain a useful function as they contribute to the regulation of society and thus to human happiness.

WRITINGS

Système de la nature 2 vols (London and Amsterdam: 1770); published under the name 'Jean Baptiste Mirabaud', trans. *The System of Nature* 3 vols, ed. B. Feldman and R. Richardson (New York: Garland, 1984).
Common Sense: or Natural Ideas Opposed to Supernatural (1772); (New York, 1836).

BIBLIOGRAPHY

Kors, A.: *D'Holbach's Coterie: An Enlightenment in Paris* (Princeton, NJ: Princeton University Press, 1976).

Naville, F.: *Paul Thiry d'Holbach et la philosophie scientifique au XVIIIe siecle* (Paris: Gallimard, 1943).

GEORGE S. PAPPAS

holism A property is *anatomic* just in case if anything has it, then at least one other thing does as well. Consider, for an untendentious example, the property of being a sibling. My being a sibling is metaphysically dependent upon someone else's being a sibling. A property is *atomic* just in case it might in principle be instantiated by only one thing. So, for example, all properties expressed by predicates like 'is a table' or 'weighs 20 kilograms' are atomic. A property is *holistic* just in case if anything has it then indefinitely many other things have it as well. Consider the property of being a natural NUMBER. Some philosophers doubt that anything has this property. But nobody could coherently doubt that if there are any numbers, then there must be quite a few. Nothing is a natural number unless there is a natural number that is its successor. No number is its own successor; so if anything is a natural number, something else must be as well. So far the number case is quite like the sibling case. But whereas every sibling is his sibling's sibling, no number is its successor's successor (or its successor's successor's successor . . . , etc.). So, if there are any numbers, then there must be an infinity of them.

Why does this matter? One way of formulating the main issue about holism in contemporary philosophy of language and philosophy of mind is whether being a symbol belonging to language L, having an intentional object, expressing a proposition, having a referent, and the like are atomic properties (*see* CONTENT; REFERENCE). The received philosophical view is that these sorts of properties are not atomic but anatomic. The question whether such properties are anatomic suffices to distinguish two great traditions in the philosophy of language. The atomist tradition proceeds from the likes of the British empiricists, via pragmatists such as PEIRCE and JAMES (*see* EMPIRICISM; PRAGMATISM). The locus classicus is the work of the Vienna circle (*see* LOGICAL POSITIVISM). This tradition's contemporary representatives are most model theorists (Richard Montague, John Perry and Jon Barwise), behaviourists (J.B. Watson, B.F. Skinner), and informational semanticists (Fred Dretske, Jerry Fodor, Ruth Garrett Millikan). Whereas people in this tradition think that the semantic properties of a symbol are determined solely by its relations to things in the non-linguistic world, people in the second tradition think that the semantic properties of a symbol are determined, at least in part, by its role in a language. If what a symbol means is determined by its role in a language, the property of being a symbol is anatomic. This second tradition proceeds from the likes of the structuralists in linguistics and its contemporary representatives are legion (*see* STRUCTURALISM). They include QUINE, DAVIDSON, David Lewis, Daniel Dennett, Ned Block, Michael Devitt, Hilary Putnam, Richard Rorty, SELLARS, among philosophers; and they include almost everybody in artificial intelligence and cognitive psychology.

According to Quine, there is no non-question-begging way of distinguishing (analytic) statements that are true in virtue of meaning alone from (synthetic) statements whose truth depends on facts about the world. This contention serves as a premise in practically all arguments for holism about meaning: if the meaning of a symbol is determined by its role in a language and if the analytic/synthetic distinction is infirm, then there is no principled distinction between those aspects of a word's linguistic role that are relevant to determining its meaning and those that are not. The invited inference is that the meaning of a word is a function of its *whole* linguistic role. This is meaning holism. Consider just a few of its more startling implications. You think that Abraham Lincoln owned a dog; I think that he did not. So there are some inferences about dogs you are prepared to accept and I am not. But holism says that what 'dog' means in your mouth depends on the totality of your beliefs about dogs. It seems to follow that you and I mean different things when we say 'dog'. This line of argument leads, more or less directly, to such surprising claims as that natural languages are not, in general, intertranslatable (Quine, Ferdinand de Saussure); that there may be no fact of the matter about the meanings of texts (Hilary Putnam, Jacques Derrida); and that scientific theories that differ in their basic postulates are 'empirically incommensurable' (Paul Feyerabend, Thomas Kuhn). Moreover, meaning holism seems to imply that there cannot be a science of mental phenomena. For, if meaning holism is true, then no two people have the same beliefs or desires. But then no two people can fall under the same psychological law; indeed, no two time-slices of one person can fall under the same psychological law.

Philosophers react to this situation in a variety of ways. A surprising number bite the bullet; strictly speaking, they say, there are no such things as mental states. Variations on this theme can be found in work by philosophers as influential as Quine, Davidson, Daniel Dennett, Hilary Putnam, Stephen Stich, Paul and Patricia Churchland and many others. Other philosophers have sought to develop a sort of mitigated holism according to which a notion of similarity of meaning (of mental content) somehow replaces the notion of semantic identity that appeals to the analytic/synthetic distinction. This approach is also popular among cognitive scientists (Hartry Field, Gilbert Harman, Paul Smolensky). And still other philosophers suggest that perhaps the analytic/synthetic distinction can be preserved from Quine's attack by developing a 'graded' notion of analyticity (Ned Block, Michael Devitt) or by arguing that there must be a viable analytic/synthetic distinction because the consequences

of there not being one are simply too awful to contemplate (DUMMETT).

BIBLIOGRAPHY

Block, N.: 'Advertisement for a semantics for psychology', *Midwest Studies in Philosophy* 12 (1988), 615–78.
Davidson, D.: 'Belief and the basis of meaning', in his *Inquiries into Truth and Meaning* (Oxford: Oxford University Press, 1984), 141–54.
Fodor, J.A. and LePore, E.: *Holism: A Shopper's Guide* (Oxford: Blackwell, 1992).
Quine, W.V.: 'Two dogmas of empiricism', (1951); in his *From a Logical Point of View* (Cambridge, MA: Harvard University Press, 1953), 20–46.

ERNEST LEPORE

Hume, David (1711–76) Scottish philosopher, historian and essayist, is customarily classified, along with LOCKE and BERKELEY as one of the leading figures of eighteenth-century British EMPIRICISM. Many regard Hume as the greatest philosopher ever to write in English. His philosophical works include *A Treatise of Human Nature* (1739–40), *An Enquiry concerning Human Understanding* (1748), *An Enquiry concerning the Principles of Morals* (1751) and *Dialogues concerning Natural Religion* (1779).

Hume has often been characterized – especially by logical positivists seeking a forerunner – as an implacable enemy of metaphysics (*see* LOGICAL POSITIVISM). Frequently cited in illustration of his alleged enmity is the famous concluding paragraph of his *An Enquiry concerning Human Understanding*:

When we run over libraries, persuaded of these principles, what havoc must we make? If we take in our hand any volume; of divinity or school metaphysics, for instance; let us ask, *Does it contain any abstract reasoning concerning quantity or number?* No. *Does it contain any experimental reasoning concerning matter of fact and existence?* No. Commit it then to the flames: for it can contain nothing but sophistry and illusion.

Yet Hume did not consider himself an enemy of metaphysics as such. For he understood 'metaphysics' to consist simply of all 'abstract and profound reasonings' – a definition broad enough to include much of his own philosophy. He did assert (in *An Enquiry concerning Human Understanding*, Sect. I) that the 'justest and most plausible objection against a considerable part of metaphysics' is that it is 'not properly a science; but arise[s] either from the fruitless efforts of human vanity, which would penetrate into subjects utterly inaccessible to the understanding, or from the craft of popular superstitions' (by which he meant organized religion). His proposed response to this objection, however, was not to abandon all metaphysics, but rather to 'cultivate true metaphysics with some care, in order to destroy the false and adulterate'.

Such cultivation, he maintained, requires a serious enquiry into the nature of the human understanding – i.e. into what we would call human cognitive psychology. According to Hume, this enquiry must be based on the experimental method. One of the conclusions of his enquiry was that all genuinely substantive reasoning is either experimental reasoning concerning matters of fact and existence, or abstract reasoning concerning quantity or number; hence his rejection of those works of divinity and 'school' metaphysics whose arguments he regarded as being neither. Because of the limitations of our representational and inferential faculties, he also recommended a 'mitigated scepticism' that involved both a degree of modest diffidence about all of one's own conclusions and a restriction of philosophy to topics of 'common life'. This mitigated scepticism – which he regarded as the natural outcome of the conflict between Pyrrhonian sceptical arguments and our natural, irresistible mechanisms of belief – was intended to forestall positive theorizing both about the ultimate nature of the universe beyond our experience of it, and about

matters of speculative theology. In his broad sense of 'metaphysics', however, there is no contradiction in saying that his own philosophy was metaphysical as well as experimental.

REPRESENTATION AND IMAGINATION

Those seventeenth-century continental philosophers who are generally classified as 'rationalists' – such as DESCARTES, SPINOZA and LEIBNIZ – emphasized a distinction between two radically different representational faculties of the mind (in addition to sensation and memory). (*See* RATIONALISM.) These two faculties were the imagination and the intellect. They understood the imagination to be a faculty of having image-like ideas, while they understood the intellect to be a faculty of having non-imagistic ideas, far richer in content than those of the imagination. Hume, in contrast, rejected the distinction, treating the imagination as the only representational faculty beyond sensation and memory. He thus construed all human cognitive processes as operations with image-like ideas. This rejection of intellect had several crucial and closely related consequences for the nature of his metaphysics.

First, it led Hume to try to explicate the content of many of the main concepts employed in metaphysics – such concepts as 'cause', 'real existence', and 'self', for example – in a way that would be consistent with their assigned status as ideas in the imagination. Furthermore – since he also held on empirical grounds that the simple elements of all ideas are always copied from the simple elements of the 'impressions' perceived in experience – he was led to approach the explication of the content of these metaphysical concepts by seeking the experiences from which their elements are derived. His attempt to explicate these metaphysical concepts as ideas of the imagination was facilitated by his theory of abstract ideas, according to which determinate image-like ideas acquire a more general signification by their association

HUME, DAVID

with a general term of a language, a term that in turn serves to excite a disposition to call up other related determinate ideas in the mind as needed.

Second, the rejection of intellect, by imposing limitations on the potential richness of content of the main ideas of metaphysics, encouraged Hume to deny the validity of many a priori arguments for specific metaphysical theses. These included ontological arguments for the existence of God, alleged demonstrations of the need for an underlying SUBSTRATUM to support the qualities of objects, and alleged a priori proofs of the necessity of a cause for every beginning of existence.

Third, Hume's rejection of intellect radically expanded the realm of the metaphysically possible. Like most of his predecessors and contemporaries, he accepted the use of conceivability as a criterion of possibility. But whereas 'conceivability' for seventeenth-century rationalism meant conceivability in the intellect (a potentially strict standard that, in the case of Spinoza, arguably excluded everything but the actual), for Hume it meant simply conceivability in the imagination – i.e. imaginability. Thus, he regarded a very wide range of things as metaphysically possible, including causal laws of nature other than the actual laws (*see* LAW OF NATURE). Because he held that the actual laws of nature could only be discovered by experience and could not be explained as the only *possible* laws, the actual laws were for him what later writers called 'brute facts'.

CAUSATION

Of all Hume's treatments of metaphysical topics, his treatment of CAUSATION (in *A Treatise of Human Nature*, Bk I, Pt iii, and *An Enquiry concerning Human Understanding*, Sects VI–VII) is perhaps the most famous. He began by examining in detail the nature of causal inferences, arguing that they are based on the mental mechanism of 'habit' or 'custom', operating on repeated experience of the conjunction of members of one class of resembling objects or events with

members of another. He then turned his attention to the relation of 'necessary connexion' that seems so essential to causation. He argued that this necessary connexion cannot be understood or represented as a quality within the cause itself (nor as a relation between the cause and effect themselves) that entails the effect, or guarantees inferences from the occurrence of the one to the occurrence of the other. On the contrary, he held, the idea of necessary connexion is merely copied from an internal 'impression of necessary connexion' or determination that arises within the mind when custom or habit, operating on 'constant conjunction', has mentally associated the representations of two kinds of objects or events in a way that leads to inference. Our sense of a 'necessary connexion' is thus a *product* of inference and association, rather than a *basis* for it.

These considerations led Hume to offer two definitions of 'cause', one in terms of constant conjunction and one in terms of the resulting association and inference:

An object precedent and contiguous to another, and where all the objects resembling the former are plac'd in like relations of precedency and contiguity to those objects, that resemble the latter.

[A]n object precedent and contiguous to another, and so united with it, that the idea of the one determines the mind to form the idea of the other, and the impression of the one to form a more lively idea of the other. (Hume, *A Treatise of Human Nature*, Bk I, Part iii, sect. xiv)

Hume readily granted that these definitions may not be fully satisfying to us, because they are 'drawn from objects foreign to the cause' – that is, they define the causal relation by appeal to objects other than the cause and effect themselves (in the first definition, to objects resembling the cause and objects resembling the effect; in the second definition, to ideas, impressions, and the mind). Moreover he was careful – particularly in *An Enquiry concerning Human Under-*

standing – not to deny that there may be qualities in causes, or relations between causes and effects, that we cannot represent or understand. He did insist, however, that his two definitions were 'just', and the best that could be provided.

LIBERTY AND NECESSITY

Hume believed that one beneficial outcome for metaphysics of his analysis of causation was its ability to shed light on the problem of the freedom of the will (*see* FREE WILL) which he called 'that long disputed question concerning *liberty and necessity*' (*Treatise*, Bk II, Pt iii, Sects i–ii; *An Enquiry concerning Human Understanding*, Sect. VIII). Causal necessity, he claimed to have shown, could only be defined in terms of constant conjunction or the resulting association and inference in the mind. Since both of these characteristics are universally allowed to pertain to human actions, he argued, it is also universally agreed, in fact if not in words, that human actions are necessary. The resistance to calling human actions 'necessary' arises in part, he held, from the mistaken view that there is a *further* kind of necessity present in physical interactions but absent in the case of human actions. Liberty or freedom should be understood not as an absence of causal determination (the 'liberty of indifference') but rather as an absence of coercion (the 'liberty of spontaneity'). Properly understood, then, liberty and necessity are compatible. Moreover, he argued, both are required for moral responsibility, since in their absence, actions will not properly reflect the enduring character of the agent.

GOD AND RELIGIOUS HYPOTHESES

Hume believed that his analysis of causal reasoning also shed light on several disputes concerning religious hypotheses. His acceptance of imaginability as the criterion of metaphysical possibility required him to grant that miracles are metaphysically possible. However, he argued in *An Enquiry concerning Human Understanding* (Sect. X)

that no testimonial evidence could establish the occurrence of a miracle, unless the falsehood of the testimony would be more miraculous than the miracle it was intended to establish; and he argued on empirical grounds that no human testimony for any miracle tending to establish a religion ever had or ever could meet that standard. In Section XI of the same work, he considered (without explicitly endorsing) an argument concerning the afterlife based on a Humean conception of causal reasoning; the argument concludes that there can be sufficient evidence for an afterlife in which good is rewarded and evil is punished, *only* if such evidence is unnecessary to provide a motive for good behaviour. In a later essay which he attempted to suppress ('Of immortality'), he argued more directly against the IMMORTALITY of the human SOUL. And although his own position is cloaked in the posthumously published *Dialogues concerning Natural Religion* by his artful use of the dialogue form, the Hume-like character Philo uses a Humean account of causal reasoning to criticize arguments for the existence of God (particularly the Argument from Design), and provides a version of the argument from evil against the hypothesis of an omnipotent and benevolent deity.

REAL EXISTENCE AND THE EXTERNAL WORLD

Unlike Locke, Hume did not recognize a separate idea of 'real existence' involved in beliefs about the external world. Instead, he analysed the belief in external objects, or 'bodies', as a belief in 'continued and distinct existences' – continued in the sense that they continue to exist when not perceived, and distinct in the sense that they have a position external to the mind and are causally independent of it in their existence and operation (*Treatise*, Bk I, Pt iv, sect. ii). He distinguished three different positions or views that could be taken towards such existences. The 'vulgar' do not draw a distinction between impressions and objects, and thus they take the very things they perceive (which are in fact impressions) to have a continued and distinct existence. They do so not through any rational insight, but rather as a result of an irresistible cognitive illusion. Furthermore – and despite the fact that everyone holds the vulgar view at least most of the time – the vulgar view can be shown to be false, Hume held, by such experiments as pressing one's eyeball so as to double the visual image. This realization leads those who achieve it to propose the 'philosophical' view of 'double existence', according to which continued and distinct objects cause resembling but interrupted and dependent impressions in the mind. This philosophical view allows one to reconcile the irresistible belief in continued and distinct existences with the results of simple experimentation; but unfortunately, the philosophical view cannot be rendered probable by any argument, since it postulates a causal relation in which the causes themselves can never be observed. *That* realization, in turn, leads temporarily to a radical scepticism about the existence of any continued and distinct existences – a position that is, however, psychologically unmaintainable except by intense reflection on the defects of the vulgar and philosophical positions. When one's attention passes to other matters, Hume claimed, one naturally returns to the vulgar view.

THE SELF AND PERSONAL IDENTITY

Like Berkeley, Hume rejected the intelligibility of an underlying SUBSTANCE in which the qualities of material objects might inhere; for Hume, the notion of such a substance was a 'fiction', an unrepresentable *something* introduced in the attempt to justify the irresistible tendency to treat a collection of closely related qualities as something single and individual. Unlike Berkeley, however, Hume also denied that mental contents can be understood to inhere in any underlying mental substance or 'self'. Instead, he maintained in the main body of the *Treatise* (Bk I, Pt iv, Sec. vi) that the mind must be understood as a 'bundle of perceptions' (i.e. impressions and ideas)

related to one another by causation and resemblance. These relations cause the bundle of related perceptions to be taken for an unchanging and uninterrupted object, and hence cause the bundle to be treated, mistakenly, as something possessing a real simplicity at one time and identity through time. In the Appendix to the *Treatise*, however, he expressed dissatisfaction with the 'uniting principles' of his own earlier account, and pronounced the problem of personal identity 'too hard for my understanding'. (*See* PERSONS AND PERSONAL IDENTITY.)

HUME'S AIMS

Because of his professed mitigated scepticism, his liberal use of irony, and his free admission (in 'My own life' (1776)) that 'love of literary fame' was his guiding passion, many critics have supposed that Hume's philosophical intentions were not fully serious. Upon examination, however, his philosophical works reveal a thinker not only deeply concerned with empirical enquiry into human cognitive psychology, but also convinced of the ability of such enquiry to clarify the sciences, improve the understanding of morals, and free humanity from the abstruse, oppressive metaphysics of 'superstitious' organized religion. It was towards the achievement of these goals that he directed his 'experimental' yet 'metaphysical' philosophy.

WRITINGS

A Treatise of Human Nature (London: 1739–40); ed. L.A. Selby-Bigge (Oxford: Clarendon Press, 1888); 2nd edn rev. P.H. Nidditch (Oxford: Clarendon Press, 1978).
Essays, Moral and Political (London: 1741–77); ed. E.F. Miller (Indianapolis, IN: Liberty Classics, 1985).
An Enquiry concerning Human Understanding (London and Edinburgh: 1777); in *Enquiries concerning Human Understanding and concerning the Principles of Morals* ed. L.A. Selby-Bigge (Oxford: Clarendon Press,

1893); 3rd edn rev. P.H. Nidditch (Oxford: Clarendon Press, 1975).

An Enquiry concerning the Principles of Morals (London and Edinburgh: 1777); in *Enquiries concerning Human Understanding and Concerning the Principles of Morals* ed. L.A. Selby-Bigge (Oxford: Clarendon Press, 1893); 3rd edn rev. P.H. Nidditch (Oxford: Clarendon Press, 1975).

Dialogues concerning Natural Religion (London: 1779); ed. N. Kemp Smith (Edinburgh: Nelson, 1947; Indianapolis, IN: Bobbs-Merrill, 1947).

BIBLIOGRAPHY

Beauchamp, T. and Rosenberg, A.: *Hume and the Problem of Causation* (New York and Oxford: Oxford University Press, 1981).

Bennett, J.: *Locke, Berkeley, Hume: Central Themes* (Oxford: Clarendon Press, 1971).

Flew, A.: *David Hume: Philosopher of Moral Science* (Oxford: Blackwell, 1986).

Fogelin, R.: *Hume's Scepticism in the Treatise of Human Nature* (London: Routledge and Kegan Paul, 1985).

Kemp Smith, N.: *The Philosophy of David Hume* rev. 2nd edn (New York: Macmillan, 1947).

Pears, D.: *Hume's System* (New York and Oxford: Oxford University Press, 1990).

Price, H.H.: *Hume's Theory of the External World* (Oxford: Clarendon Press, 1940).

Stroud, B.: *Hume* (London: Routledge and Kegan Paul, 1977).

DON GARRETT

Husserl, Edmund (1859–1938) The creator of PHENOMENOLOGY. He was born in Moravia, received a Ph.D. in mathematics, working with Karl Weierstrass (1815–97), and then turned to philosophy under the influence of BRENTANO. He took over the latter's concern with INTENTIONALITY and developed it further into what was to become phenomenology.

Husserl's development falls into three stages. He started out attempting to found mathematics on psychology, in *Philosophie der Arithmetik* (vol. 1, 1891, the second volume never came). His second stage began around 1895, when he gave up psychologism and started work on *Logical Investigations* (1900–1), his first phenomenological work. The first volume of this work is a criticism of psychologism, the second consists of six studies of basic logical notions. The third and final stage commenced in 1906, when Husserl got the idea of the transcendental reduction, or *epoché* and began developing phenomenology in an 'idealist' direction (*see* IDEALISM). *Ideas* (1913) is the first work which gives a full and systematic presentation of phenomenology. Husserl's later works remain largely within the framework of the *Ideas*. There is little change of doctrine, but Husserl takes up topics that he only dealt with briefly or not even mentioned in the *Ideas*, such as the status of the subject, intersubjectivity, time and the lifeworld.

The key idea in phenomenology, from which everything else derives, is that of intentionality. Brentano had characterized intentionality as a special kind of directedness upon an object. Husserl rejected this appeal to an object, which leads to difficulties in cases of serious misperception and hallucination, where there is no object. Instead, Husserl endeavours to give a detailed analysis of what the directedness of consciousness consists in. Husserl studies those features of consciousness that make it *as if of* an object. The collection of all these features Husserl calls the act's *noema*. The noema unifies the consciousness we have at a certain time into an act that seemingly is directed towards an object. The noema is hence not the object that the act is directed towards, but is the structure that makes our consciousness be as if of such an object.

According to Husserl 'the noema is nothing but a generalization of the notion of meaning (*Bedeutung*) to the field of all acts (*Ideas* III, 89, 2–4). Most features of the notion of meaning and its relation to the object apply as well to the noema. Note that the noema is a very rich structure, it contains constituents corresponding to all the features, perceived and unperceived, that we attribute to the object, and moreover constituents corresponding to features that we take the object as having without having ever reflected upon this or paid attention to it. All these latter features Husserl calls the *horizon* of the act. The horizon comprises many features due to our culture, features that we rarely think about and are aware of, but that are important for the humanities and for the social sciences. It is crucial for HERMENEUTICS, and generally for our attempts to study and understand other cultures, as well as our own.

Husserl distinguishes between an inner and an outer horizon. The inner horizon comprises all the various properties that we attribute to the object, while the outer horizon consists of all the objects toward which one is not now actually turned but toward which one can turn at any time, that is, all the objects one thinks there are in the spatio-temporal world.

Husserl emphasizes that our perspectives and anticipations are not predominantly factual: 'this world is there for me not only as a world of mere things, but also with the same immediacy as a world of values, a world of goods, a practical world' (*Ideas* sect. 27, *Husserliana* III.1, 58.13–19). Further, the anticipations are not merely beliefs – about factual properties, value properties and functional features – but also bodily settings, which are involved in kinaesthesis and also play an important role in perception and in the movements of our body. In numerous passages Husserl talks about practical anticipations and the role of kinaesthesis in perception and bodily activity.

The world in which we find ourselves living, with its open horizon of objects, values, and other features, Husserl, from 1917 on, calls the *lifeworld*. Our lifeworld is strongly influenced by our culture and upbringing and therefore also by the scientific views that have seeped down to us. Far from being an alternative to science, the lifeworld is connected with science in two ways: it is influenced by science and it is the testing ground for science. The lifeworld provides the ultimate justification for all our views, in science as well as in ethics. Husserl is often presented as maintaining that we could reach absolute certainty. However, he held that certainty is impossible and advocated a view on justification that anticipates ideas of GOODMAN and John Rawls.

In our natural attitude we are absorbed in physical objects and events and in their general features, such as their colour, shape, etc. These general features, which can be shared by several objects, Husserl calls essences, or eidos (*Wesen*). We get to them by turning our attention away from the individuals in their uniqueness and focusing on what they have in common. This change of attention Husserl calls the *eidetic* reduction, since it leads us to the eidos. However, we may also, more radically, leave the natural attitude altogether, put the objects we were concerned with there in brackets and instead reflect on our own consciousness and its structures, that is, the noemata, or also the noeses and the hyle (*see* INTENTIONALITY; NOEMA, NOESIS). This reflection Husserl calls the *transcendental* reduction, since it leads us to the transcendental, that is to elements which are of crucial importance to our experience, but which we are unaware of in our natural attitude. Another word for this reduction is *epoché*. Husserl uses the label the *phenomenological* reduction for a combination of the eidetic and the transcendental reduction. It leads us to the phenomena studied in phenomenology: the noemata, noeses and hyle, and focuses on their general features. Phenomenology, for Husserl, is the study of the general features of noemata, noeses and hyle and it is hence carried out by help of the phenomenological reduction.

See also INTUITION.

WRITINGS

Logische Untersuchungen vols I–II (Halle: 1900–1); *Husserliana* (the standard edition of Husserl's works) (The Hague:

Martinus Nijhoff) vols XVIII–XIX; trans. J.N. Findlay *Logical Investigations* 2 vols (London: Routledge and Kegan Paul, 1970).

Ideen Bk I (Halle: 1913); Bks I–III *Husserliana* vols III–V; Bk I trans. F. Kersten, *Ideas* (The Hague: Martinus Nijhoff, 1982).

Formale und transzendentale Logik (1929); *Husserliana* vol. XVII; trans. D. Cairns, *Formal and Transcendental Logic* (The Hague: Martinus Nijhoff, 1969).

Kartesianische Meditationen (Paris: 1931); *Husserliana* vol. I; improved edn ed. E. Ströker (Hamburg: Felix Meiner, 1977) and in *Edmund Husserl, Gesammelte Schriften* ed. E. Ströker (Hamburg: Meiner, 1992); trans. D. Cairns, *Cartesian Meditations* (The Hague: Martinus Nijhoff, 1960).

Krisis der europäischen Wissenschaften und die transzendentale Phänomenologie, Husserliana VI; trans. D. Carr, *The Crisis of European Sciences and Transcendental Phenomenology* (Evanston, IL: Northwestern University Press, 1970).

BIBLIOGRAPHY

Bell, D.: *Husserl* (London: Routledge, 1990).

Dreyfus, H. ed.: *Husserl, Intentionality and Cognitive Science* (Cambridge, MA: MIT Press, 1982).

Miller, I.: *Husserl, Perception, and Temporal Awareness* (Cambridge, MA: MIT Press, 1984).

Mohanty, J.: *The Possibility of Transcendental Philosophy* (Dordrecht: M. Nijhoff, 1985).

Smith, D. and McIntyre, R.: *Husserl and Intentionality. A Study of Mind, Meaning and Language* (Dordrecht: D. Reidel, 1982).

DAGFINN FØLLESDAL

hylomorphism　The view, first defended by ARISTOTLE that the 'soul' of living creatures is best understood as the *form* (Greek *morphē*) of their body or their matter (Greek *hulē*). It represents an attempt to do justice to the fundamental role of matter in life-activities, while at the same time recognizing the explanatory priority of structure and function. In modern terms, it can still be seen as an attractive alternative to dualism, on the one hand, and materialist reductionism, on the other.

Aristotle's hylomorphism is closely linked to his more general arguments for the priority of organization or structure to material components in explaining the natures and actions of substances of all sorts (*see* SUBSTANCE). His general argument, in a number of works, is that if we are interested in explaining CHANGE and activity in the world of nature, we need to be able to single out certain items that are both relatively enduring and relatively distinct, as the things to which changes happen. Since living things continually change their matter while retaining their identity, it would appear that their 'form' or organization is a stronger candidate for this role than their material constituents. By 'form' in these arguments Aristotle does not mean 'shape', he insists, since living things can also change their shape without ceasing to be themselves. He means, instead, the organization in virtue of which they function in the way characteristic of their kind. (*See* MATTER/FORM).

Aristotle's work *On the Soul* (*De anima*) attempts to find the best framework for explaining the life-activities of all living creatures, including plants and all animals. He announces that he takes the explananda of a theory of *psuchē* to include growth, nutrition and self-maintenance, reproduction, perception, imagination, desire and thinking. It is important to recognize that a theory of *psuchē* – unlike a theory of 'SOUL' in the modern sense – presupposes no view about whether separable non-bodily entities exist. Nor does it focus especially on the 'higher' mental functions, such as consciousness. It is, instead, an attempt to give a general answer to the question, what explains the functions of life? What makes the difference between LIFE and DEATH? And it presupposes only that this difference is interesting and that it makes sense to try to explain it.

Aristotle begins by discussing the views of his predecessors. For some thinkers, *psuchē* is a particular sort of matter, such as air or fire. For others, it is a particular balance or relation among the material constituents: thus death is understood to result from an imbalance of elements. For still others, it is a particular set of basic material particles: the small fast-moving atoms that for the early Greek Atomists performed the functions of perceiving and thinking. For PLATO, it is a separable non-bodily entity. Aristotle argues against all of these views, and then outlines his own position.

He argues, first, that the *psuchē* of living creatures cannot be equivalent to its matter: for a living creature is not just a heap of matter, but a body of a certain specific type, namely a living one – and it is this that we seek to explain. Moreover, a living creature's *psuchē* seems to be intimately connected with what it *is*, with what remains the same about it and identifies it through changes of many sorts, up until death. Matter, which changes continually in living things, cannot play this role. What, then is it that persists throughout a creature's life, only to be disrupted at death? Aristotle argues that it is the structure or functional organization characteristic of the species in question. He illustrates this idea by saying that if the living creature were an eye, *psuchē* would be its ability to see; if the living creature were an axe, *psuchē* would be its ability to cut, that is, the structure in virtue of which it is able to perform the function characteristic of an axe. Clarifying his claim, he insists that *psuchē* does not entail continuous actual activity – for living creatures frequently sleep and are inactive, without ceasing to be themselves. It is kind of organized readiness to function, which frequently issues in actual functioning.

This, however, should not be taken to imply that this functioning could go on without a suitably equipped body. *Psuchē* is the 'form' or functional organization 'of a natural body equipped with suitable organs'. The functions of life (with the partial exception of thinking, to which Aristotle gives a separate treatment) are all carried on in and by the organized body, and presupposes the presence of matter suitable to perform those functions. In short: it makes no sense to ask whether *psuchē* and matter are one: for their relation is like that of some wax and a shape impressed on the wax. Beyond this, Aristotle holds, we can say little that is informative at a high level of generality: we should turn to the examination of the characteristic functioning of each sort of creature.

Aristotle's view has consequences for the explanation of particular life-functions such as reproduction and perception, on which he focuses in other writings. Although his hylomorphism has sometimes been rejected by modern materialists, it has recently won praise from biologists for its insistence on the organic character of living systems and the importance of structural principles in explaining their workings. And his arguments still provide good reasons to consider his view as a viable alternative to dualism and reductionism.

BIBLIOGRAPHY

Aristotle: *On the Soul* (*De anima*) ed. with commentary W.D. Ross (Oxford: Clarendon Press, 1961); ed. R.D. Hicks (Cambridge: Cambridge University Press, 1907; repr. New York: Arno Press, 1976). English translations by H. Lawson-Tancred (New York: Penguin, 1986); J.A. Smith, rev. J. Barnes, in *The Complete Works of Aristotle* ed. J. Barnes, 2 vols (Princeton, NJ: Princeton University Press, 1984).

Aristotle: *Parva naturalia* ed. W.D. Ross (Oxford: Clarendon Press, 1955); trans. (various translators) in *The Complete Works of Aristotle*.

Nussbaum, M. and Rorty, A. eds: *Essays on Aristotle's De Anima* (Oxford: Clarendon Press, 1992).

MARTHA C. NUSSBAUM

hypostasis, reification A process of reasoning in which the EXISTENCE of something is accepted by virtue of its explicit role in a theory or explanation: the thing's existence is postulated within the theory or explanation in order to help understand some already accepted phenomenon or fact and its existence is accepted because the theory or explanation is thought to be a good one. Hypostasis was explicitly used initially to try to warrant belief in the existence of a SUBSTANCE underlying various groups of perceivable attributes: the substance's existence was taken to be part of the best explanation of the co-occurrence of the attributes. But its power and plausibility are perhaps better appreciated now in the area of natural science, particularly in the vindication of our beliefs in the elementary particles of physics. Their existence is accepted solely on the basis of their role in explanatorily powerful physical theories.

The reason why hypostasis seems so plausible in respect of many elementary particles is that they are postulated as causes of straightforwardly observable effects. But a number of philosophers have tried to extend the use of hypostasis to warrant acceptance of other kinds of objects to which, because of their apparent causal inertness, we would otherwise have dubious epistemological access. For example, the existence of certain mathematical objects – or their set-theoretic surrogates – is sometimes said to be warranted by their role in good physical theories about the world. (Almost all important laws of physics are mathematical in form and imply or presuppose the existence of numbers and functions of various kinds.) Equally, the existence of fictional objects is sometimes claimed to be warranted by their role in literary theory. They are part and parcel of the best explanation of the apparent truth of propositions about characters in novels, films, and so on. (*See* FICTIONAL TRUTH, OBJECTS AND CHARACTERS.)

Hypostasis is arguably therefore a powerful tool in ontological reasoning. Indeed some have argued further that it is *only* by virtue of hypostasis that something can be accepted as existing. According to this line of thought, the only alternative to hypostasis is direct (i.e. non-inferential) observation. And this seems incoherent. For it is a commonplace that all observation is 'theory-laden', and this just means that in observing something, people must inevitably base their observations on some relevant theory about it.

Tempting though this argument may seem, however, much more needs to be said before it can be accepted. For to say that observation is theory-laden is to say that when people observe something they do so by exploiting a theoretically grounded conceptual repertoire. (For instance, in observing a pig, they may observe it *as a pig*, or *as a farmyard animal*, or *as a space-occupier*, all of which concepts are underpinned by theory.) But while it may be true that all observation is theory-laden in this sense, it does not follow that in observing something, people *infer* their observations on the basis of the relevant theory. Indeed, without the fabrication of spurious 'unconscious' inferences, to suppose they did would often by contrary to plain fact. People can perfectly well observe a pig, and in so doing apprehend its existence as a pig, without reasoning from any theory of pigs. (Doubtless, in order to apprehend it as a pig, they must know certain facts about pigs. But even these facts need not form the basis of any inference.)

If this is right, then hypostasis is not the only way in which we can rationally come to accept the existence of something. And when one begins to consider the above examples in detail, doubts may begin to creep in whether it even provides *one* way. In any particular case, whatever power it has must derive from its being an instance of an inference to a good, or even the best, explanation. And this may certainly be challenged in respect of any of the above examples. Thus the argument for the existence of numbers and functions is open to the objection that if our reason for believing in them is that they play a certain role in physical theory, it becomes obscure how pure facts about them – the facts that $2 + 2 = 4$, that differentiable functions are continuous, and so on – can be both necessary and a priori. And every one of the above arguments, whether for the existence of mathematical objects, fictional objects or elementary particles, can be resisted on the grounds that it commits us to an unnecessary or profligate ontology. (Of course, for this second challenge to be successful, there must be reasonable grounds for thinking that there are alternative, equally good theories which do not entail the allegedly questionable ontologies; otherwise, the ontologies will not have been shown to be questionable.)

In themselves, none of these criticisms calls hypostasis as such into question. But even this is possible. Thus certain philosophers have objected to it by questioning the very idea of an inference to a good, or the best, explanation – at least in so far as it is conceived of as a way of reaching approximate or probable truth. The virtues of an explanation are generally agreed to include such features as simplicity, economy and comprehensivity. But it is a considerable jump (they say) from the fact that an explanation possesses these features to the conclusion that it is approximately or probably true. Although we all make such jumps, the question remains why simplicity, economy and comprehensivity should be guides to the truth. More radical still are those who argue that we cannot understand putative descriptions of the unobservable. Nothing (they say) could count as manifesting such understanding (as distinct from understanding descriptions of associated observable phenomena); and if no one can manifest such understanding, no one can gain it either. (For discussion of arguments of this sort, *see* ANTIREALISM; SIMPLICITY, PARSIMONY.)

See also ONTOLOGY.

BIBLIOGRAPHY

Hale, B.: *Abstract Objects* (Oxford: Blackwell, 1987).

Lipton, P.: *Inference to the Best Explanation* (London: Routledge, 1991).

Quine, W.V.O.: 'On what there is', in his *From a Logical Point of View* (New York and Evanston: Harper and Row, 1963), 1–19.

van Fraassen, B.C.: *The Scientific Image* (Oxford: Oxford University Press, 1980).

van Inwagen, P.: 'Creatures of fiction', *American Philosophical Quarterly* 14 (1977), 299–308.

S.G. WILLIAMS

I

idea A term prominent in early modern philosophy, but explicated in the context of radically diverse theories of perception and thought. Despite later attacks on the 'theory of ideas', for example, by REID, no single position can be associated with that phrase. The term 'idea' caught on, because DESCARTES's use of it signalled a sharp break from the scholastic doctrine of intentional species. Moreover, the term had antecedents in both NEOPLATONIST metaphysics, where it was used for eternal archetypes of creatures' essences, and materialist theories of perception, where it meant corporeal impressions constitutive of sense perception. Early moderns felt free to use it for diverse sorts of entities. (*See* ARCHETYPE; ESSENCE/ACCIDENT.)

The central notion was that ideas account for the INTENTIONALITY, or object-directedness, of perception and thought. Descartes defined idea as the 'form' of a thought, by 'immediate awareness' of which we are aware of that thought. This suggests ideas are contents *intrinsic* to cognitive acts. Sometimes the content *represents* something actual, for example, when one perceives the sun. But Descartes also said objects of cognition have 'objective existence' in the intellect. He may sometimes have meant that all cognitive acts are *extrinsically* related to objects with non-actual existence; and when we perceive the sun, for example, the sun that exists objectively (in mind) is *identical* to the sun existing actually.

ARNAULD argued for the intrinsic-content notion of ideas. As he explained, we do not *perceive* the contents of perceptual acts although we are 'immediately aware' of them. When we perceive actual things, we do so directly without perceiving intermediary objects. He opposed MALEBRANCHE, who claimed particular bodies cannot be directly 'present to mind'. Malebranche took the Neoplatonist view that UNIVERSALS are intelligible, whereas particulars are unknowable; and he supposed we *know* the essence of body (extension). Thus, since actual bodies are entirely particular, all we can perceive is universal extension. This is an Idea existing in God that represents actual bodies as archetype. (*See* UNIVERSALS AND PARTICULARS.)

LOCKE defined ideas epistemically: whatever is the 'immediate object' of awareness when one thinks. Ideas mediate thoughts of things in two ways: as signs of actual things and as specifications to which things may 'conform'. The former suggests a mental-object view of ideas and the latter, an intrinsic-content view. On that question, Locke apparently remained neutral (although he rejected Malebranche's Ideas). Unlike these others, LEIBNIZ posited *non-conscious* cognition, sometimes locating intentionality in a natural analogy (relation of 'expression') between mental modifications and objects. Ideas, he said, are DISPOSITIONS to perform various cognitive operations; for example, the idea of triangle is the tendency to regard particular triangles as 'the same', affirm the definition of triangle, etc.

Ideas were central in accounts of the metaphysical and epistemic basis of necessary truths. Descartes maintained we have ideas of 'immutable natures' with a mode of being independent of whether they exist outside the mind and whether we think of them. Malebranche's Ideas are subjects of necessary truths with non-actual existence in the mind of God, an infinite Being without modifications that 'contains' all forms of undetermined (universal) being. Leibniz grounded necessary truths in God's ideas, which he probably construed as actual modifications of God.

Arnauld and Locke recognized neither eternal nor non-actual grounds of necessary truths. They said we know such truths by discovering what is contained in ideas (Arnauld) or necessary relations between ideas (Locke). Both explicated linguistic meaning by reference to ideas. Locke held that a name 'immediately' signifies an idea and thereby signifies what the idea does.

Sense perception posed a special problem for early moderns who ascribed nothing but 'mechanical affections' to bodies. Colours, and so on, as we perceive them, are *not* modifications of bodies; nevertheless we perceive bodies when we perceive colours. Descartes and Arnauld said ideas of colours are confused and obscure. With such ideas, immediate awareness is often erroneous; for example, we mistake an idea of red-caused-by-a-body for an idea of red-modifying-a-body. Thus some ideas are *not* what they are immediately perceived to be. But Locke insisted it is the nature of ideas to be as they are immediately perceived; otherwise knowledge is impossible. (Malebranche agreed, as did BERKELEY and HUME.) For Locke, all sensory ideas are natural signs of the objects that cause them; but ideas of colours, and so on, are not representations (resemblances) of what they signify (unlike ideas of extension, motion, etc.). Malebranche denied that sensations of colours are Ideas with representative function. They are particular modifications of finite minds that serve to reduce perceptions of universal extension to particular bodies.

Berkeley later contended that mind-dependent ideas are the *only* objects of sense. (We have notions, not ideas, of non-sensible things.) Refusing altogether to distinguish perceptual acts and their objects, he insisted we cannot conceive an object (e.g. a book) existing unconceived. He said ideas are modifications of minds; like all actual things, they are entirely determined. Thus if 'abstract ideas' are contents (objects) partially determined relative to actual things, they are *logically* impossible; e.g. the 'abstract idea' of triangle would be an actual triangle (mental modification) with indeterminate altitude, area, etc. One of Berkeley's arguments for IDEALISM claims the determinate qualities of a sensible object, for example, exact colour or motion, are relative to circumstances of perception. Thus an *unperceived* object would have indeterminate qualities, but that can neither be nor be conceived.

Berkeley dismissed key elements in previous accounts of ideas: the act/content distinction, the representative nature of ideas, and theories of non-actual being. Thereby he fostered the mistaken view that his predecessors shared a single 'theory of ideas' vulnerable to idealist and skeptical arguments. Hume accepted many of the main points of Berkeley's account of ideas. He argued, further, that an idea is not perceived *by* anything and can possibly exist apart from any mind. This tended to compound the stigma later associated with ideas.

See also SENSA.

BIBLIOGRAPHY

Ayers, M.R.: *Locke* 2 vols, Vol. I *Epistemology* (London: Routledge, 1991), 13–80.

Doney, W. ed.: *Berkeley on Abstraction and Abstract Ideas* (New York: Garland Publishing, Inc., 1989).

Jolley, N.: *The Light of the Soul: Theories of Ideas in Leibniz, Malebranche, and Descartes* (Oxford: Clarendon Press, 1990).

Lennon, T.M.: 'Philosophical commentary', in N. Malebranche, *The Search After Truth* trans. T.M. Lennon and P.J. Olscamp (Columbus: Ohio State University Press, 1980), 781–809.

Nadler, S.M.: *Arnauld and the Cartesian Philosophy of Ideas* (Princeton, NJ: Princeton University Press, 1989).

Yolton, J.: *Perceptual Acquaintance from Descartes to Reid* (Minneapolis: University of Minnesota Press, 1984).

M.B. BOLTON

idealism The term 'idealist' was first used in the early eighteenth century by Christian Wolff (1679–1754) who wrote: 'Those thinkers are called "idealists" who acknowledge only ideal objects existing in our minds, denying the independent reality of the world and the existence of material bodies' (*Psychologia rationalis* sect. 36). But as now understood, the doctrine is broader.

Metaphysical idealism is the philosophical position that reality is somehow mind-correlative or mind-coordinated – that the real objects comprising the 'external world' are not independent of cognizing minds, but have an existence correlative to mental operations. The doctrine centres around the conception that reality as such reflects the workings of mind. And it construes this as meaning that the inquiring mind itself makes a formative contribution not merely to our understanding of the nature of the real but even to the resulting character we attribute to it.

The ontological idealism that is at issue in metaphysics takes one of two principal alternative forms: (1) *causal idealism*: everything there is, apart from minds themselves, arises causally from the operations of minds; and (2) SUPERVENIENCE *idealism*: everything there is, apart from minds themselves, is supervenient upon the operations of minds (i.e. somehow inheres in them in ways that are not necessarily *causal* but involve some other mode of existential dependency). Perhaps the most radical form of idealism is the ancient Oriental spiritualistic or panpsychistic idea – renewed in Christian Science – that minds and their thoughts are all there is; that reality is simply the sum total of the visions (or dreams?) of one or more minds. BERKELEY's immaterialism is a position much along these lines.

There has been disagreement within the idealist camp over whether 'the mind' at issue in formulating the doctrine is a mind emplaced outside of or behind nature (*absolute* idealism), or a nature-pervasive power of rationality of some sort (*cosmic* idealism), or the collective impersonal social mind of people-in-general (*social* idealism), or simply the distributive collection of individual minds (*personal* idealism). Over the years, the less grandiose versions of the theory came increasingly to the fore, and in recent times virtually all idealists have construed 'the mind' at issue in their theory as a matter of separate individual minds equipped with socially engendered resources. Idealism thus comes down to a view about the nature of reality as we humans can and do conceive of it.

There are certainly versions of idealism short of the spiritualistic position of an ontological idealism which holds that reality is somehow spiritual or even maintains that (as KANT formulated it at *Prolegomena* sect. 13, n. 2) 'there are none but thinking beings'. Idealism need not go so far as to affirm that mind *makes or constitutes* matter; it is quite enough to maintain (for example) that all of the characterizing properties of physical existents resemble phenomenal sensory properties in representing dispositions to affect mind-endowed creatures in a certain sort of way, so that these properties have a nature that must be understood with reference to minds. A particularly interesting version of idealism is the 'ideal-realism' of FICHTE and F.W.J. Schelling (1775–1854): a doctrine to the effect that any explanation of the real must use principles of idealization – that the nature of reality can be accounted for adequately only if mind-derived principles of aesthetic or other valuation (elegance, simplicity, economy or the like) are brought into play (*See* SIMPLICITY, PARSIMONY). A position of this sort can, but need not, be explicitly teleological. (*See* TELEOLOGY.)

Idealists need not deny matter – they need not be immaterialists. The central point of their doctrine is simply that matter-as-we-know-it is something in whose nature

227

traces of the operation of mind can be detected: that at least some of its aspects have to be seen as mind-originated: that matter has features that are inextricably rooted in the operations of mind. In the final analysis, any doctrine that denies the existence of in-principle unknowable 'things-in-themselves' and insists that the only reality there is a potentially knowable reality is a form of idealism (seeing that its in-principle knowability will render reality mind coordinated).

But how can the idealist maintain the fundamentality of mind when all the world knows that a mind's operations hinge upon those of matter? (As Mark Twain asked: 'When the body gets drunk, does the mind stay sober?') The response lies in noting that while the mind's operations may indeed involve a *causal* dependency on the operations of matter, this nowise prevents a reciprocal *conceptual* relationship through which the very conception of what matter is is something that the mind grasps in self-referential terms, thereby endowing matter with features modelled on the workings of minds. Thus while *causal* subordination moves from mind to matter, *conceptual* subordination moves from matter to mind. This particular sort of supervenience idealism averts many of the difficulties that afflict the doctrine's causal form. To be sure, it is a weak form of idealist doctrine that is, in the final analysis, compatible with a materialism that sees the operations of matter as the causal source of mental processes. (*See* PHYSICALISM/MATERIALISM.)

It is sometimes said that idealism is predicated on a confusion of objects with our knowledge of them and conflates the real with our thought about it. But this charge misses the pivotal point. The only reality with which we inquirers can have any cognitive commerce is reality as we conceive it to be. What idealists maintain is not (trivially that) minds alone can know reality, but more interestingly that the reality we come to know is itself shaped by the operations of mind.

Historically, positions of the generally idealistic type have been espoused by numerous thinkers. For example, Berkeley maintained that 'to be (real) is to be perceived' (*esse est percipi*). And while this does not seem particularly plausible because of its inherent commitment to omniscience, it seems more sensible to adopt 'to be is to be perceivable' (*esse est percipile esse*). For Berkeley, of course, this was a distinction without a difference: if something is perceivable at all, then God perceives it. But if we forgo philosophical reliance on God, the issue looks different, and now comes to pivot on the question of what is perceivable for perceivers who are *physically realizable* in 'the real world', so that *physical* existence could be seen – not so implausibly – as tantamount to observability-in-principle.

Over the years, many objections to idealism have been advanced. Samuel Johnson (1709–84) thought to refute Berkeley's PHENOMENALISM by kicking a stone. He conveniently forgot that Berkeley's theory goes to great lengths to provide for stones – even to the point of invoking the aid of God on their behalf. MOORE pointed to the human hand as an undeniably mind-external material object. He overlooked that, gesticulate as he would, he would do no more than *induce people to accept* the presence of a hand on the basis of the hand-orientation of their *experience*. PEIRCE's 'Harvard Experiment' of letting go of a stone held aloft was supposed to establish scholastic realism because his audience could not control their expectation of the stone's falling to earth. But an uncontrollable expectation is still an expectation, and the realism at issue is no more than a realistic thought-posture.

Kant's famous 'Refutation of Idealism' argued that our conception of ourselves as mind-endowed beings presupposes material objects because we view our mind-endowed selves as existing in an objective temporal order, and such an order requires the existence of periodic physical processes (clocks, pendula, planetary regularities) for its establishment. At most, however, this argumentation succeeds in showing that such physical processes *have to be assumed by minds*, the issue of their actual mind-independent existence remaining unaddressed.

(Kantian realism is an intra-experiential, 'empirical' realism.)

Moore criticized BRADLEY's form of absolute idealism by insisting that if matter and time are unreal then there are no such things as human hands or clocks, and that temporal transactions (like people being late for trains) would be abolished. What this ignores is that idealists do not seek to deny the things or facts at issue, but only to characterize their *status* (as somehow phenomenal and involving the workings of mind rather than as part of the paraphernalia of mind-external reality).

Perhaps the strongest argument favouring idealism is that any characterization of the real that we can devise is bound to be a mind-constructed one: *our* only access to information about the real is through the mediation of mind. Clearly, our only information about reality is via the operations of mind – our only cognitive access to reality is through the mediation of mind-devised models of it. What seems right about idealism is inherent in the fact that, in investigating the real, we are clearly constrained to use our own concepts to address our own issues; we can only learn about the real in our own terms of reference, so that any view of reality we can obtain is the view of a reality shaped by the operations of mind. But what seems right about realism is that the answers to the questions we put to the real are provided by reality itself – whatever the answers may be, they are as they are rather than otherwise because it is – ultimately – reality that determines them to be that way. Mind proposes but reality disposes.

See also REALISM.

BIBLIOGRAPHY

For the history of idealism:
Willmann, O.: *Geschichte des Idealismus* 3 vols (Braunschweig: Vieweg, 1894–7).

For the German tradition:
Hartmann, N.: *Die Philosophie des deutschen Idealismus* 2 vols (Berlin: De Gruyter, 1923 and 1929).
Krönenberg, M.: *Geschichte des deutschen Idealismus* 2 vols (Munich: Beck, 1909 and 1912).

For British idealism:
Ewing, A.C.: *Idealism: A Critical Survey* (London: Macmillan, 1934).
Ewing, A.C.: *The Idealist Tradition* (Glencoe: Free Press, 1957).
Pucelle, J.: *L'Idéalisme en Angleterre de Coleridge à Bradley* (Paris: Presses Universitaires de France, 1955).

For contemporary defences of idealist doctrines:
Foster, J.: *The Case for Idealism* (London: Routledge and Kegan Paul, 1982).
Rescher, N.: *Conceptual Idealism* (Oxford: Blackwell, 1973).
Sprigge, T.: *The Vindication of Absolute Idealism* (Edinburgh: Edinburgh University Press, 1983).

NICHOLAS RESCHER

identity Typically used in philosophy to mean 'numerical identity'. A thing x is numerically identical with a thing y if x and y are *one and the same*. Numerical identity is standardly contrasted with 'qualitative identity', the relationship that holds between two things that are qualitatively similar to a high degree. Identical twins are not numerically identical but they may be qualitatively identical (to a high degree). The present essay is a discussion of numerical identity.

STRICT AND NON-STRICT IDENTITY

It is arguable, however, that even 'numerical identity' is ambiguous. Most philosophers hold that identity satisfies *Leibniz's Law* (see IDENTITY OF INDISCERNIBLES), which says that if x is identical with y then x and y share all of their properties. But there seem to be ordinary examples in which identity does not satisfy Leibniz's Law. Suppose that a piece of rubber is used to make a rubber ball. It then seems correct to say, 'The piece of rubber and the ball are one and the same.' But the piece of rubber and the ball do not share all of their properties; for example, only the former has the property of having existed before the ball was created. So here we seem to have a case of (numerical) identity which violates Leibniz's Law.

The simplest response to this point is to distinguish between two senses of '(numerical) identity'. In the sense relevant to Leibniz's Law, the piece of rubber and the ball are not one and the same; in another sense they are one and the same. We can call the first sense 'strict identity' and the second sense 'temporary identity'. Temporary identity might be characterized as that relationship which holds between a pair of strictly distinct things during a period of time when they are made up of the same matter; alternatively, during a period of time when they occupy the same place; alternatively, during a period of time when they share the same stages or parts of their history (*see* TEMPORAL PARTS/STAGES). These characterizations generally amount to the same thing but they may diverge in some problematical cases (such as cases of things that occupy space but are not made up of matter). It may be noted that though temporary identity does not satisfy Leibniz's Law, it does satisfy a weakened version of the law, in that, during a period when things are temporarily identical, they must share all of their properties that are intrinsic to that period.

It seems pointless to insist that what is here being called temporary identity is not *really* identity, for it seems plain enough that, in ordinary English, the sentence 'The piece of rubber is identical with (is one and the same as) the ball' expresses a truth in the envisioned circumstances. Indeed, one must not be misled by our saying that the kind of identity expressed in this sentence is not 'strict'. This technical remark should not be taken to imply that the sentence exhibits loose usage in the sense of sloppy or metaphorical usage; there appears to be no evidence of loose usage in this sense. To say that the kind of identity expressed in the

sentence is not 'strict' means primarily that this kind of identity does not satisfy a certain stringent requirement, Leibniz's Law, which another kind of identity does satisfy. A further suggestion might be that strict identity, the kind that satisfies Leibniz's Law, is more fundamental than temporary identity. It seems impossible to think coherently about any subject matter without employing the notion of strict identity; the notion of temporary identity seems in most instances expandable. Whereas temporary identity can be defined in terms of strict identity, by reference to the strict identity of matter or places or stages, a definition in the reverse direction seems either impossible or highly artificial.

Strict identity and temporary identity may not exhaust the ordinary senses of '(numerical) identity'. Suppose that the ball in the previous example is destroyed and the piece of rubber is used to make a doorstop. In this case, the doorstop is neither strictly identical with, nor even temporarily identical with, the ball. Still, it may seem in a sense correct to say, 'The doorstop is identical with (is one and the same as) the ball.' This seems correct in the following sense: 'The doorstop is (now) *the same matter as* the ball (was earlier).' The latter statement seems easily explainable in terms of temporary identity: it means that some matter z is such that z is temporarily identical with the ball at one time and z is temporarily identical with the doorstop at another time. In general, it seems correct to say something of the form, 'a is the same F as b' whenever it is either correct to say, 'Some F is such that it is strictly identical with a and it is strictly identical with b' (in other words, 'a is F and a is strictly identical with b') or it is correct to say, 'Some F is such that it is temporarily identical with a at one time and it is temporarily identical with b at another time'.

SORTAL RELATIVITY

Geach (1962, p. 157) advanced the following *relativity thesis*: we cannot simply ask whether a thing x and a thing y are one and the same; it must always be specified *the same what*; for *x* may be the same *F* as *y* though *x* is a different *G* than *y*. Part of Geach's point seems to be supported by the example of the doorstop and the ball: the doorstop is the same matter as the ball but the doorstop is a different ARTEFACT from the ball. Wiggins (1980, pp. 18–20) argued that Geach's relativity thesis is incompatible with the assumption that identity satisfies Leibniz's Law. As adapted to the example of the doorstop and the ball, Wiggins's argument is this. Suppose that Leibniz's Law applies to the statement 'The doorstop is the same matter as the ball.' Then the doorstop and the ball have the same properties. Since the ball obviously has the property of being the same artefact as the ball, the doorstop must have that property. Hence it could not be true that the doorstop is a different artefact than the ball.

There are several different issues to be disentangled here. Let us say that 'relative identity' is expressed by a true statement of the form '*a* is the same *F* as *b* and *a* is a different *G* than *b*'. One conclusion that might be drawn from Wiggins's argument is that instances of relative identity are not instances of strict identity; since relative identity holds between the doorstop and the ball, strict identity does not hold. That, of course, would not be denied by Geach. Perhaps Wiggins wants to deny that what Geach treats as relative identity is properly called identity. But that seems like a marginal point of terminology, which is, in any case, not obviously supported by the ordinary use of the terms 'identical with' or 'one and the same as'. The crucial issue is not whether there are instances of relative identity; it seems permissible to say that there are such instances. The crucial issue is rather whether there are instances of strict identity. Geach's relativity thesis implies that the *only* notion of (numerical) identity we have is that of relative identity; the notion of strict identity is incoherent. It is this claim which seems highly implausible. The notion of strict identity is simply the notion of a relation that holds only between *a thing and itself*. This notion seems as clear, and as

fundamental to our thinking, as any that we possess.

SORTAL DEPENDENCE

While Wiggins rejects Geach's relativity thesis, he advocates the *thesis of the sortal dependency of identity* (Wiggins, 1980, ch. 2). What this amounts to, however, is elusive. A 'sortal' is supposed to be a term which in some sense tells us 'what the thing is'. One of Wiggins's examples of a sortal is the term 'tree'; such adjectives as 'brown' and 'wooden' are not sortals. If *a* is a brown wooden tree, the thesis of sortal dependency evidently implies that *a*'s identity somehow depends on *a*'s being a tree in a way that *a*'s identity does not depend on *a*'s being wooden or brown. A partial explication of this (as suggested in Hirsch, 1982, Ch. 2) might be in terms of the following principle: whereas a continuous succession of stages of trees typically must add up to stages of one and the same tree, a continuous succession of stages of brown or wooden things may jump from one brown or wooden thing to another. This principle exhibits a sense in which *a*'s identity might be said to depend on *a*'s being an instance of 'tree' rather than on *a*'s being an instance of either 'brown' or 'wooden'.

The difficulty is to find a clear way of moving from this sort of example to Wiggins's general idea that any thing's identity must depend on 'what it is'. One aspect of this difficulty can be brought out by contrasting a thing's 'identity through time' (its 'diachronic unity') with the thing's 'identity through space' (its 'synchronic unity'). If *a* is a brown wooden tree, the principle of sortal dependency in the last paragraph provides a rough analysis of what the diachronic unity of *a*'s successive stages consists in, and this analysis depends in a certain way on *a*'s being a tree. There appears, however, to be no comparable analysis of the synchronic unity of *a*'s contemporaneous parts which depends on *a*'s being a tree. But the thesis of sortal dependency, as Wiggins apparently intends it, would imply that *a*'s identity through space as well as its identity through time depends on 'what it is'.

Suppose we view the world as made up of various space-time portions of reality, most of which are discontinuous and heterogeneous, but a select number of which count as 'genuine things' or 'substances'. All trees enjoy this special status but not all brown or wooden portions of reality do, since most of these will combine stages of different brown or wooden things. Looked at in this way, 'what a thing is' provides it with the credentials required to count as a genuine thing, and any genuine thing must have such credentials. This may be one way to explain the thesis of sortal dependency. On this explanation, the thesis would not imply that we can give any analysis of a thing's diachronic or synchronic unity, let alone an analysis which depends in some special way on the thing's sortals. We appeal to the thing's sortals, rather, in justifying its status as a genuine thing.

But there is the risk that the thesis so understood trivializes the distinction between a 'genuine thing' and a 'mere portion of reality'. There seem to be three positions that can be adopted with respect to this distinction. First, it may be accepted as ultimate and unanalysable. But that would seem to imply that the distinction does *not* depend on sortals. Second, one may attempt to provide a general sortal-independent analysis of this distinction. A first approximation to such an analysis (as suggested in Hirsch, 1982, ch. 3) is that a portion of reality qualifies as a genuine thing if its boundary is at any moment highly articulated, and in tracing it through time one follows a continuous path in which changes are minimized as far as possible. Of course, if any such sortal-independent analysis can succeed, the thesis of sortal dependency is rejected. The third possibility, which is the one implied by the thesis, is that genuine things are analysed as things that are instances of a certain list of sortals. The trouble is that this third position seems to imply that genuine things really have nothing in common which sets them apart from other portions of reality. It

is as if a genuine thing is being defined as any portion of reality that is either a cat, or a dog, . . . , or a mountain or a river, . . . or (fill in for the rest of the sortals). This makes it difficult to see how there could be anything deep or important in the distinction between genuine things and portions of reality that do not so qualify.

NECESSARY AND CONTINGENT IDENTITY

The different senses of 'identity' indicated above have a bearing on the question whether identity statements are necessary or contingent. Kripke's *thesis of the necessity of identity* says that if a thing x is identical with a thing y then it is necessarily the case (it holds in all POSSIBLE WORLDS) that x is identical with y (Kripke, 1980, pp. 3–5). The argument for this follows directly from Leibniz's Law. If x is identical with y then, since y evidently has the property of being necessarily identical with y, x must have the property of being necessarily identical with y.

It is clear that Kripke intends his thesis to apply to strict identity. It will not, however, apply to temporary identity or to relative identity, since in these cases Leibniz's Law does not apply. If the ball x is temporarily identical with the piece of rubber y (or if x is the same matter as the doorstop z) then this is only a contingent fact at least in the following sense: there might have been a situation in which y existed without x ever existing (or a situation in which z existed without x existing). These examples should tempt no one to deny Kripke's thesis with respect to strict identity. There is another kind of example, however, which may seem more challenging.

Imagine that God creates a rubber ball *ex nihilo*, so that the ball and its matter come into existence simultaneously. A few minutes later God annihilates the ball and its matter. In this example the ball and the piece of rubber that makes it up are not just *temporarily* identical. They occupy the same places and are made up of the same matter throughout their entire histories; they seem indeed to share the same history. It may be tempting to think, therefore, that this is a case of strict identity. But surely the identity between the ball and piece of rubber is contingent, in the sense that there might have been a situation in which the latter existed without the former existing.

This is, however, not really a counter-example to the thesis of the necessity of (strict) identity. The ball and the piece of rubber have different properties, for the piece of rubber but not the ball has the property of being such that it might have existed without the ball existing. Since they have different properties they are not strictly identical. They are, it might be said, as *close* to being strictly identical as two things can be. Perhaps we should have a name for this relationship; we might call it 'total coincidence'; or we might even be tempted to call it 'contingent identity'. But contingent identity in this sense is not strict identity, and hence does not threaten Kripke's thesis. It should especially be stressed that the relationship between the ball and the piece of rubber does not generate any paradoxes such as 'A thing might have been two things (or might have had contradictory properties).'

It may still be wondered whether some of the applications Kripke makes of the thesis of the necessity of identity is threatened by the contingency of non-strict identity. One important application is to various theoretical identities in science and metaphysics. Traditional materialists, to take one example, have claimed that any mental property M is identical with some physical property P. Often materialists have seemed to imply that the identity of M and P is contingent, but Kripke argues that, if the identity holds, it must be necessary (Kripke, 1980, pp. 148–50). Might it be suggested, however, that the kind of identity intended by the materialist is non-strict and hence contingent? Perhaps the relationship with the materialist means to be attributing to M and N is the 'total coincidence' or 'contingent identity' of the last paragraph.

This suggestion does not seem plausible. For one thing, the arguments typically presented by materialists seem to be, if anything, arguments for the strict identity of M and P. Furthermore, since M and P are abstract properties, which are not literally composed of matter and do not literally occupy space, it seems unintelligible to say that they 'totally coincide' without being strictly identical. One would, at any rate, have to struggle to understand this on the model of the example of the ball and the piece of rubber. (*See* MODALITIES AND POSSIBLE WORLDS.)

BUTLER'S DOCTRINE

The notion of 'strict' identity has been employed in some influential literature in a way that seems quite different from that in the above discussion. BUTLER (1736) claimed that when an ordinary object such as a tree alters its material composition it retains its identity only in a 'loose and popular' sense; in a 'strict and philosophical' sense, the later tree is not identical with the earlier one. (This doctrine has also been defended by CHISHOLM (1976).) This distinction between 'strict' and 'loose' identity seems to have little to do with the distinction between senses of identity which do, and senses of identity which do not, satisfy Leibniz's Law. What Butler seems to mean is that, strictly speaking, there do not exist any objects that persist through a change of material composition. But even if such objects are 'fictions', as HUME (1739) said, they are fictions to which we apply the notion of strict Leibnizian identity. Butler would apparently allow that if it is 'loosely' correct to say that a certain tree that exists at one time t is identical with a certain tree that exists at another time t', then it must also be 'loosely' correct to ascribe to the former tree all the properties ascribed to the latter. Of course this does not mean that the tree has the same properties at t that it has at t'; rather, any properties possessed at a given time by the tree that exists at t are possessed at the given time by the tree that exists at t'. Hence, Butler's 'loose' identity is

233

not the antithesis of what we have been calling throughout the present discussion strict (Leibnizian) identity.

Although it is perhaps impossible to conclusively refute the paradoxical position that, strictly speaking, objects cannot retain their identities when they alter their material composition, one can try to formulate a more moderate position which captures all that may seem tempting in the paradoxical one. The moderate position would say that things that alter their material composition are in some important sense *derivative* of, *supervenient* upon, things that do not alter their material composition. The substantial task that would remain for this position is to make clear the relevant sense of derivativeness. (*See* SUPERVENIENCE.)

See also PERSONS AND PERSONAL IDENTITY; PHYSICALISM, MATERIALISM; SUBSTANCE.

BIBLIOGRAPHY

Butler, J.: First Dissertation to *The Analogy of Religion* (London: 1736); repr. in *Personal Identity* ed. J. Perry (Los Angeles: University of California Press, 1975), 99–105.
Chisholm, R.: *Person and Object* (London: Allen and Unwin, 1976), ch. 3.
Geach, P.T.: *Reference and Generality* (Ithaca, NY: Cornell University Press, 1962).
Hirsch, E.: *The Concept of Identity* (New York: Oxford University Press, 1982).
Hume, D.: *A Treatise of Human Nature* (London: 1739), Bk I, Pt IV, s. 6; repr. in *Personal Identity* ed. J. Perry (Los Angeles: University of California Press, 1975), 159–76.
Kripke, S.: *Naming and Necessity* (Cambridge, MA: Harvard University Press, 1980).
Munitz, M. ed.: *Identity and Individuation* (New York: New York University Press, 1971).
Perry, J. ed.: *Personal Identity* (Los Angeles: University of California Press, 1975).
Quine, W.V.: 'Identity, ostension, and hypostasis', in his *From A Logical Point of View* (New York: Harper and Row, 1963), 65–79.
Wiggins, D.: *Sameness and Substance* (Cambridge, MA: Harvard University Press, 1980).
Yablo, S.: 'Identity, essence, and indiscernibility', *Journal of Philosophy* 84 (1987), 293–314.

ELI HIRSCH

identity of indiscernibles A metaphysical thesis usually associated with the philosophy of LEIBNIZ. For this reason, it is sometimes referred to as 'Leibniz's Law'. Here is a bland formulation of the principle by Leibniz.

There is no such thing as two individuals indiscernible from each other.

Although this seems to say no more than that if individual x is distinct from individual y then there is some property F that x has and y lacks, or vice versa, Leibniz meant something considerably less bland, which comes to this: if individual x is distinct from individual y then there is some intrinsic, non-relational property F that x has and y lacks, or vice versa. The bland version is guaranteed by logic; Leibniz's version involves weighty metaphysics.

BIBLIOGRAPHY

Black, M.: 'The identity of indiscernibles', *Mind* 61 (1952), 153–64.
Leibniz, G.: 'On the principle of indiscernibles', in *Leibniz: Philosophical Writings* trans. and ed. M. Morris and G.H.R. Parkinson (London: Dent, 1973), 133–5.

ROBERT C. SLEIGH, JR

image, imagination In one sense, imagination is the power to form mental images. But it is certainly possible to imagine something without having any image of it, as, for example, when one reflects in words upon what would happen in certain circumstances. In the latter sense, which is common in ordinary speech, 'imagine' seems to mean merely 'suppose' or 'conceive'.

We normally think of mental images as being inner pictures. Here we have in mind visual images. But philosophers have sometimes used the term 'image' more broadly to cover inner representations experientially like those produced by all five senses. Thus, it is not unusual to find talk of tactual and olefactory images, for example. The question of whether visual images really are pictorial in the manner in which they represent things has been much discussed in recent cognitive psychology. Many fascinating experiments have been performed, experiments which suggest that visual images, like pictures, can be scanned and rotated. However, the results of these experiments are also open to alternative interpretations.

BIBLIOGRAPHY

Block, N. ed.: *Imagery* (Cambridge, MA: MIT Press, 1981).
Kosslyn, S.: *Image and Mind* (Cambridge, MA: Harvard University Press, 1980).
Ryle, G.: *The Concept of Mind* (New York: Barnes and Noble, 1949).
Tye, M.: *The Imagery Debate* (Cambridge, MA: MIT Press, 1991).

MICHAEL TYE

immanent/transcendent These terms are often used to mark the rather ordinary difference between being within something and being outside of it, but they are also employed in a more special and philosophical way to indicate both a separation and a connection between two subject matters, or entities. The Latin roots of the terms provide the basis for the ordinary usage: *in + manere*, to remain, and *trans + scendere*, to climb over. In the metaphysical application of this ordinary distinction the denomination of

something as 'transcendent' typically carries with it the notion of its being higher or more exalted than that which it lies beyond, for example, in theological contexts it is often said that God transcends the world but seldom said that the world transcends God. The more special philosophical usage of the distinction may be expressed as follows: for any x and any y, x is immanent to y, if, and only if, x is either a proper part of y or a character (proper or inherent property) of y, whereas x is transcendent to y if, and only if (1) x is not immanent to y; and (2) there is something z which is immanent to y such that z serves to refer to, signify, suggest, or otherwise indicate x. The additional notion of the transcendent as being higher or more exalted is seldom involved in this usage.

The term 'transcendent' in either of the above usages should not be confused with the term 'transcendental' as employed among mediaeval scholastics or by KANT. Among scholastics certain properties (and sometimes distinctions) which were thought applicable to all entities which fall within the ten Aristotelian CATEGORIES and thus go beyond them in their universality (a possibility which Aristotle expressly denied) were called *transcendentals*. These included, typically, unity (*unum*), truth (*verum*), goodness (*bonum*), being (*ens*), thing (*res*) and something (*aliquid*), but sometimes also such distinctions as contingent/necessary and actual/potential. Kant employed the term 'transcendental' quite differently. Distinguishing its sense from that of 'transcendent' (Kant, 1787, A 296/B 352), he employs it to indicate necessary presuppositions of the understanding which are applicable to all possible experiences and therefore, in such application, immanent to experience.

It appears that the special philosophical use of the distinction derives from a distinction in Aristotle (e.g. *Metaphysics* 1050a24–9) regarding actions, namely, between an action which is such that the achievement of its end follows upon the performance of the action as a product (later termed a transitive or transient action) and an action which is such that its performance is itself the achievement of its end (later termed an immanent action). These sorts of actions can therefore be distinguished by determining whether the realization of the end transcends or is immanent to the action when performed, though it is important to see that in both sorts of cases the intending of the realization of the end is immanent to the action. The scholastics adopted this distinction (see, e.g., Aquinas, *Quaestiones disputatae de veritate* XIV, a. II) and often employed it in controversy regarding God, usually with respect to whether his acts of creation were transitive or not.

Today the special philosophical use of the distinction is applied in metaphysics, not merely to action, but to experience, states of consciousness, and language. Perhaps the most common application derives from Kant. As he put it, 'it is not the idea in itself, but its use only, that can be either transcendent or immanent (that is, either range beyond all possible experience or find employment within its limits)' (Kant, 1787, A 643/B 671). In speaking of substance, causality, or God, for example, we may be said to employ ideas immanent to our experience in order to refer to things which, if real, transcend any experience which we could have. Since Kant this application has gained a broad and a narrow employment. Broadly, it is employed much as Kant introduced it to apply to claims regarding reality which are based upon experience in general, both actual and possible; more narrowly, it is applied to such claims as might be made on the basis of a specific sort or particular case of experience.

A noteworthy development of this narrow employment of the distinction can be found in the work of HUSSERL and his followers. An act of consciousness is said to be intentional, i.e. directed to an object, and though this INTENTIONALITY or directedness is immanent to the act, the object intended is not. Thus, in an act of perceiving an apple, the intentional object *apple* is not to be taken as something, such as an image or representation, which is immanent to the perceiving and which may or may not match up with a 'real' apple. Rather, the object intended just is an object which, if it were 'real', would transcend the act.

A similar sort of application to language, though usually invoked without the traditional terminology, indicates that the distinction is still alive and well in much current ontological work. Signs, referring expressions, or other semantical devices which are taken to be constituents of or identical to linguistic utterances of a certain sort are said to indicate items which, whether or not they exist or obtain, are not themselves constituents of or identical to such utterances. Such extra-utterance items clearly satisfy the conditions in the special philosophical use of the distinction on being transcendent.

BIBLIOGRAPHY

Aquinas, St Thomas: *Quaestiones disputatae de veritate* (1256–9); trans. J.V. McGlynn, *Truth* 2 vols (Chicago: Henry Regnery Co., 1953).
Aristotle: *Metaphysics*; trans. W.D. Ross, in *Complete Works of Aristotle* ed. J. Barnes (Princeton, NJ: Princeton University Press, 1984).
Husserl, E.: *Logische Untersuchungen* (Halle, 1900); trans. J.N. Findlay, *Logical Investigations*, vol. II (New York: Humanities Press, 1970), 593–6.
Kant, I.: *Kritik der reinen Vernunft* 2nd edn (Riga: 1787); trans. N. Kemp Smith, *Immanuel Kant's Critique of Pure Reason* (London: Macmillan, 1953).

DOUGLAS BROWNING

immortality PLATO tried to prove the immortality of the soul by arguing that the SOUL (animator), being essentially alive, cannot suffer DEATH, and also that the soul, being perfectly simple, cannot decompose.

AQUINAS, drawing on ARISTOTLE's idea that the soul is the form of the body, argued that the soul, though not by itself a complete SUBSTANCE, is nevertheless a 'subsistent thing' with no possibility of decomposing. After death, it awaits recompletion, he thought, at the resurrection of the body.

Rejecting Platonic reasoning, KANT argued for the immortality of the soul as a postulate of practical reason; immortality is required, he thought, for the soul to continue its endless progress toward moral perfection. NIETZSCHE, by contrast, espoused a doctrine of eternal recurrence, which seems to guarantee endless repetition of this life just as it is.

Recent philosophers have sought criteria of personal identity that could underwrite, or else rule out, the possibility of personal survival. They have also asked what disembodied experience would be like and whether infinitely extended life would even be desirable.

See also PERSONS AND PERSONAL IDENTITY.

BIBLIOGRAPHY

Aquinas, St Thomas: *Summa theologiae*, 1a, QQ 75, 89; 3a, Supplement, QQ 69–86 (many editions).
Kant, I.: *Critique of Practical Reason* (many editions).
Penelhum, T.: *Survival and Disembodied Existence* (London: Routledge and Kegan Paul, 1970).
Plato: *Phaedo* (many editions).
Williams, B.: 'The Makropulos case: reflections on the tedium of immortality', in his *Problems of the Self* (Cambridge: Cambridge University Press, 1973), 82–100.

GARETH B. MATTHEWS

indexicals An *indexical* expression is one whose extension varies with variation in features of its context of use, but which is otherwise rigid. For example, consider the sentence

(1) Jones will remember everyone now in the room.

The function of 'now' (a temporal indexical) in this sentence is to shift the temporal point at which 'everyone in the room' is evaluated from the future point at which Jones's remembering takes place to the point at which (1) is asserted. Thus, the occurrence of 'now' in (1) is unaffected by the tensed verb in whose scope it occurs, and in this sense it is rigid. Similarly, if I say, 'I might have been a fisherman' I invoke a possible situation in which *I* am a fisherman; so the extension of 'I' remains fixed in the shift from the actual situation of my utterance to a possible one in which 'I am a fisherman' is true. (Contrast: 'The first person on Mars might be a woman.') But of course the extensions of 'now' and 'I' will vary from speaker to speaker and from one moment to another. Kaplan (1988) develops a semantics which accounts for the combination of rigidity and context sensitivity characteristic of indexicals.

The first person indexical 'I' gives rise to the following interesting puzzle. My belief that I will get hit if I do not duck differs from your belief to the same effect (that I will get hit if I do not duck) since they issue in different behaviours: you shout and I duck. But it appears that each of us believes the same proposition, and so this seems to call into question the standard view of belief as a dyadic relation between an agent and a proposition (see Chisholm, 1981; Perry, 1979).

BIBLIOGRAPHY

Chisholm, R.M.: *The First Person* (Minneapolis: University of Minnesota Press, 1981).
Kamp, J.A.W.: 'Formal properties of "now"', *Theoria* 40 (1971), 76–109.
Kaplan, D.: 'Demonstratives', in *Themes from Kaplan* ed. J. Almog, J. Perry and W. Wettstein (Oxford: Oxford University Press, 1988), 481–563.
Perry, J.: 'The problem of the essential indexical', *Noûs* 13 (1979), 3–21.

Richard, M.: 'Direct reference and ascriptions of belief', *Journal of Philosophical Logic* 12 (1983), 425–52.

HARRY DEUTSCH

individual Translation of the Latin *individuum*, introduced by Boethius in philosophical discourse as a translation of the Greek *atomon* in his commentaries on Porphyry's *Isagoge*. It is opposed to 'universal' and is frequently considered synonymous with 'singular' and 'particular'. Some philosophers use it as a synonym of 'person'.

There are four metaphysical issues related to this notion: (1) the intension of 'individual'; (2) the extension of the term; (3) the ontological status of individuality in the individual and its relation to the individual's nature; and (4) the principle of individuation.

The intensional issue involves determining the necessary and sufficient conditions for something to be individual. These conditions are usually understood to involve one or more of the following: indivisibility, distinction, division, IDENTITY, impredicability and non-instantiability. The first is most often understood as indivisibility into entities specifically the same as the original (*see* SUÁREZ). The second is understood in terms of distinction or difference from other things (*see* AYER). Division is taken to refer to the capacity of individuals to divide the species (*see* OCKHAM; SELLARS). By identity is meant the capacity of individuals to remain the same through time and changes. Impredicability may be understood metaphysically or logically, giving rise to two different views of individuality. The first is defended by those who identify individuals with substances (Loux, 1978); the second by those who approach individuality linguistically (Strawson, 1959). Finally, individuality may also be understood in terms of the primitive notion of non-instantiability, that is, as the inability of individuals to become instantiated in the way UNIVERSALS can (Gracia, 1988).

The extensional issue involves determining which things, if any, are individual. This issue is closely related to the problem of universals, namely, the problem of determining which things, if any, are universal. There are three fundamental views concerning the extensional issue. One, inspired by PLATO, maintains that nothing that exists is individual and, therefore, that everything that exists is universal. A second view, inspired by ARISTOTLE, holds that everything that exists is individual and, therefore, that there are no such things as universals. A third position, most favoured today, finds a place in existence for both individuals and universals; it usually identifies individuals with Aristotelian primary substances and universals with the features of those substances. Traditionally, the first view has been regarded as a very strong form of REALISM, the second has been given the name of NOMINALISM, and the third has been regarded as a moderate form of realism.

The ontological issue involves two questions. The first asks for an ontological characterization of individuality; the second asks for the kind of distinction that obtains between individuality and the nature of an individual. In answer to the first question, individuality has been characterized as a SUBSTRATUM (*see* BERGMANN), a simple or complex feature (*see* BOETHIUS; RUSSELL), a relation (*see* CASTAÑEDA), a mode (Gracia, 1988), and nothing but the individual itself (*see* OCKHAM). Answers to the second question can be grouped into three. The first holds that individuality is really distinct from the nature of the individual, so that one can distinguish in an individual two realities, the nature and individuality, which come together to constitute the individual (*see* DUNS SCOTUS). The second holds that between the individuality of the individual and its nature there is a conceptual distinction only. In reality the individuality and the nature of the individual are one and the same, although conceptually they can be separated (Ockham). The third holds that the distinction between the nature and the individuality of an individual is something less than real but more than conceptual (formal for Scotus, modal for Suárez).

The most frequently discussed issue concerning individuals is the principle of the INDIVIDUATION of substances and their features (properties and accidents). There are four main theories of substantial individuation: bundle, accidental, essential and existential. The BUNDLE THEORY holds that the principle of individuation is the bundle of all the features of an individual (LEIBNIZ; Russell). The theory of accidental individuation holds that it is only certain accidents that are responsible for the individuality of things; most such views identify spatio-temporal location as the individuator (Boethius, STRAWSON). Among essential theories are those that identify matter (ANSCOMBE, Aristotle), form (AVERROES, Wiggins, 1980), or a *sui generis* principle (*haecceitas* for Duns Scotus, BARE PARTICULAR for Bergmann) as individuators. Much less popular than these theories is the theory of existential individuation. According to this position, the principle of individuation is existence (AVICENNA, Gracia, 1988). Some views mix essential and accidental features. For example, for AQUINAS the principle of individuation is matter taken under certain dimensions.

There are three main views of the individuation of features. The first maintains that features are individuated through the substance which has them (Aquinas). The second holds that the features of a substance are individuated through other features of that substance (Boethius). The third holds that features are individual through themselves (Suárez).

See also HAECCEITY; IDENTITY OF INDISCERNIBLES; QUIDDITY; SUBSTANCE; UNIVERSALS AND PARTICULARS.

BIBLIOGRAPHY

Armstrong, D.M.: *Nominalism and Realism*, 2 vols (Cambridge: Cambridge University Press, 1980).

Gracia, J.J.E.: *Individuality: An Essay on the Foundations of Metaphysics* (Albany, NY: SUNY Press, 1988).

Loux, M.J.: *Substance and Attribute: A Study in Ontology* (Dordrecht and Boston: Reidel, 1978).

Sidelle, A.: *Necessity, Essence, and Individuation: A Defense of Conventionalism* (Ithaca, NY: Cornell University Press, 1989).

Strawson, P.F.: *Individuals* (London: Methuen, 1959).

Wiggins, D.: *Sameness and Substance* (Oxford: Blackwell, 1980).

JORGE J.E. GRACIA

individuation Many different, sometimes related, problems have come to be known as 'problems of individuation'. Perhaps the original and central version of the problem of individuation is this: what is it, if anything, that makes some object the particular object that it is? What makes this so-and-so *this* so-and-so?

The problem may arise in the following way. Consider the quality (a non-relational property) of being blue. Since many things might be blue, what makes this blue thing *this* blue thing cannot be the fact that it is blue. Now, while many things can be blue, fewer things will be both blue and round; and fewer things, still, will be blue, round, and woollen; and so on. It may thus be asked whether there is a group consisting of some or all of the purely qualitative features of a given thing such that no thing other than it has just those qualities? If so, then what makes this thing *this* thing is the possession of just those qualities. In that case, a restricted version of the principle of the IDENTITY OF INDISCERNIBLES, cast in terms of qualities, will be true: for any object, x, and any object, y, if, for every quality Q, x has Q if, and only if, y has Q, then $x = y$. However, while it might be the case that some object, x, is in fact the one and only object that possesses a certain, perhaps complex, quality, it is compatible with this that there *could* be some object, y, that is the one and only object that possesses that very same, perhaps complex, quality, and yet is distinct from x. What individuates a given object *in fact* need not individuate it *of necessity*.

On the other hand, it might be argued that some or all of a thing's qualities are not only in fact unique but also constitute that thing's 'individual essence', and thus individuate of necessity. LEIBNIZ's view seems to be that what constitutes a thing's individual essence is comprised of *all* a thing's qualities.

If it is not the case that there is any quality, however complex, that is, either necessarily or in fact, unique to each thing, then the question of what, if anything, individuates each thing remains. Some philosophers might argue that, for each thing, x, there is not a purely qualitative property (e.g. Socrateity, in the case of Socrates) that x has in each of the POSSIBLE WORLDS in which x exists and which is such that in any possible world in which something has that property, that thing is x. Such philosophers apparently accept a less restrictive version of the principle of the identity of indiscernibles according to which two things cannot be alike with respect to all of their properties.

One might deny both the existence of not purely qualitative properties and the truth of the more restrictive version of the principle of the identity of indiscernibles. It might then be held that different, though qualitatively similar, things are simply distinct, that difference is *sui generis*. It might also be held that something other than a property individuates; for example, a thing's matter (this appears to be ARISTOTLE's view) or its spatio-temporal location (though clearly that cannot individuate of necessity).

The phrase, 'principle of individuation', is also used to refer to principles serving other, related metaphysical purposes. For example, DAVIDSON's search for a 'principle of individuation' for events is a search for an 'indiscernibility principle', a 'criterion of identity' that specifies conditions that are both necessary and sufficient for any events, e and e' to be the same event (*see* EVENT THEORY). A criterion of identity, for the

members of some metaphysically interesting kind K, has the following form: $(x)(y)$ (if x is a K and y is a K, then $(x = y$ iff $R(x,y))$, where '$R(x,y)$' is satisfied just in case x and y are indiscernible with respect to certain properties. (The properties are usually thought to be ones in terms of which one can express the idea of what it is to belong to the kind K.) Thus, for example, the claim that sets are identical if, and only if, they have the same members is said to be a principle of individuation, or a criterion of identity, for sets.

Often a criterion of identity will lead to a principle that individuates of necessity the members of the kind for which it is given. For example, it is true not only that sets are identical if, and only if, they have the same members, but also that sets necessarily have the members they in fact have. (It should be noted, however, that the latter claim does not follow from the former and must be justified independently.) By contrast, while it may be that two physical objects cannot have the same spatio-temporal history, it seems clearly possible for a physical object to have had the spatio-temporal history in fact had by another.

The phrase 'principle of individuation' is also sometimes used to apply to principles of *persistence*. There is a difference between (1) those properties a thing has the having and then lacking of which would be a CHANGE that that thing survives; and (2) those properties a thing has, the having and then lacking of which would result in that thing's going out of existence. A principle of persistence is particularly concerned to pick out the latter class of properties, since they are the ones that a persisting object must possess at every moment at which it exists. It may be that persistence principles are specific to the different kinds or sorts of persisting things. And it may well be that a thing's temporally essential properties are the very ones employed in individuating things belonging to those kinds; this would explain the use of the phrase 'principle of individuation' for persistence principles.

Some philosophers (e.g. STRAWSON) use the expression 'principle of individuation' to refer to *epistemological* principles that specify some feature that an object has in virtue of which one can tell whether or not it is the same object that one encounters on two or more occasions. It is not at all clear that such a principle of 're-identification' is just an epistemological version of a persistence principle, for it may not be the case that the properties in terms of which we pick out the same object again are the very properties in virtue of which what is picked out again is the object picked out earlier.

Lastly, the expression 'principle of individuation' is sometimes used to refer to principles that determine where one object, belonging to a certain kind, leaves off and other object, belonging to the same kind, begins. This seems to be what Wiggins had in mind in saying that 'every sortal term carries with it a principle of individuation'. Such a principle would, for example, determine how much of the world counts as *one* cat.

See also ESSENCE/ACCIDENT; IDENTITY; PERSONS AND PERSONAL IDENTITY.

BIBLIOGRAPHY

Aristotle: *Metaphysics* ed W.D. Ross (Oxford: Clarendon Press, 1928), Bk 7, ch. 8.
Davidson, D.: 'The individuation of events', repr. in his *Essays on Actions and Events* (New York: Oxford University Press, 1980).
Leibniz, G.W.F.: *Discourse on Metaphysics* (IX); *Monadology* (9).
Lombard, L.B.: *Events: A Metaphysical Study* (London: Routledge and Kegan Paul, 1986), ch. II.
Munitz, M.K. ed.: *Identity and Individuation* (New York: New York University Press, 1971).
Strawson, P.F.: *Individuals* (London: Methuen, 1959).
Wiggins, D.: *Sameness and Substance* (Cambridge, MA: Harvard University Press, 1980).

LAWRENCE BRIAN LOMBARD

infinite   *see* FINITE/INFINITE

Ingarden, Roman Witold (1893–1970) Polish philosopher, principally known for his contributions to aesthetics and the theory of literature, and above all for his *The Literary Work of Art* of 1931. As the subtitle of the latter reveals, however, Ingarden's primary interests were ontological, and his main work – *The Controversy over the Existence of the World* (1964–74) – is devoted to a detailed analysis of ontological categories as part of an attempted solution to the so-called 'problem of idealism-realism'.

Ingarden's interest in this problem had been awakened by the move to idealism on the part of his teacher HUSSERL, Ingarden himself having sided with the realist (Munich–Göttingen) wing of the phenomenological movement. The idealist maintains, crudely, that the external world is dependent for its existence upon the existence of mind or consciousness. The realist, in contrast, maintains that the world exists independently of mind (that the world would still exist even if all minds should be destroyed). For the idealist, therefore, the external world possesses something of the character of a world of fiction, a view which Ingarden sought to refute through his investigations of the ontology of literature. Broadly, he sought to demonstrate that there are radically different sorts of structures manifested by fictional and by real objects, above all in virtue of the fact that the former manifest certain 'loci of indeterminacy' where the latter are in all respects fully determinate down to the lowest specific differences.

In *The Controversy over the Existence of the World* Ingarden sets forth a systematic analysis of the various possible meanings of 'dependence' which are of relevance to the idealism/realism debate. In this way he is able to distinguish a range of alternative positions on a spectrum between extreme idealism on the one hand and extreme realism on the other. The delineation of such positions is a matter for 'ontology', which is in Ingarden's terms a discipline (preparatory to metaphysics) which analyses alternative possible structures of reality. ONTOLOGY is divided further into the three subdisciplines of existential, formal and material ontology. Here existential ontology investigates the modes of being of different kinds of objects (for example of past, present and future objects; of events and processes and other objects existing in different ways in time; of real and intentional objects, and so on), formal ontology investigates the different forms of objects (of properties, relations, states of affairs, etc.), while material ontology investigates the specific qualitative structures in reality which are involved, for example, in physical systems and in CONSCIOUSNESS.

The spectrum of alternative idealist and realist positions having once been established, it is then the task of 'metaphysics', as Ingarden conceives it, to establish which of these is in fact true of reality. Ingarden's proposed solution to the idealism/realism problem was to have consisted in demonstrating how all but one of the different projected alternatives fail through internal incoherence on the levels of formal, material or existential ontology. Volume 3 of the work was left uncompleted on Ingarden's death. The wealth of ontological analyses which the work contains, however, makes it one of the great masterpieces of contemporary metaphysics.

See also FICTIONAL TRUTH, OBJECTS AND CHARACTERS; IDEALISM; ONTOLOGY; PHENOMENOLOGY; REALISM.

WRITINGS

Das literarische Kunstwerk. Eine Untersuchung aus dem Grenzgebiet der Ontologie, Logik und Literaturwissenschaft (Halle: 1931); trans. G.G. Grabowicz, The Literary Work of Art: An Investigation on the Borderlines of Ontology, Logic and Theory of Literature (Evanston, IL: Northwestern University Press, 1973).
Der Streit um die Existenz der Welt 3 vols. (Tübingen: Niemeyer, 1964–74); partial trans. of Vol. 1, H.R. Michejda, Time and Modes of Being (Springfield, IL: Charles Thomas, 1964).

BARRY SMITH

inherence (*inesse*) is often used in a loose sense to describe the formal or topic-neutral relation between a property and the object that 'has' it. A narrower use of the word refers to the relation between an individual accident and the SUBSTANCE it belongs to. By 'individual accident' many writers meant entities such as the greenness of a plant or Sam's sadness where these were taken to be numerically distinct from, although exactly alike, the greenness of some other plant or the sadness of Maria. The relation of inherence was taken to involve at least one of the following two relations: dependence and being in. Each of these notions, like that of an individual accident, goes back to ARISTOTLE.

Dependence is often understood modally: an individual accident cannot exist unless its substance exists. This contrasts with the relation of exemplification that holds between a property and an object, for on one view a property must be exemplified, although it need not be exemplified by a given object; on another common view a property need not be exemplified.

When an accident is said to be in a substance it is often claimed, following Aristotle, that the accident is not in the substance as a part is in a whole. This rather negative characterization led some philosophers to talk of accidents as 'abstract parts' of substances. On some bundle theories of substance inherence turns out to be a more straightforward sort of mereological notion. (See BUNDLE THEORY.)

Controversies about the existence of relational accidents make clear how important it is to distinguish dependence and being in. Consider the dynamic, relational accident which is Mary's hitting Sam. It is not clear what it might mean to say that it is in both Mary and Sam. But it has been argued that the hit in question does depend on Mary and on Sam.

Accidents are particular, temporal entities, unlike properties. The list of particular, temporal entities can be extended to include, in addition to such creatures as Sam's sadness, his humanity, a humanity numerically distinct from that of Maria. We might then want to say that although Sam's sadness depends unilaterally on Sam, he and his humanity are bilaterally dependent.

Nowadays many of the entities traditionally called 'accidents' are discussed under such headings as 'tropes' (*see* TROPE), 'moments' (Momente), 'quality instances', 'individualized forms', 'characters' and 'concrete properties'. Amongst the many roles attributed to such entities are those of being truth-makers, of being constituents of the type of truth-maker called a state of affairs, of providing domains of quantification for many different types of truth-bearer, of being the objects of direct perception and the constituents of material things. Since many, if not all such entities are often held to be events, processes or states, including such subcategorizations of these as accomplishments, acts, activities and achievements, questions about the nature of the relation of inherence and of its terms turn out to be questions about what are now called the participants in events and states. Work in case and cognitive grammar and elsewhere distinguishes such participants as agents, patients, experiencers, instruments, goals and benefactives and the corresponding relations between these and events or states – distinctions which have a more than merely accidental relation to the Aristotelian tradition.

BIBLIOGRAPHY

Angelelli, I.: *Studies on Gottlob Frege and Traditional Philosophy* (Dordrecht: Reidel, 1967).

Ebert, T.: 'Aristotelischer und traditioneller Akzidenzbegriff', in *Logik, Ethik, Theorie der Geisteswissenschaften* ed. G. Patzig, E. Scheibe and W. Wieland (Hamburg: Meiner, 1977), 338–49.

Fine, K.: 'Husserl's theory of part and whole', in *Husserl* ed. B. Smith and D.W. Smith (Cambridge and New York: Cambridge University Press, 1994) forthcoming.

Mulligan, K., Simons, P. and Smith, B.: 'Truth-makers', *Philosophy and Phenomenological Research* XLIV (1984), 287–321.

Parsons, T.: *Events in the Semantics of English. A Study in Subatomic Sentences* (Cambridge, MA: MIT Press, 1990).

Simons, P.: 'Relational tropes', in *Analytic Phenomenology. Festschrift for Guido Küng* eds. G. Haefliger and P. Simons (Dordrecht: Kluwer, 1994) forthcoming.

KEVIN MULLIGAN

intension *see* EXTENSION/INTENSION

intention There are two relevant aspects of intention': (1) a characteristic of action, as when one acts *intentionally* or *with a certain intention*; (2) a feature of one's mind, as when one *intends* (*has an intention*) to act in a certain way now or in the future. An important question is: how are (1) and (2) related? (See Anscombe, 1963.) Some philosophers see acting with an intention as basic and as involving: (a) the action; (b) appropriate desires and beliefs; and (c) an appropriate explanatory relation between (a) and (b) (Davidson, 1980, essay 1). In explaining (a) in terms of (b) we give an explanation of the action in terms of the agent's reasons for so acting. What about intentions as states of mind? Some see them simply as complexes of desires and beliefs, some as evaluations (Davidson, 1980, essay 5), some as special kinds of beliefs (Velleman, 1989), some as involving a special attitude of 'willing' (Grice, 1971), and some as distinctive attitudes with important roles in practical reasoning (Castañeda, 1975; Harman, 1986) and planning (Bratman, 1987).

BIBLIOGRAPHY

Anscombe, G.E.M.: *Intention* 2nd edn (Ithaca, NY: Cornell University Press, 1963).

INTENTIONALITY

Bratman, M.E.: *Intention, Plans, and Practical Reason* (Cambridge, MA: Harvard University Press, 1987).

Castañeda, H.N.: *Thinking and Doing* (Dordrecht: Reidel, 1975).

Davidson, D.: *Essays on Actions and Events* (New York: Oxford University Press, 1980).

Grice, H.P.: 'Intention and uncertainty', *Proceedings of the British Academy* 57 (1971), 263–79.

Harman, G.: *Change in View* (Cambridge, MA: MIT Press, 1986).

Velleman, J.D.: *Practical Reflection* (Princeton, NJ: Princeton University Press, 1989).

MICHAEL E. BRATMAN

intentionality An aspect – perhaps an (or the) essential aspect – of the mental: the directedness of mind as manifest through various states, activities or attitudes (not limited to the intending of actions or consequences), particularly in so far as such directedness admits of bi- or multivalence with respect to ontological status. Contemporary discussion has been influenced by BRENTANO's extension of the mediaeval notion of the intentional 'inexistence' of objects. Metaphysical issues concern the apparent fact that the object of intention may be imaginary, abstract, relatively indeterminate or even contradictory.

Some construe intentionality relationally, thereby apparently countenancing special entities or ontological categories on the side of the 'object': for example, NON-EXISTENT OBJECTS. It is debated to what extent this is done by Brentano or MEINONG (see the latter on the *Aussersein* of 'pure objects' and on 'incomplete objects'). Similar issues are raised regarding intentional relations with facts, propositions, states of affairs, or with what Meinong calls 'objectives'. To avoid recourse to the latter, RUSSELL proposed n-termed mental relations connecting subjects and the $n - 1$ *constituents* of such would-be objects. (*See* FACT; PROPOSITION/STATE OF AFFAIRS.)

There are debates concerning the extent to which CONSCIOUSNESS is fundamental for intentionality and also to which intentionality may be essentially linguistic. There is therefore debate as well as to the intentionality of sensory and feeling states. The introduction of SENSA may be regarded as part of a metaphysical approach to the latter. However, if all sensa have the same ontological status (with no difference for the apprehension of existent and non-existent ones), this may be regarded as tantamount to denying intentionality on the level of sensation or feeling. It would in any case not involve recourse to special 'intentional relations'. The same holds for certain views as to the role of 'ideas' or concepts in intentionality (*see* CONCEPT).

Some explain intentionality by appeal to intentional CONTENT. Such content might be viewed metaphysically: for example, as unique characters instantiable by mental states. Thus the earlier HUSSERL (1900–1) posits a realm of ideal meaning (*Bedeutung*) in which components of a person's mental life 'participate'. (BERGMANN's approach is similar but also requires an intentional 'nexus' between meaning-contents and actual/non-actual states of affairs.) Although FREGE does not describe it as either intentional 'object' or 'content', nor its connection with mind as a species of participation or instantiation, the sense or meaning (*Sinn*) that plays a role in his theory of REFERENCE is often discussed in this context (Addis, 1989; Searle, 1983). In some cases, one is also said to ascribe intentional content to systems to which one would not ordinarily ascribe mentality. Many regard this as merely 'as-if' ascription. However, some (e.g. Daniel Dennett) suppose the same with regard to the ascription of intentional content to human beings in the first place.

Depending on one's ontology of POSSIBLE WORLDS, appeal to the latter might provide either a metaphysical or a nonmetaphysical approach to intentionality. Some avoid metaphysics by way of FUNCTIONALISM or some other type of reductionism, or through an ADVERBIAL

244

THEORY. Others (e.g. SELLARS) hold that the ascription of content is simply a type of 'translation'. This may lead to the view (see QUINE) that ascription of content is in principle indeterminate.

Through Husserl (1913), intentionality has become the central notion in PHENOMENOLOGY. Perhaps the most fruitful approach lies in his theory of the NOEMA, NOESIS correlation. Two approaches to Husserl tend to be adopted. One compares the role of the noema to that of Frege's *Sinn*. The other emphasizes the structure of the noesis (= mental act), construing the noema as the intentional 'correlate', or a kind of 'reflection', of the act itself, not as an entity of any sort.

Husserl used the term *hyle* for the 'material' component of mental states relative to intentional 'forming'. On the most basic level, this comprises non-intentional sensory or feeling states as well as primitive drives, dispositions, and pre-intentional anticipations and retentions. Intentional states are then viewed as structures formed in so far as intentionality 'animates' or operates through a body of such material. Such states may also serve as material for higher-level states. The noema may be construed as the 'intentional object' in a non-ontological sense, purely as a correlate of the noesis: generally, as a field of consciousness of indeterminate boundary surrounding a 'nucleus' correlative with a relatively determinate or indeterminate directedness of consciousness.

SARTRE rejects the distinction between matter and intentional form. However, his own approach in terms of a distinction between 'facticity' and 'transcendence' might be regarded as employing the distinction in different terms. He argues that intentionality presupposes, not a realm of intentional objects, nor of ideal meaning-contents, but an undifferentiated background of Being-in-itself.

The term 'intentionality' is also used more broadly, in connection with intensionality, a logical feature of sentences or propositions. In general, the criteria involve failure to preserve either truth value or modal status under certain transformations. CHISHOLM and others (see Marras, 1972) have attempted to discover a relationship between such criteria and sentences whose subject matter is mental. In some cases, the use of intensional sentences may be regarded as tantamount to the ascription of 'intentional content'.

See also CONTENT; EXTENSION/INTENSION; IDEA; REDUCTION, REDUCTIONISM.

BIBLIOGRAPHY

Addis, L.: *Natural Signs: A Theory of Intentionality* (Philadelphia, PA: Temple University Press, 1989).

Aquila, R.E.: 'Intentionality, content, and primitive mental directedness', *Philosophy and Phenomenological Research* 49 (1989), 583–604.

Husserl, E.: *Logische Untersuchungen* (Halle: 1900–1); trans. J.N. Findlay, *Logical Investigations* (New York: Humanities Press, 1970).

Husserl, E.: *Ideen zu einer reinen Phänomenologie und phänomenologischen Philosophie, I. Buch* (Halle: 1913); trans. F. Kersten, *Ideas Pertaining to a Pure Phenomenology and to a Phenomenological Philosophy, First Book* (The Hague: Martinus Nijhoff, 1983).

McIntyre, R. and Smith, D.W.: *Husserl and Intentionality* (Dordrecht: Reidel, 1982).

Marras, A. ed.: *Intentionality, Mind, and Language* (Urbana, IL: University of Illinois Press, 1972).

Searle, J.R.: *Intentionality: An Essay in the Philosophy of Mind* (Cambridge: Cambridge University Press, 1983).

RICHARD E. AQUILA

internal relations According to RUSSELL all relations are external. According to a view associated with German and British IDEALISM, all relations are internal. Against these two monisms, philosophers such as MEINONG, HUSSERL and MOORE allow for both types of relation in their ontologies. WITTGENSTEIN, too, frequently relies on the distinction. A relation is said to be external if it need not relate the entities it does relate (Maria need not be next to Sam); if two or more entities must stand in some relation then it is said to be internal (Orange must be between yellow and red, 4 must be greater than 3). A non-modal characterization may be preferred, replacing 'need not' by 'does not always'. The two examples given of internal relations relate abstract or ideal entities, properties and numbers. Spatial and/or temporal points and regions are also often held to stand in internal relations to one another. A nominalist ontology (see NOMINALISM) that works with tropes (see TROPE) can also allow for internal relations: this orange trope (and all tropes that exactly resemble it) must be between some yellow trope and some red trope. Johansson (1989) and Campbell (1990) describe a second type of non-external relation: if a relation supervenes on (see SUPERVENIENCE) or is dependent on the properties or tropes of two things then it is a founded or grounded relation. The relation ascribed by 'Sam is sadder than Hans' is founded on the sadnesses of Sam and Hans. It is a contingent fact that they have the sadnesses they have. But between any two sadness tropes the relation of greater than or equal to must obtain.

The terms of all the examples of non-external relations given so far are non-things. Are there any such relations between things? Meinong and Saul Kripke suggest that numerical difference would be one such: if a differs from b then necessarily so. The relation of origin described by INGARDEN and Kripke is another possible example: if a is a son of b then necessarily so.

Three basic types of non-external relations are determination, distance and dependence. Determination relations hold in the first instance between concepts such as *red* and *coloured*, *rabbit* and *animal*, *strangle* and *kill*. The subordinate concept determines or specifies the superordinate concept. Where properties and kinds are admitted in addition to concepts then the property of being red is said to be a determinate of the determinable property of being coloured, and the kind denoted by "rabbit" is said to be a species of the genus denoted by "animal". Since whatever is red must be coloured, relations between subordinates and their superordinates, whether concepts or properties, are not external. Incompatibility relations between subordinates of a superordinate are also held to be internal relations. Since tropes are completely determinate there can be no determinable tropes. Examples of distance relations are provided by relations of more or less within the different quality orders, between quantities, numbers, by relations between spatial and temporal regions and by relations of structural similarity. The simplest sort of dependence relation is provided by the INHERENCE relation between a trope and its bearer (on one view of these). Sam's sadness, say, could not exist without Sam. Individual dependence of this sort is distinguished from both generic dependence (a cannot exist without some A) and notional (de dicto) dependence. The traditional specifications of external and internal relations in the first paragraph above actually employ a notion of dependence.

BIBLIOGRAPHY

Bigelow, J. and Pargetter, R.: 'Quantities', in *Science and Necessity* (Cambridge: Cambridge University Press, 1990), ch. 2.

Campbell, K.: 'Relations, causation, space-time and compresence', in *Abstract Particulars* (Oxford: Blackwell, 1990), ch. 5, 97–134.

Johansson, I.: 'External, internal and grounded relations', and 'Existential dependence', in *Ontological Investigations: An Inquiry into the Categories of Nature, Man and Society* (London: Routledge, 1989), chs 8, 9, 110–44.

Moore, G.E.: 'External and internal relations', in his *Philosophical Studies* (Paterson, NJ: Littlefield, 1959), 276–309.

Simons, P.: 'Ontological dependence', in his *Parts: A Study in Ontology* (Oxford: Clarendon Press, 1987), 290–323.

KEVIN MULLIGAN

intuition Used in a variety of ways, mostly about some sort of direct, non-inferential insight. Perception is usually classified as a kind of intuition. A key issue in mediaeval philosophy as well as in RATIONALISM and EMPIRICISM is whether there are other sorts of such insight. KANT defines 'intuition' (*Anschauung*) as a representation which 'relates immediately to its object and is singular' (1781, A320, B376–7). BOLZANO developed this idea with great precision. For HUSSERL, an intuition is an act where we are constrained in how we constitute the act's objects, such as we typically are in perception, which is one of his two varieties of intuition. The other variety Husserl calls essential insight (*Wesensschau*). The object is here a general feature, an essence (*Wesen*), such as for example, triangularity. For Husserl, as for Kant, intuition is a key kind of evidence in mathematics.

See also PHENOMENOLOGY.

BIBLIOGRAPHY

Hintikka, J.: 'On Kant's notion of intuition (*Anschauung*)', in *The First Critique: Reflections on Kant's Critique of Pure Reason* ed. T. Penelhum and J.J. MacIntosh (Belmont, CA: Wadsworth, 1969), 135–52.
Kant, I.: *Critique of Pure Reason* (Riga: 1781); trans. N. Kemp Smith (London: Macmillan, 1964).
Parsons, C.: *Mathematics in Philosophy* (Ithaca, NY: Cornell University Press, 1983), esp. 22–6, 111–15 and 142–9.

DAGFINN FØLLESDAL

intuitionism in logic and mathematics A doctrine about the nature of mathematical objects, knowledge and reasoning; and in part a doctrine about which logic is the right logic. Indeed, intuitionists regard logic as a proper part of mathematics – as concerned with proofs as constructions.

The name 'intuitionism' derives from KANT's account of temporal intuition as a priori. The early intuitionists, such as L.E.J. Brouwer, took the notion of natural number to arise out of our a priori conception of successive moments in time. Intuitionists tend, in the spirit of Kronecker (1823–91), to take the natural numbers as primitively generable and primitively graspable mental constructions. They seek then to construct other kinds of mathematical object in a suitably constrained way out of the natural numbers as their 'ground type'. Neither the natural numbers, however, nor any other infinitely numerous objects of any other kind, can be thought of as comprising a completed totality to be treated as an object in its own right.

Mathematical objects, because they are mental constructions, depend for their identity on their mode of construction, or presentation, or description: they have intensional identity conditions. This means that the identity relation among them is effectively decidable. But *extensional* identity among mathematical objects is not in general decidable.

What can in principle be known – hence, be true – about the mathematical realm of mentally constructible objects arises from their very nature as mental constructions. Mathematical *proof* is both the vehicle of knowledge and the ground of truth. Any intuitionistic proof of a mathematical statement must be effectively recognizable as such. Since the truth of a statement equates with constructive existence of a proof of it, the Law of Excluded Middle fails. For, given any statement a, one is not generally in possession of an effective means of finding either a proof of a or a refutation of a.

A unified intuitionism, such as that pursued by Martin-Löf, accordingly seeks to account for the licit methods of construction both of mathematical objects and of proofs of statements about them. This form of intuitionism represents a mature stage in the evolution of the doctrine. It began (ironically) with solipsistic ideas of Brouwer's about the incommunicability of mathematical thoughts. This led, famously, to his rejection of the Law of Excluded Middle (either p or not-p) as a logical axiom. In due course Heyting gave an account of intuitionistic logic as the logic of mental constructions.

This account was later deepened by DUMMETT's theory of meaning according to which mathematical thoughts were essentially communicable, and indeed communicable on the basis of observable behaviour. The so-called *manifestation requirement* on the theory of meaning was that grasp of meaning should be exhaustively manifestable in observable behaviour. This requirement led, in Dummett's view, to intuitionistic logic as the right logic for the logical operators. On this view the operators had only such graspable content as could be exhausted by the inference rules of intuitionistic logic. Dummett has sought also to generalize this approach to other areas of discourse besides the mathematical. The resulting doctrines have come to be labelled as *antirealist* for the areas of discourse concerned.

A sophisticated recursive account (initially due to Prawtiz) can be given of how the intuitionistic validity of proofs is grounded ultimately on *canonical* proofs, which establish their conclusions directly. Thus, for example, a canonical proof of an existential statement 'There is a number n such that $F(n)$' would consist of a valid proof of *some particular instance $F(t)$*. More exactly, such a canonical proof would provide a *recognizably effective means of constructing* such an instance t, and a valid proof of $F(t)$. Likewise, a canonical proof of a disjunction 'a or b' would consist of a valid proof of a or a valid proof of b. Knowing *which* instance or *which* disjunct justifies an existential or disjunctive claim, respectively, is essential to the intuitionist.

Martin-Löf's intuitionistic type theory represents an attempt to extend these meaning-theoretic ideas to a significant variety of operators, functions and predicates (both logical and mathematical). His rules are designed so as to permit the understanding of a mathematical statement in computational terms: as a program specifying an effective method for carrying out a constructive task. A proof, in his type theory, of such a statement, is then a proof *that the program encoded by the statement works*. As a result, his intuitionistic type theory provides a foundation for all high-level programming languages.

It is important to appreciate that intuitionism involved a re-thinking of the nature of mathematical objects and mathematical proofs that in due course occasioned this deepening of meaning-theoretic foundations. The process began with the theory of species in place of the classical theory sets, and the theory of free choice sequences in place of the classical theory of real numbers. It is important also to realize that intuitionists are unwilling to commit themselves in advance to a formally delimited class of methods of proof and construction as *exhaustive*. For the intuitionist, the notion of correct inference and correct proof is an *open-textured* one.

An inadequate but convenient way for the classical logician and mathematician to appreciate what the intuitionist holds is to consider first what would have to be sacrificed were one to be prevented from using non-constructive, or strictly classical, methods of proof. These are the methods of proof rejected as invalid by the intuitionists. Not only is the Law of Excluded Middle forbidden; one must also eschew related rules concerning negation, such as Double Negation Elimination (from not-not-p you may infer p), and classical *reductio* (you may infer p if you have reduced not-p to absurdity). This latter rule, for example, would allow one to infer the existential statement 'There is a number n such that $F(n)$' merely by reducing its negation to absurdity, rather than by constructing a particular instance t for which one could show $F(t)$. Once one eschews the strictly classical negation rules, one sacrifices many other familiar logical principles as well. One has to give up, for example, the de Morgan Law 'not both a and b, therefore either not a or not b'. One has also to give up the familiar classical quantifier dualities. In particular, 'for some x $F(x)$' no longer entailed by 'not for every x not $F(x)$'. No longer can one convert any given quantified statement into a logically equivalent one in prenex normal form.

Indeed, such is the sacrifice of classical logical principles that the intuitionistic logician is not able, as the classical logician is, to define all connectives in terms of just negation and one other binary connective. In intuitionistic logic one needs negation, implication, conjunction and disjunction as primitive connectives; and both the existential and the universal as primitive quantifiers. Results due to Prawitz and Schroeder-Heister show that these indeed suffice to define all other intuitionistically meaningful operators.

Intuitionistic logic, then, is a proper subsystem of classical logic. One could take an extant axiomatization of a mathematical theory, possibly reworking the axioms slightly so that they were acceptable to the intuitionist; and then regard the corresponding intuitionist mathematical theory as simply the deductive closure, under the restricted rules of intuitionistic logic, of those reworked axioms. Thus, for example, one might take intuitionistic Zermelo-Fraenkel set theory to be the intuitionistic closure of the axioms, which would be reworked so that they expressed intuitionistically acceptable principles. Intuitionists have also isolated various special principles with a classical flavour that might be used to extend their axiomatizations. A good example is Markov's Principle in the theory of natural numbers: for quantifier-free F, you may infer 'There is a number n such that $F(n)$' if you have reduced its negation to absurdity. Markov's Principle represents a slight concession to the non-constructivists. It allows Σ_0-statements to feature as conclusions of classical *reductio ad absurdum*. Generally, theories become less constructive as more extensive (syntactically characterized) classes of sentences become eligible to be conclusions of applications of classical *reductio ad absurdum*.

This method of construing intuitionism (old axioms, new logic) gives only an approximate understanding of its content; such understanding is not thorough enough.

An example of the difficulties with this limited approach is to be found in intuitionistic real number analysis. Here we have the theorem that all real-valued functions on the unit interval are continuous – a result that fails classically. The reason for this discrepancy is that the intuitionist analyses the notion of *function* differently. On their revised understanding of functions, furthermore, Church's Thesis becomes obviously true. Another example is the Axiom of Choice. This is classically moot, and independent of the standard axiomatizations of set theory. For the intuitionist, however, it expresses an obvious truth. Intuitionistic mathematics, then, is not arrived at simply as a deductive restriction of classical mathematics.

There is a great variety of formal semantics for intuitionistic logic. The best-known of these, due to Kripke and to Beth, attempt to model the notion of a state of knowledge that grows by accretion over time. This enables one to give an account of the 'strong' negation of the intuitionists. A statement 'not p' is made true at a world (state of knowledge) just in case the statement p is made true *at no subsequent worlds*. Likewise, a conditional statement 'if p then q' is made true at a world just in case, for any subsequent world, if p is made true, then q is made true also. This is an attempt to model the idea that a proof of a conditional 'if p then q' should provide a method that will transform any proof of its antecedent p into a proof of its consequent q.

With respect to semantics such as these, it is possible to provide soundness and completeness proofs for intuitionistic logic. Originally these completeness proofs followed the classical Henkin method that had been employed to prove the completeness of classical logic. More recently, completeness proofs have been provided that are acceptable to the intuitionist. These are due to Veldman and de Swart. They establish *weak completeness* – that every logically true sentence is a theorem of intuitionistic logic. There is, however, an argument due to Troelstra that shows that there can be no intuitionistically acceptable proof of *strong* completeness. For strong completeness we require that any consequence of *any* set of premises (even an infinite set) can be deduced from (finitely many of) those premises.

There is a variety of effective translations f for which, if p can be deduced classically from x, then $f(p)$ can be deduced intuitionistically from $f(x)$. The best-known of these is the double-negation translation. Such results show immediately that, since classical first-order logic is undecidable, then so too is intuitionistic first-order logic.

Intuitionistic *propositional* logic, like classical propositional logic, can be shown to be decidable. By contrast, we remark on two metalogical anomalies. First, the complexities of these decision problems are different: that for classical logic is NP-complete, whereas that for intuitionistic logic is PSPACE-complete. Second, intuitionistic propositional logic, unlike classical propositional logic, has no finite characteristic matrix of truth values. An active area of contemporary investigation is that of *intermediate* logics: logics lying between intuitionistic and classical (propositional) logic.

Another metalogical anomaly, this time at the level of first-order logic, is that there is no intuitionistically acceptable analogue of the classical downward Löwenheim-Skolem theorem. This is the theorem that states that if a set of sentences has a model then it has a countable model. It can be shown that no *intuitionistic* extension of intuitionistic Zermelo-Fraenkel set theory, no matter how strong, can deliver a countable models result, no matter how weak.

Intuitionistic and classical mathematical theories have been related by various relative consistency results. Perhaps the most remarkable of these are due to GÖDEL and Gentzen, to Friedman and to McCarty. Gödel and Gentzen provided a translation γ (essentially mapping disjunction and existential quantification to their classical duals) such that a sentence a is a theorem of classical Peano arithmetic just in case $\gamma(a)$ is a theorem of intuitionistic ('Heyting') arithmetic. Friedman showed that if intuitionistic Zermelo-Fraenkel set theory is inconsistent,

then so too is its classical counterpart. McCarty showed that intuitionistic Zermelo-Fraenkel set theory is equivalent to classical recursive number theory. There are also relative consistency results for systems of real number analysis.

What these results collectively show is that the kind of 'profligacy' of which the classical mathematician stands accused by his or her intuitionistic counterpart is not such as to lead to any greater risk of *inconsistency*. Rather, the dispute has to turn, ultimately, on a philosophical account of the meanings of mathematical statements and the grounds for their assertion. 'Intuitionists are engaged in the wholesale reconstruction of mathematics, not to accord with empirical discoveries, nor to obtain more fruitful applications, but solely on the basis of philosophical views concerning what mathematical statements are about and what they mean' (Dummett, 1977, p. viii).

See also ANTIREALISM; CLASS, COLLECTION, SET; REALISM.

BIBLIOGRAPHY

Beth, E.W.: *The Foundations of Mathematics* (Amsterdam: North-Holland Publishing Co., 1959).

Brouwer, L.E.J.: *Collected Works*, Vol. 1 *Philosophy and Foundations of Mathematics*, ed. A. Heyting (Amsterdam: North-Holland Publishing Co., 1975).

Dummett, M.A.E. with the assistance of Robert Minio: *Elements of Intuitionism* (Oxford: Clarendon Press, 1977).

Friedman, H.: 'The consistency of classical set theory relative to a set theory with intuitionistic logic', *Journal of Symbolic Logic* 38 (1973), 315–19.

Gentzen, G.: *Collected Papers* trans. and ed. M.E. Szabo (Amsterdam: North-Holland Publishing Co., 1969).

Gödel, K.: 'Zur intuitionistischen Arithmetik und Zahlentheorie', *Ergebnisse eines mathematischen Kolloquiums* 4 (1933), 34–8.

Heyting, A.: *Intuitionism: An Introduction* 3rd edn (Amsterdam: North-Holland Publishing Co., 1982).

Kripke, S.: 'Semantical analysis of intuitionistic logic I', in *Formal Systems and Recursive Functions* ed. J.N. Crossley and M.A.E. Dummett (Amsterdam: North-Holland Publishing Co., 92–130).

McCarty, D.C.: *Realizability and Recursive Mathematics*, D.Phil. thesis, University of Oxford; released as a technical report by the Department of Computer Science, Carnegie-Mellon University, Pittsburgh, No. CMU-C2-84-131.

Martin-Löf, P.: *Intuitionistic Type Theory* (Padua: Bibliopolis, 1984).

Minc, G.E.: 'The Skolem method in intuitionistic calculi', *Proceedings of the Steklov Institute of Mathematics* 121 (1972); Logical and Logico-Mathematical Calculi 2 (American Mathematical Society, 1974), 73–109.

Prawitz, D.: 'On the idea of a general proof theory', *Synthese* 27 (1974), 63–77.

Prawitz, D.: 'Proofs and the meanings and completeness of the logical constants', in *Essays on Mathematical and Philosophical Logic* ed. K.J.J. Hintikka *et al.* (Dordrecht: Reidel, 1978), 25–40.

Schroeder-Heister, P.: 'Proof-theoretic Validity and the Completeness of Intuitionistic Logic', in *Foundations of Logic and Linguistics: Problems and their Solutions* ed. G. Dorn and P. Weingartner (New York: Plenum Press, 1985), 43–87.

de Swart, H.: 'Another intuitionistic completeness proof', *Journal of Symbolic Logic* 41 (1976), 644–62.

Tennant, N. and McCarty, D.C.: 'Skolem's paradox and constructivism', *Journal of Philosophical Logic* 16 (1987), 165–202.

Troelstra, A.: *Principles of Intuitionism. Lecture Notes in Mathematics No. 95* (Berlin, Heidelberg and New York: Springer, 1969).

Veldman, W. 'An intuitionistic completeness theorem for intuitionistic predicate logic', *Journal of Symbolic Logic* 41 (1976), 159–66.

NEIL TENNANT

isomorphism An ordered pair $<A, R>$ (a 'relational structure') consisting of a set of elements A and a relation R (defined on A), is *isomorphic* to a relational structure $<B, S>$ (B a set and S a relation defined on B and of the same degree as R) if there is a one-to-one function f mapping A onto B such that: for all x and y belonging to A, xRy if, and only if, $f(x)Sf(y)$. Then f is an *isomorphism* between the structures $<A, R>$ and $<B, S>$. The generalization of this to structures involving more than one relation proceeds in the obvious way.

LEIBNIZ's view that every monad mirrors every other monad might be explicated using the notion of an isomorphism (although he seems to have had a more general relation in mind). SPINOZA maintained that the mental and the physical are correlated in a way that preserves 'order and connection'. RUSSELL (1927) argued that all we can know is that there is an isomorphism between our percepts and their physical causes (see Demopoulos and Friedman, 1989). According to Church (1954) *synonymous isomorphism* can be used as a criterion of synonymy and thus indirectly as a criterion of identity for propositions.

See also PROPOSITION, STATE OF AFFAIRS.

BIBLIOGRAPHY

Church, A.: 'Intensional isomorphism and identity of belief', *Philosophical Studies* 5 (1954), 65–73.

Demopoulos, W. and Friedman, M.: 'The concept of structure in *The Analysis of Matter*', in *Rereading Russell: Essays in Bertrand Russell's Metaphysics and Epistemology* ed. C.W. Savage and C.A. Anderson (Minneapolis: University of Minnesota Press, 1989), 183–99.

Russell, B.: *The Analysis of Matter* (London: Kegan Paul, Trench, Trubner, 1927).

C. ANTHONY ANDERSON

J

James, William (1842–1910) American philosopher and psychologist. According to James, metaphysics cannot reveal the inner nature of the universe; its task is to explain the meaning and purpose of conceptual organizations of experience and methodically evaluate competing interpretations. A satisfactory account would harmonize each person's entire intellectual, affective and volitional nature. RUSSELL's claim that the criterion of satisfaction is indefensibly subjectivistic began a persistent line of criticism. Pragmatists point out that his objection only makes sense on the assumption of a psychology of inner states of consciousness reflecting on an external world of objects, the dualistic paradigm which PRAGMATISM refutes. The contributions of intellect and sense which constitute the world as experienced can only be retrospectively distinguished. In doing so, there is no recovery of a distinct subjective contribution and objective sense data (*see* SENSA), but rather their postulation as a useful way of interpreting EXPERIENCE. James's postulate of pure experience is a conceptual reconstruction of his concrete or phenomenological investigation in *The Principles of Psychology* (1890) of the unique manyness-in-oneness which constitutes mental states. Pure experience means either lived experience, in which we focus on an object or are otherwise engaged in doing something, and are not conscious of the fringe of beliefs and relations which structure the object or activity; or it means a limit concept, whose function is to remind us that we contribute to the character of the seemingly already structured world which we take for granted, such that if we lost our ability to do so, we would fall back into an undifferentiated chaos. In the first case, our experience is 'pure' of conscious knowledge of the background relations, but not of their operation; and in the second, we are reminded that an experience 'pure' of all subjective contributions would not be objective, but chaotic.

James's metaphysics of radical EMPIRICISM postulates that reflection be limited to experience, and he begins with the demonstrated fact that relations are directly experienced. His metaphysics is empirical because it regards conclusions about matters of fact as hypotheses modifiable in the course of future experience, and it is radical in its non-reductive pluralism because finite limitations of the human condition ensure that no point of view can ever be comprehensive. (*See* MONISM/PLURALISM; REDUCTION, REDUCTIONISM.) Darwin's evolutionary discovery that species evolve problematized the notion of natural kinds and motivated a conceptual shift away from a metaphysics of *ens qua ens* to genetic analyses of the process of becoming (*see* NATURAL KINDS). In reflecting on what it means to become human as one species among others in a changing environment, and rejecting the obsolete metaphysical search for essential natures, James developed a concrete analysis of the human condition. (*See* ESSENCE/ACCIDENT; ESSENTIALISM.) In an evolutionary model of human consciousness in which our odds of survival as a species are increased through the development of a brain and nervous system more flexibly responsive to changes in the environment, it is not passive reception of sense stimuli that distinguishes human intelligence, but the ability to select out of many alternative possibles the reality most favourable to our interests. Since interests vary, there results a pluralism of worlds of reality, for example, the worlds of common sense, of physics, of religion, and of drama. The efficacy of human decisions underlies James's arguments for freedom and against determinism (*see* FREE WILL). The self is a complex organizing centre exhibiting functional rather than substantial identity (*see* PERSONS AND PERSONAL IDENTITY). Continuity over time is substituted for identity of substance, and the integration of our varied material and social selves is an ongoing task.

James's metaphysics of radical empiricism can best be understood as an attempt to bring all his reflections together into a single paradigm. The natural history finding of the psychological sense of reality developed through the reflex arc is reformulated into the '*full* fact' of his metaphysics. The physiological fact that incoming stimuli are adjusted by the nervous system and brain in executing action demonstrates both the selective nature of our responses even at the level of sensation and that thinking and feeling are for the sake of action. The *full* fact, which also determines the character of reality, is 'a conscious field *plus* its object as felt or thought of *plus* an attitude towards the object *plus* the sense of self to whom the attitude belongs' (James, 1985, p. 393). The synthesis of apperceptive categories and phenomena yield those facts, which in James's formulation of a pragmatically hermeneutic circle, determine beliefs provisionally and acting upon these beliefs brings about new facts. According to this radically empiricist REALISM, the facts of any situation cannot be determined without evaluation of the selective interests operative and of the consequences of acting on them.

James begins his genealogy of metaphysical categories with a concrete analysis of change taking place, since it is synonymous with our sense of life. This felt sense of activity is interrogated as it is lived through in order to develop and criticize the intelligible structures by which it is known-as. We discover on this phenomenal level the experiences of process, obstruction and release, of sustaining a felt purpose against felt obstacles, which are the original experiences underlying such conceptual reconstructions as the category of cause and effect. If one assumes that phenomena and noumena are ontologically distinct, these activity situations can be criticized as the mere appearances of an underlying reality (*see* NOUMENAL/PHENOMENAL). But James appeals to the pragmatic method according to which differences in practice are indistinguishable, except speculatively, from differences in reality and, in fact, are what we can justifiably mean by such differences. There are as many ways to explain activity as there are ends-in-view, but they all demonstrate the fact that they are our explanations and answerable to our criteria. In order for anything to be real for us, it must affect us in some way and be recognized as so doing.

Sensations elicit our beliefs most strongly because they coerce attention. But they are radically underdetermined and become objects for us only to the extent that they satisfy our concretely rational demands. Rationality, the drive to organize our experiences meaningfully, consists in the satisfaction of both aesthetic and practical criteria. The two aesthetic demands of our logical nature are (1) simplicity or unity, which is a drive to unify the multiplicity of sensations, and (2) clarity, the identification of the myriad distinctive aspects of sensations. The third, practical demand is to secure a solid outward warrant for our emotional ends. The goal of metaphysics is to harmonize these three rational criteria, and James argues that the two aesthetic criteria remain inconclusive unless guided by the practical one. Although James incompletely transformed a realist metaphysics into a pragmatically concrete HERMENEUTICS, he gave good reason for doing so. They have been developed in this account to show the radical turn his radical empiricism introduced into classical American philosophy.

WRITINGS

The Principles of Psychology 2 vols (New York: 1890); repr. 3 vols (Cambridge, MA: Harvard University Press, 1981).

The Varieties of Religious Experience (New York: 1902; repr. Cambridge, MA: Harvard University Press, 1985).

Pragmatism (New York: 1907; Cambridge, MA: Harvard University Press, 1975).

A Pluralistic Universe (New York: 1909; repr. Cambridge, MA: Harvard University Press, 1977).

Some Problems of Philosophy (New York: 1911; repr. Cambridge, MA: Harvard University Press, 1979).

Essays in Radical Empiricism (New York: 1912; repr. Cambridge, MA: Harvard University Press, 1976).

BIBLIOGRAPHY

Flower, E. and Murphey, M.G.: 'William James, the toughminded: an appraisal', in *A History of Philosophy in America* vol. 2 (New York: Capricorn Books, 1977), 635–92.

McDermott, J.J.: 'William James', in *Classical American Philosophy* ed. J.J. Stuhr (Oxford: Oxford University Press, 1987), 93–107.

Myers, G.E.: *William James: His Life and Thought* (New Haven: Yale University Press, 1986).

Seigfried, C.H.: *Chaos and Context: A Study in William James* (Athens, OH: Ohio University Press, 1978).

Seigfried, C.H.: *William James's Radical Reconstruction of Philosophy* (Albany, NY: SUNY Press, 1990).

Suckiel, E.K.: *The Pragmatic Philosophy of William James* (Notre Dame, IN: University of Notre Dame Press, 1982).

CHARLENE HADDOCK SEIGFRIED

K

Kant, Immanuel (1724–1804) Often regarded as the greatest of the modern philosophers, Kant spent most of his life in or near the East Prussian city of Königsberg. His contributions to metaphysics occur mainly in the first of his three *Critiques*, the *Critique of Pure Reason* (1781; 2nd edition, 1787).

In the prefaces to the *Critique of Pure Reason*, Kant characterized metaphysics as previously practiced as a 'battlefield of . . . endless controversies' (A viii) in which 'no participant ha[s] ever yet succeeded in gaining even so much as an inch of territory' (B xv). Metaphysicians had failed to reach secure results, he suggested, because they had sought to attain knowledge of objects (such as God and the soul) that could never be given in EXPERIENCE. In order for metaphysics to enter upon 'the secure path of a science', it would have to concern itself henceforth only with objects of possible experience. Transcendent metaphysics (as he called the old unsuccessful variety) would have to give way to immanent metaphysics (whose principles apply only within the world of experience).

This prognosis was reinforced by Kant's investigations into the conditions of synthetic a priori knowledge. Kant believed that the interesting propositions of metaphysics were both synthetic (i.e. not true simply because their predicate concepts were contained in their subject concepts) and, if knowable at all, a priori (i.e. knowable without relying on empirical evidence). He therefore saw the possibility of metaphysics as bound up with the central question of the *Critique of Pure Reason* – how are synthetic a priori judgements possible? Kant's answer to this question implies that a synthetic judgement is knowable a priori only if it concerns actual or possible objects of experience. The judgement need not be *validated* by experience, but it must have something experienceable for its subject matter. It follows that immanent metaphysics alone is a legitimate field of metaphysical inquiry.

This article will discuss Kant's views on each of the two varieties of metaphysics he distinguishes, as well as one of the main metaphysical doctrines of his own philosophy, transcendental IDEALISM.

TRANSCENDENTAL IDEALISM

This is the view that things in space and time are only appearances or phenomena, i.e. items that exist only as the contents of actual or possible representations. Kant stated one consequence of this view as follows: 'if the subject, or even only the subjective constitution of the senses in general, be removed, the whole constitution and all the relations of objects in space and time, nay space and time themselves, would vanish' (A 42/B 59). Transcendental idealism is not *total* idealism, for Kant allowed (and at times insisted) that there must be some things that do not depend for their existence on being represented or cognized; these he called things in themselves or noumena. But he was nonetheless an idealist regarding everything existing in space and time. (*See* NOUMENAL/PHENOMENAL.)

Kant offered four arguments for his idealism, two epistemological and two ontological.

1. He maintained that a priori knowledge of synthetic propositions (such

as we possess in geometry) is explainable only on the assumption that the objects of such knowledge must 'conform to our knowledge' rather than our knowledge having to conform to them (B xvi). For example, we know a priori that geometrical figures will obey Euclid's laws because our minds impose a Euclidean organization on any objects that come before it. But it is very difficult to see how we could impose any features on things in themselves, which by definition are mind-independent. Kant concluded that the objects concerning which we can have geometrical knowledge – things in space – must not be things in themselves, but only appearances. This argument is to be found in the Transcendental Aesthetic (e.g. at A 48/B 65).

2. Like DESCARTES and LOCKE, Kant believed that our immediate awareness extends no further than our own representations. Unlike Descartes and Locke, however, he believed that human beings have immediate awareness of an external world in space – we need only open our eyes to be assured of the existence of rivers and mountains and stars. How can these two seemingly contradictory views be combined? Only by making the following assumption: that objects in space are nothing but patterns of representations. This Berkeleyan side of Kant's views is most forcefully expressed in the Fourth Paralogism (A 366ff.) (see BERKELEY).

3. Kant hit upon another argument for idealism by reflecting on certain puzzling features of incongruent counterparts – objects that are perfectly similar except for being mirror images of each other, such as left and right human hands. The argument may be put thus:

(a) Any relations among things in themselves must be reducible to intrinsic or non-relational properties of the relata (a premise Kant shared with LEIBNIZ).

(b) The relation of incongruence between two counterparts is not thus reducible (as shown by the fact that a right hand and a left may be as alike in their intrinsic properties as two rights or two lefts).

Therefore

(c) Hands (and by extension all objects in space) are not things in themselves.

This argument occurs in section 13 of the Prolegomena (1783).

4. Finally, Kant marshalled his famous ANTINOMIES as indirect proof of transcendental idealism. He argued that if the world in space and time were a world of things existing in themselves (apart from human cognition), it could be demonstrated to have various contradictory properties. For example, it would have to be either finite or infinite in spatial extent, yet Kant thought that either alternative led to logical absurdity. More will be said below about the antinomies.

IMMANENT METAPHYSICS

Kant believed there were legitimate synthetic a priori principles involving each of his twelve famous categories. Here we will discuss just the principles involving the most important categories, SUBSTANCE and cause (See CAUSATION); these principles are known as the Analogies of Experience.

The First Analogy of Experience, or principle of the permanence of substance, may be put thus: all change (defined technically to mean all coming to be or ceasing to be) is alteration in the properties of one or more everlasting substances. For example, if a log is consumed by flames, this is not a case of something's reverting to nothing, but is rather a case of the underlying matter's being transformed into smoke and ashes. There is no absolute perishing, but only a change of form. Kant held that all ceasing to be must be like this, and that the underlying substances themselves never cease to be. The gist of one of his lines of argument is as follows:

(1) Any change in the phenomenal world must be perceivable.
(2) A change is perceivable only if it is an alteration in the properties of an underlying substance.
(3) A substance, by traditional definition, is 'something which can exist as subject and never as mere predicate' (B 149), so a substance cannot be adjectival upon any deeper substance.

Hence

(4) Substances themselves cannot pass away, for if they did we would need deeper substances for them to be adjectival upon.

So finally

(5) All changes in the phenomenal world are alterations in the properties of everlasting substances.

The Second Analogy of Experience is the principle that every event has a cause. HUME had contended that this principle can never be established by human reason, thereby rousing Kant from his 'dogmatic slumber'. Kant maintained on the contrary that the causal principle can be demonstrated by showing its truth to be necessary for experience. In particular, he sought to show that we can know on the basis of experience that an event has occurred only if the event has a cause. He began by pointing out that whether we are observing an event (e.g. a ship moving downstream) or a static object (e.g. a house) our perceptions occur successively: we see the ship first here, then there; we see first one part of the house, then another. Hence the mere successiveness of our perceptions does not tell us whether what we are observing is an event or a non-event. (Incidentally, this shows that Kant's idealism does not take the simple form of identifying external objects and events with perceptions; instead, external items are logical constructions out of perceptions.) So what more is required before we can say that we have witnessed an event, the giving way of one state to another in nature? Kant argued that we can know that succession in our perceptions corresponds to succession in the states of an external object (i.e. an event in nature) only on the assumption that something caused the states to occur in the order they did. By this strategy, he hoped to have shown that the principle of universal causation is a necessary condition of the possibility of experience – in this case, the experience of events.

TRANSCENDENT METAPHYSICS

This divides into three main areas: rational psychology, rational cosmology, and rational theology, which endeavour to prove by reason important attributes of the soul, the cosmos, and God.

The three principal contentions of rational psychology were these: (1) the soul (or thinking self) is a substance; (2) it is simple, i.e. without parts, and therefore immaterial; and (3) it has genuine identity through time, rather than being a succession of distinct entities. Besides criticizing in detail specific arguments by which rational psychologists had sought to prove these conclusions, Kant put forth a general critique of any possible attempt to prove things about the soul. One of its premises is that the self is not an object of awareness, a point on which Kant agreed with Hume. Another is that the propositions of rational psychology are synthetic and, if knowable at all, a priori. A third is the doctrine mentioned above that synthetic a priori knowledge can be had only of objects of possible experience. From these three premises it

KANT, IMMANUEL

follows that rational psychology can teach us nothing about the self.

We pass now to rational cosmology and Kant's antinomies. An antinomy is a pair of conflicting propositions for which equally cogent proofs can be given on either side. Kant believed that antinomies were generated whenever human reason applied itself to any of the following four questions: (1) Does the world have a beginning in time and a boundary in space, or is it without beginning and without bound? (2) Are composite substances made up of simple substances, or do they contain parts within parts *ad infinitum*? (3) Are there any actions that are free, in the sense of being caused by volitions that are themselves uncaused, or are all actions caused by causes that have their own causes and so on *ad infinitum*? (4) Is there an absolutely necessary being to serve as ground of the rest of what exists, or are all beings contingent?

Kant believed that his own philosophy of transcendental idealism could resolve the antinomies, whereas the opposing philosophy of transcendental realism could not. In the case of antinomies (1) and (2), a transcendental realist – one who believes that things in space and time exist independently of human cognition – would have to accept the antinomial alternatives as exhaustive. For example, he would have to hold that the extent of the material universe in space is either finite or infinite. But each of the two alternatives could be shown to lead to absurdity, Kant thought, thereby refuting transcendental realism. The transcendental idealist, however, need not accept the alternatives as exhaustive. Believing that things in space exist only in being apprehended, he can believe that the series of ever remoter regions of the universe (or of ever smaller parts of matter) is potentially infinite (always further prolongable), but neither actually finite nor actually infinite. He thus escapes the absurdities that refute the realist.

In the case of antinomies (3) and (4), Kant sought to show that the two conflicting propositions (thesis and antithesis) could both be true (in different connections), pro-

vided one accepted his distinction between phenomena and noumena. The antithesis is true in each case of phenomena – every phenomenal event has a phenomenal cause, and every phenomenal being is contingent. But the thesis may be true of noumena: it is not excluded by what has been said so far that some actions have noumenal causes that are free, or that there is a necessarily existing noumenal ground of the entire phenomenal world. We cannot prove that these things are so, but we can make room for their possibility.

We come finally to rational theology. Kant maintained that there were only three possible proofs of the existence of God: the ontological proof, or argument from the definition of God, the cosmological proof, or argument from the existence of a cosmos, and the physico-theological proof, or argument from design. The ontological argument may be set forth very simply: God is by definition the *ens realissimum*, the most real or perfect being; nothing can satisfy the requirements of that definition unless it exists; therefore, God exists. Kant is generally credited with having shown definitively what is wrong with the ontological argument. Even if we concede that one cannot without contradiction speak of a most perfect being who does not exist, the possibility remains of 'reject[ing] subject and predicate alike' (A 594/B 622), i.e. saying that there is no perfect being. In effect, Kant pointed out that the argument can only reach a conditional conclusion – *if* anything is a perfect being, it must exist. This criticism is more to the point than his more famous criticism involving the slogan 'existence is not a real predicate'. Kant went on to criticize the other two classical arguments by maintaining that in the end they presuppose the ontological proof.

See also CAUSATION; KANTIANISM.

WRITINGS

Critique of Pure Reason (Riga: 1781; 2nd edn 1787); trans. N. Kemp Smith (New York: St Martin's Press, 1965).

Prolegomena to Any Future Metaphysics (1783); trans. L.W. Beck (Indianapolis, IN: Bobbs-Merrill, 1950).

BIBLIOGRAPHY

Allison, H.: *Kant's Transcendental Idealism* (New Haven: Yale University Press, 1973).
Ameriks, K.: *Kant's Theory of Mind: An Analysis of the Paralogisms of Pure Reason* (Oxford: Clarendon Press, 1982).
Bennett, J.: *Kant's Analytic* (Cambridge: Cambridge University Press, 1966).
Bennett, J.: *Kant's Dialectic* (Cambridge: Cambridge University Press, 1974).
Broad, C.D.: *Kant: An Introduction* (Cambridge: Cambridge University Press, 1978).
Harper, W. and Meerbote, R. eds: *Kant on Causality, Freedom, and Objectivity* (Minneapolis: University of Minnesota Press, 1984).
Kemp Smith, N.: *A Commentary on Kant's Critique of Pure Reason* 2nd edn (London: Macmillan, 1923).
Sellars, W.: *Science and Metaphysics: Variations on Kantian Themes* (London: Routledge and Kegan Paul, 1968).
Strawson, P.F.: *The Bounds of Sense* (London: Methuen, 1966).
Van Cleve, J. and Frederick, R. eds: *The Philosophy of Right and Left: Incongruent Counterparts and the Nature of Space* (Dordrecht: Kluwer, 1991).
Wood, A.W. ed.: *Self and Nature in Kant's Philosophy* (Ithaca, NY: Cornell University Press, 1984).

JAMES VAN CLEVE

Kantianism The philosophy of KANT has influenced a wide range of philosophical movements in modern philosophy, from German IDEALISM and PHENOMENOLOGY to PRAGMATISM and LOGICAL POSITIVISM. The 'critical philosophy' or 'criticism' (as both Kant and his followers would prefer to call it) attempts to overcome the opposition between RATIONALISM and EMPIRICISM, by limiting the field of our knowledge to objects of experience, yet providing an a priori basis for those propositions, such as the principle that every event has a cause, which are required for empirical science but which, as HUME showed, cannot be justified on the basis of experience. By bringing to light the active role of the mind in the process of knowing, Kant's philosophy is also one principal source of modern ANTIREALISM.

Yet if 'Kantianism' or 'criticism' is the name for a distinctive philosophical movement, then it would have to be one whose identity has been a matter of constant dispute over the past two centuries. Nor would strict fidelity to the letter of Kant's own doctrines ever be the chief criterion used in such disputes. Rather the issue has always been: in what direction should one depart from the letter of Kant's writings if one wants to realize the spirit of the critical philosophy?

THE FIRST KANTIANS AND GERMAN IDEALISM

Kant's earliest followers were already concerned to 'go beyond Kant' in at least two ways. First, Kant had described the *Critique of Pure Reason* (1781) as a 'treatise on method' as distinguished from the 'system' of philosophy which was to be built on it. The first Kantians, such as Karl Leonhard Reinhold (1758–1823) and FICHTE, sought to use the method to produce the system Kant had never completed. Second, they thought the *Critique*'s reply to Humean scepticism had not been thorough enough; this was partly through sceptical challenges directed against the critical philosophy by two philosophers who had already absorbed it and were sympathetic to it: Gottlob Ernst Schulze (1761–1833) and Salomon Maimon (1754–1800). Reinhold and Fichte sought to provide a transcendental deduction of the whole critical system from a single fundamental principle whose self-evidence would render the system immune to sceptical attack. For Reinhold, this was the 'principle of consciousness': that every mental representation refers to a subject and an object, which are both distinguished from the representation and related to one another through it. For Fichte, the principle was the 'I': the original act which, in freely positing itself, makes itself its own object.

Fichte's version of the Kantian system was the source of the German idealist movement. It inspired a generation of German philosophers convinced that Kant had set in motion a whole new way of thinking still in search of its telos. In the hands of F.W.J. Schelling (1775–1854) 'critical' philosophy was succeeded by a 'speculative' philosophy, and the German idealist movement was generally regarded as having received its final form in the system of HEGEL. Fichte's version of the critical philosophy was also the source of German Romanticism and of the philosophy of Schulze's student SCHOPENHAUER, who always considered himself to be Kant's only true heir.

NEO-KANTIANISM

'Back to Kant!' (drawn from Otto Liebmann's *Kant and the Epigones* (1865)) was the motto of the so-called 'neo-Kantian' movement in late nineteenth- and early twentieth-century philosophy. The various (often mutually hostile) philosophers and schools usually subsumed under this title were not, as is often thought, calling for a return from the speculative metaphysics of German idealism, which by mid-century had long been out of fashion. Instead, their main opponents were the eclecticism and the often crudely speculative yet largely anti-philosophical scientistic materialism which dominated European intellectual life in the middle of the nineteenth century (*see* PHYSICALISM/MATERIALISM). Some precursors of neo-Kantianism, such as the physicist and physiologist Hermann von Helmholtz (1821–94) and the forerunner of Marburg neo-Kantianism Friedrich Albert Lange (1828–75), were strongly influenced by scientific materialism; and the neo-Kantians themselves were thinkers of rationalistic, even scientific temperament. Yet like Kant they were convinced that empirical science both admits of and requires a systematic grounding in a philosophical theory distinct from it, which would ground a scientific knowledge of the world and also help to secure the place of science within the wider concerns of human culture.

Perhaps the chief school of neo-Kantian philosophy was the Marburg School, founded by Hermann Cohen (1842–1918) and continued by Paul Natorp (1854–1924), Karl Vorländer (1860–1928) and Ernst Cassirer (1874–1945). Also important was the so-called Southwest German or Heidelberg School, whose most prominent representatives were Wilhelm Windelband (1848–1915) and Heinrich Rickert (1863–1936). Two other leading neo-Kantians were Alois Riehl (1844–1924), whose version of criticism has much in common with recent scientific REALISM, and Leonard Nelson (1882–1927), whose psychologistic Kantianism was strongly influenced by Jakob Friedrich Fries (1773–1843), a contemporary of Hegel (and his most bitter rival).

CRITICISM AND METAPHYSICS

Etymologically, 'metaphysics' means 'beyond nature'; but it is generally the critical position that human cognition is limited to the natural world of sense. Thus 'metaphysics' is often used pejoratively by critical philosophers, as it is by positivists. Kant, however, proposed to turn metaphysics into a science, and critical philosophers distinguish a transcendent metaphysics, which fails to respect the limits of our faculties of cognition, from an immanent or critical metaphysics, which is founded on an awareness of them.

Kant's official definition of metaphysics is: 'Synthetic a priori cognition from concepts'; a 'cognition' is a representation which refers to an object, and not merely to the state of the subject. This distinguishes *metaphysics* from three other species of knowledge: (1) *mathematics*, which in Kantian doctrine is synthetic a priori cognition of objects based on the pure intuitions of

SPACE AND TIME rather than on concepts; (2) *logic*, which is not a form of cognition because it refers only to forms of thought and does not deal with objects; and principally (3) *empirical science*, whose cognition of objects is a posteriori. Thus when critical philosophy uses 'metaphysics' in a positive sense, 'beyond nature' is taken in an exclusively epistemic significance: metaphysics goes 'beyond nature' not in the sense that its objects are supernatural, but in the sense that the cognition itself is independent of experience.

The critical question then is: how is metaphysics possible? The critical answer is that it is possible because our cognition of objects is dependent not only on those objects, but also on our faculties of cognition, which therefore determine the objects we can know in certain ways a priori. The apriority of a cognition consists in the fact that it is based not on the objects known but on the contribution made to knowledge by our cognitive faculties. Thus a priori knowledge is utterly different from *innate* knowledge (whose existence Kant rejects): innate knowledge would have to be implemented in us at birth, by nature or God, whereas we ourselves produce a priori knowledge through the exercise of our own faculties.

Cognition arises through both passive and active faculties. Objects affect us, providing sensible intuitions, and our understanding brings about a synthesis, according to rules, making possible a unified experience. Our sensibility can receive intuitions only as ordered in certain relations, in space and time. This gives rise to the a priori intuitive cognitions of mathematics. The necessary forms of our understanding yield the fundamental a priori concepts, or categories according to which empirical objects are necessarily subject to certain conditions, such as that all changes are modifications of substance and follow causal laws.

Metaphysics is possible because the nature of our faculties conditions the possibility of experience. Kant calls the cognition of objects which makes experience possible *transcendental* cognition. Thus metaphysics

cannot be *transcendent* but it is necessarily *transcendental*. To prove that a principle (for example, that every alteration has a cause) is known a priori, we provide a 'transcendental deduction' for the principle, which shows that it is a condition for the possibility of experience. (*See* TRANSCENDENTAL ARGUMENTS.)

Since transcendental cognition conditions the possibility of objects of experience, even empirical knowledge of these objects is only relative to our capacities. Thus empirical objects are only appearances or phenomena; they are empirically real, but transcendentally ideal. Objects in themselves (or noumena – objects of a pure intellect) are unknowable by us (see NOUMENAL/PHENOMENAL). This position Kant calls 'transcendental (or critical) idealism' which he distinguishes both from transcendental realism, which holds that the objects of our cognition are things as they exist in themselves and from empirical idealism which holds either that such real objects are nonexistent or that their existence is uncertain. Indeed, Kant argues that transcendental realism is the most direct path to empirical idealism, and that the surest way to avoid the sceptical paradoxes of empirical idealism is to embrace transcendental idealism. The varieties of Kantian or critical philosophy derive mainly from the questions, tensions and unclarities besetting Kant's transcendental theory of experience and his transcendental idealism. There are two basic issues in terms of which we can understand much of the dynamics of critical philosophy: the status of a transcendental theory of experience, and the relation of appearances to things-in-themselves.

TRANSCENDENTAL PSYCHOLOGY

Kant's theory of experience seems to be based on a number of givens: that there are objects outside us which are given to us by affecting our senses, that our sensibility receives intuitions through the forms of space and time, and that our understanding thinks objects through twelve fundamental a priori concepts (categories). The theory is apparently based on knowledge we happen to possess about our cognitive faculties and how they interact with reality. But where do we get this knowledge?

Suppose *e* is an a priori cognition. Does it follow that our knowledge that *e* is a priori must also be a priori? Apparently not; for if what makes *e* a priori is that *e* depends on the constitution of our faculties, then we can know a priori that *e* is a priori only if we have a priori cognition of the way our faculties are constituted, i.e. only if the self-knowledge of our faculties is derived solely from these faculties themselves. On the face of it, though, it might seem more likely that knowledge of our faculties is a species of empirical knowledge, obtained either through an introspective or a physiological psychology. This plausible view was the basis of Fries's 'anthropological' critique of reason, later taken up by Nelson, which abandoned transcendental arguments and put in their place the discovery of self-evident metaphysical principles through psychological introspection. An even more naturalistic version is found among scientistic Kantians such as Helmholtz, who held that the constitution of space depends on the organization of the human nervous system. Kantian psychologism in the late nineteenth century provided the main background for the anti-psychologism of both FREGE and HUSSERL.

But it was just the thought that Kantianism might be this kind of position that provoked the metacritical scepticism of Schulze. Humean scepticism rested on the fact that our knowledge is founded on experience. If Kant's reply to Hume presupposes a theory of mind with an empirical basis, Schulze argued, then the Humean may easily renew the sceptical challenge by directing it at the empirical basis of Kant's transcendental philosophy. Perhaps for this reason, the commonest Kantian position is not that of Fries or Helmholtz, but rather one which attempts to maintain that the theory of experience behind the critical philosophy is itself composed entirely of transcendental cognitions, and therefore itself possesses an a priori status. In other words, not only are

the objective validity of the categories and the principles of pure understanding (such as the principle of causality) to be transcendentally deduced from the conditions for the possibility of experience, but the Kantian account of these conditions is also to be transcendentally deduced from some basic concept of experience. This was the approach of Reinhold and Fichte, when they tried to provide the critical philosophy with a more secure basis by grounding it on a single self-evident principle (Reinhold's 'principle of consciousness' or Fichte's self-positing I).

The problem here is that this burdens the critical philosopher with transcendental psychology, as an a priori science of the human mind. It is not clear that such a science is possible at all, or that it is even compatible with critical principles. This makes it understandable that STRAWSON should have preferred to reconceive the Kantian project as a 'descriptive metaphysics' which retains transcendental arguments while ridding itself of the albatross of transcendental psychology. Transcendental philosophy was also reconceived non-psychologistically by Cohen and Natorp as a rational reconstruction based on the 'fact of science', and by Rickert as a normative science based not on the *existence* of any thing which *is* but on the *validity* of a *value*, namely, the value of truth. But these approaches, which seek to free transcendental philosophy from psychology, whether a priori or empirical, seem tenable only if we take Humean scepticism less seriously than did Reinhold, or Schulze, or Fichte – or Kant himself.

THE THING IN ITSELF

Kant maintains that the objects of our knowledge are only appearances, and that things in themselves are unknowable. It was the acute philosophical critic Friedrich Heinrich Jacobi (1743–1819) who said that one cannot enter the critical philosophy without the thing in itself, but with the thing in itself one cannot remain in it. The doctrine of the thing in itself was denied by some of Kant's earliest and most significant followers, including Fichte and Jakob Sigismund Beck (1761–1840), and by such important later Kantians as Cohen and Natorp. Both sides in the dispute lay claim to the modest and anti-metaphysical spirit of the critical philosophy. Those who favour the thing in itself say that it is needed as a limiting concept (*Grenzbegriff*) to indicate the bounds of our knowledge; its opponents regard it as a metaphysical monstrosity encumbering criticism with a realm of unknowable speculative entities beyond the empirical world.

Resistance to the thing in itself has many sources. One is that a doctrine which admits extra-mental reality only to declare it unknowable may seem more like an unconditional capitulation to scepticism than a triumphant refutation of it. Jacobi argued that the positing of a supersensible object as the cause of sensible representations is inconsistent with the basic tenets of the critical philosophy, since it obviously violates the critical stricture that the principle of causality is applicable only to relations between appearances. Perhaps the subtlest and most authentically Kantian objection to the thing in itself is the sceptical worry raised by Maimon. According to Kant's transcendental deduction of the categories, things produce sensations in us, which the transcendental imagination then synthesizes in such a way that the sensations are referred to objects conceptualizable by the understanding under the categories. But what reason do we have for thinking that there is any resemblance or correspondence at all between these imagined objects and the things producing the sensations? Maimon concluded that sensations themselves have meaning only in relation to empirical objects, and might as well be regarded as themselves products of the transcendental imagination, rendering things outside the mind entirely superfluous in the Kantian account of cognition. It was this line of thought, taken up by Fichte, which led most directly to German idealism's denial of the thing in itself.

Problems about the thing in itself have their source in ambiguities within Kant's own formulations of transcendental idealism. Kant sometimes refers to the empirical object as an 'appearance of' a transcendental object distinct from it (perhaps standing to it in a relation of cause to effect). But he also speaks of the appearance and the corresponding thing-in-itself as though they were one and the same entity, as when he says that we know things only 'as they appear' but not 'as they are in themselves'. The former way of speaking leads to what we could call a 'causal' interpretation of transcendental idealism, whereas the latter leads to an 'identity' interpretation. Kant speaks interchangeably in both these ways, sometimes in the course of a single sentence; but it is far from clear how a thing in itself can be *identical* with an appearance if it is also its *cause* or ground.

Then there is a further question about the relation of appearances to the subjective representations through which we know them. Sometimes Kant says that empirical objects or appearances are 'only representations' having 'no existence in themselves'. This talk leads naturally to phenomenalist interpretations of Kant (*see* PHENOMENALISM). But if appearances have *no* existence in themselves, how can Kant claim that our knowledge is bounded because we do not know them *as* they are in themselves? Moreover, Kant sometimes speaks as if empirical objects are the empirical causes of representations in us; and he describes his opposition to empirical idealism as a 'dualistic' position, which holds that experience must contain both subjective representations and their empirical causes in outer objects (appearances) distinct from them. But are there *two* causal relations, then, one between unknown things-in-themselves and knowable appearances, the other between appearances and the subjective representations they empirically cause? An affirmative answer to this question was famously defended in Erich Adickes, *Kant's Doctrine of the Double Affection of Our I as the Key to his Theory of Cognition* (1929).

Finally, Kant is not clear about the relation between the mind and the a priori necessary features of empirical objects. Does the mind *impose* space, time and categorial synthesis on empirical objects? Or is it merely that our faculties *restrict* our cognition to those objects which (independently of our mental activity) stand in spatio-temporal relations and conform to the understanding's a priori laws?

The imposition view goes well with the interpretation which reduces empirical objects phenomenalistically to subjective representations ordered a priori in certain ways by the subjective forms of space and time and the rules imposed by the understanding. This can then be combined with the causal interpretation, making mind-constituted orderings of representations, which have no existence at all in themselves, dependent on an unknown alien cause in the noumenal world. But this interpretation of transcendental idealism surely does make the thing in itself look superfluous and absurd. Getting rid of it seems to be the only way to save transcendental idealism from the appearance of radical scepticism, as well as from the objections of Jacobi and Maimon.

On the other hand, if we combine the restriction view and Kant's dualism with an identity interpretation, then transcendental idealism is quite a different doctrine, looking very much like Riehl's version of Kantian realism. Not only do empirical objects have an existence in themselves but we actually know these independently existing things themselves (and not merely their effects or ghostly replicas) through their (empirical) causality on us, though we do not know them *as* they are in themselves, since our knowledge is limited in certain ways by the constitution of our faculties. That seems to be Kant's position in the B Edition 'Refutation of idealism'; it is not in the least phenomenalistic, it is epistemically modest without being radically sceptical, and it avoids Jacobi's charge that Kant makes transcendent use of the causal principle.

The problem with this sensible view is not only that it contradicts some of Kant's formulations – and especially the A Edition 'Refutation of idealism' (in the Fourth Paralogism). It also not clear that it is compatible with Kant's use of transcendental idealism to resolve the mathematical ANTINOMIES of Pure Reason, since that seems to depend on treating empirical objects as consisting in nothing more than actual or possible subjective representations. Besides, can we still defend the view that space and time have no existence in themselves if we hold that spatio-temporal objects themselves and not merely their noumenal causes have such an existence? Perhaps rival versions of the critical philosophy have arisen partly because Kant's revolutionary metaphysical hypothesis of transcendental idealism was formulated in a variety of ways. Kant availed himself of each in turn as needed, but did not realize that the different formulations cannot be equated and lead ultimately to mutually incompatible theories.

BIBLIOGRAPHY

Beiser, F.C.: *The Fate of Reason: German Philosophy from Kant to Fichte* (Cambridge, MA: Harvard University Press, 1987).

Cohen, H.: *Logik der reinen Erkenntnis* (Berlin: Bruno Cassirer, 1914); *Werke* (Hildesheim: Olms, 1977), vol. 6.

di Giovanni, G. and Harris, H.S. eds: *Between Kant and Hegel* (Albany, NY: SUNY Press, 1985).

Fries, J.F.: *Neue oder anthropologische Kritik der Vernunft* (Heidelberg: Mohr & Zimmer, 1807, 2nd edn 1838); *Sämmtliche Schriften* (Darmstadt: Scientia, 1982), vol. 4.

Maimon, S.: *Versuch über die Transzendentalphilosophie* (Berlin: Voss und Sohn, 1790); *Gesammelte Werke* ed. Verra (Hildesheim: Olms, 1970), vol. 2.

Ollig, H.L.: *Der Neukantianismus* (Stuttgart: Metzler, 1979).

Reinhold, K.L.: *Beiträge zur Berichtigung bisheriger Missverständnisse der Philosophen* 2 vols (Jena: Mauke, 1790, 1794).

Riehl, A.: *Der philosophische Kritizismus und seine Bedeutung für die positive Wissenschaft* (Leipzig: Engelmann, 1887).

Ritzel, W.: *Studien zum Wandel der Kantauffassung* (Meisenheim/Glan: Westkulturverlag, 1952).

Schulze, G.E.: *Aenesidemus, oder über die Fundamente der von Herrn Prof. Reinhold in Jena gelieferten Elementar-Philosophie* (1792), *Aetas Kantiana* (Brussels: Culture and Civilisation, 1969).

Willey, T.E.: *Back to Kant* (Detroit: Wayne State University Press, 1978).

ALLEN W. WOOD

L

---

law of nature It is widely held by both scientists and philosophers that our universe is governed by scientific laws and that it is one of the primary aims of science to discover these laws. Particular scientific subjects are often organized around laws stated in the vocabulary of that subject. For example, Schrödinger's equation is central to physics, the Hardy–Weinberg law to genetics, and equilibrium laws to economics. It is also widely held that the concept of a scientific law is intimately related to other important concepts including CAUSATION, NATURAL KIND, explanation, confirmation, reduction, necessity and probability. (*See* REDUCTION, REDUCTIONISM.) It is not surprising then that the task of elucidating the concept of a scientific law figures prominently within contemporary metaphysics and philosophy of science.

Most writers on laws agree that law statements express regularities of some sort or other. For example, Boyle's Law, $PV = kT$, expresses a regularity relating the pressure, volume and temperature of 'ideal' gases. One way of formulating the problem of laws is by asking what distinguishes lawful from accidental regularities. Lawful regularities are said to be in some sense necessary and capable of bestowing some kind of necessity on events which they subsume. The necessity involved is sufficient to support COUNTERFACTUALS. For example, Boyle's law supports the counterfactual that if an ideal gas in a container were heated the pressure exerted by the gas on the walls of the container would increase. But this way of distinguishing laws only seems to connect laws to another problematic notion. The question then is what is it about laws that endows them with the necessity that enables them to support counterfactuals.

There are various accounts of the nature of laws which have been considered. The main distinction is between Humean and non-Humean accounts. According to Humean accounts lawful regularities are distinguished by the roles they play in our theorizing and not in virtue of describing some metaphysical reality over and above the events which actually occur. Thus Humean accounts locate the grounds of nomological necessity in our minds or practices. In contrast non-Humean accounts hold that lawful regularities hold independently of their roles in our theorizing and in virtue of some reality over and above actual events. The two kinds of accounts typically divide over the following SUPERVENIENCE principle:

Humean supervenience
Two POSSIBLE WORLDS exactly alike in their actual course of events have the same laws.

Hempel's view (1965) that laws are true generalizations containing predicates which make no reference to specific individuals and GOODMAN's view (1955) that laws are true generalizations containing entrenched predicates are both Humean. The most sophisticated Humean account is due to David Lewis (1973). He holds that the laws of a world are the regularities described by generalizations which are entailed by the theory (or all the theories) of that world which exhibits the best combination of strength and simplicity (*see* SIMPLICITY, PARSIMONY). A theory is strong to the extent that it entails many particular facts and simple to the extent that it can be formulated with few basic principles. This account is Humean since worlds alike in particular facts are alike in their laws. Nomological necessity is grounded partly in the nature of the world but also partly in what counts as a simple (for us) theory. Lewis is able to connect this characterization of laws with his accounts of counterfactuals, causation, explanation and necessity so as to recapture a number of the important connections among these notions.

There are two main difficulties with Lewis's (and other Humean) views. The first is that the necessity it assigns to laws seems less than the necessity they possess and seem to bestow on events which conform to them. The second is a symptom of the first. It is that there seem to be straightforward counterexamples to Humean Supervenience. It is not difficult to imagine two worlds in which different laws obtain but in which the course of events are the same. For example in one world it is a law that when k and k' particles interact they annihilate one another but this is not a law in another world. In both worlds k and k' particles never interact (although it is nomologically possible for them to do so) and the two worlds are exactly the same with respect to particular events.

There are two kinds of non-Humean views which have been proposed. One account attempts to explain laws in terms of some other concepts. The other takes lawhood as primitive. ARMSTRONG proposes an account of the first kind according to which a law statement expresses a relation of 'nomic necessity' between properties. For example, it is a law that Fs are followed by Gs which says that exemplification of F-hood brings about exemplification of G-hood. Relations of nomic necessity do not supervene on the actual course of events but in some way bring about the course of events. There are two chief difficulties for non-Humean views. One is providing an epistemology for laws since it is not easy to see how we can have epistemological access to laws metaphysically construed. Another

is clarifying how laws are related to events which conform to them so that they bestow on them the appropriate necessity. The relation seems to be neither a logical nor a causal one.

In view of problems with Humean and non-Humean views a radical eliminativist view of laws has recently been advocated by Bas van Fraassen (1989). According to him the non-Humean account of laws is close to being a correct account of the philosopher's concept of law but we have no reason to believe that there are such laws. Van Frassen thinks that scientific practice can be accounted for without employing any metaphysically charged notion of law. The trouble with van Fraassen's sceptical view is that the concept of a law and related notions seem to be involved at every level of description and so disbelieving in laws may entail disbelieving in much else. For example, according to functionalist accounts pain is analysed in terms of a state's lawful relations to other states. If this analysis is correct and if we have no reason to believe in laws then we also have no reason to believe in pains. (*See* FUNCTIONALISM.)

BIBLIOGRAPHY

Armstrong, D.: *What is a Law of Nature?* (Cambridge: Cambridge University Press, 1989).

Carroll, John: Laws of Nature (Cambridge, 1993)

Davidson, D.: 'Causal relations', *Journal of Philosophy* 64 (1967), 691–703.

Dretske, F.: 'Laws of nature', *Philosophy of Science* 44 (1977), 248–68.

Earman, J.: *A Primer of Determinism* (Dordrecht: Reidel, 1986).

Goodman, N.: *Fact, Fiction, and Forecast* (Cambridge, MA: Harvard University Press, 1955).

Hempel, C.G.: *Aspects of Scientific Explanation* (New York: The Free Press, 1965).

Lewis, D.: *Counterfactuals* (Cambridge: Harvard University Press, 1973).

Schiffer, S.: 'Ceteris paribus laws', *Mind* 100 (1991), 1–17.

Tooley, M.: *Causation: A Realist Approach* (Oxford: Clarendon Press, 1987).

van Fraassen, B.C.: *Laws and Symmetry* (Oxford: Oxford University Press, 1989).

BARRY LOEWER

Leibniz, Gottfried Wilhelm (1646–1716) Born in Leipzig, where he received most of his education. Leibniz declined the offer of a professorship at the University of Altdorf, from which he received his doctorate in law in 1667. He sought more interesting opportunities in the career of a legal and intellectual advisor to German princes. His first patron, Baron Johann Christian von Boineburg, sent him on a mission to Paris, where he lived from 1672 to 1676, deepening his understanding of Cartesianism and other movements in contemporary French thought, and studying mathematics. During this period he did a large part of the work that made him an inventor of the calculus of infinitesimals. After brief visits to England and Holland, he settled in Hanover at the end of 1676, to enter the service of the Dukes (later Electors) of Hanover. He made his home there for the rest of his life, though he travelled once to Italy, and often to other parts of Germany, becoming in 1700 the first president of what would develop into the Prussian Academy in Berlin.

Though it is probably his contributions to metaphysics that command the most attention today, Leibniz was occupied with almost the whole range of intellectual activity of his time, including geology, physics, mathematics, theology, jurisprudence, German history, and historiography, as well as the political and other practical interests of his employers. With such diversity of interests, he never found the time to write a comprehensive, book-length statement of his philosophy. The two best known of the books that he did write (Leibniz, 1710 and 1705; the latter not published during his lifetime), are composed in the form of commentaries on the work of Pierre Bayle (1647–1706) and LOCKE, respectively.

Leibniz's philosophy is found chiefly in shorter papers, only a few of them published in his lifetime, and in some of the thousands of letters that he wrote to most of the leading European intellectuals of his day. Thousands of pages of his manuscripts, mostly written in Latin and French, rarely in German, are preserved in the state library at Hanover. Some that bear on metaphysics have never been published at all, and many that are published have never been translated into English.

Despite the largely fragmentary form of his literary remains, Leibniz's metaphysics is strikingly systematic. During most of the twentieth century the deservedly influential work of RUSSELL (1900) and Couturat (1901) has focused the attention of interpreters on papers written in the 1680s but not published until the nineteenth and twentieth centuries, in which Leibniz appears to derive many of his characteristic metaphysical theses from a remarkable doctrine about the nature of *truth* (Leibniz, 1969, pp. 267–70, 307–14). He held that 'in every true affirmative proposition, necessary or contingent, . . . the notion of the predicate is in some way included in that of the subject . . . ; otherwise I do not know what truth is' (Leibniz, 1969, p. 337). Leibniz infers that there is a reason for every truth (the principle of sufficient reason); and from that he infers that no two individual things can differ only in number (the principle of the identity of indiscernibles).

An individual substance, on this view, must have (in God's mind) a concept so complete that every thing that will ever be true about the substance follows from its concept. From this Leibniz infers that 'there are no purely extrinsic denominations', but that all of a substance's relational predicates must be expressed by internal properties that it has. And since it has relations (at least trivial ones) with every other substance in, and every fact about, the whole world of which it is a part, it follows that each substance contains within itself a complete expression of its universe, and thus corresponds perfectly with every other substance. Inasmuch as 'all the future states of each thing follow from its own concept', Leibniz argues further, all created substances are causally independent of each other. None of them acts, in metaphysical strictness, on another. Their perfect correspondence is explained, according to Leibniz, by his famous doctrine of pre-established harmony. God alone does act on created substances, causing their *existence*, though their *states* are normally produced by their own natures. God has created a set of substances whose natures are so harmonious that each successive state of each substance, though determined by the nature of that individual substance alone, mirrors the corresponding states of all the others (Leibniz, 1969, pp. 268–9).

Now these consequences certainly do not all follow logically from Leibniz's theory of truth considered by itself. The mutual causal independence of created substances, for example, does not follow from the completeness of their individual concepts apart from some concrete causal structure in the substance, isomorphic with its concept. That Leibniz believed in such a structure is clear. He identified it with the *substantial forms* of scholastic Aristotelianism (Leibniz, 1969, pp. 307–8), and no turning point was more important for the development of his metaphysics than his decision, in the late 1670s, to try to rehabilitate that scholastic notion (Robinet, 1986, pp. 245–51). The substantial form, for Leibniz, is an internal, active causal principle in an individual substance. The individual concept of the substance is to express the substantial form, and the completeness of the concept mirrors the causal determination of all the states of the substance by the form.

In keeping with his Aristotelian inspiration, Leibniz saw the substantiality of a thing as constituted primarily by this principle of activity. This grounded one of his main objections to the occasionalism of MALEBRANCHE. The latter's denial of metaphysical reality to all the apparent causality in created things threatened, in Leibniz's eyes, to deny all substantial reality to the things themselves (Leibniz, 1956, p. 502).

For Leibniz as for ARISTOTLE, the substantial form is a *teleological* principle (*see* TELEOLOGY). Much more than Aristotle, Leibniz conceived the causal and teleological action of the form on the model of the purposive action of a soul. It is as if each substance sings its parts in the universal harmony by knowing and intentionally following a 'score', corresponding to its complete individual concept, that is built into its substantial form – though such knowledge and intentionality is wholly or partly unconscious in all finite substances (Leibniz, 1989, pp. 84–5). Being constituted by such forms, all substances have 'something analogous to sense and appetite' (Leibniz, 1969, p. 454).

Leibniz had several reasons for this rather mentalistic conception of substances. Of these the most important for the structure of his philosophy – fully as important as the predicate containment theory of truth – is an argument about simplicity and complexity (*see* SIMPLICITY, PARSIMONY). If a whole is divided, or divisible into parts – parts that are, or would be, as substantial as the whole is – then the reality of the whole, Leibniz argued, consists in the reality of the parts, and the reality of the parts is prior to the reality of the whole. Hence if a thing is divided, or divisible, to infinity, and is not ultimately composed of anything indivisible, there will be an infinite regress. The reality of the thing will consist in the reality of parts whose reality consists in the reality of parts whose reality consists in the reality of parts whose reality consists in the reality of parts . . . and so on to infinity. This regress will be vicious because there will be in the whole hierarchy of parts of parts no 'reality not borrowed', as Leibniz put it (Russell, 1900, p. 242). That is, nothing in this thing will possess reality in its own right; and where nothing has reality in its own rights. Leibniz inferred, there is no reality at all. In order to have any reality in itself, a composite thing must be composed ultimately of indivisible things, because only indivisibles can have reality in their own right (Leibniz, 1989, p. 85; 1969, pp. 535–9, 643). (*See* PART/WHOLE.)

Leibniz used this argument to attack DES-CARTES's conception of body as a substance whose essence is extension. It belongs to the essence of extension, as traditionally conceived, that every extended thing is composed of extended parts, which, as extended, are themselves composed of extended parts, and so on to infinity. Because of this regress, the extended as such has no reality in its own right, Leibniz argued; and if bodies have metaphysical reality in them at all, they must be composed ultimately of indivisible, and hence unextended, entities. These indivisible, ultimately real entities are the simple substances or *monads* of Leibniz's metaphysics. (*See* ATOMISM.)

What qualities can these simple, unextended substances have in themselves? Surely they must have some, but these can hardly be the 'mechanical' qualities of Cartesian physics, which presuppose extension. Our own souls are for Leibniz our one accessible model of a simple substance, and he accordingly proposes perceptions and appetitions as the intrinsic qualities of all simple substances – though with the qualification that all the perceptions of most substances, and most of the perceptions of all finite substances, are so confused as to be wholly subconscious. In some contexts Leibniz speaks of 'primitive forces' as the most fundamental properties of simple substances (the 'primitive active force' being identified with the substantial form). But primitive forces intrinsic to a substance must be tendencies of the substance to have certain intrinsic qualities; what could these be? At bottom, in a simple substance, they can only be perceptions, Leibniz seems to have thought; and the internal forces of simple substances he conceived as appetites. 'Indeed, considering the matter carefully, we must say that there is nothing in things but simple substances, and in them, perception and appetite' (Leibniz, 1989, pp. 180–1; cf. ibid., pp. 214–15).

Extended bodies can be viewed, in the Leibnizian system, as *aggregates* of simple substances. At the same time they can be viewed as mere *phenomena*, albeit 'well founded phenomena', having a double dependence on the perceptions of the simple substances. (1) Leibniz was a sort of conceptualist about UNIVERSALS, numbers, relations, and in general about abstract objects and indeed about all sorts of object other than concrete, actual individuals (*see* CONCRETE/ABSTRACT). All such entities, he thought, exist only as objects of perception or thought. He held, accordingly, that aggregates as such, even aggregates of simple substances, depend for their existence on beings that perceive them (Leibniz, 1989, p. 89). (2) Bodies, as aggregates, are further dependent on perception inasmuch as the grouping of simple substances into corporeal aggregates (which monads belong to which aggregates) depends on relations among their perceptions. (For fuller development of this interpretation of Leibniz's philosophy of body, see Adams, 1994, chs 9–12; and for a contrasting interpretation see Garber, 1985.)

God has several foundational roles in the Leibnizian metaphysics. The simple, purely positive properties, from which all the properties of other things are derived by limitation or logical construction, are identified with the perfections of God. Necessary truths and pure possibilities, independent of human thought and of actual exemplification, have their being in God's understanding of them. The pre-established harmony depends on God's creative power and wisdom. Indeed the harmony of things in general is explained by God's selection and creation of the 'best of all possible worlds'. These metaphysical roles of the deity play a central part in several arguments that Leibniz offers for the actual (and indeed necessary) existence of God (Leibniz, 1969, pp. 303–6, 484–91, 646–8).

It is clear, especially in Leibniz's discussions of the ontological argument, that he sees a deep metaphysical connection between perfection and EXISTENCE. This led him into inconclusive speculation about the nature of existence. In various places he suggests that for a thing to exist *is* for it to be chosen by God, or, alternatively, to be more perfect (or part of a more perfect whole) than anything inconsistent with it.

But these definitions, which threaten to trivialize Leibniz's conception of creation, do not ultimately form part of his philosophy (Adams, 1994, ch. 6).

An extensive DETERMINISM follows from several fundamental features of Leibniz's philosophy. God's choice of the best of all POSSIBLE WORLDS would not be assured of having its perfectly optimific effect, if it did not determine every detail of the actual world, for even the slightest deviation from the divine plan would yield an inferior world. The effect of God's creative choice is simply the existence of certain finite substances (infinitely many of them); but this suffices, in Leibniz's system, to determine the world in every detail. For every state of every substance follows from its complete individual concept, and is determined by its substantial form. The pre-established harmony depends on this determinism. If the states of created substances were not all determined by their natures, God would have to keep intervening to assure their continued coordination.

Leibniz explicitly acknowledges the deterministic character of his thought. He maintains that determinism is compatible with FREE WILL, which he understands in terms of the intelligence and self-determination of the agent and the contingency of the event (Leibniz, 1710, p. 303). There are two main lines of argument by which he tries to make room in his system for contingent truths. (1) He holds that actual facts are contingent in so far as they have alternatives that are possible in themselves even if they could not have been chosen by the perfect deity who necessarily exists (Leibniz, 1989, p. 21). (2) He recognizes only formally demonstrable truths as necessary, and only finite proofs as demonstrations. So although the concept of the predicate is contained in that of the subject in every truth, only those that can be proved by a finite analysis are necessary; the others, which depend on an infinite complexity of factors, are contingent in Leibniz's view (Leibniz, 1989, pp. 28–30, 94–8; cf. Adams, 1994, ch. 1, and Sleigh, 1990, ch. 4).

See also MONAD, MONADOLOGY.

WRITINGS

Nouveaux essais sur l'entendement humain (MS of 1705); trans. and ed. P. Remnant and J. Bennett, *New Essays on Human Understanding* (Cambridge: Cambridge University Press, 1981).

Essais de théodicée (Amsterdam: 1710); trans. E.M. Huggard, *Theodicy* (London: 1951; repr. La Salle, IL: Open Court, 1985).

Philosophical Papers and Letters ed. and trans. L.E. Loemker (Chicago: 1956); 2nd edn (Dordrecht: Reidel, 1969).

Philosophical Essays ed. and trans. R. Ariew and D. Garber (Indianapolis, IN: Hackett, 1989).

BIBLIOGRAPHY

Adams, R.M.: *Leibniz: Determinist, Theist, Idealist* (New York: Oxford University Press, 1994).

Couturat, L.: *La logique de Leibniz* (Paris: Presses Universitaires de France, 1901).

Garber, D.: 'Leibniz and the foundations of physics: the middle years', in *The Natural Philosophy of Leibniz* ed. K. Okruhlik and J.R. Brown (Dordrecht: Reidel, 1985), 27–130.

Robinet, A.: *Architectonique disjonctive, automates systémiques, et idéalité transcendentale dans l'œuvre de G.W. Leibniz* (Paris: Vrin, 1986).

Russell, B.: *A Critical Exposition of the Philosophy of Leibniz* (London: 1900); 2nd edn (London: George Allen and Unwin, 1937).

Sleigh, R.C., Jr.: *Leibniz and Arnauld: A Commentary on Their Correspondence* (New Haven, CT: Yale University Press, 1990).

ROBERT MERRIHEW ADAMS

Leibniz's Law *see* IDENTITY OF INDIS-CERNIBLES

Leśniewski, Stanisław (1886–1939) Leader of the Warsaw school of logic and philosophy between the wars, where he taught many excellent logicians, most notably TARSKI. Leśniewski's publications and unorthodox logical systems are characterized by extreme care and rigour. His major efforts went into constructing and improving his three logical systems. These are: protothetic, a system of propositional logic with quantifiers and higher-order functors; ontology, a generalized term logic also constructible to any finite order; and mereology, a formal theory of PART/WHOLE and aggregates. Leśniewski created his system in response to RUSSELL's Paradox, as a foundation for mathematics without the PLATONISM and sloppiness of WHITEHEAD and Russell's (1910–13) *Principia Mathematica* or the intuitive incomprehensibility of Zermelo's sets. (*See* CLASS, COLLECTION, SET.)

Like his hero FREGE, Leśniewski decried formalism, insisting that his logical systems are interpreted and true. He believed logic should be ontologically neutral, and took care that no thesis of his system imply the existence of anything. This caution extended to his metalogical presentation: systems are taken not as tendentious abstract structures but as visible collections of marks growing in time by the addition of new theses (theorems and definitions) according to perfectly exact metalogical directives.

Ontology (so called because in it many senses of 'to be' are definable) allows, besides the singular terms of standard logic, also empty and plural terms, and permits quantifiers to bind variables of any syntactic category, so it is potentially as powerful as *Principia*. This would seem to contradict ontological neutrality, but Leśniewski clearly did not consider quantification to carry ontological weight: it is a theorem of first-order ontology that *For some* a, *no* a *exists*. Whether the quantifiers are understood substitutionally or in some other way is not clear from his writings. Numerous useful formal ontological concepts are rigorously defined in ontology, and many more can be found in mereology.

See also NOMINALISM.

WRITINGS

Collected Works ed. S.J. Surma, J.T. Srzednicki, D.J. Barnett and V.F. Rickey (The Hague: Martinus Nijhoff, 1992).

PETER SIMONS

life For the metaphysician, the fundamental question concerning life is the question about the nature of life itself. For many contemporary philosophers, the most satisfying answer to this question would be formulated as a philosophical analysis of the meaning of the phrase '*x* is alive at *t*'. Some hold that a satisfactory analysis would reveal the nature of the property we ascribe to things when we say that they are alive. Others feel that analysis serves primarily to introduce a new, clear, and precise concept that might replace confused predecessors.

VITALISM

Vitalists maintained that living things differ from non-living things in virtue of the fact that the former contain a non-physical element by which they are animated. Some vitalists (e.g. Hans Driesch (1867–1941)) claimed that this element somehow enables the organism to become 'purposive', so that it strives to develop toward its natural end. Following ARISTOTLE, Driesch referred to the alleged entity as an 'entelechy'. Others held that the life-giving element is an individual substance endowed with psychological characteristics. They called the entity a SOUL, and their view is a form of spiritualism. Yet others spoke more obscurely of 'vital fluid' or *élan vital*.

One difficulty for vitalism is that there is no direct evidence for the existence of souls or other suitable non-physical animating entities. Carl Hempel claimed that vitalism is nonsensical in virtue of the unverifiability of statements about entelechies. Vitalists also have difficulty explaining precisely how the presence of a non-physical element could influence chemical and physical processes in an organism.

STRUCTURALISM

Typical living organisms display a complex hierarchical structure. The organism as a whole consists of a set of systems (e.g. digestive, nervous, skeletal, etc.). Each system consists of a set of organs. Each organ consists of a set of tissues. Each tissue consists of a set of cells. It might therefore be thought that to be alive is to be thus hierarchically structured.

The most serious objections to any such view are (1) that recently dead organisms have the same hierarchical structure; (2) complex machines may have hierarchical structures quite similar to those of living organisms; and (3) it is at least conceivable that there might be living things that do not display this sort of structure.

SYNTROPISM

One important difference between a typical machine and a typical living organism is that the normal operation of the machine inevitably involves the machine's destruction. Friction, metal fatigue, oxidation and other factors may eventually reduce the machine to a homogeneous pile of rust. But a living organism has the capacity to maintain – and even increase – its structural complexity. Reflection on this fact has led some (e.g. Erwin Schrödinger (1967), Jay Rosenberg) to maintain that life is precisely this 'entropy-evading' internal capacity to maintain this self-regulating organization.

This approach confronts several difficulties. Living organisms are 'open systems'; they receive inputs of energy from their environments. If machines are given the same advantage, some of them will be able temporarily to evade disintegration. On the other hand, when in advanced stages of decrepitude, living organisms seem to lose the cited power.

LIFE FUNCTIONALISM

Many philosophers and biologists have noted that there are certain activities that seem to be distinctive of living things. Aristotle mentioned nutrition, reproduction, self-induced motion (including growth), perception, and thought. He attributed each of these 'vital functions' to the operation of a 'soul', and so his view is a form of vitalism. However, if we delete the appeal to souls the resulting view is a form of life functionalism: to be alive is to be able to perform the life functions.

Aristotle's list of life functions is problematic. Many living organisms cannot engage in perception or rational thought. Many cannot reproduce. Some continue to live after they have lost the ability to acquire and digest food. So we cannot identify life with the ability to engage in *all* of the Aristotelian life functions. Since non-living machines may be capable of self-induced motion, we cannot identify life with the ability to engage in *at least one* of these life functions.

Some have suggested that the most crucial life function is metabolism. An entity engages in metabolism when it acquires inputs of food from its environment, transforms the food into forms useful for growth and activity, and releases the waste products back to the environment. This approach confronts several difficulties. (1) Some non-living entities, such as gasoline engines, engage in activities quite like metabolism. (2) Some living entities, such as final stages in the life-cycle of moths, lack the capacity to acquire inputs of food.

Others, perhaps influenced by Charles Darwin, have suggested that the crucial life functions are all somehow related to evolution. In order for evolution to occur, there must be reproduction. Furthermore, when reproduction occurs, offspring must be quite like their parents, but they must also display a range of slight variations. Some have hinted that this capacity for variable reproduction is the essential life function. But since there are sterile living things, it cannot be identified with life itself.

273

A more complex form of the life-functional approach notes that each *species* has its distinctive form of metabolism, reproduction, and perhaps other life functions. Some *individuals* may lack the relevant capacities. However, it has been suggested (by Gareth Matthews (1992)) that to be alive is to be a member of a species that has a suitable set of life functions. This approach is also problematic. It may misrepresent the vital status of dead organisms. If they are still members of their species, the proposal implies that they are still alive. Another problem is that hybrids and 'one-off' organisms produced by genetic manipulation seem not to be members of any species. The view implies that such individuals are not alive even if they move, grow and metabolize.

In light of the difficulties confronting the various proposals, it appears that life itself may be indefinable. Some conclude that it is a 'family-resemblance concept'. Living things have no single property in common, but are linked by a network of resemblances. Others say that life is an indefinable property usually, but not necessarily, associated with the 'life functions'. In this case, it would indeed be correct to say that life is a mystery.

See also DEATH; VITALISM.

BIBLIOGRAPHY

Aristotle: *De anima* (*On the Soul*), in *The Basic Works of Aristotle* ed. R. McKeon (New York: Random House, 1941).
Driesch, H.: *The Science and Philosophy of the Organism*, The Gifford Lectures delivered before the University of Aberdeen in the year 1907 (London: Adam and Charles Black, 1908).
Matthews, G.: '*De Anima* B2–4 and the meaning of *life*', in *Essays on Aristotle's De Anima* ed. M. Nussbaum and A. Rorty (Oxford: Oxford University Press, 1992), 185–93.
Mayr, E.: *The Growth of Biological Thought* (Cambridge, MA: The Belknap Press of Harvard University Press, 1982).
Schrodinger, E.: *What is Life? & Mind and Matter* (London and New York: Cambridge University Press, 1967).

FRED FELDMAN

light of nature [natural light (of reason)] In their general usage these phrases refer to a faculty of knowledge God gives to all people, by which they can know truths independently of divine revelation. In this sense, the reference is not to a faculty whose knowledge must be a priori (AQUINAS, *Summa theologiae* I. xii. 13; LOCKE, *Essay concerning Human Understanding* (1690) I, iii, 13.

In DESCARTES and philosophers influenced by him, there is often the additional connotation that the faculty needs no instruction to operate properly, has not been corrupted by miseducation and is not open to doubt (*The Search After Truth* (1701) (*Œuvres de Descartes*, vol. X, p. 506); *Rules for the Direction of the Mind* (*Œuvres*, vol. X, p. 442); *Meditations* (*Œuvres*, vol. VII, pp. 38–9)). In this sense, the faculty is conceived as one whose knowledge must be a priori, and is supposed to provide knowledge of the first principles of logic, mathematics, and metaphysics. (See 'Third Meditation', *passim*; and LEIBNIZ's Letter to Queen Sophie Charlotte of Prussia (Gerhardt, *Die philosophischen Schriften* (1875–90) VI, pp. 503–4).)

BIBLIOGRAPHY

Descartes, R.: *Œuvres de Descartes*, vols I–XII, ed. C. Adams and P. Tannery (Paris: Leopold Cerf, 1897–1913).

EDWIN CURLEY

Locke, John (1632–1704) Locke's metaphysics is largely determined by his theory of knowledge. While he accepted the traditional view that a genuine science must be based on knowledge of essences, he argued that we cannot know real essences in the natural domain. EXPERIENCE, our only source of information about the natural world, underdetermines essences. Still by experimentation and reasonable inference, we may construct probable hypotheses short of genuine science. Locke supposed corpuscular theory was the best hypothesis about the material world we are likely ever to have. The broad mechanist thesis that what happens in the corporeal realm is reducible to insensible particles in motion is one tenet of Locke's metaphysics. An equally important tenet is that with respect to the *fundamental* constitution of nature we cannot expect to have even a probable hypothesis.

According to Locke, everything that exists is entirely particular and we make general ideas (universals) by abstracting from experience of particulars (*see* UNIVERSALS; UNIVERSALS AND PARTICULARS). Locke's classification of general ideas is a catalogue of sorts of beings. There are simple ideas and complex ones. Simple ideas include, not just sensations (e.g. red, pain), but also ideas of sensible qualities (i.e. powers to produce sensations), other causal powers (e.g. malleability, power to attract iron), and abilities (e.g. to think, to will). Complex ones are divided into ideas of substances, modes and relations. Ideas of substances, meant to represent things that 'subsist by themselves', are composed of ideas of qualities and other causal powers found to coexist in things plus the obscure idea of SUBSTRATUM; particular sorts of substances include gold, horse, man, body, spirit (*see* SUBSTANCE). Ideas of substance are intended to represent natural unities with indefinitely many causal powers; because only some of these powers can be included, substance ideas are inadequate. In contrast, ideas of modes represent things whose existence depends on substances. Locke discusses two sorts of modes: simple and mixed. Simple modes are said to be variations of one simple idea, for example, numbers, infinity, temporal durations, spatial distances, also sorts of pleasures, pains, thoughts, volitions, bodily motions. (Locke supposed that SPACE AND TIME exist independently of finite things in the being of God.) Mixed modes include geome-

trical ideas and ideas of actions, institutions, etc. whose names 'are made use of in Divinity, Ethicks, Law, and Politicks, and several other Sciences' (Locke, 1690, p. 294). Mixed modes have no archetypes (*see* ARCHETYPE) and represent a unity (e.g. one action, discriminated within the flow of bodily motion) due to the mind's making the complex idea. Thus, Locke argues, these ideas are adequate, specify real essences, and support genuine demonstrative sciences (e.g. mathematics, morals). Finally, ideas of relations are ways of comparing that presuppose the existence of two or more things, e.g. cause, father, identity over time, conformity of action to law. Critics find this catalogue to have omissions, notably non-natural kinds of material objects (e.g. table, hat) and natural events and processes (e.g. lunar eclipse, fermentation) (see e.g. Ayers, 1991, pp. 91–109).

Substances are enduring bearers of causal powers and presumptive subjects of prediction and explanation. Qualities by which we apprehend substances are supposed to 'subsist in' an unknown substratum from which 'they do result' (Locke, 1690, p. 295). Apparently substratum in general is whatever ultimately accounts for causal powers as a standing condition and at least partial cause of their actualization. Our best hypothesis posits particulate constitutions that actualize powers by mechanical means. We can accordingly say that 'the subject wherein Colour and Weight inheres [is] . . . the solid extended parts' (Locke, 1690, p. 295; also p. 545). Locke presses the question what solidity and extension inhere in, apparently because we cannot warrantedly conclude that solidity and extension are ultimately basic in explanation (*contra* DESCARTES). Those attributes afford no solution to fundamental problems of physics: communication of motion, coherence and continuity of parts, production of sensation by impulse. Lacking a reasonable hypothesis, we are reduced to saying solidity and extension inhere in 'something, I know not what'.

Some have interpreted substratum as featureless prime matter or bare subject of predication (see e.g. Bennett, 1987). Locke said: 'when we speak of any sort of Substance, we say it is a *thing* having such or such Qualities, as Body is a *thing* that is extended, figured, and capable of Motion' (Locke, 1690, p. 297). But he was using 'thing', not to signify a bare subject (*see* BARE PARTICULAR), but rather to express the fact that we cannot fully specify the natures of substances which we identify by some of their causal powers. Locke's willingness to ridicule the emptiness of the idea of substance has also seemed to support the 'bare substratum' interpretation. He meant, however, to oppose those who thought our idea enabled us to define substance as such. Locke asks whether a single idea is associated with the word 'substance' when applied to God, finite spirits, and bodies; if so, then all three have 'the same common nature of *Substance*' and 'differ not any otherwise than in a bare different modification of that *Substance*'; but if the word signifies different ideas, the idea of substance must be precised before we use it in reasoning (Locke, 1975, p. 174). LEIBNIZ objected that if God, finite spirits, and bodies satisfy the same definition of substance they share a logical genus, but it does not follow that they share a real genus or nature (Leibniz, *c*.1705, p. 64). According to Locke, however, we must establish the natures of things in order to explicate what 'support' and 'inherence' mean in each case. (The same idea of substance applies to God, etc., only if God, etc., have the same nature which functions in the same way as 'support'.) Locke rejected what Leibniz (and the scholastics) contended for, a demonstrative science of metaphysics as such.

Operations we discover by reflection, for example, thinking, willing, also inhere in unknown substance. Citing ignorance of substance, Locke rebuts the Hobbesian argument that immaterial substance is impossible, because we lack its conception, and the Cartesian conclusion that thinking substance is immaterial (*see* HOBBES; DESCARTES). No available hypothesis is fully intelligible, Locke contends. An immaterialist view cannot explain how spirit moves body or is affected by impulse. We cannot understand how *anything* thinks, whether immaterial substance or system of matter. (Locke is clearly agnostic on substance-dualism, but does not address attribute- or event-dualism.) Some take Locke to mean that God gave substances unfounded, ultimately inexplicable powers (Leibniz, *c*.1705, pp. 65–8; Wilson, 1979). But the supposition of substratum assumes that powers have and cause foundation of union. Some maintain Locke even supposes there is a demonstrative essence-based science of nature (Ayers, 1991, pp. 142–53). Others hold he supposes there is a contingent connection between essence and some powers, due to the will of God.

In discussing identity, Locke bases INDIVIDUATION of substances on the principle: it is impossible for two things of the same kind to be in the same place at the same time. For instance, two atoms or horses cannot be coincident, but an atom and an immaterial substance may coincide and so may a mass of atoms and an individual horse. Locke also says a substance cannot begin to exist in different places or times; so apparently he does not anticipate Peter Geach's theory that one substance has multiple kind-relative identities, as some have thought (Mackie, 1976, pp. 160–1) (*see* IDENTITY). Times and places are individuated in relation to bodies, but the circularity is arguably benign. Diachronic identity must be specified in terms of the substance-kind to which an individual belongs. An atom begins to exist at a certain time and place and endures just as long as an atom is spatio-temporally continuous with the atom in that location. A mass of atoms joined together continues to exist if and only if no atom is lost and none is gained. In contrast to these *simple* substances, a compound substance survives change of parts. An oak (horse, man) continues to exist just as long as there is a continuous series of individually different masses of particles that sustain the specific life-functions of oak (horse, man). An oak and the particle-mass that constitutes it at a certain time are individually different subjects of qualities, for example, a colour-particular. Backed by mechanist reduction, Locke apparently held that one colour-particular belongs to both.

A person, according to Locke, is a thing that thinks, reflects, and is conscious of itself existing at different times. It is a compound consisting of (one or more) bodies and one or more simple thinking substances, which are either finite immaterial substances or thinking particle-masses. Personal identity is determined by a person's ability to 'extend consciousness' to remember performing past actions. (All possible means of recall, even God's power, underwrite the ability.) Locke's main contention is that personal identity is conceptually independent of identity of substance. That is, we know nothing that precludes the possibility that a person is a series-being constituted of a sequence of individually different simple substances whose cognitive abilities are transferred rather as life functions are continued in an oak. Transmigration is not precluded; neither is a plurality of persons in one man or in one immaterial substance. (See PERSONS AND PERSONAL IDENTITY.)

Critics charge Locke's claim that a thinking thing can represent itself as having done an act it did not do contradicts his doctrine that personal identity extends to all acts a thinking thing can represent itself as having done (Flew, 1968, pp. 163–4). The objection conflates simple thinking substances, which perhaps can falsely represent past actions, and persons, who cannot. Each act done by a given person is also done by some simple substance, but perhaps not all by the same simple substance (compare the colour-particulars belonging to an oak). Persons alone are said to bear moral responsibility. Yet Locke doubts God's goodness permits responsibility-bearing consciousness to be transferred among substances. Many take this to undo his conceptual distinction between identity of person and substance (Flew, 1968, p. 164; Mackie, 1976, p. 184). But perhaps Locke simply thought consciousness-transfer would needlessly complicate rational pursuit of self-interest, on which he grounds morality. Another

objection is that an adequate explication of a person's remembering x states it as a necessary condition that the person actually did x (Flew, 1968, p. 161). In fact, this has no force against Locke. He explicates the identity of simple substances, whether immaterial or material, without reference to memory. A *person*'s ability to extend consciousness can then be constructed from the mnemonic abilities of the simple thinking substance(s) that constitute the person.

A distinction between primary and secondary qualities was implicit in seventeenth century MECHANISM. Locke defended it by arguing that we cannot conceive a body with no size, shape, motion or rest, or solidity; primary qualities are in bodies whether we perceive them or not, and bodies resemble the primary-quality ideas they cause. In contrast, secondary qualities are nothing but powers to produce sensations of colour, taste, and so on, by the primary qualities of insensible parts; these sensations do not resemble their causes. These claims pose several questions of interpretation (for example, Alexander, 1985, pp. 91–182; Mackie, 1976, pp. 7–36). But the main point is that primary qualities characterize the world as it is apart from its appearance to sense, whereas colours, etc., are inextricable from specific modes of perception. Locke suggests we cannot conceive what it would be for all or part of the content of an idea of red, say, to exist apart from visual perception. (See QUALITY, PRIMARY/SECONDARY.)

In place of received theories of essence, Locke proposed to distinguish real and nominal essences of a kind. Nominal essence is the general idea signified by the name of the kind. The content of a general idea sets the basic membership conditions for the kind the idea represents. Thus we cannot use a name to signify a kind whose boundary we do not know.

Real essence is what gives rise to the properties of the kind defined by a nominal essence and explains the general truths of which the kind is subject. Locke repudiated the Aristotelian view that species of substances are determined by certain 'forms and molds', arguing it is refuted by idiots and monsters (*see* ARISTOTLE). Apparently his point is that Aristotelian species-essences were supposed to ground a necessary union among certain *propria* (e.g. ability to learn grammar, upright posture), whereas in fact those qualities are not always united in nature. Locke himself urged that real essences of corporeal substances are the corpuscular constitutions that give rise to the qualities collected in the nominal essences of substance-kinds. Although nominal essences of substance-kinds are copied from nature, they are to some extent 'arbitrary'. This is inevitable, given our ignorance of qualities and constitutions; but it is equally important that mechanism (unlike Aristotelianism) was not committed to natural kinds of plants, animals, minerals, etc. (*see* NATURAL KIND). Locke was apparently agnostic on whether substances have a uniquely natural classification. As for mixed modes, their real essences are specified by our ideas and thus identified with nominal essences.

Locke also opposed received views on individual essence, saying that individuals 'considered barely in themselves' have no essential qualities. *He*, for example, could loose health, sense, reason and life. These qualities are essential to him, only as conditions of being in some kind (nominal essence) (Locke, 1690, p. 441). It is unclear whether Locke meant literally that a corporeal being could loose *any* quality it has, including solidity and extension. Some suggest he meant instead the anti-Aristotelian thesis that matter is a substance more enduring than a living animal, which we carve from the flux of matter by a general idea made 'arbitrarily' (Ayers, 1991, pp. 206, 216–28). But for Locke, substances are natural unities that our ideas inadequately represent. Probably he is best taken to mean that we cannot *know* a quality is essential to an individual without reference to a nominal essence.

See also EMPIRICISM; IDEA; SUBSTANCE.

WRITINGS

An Essay Concerning Human Understanding (London: 1690); ed. P.H. Nidditch (Oxford: Clarendon Press, 1975).
Correspondence between Locke and Stillingfleet, in *The Works of John Locke*, 10 vols, Vol. 4 (London: Otridge, 1812).

BIBLIOGRAPHY

Alexander, P.: *Ideas, Qualities and Corpuscles* (Cambridge: Cambridge University Press, 1981).
Ayers, M.: *Locke*, 2 vols, vol. 2 *Ontology* (London: Routledge, 1991).
Bennett, J.: 'Substratum', *History of Philosophy Quarterly* 4 (1987), 197–215.
Bolton, M.B.: 'Locke on identity: individuation in a mechanist universe', in *Individuation and Identity in Early Modern Philosophy* ed. K. Barber and J. Gracia (Albany, NY: SUNY Press, 1994).
Chappell, V.: 'Locke on the ontology of matter, living things and persons', *Philosophical Studies* 60 (1990), 19–32.
Flew, A.: 'Locke and the problem of personal identity', in *Locke and Berkeley* ed. C.B. Martin and D.M. Armstrong (Garden City, NY: Doubleday, 1968), 155–78.
Leibniz, G.W.: *New Essays on Human Understanding* (*c.*1705); trans. P. Remnant and J. Bennett (Cambridge: Cambridge University Press, 1981).
Mackie, J.L.: *Problems from Locke* (Oxford: Clarendon Press, 1976).
Wilson, M.D.: 'Superadded properties: the limits of mechanism in Locke', *American Philosophical Quarterly* 16 (1979), 143–50.

M. B. BOLTON

logical atomism RUSSELL coined this name for the philosophy which he was developing just before the First World War when he met and worked with WITTGENSTEIN. He explained it at the beginning of the lectures that he gave in London under the title 'The philosophy of logical atomism' in 1917–18:

> The reason that I call my doctrine *logical* atomism is because the atoms that I wish to arrive at as the sort of last residue in analysis are logical atoms and not physical atoms. Some of them will be what I call 'particulars', . . . such things as little patches of colour, momentary things . . . and some of them will be predicates or relations, and so on. (Russell, 1918, p. 179)

This theory, later abandoned by Russell, can be seen as a reaction against the holism of HEGEL's British idealist followers. Holism includes the connections between things among their essential properties and so by a process of aggrandizement like expanding federation it tends to develop into the theory that *au fond* there is only one thing, the most extreme kind of monism. (*See* ESSENCE/ACCIDENT; ESSENTIALISM; MONISM/PLURALISM.) So when Russell rejects the holism of the British idealists, he describes this stage of his philosophy as a revolt into pluralism (Russell, 1959, p. 54). It was really a movement of thought with two distinguishable steps. First, there was the claim that reality consists of many separate things externally (non-essentially) related to one another (*see* INTERNAL RELATIONS); then follows the further claim that if some of these things have a complex structure, we can analyse them and reanalyse them until we are left with things that are absolutely simple. Atomism is the ultimate development of pluralism, just as extreme monism is the ultimate development of holism.

Since Russell's atoms are logical rather than physical, the process that leads to their disclosure is not physical division but logical ANALYSIS. The sense data which constitute a physical object will be displayed in its logical analysis but they are not its physical parts, and a shape like *elliptical* will be analysed into the basic properties which provide its definition (*see* SENSA). Russell was convinced that this kind of analysis would lead to particulars, properties and relations which would not be further analysable and so the chain of definitions would terminate with indefinables.

His belief in logical atoms rested in part on an intuition which seemed to be supported by science, the intuition that the complexity of structure of some things presupposes other things with no internal structure (Russell, 1924, p. 337). It was also supported by his theory of language. For he held that there are two ways in which the meanings of words can be learned: either they will be defined in terms already familiar to us, or else we will have to achieve ACQUAINTANCE with the things designated by them. But, he argued, we will find that many words prove to be learnable only in the second of those two ways. Now a definition which gives the meaning of a word counts as its analysis. So if his theory of the learning of meanings can be trusted, the words which force us to have recourse to acquaintance will be unanalysable and will, therefore, designate logical atoms. He believed that words for precise shades of colour and words designating particular sense data were examples of forced acquaintance, and so of atomicity (Russell, 1912, p. 58).

The argument that logical atomism is discovered to be true empirically rather than established a priori is a repetition of HUME's argument for his earlier version of atomism. According to Hume, we find that there are ideas which we cannot acquire in any other way than by getting the corresponding impressions and these are simple ideas (Hume, 1739, pp. 1–7). This is a psychological version of atomism rather than a logical one and Hume confined it to ideas of properties and relations, excluding ideas of particulars. Nevertheless, the structure and argument for his theory evidently influenced Russell (Hume, 1739–40, pp. 1–7).

Wittgenstein's logical atomism had a different structure and a different motivation and his criterion of atomicity was stricter than Russell's. According to Russell, an atomic word was one which could not be defined in a way that would enable anyone to learn its meaning without acquaintance with the thing designated by it. For example, 'scarlet' would be an atomic word, because though it might be definable, no definition of it would provide a would-be learner with an alternative resource to take the place of acquaintance. Wittgenstein gave the screw a further turn and required that atomic words should not be definable in any way – not even in a way that would not help a would-be learner of their meanings. So his atomic words did not generate any logical connections between the sentences in which they occurred and any other sentence belonging to the same level of analysis (elementary sentences). It followed that in his theory, colour words were not atomic, and, surprisingly, he did not claim to be able to identify any atomic words in natural languages (Wittgenstein, 1922, 6.3751).

The motivation for this extreme development is clear. If logical atomism requires that *au fond* all the relations between things should be non-essential to them, then atomic words ought to generate no logical connections whatsoever between the sentences in which they occur. So the difference exploited by Russell between logical connections which would help the would-be learner of meanings and logical connections which would not help him ought to be irrelevant. Wittgenstein's more rigorous theory also had another advantage. He held that all necessary truths are tautologies and so a logical atomism which allows necessary truths that could not be explained in this way, like the specifications of the essences of Russell's logical atoms, struck him as an unintelligible compromise. He, therefore, severed the link between logical atomism and the empiricist account of the learning of language.

He then needed a new argument for logical atomism and he extracted one from his theory of meaning (but not from any theory about our learning of meanings). If, as he maintained, sentences are pictures, the words in them must get their meanings by standing for things (the things *are* their meanings). Now if all things were complex, then whenever a word stood for a thing, the essential composition of the thing would need to be specified in further words, and the sense of any sentence would always depend on the truth of further sentences. But in that case no sentence would ever possess the definiteness of sense that FREGE rightly demanded. For the mechanism of picturing would generate an infinite regress of sense and truth. So reversing the argument he rejected the hypothesis that all things are complex (Wittgenstein, 1922, 2.021–2.0212).

In his later work Wittgenstein abandoned the premises of this argument one by one. First, he reverted to a logical atomism closer to Russell's, without the impossibly strict requirement that there should be no logical connections whatsoever between elementary sentences (Wittgenstein, 1929), and then he gave up the theory altogether. It was a theory that ran counter to the general tenor of his thought, which even in his first book, the *Tractatus Logico-Philosophicus*, showed strong holistic undercurrents. His discussion of logical atomism in his *Notebooks 1914–1916* (Wittgenstein, 1914–16, pp. 45–71) leaves little doubt that his adoption of it was largely attributable to the influence of Russell.

BIBLIOGRAPHY

Hume, D.: *A Treatise of Human Nature* (London: 1739–40); ed. L.A. Selby-Bigge, 2nd edn rev. P.H. Nidditch (Oxford: Oxford University Press, 1978).

Russell, B.: *The Problems of Philosophy* (Oxford: Oxford University Press, 1912; repr. 1959).

Russell, B.: 'The philosophy of logical atomism' (1918); repr. in his *Logic and Knowledge, Essays 1901–50* ed. R.C. Marsh (London: Allen and Unwin, 1956), 175–281.

Russell, B.: 'Logical atomism' (1924); repr. in his *Logic and Knowledge, Essays 1901–50* ed. R.C. Marsh (London: Allen and Unwin, 1956), 321–43.

Russell, B.: *My Philosophical Development* (London: Allen and Unwin, 1959).

Wittgenstein, L.: *Notebooks 1914–1916* (1914–16); trans. G.E.M. Anscombe (Oxford: Blackwell, 1961).

Wittgenstein, L.: *Tractatus Logico-Philosophicus* (1922); trans. C.K. Ogden (London: Kegan Paul, 1922); trans. D.F. Pears and B.F. McGuinness (London: Routledge and Kegan Paul, 1961).

Wittgenstein, L.: 'Some remarks on logical form', *Proceedings of the Aristotelian Society* supp. vol. 9 (1929), 162–71; in *Essays on Wittgenstein's Tractatus* ed. I. Copi and R. Beard (London: Routledge and Kegan Paul, 1966), 31–7.

DAVID PEARS

logical positivism A philosophical movement that emerged and flourished in the 1920s and 1930s among scientifically oriented philosophers in Europe. In light of important doctrinal modifications, many adherents in the 1940s and 1950s came to prefer the label 'logical empiricism'. The centre of the movement was the Vienna Circle, a discussion group of philosophers, scientists and mathematicians convened by Moritz Schlick (1852–1936), who from 1922 until his murder in 1936 held the Chair in the Philosophy of the Inductive Sciences at Vienna, a chair previously held by MACH and Ludwig Boltzmann (1844–1906). Other prominent figures associated with the movement include REICHENBACH, CARNAP, Otto Neurath (1882–1945) and Carl Hempel. The threat posed by Nazism ended the European phase of the movement in the late 1930s. A number of the leading positivists emigrated to the United States. Abetted by affinities between positivism and PRAGMATISM, these emigrés together with their students and sympathizers emerged as leading figures in American philosophy in the 1940s and 1950s. With its absorption into the mainstream of Anglo-American philosophy, logical positivism ceased to be an identifiable philosophical movement. However, both the refinement and the critical evaluation of ideas associated with logical positivism on the part of those most

sympathetic with the movement was a prominent feature of post-1945 American philosophy.

BACKGROUND

The historical sources of logical positivism are varied and complicated.

Neo-Kantianism

Neo-Kantian philosophers like Ernst Cassirer (1874–1945) around the turn of the century attempted to refurbish KANT's philosophy of science to take account of nineteenth-century developments. The neo-Kantians influenced especially the earlier writings of Schlick, Reichenbach and Carnap, as each of these thinkers groped for alternatives to Kantian accounts of the objectivity of empirical science. Especially influential was the neo-Kantian emphasis on the subjectivity of mere sensation and the view that objective knowledge arises from the synthesis of subjective sensation into the system of science in accordance with the necessary and normative rules (categories) governing thought. Furthermore, on this view the identity of abstract scientific concepts is constituted by their position in the system of objective knowledge.

Poincaré and Hilbert on geometry

Henri Poincaré (1854–1912) argued that, given a physical theory built around Euclidean geometry, by making compensating adjustments in the physical theory, one could devise an experimentally equivalent physical theory built around a non-Euclidean geometry. He concluded that the choice between Euclidean and non-Euclidean geometry is a matter of convention. David Hilbert's work in foundations of geometry was taken to reinforce Poincaré's conventionalism. Hilbert (1862–1943) maintained that the axioms of a geometry implicitly define the concepts of that geometry, and he accordingly treated Euclidean and non-Euclidean geometries, from the vantage point of pure mathematics, as equals. In Poincaré and Hilbert, positivists

281

found material for an account of geometry and its application in physics that breaks sharply with Kant.

Relativity theory

Einstein's Special and General theories of relativity are the single most important spur to logical positivism. First, Einstein's work discredits Kant's synthetic a priori, as Schlick prominently and persuasively argued in papers from 1917–22. Kant maintained that Euclidean geometry and Galilean kinematics, while synthetic, are necessary presuppositions for objective empirical knowledge. Einstein's work exhibits that these principles lack the necessity Kant claims for them. Schlick sees no prospect of locating comparably precise principles to replace these as necessary presuppositions for knowledge. Positively, Einstein's work appeared to Schlick to support a shift toward empiricism. Schlick thought (mistakenly) that General Relativity supports the view that the choice of a metrical geometry is a matter of convention. It thus began to look to him as if the constitutive principles presupposed in the formulation and testing of basic physical theories are conventions, not unavoidable synthetic a priori truths. The facts, the measurements, by which theories are tested are space-time coincidences of points. Schlick extracts from Einstein the methodological principle that every scientific hypothesis must make a measurable difference and that theories that agree as regards point-coincidences are equivalent. This methodological principle anticipates Schlick's later verificationism.

Mathematical logic and logicism

The absorption and application of mathematical logic gives logical positivism its distinctive flavour. First, mathematical logic opens the way for a new and non-psychological understanding of logic. Kantian transcendental logic with its notion of form as something imposed on what is given to the mind is abandoned. Furthermore, the formalization of quantificational logic introduces a powerful conception of proof that arguably covers the forms of argument exhibited in mathematics and the natural sciences. We find here a new model of what it is to be fully explicit in the statement of claims and rigorous in the conduct of argument. Second, WHITEHEAD and RUSSELL's *Principia Mathematica* (1910) is influential in two ways. *Principia* attempts to establish logicism, to derive of mathematics from logic. This assimilation of mathematics to logic promised to ground a precise and persuasive alternative to Kantian accounts of mathematics. As important, is the example *Principia* gives of a scientific way to do philosophy. Russell held out hopes that the application of mathematical logic to the empirical sciences might yield similar results.

Wittgenstein's Tractatus

The Vienna Circle read and discussed Wittgenstein's *Tractatus* (1922) in the late 1920s. First, the *Tractatus* articulates a philosophy of logic that promises to give logicism the desired significance as a philosophy of mathematics. According to the *Tractatus*, logical truths are tautologies that lack sense and say nothing about reality. Their truth, so to speak, is linguistically secured independently of the facts. If mathematics could be reduced to tautologies, mathematics would share this status, a status that promises to dissolve philosophical problems about the ontology, epistemology, and application of mathematics. Second, the *Tractatus* maintains that there are no truths apart from those of the natural sciences. The task of philosophy is to clarify the statements of science through analysis. This view prompts a linguistic turn that makes questions of meaning prior to all others. It also reinforces and gives shape to antimetaphysical impulses from other sources: according to the *Tractatus*, metaphysics is nonsense.

GENERAL FEATURES

There is no unified logical positivist position. Between 1920 and 1940 Schlick, Carnap, Reichenbach and Neurath repeatedly modified their positions in significant ways under the pressure of philosophical criticism and new developments in physics and logic. There is, though, a general philosophical orientation, that makes logical positivism, especially the mature logical positivism of the 1930s, a cohesive movement.

Science and scientific philosophy

The Vienna Circle came to think of themselves as representing a decisive turning point in philosophy, a turning point which would transform philosophy into a collaborative scientific enterprise. They shared a hostility toward much prior philosophy, especially speculative metaphysics. There is no knowledge other than that to which the formal and empirical sciences aspire; there is no realm of extra-scientific truths that philosophy investigates.

The positivists assert the UNITY OF SCIENCE, rejecting dichotomies between the natural and social sciences. The concepts of the sciences are analysed in the same way; theories and hypotheses are confirmed and disconfirmed in the same way. In mature positivism, Schlick's verificationist view of meaning and Carnap's empiricist languages represent alternative accounts of this unity.

According to the positivists, philosophy does not sit in judgement of science; nor does it aim to provide science with 'foundations'. Rather, philosophy must orient itself to the sciences and test its claims about science against the best science of the day. This regard for science urgently raises the question of the task of philosophy. Most of the positivists sharply distinguish their investigations from those of empirical psychology. They gravitate to the position that philosophy analyses the meaning of scientific statements, and that meaning is a matter of logic.

Analyticity

There is a sharp distinction between analytic truths and synthetic truths. Kant's explanation of this distinction is rejected. Synthetic truths are factual truths, i.e. empirically testable truths. There are no synthetic a priori truths and no synthetic

necessities. Analytic truths do not set forth any facts. Their truth is linguistically secured by logical form and/or linguistic convention. Among these conventions are Reichenbach's coordinating definitions that assign experimental significance to abstract vocabulary. The only a priority and the only necessity is that which is somehow grounded in language.

Mathematics is supposed to be analytic. It proves difficult, however, to arrive at a notion of analyticity that sustains this position. Some of the axioms required in Russell's logic for the derivation of mathematics patently fail to be tautologies in Wittgenstein's sense. Restriction to Wittgenstein's logical resources would deny the natural sciences the mathematics they require. The development of metamathematics appears to open the way for a sophisticated conventionalism. A language formalizing a body of mathematics can be described syntactically by setting forth formation rules, axioms, and inference rules. Such a syntactic description can be the content of a convention by which an investigator adopts a language: the theorems of the language thus become truths by this convention. The use of this language enables an investigator to infer empirical truths from empirical truths. The conventional truths are contentless auxiliaries for such inferences. GÖDEL argued against this conventionalism (Gödel, 1993). To justify such a syntactic convention – i.e. to justify the claim that the theorems of the language are contentless auxiliaries – it must be shown that no empirical sentence is a theorem of the language. A proof that a language satisfies this condition would be a proof of the consistency of the mathematics the language formalizes. On the basis of his second incompleteness theorem, Gödel notes that this proof requires mathematics stronger than that formalized in the language. Since the justification of the convention requires the use of mathematics stronger than that stipulated by the convention, mathematics cannot be taken to be true by syntactic convention without vicious circularity.

Empiricism

The view of analytic truths as linguistically secured and the rejection of both the synthetic a priori and the synthetic necessary supports an empiricist position: synthetic truths set forth empirically testable matters of fact. There are important differences among the positivists as to how this empiricism is to be worked out. In the early 1930s in papers like 'Positivism and realism' (Schlick, 1979), Schlick, giving Wittgenstein's *Tractatus* a phenomenalist interpretation, arrives at the view that subsequently is taken as the classical expression of logical positivism (*see* PHENOMENALISM). Schlick maintains that the concepts of the empirical sciences are definable in terms immediately applicable to what is given in experience. He emphasizes the role ostension plays in grounding chains of definition by linking undefined names with these given elements. Schlick thus embraces a verificationist conception of meaning. A non-logical statement is meaningful just in case it has verification conditions. A non-logical statement is tested by 'comparing it with the facts', by observationally checking whether its verification conditions hold. The statements that formulate these observational checks are, as the end points of analysis and testing, empirically certain: they are not themselves subject to further verification by later observations. Schlick's theory of meaning does not lead him to take an instrumentalist attitude toward the theoretical posits of natural science. Existence claims like 'There are electrons', are shown to be flatly true, if the truth-conditions analysis reveals do indeed obtain. Any statement of an instrumentalist position would contain metaphysical pseudo-statements that lack verification conditions. Similarly, the REALISM that maintains there is something more to existence claims than satisfaction of verification conditions is rejected. Schlick thus takes his position to overcome the opposition between realism and previous positivist positions.

Schlick's verificationism, however, makes the characterization of the bottom level of analysis, of the given, a pressing matter. Neurath, joined by Carnap and Hempel, objected to Schlick's account, arguing that it reintroduces the metaphysics that should be banished from scientific philosophy. In particular, Neurath rejected the view that reports of observation are unrevisable empirical certainties about the observer's experiences. Neurath urges that observation reports are statements reporting the observationally ascertainable properties of physical bodies. In the formulation of the system of science, investigators aim to arrive at a consistent set of statements that includes both the theoretical hypotheses of science as well as reports of observations. There are no non-logical statements that are immune from revision, should an inconsistency emerge in the system. In particular, when an isolated observation is at odds with a well-entrenched, comprehensive theory, consistency may be restored to the system by denying the report of the observation. Neurath thus advocates a holistic view of hypothesis testing: the unit of epistemic evaluation in science is a comprehensive theory, including observation reports, not an individual hypothesis. Moreover, in all this, Neurath adopts a naturalistic approach to discussions of language, meaning, and observation. The use of language in the formulation and testing of scientific hypotheses is a human social phenomenon that calls for empirical investigation. Neurath thus denies that meaning and the analysis of meaning is the task of scientific philosophy, a task that separates it both from empirical science on the one side and empirically vacuous metaphysics on the other.

Carnap's logical syntax programme

Carnap's logical syntax programme was the most sophisticated attempt to combine various positivist themes into a coherent position. The programme was set forth initially in *Logische Syntax der Sprache* (1934). With modifications prompted by Carnap's acceptance of TARSKI's semantical techniques, Carnap adhered to the programme for the rest of his career. Central to the programme is the notion of a linguistic framework. A linguistic framework can be described syntactically by definitions of well-formedness and consequence. Carnap maintained (Carnap, 1934) that analyticity can be defined in logical syntactic terms so that the vague notion of linguistically secured truth can be replaced by a purely formal notion. He exhibited languages whose mathematical truths satisfy the formal definition of analyticity. There are any number of different linguistic frameworks. Carnap held that there is no right or wrong in the choice of a language, no language-transcendent facts that justify the choice of one language over another. This is Carnap's principle of tolerance. It supports a sweeping relativism in logic, and it arguably enables Carnap to sidestep standard objections to conventionalism in mathematics, including Gödel's. Scientific philosophy, Carnap urges, is the logic of the languages of science. The scientific philosopher describes languages suitable for the formalization, the rational reconstruction, of scientific theories and investigates their formal features. Here we have an enterprise that is free from metaphysical involvements, distinct from empirical science, but informed by scientific standards of clarity and rigour.

For Carnap, basic ontological issues concern the choice of a language. The investigation of any issue is a matter of accepting or rejecting statements *within* a linguistic framework one has adopted, for only within the context of a language do questions of fact or logic acquire a definite sense. So, for example, the question of the existence of numbers can be trivially answered by proving an arithmetic existence claim within a language. A person who refuses to accept this answer to the question, shows that he or she is asking what Carnap calls an external question. According to Carnap, what is really at issue in external questions is the advisability of adopting a language that contains numerical terms and variables. By the principles of tolerance, there is no right or wrong in this choice. Carnap believes that ontological pseudo-questions arise as a result of the conflation of assertion of statements within a framework with advocacy of the adoption of a language (see Carnap, 1949).

Carnap's logical syntax programme avoids the features of Schlick's verificationism that Neurath rejects. Under Neurath's influence, Carnap gives up a phenomenalist construal of observational reports and decides that observation predicates are to be characterized behaviourally in terms of observation-based agreement in the application of the predicates to demonstrated items. Empirical scientific theories can be rationally reconstructed using languages that contain observation predicates. Carnap comes to realize that the theoretical vocabulary of science cannot be explicitly defined using only observation predicates. In (Carnap, 1936, 1937), he proposes a logically looser relation between theoretical and observation predicates – one compatible with a holistic view of theory testing and also intended to insure that comprehensive theories whose theoretical predicates satisfy his loose condition have a rich array of observational consequences. Empiricism becomes the recommendation that only languages whose theoretical predicates are so related to observation predicates be used for the statement of scientific theories.

In the 1950s QUINE subjected Carnap's analytic/synthetic distinction to penetrating criticism. Carnap's programme of rational reconstruction assumes the availability of a criterion for attributing a formal language to an individual, and so for distinguishing his or her analytic from his or her synthetic sentences. Such a criterion is a prerequisite for applying the distinction between investigations within a language and advocacy of a language, between scientific issues and pseudo-questions. Quine challenged this assumption. He observed that no purely formal demarcation of a class of sentences of a language supplies the desired criterion. He surveyed plausible criteria of analyticity framed in terms of logical form, convention, definition, semantic rules and empirical revisability, arguing that the attempted criteria either fail to draw the intended distinction or are couched in terms that presuppose it. Quine, although sharing the positivist orientation toward science, concluded that there is no analytic/synthetic distinction and no sharp principled boundary between substantive scientific questions and logical-linguistic matters. Quine thus rejected Carnap's understanding of ontological disputes as optional linguistic differences.

See also LOGICAL ATOMISM; PRINCIPLE OF VERIFIABILITY.

BIBLIOGRAPHY

Carnap, R.: *Logische Syntax der Sprache* (Vienna: 1934); trans. A. Smeaton, *The Logical Syntax of Language* (London: Routledge and Kegan Paul, 1937).

Carnap, R.: 'Testability and meaning', *Philosophy of Science* 3 (1936), 419–71; 4 (1937), 1–40.

Carnap, R.: 'Empiricism, semantics, and ontology', *Revue internationale de philosophie* 4 (1949), 20–40; repr. in his *Meaning and Necessity* (Chicago: University of Chicago Press, 1956) Appendix 1, 205–21.

Coffa, A.: *The Semantic Tradition from Kant to Carnap* (Cambridge: Cambridge University Press, 1991).

Friedman, M.: 'Critical notice: Moritz Schlick, *Philosophical Papers*', *Philosophy of Science* 50 (1983), 498–514.

Friedman, M.: 'The re-evaluation of logical positivism', *Journal of Philosophy* 88 (1991), 505–19.

Gödel, K.: 'Is mathematics syntax of language?', in his *Collected Papers*, vol. 3, ed. S. Feferman *et al.* (Oxford: Oxford University Press, 1993).

Neurath, O.: *Philosophical Papers 1913–1946* (Dordrecht: Reidel, 1983).

Quine, W.V.: 'Carnap and logical truth', in *The Philosophy of Rudolf Carnap* ed. P. Schilpp (La Salle, IL: Open Court, 1963).

Reichenbach, H.: *Hans Reichenbach: Selected Writings 1909–1953* 2 vols (Dordrecht: Reidel, 1978).

Ricketts, T.: 'Carnap's principle of tolerance, empiricism, and conventionalism', in *Reading Putnam* ed. P. Clark (Oxford: Blackwell, forthcoming).

Schlick, M.: *Moritz Schlick: Philosophical Papers* 2 vols (Dordrecht: Reidel, 1979).

Whitehead, A.N. and Russell, B.: *Principia Mathematica* (Cambridge: Cambridge University Press, 1910).

Wittgenstein, L.: *Tractatus Logico-Philosophicus* (1921); trans. C.K. Ogden (London: Routledge and Kegan Paul, 1922).

THOMAS RICKETTS

M

Mach, Ernst (1835–1916) Physicist, physiologist and perceptual psychologist who wrote extensively on philosophy and the philosophy of science. Mach's world contains only elements. Elements are more or less strongly independent. Elements can be called sensations, provided it is borne in mind that these are neither physical nor psychological. To forget the proviso is to fall back into a one-sided theory. Because all elements are of the same type Mach's view has been described as neutral monism, a position also defended by Russell in the *Analysis of Mind* (1921) (*see* MONISM/PLURALISM). Because Mach rejects the distinction between sense perception and objects independent of such perceptions his view is also phenomenalist (*see* PHENOMENALISM). The most influential and important formulations of Mach's monism and phenomenalism are to be found in *Contributions to the Analysis of Sensations* (1886) and in *Knowledge and Error* (1905).

Selves, substances, physical and psychological entities have no place in Mach's world (*see* SUBSTANCE). We describe certain elements as psychological in some contexts and physical in others. The task of science is to tabulate the relations of dependence among entities, usually by describing functional connections amongst elements. Mach's emphasis on interdependence in his writings on perceptual psychology allowed him to break with prevailing atomist assumptions (*see* ATOMISM), to anticipate the discovery of perceptual Gestalt qualities by Christian von Ehrenfels (1859–1932) and to influence a number of anti-atomist philosophies of mind, such as that of HUSSERL.

In *The Science of Mechanics: A Critical and Historical Account of its Development* (1883), *Principles of the Theory of Heat: Historically and Critically Elucidated* (1896) and elsewhere Mach undertook extensive comparisons between the epistemological, metaphysical and methodological commitments of scientific theories past and present, on the one hand, and his own phenomenalist monism, on the other hand. These comparisons often have at least two goals. First, Mach is concerned to describe, from a naturalistic point of view, how scientific enquiry, conceived as a biological phenomenon, actually functions (*see* NATURALISM). Secondly, he has a critical goal. With respect to a range of scientific ideas he asks what the cash value of these ideas is in terms of elements and their interconnections and seeks to show where they go beyond the bare descriptive minimum which, Mach thinks, is all science should allow itself. Amongst the many casualties of this penetrating examination are mechanistic conceptions of space, time, mass, energy, movement and temperature. Thus whether a motion is uniform is a question that can only be raised with respect to some other motion. Mach's examination of NEWTON's account of absolute space prepared the way for Einstein's theory of relativity. Another casualty is the notion of an asymmetric causal nexus, which is rejected in favour of functional interdependence amongst elements, in particular by systems of differential equations. A similar refinement of HUME's views about causality was put forward by Russell in 'On the notion of cause' (1912).

The sceptical and verificationist strands in Mach's critical examinations of a variety of scientific claims have often been felt to be compatible with philosophical positions other than those espoused by Mach. In their scope and combination of conceptual criticism with historical insight Mach's scrutinies of the credentials of a variety of scientific notions, to be found in nearly all his writings, are unmatched.

Mach's conviction that elements are interdependent manifests itself in his views about the relations between different branches of science and between philosophy and science. Like BRENTANO and Otto Neurath (1882–1945) he defended the UNITY OF SCIENCE. And in the last analysis he thought that distinctions between science and philosophy were likely to be simply an obstacle to the advance of knowledge.

Mach was one of the very few antirealists within Austrian philosophy and philosophy of science. He was also one of the most influential Austrian philosophers outside philosophy and science. His slogan *Das Ich ist unrettbar* ('The self cannot be salvaged or saved') and his contextualism were widely felt to capture part of the Zeitgeist within Austro-Hungarian culture at the turn of the century and his philosophy made its mark on Viennese Impressionism. (*See* ANTI-REALISM; REALISM.)

BIBLIOGRAPHY

Blackmore, J.T.: *Ernst Mach – His Life, Work and Influence* (Berkeley: University of California Press, 1972).

Bradley, J.: *Mach's Philosophy of Science* (London: Athlone Press, 1971).

Cohen, R.S. and Seeger, R.J. eds: *Ernst Mach. Physicist and Philosopher*, Boston Studies in the Philosophy of Science, vol. VI (Dordrecht: Reidel, 1970).

Ernst Mach – Werk und Wirkung ed. R. Haller and F. Stadler (Vienna: Hoelder-Pichler-Tempsky, 1988).

Mulligan, K. and Smith, B.: 'Mach and Ehrenfels: the foundations of Gestalt theory', in *Foundations of Gestalt Theory* ed. B. Smith (Munich: Philosophia Verlag, 1988), 124–57.

Musil, R.: *On Mach's Theories* (1908); (Munich: Philosophia Verlag, 1982) trans. K. Mulligan.

Russell, B.: 'On the notion of cause', *Proceedings of the Aristotelian Society* XII (1912–13); repr. in his *Mysticism and Logic* (New York: Longmans, 1918).

KEVIN MULLIGAN

McTaggart, John McTaggart Ellis (1866–1925) British metaphysician. In *The Nature of Existence* (1921, 1927), McTaggart deduces from allegedly synthetic a priori propositions, with a couple of innocuous contingent propositions thrown in, that reality is a mutual admiration society comprised only of timeless, immaterial spirits and their loving perceptions of themselves and each other. He begins with the contingent fact that something exists, for which he gives the Cartesian justification that one could not truly deny this, since the act of denying is one kind of existent, together with the required denier, thereby assuring that at least two things exist. Whatever exists must have positive characteristics, i.e. qualities or relations, other than just existence and therefore must qualify as a SUBSTANCE in the sense of being a subject of characteristics without being a characteristic. Furthermore, we know on a priori grounds that a substance is made up of parts that are themselves substances, thereby entailing that the universe contains substantial parts of substantial parts ad infinitum of these existent substances.

Every substance must have at least one characteristic that is unique to it, thereby permitting an 'exclusive description' of it. Since no restriction is placed on what counts as a characteristic, it is obvious that given any two substances, *a* and *b*, *a* will have the 'characteristic' of being identical with *a* while *b* will not. Furthermore, a substance cannot have an exclusive description without also having a 'sufficient description', i.e. one that employs only fully general or multiply instantiable descriptions devoid of any purely designative singular term, such as a proper name or demonstrative (*see* INDEXICAL). McTaggart offered a vicious infinite regress argument (an argument form of which he was the master, though he often saw viciousness where others did not, possibly because he scared too easily) for this. Take any substance A. A is supposed to have an exclusive but not a sufficient description. Because A does not uniquely possess some quality, its dissimilarity depends on its uniquely having some relation to another substance B. 'And the existence of B depends on its dissimilarity to all other substances. And this depends on the existence of C, and this on its dissimilarity to all other substances, and so on. If this series is infinite, it is vicious.'

The regress appears to be based upon existential dependency, and thus will be no more vicious than that in the second way of AQUINAS (which infers the existence of a first cause from the alleged impossibility of an infinite chain of efficient causes). The argument, however, becomes more powerful when it is realized that the role played in McTaggart's system by the principle that every substance has a sufficient description is to explain the ultimate ground of INDIVIDUATION of substances without having to invoke non-empirical individuators whose own individuation is mysterious, such as a receptacle, prime matter, SUBSTRATUM, or BARE PARTICULAR. The regress is vicious because it is one of explanation – the individuation of A being explained by reference to another substance B, whose individuation in turn is explained by reference to another substance C, *ad infinitum*. But given that McTaggart's individuators are fully general characteristics, we seem to be able to imagine counterexamples to the principle of sufficient reason consisting of *dopplegänger* empirical objects, to which his response was that they must occupy different places and/or times in order to be numerically distinct; however, he failed to see that this seems to bring back in the non-individuated individuators, in this case space–time regions, and, further-

more, would be of no avail in meeting a counterexample to the spirits in his system of ontological IDEALISM involving coexistent but qualitatively indistinguishable immaterial spirits. McTaggart responded by showing how such spirits *might* be individuated, but he failed to show that they *must* be so individuated.

The principles of sufficient description and the infinite differentiation of substance into substantial parts, together with another a priori principle, that reality is completely determinate, form the premises of a vicious infinite regress argument against the existence of MATTER. Any substance A will consist of an infinite regress of parts. If it is material, the required sufficient description of its parts on any level n will fail to be completely determinate or specific, since it will fail to specify the parts of the level-n parts. But, since the regress is infinite, there is no completely determinate description of A, which violates the principle of determinateness of reality. The same argument applies against the existence of sense data. (*See* SENSA.)

A community of at least two spirits can satisfy the above three a priori principles provided their parts consist of clear and distinct (and coexistent, since time has been shown to be unreal) perceptions that stand to each other in an intricate relation of 'determining correspondence' which would allow for a sufficient description of any one of the spirits to *entail*, and thereby specify, sufficient descriptions of its parts within parts to infinity, which satisfies the principle of the determinateness of reality. Each would perceive the other's perceiving the other in a mirroring manner to any degree of complexity you please. Given that substances exist and are either a material object, a sense datum or a spirit, and that only the latter is possible, it follows that spirits alone exist. This conclusion is not necessary, since the disjunction is only contingently true, being relative to our powers of imagination. The conclusion, however, has as great a degree of certainty as we finite beings can hope to achieve. Our delusory perceptions of a world of changing objects really form a timeless C series whose generating relation is *being a more adequate perception of* that converges toward the heavenly state in which all spirits stand to each in the relation of determining correspondence.

WRITINGS

Studies in the Hegelian Dialectic (Cambridge: Cambridge University Press, 1896).

Studies in the Hegelian Cosmology (Cambridge: Cambridge University Press, 1901).

Some Dogmas of Religion (London: 1906); repr. with an introduction by C.D. Broad (London: E. Arnold, 1930).

A Commentary on Hegel's Logic (Cambridge: Cambridge University Press, 1910).

The Nature of Existence vol. 1 (Cambridge: Cambridge University Press, 1921); vol. 2, ed. C.D. Broad (Cambridge: Cambridge University Press, 1927).

BIBLIOGRAPHY

Broad, C.D.: *Examination of McTaggart's Philosophy* (Cambridge: Cambridge University Press, vol. 1, 1933, vol. 2, printed as two volumes, 1938).

Geach, P.: *Truth, Love and Immortality* (Berkeley: University of California Press, 1979).

RICHARD M. GALE

Maimonides [Moses ben Maimon] (1138–1204) A towering rabbinic authority of Hispano-Jewish culture, Maimonides is also recognized as the greatest and most significant of Jewish philosophers. Deciphering his metaphysical theories is difficult. He wrote his main philosophic work, *The Guide of the Perplexed* (c.1190), in the 'esoteric' style also cultivated by Moslem thinkers. Accordingly, he eschews laying out his views explicitly, even to the point of deliberately inserting contradictions that veil his true intent (or, as recent scholars suggest, reflect his own uncertainty). In addition, the *Guide* is not designed primarily to expound a systematic theory, but instead to interpret biblical and rabbinic texts, especially those dealing with *maaseh bereshit* ('work of the creation', i.e. natural science) and *maaseh merkavah* ('work of the chariot', i.e. metaphysics), in philosophic terms, thereby merely 'opening the gates' of apprehension to capable readers.

Notwithstanding these methodological impediments, we may identify Maimonides' system as a 'Neoplatonized Aristotelianism' (*see* ARISTOTLE, NEOPLATONISM). There are ten emanated intellects and spheres. The lowest of the intellects, the Active Intellect, causes sublunar phenomena, including human cognition. God is identified as either an Aristotelian 'First mover' or as an even more transcendent neo-Platonic 'Necessary Existent'.

The essence of God is unknowable. Hence, terms like 'knowing', 'powerful', 'willing' and 'living', are to be understood as negative attributes when predicated of God – indeed, as negating of God not only determinates but determinables (*see* DETERMINATE/DETERMINABLE). Human conceptual categories thus do not apply to God at all. God's 'actions' and the moral characteristics they exemplify *are* knowable, but 'God's actions', for Maimonides, refers to *natural* events. This reading is symptomatic of a broader naturalistic sensibility. For example, Maimonides tries to reduce the number of miracles and views those that occur as part of the original natural order. Also, he regards prophecy and providence as natural processes that ensue upon proper development of the intellect. Maimonides is sharply critical of Islamic occasionalists (*see* OCCASION, OCCASIONALISM) for their extreme belief in constant divine interventions.

Regarding whether the world was created from nothing, created from eternal matter, or has existed eternally, Maimonides declares that no side in the controversy can be demonstrated, and that it is appropriate to follow the biblical account (i.e. *creation ex nihilo*) on this major issue. Scholars debate, however, whether this stated position is an 'exoteric' guise for a more radical, 'esoteric' view.

Human beings are distinguished by their intellect, the 'image of God' in Maimonides' philosophic construal of Genesis. As in Platonic thought, however, they are prone to suffer cognitive limitations and appetitive interference as a result of matter. Our knowledge of metaphysics and celestial physics is, consequently, limited. Whether human beings can know immaterial beings at all according to Maimonides is an oft discussed question; the answer would have large repercussions with respect to such issues as IMMORTALITY, providence, prophecy and human perfection.

See also ALFARABI; AQUINAS; AVERROES; AVICENNA.

WRITINGS

Guide of the Perplexed (c.1190); trans S. Pines (Chicago: University of Chicago Press, 1963).

BIBLIOGRAPHY

Altmann, A.: 'Essence and existence in Maimonides', Bulletin of the John Rylands Library 35 (1953), 294–315; repr. in Maimonides: A Collection of Critical Essays ed. J.A. Buijs (Notre Dame, IN: University Notre Dame Press, 1988), 148–65.

Altmann, A.: 'Maimonides on the intellect and the scope of metaphysics', in his Von der mittelalterlchen zur modernen Aufklarung: Studien zur judischen Geistesgeschichte (Tübingen: J.C.B. Mohr (Paul Siebeck), 1987), 60–129.

Buijs, J.A. ed.: Maimonides: A Collection of Critical Essays (Notre Dame, IN: University of Notre Dame Press, 1988), esp. Pts I and II.

Fox, M.: Interpreting Maimonides (Chicago: University of Chicago Press, 1989), esp. Pts I and III.

Harvey, W.Z.: 'A third approach to Maimonides' cosmogony-prophetology puzzle', Harvard Theological Review 74 (1981), 287–301; repr. in Maimonides: A Collection of Critical Essays ed. J.A. Buijs (Notre Dame: IN: University of Notre Dame Press, 1988), 71–88.

Hyman, A.: 'Maimonides on causality', in Maimonides and Philosophy ed. S. Pines and Y. Yovel (Dordrecht: Martinus Nijhoff, 1986), 157–72.

Ivry, A.: 'Providence, divine omniscience, and possibility: the case of Maimonides', in Divine Omniscience and Omnipotence in Medieval Jewish Philosophy ed. T. Rudavsky (Dordrecht: Reidel, 1985), 143–59; repr. in Maimonides: A Collection of Critical Essays ed. J.A. Buijs (Notre Dame, IN: University of Notre Dame Press, 1988), 175–91.

Pines, S.: 'Translator's introduction: the philosophic sources of the Guide of the Perplexed', in Guide of the Perplexed trans. S. Pines (University of Chicago Press, 1963), lvii–cxxiv.

Reines, A.: 'Maimonides's concepts of providence and theodicy', Hebrew Union College Annual 43 (1972), 169–206.

Wolfson, H.A.: 'Maimonides on negative attributes', in Louis Ginsberg Jubilee Volume on the Occasion of His Seventieth Birthday (New York: American Academy for Jewish Research, 1945), 411–46.

DAVID SHATZ

Malebranche, Nicolas (1638–1715) French Oratorian priest, whose theocentric metaphysics, although unique, owed much to AUGUSTINE and DESCARTES. Like Descartes, Malebranche held that we can conceive a being to be *finite* only by thinking some limitation in *infinite* being. But unlike Descartes, he denied that any *idea* can *represent* infinite being to us, from which he concluded that we can form the ideas of finite beings only because the infinite being itself (God) is *immediately present* to our minds. We do not, however, perceive God's essence in itself; instead, we perceive 'infinite intelligible extension' – God's archetypal idea of the material world (*see* ESSENCE/ACCIDENT). Thereby we can have those CLEAR AND DISTINCT ideas of extended things that make science possible. But though we thus know the essence of extension, Malebranche denied that reason can demonstrate that God has created a material universe corresponding to intelligible extension; only faith in Scripture makes such a material creation certain. In short, we can have knowledge of the essence, but not of the EXISTENCE, of bodies. With minds the case is reversed. Self-consciousness makes indubitable our mind's existence, but – as God has not disclosed his archetypal idea of the mind to us – we do not know its essence. SELF-CONSCIOUSNESS reveals enough to assure us that mind is not an extended thing, but not enough to make its nature clearly known.

Not just the mind but all things depend immediately on God for their existence and for any change in their states, argued Malebranche; for nothing occurs unless God wills it and whatever God wills, occurs. He concluded that God's will is the sole necessary and sufficient condition of any occurrence, so the only true cause of all events. 'Natural causes' are really just the *occasions* on which God causes events to occur; for between a *true cause* and its effect there is a necessary connection, but no two finite things are *necessarily connected*, for it is in God's power to produce one without the other. God's will alone is necessarily followed by whatever he wills, so God is the sole true cause.

See also OCCASION, OCCASIONALISM.

WRITINGS

De la recherche de la vérité 2 vols (Paris: 1674–5); trans. T.M. Lennon and P. Olscamp, *The Search after Truth* (Columbus, OH: Ohio State University Press, 1980).
Entretiens sur la métaphysique (Rotterdam: 1688); trans. W. Doney, *Dialogues on Metaphysics* (New York: Abaris Books, 1980).
Œuvres complètes ed. A. Robinet, 20 vols (Paris: Vrin, 1958–68).

BIBLIOGRAPHY

Gueroult, M.: *Malebranche* 3 vols (Paris: Aubier, 1955–9).
Radner, D.: *Malebranche: A Study of a Cartesian System* (Amsterdam: Van Gorcum, 1978).
Robinet, A.: *Système et existence dans l'œuvre de Malebranche* (Paris: Vrin, 1965).

CHARLES J. McCRACKEN

Marcus, Ruth Barcan (1921–) One of the principal founders of modern modal logic and a leading contributor to the philosophy of logic. Marcus has taught at University of Illinois at Chicago, Northwestern University, and Yale. She has also made seminal contributions to metaphysics, ethics, and philosophy of language.

Ruth Barcan Marcus published the first systematic treatise on quantified modal logic (1946). The first-order formalization was extended to second order with identity (1947) and to modalized set theory (1963 and elsewhere). Among widely discussed features of the formalization were the axiom $\Diamond \exists x Fx \rightarrow \exists x \Diamond Fx$ (the Barcan formula) and the theorem about the necessity of IDENTITY (NI).

In more discursive papers, Marcus (1) advances a flexible notion of extensionality (1960, 1961); (2) defends the plausibility of NI (1961); (3) argues that proper names function as contentless directly referential tags (1961), paving the way for theories of direct reference later elaborated by Keith Donnellan, Saul Kripke, David Kaplan and others; (4) proposes, for certain uses, a substitutional interpretation of quantifiers (1961, 1962); (5) dispels putative puzzles about substitutivity and quantifying into modal contexts (1961 and elsewhere); (6) dispels putative claims about modal logic's *commitment* to ESSENTIALISM (1961 and elsewhere); (7) develops an account of Aristotelian essentialism within a modal framework (1967, 1971); and (8) defends metaphysical actualism (1985–6).

In ethics, an influential paper on moral dilemmas (1980) argues from a straightforward analogue with semantic consistency, that moral dilemmas are compatible with the consistency of the general principles or rules from which they derive. Dilemmas therefore are not evidence for ethical ANTIREALISM. (*See also* ANTIREALISM.) The analysis suggests second-order principles of conflict avoidance.

In some papers on belief (1981, 1983, 1990) Marcus rejects language-centred theories where beliefs are taken to be attitudes to linguistic or quasi-linguistic entities. Her proposal is that *x* believes that *s* if, and only if, *x* is disposed to respond as if *s* obtains, where *s* is a state of affairs and responses are functions of internal and external factors including needs and desires. The view accommodates unconscious beliefs and beliefs of non-linguals. Also accommodated is a richer notion of rationality where rational agents among other things seek to maintain coherence of all belief indicators including speech acts such as sincere avowals.

WRITINGS

'A functional calculus of first order based on strict implication', *Journal of Symbolic Logic* 11 (1946), 1–16.
'The identity of individuals in a strict functional calculus', *Journal of Symbolic Logic* 12 (1947), 12–15.
'Extensionality', *Mind* LXIX (1960), 55–62.
'Modalities and Intensional Languages', *Synthése* XIII (1961).
'Interpreting quantification', *Inquiry* 5 (1962), 252–9.
'Classes and attributes in extended modal systems', *Proceedings of the Colloquium in Modal and Many Valued Logic. Acta Philosophica Fennica* 16 (1963), 123–36.
'Essentialism in modal logic', *Noûs* (1967), 91–6.
'Essential attribution', *Journal of Philosophy* LXVII (1971), 187–202.
'Moral dilemmas and consistency', *Journal of Philosophy* LXXVII (1980), 121–35.
'A proposed solution to a puzzle about belief', *Midwest Studies in Philosophy: Foundations of Analytical Philosophy VI* ed.

P. French, T. Vehling, H. Wettstein. (1981), 501–37.
'Rationality and believing the impossible', *Journal of Philosophy* LXXV (1983), 321–37.
'Possibilia and possible worlds', *Grazer Philosophische Studien*, ed. R. Haller, v. 25, 26, 1985–6, 107–32.
'Some revisionary proposals about belief and believing', *Philosophy and Phenomenological Research* (1990), 133–54.
Modalities: Philosophical Essays (New York and Oxford: Oxford University Press) (1993).

DIANA RAFFMAN
GEORGE SCHUMM

Marx, Karl (1818–83) Social theorist, born in Trier, Germany and died in London. His great uncle was the chief rabbi of Trier; his father, a lawyer, had converted to Christianity in order to be able to continue in the legal profession. His wife's family belonged to the lower ranks of Prussian landed gentry.

At the university, first in Bonn and then in Berlin, Marx studied law to please his father, and history and philosophy because those were his real interests. He had intended to pursue a career of teaching in a university. But having early displayed his tendency towards radicalism, the Prussian government – which controlled all universities – was not inclined to employ him. Marx turned to journalism, to begin a life long career as a writer. In 1842, he became the editor of the *Rheinische Zeitung* until it was suppressed by the Prussian government in the next year. He then moved to Paris where he worked on the *Deutsch-Franzoesische Jahrbuecher*. Due to the pressure from the Prussian government, Marx was expelled from France in 1846 and moved to Brussels. During the years of revolution, 1847–9, Marx lived in Paris again, and for a short time in Germany. Expelled from France for a second time, he moved to London in 1849 where he spent the remaining 34 years of his life.

From the very beginning of his career, Marx was a political radical. His very first contributions to the *Rheinische Zeitung* about the plight of Rhenish woodcutters and Moselle wine growers, led him to the study of economics that occupied him for the remainder of his life. The most immediate results of his early economic studies are recorded in the *Economic and Philosophic Manuscripts of 1844*. First, however, he needed to come to terms with HEGEL, who was the dominant German philosopher when Marx was a student, and whose thinking deeply affected all of Marx's writings. The philosophical separation from Hegel was made in the *German Ideology*, written jointly with Friedrich Engels in 1845. A first outline of his economic and political views was suggested in the *Communist Manifesto* (1847).

In so far as he had views about metaphysical topics, such as the nature of persons, the existence of God, the nature of reality, and the basic furniture of the universe, Marx was always a metaphysician. But what makes Marx's views on metaphysics particularly interesting is the fact that he also had views about what sort of knowledge we can have about topics of this sort. Many metaphysicians lay claim to knowledge that is timeless. The truths they claim to have found are true everywhere and for all time. This presupposes certain other views, such as:

(1) There are certain features of the universe that are unchangeable, such as e.g. the existence (or non-existence) of a deity.

(2) The nature of such features of the universe, which metaphysicians try to discover, is, therefore, unaffected by human agency.

(3) Among those basic features are, a.o., the nature of persons and their identities, i.e. their self, as philosophers call it.

Given those assumptions, and the additional belief that the metaphysician's quest is not futile, traditional metaphysics also presupposes that

(4) Human reason is able to apprehend eternal truths. The faculty of thought can transcend the historical and geographical limitations of the thinker's existence. One way of making out that claim is to assert that

(4a) The truth of what we think is independent of truths about the thinker.

Marx is not alone in being very suspicious of these presuppositions. Hegel before him rejected them, as did Søren, Kierkegaard (1813–55), NIETZSCHE, HEIDEGGER and DEWEY, as well as the post-modernists such as Michael Foucault (1926–84) and Jacques Derrida in France, or Thomas Kuhn and Richard Rorty in the United States. Marx supports his suspicions by citing the following considerations:

(4′) Thinking is a social activity. That means that it takes place only in human groups and that it serves a function in those groups (Marx, 1947, p. 19). (Robinson Crusoe is not a counterexample to that claim.)

(4a′) Thoughts are not timeless entities but human artefacts, shaped by the social situation in which thinking takes place.

We may ask Marx, whether there is not impartial and disinterested scientific and scholarly activity that transcends local social interests and concerns. Marx replies that in certain cultures intellectual activity becomes the task of a particular stratum of society. The intellectuals in such a society appear to be divorced from the ordinary concerns, and thus appear to be apart from the ephemeral concerns of the rest of society. They may then also appear to be preoccupied with timeless truths such as those in traditional metaphysics.

Marx is not denying that we make truth-claims, or that truth is important and preferable to error. But he is pointing out to us that we are not omniscient, but fashion a picture of the world in the light of partial information. In any given social situation, some facts loom very large, others are practically invisible.

What is more, Marx insists that what we think about the world is important. Once we acknowledge that thinking plays a distinct role in our social organization, we can begin to see that our thinking shapes, maintains, and at times transforms social formations. Marx, for instance, would not have disagreed with Weber's claim in *The Protestant Ethic and the Spirit of Capitalism* (1958) that the Protestant Ethic had an important effect on the growth and development of capitalism in England. The transition from feudalism to capitalism involved, among others, a transition to a new conception of what it meant to be a person, and what the goals of human life are. Those connections change only in so far as people think about them.

This implies that social orders change, in part as a result of human intellectual activity. But Marx also thinks, as we have seen already, that as social orders change so does the nature of persons. Thus human beings have some effect on what it means to be a person. Their nature is shaped by their social organization, but they themselves have a hand in creating that social organization, and thereby shape their own nature (Marx, 1947, p. 7).

This view is in direct contradiction to theses (1)–(3) above: on a metaphysical question, such as the nature of persons, there are no eternal truths because the nature of persons changes throughout human history and is, moreover, not independent of what persons think about their own nature.

An example may help to make this clearer. Anglo-American metaphysicians since the eighteenth century have thought about persons as owners of their own attributes (Chisholm, 1976; Cohen, 1986; Locke, 1690; Nozick, 1974). Such a conception, Marx argued, is plausible in a world where persons are separate economic agents. Until the rise of capitalism, however, ownership of land came with membership in a community. Ownership presupposed membership in a group; there were no individual owners, because one owned only through and with one's fellow group members. In such a world, it would have made little sense to think of individuals as owners of themselves since they could not even think of themselves as individual owners of land. Only with the emergence of 'free labour' – a person who owned nothing but her or his ability to work – could the notion of a persons as owners of their own attributes make sense (Marx, 1857–8). (Marx provides hints of similar arguments about the existence of God (Marx, 1978, p. 54) and causality (Marx, 1973).)

Nor is this only a view of his early years. It is elaborated in the preliminary draft of the work which he finally published as volume I of *Capital* (1867), and most familiarly in the Introduction to the *Critique of Political Economy* (1859).

Does such a view commit Marx to relativism and thus make his stance self-contradictory? Marx is quite prepared to assume the same modesty with respect to his own views that he urges on other metaphysicians. He does not assert the implication of social conditions in our thoughts as a timeless truth. He is quite willing to say that social science, and hence the investigation of the connections between the thoughts of a given period and the social conditions of that period, is a temporary phenomenon and that in a future, better time, social science would not be necessary. The implication is that what Marx claims to be true in his day may, in other times, be of no more than historical interest (Marx, 1894, p. 817).

While there is no reason to think that Marx retreated from his critique of traditional metaphysics in his later years, his interests certainly shifted to more detailed studies of economics. At the same time, he remained a revolutionary. After the defeat of the revolutions of 1848, he withdrew from political activity for about ten years. In 1864 he was the moving spirit behind the founding of the International Working Men's Association. After the defeat of the

Paris Commune, he praised and defended that experiment in popular democracy in *The Civil War in France* (1871). In his later years, he taught himself Russian in order to be able to study the history and social conditions of Russia, which, he believed, required considerable modifications of his earlier views about the pattern of historical change (Shanin, 1983).

WRITINGS

Capital Vols I–III (Hamburg: Otto Meissner, 1894).

Marx, K. and Engels, F.: *The German Ideology* (1845); (New York: International Publishers, 1947).

Grundrisse (1857–8); (Harmondsworth: Penguin Books, 1973).

The Marx–Engels Reader ed. R. Tucker (New York: Norton, 1978).

BIBLIOGRAPHY

Chisholm, R.M.: *Person and Object* (La Salle, IL: Open Court, 1976).

Cohen, G.A.: 'Self-ownership, world ownership, and equality', in *Justice and Equality Here and Now* ed. F.S. Lucash (Ithaca, NY: Cornell University Press), 108–35.

Locke, J.: *The Second Treatise of Government* (1690); (Oxford: Blackwell, 1948).

Nozick, R.: *Anarchy, State and Utopia* (New York: Basic Books, 1974).

Shanin, T.: *Late Marx and The Russian Road* (New York: Monthly Review Press, 1983).

Weber, M.: *From Max Weber: Essays in Sociology* (New York: Oxford University Press, 1958).

RICHARD SCHMITT

Marxism The two major metaphysical influences on MARX were HEGEL's philosophy, which Marx studied in Berlin and to which he at first subscribed as a member of the circle of Left Hegelians, and Greek philosophy, especially ARISTOTLE and the ATOMISM of Democritus and EPICURUS,

the latter of which formed the subject of his doctoral dissertation. Marx was also acquainted with, and wrote about, the materialist philosophies of HOBBES, of Ludwig Andreas Feuerbach (1804–72), and of the French encyclopedists, especially HOLBACH.

Marx's metaphysical views emphasized two points: a rejection of the IDEALISM of Hegel, which held that everything that existed was essentially dependent on consciousness or mind, and, in his *Theses on Feuerbach* (1845), a rejection of materialist philosophies which eliminated or reduced the category of human action (*see* PHYSICALISM/MATERIALISM). Insofar as Marx rejected Hegelian idealism, he insisted on the irreducible existence of some things which are essentially independent of consciousness or mind. Thus, his metaphysical views should be described as realist (*see* REALISM). His insistence on the centrality and irreducibility of action, and specifically of labour or work, is entirely consistent with his realist philosophy. His view is that what makes persons special, and sets them apart from the rest of nature, is their capacity for intentional action, action undertaken according to a plan. The metaphysical uniqueness of agency underpins his labour theory of value, the insistence that only human labour, but not the motions of animals or machines, can create value.

Two important metaphysical ideas that Marx borrowed from Hegel were the distinction between essence and appearance, akin to KANT's distinction between noumena and phenomena (*see* NOUMENAL/PHENOMENAL), and the idea of dialectics. Marx's view is that there is a discrepancy, both in the natural world generally and in the social world at least under capitalism, between how things really are and how they merely seem to be. Indeed, the capitalist mode of production, according to him, causes that discrepancy within the social realm. It is for this reason, Marx claims, that the capitalist social relations into which persons enter are not transparent to them, and bring about the need for a science of society, whose job it is to reveal the truth about the way in which capitalist society works.

By 'dialectical change', Hegel intended not just change or movement, but self-movement, when a 'thing' is its own source of movement and moves in such a way that it transforms itself into its very opposite. Marx, following Hegel, held that the source of this inner propulsion was 'contradiction'. Marxists have sometimes thought that this commits Marx to a denial of the logical Law of Non-contradiction. However, none of Marx's examples of contradiction so commits him. For example, Marx held that the proletariat and the bourgeoisie constitute a contradiction, and that the struggle between them provides the driving force that moves capitalism into its own opposite, socialism. For Marx, a contradiction is akin to a necessary opposition. Marx also embraced the idea of INTERNAL RELATIONS; necessarily, the bourgeoisie could not be unless the proletariat existed. Marx was attracted to the fluidity of dialectics, the way in which it dissolved rigid things into things-in-constant-flux. Marx believed that a metaphysics of flux provided a better methodology for understanding society than did a metaphysics of stable things.

Once he had made his break with Hegelian philosophy, Marx spent little time further developing or refining his general metaphysics. His attention was directed to propounding a view of history, but his writings are sufficiently ambiguous on this score to bear more than one interpretation. It is clear, however, that he assigned some sort of primacy to the conditions of mankind's 'material existence' in the explanation of historical change. He seems to be denying explanatory efficacy, or anyway primary explanatory efficacy, to philosophical, political and religious ideas, legal and political systems, institutions, etc. ('superstructural' features of a society) in accounting for historical development. Marx thought that history was governed by laws, but for the most part he thinks of these laws as describing tendencies only. Hence, he does not generally attempt to offer categorical predictions about the future course of history. He

seems to have thought that all human actions, including presumably acts of will, were caused, and so he can be classified as a soft determinist (*see* FREE WILL).

Marx was not inclined to give a name to his philosophical system, but on at least one occasion he referred to it as 'the materialist conception of history'. In his *Theses on Feuerbach*, he implied, but did not quite say, that his philosophy was a new kind of materialism. Friedrich Engels, Marx's life-long political and intellectual associate, asserted categorically that Marx's metaphysical system was materialist and developed this interpretation in his *Dialectics of Nature* (1927). Engels also attempted to provide universal laws of dialectical change, partly based on Hegel's views, which would be valid for all of reality, natural as well as social, and which therefore could be used to understand history.

This interpretation of Marx's thought, often called 'dialectical materialism' or 'diamat', attempted to combine traditional materialism with Hegel's emphasis on self-movement. Traditional materialism is a reductive doctrine, which holds that ultimately all that irreducibly exists is what (true) physics must postulate. Movement is so important in Engels's thought that he replaces the category of material thing or object with the category of material process as the foundation of the metaphysical system. Officially sanctioned by the Soviet Union, dialectical materialism or diamat provided the orthodox and dominant interpretation of Marx's metaphysics, until about 1968. V.I. Lenin's *Materialism and Empirio-Criticism* (1909) and Georgi Plekhanov's *Fundamental Problems of Marxism* (1969) provide further examples of this school of Marx interpretation.

There is no inconsistency between materialism as a metaphysical thesis and the retention of the idea of change or movement. However, in Hegel, dialectical change is that change the source of which is within the changing thing itself, i.e. *self*-movement. In many philosophical systems, the only sort of change that meets that description is action, the kind of change initiated by a person or actor (in Hegel for example, God is the agent who ultimately accounts for dialectical change). No physical theory as such provides room for the idea of agency. Dialectical materialism struggled with the difficulty of how a metaphysical view could be both authentically materialist on the one hand and non-reductionist with regard to the category of human action on the other.

Dialectical materialism may have provided the orthodox interpretation of Marx's metaphysics, but it did not provide the only interpretation. As early as the turn of the century, other Marxists, influenced for example by Kantian philosophy, or by the writings of MACH and by Richard Avenarius (1843–96), developed non-materialist interpretations of Marx's metaphysics. At first, these non-materialist Marxist philosophers (one such philosopher important for the history of Marxism was Alexander Bogdanov (1873–1928)) were to be found both within and outside Russia, but after the Bolshevik revolution, these developments were no longer possible within the Soviet Union itself.

Since there was in any case something of a tension within dialectical materialism between the self-movement appropriate to agency and traditional materialism, Marxist philosophers who emphasized work or labour (forms of agency) tended to adhere to non-materialist interpretations of Marx, or, more frequently, interpretations with unnoticed and unremarked non-materialist strands; examples of work in this genre include some of the writings of Anton Pannekoek, Karl Korsch (1972), Georg Lukács (1978) and the works by the 'humanist Marxists' of the post-Stalin period. In many cases, the momentum for the development of humanist Marxism was as much political as intellectual, as a way for Eastern European intellectuals to express their opposition to Stalinism and its aftermath.

Unfortunately, the debate between dialectical materialists and their opponents was trapped by the distinction between materialism and idealism which they wrongly took to be exhaustive of the metaphysical possibilities, so that every opponent of dia-

lectical materialism had to wrestle with the problem of why he was not an 'idealist' (an unthinkable view for most Marxist philosophers). The debate was born only out of mistaken nomenclature. If they had remembered that the negation of idealism (that everything is essentially dependent on consciousness) is realism (the view that at least some things are not essentially dependent on consciousness), and that reductive materialism is only one specific variety of realism, the anti-diamat point of view might have been more widely held much earlier by Marxist philosophers.

BIBLIOGRAPHY

Dietzgen, J.: *The Positive Outcome of Philosophy* (Chicago: Charles Kerr, 1906).

Engels, F.: *Dialectics of Nature* (Frankfurt: 1927); ed. and trans. C. Dutt (New York: International Publishers, 1973).

Geras, N.: 'Essence and appearance: aspects of fetishism in Marx's *Capital*', *New Left Review* 65 (1971), 69–85.

Korsch, K.: *Marxism and Philosophy* (London: New Left Books, 1972).

Lenin, V.I.: *Materialism and Empirio-Criticism* (Moscow: 1909); (Moscow: Progress Publishers, 1970).

Lukács, G.: *Marx's Basic Ontological Principles* (London: Merlin Press, 1978).

Marx, K.: *Critique of Hegel's 'Philosophy of Right'* (Berlin and Frankfurt am Main: 1927); ed. J. O'Malley, trans. A. Jolin (Cambridge: Cambridge University Press, 1970).

Marx, K.: *Economic and Philosophic Manuscripts of 1844* (Moscow: Progress Publishers, 1967).

Plekhanov, G.: *Fundamental Problems of Marxism* (London: Lawrence and Wishart, 1969).

Ruben, D.-H.: *Marxism and Materialism* 2nd edn (Brighton: Harvester Press, 1979).

DAVID-HILLEL RUBEN

mass terms Nouns in many languages divide roughly into two groups, distinguished grammatically and semantically.

Count nouns like 'dog' designate individuals that can be counted. We can speak of one dog, two dogs, or ask 'How many dogs?' Mass terms like 'water' typically designate not things but stuff; we can ask 'How much water?' but not 'How many water?' Stuffs are measured, not counted. Some terms for processes, for example 'running', and abstractions, for example, 'justice', act grammatically like mass terms. There are also definite mass terms like 'this milk', designating particular portions of a stuff. Mass terms for stuffs are mereologically cumulative: any sum of portions of gold is itself gold. A portion (e.g. some gold) is distinct from an individual (e.g. a golden statue) it may make up, but philosophers reluctant to accept portions of stuff have variously suggested unadorned mass terms denote properties of individuals, or sets of individuals, or a single scattered individual.

BIBLIOGRAPHY

Jesperson, O.: *The Philosophy of Grammar* (London: Allen and Unwin, 1924), esp. 'Mass-Words', 198–201.

Pelletier, F.J. ed.: *Mass Terms: Some Philosophical Problems* (Dordrecht: Reidel, 1979). This includes a bibliography.

Quine, W.V.: *Word and Object* (Cambridge, MA: MIT Press, 1960), esp. 90–124.

PETER SIMONS

materialism *see* PHYSICALISM, MATERIALISM

matter The concept of matter may plausibly be regarded as the first and most basic of explanatory concepts in the intellectual enterprise that came to be called 'philosophy'. The speculative issues that defined the earliest Ionian quest concerned origin and CHANGE. Is there a single 'stuff' underlying the myriad changes in the physical world? Did all things originally come to be from such a stuff? (*See* PRESOCRATICS.) Until ARISTOTLE converted the term used for

construction-timber (hyle) to his own technical usage, there was no specific word to denote the kind of answer sought to questions such as these. Aristotle made this notion of matter a key to his natural philosophy and eventually to his metaphysics. Later, the notion was extended in ways that were not always consistent with its first usage.

SUBJECT OF CHANGE

Aristotle begins not from an inductive review of observed changes but from the ways we *speak* about change. Analysis shows that three terms are necessary and sufficient: the subject that changes (the 'matter' of the change), lack of a particular predicate (privation), and possession of that predicate (form). This simple analysis enables Aristotle to respond to Parmenides' challenge. The attempt to express change in two terms (Being and Non-Being) had ended in paradox. The analysis here is in the first instance semantic; the matter defined by it ('second matter') is not a stuff but simply whatever is designated by the subject term of the proposition describing the change. The matter here provides the element of continuity; it is that which ensures that the change *is* a true change and not replacement. Matter and form are thus correlative aspects of *any* change. To explain (to specify the causes of) any change is, in part, to specify what serves as matter for that change.

SUBSTRATUM AND STUFF

The Ionian students of nature (the 'physicists') had already proposed to explain the diversity of the natural world by means of one or more underlying constituents of a familiar sort, like water, say. Aristotle objects: such an underlying stuff would already itself constitute a SUBSTANCE, and the forms it takes on would thus differ only accidentally from one another. Properly 'unqualified' (substantial) change would then be barred, the sort of change that occurs when, for example, an element (like fire) changes into another element (like air). In such a change, the substrate (*see* SUB-STRATUM) could not itself constitute a substance. Though a real 'principle' (the notion of *principle* here becomes all important), it must lack any properties on its own account. At this point, the analysis is no longer a semantic one since there is no subject term corresponding to this unqualified 'primary' matter. Aristotle did not develop this notion in any detail, but it became the cornerstone of the medieval doctrine of HYLOMORPHISM in which primary matter and substantial form are regarded as the ontological constituents of all physical things. In this perspective, matter is also the locus of *potentiality*: it is the determinable, that which enables a thing to take on different forms.

SUBJECT OF PREDICATION

Though matter was originally postulated in the context of CHANGE, Aristotle extended this analysis to predication generally. Analysing the subject–predicate relation, he characterizes the subject of predication as the 'matter'. Thus, accidents are predicated of substance as of their matter. Of what is substance itself predicated? Of matter, considered as lacking in itself all predicable properties. Thus, matter becomes the ultimate subject of predication, and the analysis of predication is assumed to be the key to ontology. This will provide the matter (in another sense) for much later discussion.

PRINCIPLE OF INDIVIDUATION

The individual sense-object poses a problem for PLATO. If form is the ultimate reality, how can there be many individuals, each of them presumably instances of the same form? What is the basis for the uniqueness of sensible things, since it obviously cannot be form? Plato answered in terms of a 'Receptacle', a matrix of becoming, that allows image-individuals to be differentiated on the basis of internal relatedness. Aristotle, on the other hand, associates individuation with an ontological constituent of

physical things, co-principle with form. The matter principle enables form to be instantiated indefinitely often. But how can a matter itself lacking in all determination serve to differentiate? This question gave rise to much debate in medieval philosophy. Something else, it was said, must be involved: the accident of quantity. It is matter as quantified (*materia signata quantitate*) that individuates. What does matter contribute to this, and how are its roles as substrate of change and individuating principle to be reconciled? Are two separate principles being conflated under a single label? (*See* MATTER/FORM.)

DEFECT AND CHANCE

One of the most obvious features of the sensible world, in Plato's view, is the presence within it of defect, of things that manifestly fall short of their goals. There must, then, be a source of resistance to the full embodiment of form in the domain of sense. The Receptacle must not be wholly receptive of form; the material element cannot, it seems, be entirely governed by Reason. In later PLATONISM, this tracing of evil and defect to the matter-element was often linked with religious beliefs. Aristotle looked at the world differently. There is no barrier in matter *per se* to the embodiment of form. But the mere *fact* of embodiment involves the physical individual, the matter–form composite, in a complex network of interlocking causalities where chance outcomes may easily frustrate the natural ends of individuals. Material things are liable to teleological failure precisely in so far as they *are* material, that is, involved in a common arena, that is, in space and time. (*See* TELEOLOGY.)

SOUL AND BODY

Living things, most Greek philosophers agreed, have within themselves a principle of self-motion, a SOUL. When death occurs, only the body, the material element, remains. Soul and body are thus mover and moved. The contrast is even sharper when the human soul is in question. The abilities of reason and will appear to transcend the material order. Plato and Aristotle disagree as to how this transcendence is to be understood. Plato treats the human soul as an immaterial substance; from this many later forms of strong dualism will take their inspiration. Aristotle, more cautiously, regards the soul as the form of a particular matter, and hence as dependent on matter for its existence; its most distinctive faculty, that of intellect, is not, however, constrained by materiality. Later Christian Aristotelians will attempt to enlarge this opening. In the debates, matter will often be treated as the principle of corruptibility, by contrast with soul or mind, of its nature incorruptible.

ALL THERE IS

The ancient atomists were 'materialists' in the sense of claiming that atoms and the void are all there is. The distinguishing mark of materialism is the denial of transcendence; the human is unique only in being more complex and there are no gods operating outside or above the ordinary relationship of space and time. Matter here is the causally connectible complexus of physical objects. This sense of the term became prominent in the seventeenth century. The new science of mechanics prescribed the 'primary' properties that something should have to make it 'material', that is, subject to mechanical law. The matter of later materialism is no indefinite principle, but the extended solid dynamic sum of all there is. (*See* PHYSICALISM/MATERIALISM.)

THE OBJECT OF SENSATION

What is it that we sense? An innocuous question, it might seem, but one that proved more and more daunting as empiricist philosophers attempted, from the late seventeenth century onwards, to find a starting-point for knowledge (*see* EMPIRICISM). According to LOCKE, modifications of matter causes ideas in us; what we know are the ideas which in turn signify the objects through their primary qualities (*see* QUALITY, PRIMARY/SECONDARY). BERKELEY attacks the distinction between primary and secondary qualities; all are alike ideas and they cannot exist in an 'unthinking substratum'. The notion of matter thus involves a contradiction. Only spirit can truly cause; even if matter as substratum were to exist, it could never be known. HUME carried the PHENOMENALISM of Berkeley one stage further: material objects are dissolved into strings of sense-data, lacking any intrinsic principle of ordering, any *nature*. But this dismissal of the traditional concept of matter exacted a high price: what is to provide the continuity and autonomy which the objects we perceive seem to possess? Although KANT retained many features of phenomenalism, he restored matter as the main physical category. In this view, matter is that which is encountered, that which cannot be anticipated. The necessity for a 'matter given in sensation' is what prevents the elaborate apparatus of forms and categories that he proposes for the understanding from reducing to another species of RATIONALISM. Matter is represented as being in space, a space which is somehow in us as a form of sensibility while also being that in which sensible objects are externally related to one another. It is thus not the empiricist thing-in-itself that the phenomenalists had rejected but the appearance considered as external.

QUANTITY OF MATTER

Even though primary matter was held to be indeterminate, natural philosophers in the late Middle Ages saw that the mechanical behaviour of a body is dependent on a factor that is conserved even in fundamental changes, a factor that is dependent on density and volume taken conjointly. This they called the 'quantity of matter'. After a failed attempt on DESCARTES's part to reduce it to extension only, quantity of matter (or *mass*, as it came to be called)

301

became one of the central ideas in NEWTON's system of mechanics. Indeed, the correlative ideas of *mass* and *force* may be said to have defined that mechanics. The matter of which mass is the measure is assumed to have three interrelated properties: inertia, the ability to attract gravitationally, and the ability to be acted upon gravitationally. The measure of each is the same, though Newton was unable to give a reason for this. Einstein later had more success in devising a single coherent concept of mass. And his Theory of Relativity implies that mass and energy have quantitatively the same measure. This does not mean (as is sometimes supposed) that 'matter' is now shown to be capable of transformation into 'energy'. Rather, the new theory has redefined both *mass* and *energy* in such a way that when, for example, a system loses rest-mass, conservation principles show that a large amount of radiation will be liberated. The radiation in this case is, of course, 'material' in the philosopher's sense of that term, though it would not count as 'matter' for the physicist.

The long and tangled development of the concept of matter has left us with many tensions of which this last is but one instance. Is this something to be deplored and, so far as possible, rectified? Or is the fascinating multiplicity of the concept of matter a necessary part of the service it renders to philosophers and scientists?

BIBLIOGRAPHY

Lobkowicz, N. and McMullin, E.: 'Matter', in *Marxism, Communism and Western Society* (Freiburg: Herder, 1973), 383–405.
McMullin, E. ed.: *The Concept of Matter in Greek and Medieval Philosophy* (Notre Dame, IN: University of Notre Dame Press, 1965).
McMullin, E. ed.: *The Concept of Matter in Modern Philosophy* (Notre Dame, IN: University of Notre Dame Press, 1970).

ERNAN McMULLIN

matter/form The idea of the contrast and interrelation between form and MATTER was developed by ARISTOTLE, although he himself traces it back to the PRESOCRATICS (*Metaphysics* I) and adumbrations of it appear in PLATO (*Timaeus* 48–52).

In Aristotle the idea of matter involves several elements. One is the notion of that of which a thing consists or is made, as a statue is made of bronze. A second is the notion that when an individual SUBSTANCE, such as Bucephalus, comes into being or perishes there is something, namely some matter, that persists before and after and that in some sense undergoes the change (see, e.g. *Physics* I 6–9, *Gen. et Corr* ('On Generation and Corruption') I 3–4). In general it is Aristotle's view that the two aforementioned things are the same, for example, that what persists through the perishing of Bucephalus is the same as that of which Bucephalus consists (or at least, of that of which he consists right before he perishes). This idea is closely associated with the thought of matter as 'potentiality' (*dynamis*), i.e. of what *can*, of itself, either be incorporated into Bucephalus *or not*.

A third element of Aristotle's idea of matter is the notion that matter possesses less *structure* or organization, in some sense, than the thing, Bucephalus, that consists of it. Here it is appropriate to introduce explicitly the contrast of matter with form. The form of Bucephalus is in some sense his structure. In the case of relatively simple things, especially non-natural artifacts such as a bronze sphere, the form of a thing amounts simply to its static shape. But in the case of something like Bucephalus the form should be taken to be not merely his static shape at a given time, but also the pattern of organization of his activities through his life. In this connection it is common for Aristotle to call form or structure either 'activity' (*energeia*) or 'actuality' (*entelecheia*), in contrast to 'potentiality'. He also associates 'actuality' with an 'end' (*telos*) or natural goal (*Physics* I 9, *Metaphysics* IX 8–9). (*See* TELEOLOGY.)

Aristotle sometimes speaks of an object like Bucephalus or a bronze sphere as a 'compound' of form and matter, but the manner of composition is a very particular one, the description of which gives rise to severe problems (*Metaphysics* VII–VIII, esp. VII 17). First, it seems that the form somehow structures or informs the matter, not the other way around. The matter of Bucephalus is not as fully endowed with structure as it might be; the form is that further degree of structure that the matter takes on when the compound comes into being and loses when the compound perishes.

The contrast between form and matter is used by Aristotle in a way that allows him to say, for example, that water is the matter of bronze, and that bronze therefore is constituted of water as its matter and possesses a form in addition to that matter. Discredited chemistry aside, this idea indicates that in Aristotle's view bronze consists of some further kind of matter, water, which takes on further structure when the bronze comes into being, and that thus one kind of matter can be constituted of another. The contrast between form and matter therefore does not correspond straightforwardly to a contrast between the structured and the structureless, or between 'sortals' or 'terms with divided reference' and 'MASS TERMS'.

Aristotle's views also illustrate the fact that the contrast between form and matter does not have to rest on an atomistic conception of the constitution of matter, nor on the idea that the addition of structure must consist in the arrangement or rearrangement of parts, discrete or otherwise (*see* ATOMISM). Aristotle is relentlessly hostile to atomism (*Gen. et Corr.* I 2, 8). In his view, the way in which bronze amounts to water with further form imposed on it does not involve any idea of the arrangement of parts, but on a (so to speak) purely chemical imposition of more complex structure and properties than those that are found in water itself (see Furth, 1988).

Another feature of Aristotle's views shows the breadth of his conception of the contrast between form and matter. He extends it to non-physical things, in application to which there can be no thought of physical parts or physical structure, but only of structure of some other sort. For example, he suggests that the premises of a syllogism are the matter for its conclusion (*Metaphysics* V 2 with XII 4). He also suggests that triangles that we think about, as opposed to triangles made out of wood or the like, possess 'intelligible matter' (*hyle noete*) (*Metaphysics* 1036a11). He speaks, too, of the genus as the matter of the species *Metaphysics* VII 12). He also speaks of a form, such as the form of circle, as itself having 'parts', which are themselves parts neither of the matter of a particular circle nor of the compound of form and matter (*Metaphysics* VII 11).

In all of these instances Aristotle's thought seems to focus on an extremely general notion of structure, as capable of being imposed on something less structured. Thus, drawing the conclusion somehow involves imposing structure on (or discerning the structure in) otherwise unconnected propositions that are its premises.

On some interpretations, Aristotle also invokes matter to explain how two co-specific individuals are distinct: they are constituted of numerically distinct matter. This interpretation is controversial, and is difficult to reconcile with the idea of matter as what is comparatively unstructured.

According to some interpretations of Aristotle, and some views developed from his, the contrast between the form and matter of physical things can be projected to allow the notion of 'prime matter', i.e. matter that has no structure at all and underlies all changes, and of which all physical things consist. Whether Aristotle accepted such a notion is controversial. It would be the notion of a physical thing that is without all structure whatsoever, but on which structure can be imposed to yield all of the physical things that there are. (*See* SUBSTRATUM.)

The same idea can perhaps be developed in the opposite direction too, to yield the idea of something that is entirely structure, not imposed on anything. Thus, Aristotle maintains that the 'prime mover' alone is 'pure actuality' and without any potentiality (*Metaphysics* XII 7), meaning by this that the prime mover alone actually is everything that it is capable of being. (*See* POTENTIALITY/ACTUALITY.)

BIBLIOGRAPHY

Anscombe, G.E.M.: 'The principle of individuation', *Proceedings of the Aristotelian Society* Supp. Vol. 27 (1953), 83–93.
Aristotle: *The Complete Works of Aristotle* ed. J. Barnes (Princeton, NJ: Princeton University Press, 1984).
Code, A.: 'The persistence of Aristotelian matter', *Philosophical Studies* 29 (1976), 357–67.
Furth, M.: *Substance, Form and Psyche* (Cambridge: Cambridge University Press, 1988).
White, N.: 'Identity, modal individuation, and matter in Aristotle', *Midwest Studies in Philosophy* 11 (1987), 475–94.

NICHOLAS WHITE

mechanism Construed in broad terms, the doctrine that every event in the natural, physical world can be fully explained and predicted by the principles and laws of physics. A much narrower understanding of this concept results if we restrict physics to mechanics, especially classical or Newtonian mechanics, and if we think of all of the laws included within mechanics as fully deterministic laws (*see* DETERMINISM). HOBBES gave expression to something like this idea by claiming that all change 'can be nothing else but motions of the parts of that body which is changed' (Hobbes, 1910, p. 75). Essentially the same doctrine was accepted by other great figures of the seventeenth century, including DESCARTES and Christian Huygens (1629–95) (see Dijksterhuis, 1961, pp. 368–80 and 403–19).

If mechanism is conjoined with materialism (*see* PHYSICALISM, MATERIALISM), that is, with the view that every existing entity has only physical properties, the result is an even more restrictive doctrine, namely that *every* event can be fully explained and predicted by the principles and laws of mechanics. This also seems to be Hobbes's view, for at one point he says that,

> For seeing life is but a motion of limbs, the beginning whereof is in some principle part within, why may we not say, that all *automata* (engines that move themselves by springs and wheels as doth a watch) have an artificial life? For what is the *heart*, but a *spring*; and the *nerves* but so many *strings*, and the *joints* but so many *wheels*, giving motion to the whole body. (Hobbes, 1930, p. 136)

More than a century later, the same doctrine was espoused by Enlightenment philosophers, including especially Denis Diderot (1713–84) and HOLBACH.

Even in this narrow sense, however, mechanism can take different forms, primarily depending on how the science of mechanics is understood. For example, it might be demanded of a theory of mechanics that it employ only force-functions having a single form, such as that for contact forces between perfectly elastic bodies. Following Nagel, we can refer to such theories as *unitary* mechanical theories (Nagel, 1961, p. 173 I here adapt from what Nagel says about theories of mechanical explanation.) Historically, Cartesian physics was a unitary mechanical theory. On the other hand a theory of mechanics might allow different force-functions, including gravitational forces, to figure in explanations of motions and changes in bodies. Such a theory of mechanics, historically associated with the work of NEWTON, would in Nagel's terms be a *pure* mechanical theory (Nagel, 1961, p. 173). It is clear that what was referred to above as *narrow* mechanism can incorporate either a unitary or a pure mechanical theory, resulting in two different variants of narrow mechanism.

Whichever theory of mechanics is used, the narrow notion of mechanism implies strict determinism with respect to all events, including human actions. Accordingly, mechanism has always been opposed by those thinkers who have held both that some actions are free and that strict determinism does not allow for free actions (*see* FREE WILL). Mechanism also implies that every *biological* event can be fully explained by the laws of mechanics, a thesis that has met with considerable opposition, not only from vitalists within biology, but also from those wholly naturalistic thinkers who have denied that biology is in any interesting sense reducible to physics (Nagel, 1961, ch. 12 contains a good discussion of this question). (*See* VITALISM.)

See also REDUCTION, REDUCTIONISM.

BIBLIOGRAPHY

Dijksterhuis, E.J.: *The Mechanization of the World Picture* (New York: Oxford University Press, 1961).

Hobbes, T.: *The Metaphysical System of Hobbes* ed. M. Calkins (Chicago: Open Court, 1910).

Hobbes, T.: *Hobbes Selections* ed. F.J. Woodbridge (New York: Scribner's, 1930).

Nagel, E.: *The Structure of Science* (New York: Harcourt Brace, 1961).

GEORGE S. PAPPAS

Meinong, Alexius (1853–1920) Born at Lemberg, in 1853, he studied philosophy at the University of Vienna under the supervision of Franz BRENTANO, devoting himself initially to HUME's works. He wrote his *habilitation* on Hume's theory of abstraction, thus placing himself in the Anglo-Saxon tradition, a tradition in which his philosophical influence flourished. Indeed, MOORE and RUSSELL were greatly impressed by the quality and scope of his ideas. After a brief period as *Privatdozent* at the University of Vienna, he moved to Graz, a beautiful city in the Austrian province of Styria (*Steiermark*) near the borders of Hungary on the east and former Yugoslavia

on the south, eventually ascending to a Chair in the Philosophy Institute at the Karl Maximilians University. He spent the rest of his life in this enchanting environment working out his unique ontological views, and also creating one of the earliest laboratories in experimental psychology. Held in great esteem by the citizens of Graz – the street Meinonggasse is named after him – he died there in 1920.

The most distinctive principle in Meinong's ontological theory – the theory of objects (*Gegenstandstheorie*) – is the principle that there are objects which have no being. Those with a taste for paradoxical expression, he said, might prefer the statement that there are objects such that there are no such objects.

Meinong reserves the word 'existence' for spatio-temporal objects and uses the word 'being' (or '*subsistence*') more broadly to apply also to abstract objects. The number 2, for example, has being even though it does not exist. Objects having no being – the *non-subsistent* objects – include both putatively concrete objects (the golden mountain) and putatively abstract objects (the first number divisible by 0).

The principle that there are non-subsistent objects has non-trivial consequences when conjoined with the equally radical *principle of independence* which says that what an object is is independent of its being; together they imply that non-subsistent objects can have properties. Thus, not only is the humming-bird now at the feeder winged, but so are Pegasus and the winged wingless horse, even though the latter two objects lack being.

Meinong holds that the properties of an object fall into two classes, those which are part of its nature, that is, nuclear (*konstitutorische*) properties, and those which are not, that is, non-nuclear (*ausserkonstitutorische*) properties. For instance, goldenness is a nuclear property of the golden mountain, but its beinglessness is not. This leads to another important principle, the *principle of indifference*, which says that neither being nor beinglessness is part of the nature of an object. Objects are identified by

305

means of their nuclear properties; a and b are the same objects just in case they have all the same nuclear properties. To remove the apparent inconsistency generated by this principle of identification and the fact that the existent gold mountain and the golden mountain are not identical, Meinong invokes the highly complex doctrine of 'watered down' counterparts of non-nuclear properties – watered down existence, for example – and counts them among the properties comprising the nature of an object. So, the existent golden mountain has watered down existence but the golden mountain does not, and, hence, they are not the same object even though neither of them has non-nuclear existence.

Two persistent misunderstandings of Meinong's ontological doctrine are that the world of non-beings (*Aussersein*) consists only of possible objects, and that the objects of that world are a kind of intentional object. But the fact that there are – for Meinong – impossible objects such as the round square is a repudiation of the former misunderstanding, and the fact that Meinong distinguishes sharply between objects such as the *thought* of Pegasus and Pegasus, only the former of which has being, refutes the latter misunderstanding. Meinong is a realist with respect to non-subsistent objects, not an intentionalist. (*See* REALISM.)

Meinong classifies objects into two broad and important categories, objecta and objectives (*Objektive*), on the one hand, and complete and incomplete, on the other hand.

Objectives are states-of-affairs-like entities that can have objecta as constituents, but objecta can never have objectives as constituents (*see* PROPOSITIONS/STATES OF AFFAIRS). For instance, both the subsistent objective that Oslo is in Norway and the non-subsistent objective that Oslo is in Sweden have Oslo as a constituent, but the individual Oslo itself has no objective as a constituent. Objectives play an important role in Meinong's theory of truth, serving as the truth-makers, and in his prophetic and masterful work, *Über Annahmen* (1902), they serve as the 'objects' of at least some of

what would later be called propositional attitudes.

Complete objects are objects such that for every property P they either have P or the complement of P – non-redness, for example, is the complement of redness. Incomplete objects are objects such that for some property P they neither have P nor the complement of P. Incomplete objects, strictly speaking, neither have nor lack being in the primary sense, though many of them may be said to have a kind of being ('derived being'). Meinong seems to think of many if not most incomplete objects rather like Platonic forms and speaks of them as being *embedded* in objects. They play a significant role in his theory of reference and in his general theory of knowledge.

In *Über Möglichkeit und Wahrscheinlichkeit* (1915) Meinong distinguishes between a narrower and a wider sense of negation and hence a narrower and wider sense of the principle of excluded middle. In particular, to deny that an (incomplete) object neither has P nor its complement, which constitutes a rejection of excluded middle in the narrow sense, does not conflict with the *law* of excluded middle in the wider (and classical) sense that every object has P or does not have P, because the fact that an (incomplete) object does not have the property P does not exclude the possibility that it also does not have the complement of the property P. So, for example, though it is true by logic alone that the ideal triangle either has the property of equiangularity or does not have that property (wide negation), it does not follow from the fact that it does not have the property of equiangularity that, therefore, it has the property of non-equiangularity (narrow negation). This, Meinong believes, was the fundamental error in BERKELEY's attack on LOCKE's abstract ideas.

Until recently it was widely believed that Meinong's theory of non-subsistent objects – and, hence, his general theory of objects – is untenable because Russell (1905) had shown that Meinong's theory yields both the conclusion that the round square is round and is square, and the conclusion that the existent golden mountain exists and does not exist. But Russell's arguments against Meinong's theory have been vigorously challenged in the last two decades (see, for example, Lambert, 1983), and, in fact, many provably consistent formal theories of non-existent objects, some of them close to Meinong in word and spirit, have been developed (see, for instance, Parsons, 1980). Indeed, modern examination of Meinong's theory of objects has shown the infelicity of RYLE's remark that Meinong's theory of non-subsistent objects is 'dead, buried and not going to be resurrected' (Ryle, 1972, p. 7). On the contrary, in recent times Meinong's conception of non-subsistent objects has proved to have wide application in areas as diverse as the analysis of fictional discourse, on the one hand, and logic and the philosophy of physics, on the other.

See also FICTIONAL TRUTH, OBJECTS AND CHARACTERS.

WRITINGS

'Über Gegenstandstheorie', in his *Untersuchungen zur Gegenstandstheorie und Psychologie* (Leipzig: Barth, 1904), 1–50; trans. 'On the theory of objects', in *Realism and the Background of Phenomenology* ed. R.M. Chisholm *et al.* (New York: The Free Press, 1960), 76–117.
Über Annahmen (Leipzig: Barth, 1902); 2nd edn (Leipzig: Barth, 1910).
Über Möglichkeit und Wahrscheinlichkeit (Leipzig: Barth, 1915).

BIBLIOGRAPHY

Lambert, K.: *Meinong and the Principle of Independence* (London: Cambridge University Press, 1983).
Parsons, T.: *Nonexistent Objects* (New Haven: Yale University Press, 1980).
Russell, B.: 'Meinong's theory of complexes and assumptions', *Mind* 13 (1904), 204–19, 336–54, 509–24.
Russell, B.: 'On denoting', *Mind* 14 (1905), 479–93.
Ryle, G.: 'Intentionality theory and the nature of thinking', in *Jenseits von Sein und Nichtsein* ed. R. Haller (Graz: Akademische Druck u. Verlaganstalt, 1972), 7–15.

KAREL LAMBERT

mental/physical DESCARTES was the first philosopher to elaborate a systematic account of the nature of the mental and its relationship to the physical (*see* MIND/BODY PROBLEM). For Descartes, minds are unextended, thinking substances that causally interact with the extended, unthinking material substances comprising the physical world. This view is widely rejected in philosophy today in part because of its introduction of mysterious mental substances and in part because we now think of the physical as including more than material substances (for example, magnetic fields and waves). But there is no broad agreement among contemporary philosophers about exactly how the mental/physical distinction is to be drawn. Let us begin with some recent views on the physical side of the distinction.

It is sometimes supposed that a general term is physical (that is, that it picks out a physical state or property or kind) just in case it occurs in some true theory of physics. This is evidently too narrow a definition, however; for terms like 'acid', 'alkali', and 'DNA' lie outside the domain of physics and yet they would normally be classified as physical. Perhaps we should say, then, that a general term is physical just in case it occurs in some true theory of physics, chemistry, molecular biology or neurophysiology. But it is far from clear that this is a satisfactory way to characterize the physical. If 'gene' and 'neuron' are now classified as physical terms, then why not go further and classify 'tsetse fly', 'crocodile', 'mountain' and 'fossil' (terms found in entomology, zoology, geology and paleontology, respectively) as physical too? The general problem here, of course, is that we have not been provided with any account of what physics, chemistry, molecular biology and neurophysiology share in virtue of which they count as physical and the other sciences mentioned above do not (for more on this issue, see Hempel, 1970).

One way of avoiding this problem is to say that a general term is physical just in case it occurs in some true theory adequate for the explanation of the phenomena of non-living matter (see Block, 1978). But there remain serious difficulties even here. Suppose that there are properties that are tokened only in the brains of certain living creatures, and that these properties figure in neurophysiological laws. It seems *ad hoc* to deny that such properties are physical. Yet this is what we must do according to this proposed definition.

How, then, is the term 'physical' to be understood? If this question is taken to demand a fixed list of necessary and sufficient conditions for the application of 'physical', as ordinarily used, then it is doubtful that it has an answer. Necessary and sufficient conditions are hard to come by for any terms, let alone ones at this level of abstraction. Perhaps the best we can say is something like this: physics is the paradigm or prototype for the physical sciences. A given science counts as physical, then, so long as it is sufficiently similar to physics, and a given general term counts as physical so long as it occurs in a physical science. The notion of sufficient similarity at work here is vague and multidimensional. Different competent users of 'physical' may rely tacitly on different dimensions of similarity, thereby forming conflicting views about whether to count 'mountain', say, as a physical term.

The difficulties we have encountered in trying to specify the meaning of the term 'physical' multiply when we turn to the term 'mental'. Although, as I noted above, few philosophers today would endorse Descartes's view that 'mental' applies to immaterial, thinking substances, there is even less agreement about what constitutes the mark of the mental than there is about how to define the physical. One well-known proposal is that incorrigibility is the distinguishing feature of the mental (Rorty, 1970). That is to say, a report or description is classified as mental just in case it could not possibly be in error. This proposal derives from consideration of simple reports of sensations (for example, 'I am in pain') in everyday contexts. However, it is clear that people do sometimes make mistakes about their mental states, as is shown by any number of psychological experiments (see Nisbett and Wilson, 1977). Furthermore, cognitive psychologists have developed theories of our cognitive capacities which posit mental states that are inaccessible to consciousness. The claims made in such theories are empirical and are therefore subject to revision and falsification.

Another proposal is that mental states or events are those to which their subjects have privileged access. This proposal admits the possibility of error for mental reports but insists nevertheless that the subject of the report is necessarily always in the best position to discover whether it is mistaken or to confirm it. So, for example, it is now conceded that one may mistakenly think at some given moment that one is having a visual experience of blue, say, but one has final epistemological authority on the matter: no one else could be as well placed to decide whether one is really having a visual experience of blue.

This suggestion is a minor improvement on the appeal to incorrigibility, but it is still indefensible. One problem, for example, is that subjects cannot have any privileged way of knowing with respect to mental states which are inaccessible to consciousness.

A third proposal for characterizing the mental (due to BRENTANO) is that mental entities are intentional; that is, they represent states of affairs or objects, whether or not the states of affairs or objects actually exist. For example, imagining something is mental by this criterion, since a person may imagine a three headed monster even though there are no such beasts. Likewise, wanting, hoping, doubting and believing all pass the test. Unfortunately, some mental phenomena seem to fail. Consider, for example, having an itch, or experiencing a pain, or feeling happy.

It appears no easy matter, then, to discover the essence of the mental. This need not necessarily concern us, however. For it may well be that the mental has no interesting essence waiting to be discovered. After all, if there is no illuminating list of necessary and sufficient conditions that characterizes the physical, it seems plausible to suppose that there is no such list for the mental either.

So where does this leave us with the mental/physical distinction? Well, whatever else the mental may be, it is a proper object of study of the science of psychology (both cognitive and physiological). And, according to the view suggested earlier, a general term counts as physical just in case it occurs in a physical science. So, whether we count the mental as physical depends upon whether we classify psychology as a physical science. Given our earlier comments, this seems to be an issue on which there is no single, fixed, correct view. But it seems that geology is reasonably classified as a physical science. And if geology is, why not psychology?

See also INTENTIONALITY; PUBLIC/PRIVATE.

BIBLIOGRAPHY

Block, N.: 'Troubles with functionalism', in *Minnesota Studies in the Philosophy of Science* Vol. 9 *Perception and Cognition: Issues in the Foundations of Psychology* ed. C.W. Savage (Minneapolis: University of Minnesota Press, 1978), 261–325.

Hempel, C.: 'Reduction: ontological and linguistic facets', in *Essays in Honor of Ernest Nagel* ed. S. Morgenbesser, P. Suppes and M. White (New York: St Martin's Press, 1970), 179–99.

Kraus, O.: *Franz Brentano: Zur Kenntnis seines Lebens und seiner Lehre* (Munich: O. Beck, 1919).

Nisbett, R. and Wilson, T.: 'Telling more than we can know: verbal reports on mental processes', *Psychological Review* 84 (1977), 231–59.

Rorty, R.: 'Incorrigibility as the mark of the mental', *Journal of Philosophy* 67 (1970), 399–424.

MICHAEL TYE

mereology *see* PART/WHOLE

Merleau-Ponty, Maurice (1908–61) French philosopher of the period immediately following the Second World War who developed a phenomenology of perception into a comprehensive philosophy of human being-in-the-world, of embodied consciousness, emphasizing the interplay of self and world, and of self and other selves. He also examined the expressive possibilities of language, science, literature and art. He was a phenomenological critic of PHENOMENOLOGY; against the idealism of HUSSERL and the dualism of SARTRE, he held that a faithful phenomenology requires an ontology which displaces, while it saves the sense of, the traditional dualisms of subject and object, immanence and transcendence.

From the time of his most formative work, *Phenomenology of Perception* (1945), the organizing principle of Merleau-Ponty's thought is what he calls the 'primacy of perception', where the critical point is that 'perception' is taken, not as some sort of interior event, but as our way of being in (or 'at') the world, having access to the world, through our bodies. Thus, we need not wonder 'whether we really perceive a world, we must instead say: the world is what we perceive' (Merleau-Ponty, 1945, p. xvi). As Merleau-Ponty sees it, there is no 'more real' world, perhaps a 'scientifically known world', behind the world we touch and see and through which we move. Rather, there is one world, the perceived world, which we bring to expression in language and which we explore and redescribe for special purposes in the sciences. The task for philosophy is to recapture the full meaning of this primordial perceptual world and to exhibit its interplay with various cultural practices. There can be, Merleau-Ponty thinks, no 'absolute'

ONTOLOGY, none which gives us the world as it is thought to be from 'outside' human experience, but we can attempt an 'indirect ontology' – a contingent one – which evokes and elucidates the most fundamental features of things from within our situation in the midst of them.

The core of this ontology lies in the reciprocity Merleau-Ponty sees within the primordial perceptual world among the embodied self, other embodied selves, and bodily things. At a level of experience 'below' self-conscious judgement, we find ourselves caught up with things and with other selves, and they with us, in such an 'interweaving' that it is impossible to say what is contributed by us and what by them. Perceived things are both 'in themselves' and 'for us' – disclosed as transcendent, already there, but only through the limited perspectives we and others take upon them. We are both 'in ourselves' and at the same time 'for others' and 'for things' – conscious subjects, yet only as embodied and temporalized, 'intervolved' with past and future, with other selves and other things, through our bodies. So Merleau-Ponty says, 'The world is inseparable from the subject, but from a subject which is nothing but a project of the world' (1945, p. 430).

Similarly, on his view, human beings are to be understood both as 'psychic' and as 'physical', but only in a sense in which no firm line can be drawn between them: 'There is not a single impulse in a living body which is entirely fortuitous in relation to psychic intentions, not a single mental act which has not found at least its germ or its general outline in physiological tendencies' (1945, p. 88). And for human action, since the world is seen as both already constituted and at the same time never completely constituted, 'There is ... never determinism and never absolute choice' (1964, p. 453) (see FREE WILL).

In his last work, The Visible and the Invisible (1964), unfinished at his death, Merleau-Ponty sought to emphasize still further that Being subtends the distinction between subject and world. Being is 'wild', it is a 'dehiscence', a 'divergence' (écart), always beyond monistic characterization, yet it comes to intelligibility through an 'exemplar' of being, the human body as 'flesh'. Merleau-Ponty takes the experience of one hand touching and being touched by another, with its unusual interplay of self and other, identity and difference, as an expression of the interplay among beings and of the inner 'latency' and 'dimensionality' of Being itself.

See also EXISTENTIALISM; HEIDEGGER.

WRITINGS

Phénomenologie de la perception (Paris: Gallimard, 1945); trans. C. Smith, The Phenomenology of Perception (New York: Humanities Press, 1962).
The Primacy of Perception ed. J.M. Edie (Evanston, IL: Northwestern University Press, 1964).
Le visible et l'invisible (Paris: Gallimard, 1964); trans. A. Lingis, The Visible and the Invisible (Evanston, IL: Northwestern University Press, 1968).

BIBLIOGRAPHY

Dillon, M.C.: Merleau-Ponty's Ontology (Bloomington, IN: Indiana University Press, 1988).
Mallin, S.: Merleau-Ponty's Philosophy (New Haven, CT: Yale University Press, 1979).

JOHN J. COMPTON

metalanguage see OBJECT LANGUAGE/ METALANGUAGE

metaphysics: definitions and divisions There is no clear and generally accepted definition of metaphysics, no agreement on its tasks, scope or divisions. In these circumstances it is best simply to explain what influential philosophers have taken these to be.

THE NAME

Metaphysics as a discipline goes back to ARISTOTLE, but the name 'metaphysics' goes back to the Aristotelian editors of the first century BC. When Aristotle's extant works were finally ordered, fourteen assorted treatises, clearly connected with the books on nature (*ta physika*), but more general and fundamental, were collected. Placed after the physical treatises, they were called 'the [books coming] after the [books on] nature', *ta meta ta physika*. The name was later taken to connote what is beyond sensible nature, playing on an ambiguity in '*meta*'. Aristotle called what he did in these books variously 'wisdom', 'first philosophy', and 'theology'.

TASKS

Aristotle gives three different, not obviously equivalent accounts of the task of first philosophy. In Book *A* it is the science of first principles and causes, in Book *Γ* the science of being as being, and in Books *A* and E it is called theology. The treatises of the *Metaphysics* engage in all three tasks, identifying the most general laws of thought and the basic kinds of cause, talking about beings in general, their principal kinds and characteristics, and in Book *Λ* discussing the divine. There is also other material such as criticisms of Aristotle's predecessors, in particular PLATO's theory of forms. The scholastics and early moderns adopted this outline with little change, though there was at all times sharp disagreement on what there really is. The first western treatise on metaphysics other than a commentary on Aristotle was SUÁREZ's *Disputationes Metaphysicae* of 1597. With the emphasis on knowledge, promoted by Descartes and emphasized by the empiricists, claims of metaphysics to provide knowledge of first things were increasingly doubted, until HUME declared 'school metaphysics' to contain 'nothing but sophistry and illusion' (*see* EMPIRICISM). KANT attempted to rescue metaphysics by confining it to the knowable. Hume's critique was accepted wholeheartedly by nineteenth- and twentieth-century positivists; the logical positivists claimed to have shown by the PRINCIPLE OF VERIFICATION that metaphysical statements are literally meaningless (*see* LOGICAL POSITIVISM). It was soon realized that the logical positivists' own claims and the scientific laws they held up as paradigms of rationality fell by the same axe, so the way was clear for metaphysics to re-emerge in analytical philosophy, more closely tied to the philosophy of logic and language. Of the original three tasks of metaphysics, that of the discovery and justification of first principles has been carved up among philosophers of logic, science and cognition, while (rational) theology has been consigned to a corner of special metaphysics; the only branch to flourish is the study of being as being, usually under its later name ONTOLOGY.

SCOPE

Aristotle took metaphysics to have all actually existing beings as its objects, but only in respect of what belongs to them as beings. By the time of DUNS SCOTUS, metaphysics had been subtly expanded in range to deal not only with all actual beings, but also to consider purely possible beings (*see* MODALITIES AND POSSIBLE WORLDS). Christian Wolff (1679–1754) defined an entity as 'that which contains no contradiction in itself', and ontology as the science of entities as entities, echoing Aristotle in letter but not in spirit. A further notional expansion of the scope of metaphysics, foreshadowed by REID, occurred when MEINONG developed his theory of objects, which include not only the actual and possible, but also the impossible, for example, contradictory objects like the round square. Debates about whether one can sensibly ascribe 'ontological status' to what does not exist or what could not exist are part and parcel of modern metaphysics.

311

DIVISIONS

Aristotle's three tasks naturally gave rise to three divisions of metaphysics, so AQUINAS divided *sapientia* into *metaphysica* (being as being), *prima philosophia* (first principles), and *theologia*. This scheme remained intact until early modern times. It was replaced by Christian Wolff, who divided metaphysics into general and special, calling general metaphysics, the science of being as being, by the name '*ontologia*' (the term was coined by Rudolf Goclenius in 1613). Special metaphysics was now divided into the three branches of rational theology, rational psychology, and rational cosmology, namely the (rational) sciences of God, souls and bodies respectively, which in fact correspond in subject matter to the divisions of Aristotle's *second* philosophy. Kant's 'metaphysics of nature', subordinated to epistemology, was divided similarly into a general part, ontology, opposed to the physiology of reason, itself divided into two 'transcendent' parts (rational theology, rational cosmology) and two 'immanent' parts (rational psychology and rational physics). HUSSERL gave the discipline of being the name of ontology, but divided it into formal ontology and several material or regional ontologies. Formal ontology deals with formal ontological concepts, those concerned with objects in general, as distinct from formal logical concepts, those concerned with truth and inference. Regional ontologies study the most general concepts and principles of the principal regions of being, including physical nature, consciousness, mathematics and the divine. Husserl himself spent much of his time on methodological issues and his regional ontologies were only sketched. Husserl's student INGARDEN divided ontology into existential, formal and material. Existential ontology is concerned with what he called moments of existence, like forms of dependence, modality and temporality, which are combined into modes of being. Formal ontology studies different objects according to their form (thing, property, event, process, relation, state of affairs, system), material onto-

logy according to their kind (spatio-temporal, psychological, divine). For Ingarden 'metaphysics' denotes among all possible ontologies the one that is actual. Contemporary philosophy has mainly not subdivided metaphysics; an exception is WILLIAMS's division into analytic ontology ('examining the traits necessary to whatever is') and speculative cosmology ('What kinds of things are there?'), but the divide is not a sharp one. A priori divisions such as that of Husserl are found ill-justified or question-begging, so metaphysics is generally practised today as, on the one hand, general ontology or theory of objects and, on the other hand, an assortment of more or less traditional metaphysical disputes, on such topics as FREE WILL, God, UNIVERSALS, SPACE AND TIME and persons (*see* PERSONS AND PERSONAL IDENTITY). Ontology connects with questions of semantics and philosophical logic such as quantification and ontological commitment, the status of higher-order logic, modality, identity, etc., and with issues in the philosophy of science concerning such topics as relativity, quantum theory, and evolution.

BIBLIOGRAPHY

Aristotle: *Metaphysica* ed. W. Jaeger (Oxford: Clarendon Press, 1957).
Ingarden, R.: *Time and Modes of Being* (Springfield, IL: Thomas, 1964).
Meinong, A.: 'Über Gegenstandstheorie', *Alexius Meinong Gesamtausgabe* vol. 2 (Graz: Akademische Druck- u. Verlagsanstalt, 1971), 481–530.
Williams, D.C.: 'The elements of being', in his *Principles of Empirical Realism* (Springfield, IL: Thomas, 1966), 74–109.
Wolff, C.: *Philosophia prima sive ontologia* (Frankfurt: 1729; Hildesheim: Olms, 1962).

PETER SIMONS

metaphysics in Africa   What is distinctively African in metaphysics in Africa today derives from African traditional thought. This article will treat of that body of thought as interpreted and analysed from the standpoint of contemporary African philosophy. The concerns of traditional African metaphysics are, perhaps, best characterized in the phrase of KANT as 'God, freedom and immortality'. But one has not advanced one step towards understanding African thought unless one understands the radically un-Kantian connotations of these concepts. More generally, African conceptions of these great topics frequently stand in striking contrast to *much* western thought thereto.

To start with matters related to the concept of God: belief in a supreme being is common to the traditional thought of most African peoples, though it is of more than a parochial interest to note that some African peoples, such as the Luo of East Africa, do not seem to have any place for such a concept in their (highly sophisticated) traditional thought. Significantly, the reason for the a-theism of the traditional Luo is cognate with the conceptual orientation underlying the particular conceptions of the supreme being held by those African peoples who make such a postulation in their communal philosophies. That cast of thought is preeminently empirical.

The most fundamental level at which the empirical outlook of African metaphysics is manifested is in the semantics of the notion of existence. To exist is to be *somewhere*, and the so-called existential 'is' or 'to be' corresponds to no complete thought – a semantical circumstance which inspired the following animadversion on DESCARTES's *cogito* from Alexis Kagame, the famous African metaphysician and linguist: 'The celebrated axiom "I think, therefore I am" is unintelligible, as the verb "to be" is always followed by an attribute or an adjunct of place: I am good, big, etc., I am in such and such a place, etc. Thus the utterance '. . . therefore I am" would prompt the question: "You are . . . what . . . where?" ' (1976, p. 95). Kagame had in mind here specifically the linguistic situation 'throughout the Bantu zone', but the remark applies to the rendition of existence in other language areas in Africa.

The ontological implications of this semantical fact are perceivable in the homogeneity of African ontologies. Typically, they are devoid of sharp dualisms such as those of the material and the spiritual, the supernatural and the natural, and the secular and the religious. The notion of God that emerges is that of a cosmic architect, a fashioner of the world out of a preexisting manifold of indeterminacy in contradistinction to the ex-nihilo creator of Christianity. This supreme being is conceived to be good in the highest and all-powerful, though not omnipotent in all the known interpretations of this term. He or s/he – God is hermaphroditic in the thought of some West Africans – is at the apex of a cosmic hierarchy, featuring in its upper echelons a variety of extra-human beings and forces of differing moral sensibilities and causal powers, and in its middle and lower rungs human beings, the lower animals and the world of inanimate objects and phenomena.

Two things in this system of thought call for special emphasis. In view of the locative sense of existence, God cannot be said to be a *transcendent* being, and in the absence of any sharp ontological cleavages, the concept of *nature* has neither an explanatory utility nor even a basic coherence. God, the extra-humans and the sub-humans are all regarded as integral parts of a single totality of existence. Accordingly, explanatory invocations, in human affairs, of factors from the higher domains do not engender the sense of ontological border-crossing that a term like 'supernatural' is apt to communicate, and the frequent use of this and allied terms in the characterization of African explanations betokens an indiscriminating alien conceptual standpoint which has, ironically, infected even African writings in western languages.

A corollary of the trait of African metaphysics just noted is that the NATURALISM/non-naturalism antithesis, so historically important in western philosophy, does not even arise in African traditional thinking. This same trait, moreover, is connected with a thoroughgoing DETERMINISM

313

which precipitates the problem of FREE WILL in a very sharp form. The determinism, however, is not one predicated on a mechanical conception of causality; what it means is a commitment to the universal reign of law in all spheres of existence – animate and inanimate, mental and nonmental. A particularly uncompromising version of this viewpoint is encountered in the metaphysical sayings of the Akans of Ghana, some of which express the thought that even the (demiurgic) act of divine creation was subject to irreversible laws of God's own being.

As it impinges on the notion of human personality, this deterministic persuasion takes the form of a doctrine of divine predestination of human destinies in which the very principle of personal individuation consists in the unique destinies thus appointed. Details vary across the continent, but the basic conception of human personhood in Africa involves, on the ontological plane, two types of constituents, one material, the other quasi-material (see MIND/BODY PROBLEM). The first consists of the body, the second usually of a pair of breezy, ontologically versatile entities, conceived in one case as the principle of life and in the other as the basis of the complexion of individuality. In terms of imagery, both are on occasion modelled on the human person, but in terms of dynamics they are thought of as exempt from the grosser limitations of actual persons.

The crucial difference between the two quasi-material constituents of human personality is with respect to their origination. The animating element is often supposed to come directly from God and is, in fact, held to be a piece of the divine substance and also to be the recipient (from God) of the blueprint of personal destiny, while the other element is credited to mundane genetics. Basic survival, and beyond that, human flourishing presuppose the harmonious functioning of all the constituents. Impairment of that harmony may be remediable or it may not. Either contingency is fixed by destiny. But even in the fatal alternative, something is thought to survive perma-

nently, namely, the life principle, which in this post-mortem scenario eventually becomes an ancestor.

The immortality just spoken of is conceived purely in pragmatic terms. From the African point of view, survival in itself, even if blissful (which it is not quite), is of no particular value; what is of significance is the ability of the immortals to bring succour to the living sections of their families and to exercise moral leadership among them. The metaphysical implication of this level of interaction between mortals and immortals is that the world of the latter is ontologically both analogous and contiguous to that of the former. The contrast with, for example, orthodox Christian doctrines of IMMORTALITY is obvious.

Other conceptual contrasts are perhaps not so obvious. Thus it takes some noticing that in the African framework of thought the part of a person that becomes an immortal is of a different category from what in English is called the SOUL, given that a soul is supposed (in neo-Cartesian thought, for instance) also to be a mind. The disparity is because the African *mind*, as distinct from the animating element, is not a kind of entity, but rather a capacity (for doing various things) supervenient upon brain functioning in human beings and upon the functioning of whatever paraphernalia may be appropriate to any admissible plane of existence. Moreover, at no stage does mortal life or immortal survival involve any element of absolute immateriality.

An equally important difference arises in connection with the problem of free will. African thought is particularly sensitive to this problem, in view of its commitment to divine predestination. In fact, however, this predestination is only a special case of general determinism; and the question therefore is the single one of whether determinism precludes free will. A further narrowing down of the problem comes in the fact that African speculative preoccupation with this issue is predominantly normative. The question of free will reduces, in essence, to that of responsibility, namely, under what conditions is human conduct to be evaluated in moral terms? One answer, clearly arguable on the basis of well-known African attitudes and reactions to conduct, is that an action falls under this category if, and only if, the agent's behaviour is susceptible of modification through rational persuasion. On this account, some kinds of causes are deleterious to freedom, others are not. Furthermore some people are free in some respects and in some degree; others are not, relatively speaking.

Caveat: Africa is a huge continent, and while this account is likely to be found substantially valid in regard to many African peoples south of the Sahara, there is no pretence at a total continental universality. In any case, the conceptual schemes underlying these thoughts seem to me to offer promising options for contemporary metaphysical thinking in Africa and elsewhere.

BIBLIOGRAPHY

Abraham, W.E.: *The Mind of Africa* (Chicago: The University of Chicago Press, 1962).

Gyekye, K.: *An Essay on African Philosophical Thought* (New York: Cambridge University Press, 1987).

Kagame, A.: 'Empirical apperception of time and the conception of history in Bantu thought', in *Cultures and Time* ed. P. Ricoeur (Paris: UNESCO, 1976), 89–116.

Mbiti, J.: *African Religions and Philosophy* 2nd edn (London: Heinemann, 1990). Sparsely philosophical but well-established in the literature.

P'Bitek, O.: *African Religion in Western Scholarship* (Nairobi: East African Literature Bureau, 1970).

Tempels, P.: *Bantu Philosophy* (Paris: Prénce Africaine, 1959). A controversial classic.

KWASI WIREDU

metaphysics in China In China as in the West, metaphysics and theory of language go hand in hand. Their radically different language and distinctly practical philosophical projects give Chinese theory of language a wholly different character. Chinese theorists did not mention sentences or parts of speech. They thought of language as written strings of ideographic characters which could be pronounced in different ways. Ancient sage kings had invented the characters along with a code of behaviour. Traditional texts transmitted the language and practical instruction set (the sage's *dao*) together.

Classical philosophers described the problem of correct word usage as discriminating stuff in the proper way. Initially that meant the way that the sage kings intended, making distinctions so we perform as the sages would themselves have performed. The implicit role of language was to guide behaviour, not to represent reality. We learn to associate each term with parts of the instruction set called the 道 *dao*. Assigning a term to a person or an object directs our attention to the parts of guiding discourse. We are programmed by the language to adopt proper behaviour toward that person or object.

The immediate issue among early thinkers, therefore, was not 'How is the world constructed?' but 'Which is the correct way of making distinctions?' The implied view of reality reflected the linguistic procedure of distinguishing thing-types (stuffs) from a background. The implicit metaphysics had a PART/WHOLE structure – a mereological NOMINALISM, rather than an object/property or member/set metaphysics. We commonly translate 物 $wu^{\text{thing-kind}}$ as *object* but it makes the textual theories more plausible if we treat the standard phrase 萬物 $wan^{10,000}$ $wu^{\text{thing-kinds}}$ as referring to the 10,000 nameable species or stuffs.

The practical focus of early philosophy motivated an antirealist bias. All the early views of language suggested that society projected language on the world. Still, the ethical theories were *formally* realistic; only the Daoists doubted that there was *one correct* way to project distinctions on the world in guiding behaviour. They were not, however *external* realists – they did not think the distinctions carved reality at some metaphysically natural joints. They did accept nature as the source and warrant of the standards guiding how we project distinctions. The Mohists' pragmatic answer was naturalistic. It said we should mark distinctions where they will yield the best results given how the world was. (*See* ANTI-REALISM; REALISM.)

One metaphysical result emerged from Daoist linguistic IDEALISM. The realm of perspective relativity was the conventional linguistic community rather than the subjectivity of an individual. One popular analysis of this Daoist scheme is the chaos theory. Conventional language imposes order on a pre-linguistic chaos and *creates* things (thing-kinds).

Other reflections on these *dao*-based theories motivated a different route into metaphysics. The concern with projecting the correct distinction led to an analogue of rule scepticism. Any given *discourse* can result in a variety of *courses* of action when performers interpret the terms in that 道 *dao*^{guiding discourse} differently. Interpretive realism suggested that only one of these possible courses of action was correct. That led to an equivocal reading of *dao*: *discourse dao* and *performance dao*. A *dao* was both the discourse that guided behaviour and the *correct course* (road, path) that rectified performance interpretation produced.

Dispute about *dao* came to focus on the performance *dao*. The implicit goal of philosophy was to find a way to specify or identify the correct prescriptive future history – the constant *dao*. Knowledge was knowledge of that event path. Since *dao*, like other terms, was summable, one could speak of the different paths 天地 *tian-di*^{the cosmos} would trace if we executed Confucian or Mohist guiding discourse.

Each philosophical system, therefore, represented a different prescriptive possible world – a 道 *dao*^{path} the world would trace if humans followed that 道 *dao*^{guiding discourse}. An early theorist, Shendao, observed that although there are many possible courses of world history, only one *actual dao* runs from past to future. One and only one of the possible courses will be the actual course. If our goal is to follow the *natural dao*, we can relax. We will! Even a clod of earth, Shendao declared, cannot miss the *Great Dao*. He thus argued that we can dispense with knowledge (of language based *daos*). This anti-language twist on the metaphysical notion of the actual course of events blended with the notion of the pre-linguistic chaos to produce the popular view of *The Dao* as incommensurable with language.

Materialist theory identified the underlying stuff as 氣 *qi*^{material-force}. This doctrine informed Mencius' innatist theory. He assumed that *qi*^{material-force} incorporates the key moral impulse that guides correct performance interpretations. *Qi* pervades our natures and links us to the moral cosmos. A more purely metaphysical version of *qi* theory argued that the basic metaphysical distinction in *qi*^{material-force} is 陰 *Yin*^{female, cool, dark etc.} and 陽 *Yang*^{male, warm, bright etc.}.

Formal semantic and metaphysical theory flowed out of the first attempt at direct external realism. Followers of Mozi argued that the way to make distinctions was to cluster stuff according to different kinds of 同 *tong*^{same} and 異 *yi*^{different}. They analysed particulars as simply a narrow scope – the scope of a singular term. Singular terms marked only numerical difference. The Mohists noted, however, that even numerical difference was relative to levels of view. What is a whole from one scope perspective, was a collection from the lower perspective.

Chinese grammar offered only context to discriminate between two semantic effects of concatenation of names. With some terms, the concatenation *picked out* the intersection of the scopes of the two component terms. With others, it picked out the union of the scope of the components.

牛馬 *niu-ma*^{ox-horse} was an example of the summing or union of scopes. We can view *niu-ma* as a duality with *niu* and *ma* as the component individuals. We can also view *niu* as many from a lower position or we can see *niu-ma* as *one* from a higher viewpoint. The Later Mohists used a metaphysical distinction to explain the different semantic principles for interpreting those

Yin and *Yang* in *Tai-ji*

compounds. Since in sum compounds the scopes do not interpenetrate, we treat each as a 體 *ti*^part:substance:body. The compound is a 兼 *jian*^whole. 堅白 *Jian-bai*^hard-white is an example of an intersection or product compound. The scopes of the component terms *interpenetrate*; we cannot separate them. *Jian* and *bai* are not *ti*.

Speculative COSMOLOGY gradually grew in importance during the late classical period and flourished during China's philosophical dark age. Xunzi, a later Confucian, began to use the term 理 *li*^patterns of the realistic ground of distinctions and *dao*. The natural patterns or tendencies in nature both guide our distinctions of types and dictate the behaviour of each stuff. Xunzi assumed that the *li*^pattern of the three realms, heaven, earth and the human, have a natural harmony. The Confucian sage was capable of detecting the *li*^pattern of human behaviour and thus lead us into harmony with *li* of the universe.

Later, other cosmologically minded Confucian scholars focused on the 易經 *I Jing*. The *I Jing* was a divination text based on a *Ying/Yang* theory of cosmic change. 太極 *Tai-ji*^Great Ultimate divided into *Yin* and *Yang* (as shown in the Figure). Every event-state is a dynamic interplay of *Yin* and *Yang*. The *I Jing* schematized cosmic process as a constantly changing mixture of *Yin* and *Yang* forces. They represented situations-types by arranging *yin* (- -) and *yang* (–) lines in trigrams (≡) and hexagrams (䷀). Each trigram or hexagram corresponds to a

Chinese ideograph that describes the situation. There were various traditional hexagram orders, but the scheme of change was unpredictable. The act of divining randomly selects the schematic type and its successor. The scheme also embodied the famous assumption in the traditional symbol that each polar element in its purest or most concentrated form was transforming into its opposite.

Another popular cosmological scheme at the end of the classical period was the five-element (five-process) scheme. The basic five were water, earth, fire, metal and wood. Many systems of pentuples mirrored and resonated with the original five in a myriad of cosmic and social patterns. Thus in a certain season, one element, one colour, one bodily organ, one musical note, one flavour, one direction, etc. was dominant.

Five-element portentology and the scheme of correlations became the main focus of intellectual activity after the Han empire installed Confucianism as its state orthodoxy. Both portentology's philosophical value and its centrality to Chinese thought are controversial issues. Sceptical Chinese thinkers treated the correlation movement as sign of the intellectual decline that made China receptive to Buddhism.

On the cusp of that Buddhist period, interest in Daoist texts resurfaced. An unorthodox Confucian, Wang Bi, produced an interpretation of Daoism that linked Daoism to the *I Jing* and Confucian cosmology. He characterized *dao* as having 無 *wu*^not exist as its 體 *ti*^body:essence and 有 *you*^exist as its 用 *yong*^function:manifestation. The essence of any 物 *wu*^thing-kind was its 理 *li*^pattern and the *li* of the cosmic *dao* was 無 *wu*^not exist. Wang Bi's system provided a framework for adopting Buddhism and eventually the framework in which Confucianism revived after centuries of Buddhist domination.

The spread of Buddhism into China represented the invasion of an Indo-European metaphysical scheme. Buddhism brought with it the classical western notions of grammar and subject/predicate sententials, and object/property metaphysics, scepticism of the senses, truth bearing mental states (beliefs), a theory of phenomenal, mental representative items giving phonemic words meaning, and the conceptual contrasts of mind/body, one/many, and permanence/change.

Little of this appealed to Chinese intellectuals at first and Buddhism had to cast its soteriological message in the language of Wang Bi's Daoism. They presented the puzzling status of Nirvana as similar to *Dao* – a mystical dialectic between *something* and *nothing*. Buddhism and Cosmological Daoism began to blend.

Neo-Confucianism consists of a plethora of similar but rival metaphysical systems structured around 理 *li*^pattern:tendency^, 氣 *qi*^material force^ and 心 *xin*^mind^. Neo-Confucianism designed these schemes to give a naturalistic explanation of moral motivation. They resurrected Mencius' moral mysticism both for its moral content and as an alternative to Buddhist metaphysics.

The externalist school of *li* sought mastery of human motivation by coming to understand *li* in nature. The internalist school of mind saw us as projecting our morals on the world in action. We *infused* the world with *li* in acting. Differences in these Neo-Confucian moral structures are variations on the classical linguistic idealist theme of an amorphous chaos organized or divided by moral consciousness or action.

BIBLIOGRAPHY

Bao, Z.: 'Language and world view in Ancient China', *Philosophy East and West* (1990), 195–219.

Graham, A.: *Later Mohist Logic, Ethics and Science* (Hong Kong and London: Chinese University Press, 1978).

Graham, A.: *Disputers of the Tao: Philosophical Argument in Ancient China* (La Salle, IL: Open Court, 1989).

Hansen, C.: *Language and Logic in Ancient China* (Ann Arbor, MI: University of Michigan Press, 1983).

Hansen, C.: *A Daoist Theory of Chinese Thought* (New York: Oxford University Press, 1992).

Schwartz, B.: *The World of Thought in Ancient China* (Cambridge, MA: Harvard University Press, 1985).

CHAD HANSEN

metaphysics in India Positions and polemics regarding what there is have been prevalent in India since at least 1500 BC. A hymn of *ṛg veda* debates whether this cosmos came out of reality, nothingness or neither. Systematic solutions or dissolutions of problems regarding the external world, the self, creation, CAUSATION, UNIVERSALS, SPACE AND TIME, SUBSTANCE, motion, etc., were already being argued for and against when Gautama Buddha started his spiritual quest. Mutually disagreeing 'affirmers' of the Vedic orthodoxy as well as sophists, sceptics, materialists and other 'deniers' were so relentless in wrangling with each other about these issues that early Buddhism reacted by a positivistic jettisoning of all metaphysical questions as unedifying. Ironically enough, subsequent Buddhism itself branched into four fiercely metaphysical schools roughly classifiable as naive realism (*vaibhāṣika*), critical realism (*sautrāntika*), subjective idealism (*yogācāra*) and voidism (*mādhyamika*). While the so called Vedic schools all affirmed the existence of a deathless SOUL in each mortal body and the *cārvāka* physicalists rejected the idea of any self other than the perishable live body, the Buddhists reduced each 'self' into a transmigrating causal claim (set and series) of partly physical and partly psychological ephemeral *factors*. Noticing the elements of truth in both eternalism and flux theory, in physicalism and dualism – the judicious *jaina* metaphysicians defined a real substance as what originates, dies and stays on in some form or other and recognized the soul to be temporally limitless but spatially limited by (though distinct from) the body. Competing metaphysical views did not come as successive waves but flourished in parallel throughout the history of classical Indian philosophy until their growth was arrested by some foreign political aggression or other.

TYPES OF METAPHYSICS

Risking overgeneralization one could find at least ten different answers to the question 'What *really* exists?' in the history of these parallel Indian philosophies.

(M1) Nothing exists (Nihilism, reported and critiqued in *nyāya sūtras* 4.1.37 through 4.1.57).

(M2) Only strictly momentary particulars exist (*sautrāntika* Buddhism).

(M3) Numerically *one* entity exists which is pure objectless ownerless consciousness because all plurality is illusory (non-dualistic *vedānta*).

(M4) Only one sort of thing (material or mental) exists (*cārvāka* materialism or *yogācāra* Buddhist idealism).

(M5) Only one *independent* substance (= God) exists but there are other dependent attributive realities, namely individual souls and material objects (qualified monistic *vedānta*).

(M6) Two *sorts* of things exist, namely, plurality of uncaused and uncausing selves and one evolving primal matter (*sāṃkhya-yoga*).

(M7) *Seven* basic types of item exist, namely, Substance (an apple), unrepeatable Quality (the red colour of it), Motion (its rolling or falling), Universal (the fruitness or substanceness it exemplifies), Inherence Relation (which ties the apple to its parts or the colour to the apple or the colourness to the colour), Ultimate Differentiator (that which marks off one eternal atom from another of its own kind) and Not-being (the apple's *absence prior* to its coming into being, its *absence after* it has been eaten up, its *atemporal absence* on top of Mt Everest or its *otherness* from a peach) (*nyāya-vaiśeṣika*).

(M8) The answer depends on what point of view one takes. Truth lies in accepting affirmative, negative, agnostic and combined answers to each fundamental question as correct within its own presupposed conceptual framework (*jaina* non-one-edge-ism).

(M9) The correct answer dawns on you through silence following a reasoned refutation of all metaphysical views (*mādhyamika* Buddhism of Nāgārjuna).

(M10) Since all reasoning about what lies beyond current perception is essentially flawed, we should stop examining life and follow happy-go-lucky common sense (*cārvāka* naturalism).

Often, at the root of these various answers to the question about the nature and number of reals lay differences regarding *what it is to be real*. Thus existence has been *defined* by the Buddhists as capacity to cause something, by the non-dualist *vedantin* as freedom from all limitations of space, time and individuality, by the *vaiśeṣika* as possession of a determinate own-nature (which makes something knowable and designatable) and by yet other Indian philosophers (e.g. Kumārila Bhaṭṭa) as relatedness to time.

How any one of these definitions can lead to a special metaphysical worldview could be illustrated by the following reductio argument proposed for the Buddhist 'revisionary metaphysics' of universal flux (M2).

(1) *Suppose* that a endures for more than a moment (e.g. for t_1, t_2, t_3, etc.).

(2) a exists if, and only if, a is causally productive (Definition).

(3) Either a actually produces effects at both t_1 and t_2 or a has an unexercised capacity at t_1 and produces something only at t_2 (or any such later time).

(4) If a actually produces some effect at every moment of its life, it could not be producing numerically the same effect twice, so it must be producing e_1 at t_1

319

and e_2 at t_2. In that case, a splits into two: the momentary producer of e_1 which failed to produce e_2 and the distinct entity which produced e_2 but could not have produced e_1. There just remains no continuant real called 'a'.

(5) If a could produce something at $t1$ but did not do so for want of an aiding condition which brings out its latent capacity at t_2, then it is either the momentary auxiliary or its combination with a which gets the causal credit. Hence it is either the enriched a of $t2$ or an aiding factor – both momentary entities – that can claim causal efficacy and thereby existence, not a-as-such.

(6) Since a is shown to be causally sterile at all but one moment of its putative persistence, it cannot be said to be real *qua* enduring. It is close *resemblance* of the perpetually cropping up and vanishing particulars which is mistaken for diachronic identity.

(7) Therefore, only the momentary is real.

Of course, the supporting arguments for each premise above hide a number of assumptions which were challenged especially by the 'descriptive metaphysicians' of the *nyāya-vaiśeṣika* school.

REALISM VERSUS ANTIREALISM

For at least a thousand years the idea of an enduring substance has been defended by the realists who make the following four claims of irreducibility:

(1) A whole is not reducible to parts or their mere collection.
(2) The substantival seat of qualities is not reducible to the qualities or their collection.
(3) The genuine universal (e.g. substancehood or colourhood) which inheres in particular substances, events or qualities is not reducible to its substrata (*see* SUBSTRATUM).
(4) The object of experience is not reducible to someone's experience of the object.

With a series of ingenious dilemmas such as: 'Either the central atom is touched from all six sides by six other atoms to make up a bigger whole and the partless atom falls into six parts which is a contradiction, or the whole gets no bigger than and no more perceptible than a single atom' – the Buddhist idealists attacked all atomistic accounts of an extended substance (*see* ATOMISM). The particular qualities – a unique category of entities admitted by *vaiśeṣika* realists – include episodic wishes, pains, awarenesses and decisions from which the existence of a substantial self is inferred with the major premise that qualities cannot subsist without a substance. The 'Self-less' Buddhist resists this move by denying (2). Against universals Buddhist antirealism took the very distinctive form of an exclusionism which showed that e.g. humans have nothing in common except non-membership in the mixed set of non-humans.

But naturally the last irreducibility claim drew the maximum amount of dialectical attention. Both *mīmāṃsā* and *nyāya-vaiśeṣika* philosophers defended the knowledge-independence of the objects of veridical experience while *yogācāra* Buddhists like Vasubandhu used the argument from illusion and dream as well as the irrefutable point that we can never *get* a blue which is not glued to some awareness of blue. One new argument that Dignāga gives goes straight into the heart of the issue. There are two essential aspects to the notion of an *object* of veridical cognition, namely, it should be both the actual *cause* as well as the manifest *topic* of the cognitive state. Under the realist picture of an extended middle-sized body figuring as the object these two aspects will always fall apart.

Even if the atoms cause the sensory awareness, since the latter does not bear the form of those atoms they are not the (intended) topic of that cognition. (Dignāga, *Alambana Parikṣā*, verse 1)

But this falling part of the cause and the topic typically happens in illusion (the rope is the cause and the snake is the topic) and dream. So externality of the perceptual object is nothing but a beginningless error of our separative intellect.

Excellent retorts to such subjective idealistic arguments came not only from the realist but also from the transcendental idealist, Śaṃkara, who rejected the illusionism of the Buddhist by clinchers like the following:

If a thing outside awareness is as impossible as a barren woman's son how can we even feel *as if* something is outside? Nothing even *appears* to be like an impossibility.

Yet Śaṃkara himself is a non-dualist believing in nothing but one undifferentiated consciousness (M3). He would answer the question 'What is the status of the external world?' by distinguishing the practical and the noumenal level (*see* NOUMENAL/PHENOMENAL).

IS CHANGE REAL?

'The world of the real is a world in which this acts on that, changes it' remarked FREGE. CHANGE in its turn is understood in terms of cause and effect. So traditional Indian ontologists rephrased the question 'Is the changing world of ordinary experience real?' in the following canonical form:

'Is the effect real (dormant in its *stuff-cause*) before its origination?'

Answers to this question have divided philosophers into four major camps:

(1) The cause perishes before the effect can arise (Flux Theory of Buddhism).
(2) The effect is a new entity which was not there at all before its production (Beginningism of *nyāya-vaiśeṣika*).
(3) The effect slumbers in its material cause before its so-called emergence; it is stuff-wise the *same* as the cause (Alternationism of *sāṃkhya-yoga*).
(4) The cause alone is real, the effect is an insubstantial projection of variety due

to 'name and form', it is neither real nor unreal. Its apparent novelty is an inexplicable trick played on us – a magic or *māyā* (Magicism of the non-dualist Śaṃkara).

Beginningism (2), associated with (M7) turns on the literal meaning of the term 'origination', using the following arguments:

First: That yoghurt is distinct from milk, a cup from the clay is undeniably given in perception.
Second: If these effects were of the same nature as their stuff-causes they would have served the same purposes, but surely we can not drink from a lump of clay.
Third: If the effect were pre-existent in the cause the instrumental agents' effort to bring it about will be strictly redundant. Surely the weaver does not spend all that energy just to 'uncover' what is already there in the fibres! (The architect of the world according to this view, depends on pre-existent atoms and constructs a world that the eternal souls deserve. Yet he is rightly called a 'creator'. The *sāṃkhya* alternationist naturally finds such a theism otiose.)
Fourth: If the effect is merely 'manifested' rather than produced (as the alterationist insists) then at least the *manifestation* of it is one new entity which was previously absent. If the manifestation of yoghurt itself can be admitted to be absent in the milk, why not the yoghurt itself?

Alternationism (3) of (M6), on the other hand, stands on the following strong considerations:

First: A total non-entity like tortoise-wool cannot be made to exist. Since the effect is made to exist, it could not have been a non-entity. What counts as 'change' or 'origination' in common parlance is *transformation*.

When giving up old attributes new attributes are assumed by a substance which remains fixed in its essential nature – we call it *transformation*.

If the novelty of the attributes meant addition to reality then every time a crumpled piece of cloth is smoothed out an increment in reality would have to be acknowledged. Genuine efforts could be needed to *reveal* a pre-existent jar when it is buried or lost in the lumpy form of clay. (The analogy is then stretched to the cosmic level where the entire world of receiving sense organs and received gross earth, water, air, fire and their evolutes are said to have been already contained in the three basic 'affective strands' – pleasure, pain, torpor – an equipoise of which is taken as the root cause or *Nature*).

Second: If the effect even before emergence has to *be related* to its own cause and not arise randomly just from any old stuff, then it must *be* there when the cause is there.

Third: When accounting for causal regularities even the Beginningist resorts to the idiom of '*c*'s exclusive capacity to evolve as *e*'. What is *c*'s capacity for *e* except *e*'s potential *existence* in *c*?

Fourth: In spite of different purposes served (which is compatible with sameness, e.g. use of fire to burn and to cook food) the stuff-cause and the effect are ultimately of the same *nature*. To prove this *Sāṃkhya* uses physical considerations like: the table cannot be heavier than all its constituent causes put together; linguistic arguments like: if *a* and *b* are separate it makes sense to say 'bring *a* and also *b*', but to say 'bring the cloth and also its threads' is nonsense.

Of course, the debate goes on. In the crucial first argument the Alterationist is distorting the Beginningist who is not saying that the effect is a sheer unreality before its origination. It is just said to be *absent*. Absence (e.g.

of sweetness in stone) which belongs to the seventh category of existents admitted by the *nyāya-vaiśeṣika* schools has the peculiarity that it requires a real absentee (sweetness) which must be there in the past, future or some other place (e.g. in honey). The table is new only in the sense that it is an absentee to its prior not-being in the lumber. Since prior absence is not a mere nothing, Beginningism cannot be reduced to the absurdity that something comes out of pure nothing.

Now, in spite of emphasizing the essential sameness of effect and cause, *Sāṃkhya* did not impugn the *reality* of the plural world of effects which emerges from the unified three-stranded 'Nature'. Material objects were as real for them as numerous witnessing centres of pure consciousness (for *yoga* one such centre is Omniscient and Perfect and hence, worship-worthy though by no means a creator) which seems to get involved in this business of enjoying suffering and getting confused with nature. Both Alternationists and Beginningists are realists, whereas Śaṃkara, while rejecting subjective idealism, takes up the Upaniṣadic idea that only the ever-present and the changeless must be real. Being lumpy or shaped as a cup or pulverized are states which come and go (like the illusory mirage-water) whereas clay – the generic stuff – remains ever present. The only ever present stuff ultimately is pure consciousness (which is not to be confused with some*one* or someone's awareness *of* something). The plurality and objecthood displayed by the world are neither as real as this ever unnegated consciousness which is called *brahman* (All) or *ātman* (self) nor as unreal as an unpresentable impossibility. It is a presented falsehood or *māyā* which literally means magic. Śaṃkara's non-dualism has been the most well-known, though not the only, philosophical background for India's spiritual traditions but it hardly went unchallenged. Rāmānuja and Madhva attacked the notion of inexplicable presented falsity vigorously. Since empirical knowledge proceeds by limiting its object as *not-another-thing* the non-dualists' rejection of all difference as logically incoherent led to a sort of absolute scepticism. This made Vedic non-dualists sound very similar to the anti-Vedic voidists. Committed and complicated metaphysical accounts of the world thrived as they still do in India largely in the hands of the neo-*nyāya vaiśeṣika* authors whose modern disciples now try to rejuvenate the realist tradition by using critical and comparable insights from contemporary western philosophy. Vedantic monism, sceptical materialism, as well as *jaina* meta-ontological alternativism, keep contributing to the osmosis with western analytical and continental philosophy making the current Indian scene in metaphysics just as diverse as the young Buddha had once found it to be.

BIBLIOGRAPHY

Bhaduri, S.: *Studies in Nyaya Vaisesika Metaphysics* (Poona: B.O.R. Institute, 1975).

Bhattacharya, G.N.: *Essays in Analytical Philosophy* (Calcutta: Sanskrit Pustaka Bhandar, 1989).

Bhattacharya, K.C.: *Search for the Absolute in Neo-Vedanta* (University Press of Hawaii, 1976).

Chattopadhyaya, D.: *Carvaka/Lokayata* (Calcutta: I.C.P.R., 1990).

Larson, G.J. *et al.* eds: *Encyclopedia of Indian Philosophy* vol. 4 *Samkhya* (Princeton, 1983).

Matilal, B.K.: *The Central Philosophy of Jainism* (Ahmedabad: L.D. Institute, 1981).

Mookerjee, S.: *The Buddhist Philosophy of Universal Flux* (Delhi: Motilal Benarasidas, 1980).

Potter, K. ed.: *Indian Metaphysics and Epistemology* (Princeton, NJ: Princeton University Press, 1978).

Potter, K. ed.: *Advaita Vedanta upto Samkara* (Princeton, NJ: Princeton University Press, 1980).

Smart, N.: *Doctrine and Argument in Indian Philosophy* (London: Allen and Unwin, 1964).

ARINDAM CHAKRABARTI

metaphysics in Latin America The history of philosophy in Latin America may be divided into four periods of development: colonial, independentist, positivist and contemporary. Except for the second, all of them had something to contribute to the history of metaphysics in the region.

COLONIAL PERIOD (1492–1750)

This period was dominated by scholasticism. The texts studied were those of medieval scholastics, primarily AQUINAS and DUNS SCOTUS, and of their Iberian commentators, particular SUÁREZ. The university curriculum was modelled after that of Iberian universities and instructors produced both commentaries and systematic treatises. The philosophical concerns centred on logical and metaphysical issues inherited from the Middle Ages and on political and legal questions raised by the discovery and colonization of America. Examples of the former were the logic of terms and propositions and the problems of UNIVERSALS and INDIVIDUATION; among the latter were the rights of the native population.

The main philosophical centres during the period were Mexico and Peru. The first teacher of philosophy in the new world was Alonzo de la Vera Cruz (*c.*1504–84), who composed several treatises on logic and metaphysics. Perhaps the most important figure of the period was Antonio Rubio (1548–1615), author of the most celebrated scholastic book written in the new world, *Logica mexicana* (1605). Other scholastics of note were Tomás de Mercado (*c.*1530–75) and Alfonso Briceño (*c.*1587–1669).

Scholasticism exercised complete control over the intellectual life of colonial Latin America, but some authors were also influenced by humanism and therefore rejected the logico-metaphysical concerns of scholastics. Among these were Bartolomé de las Casas (1484–1566), Carlos Sigüenza y Góngora (1645–1700), and Sor Juana Inés de la Cruz (1651–1695).

INDEPENDENTIST PERIOD (1750–1850)

The leading intellectuals of this period ceased to be preoccupied with the issues that had concerned scholastics and became interested in social and political questions. They found inspiration in DESCARTES, LOCKE, Jean-Jacques Rousseau (1712–78), François-Marie Arouet de Voltaire (1694–1778), and other modern philosophers. Most of these intellectuals were men of action. As a result there is limited theoretical value in their views and no metaphysical speculation.

Among the authors who stand out are Francisco Javier Clavijero (1731–87), Francisco de Mont'Alverne (1784–1858), Simón Bolívar (1783–1830), José María Morelos y Paván (1765–1815) and Mariano Moreno (1778–1811).

POSITIVIST PERIOD (1850–1910)

During this period positivism became not only the most popular philosophy in Latin America but also the official philosophy of some countries. Latin American positivism was an eclectic point of view that included elements from the thought of such European thinkers as Comte (1798–1857), Herbert Spencer (1820–1903) and Ernst Haeckel (1834–1919). Positivists emphasized the explicative value of empirical science while rejecting metaphysics. All knowledge is to be based on experience and its value is found in its practical applications. Their motto, preserved in the Brazilian flag, was 'Order and Progress'. Positivism left little room for freedom and values, since it views the universe as moving inexorably according to mechanistic laws.

Among those who prepared the way for positivism are the Argentinians Esteban Echevarría (1805–51) and Juan Bautista Alberdi (1812–84); they had an interest in French socialism. Another precursor was the Venezuelan Andrés Bello (1781–1865), who attempted to reduce metaphysics to psychology in *Filosofía del entendimiento* (1881).

The most distinguished advocates of positivism were the Argentinian José Ingenieros (1877–1925) and the Cuban Enrique José Varona (1849–1933). Both modified positivism. Ingenieros made room in his thought for metaphysics which, according to him, studies the realm of the 'yet-to-be-experienced'. And Varona subscribed to views of human conduct that went beyond purely mechanistic explanations.

In Mexico the leading positivists were Gabino Barreda (1818–81) and Justo Sierra (1848–1912), and in Brazil Miguel Lemos (1854–1916) and Raimundo Teixera Mendes (1855–1927). The most prominent Chilean positivists were José Victorino Lastarria (1817–88) and José Valentín Letelier (1852–1919).

CONTEMPORARY PERIOD (1910 TO THE PRESENT)

The contemporary period begins with the demise of positivism. The first generation of contemporary thinkers, called the 'generation of founders' by Francisco Romero, rebelled against positivism: Alejandro Korn (1860–1936) in Argentina, Alejandro Octavio Deústua (1849–1945) in Peru, José Vasconcelos (1882–1959) and Antonio Caso (1883–1946) in Mexico, Enrique José Molina (1871–1956) in Chile, Carlos Vaz Ferreira (1872–1958) in Uruguay, and Raimundo de Farias Brito (1862–1917) in Brazil.

The aims and concerns of these philosophers were similar. In spite of their positivist training, they rejected positivism's dogmatic intransigence, mechanistic determinism, and emphasis on pragmatic values. They welcomed metaphysical ideas and some went on to develop elaborate metaphysical systems. Deústua developed a detailed criticism of positivistic determinism in *Las ideas de orden y de libertad en la historia del pensamiento humano* (1917–19). Caso proposed a view of man as a spiritual reality that surpasses nature in *La existencia como economía, como desinterés y como caridad* (1916). And

Vasconcelos developed a metaphysical system based on aesthetic principles in *El monismo estético* (1918).

One of the earliest criticisms of positivism is found in Vaz Ferreira's *Logica viva* (1910), where he rejected the abstract, scientific logic favoured by positivists in favour of a logic of life. The earliest attempt at developing an alternative to positivism, however, was produced by Farias Brito. In *Finalidade do mundo* (1895–1905), he conceived the world as an intellectual activity identified with God's thought.

Positivism was superseded by the founders with the help of ideas imported from France and Germany. The process began with the influence of Boutroux and Bergson, evident in Molina's *La filosofía de Bergson* (1916), but it was consolidated when ORTEGA Y GASSET introduced the philosophy of Max Scheler (1874–1928), Nicolai Hartmann (1882–1950), and other German philosophers during his visit to Argentina in 1916. Korn is exceptional in that he turned to KANT in his search for an alternative to dogmatic positivism in *La libertad creadora* (1920–2).

Among the thinkers who followed the founders, the most important is Francisco Romero (1891–1962), who in his *Teoría del hombre* (1952) developed a philosophical anthropology within the context of a metaphysics of transcendence. The influence of Ortega is evident in Samuel Ramos (1897–1959), who appropriated his perspectivism and the metaphysics of life in *Hacia un nuevo humanismo* (1940). Carlos Astrada (1894–1970) displays the impact of EXISTENTIALISM and PHENOMENOLOGY in *El juego existencial* (1933). And Carlos Mariátegui (1895–1930) is a representative of MARXISM. His *Siete ensayos de interpretación de la realidad peruana* seek to adapt Marxist thought to the Peruvian sociopolitical situation.

The introduction of recent European philosophy was helped in the 1930s and 1940s by the arrival of a substantial group of Spanish philosophers who were escaping the Spanish Civil War. The most important among these was José Gaos (1900–69), for he was the mentor of a generation of influential Mexican philosophers.

With the generation born around 1910, Latin American philosophy achieved what Romero called a 'state of normalcy'. Philosophy established itself as a professional discipline. The core of this generation was composed by philosophers working in the German tradition. Risieri Frondizi (Argentina, 1910–83), Eduardo García Máynez (Mexico, b. 1908), Juan Llambías de Azevedo (Uruguay, 1907–72), and Miguel Reale (Brazil, b. 1910) were all influenced by Scheler and Hartmann, and concerned themselves primarily with axiology and philosophical anthropology. They also engaged in metaphysical speculation, but only indirectly.

There were also representatives of other traditions in this generation. Following Ramos, Leopoldo Zea (Mexico, b. 1912) initiated the controversy concerning the identity of Latin American philosophy, and Francisco Miró Quesada's (Peru, b. 1918) concern with logic led him to the exploration of rationality.

The overall philosophical attitude toward metaphysics in the period that goes from 1940 to 1960 did not change substantially from the one that preceded it. Metaphysics was not the centre of attention, but metaphysical problems and views were ubiquitous. However, this attitude has changed markedly in the three decades that have passed since 1960 as a result of the progressive influence of analytic philosophy, the philosophy of liberation, and Marxism. Adherents to these philosophical currents tend to be hostile toward metaphysics. Marxists see it as a bourgeois enterprise used to preserve capitalist privilege; philosophers of liberation look upon it as an import, and thus an obstacle to intellectual and social independence; and analysts are suspicious of the language it uses and the problems it addresses. Since these three philosophical currents appear to have the upper hand in Latin American philosophy at present, the future of metaphysics in the region looks precarious at best.

BIBLIOGRAPHY

Berdtson, C.A.E. ed.: *Readings in Latin American Philosophy* (Columbia, MO: University of Missouri Press, 1949).

Crawford, W.R.: *A Century of Latin American Thought* (Cambridge, MA: 1944); rev. edn (New York: Praeger University Series-606, 1966).

Davis, H.E.: *Latin American Thought: A Historical Introduction* (Baton Rouge, LA: 1972); 2nd edn (New York: The Free Press, 1974).

Gracia, J.J.E. ed.: *Latin American Philosophy in the Twentieth Century: Man, Values, and the Search for Philosophical Identity* (Buffalo, NY: Prometheus, 1986).

Gracia, J.J.E. ed.: *Contemporary Latin American Philosophy*, double issue of *Philosophical Forum* 20 (1989–90). Articles by Cerutti-Guldberg, Gracia, Jaksić, Sánchez Vázquez, Schutte, Sobrevilla and Zea.

Gracia, J.J.E. and Camurati, M. eds: *Philosophy and Literature in Latin America: A Critical Assessment of the Current Situation* (Albany, NY: SUNY Press, 1989). Articles by Almeida, Biagini, Gracia, Martí, Sturm and others.

Gracia, J.J.E., Rabossi, E., Villanueva, E. and Dascal, M. eds: *Philosophical Analysis in Latin America* Synthese Library 172 (Dordrecht: Reidel, 1984).

Sánchez Reulet, A. ed.: *Contemporary Latin American Philosophy: A Selection*, trans. W.R. Trask (Albuquerque, NM: University of New Mexico Press, 1954).

Stabb, M.: *In Quest of Identity: Patterns in the Spanish-American Essay of Ideas, 1860–1960* (Chapel Hill, NC: University of North Carolina Press, 1967).

Zea, L.: *The Latin American Mind*, trans. J.H. Abbot and L. Dunham (Norman, OK: University of Oklahoma Press, 1963).

JORGE J.E. GRACIA

Mill, John Stuart (1806–73) British philosopher, politician and economist. The main source for Mill's metaphysical views is his *Examination of Sir William Hamilton's Philosophy* (1865), a detailed criticism of the Scottish philosopher. In it Mill endorses a doctrine which was then accepted, as he says, on all sides: 'the doctrine of the Relativity of Knowledge to the knowing mind'. It affirms that our knowledge and conception of objects external to consciousness consists entirely in the conscious states they excite in us, or that we can imagine them exciting in us.

The doctrine leaves open the question whether objects exist independently of consciousness. It may be held that there are such objects, although we can only know them by hypothesis from their effects on us. Mill rejects this view. Instead he argues that external objects amount to nothing more than 'Permanent Possibilities of Sensation', proceeding by analysis of the content and origin of our notion of an 'external substance'. We acquire from experience the idea of a possible sensation – a sensation we are not feeling, but would feel if certain conditions were present. Such a possibility is permanent, not in the sense that it cannot cease to obtain, but in the sense that it obtains whether or not it is realized. We can be confident that the sensation would occur if the antecedent condition were present. (As well as 'permanent' Mill uses other terms, such as 'certified' or 'guaranteed'.)

We discover correlations between permanent possibilities of sensation. Our ideas of CAUSATION, power and activity come to be connected not with sensations but directly with these possibilities. They are the important thing to us, in that practical consequences depend on them. Thus they acquire distinguishing names; these names come to be considered not merely as naming perdurable possibilities, existing independently of the particular sensations we happen to experience – but external substances, existing independently of sensation as such, and causing it.

Mill does not therefore claim, in the manner of twentieth-century phenomenalists, that our statements about external objects can be analysed *without remainder* into statements, including conditional statements, about sensation. His points rather are these: that facts about permanent possibilities are what the truth or falsity of statements about external objects pragmatically turn on, and that there is no need to postulate external objects to explain the origin of our concept of external objects. (*See* PHENOMENALISM.)

But even if the concept's origin can be explained as Mill suggests, why should the *existence* of Permanent Possibilities of Sensation, and their correlations, not be explained by appeal to external causes? It is at just this point that the inductivism Mill develops in his *System of Logic* (1843) comes in. Such an inference would be a case of hypothetical reasoning, to an explanation of experience which transcended all possible data of experience – and that is what inductivism rejects.

But Mill does not highlight this point. His own stress is on the alleged fact that our perceptual concepts can be explained without supposing perception to be a mode of knowledge of external objects. Memory, in contrast, he acknowledges in the manner of REID to be 'ultimate' – the point seems to be that it and other phenomena cannot be explained without assuming that memory does yield knowledge of past events, and thus acknowledging it as an ultimate source of knowledge.

Our knowledge of mind, like our knowledge of matter, Mill thinks to be 'entirely relative'. But he finds a difficulty in the view that it can be resolved into a series of feelings and possibilities of feeling. For 'the thread of consciousness' contains memories and expectations as well sensations. But to remember or expect a feeling is not simply to believe that it has existed or will exist; it is to believe that *I myself* have experienced or will experience that feeling. Thus if the mind is to be a series of feelings, we seem forced to conclude that it is a series that can be aware of itself as a series.

So despite his reluctance to accept that Mind is a 'so-called substance', the fact of SELF-CONSCIOUSNESS drives Mill to recognize in it a reality greater than the existence as a Permanent Possibility which is the only

reality he concedes to Matter. Yet he misstates the difficulty, because he does not fully think through the paraphrasis which is required. (The method of paraphrasis was familiar to him from BENTHAM.) The view that mind resolves itself into a series of feelings need not literally identify selves with series: it paraphrases talk of selves in terms of talk of series.

Ultimately, on Mill's view, and discounting his uncertainty about what to say of the self, all that exists are experiences in a temporal order. But he claims that this metaphysics is consistent with common-sense realism, and his general standpoint is thoroughly naturalistic; he sees minds as proper parts of a natural order. The difficulties of this begin to emerge when we ask whether the feelings referred to in Mill's metaphysics are the very same as those referred to by common sense – and explained by physical antecedents. Must there not be a Kantian distinction here, between transcendental and empirical levels, a distinction which would run against the NATURALISM of Mill's philosophy? The same difficulties emerge for later phenomenalists, but Mill never addresses them. (*See* KANT.)

WRITINGS

System of Logic (London: Longmans, 1843).
Examination of Sir William Hamilton's Philosophy (London: Longmans, 1865).

BIBLIOGRAPHY

Scarre, G.: *Logic and Reality in the Philosophy of John Stuart Mill* (Dordrecht: Kluwer Academic Publishers, 1989).
Skorupski, J.: *John Stuart Mill* (London: Routledge, 1989).

JOHN SKORUPSKI

mind/body problem There is a philosophical mind/body problem because, on the one hand, mental phenomena seem to be *sui generis* and not reducible to or explicable in terms of physical phenomena and, on the other hand, the mental and the physical seem to interact causally, nomologically and explanatorily. The resulting tension can be formulated in terms of the following principles:

(1) Mental events and properties are not reducible to or explicable in terms of physical events and properties.
(2) Mental events and properties are involved in causal explanations of other mental events and physical events.
(3) The physical is causally and explanatorily closed.

Principle (1) has been supported by appeals to intuition, argument, and failures to produce an account of mental phenomena in purely physical terms. These all turn on the central features of the mental, CONSCIOUSNESS and INTENTIONALITY. Conscious mental states are subjective, private and possess a qualitative or 'what it is like to be' character (see PUBLIC/PRIVATE). For example, a person's feeling of fear when looking down from a great height has a qualitative character of which only that person is directly aware. It has been argued that these features of consciousness cannot be reduced to and defy explication in terms of physical properties since the physical is inherently objective, intersubjectively accessible, and seems to lack anything corresponding to qualitative character. Intentionality refers to the fact that certain mental states, for example, thinking that mangoes are tasty, possess semantic properties; it is about mangoes and has the truth condition that they are tasty (see CONTENT). It has been argued that such semantic properties are normative, for example, one *ought* to apply 'mango' only to things which are mangoes. And nothing purely physical can give rise to this normativity. Whether or not this is correct, it is difficult to see how intentionality can emerge from physical states and processes.

Until relatively recently it was almost universally held that consciousness and intentionality are inextricably connected. Consciousness seems always to be conscious of something and some writers see consciousness as the source of intentionality. But after FREUD, these two marks of the mental are frequently separated and cognitive psychologists feel no qualms positing intentional states which are not conscious and not even accessible to consciousness.

DESCARTES, whose writings shaped our current understanding of the mind/body problem, argued that since he could clearly and distinctly (see CLEAR AND DISTINCT) conceive of his mind existing without body and body without mind, these are different and separable substances. He claimed that mental substance is essentially thinking and non-extended while physical substance is essentially extended and non-thinking. By 'thinking' Descartes referred to a process which is both essentially conscious and intentional. He rejected principle (3) and believed that certain behaviour – specifically linguistic and mathematical behaviour which exhibit a certain creativity – cannot be accounted for causally entirely in terms of physical events. Descartes' position, *interactive dualism*, encounters a number of difficulties. One is that within his framework it is difficult to understand how mental events and physical events causally interact since in his mechanistic physics causation is by contact. Descartes' well-known attempt at a solution is that mind and body are joined in the pineal gland. At best this localizes the problem rather than solves it since it fails to explain how non-extended substance can be in contact with extended substance. A more serious problem is that as the physical sciences advanced the following version of principle (3) became increasingly plausible

(3′) To the extent that a physical event (i.e. the change in the value of a physical property) can be causally explained, it can be to that extent causally explained by reference only to other physical events.

(3′) contradicts (1) and (2). If the most complete causal explanation of a physical event makes reference only to other physical events, and if mental events are distinct from physical events then, contrary to (2), they cannot be causes of physical events.

After Descartes, philosophers formulated alternatives to interactive dualism which attempt to accommodate (3'). LEIBNIZ's *parallelism* rejects (2) and holds that although the mental and the physical are causally isolated from each other they evolve in a pre-established harmony which gives rise to the illusion of causal interaction. MALEBRANCHE's *occasionalism* maintains that neither mental nor physical events are causes but that they are both the effects of a common cause, God's will (*see* OCCASION, OCCASIONALISM). And *epiphenomenalism* claims that physical events are causes of both physical and mental events but mental events are causally inert. In contrast to these views which endorse (1), HOBBES and GASSENDI claimed that all states and processes including mental ones are physical. This latter position is *physicalism* or *materialism* and some version or other of it has dominated twentieth-century approaches to the problem.

Two versions of *physicalism* were popular in the 1950s, *analytical behaviourism* and *the identity theory*. According to crude analytical behaviourism, each mentalistic statement (e.g., 'John has a toothache') is equivalent in meaning to a statement referring to patterns of behaviour or dispositions to behave (e.g., 'John is writhing and pointing to his tooth and . . .'). Analytic behaviourism rejects (2). According to RYLE, a proponent of a sophisticated version of this view, it is a 'category mistake' to say that a mental event causes behaviour since mentalistic statements do not describe the neural events which cause the behaviour but describe either patterns of behaviour or dispositions to behave. Analytic behaviourism can be formulated less crudely but even in its most sophisticated forms it strikes most philosophers as immensely implausible.

The 'identity theory' says that mental predicates differ in meaning from behavioural predicates and other physical predicates but that, as a matter of contingent fact, they refer to neurophysiological properties, and descriptions of mental events

refer to neurophysiological events. Identity theorists hoped to discover these identities by finding 'bridge laws' connecting mental with physical predicates – for example, when, and only when, x has the experience of a toothache x's C-fibres fire in such and such a way. It was supposed that such bridge laws justify the identities. According to the identity theory mental events cause behaviour (since neurophysiological events cause behaviour) and mental properties enter into the laws which explain behaviour since they are neurophysiological properties and these enter into laws. So the identity theory rejects (1) but is compatible with (2) and (3/3').

The identity theory came under severe criticism during the 1970s. It seems to have the implausible consequence that members of different species do not share mental properties since they do not share neurophysiological properties. Another problem is that nothing like the system of bridge laws required to support the identity theory has been forthcoming. But the objection that probably has been most persuasive against the identity theory is that it fails to explain how neurophysiological properties exemplify consciousness and intentionality. It has been argued by Thomas Nagel (1974) and Frank Jackson (1986) that even a complete understanding of a person's neurophysiology would leave the qualitative character of consciousness unexplained. It is also doubtful that intentional states can be explained in neurophysiological terms. One reason for this, as Hilary Putnam (1967) has argued, is that a person's thoughts and other intentional states possess their semantic properties in virtue of relations between that person and various features of that person's environment. For example, Putnam argued that a person's concept 'water' can only refer to a substance which is causally related to it. If this is correct then two people could be exactly alike with respect to their neurophysiological properties but differ with respect to what they think, believe, and so on since their concepts 'water' may be causally connected to different substances.

There have been a number of responses to the failures of analytic behaviourism and the identity theory. One, extreme response is *eliminativism*. Eliminativists deny that mental properties are ever instantiated (or that there are any such properties). According to eliminativism, statements which attribute mental states are, like statements which attribute supernatural powers, strictly false. This view resolves the tension among (1), (2) and (3/3′) by maintaining (1) and (3) but rejecting (2), since it says that nothing has mental properties. One may wonder whether eliminativism is a coherent view. But even if it is, it is a drastic resolution to the mind/body problem since it involves such a radical revision in our conception of ourselves.

A less drastic response is DAVIDSON's (1970) *anomalous monism*. Davidson argued that the laws required to reduce intentional mental properties to neurophysiological (or other physical) properties do not exist just because intentionality is so different from physical features. Thus, anomalous monism rejects the type-identities assumed by the identity theory. On the other hand, Davidson pointed out that this does not preclude causal interactions between mental and physical *events* since the former are token-identical to physical events and so are subsumable under physical laws. Nor does it preclude, Davidson claims, the mental from *supervening* on the physical (*see* SUPERVENIENCE).

Anomalous monism rejects (1) and endorses (2) and (3) with regard to mental events but endorses (1) with respect to mental properties. This may seem like an appealing compromise but there are some problems. One is that it has seemed to a number of commentators that Davidson's account is a form of *epiphenomenalism* with respect to mental properties (or predicates) since it seems to deny them a role in laws. A second is that it provides no account (and may even be incompatible with there being an account) of the physical basis of intentionality. In fact some philosophers see a tension in Davidson's position since it is not clear that the supervenience of the mental on the physical is compatible with there being no physical account of intentionality.

Another response to the mind/body problem is FUNCTIONALISM. According to the dominant version of this view, types of mental states are functional properties. A functional property is a property which is exemplified by an individual in virtue of that individual's causal and/or nomological relation to other individuals' possessing other properties (which also may be functional properties). It also may be a property such that something which has it performs a function but this is a different use of the word. For example, the property of being a heart is a functional one (in both senses) since something is a heart in virtue of its causal relations to other organs, blood, and so on. Applied to mental properties the idea is that these are characterized in terms of their causal relations to other mental states, to stimuli, and to behaviour. For example, a mental state is a belief in virtue of the ways in which it interacts with perception, desire, behaviour and so on.

Functionalism is compatible with physicalism since it is compatible with the view that functional states are always *realized* in physical mechanisms. The realization relation requires elucidation. One suggestion is that a physical state realizes a functional state just in case it engages in the causal relations which constitute the functional state under appropriate conditions. It also endorses (1) since it does not identify mental states with physical states. It answers one of the objections against the identity theory since it allows for the possibility that different physical states realize the same functional state. Whether or not it allows for a causal and explanatory role for mental properties depends on how property causation and explanation are characterized. But however they are characterized, if mental properties are functional properties then unless they have special problematic features they would be no worse off as far as causation is concerned than non-mental functional properties, for example, being a heart.

It is plausible that functionalism provides a framework for resolving the mind/body problem only if mental properties are functional properties and there are physical states which realize these functional properties. Consciousness and intentionality present different difficulties. Some philosophers have doubted that properties involving consciousness are functional properties at all. They have argued that for any functional property it is possible that it is exemplified without consciousness being exemplified. This kind of argument echoes Descartes's claim that he can clearly and distinctly conceive of body existing without mind and mind existing without body. If this is correct then functionalism cannot provide a complete solution to the mind/body problem. While the same kind of objection has sometimes been made against intentional states a different problem has more usually been stressed. A functionalist account of mental properties should specify for each mental property the functional property with which it is identified and then to explain how such a state can be physically realized. The latter is a problem for intentional states since it is not at all obvious how physical mechanisms can produce the range of human reasoning and behaviour. Specifically, what needs explanation is how physical processes can be sensitive to the semantic properties of intentional states in the way that reasoning clearly is.

The most prominent functionalist approach to intentional mental states, the *representational-computational theory of mind* (RCTM), is designed to solve the problem just mentioned. According to the RCTM, an intentional state – for example the belief that mangoes are tasty – is a functional state which involves a relation between the thinker and a sentence s in a hypothesized language of thought, usually called 'mentalese'. The state is a belief because it satisfies a certain pattern of causal relations to stimuli, other beliefs, desires and behaviour. It is the belief *that mangoes are tasty* because s has the truth condition that mangoes are tasty. According to the RCTM, the mind is a kind of computer or Turing machine and the causal interactions involving mental states are implemented by computations on the syntactic properties of mentalese sentences. Turing machine computations can be sensitive to the semantic properties of the symbols since these can be encoded in the symbols' syntactic properties. A clear example of this is theorem-proving. Since any Turing machine can be implemented by a physical mechanism (e.g. a digital computer) the RCTM is apparently capable of accounting for how physical processes can implement rational mental processes. Because of this the RCTM seems to be a very promising solution to the mind/body problem.

However, there are some difficulties with the RCTM. While credible computational accounts of certain specific mental processes – for example, the perception of the relative distances of objects and the parsing of speech – have been discovered, human cognitive processes in general – for example, the process of reasoning from evidence – have so far resisted computational accounts. The heart of the difficulty is the so called 'frame problem'. The problem is that it seems that just about any belief may be relevant to how someone changes belief upon receipt of new information. It is difficult to see how any program which is actually implemented by the mind can accomplish the required calculations, since every belief will need to be checked for relevance and that, it appears, would require an inordinate number of calculations.

There is an alternative to the RCTM account of mental causation which is alleged to avoid the frame problem. This is the *connectionist* theory of mind. A connectionist network is a collection of nodes in various states of activation connected to one another in something like the manner in which neurons are connected to each other. A change in the level of activation of one node, which may be initiated by a stimulus, causes changes throughout the network resulting in a new global state. Connectionists who are realists about intentional states identify them with features of the network. This kind of model may seem to avoid the frame problem by being able to model how all of a person's beliefs (as represented by the global state of activation of the nodes) may be brought to bear in the process of belief change. But it is far from clear that this model really works since changes in belief typically involve changes in the relevance relations among beliefs and it is not clear how these are to be accounted for by connectionist models. Further, by rejecting the idea that mental processes are sensitive to the syntactic properties of mentalese sentences, connectionism rejects the only account of how mental processes can be sensitive to semantic properties which we have.

Whether the causal processes are computational or connectionist, an intentional realist account compatible with physicalism must explain how physical events can exemplify semantic properties. A number of accounts have been suggested. One, *information theoretic semantics* says that a mentalese predicate $ refers to a property *P* if under suitable conditions instances of *P* causally covary with tokenings of $. Suitable conditions have been characterized in various ways including the proper functioning of cognitive systems. Another kind of account, *inferential role semantics*, says that the content of a mentalese term is a function of its role in inferences and its causal connections with external objects and behaviour. As of this writing, neither of these approaches has been sufficiently developed to evaluate its prospects of success.

The situation with respect to consciousness is bleaker. While not every philosopher accepts the arguments that allegedly show that conscious properties cannot be neurophysiological properties or functional properties, no account which explains how physical properties can be or realize conscious properties has received much support. It has even proved difficult to make explicit the adequacy conditions of an account of consciousness. Recently some philosophers have attempted to make the best of this situation by suggesting that the problem with consciousness lies not with it but with our own cognitive abilities. Colin McGinn (1991) has argued that the failure of philosophers to resolve the mind/body problem suggests that while conscious properties are identical to neurophysiological properties, we are prevented from seeing this since we lack and are biologically incapable of acquiring the concepts required to understand how this can be so. However, in view of the fact that philosophers have been thinking about the problem for only a little more than 300 years, McGinn's pessimism may be a bit premature.

BIBLIOGRAPHY

Block, N.: *Readings in the Philosophy of Psychology* vol. I (Cambridge, MA: Harvard University Press, 1980).

Davidson, D.: 'Mental events' (1970); in his *Essays on Actions and Events* (New York: Oxford University Press, 1980).

Descartes, R.: *Meditating on First Philosophy* (1641).

Fodor, J.A.: *Psychological Explanation* (New York: Random House, 1968).

Fodor, J.A.: *The Language of Thought* (New York: Crowell, 1975).

Fodor, J.A.: *Psychosemantics* (Cambridge, MA: MIT Press, 1987).

Jackson, F.: 'What Mary didn't know' (1986); repr. in *The Nature of Mind* ed. D. Rosenthal (Oxford: Oxford University Press, 1991).

McGinn, C.: *The Problem of Consciousness: Essays Towards a Resolution* (Oxford: Blackwell, 1991).

Nagel, T.: 'What is it like to be a bat?' (1974); repr. in *The Nature of Mind* ed. D. Rosenthal (Oxford: Oxford University Press, 1991).

Putnam, H.: 'The nature of mental states' (1967); repr. in *The Nature of Mind* ed. D. Rosenthal (Oxford: Oxford University Press, 1991).

Rosenthal, D. ed.: *The Nature of Mind* (Oxford: Oxford University Press, 1991). This volume has an extensive bibliography on the mind/body problem.

Ryle, G.: *The Concept of Mind* (New York: Barnes and Noble, 1949).

BARRY LOEWER

modalities and possible worlds Propositions are evaluated not only as true or false, but as necessarily or contingently true or false (*see* PROPOSITION/STATE OF AFFAIRS). That seven plus five equals twelve is necessary; that the Queen of England had seven brothers is merely possible. What sort of fact makes it true that these propositions have the modal status that they have? The problem is sometimes put in epistemological terms: empiricists, for example, ask how experience could give us reason to believe that a proposition is not just true, but necessary (*see* EMPIRICISM). But the real problem behind this question is not epistemological, and not dependent on any thesis about the sources of our knowledge. Even if an oracle gave us unlimited access to matters of fact about the world, we would still face the question, what could make it the case that some fact was not just true, but *had* to be true?

According to one traditional response to this problem, modal propositions are made true by relations of ideas or linguistic convention – not by the way the world is, but by the way we conceive or describe it. But what is necessary is not that we conceive or describe the world as we do. If it is necessary that all uncles are male, it is not because it is necessary that we should have adopted certain conventions to use the words 'uncle' and 'male' in certain ways. What is said to be a matter of convention – that a certain sentence be used to say something that is true no matter what the facts are – is not the same as what is said to be necessary – the proposition itself that this sentence is used to express. So how can linguistic convention explain necessity and possibility? In any case, it is hard to see how some statements widely thought to be necessary could be true by convention. How could the way we talk or think make it true that something (infinitely many primes, or God) exists, or that a particular thing (Joe DiMaggio, say) is a member of a particular kind (human being)?

Necessity, according to a familiar slogan, is truth in all POSSIBLE WORLDS. Contemporary philosophers and logicians have built an intuitive semantics and a formal model theory for modal logic on this traditional idea, and have used freely the imagery of possible worlds in formulating modal theses and arguments. (The most influential early work on both the development of 'possible worlds' semantics and its application to philosophical problems was by Saul Kripke (see Kripke, 1963, 1980).) The framework of possible worlds provides both a representation of the propositions to which modal status is assigned, and an account of the modal status itself. Propositions are understood as sets of possible worlds, or functions from worlds into truth values. The idea is that what is essential to the content of a judgement is its truth conditions, which can be represented by the set of possible circumstances, or worlds, which would make the judgement true. A judgement is a necessary truth if it would be true in any possible circumstances, or if its content is represented by the set of all possible worlds.

The possible worlds representation of content and modality should be regarded, not as a proposed solution to the metaphysical problem of the nature of modal truth, but as a framework for articulating and sharpening the problem. The framework provides only a paraphrase of problematic modal claims in a language in which ambiguities and equivocations are more easily avoided, in which the structure of modal claims and questions are more perspicuously displayed. The thesis that necessity is truth in all possible worlds is like the thesis that to be is to be the value of a bound variable, which is not a claim about what there is, but an attempt to get clearer about what such claims come to. The paraphrase of modal claims and questions into the language of possible worlds solves some of the more superficial puzzles about referential opacity and merely possible individuals by diagnosing scope ambiguities and by separating questions about names and words from questions about the individuals, kinds and properties that the names and words designate. And it brings to the surface and gives new form to the underlying metaphysical questions about the nature of modality.

The central question about the source of modal truth becomes, in the context of the possible worlds framework, a question about the nature of possible worlds. What are possible worlds, and what makes it true that there are just the possible worlds that there are? Different philosophers using the possible worlds framework give radically different answers to this question. Specifically, there is a contrast between *actualist* and *possibilist* accounts of possible worlds, a contrast that comes out in the divergent answers that are given to the following general challenge to the coherence of the idea of a merely possible world:

A merely possible world is a world that is not actual, which is to say a world that does not exist. But the possible worlds account of modality is committed to the existence of merely possible worlds, which seems to mean that it is committed to the existence of things that do not exist.

Any response to this challenge that defends possible worlds must distinguish a sense in which merely possible worlds do not exist and a sense in which they do, but there are two quite different distinctions that do this. The possibilist response (Lewis, 1986) distinguishes two different ranges for the quantifier. There really is a plurality of universes, it says, and they really are universes – things of the same kind as the cosmos in which we live. The actual world is just a part of reality – the part that is temporally and spatially related to us – but we most commonly use the quantifiers with a range restricted to this part of reality. 'There exist merely possible worlds' is false, according to the possibilist, when the existential quantifier ranges over actuality, but true when it is unrestricted, ranging over all of reality. The actualist response finds the ambiguity in a different place: there are two ways of understanding the term 'possible world': first, a possible world may be understood as a way things might be, a state that the

world might be in, a property of a certain kind that the world might have had; alternatively 'possible world' may be taken more literally to denote a world or universe – something that is in the state, or that has the property in question. According to the actualist, the sense in which there are merely possible worlds is the first sense – there are many ways things might have been, many states the world might have been in. But all but one of these ways or states are uninstantiated, since there is only one possible world in the second sense – only one world that instantiates one of the many ways that the world might be. The quantifier, according to the actualist, ranges unambiguously over what is real, which is to say over what is actual. So merely possible worlds, in the sense in which merely possible worlds exist, are part of the actual world – things that actually exist (see Adams, 1974; Kripke, 1980; Plantinga, 1976; and Stalnaker, 1976 for actualist accounts of possible worlds).

The contrast between actualism and possibilism has consequences for a range of more specific metaphysical questions about modality that arise in the context of the possible worlds framework. We will consider some issues concerning the status of merely possible individuals and the relations between particular individuals and their properties before concluding with some remarks about the possible worlds conception of content, and its consequences for our understanding of the more general issue about the nature of modal truth.

Intuitively, it seems clear that there might have been things other than any that actually exist. For example, the Queen might have had seven brothers, and if she had, seven people who did not in fact exist at all would have been born to her parents. The possible worlds account represents this general thesis as the claim that the domains of some possible worlds contain things that are not in the domain of the actual world. The possibilist has no problem with this thesis; the actual world is just one place among others, and non-actual individuals are just individuals that are located at one of the other places. But what does the actualist, who claims that the domain of the actual world is the domain of everything that exists at all, say about merely possible individuals – the entities that belong to the domains only of merely possible worlds? Actualists, if they are to accept the intuitively plausible thesis, must make a distinction that parallels the distinction between the two senses of 'possible world'. A merely possible individual, like a merely possible world, cannot be a thing that does not exist, but must be some kind of conception that is uninstantiated. Just as we can distinguish the way the world is from the world that is that way, so we can distinguish an individual from the property of being that individual. To say that there are merely possible individuals is to say that there are properties of this kind that are uninstantiated. The domains of possible worlds that the actualists quantify over in their theory are domains of such properties. Alvin Plantinga calls them 'essential domains', domains of *haecceities* (*see* HAECCEITY), or *individual essences* (see Plantinga, 1976).

The property of being a certain individual – for example the property of being identical to Joe DiMaggio – is relatively unproblematic for actual individuals, since such properties are definable in terms of the individual itself. But is it reasonable to believe that there exist uninstantiated properties of this kind, properties that are UNIVERSALS in the sense that they are the kind of thing that is instantiated or uninstantiated, but that also have a kind of irreducible particularity, 'primitive thisness'. (See Adams, 1979.) Even a Platonic realist (*see* PLATONISM) who is comfortable with ordinary universals may be sceptical of uninstantiated individual essences, and so may look for some kind of reduction of merely possible individuals. One such reductionist strategy argues that all possibilities are to be explained as rearrangements of the materials that are found in the actual world. Merely possible individuals are merely possible configurations of parts that make up actual things. Perhaps the Queen's possible brothers are defined in terms of actual

sperms and eggs that never in fact got together, but might have. And if there are merely possible sperms and eggs, they will be constituted by actual atoms that might have had different histories than they in fact had.

An alternative reductionist strategy rejects primitive thisness altogether. The fact that a particular individual exists, according to this strategy, is just the fact that a certain set of properties is instantiated at a certain place. The conception of individuals as bundles of qualities must be supplemented by an account of the modal properties of individuals. If there is no more to Joe DiMaggio than the configuration of properties that he in fact has, had and will have, then how can we talk coherently about what *he* might have done but did not? The answer requires a counterpart relation between configurations of properties, about which more will be said below.

Both of these strategies are metaphysically restrictive, with conclusions about the way the world might have been limited by ontological scruples about the kinds of things that actually exist. But one might think that the range of possibility is not constrained by what really exists. Intuitively, it does not seem that the belief that there might have been individuals other than any that actually exist commits one to the existence of particular conceptions of any individuals who would have existed had that possibility been realized. But to say this is to make a modest retreat from the conception of possibility suggested by the possible worlds framework, which models possibilities by a set of objects that represent the realization of those possibilities; it is to admit that in some cases the fact that a certain possibility might be realized in different ways (for example by different particular individuals) is not grounded in the actual existence of different ways that it might be realized.

Even if we ignore merely possible individuals, there are problems with attributions of modal properties to actual individuals. *De re* modal claims, claims about what could or could not have been true of some particular thing, seem especially problematic since it is not clear how they could be true by convention, or in virtue of relations of ideas. The possible worlds account seems to offer a straightforward paraphrase of such claims: to say that Joe DiMaggio might have been a philosopher, but could not have been a flatworm, is to say that there is a possible world in which he is a philosopher, but no possible world in which he is a flatworm. But is the philosopher in the other possible world really our Joe DiMaggio? And what about him explains the difference between his metaphysical capacity to be a philosopher and his incapacity to be a flatworm? Possibilists and actualists answer these questions in very different ways.

If possible worlds are ways the world might have been, then there is no implausibility in accepting the straightforward assumption that Joe himself inhabits other worlds, since this is only to say that among the ways the world might have been but was not are ways that Joe might have been. (Kripke (1980) attempts to demystify counterfactual suppositions about particular individuals.) On the other hand, if other possible worlds are like other places, then it is not plausible to believe that inhabitants of the actual world are also to be found in other possible worlds. The possibilist must explain the modal properties of an individual, its potentialities, powers and dispositions, in terms of the existence in other possible worlds of *counterparts*, which are individuals that are similar in relevant respects. According to possibilist counterpart theory, Joe himself exists only in the actual world, but he still might have been a philosopher if there is a possible world in which one of his counterparts is a philosopher (Lewis, 1986).

Counterpart theory may also be used by actualists, but for them there is no conflict between the counterpart analysis and the thesis that the philosopher in the other possible world really is our Joe. Recall that for the actualist, the domains of other possible worlds are not literally domains of individuals, but are domains of individual essences, or of some kind of property that may be

instantiated by an individual. The sceptic about primitive individual essences might analyse these in terms of clusters of properties and counterpart relations between them. Such an analysis would be compatible with saying that the individual who instantiates Joe's essence in a possible world in which Joe is a philosopher, is literally Joe himself (Stalnaker, 1986).

Counterpart theory has been criticized as a semantic cover-up of a metaphysically implausible thesis – the thesis that all of an individual's properties and relations are essential to it. The charge is that the theory avoids the implausible essentialist consequence only by changing the interpretation of the language so that the words used to state this consequence become false by saying something else. (This criticism is developed in Plantinga, 1973; and Salmon, 1981, pp. 232–8.) Defenders of counterpart theory respond that this criticism begs the question by assuming that their semantic analysis is a change in the language rather than, as they claim, an account of what the language has always been used to say. But even if the critic's assumption were correct as directed at the possibilist version of counterpart theory, it would not apply to the actualist version. What is really at issue between counterpart theorists and their opponents is not whether individuals have all their properties essentially, but whether particular individuals are in some sense reducible to their qualitative characteristics.

The possibilist has a clear and simple answer to the central metaphysical question about modality: what is the source of modal truth? The merely possible worlds that make propositions necessary or possible have the same status as the actual world whose existence and character explain the truth of ordinary contingent propositions. It is true that some tigers have teeth because of the existence, in the universe in which we find ourselves, of tigers with teeth. According to the possibilist, it is possible that some tigers wear trousers for a similar reason: because of the existence in a part of reality (though perhaps not the part we find ourselves in) of tigers that wear trousers. Modal truths are made true by the same kind of correspondence with reality that makes empirical claims true; the difference is that contingent truths must be made true by local circumstances, while claims about what is necessary or possible concern reality as a whole.

Actualists disagree about the kind of thing a possible world is, but they, it seems, also take modal claims to be claims that are made true or false by the characteristics of the members of a domain of entities, which suggests that there is something substantive to be said about what is necessary – about what is common to all possible worlds. This suggestion seems to conflict with the picture of necessary truths as empty of content, true not because of the way the world has to be, but because the semantic rules for interpreting them make them true no matter how the world is. But the contrast is not so clear for the following reason: both actualists and possibilists accept the possible worlds analysis of the propositions to which modal status is assigned. The idea is that to say something – to characterize the world as being a certain way – is to locate the world in a space of possibility, to distinguish the way it is from alternative ways that it might be. But if that is how content is to be understood, then the idea of a substantive (contentful) characterization of necessary truth is incoherent. To say something substantive about what is common to all possible worlds would be to contrast them with alternative ways that all possible worlds might have to be. But actualists and possibilists agree that there are no such ways, so both will agree that all necessary truths are, like tautologies, empty of content. However metaphysical a statement may appear to be, to understand that it is necessary is to see that the rules that determine what the statement says also determine that it will be true whatever the possible worlds are like.

See also ESSENCE/ACCIDENT; ESSENTIAL-ISM; EXISTENCE; THEORIES OF TRUTH.

BIBLIOGRAPHY

Adams, R.M.: 'Theories of actuality', *Noûs* 8 (1974), 211–31; repr. in *The Possible and the Actual* ed. M.J. Loux (Ithaca, NY: Cornell University Press, 1979), 190–209.

Adams, R.M.: 'Primitive thisness and primitive identity', *Journal of Philosophy* 76 (1979), 5–26.

Kripke, S.: 'Semantic considerations on modal logic', *Acta Philosophica Fennica* 15 (1963), 83–94; repr. in *Reference and Modality* ed. L. Linsky (London: Oxford University Press, 1971), 63–72.

Kripke, S.: *Naming and Necessity* (Cambridge, MA: Harvard University Press, 1980).

Lewis, D.K.: *On the Plurality of Worlds* (Oxford: Blackwell, 1986).

Plantinga, A.: 'Transworld identity or worldbound individuals', in *Logic and Ontology* ed. M. Munitz (New York: New York University Press, 1973); repr. in *The Possible and the Actual* ed. M.J. Loux (Ithaca, NY: Cornell University Press, 1979), 146–65.

Plantinga, A.: 'Actualism and possible worlds', *Theoria* 42 (1976), 139–60, repr. in *The Possible and the Actual* ed. M.J. Loux (Ithaca, NY: Cornell University Press, 1979), 253–73.

Salmon, N.U.: *Reference and Essence* (Princeton, NJ: Princeton University Press, 1981).

Stalnaker, R.: 'Possible worlds', *Noûs* 10 (1976), 65–75; repr. in *The Actual and the Possible* ed. M.J. Loux (Ithaca, NY: Cornell University Press, 1979), 225–34.

Stalnaker, R.: 'Counterparts and identity', *Midwest Studies in Philosophy* 11 (1986), 121–40.

ROBERT STALNAKER

mode The term 'mode' derives from the Latin *modus*, meaning 'measure', 'standard', 'manner' or 'way'. Scholastic philosophy used the term *modus* in each of these senses. One scholastic use of the term, in the sense of 'manner' or 'way', referred to the qualities, affections, or accidents of a SUB-STANCE; and the writings of DESCARTES helped to fix this as the canonical use of 'mode' for modern philosophy. 'By mode', he affirmed, 'we understand exactly the same as what is elsewhere meant by an *attribute or quality*. But we employ the term *mode* when we are thinking of a substance as being affected or modified' (*Principles of Philosophy*, I 55). Descartes held that each substance has a *principal attribute – thought* in the case of minds, *extension* in the case of physical objects, or 'bodies' – and that everything else attributable to a substance is a modification, or *mode*, of that substance's principal attribute.

Modes play a central role in Descartes's theory of distinctions. In addition to *real distinctions* (between different substances) and *conceptual distinctions* or *distinctions of reason* (between a substance and one of its essential attributes, or between two essential attributes of the same substance), there are two kinds of *modal distinctions*. The first holds between a non-essential mode and the substance of which it is a mode, while the second holds between two non-essential modes of the same substance. In the former case, we can conceive the 'substance apart from the mode which we say differs from it, whereas we cannot, conversely, understand the mode apart from the substance'; in the latter case, 'we are able to arrive at knowledge of one mode apart from the other, and *vice versa*, whereas we cannot know either mode apart from the substance in which it inheres' (*Principles of Philosophy* I 61).

SPINOZA employed a definition of 'mode' very similar to Descartes: 'By *mode* I understand the affections of a substance, or that which is in another through which it is also conceived' (*Ethics* Id5). However, his application of the concept was radically different. Because he held that God (which he identified with Nature) is the only substance, Spinoza concluded that individual things, such as minds and bodies, are not themselves created substances – as Descartes had held – but instead modes of the one substance. Thus, individual things must be conceived as being among the affections of

God – that is, as among the ways in which God or Nature is modified, qualified, or expressed. The distinctions between God and individual things, as well as those among different individual things, cannot be *real distinctions*, and must instead be merely modal distinctions.

Spinoza regarded thought and extension as two *attributes* (in the sense of Cartesian 'principal attributes') of a single substance. Accordingly, he affirmed that minds and bodies are modes of the same substance. But he also went further, claiming that every mode of extension is actually identical with a corresponding mode of thought, which is the *idea* (or, especially in the case of highly complex individuals such as human beings, the *mind*) of that mode of extension. In his view, God has infinitely many *attributes*, although thought and extension are the only two known to us. God must therefore have modes of these other attributes in addition to modes of thought and extension. Spinoza also drew an important distinction between finite modes and infinite modes. Finite modes – such as finite minds and bodies – are local and temporary affections of God, whereas infinite modes are pervasive and unending affections of God. The infinite modes include the infinite intellect of God, the infinite individual composed of all finite bodies, the formal essences of things, and the general features of the universe that correspond to the laws of nature (*see* LAW OF NATURE).

The term 'mode' also plays a prominent role in the philosophy and cognitive psychology of LOCKE. Locke distinguished all ideas into the simple and the complex, and further distinguished complex ideas into ideas of substances, modes, and relations. Ideas of modes differ from ideas of substances, according to Locke, by not containing as a part the 'supposed, or confused' idea of a substantial SUBSTRATUM; they therefore 'contain not in them the supposition of subsisting by themselves; but are considered as Dependences on, or Affections of Substances' (*An Essay concerning Human Understanding* (1690) II, xii, 4–6). Lockean modes are either *simple* or *mixed*. Ideas of simple modes involve either a repetition of a simple idea (as the idea of *dozen* repeats the simple idea of *space*) or a variation of a simple idea (as the ideas of different *degrees* or *shades* of blue vary the simple idea of *blue*). Ideas of mixed modes combine more than one simple idea (as in the ideas of *obligation, justice, drunkenness, a lie*). Unlike ideas of substances, which are patterned on nature, ideas of mixed modes are arbitrary combinations of ideas made by the mind. Hence, although the *real essence* of a substance – i.e. that from which its properties flow – lies in the imperceptible constitution of its corpuscular parts, the real essence of a mixed mode is the idea of the mixed mode itself. It is for this reason, Locke thought, that our knowledge of modes can be more thorough than our knowledge of substances.

BIBLIOGRAPHY

Descartes, R.: *The Philosophical Writings of Descartes* 3 vols, ed. and trans. J. Cottingham, R. Stoothoff and D. Murdoch (Cambridge: Cambridge University Press, 1985).
Hume, D.: *A Treatise of Human Nature* (London: 1739–40); ed. L.A. Selby-Bigge (Oxford: Clarendon Press, 1888); 2nd edn rev. P.H. Nidditch (Oxford: Clarendon Press, 1978).
Locke, J.: *An Essay concerning Human Understanding* (London: 1690); ed. P.H. Nidditch (Oxford: Clarendon Press, 1975).
Spinoza, B.: *The Collected Writings of Spinoza* Vol. 1, ed. and trans. E. Curley (Princeton, NJ: Princeton University Press, 1985).

DON GARRETT

monad, monadology Monadology is a doctrine usually associated with the mature ontological position of LEIBNIZ, perhaps best expressed by him in a letter to De Volder:

considering matters accurately, it must be said that there is nothing in things except simple substances, and, in them, nothing but perception and appetite. Moreover, matter and motion are not so much substances or things as they are the phenomena of percipient beings, the reality of which is located in the harmony of each percipient with itself (with respect to different times) and with other percipients.

The basic thesis, then, is this: the ultimate individuals of an acceptable ONTOLOGY are all soul-like entities, the monads, whose intrinsic properties are characterizable in terms of the perceptions and appetites of the monads. Any other entities that have a claim to reality must be, at best, well-founded phenomena analysable in terms of properties attributable to the monads.

BIBLIOGRAPHY

Leibniz, G.W.: *Principes de la nature et de la grâce fondés en raison. Principes de la philosophie ou Monadologie* ed. A. Robinet, 3rd edn (Paris: Presses Universitaires de France, 1986).
Rescher, N.: *G.W. Leibniz's Monadology – an edition for students* (Pittsburgh: University of Pittsburgh Press, 1991).

ROBERT C. SLEIGH, JR

monism/pluralism The issue of whether, using 'thing' in the broadest sense, all things or kinds of thing are reducible to, derivable from, caused by, or explicable in terms of some one thing or kind of thing (*see* REDUCTION, REDUCTIONISM). Monists answer this question affirmatively, pluralists negatively. If there are at least two things or kinds of thing, neither of which is explicable in terms of the other or in terms of some third thing or kind of thing, pluralism is true; if there are not, monism is true. Monists, like pluralists, admit that there is a plurality of things and kinds, at least at the level of appearance. The issue at stake between the two positions is therefore not that of whether there is a plurality of at least apparent things and kinds, but rather whether this plurality is explicable in terms of one thing or kind.

The issue of monism versus pluralism arose at the beginning of the history of western philosophy (*see* PRESOCRATICS). Thales, generally credited with being the first western philosopher, rejected the view that there are four fundamental material substances, elements or stuffs – earth, air, fire and water – that are such that none are reducible to any of the others, and held instead that earth, air and fire are all forms of water, so that anything composed of any combination of these other elements at bottom is composed of water. His successor Heraclitus chose fire as his fundamental substance, so that all other elements are forms of fire and anything composed of any combination of other elements is ultimately a manifestation of fire. Contemporary chemists, by contrast, are pluralists, since they hold that there are over a hundred chemical elements, none reducible to any combination of any of the others. This indicates that the issue of monism versus pluralism is significant not only for metaphysics but also for chemistry and natural science in general.

Each of the four elements mentioned above differs qualitatively from one another. For the Greek atomists, however, such as Democritus (*c*.460–*c*.370 BC) and Leucippus (*fl*.450–420 BC), all qualitative differences are manifestations of and explicable in terms of various combinations of atoms, none of which differs qualitatively from any of the others (*see* ATOMISM). Although the atomists were pluralistic in positing a multiplicity of atoms, they were monistic in maintaining that qualitatively atoms are the same in kind, given that there are no qualitative differences between them. The qualitative differences between the phenomena we perceive are all subjective and have no ontological status in reality independently of our sensing or perceiving them. Such atomism, while again pluralistic in positing a multiplicity of atoms, is thus a form of monism in maintaining that everything

objectively real is the same in kind qualitatively. Such atomism is the precursor of much of modern physics, which is also at once pluralistic and monistic in the senses in question. It is also the precursor of contemporary materialistic approaches to the MIND/BODY PROBLEM, which hold that mental acts, events and states are all reducible to, caused by, or supervenient upon and explicable in terms of events in and states of the brain and central nervous system (*see* PHYSICALISM, MATERIALISM; SUPERVENIENCE). Such approaches to this problem are also at once pluralistic and monistic in the senses in question.

The extreme opposite of these forms of materialism is Berkeleyan (*see* BERKELEY) IDEALISM, according to which the only things that exist are minds and their ideas. Such immaterialism, while pluralistic in asserting a plurality of minds and ideas, is monistic in denying the existence of matter. An intermediate position between those of materialism and Berkeleyan immaterialism is that of Cartesian (*see* DESCARTES) dualism, which is explicitly dualistic and therefore pluralistic in maintaining that the human being is a composite of two substances – mind and body – neither of which is reducible to or explicable in terms of the other. Such a position is pluralistic not only in maintaining that there is a plurality of minds and bodies but also in holding that there are two types of SUBSTANCE – mental and material.

Perhaps the outstanding example of monism in the history of western philosophy is the position of SPINOZA, according to which anything finite that in any way exists or is real is either an attribute or MODE of one substance, which he calls not only Substance but also Nature and God. His position is therefore a form of PANTHEISM, which is monistic in a way in which theism is not. Indeed, there is a form of theism – polytheism – that is explicitly pluralistic, since it asserts the existence of a plurality of gods. Yet even that form of theism – monotheism – that accepts the existence of only one God is pluralistic in holding that there is a radical difference between God and the world. According to various monotheistic theologians, although God is immanent in and indeed omnipresent in the world, and although everything natural in the world is a theophany or manifestation of God, the world and everything in it is created by God from nothing and depends constantly for its continuing existence from moment to moment upon the continuing conserving action of God, who exists necessarily through His own nature or essence independently of the world. Despite, however, the difference between God and the world, monotheism is monistic in holding that the existence of the world is explicable ultimately only through appealing to the creative and conserving action of God.

One of the central motives animating monists is a desire for simplicity (see SIM-PLICITY, PARSIMONY). The world is simpler in those respects in which a plurality of things or kinds of thing are explicable in terms of one thing or kind of thing. On the other hand, one of the central motives animating the pluralist is a desire to avoid the kind of oversimplification that consists in maintaining that a given plurality of things or kinds is explicable in terms of a single thing or kind when in fact they are not. One of the central *desiderata* in metaphysical investigations is to seek simplicity, but not at the cost of over-simplification.

See also SUBSTANCE.

BIBLIOGRAPHY

Berkeley, G.: *The Principles of Human Knowledge* (many editions).
Bradley, F.H.: *Appearance and Reality* (Oxford: 1893); 2nd edn (Oxford: Clarendon Press, 1897).
Descartes, R.: *Meditations on First Philosophy* (many editions).
Plato: Parmenides (many editions).
Spinoza, B.: *Ethics* (many editions).

RAMON M. LEMOS

Moore, George Edward (1873–1958) British philosopher who first made his reputation as a critic of idealist metaphysics. Moore's influential 'refutation' of IDEALISM rested on two lines of criticism. (1) KANT and his followers are accused of a refined psychologism, whereby both a priori and empirical truths are wrongly regarded as dependent upon the nature of the mind's activities. By contrast, Moore held that in all cases, the objects of thought and experience (propositions and simpler objects) are independent of our consciousness of them, as is also their status (true/false, real/imaginary). (2) Hegelians such as BRADLEY and McTAGGART are criticized for their extreme holism – their conception of the universe as an organic whole and their rejection of all merely external relations (see INTERNAL RELATIONS). In opposition Moore argued that pluralism and contingency are inescapable features of the world to which we must accommodate our metaphysics.

Moore's early metaphysics is, therefore, an atomist REALISM concerning the objects of thought and experience. But one further theme is a residue of his youthful idealism: this is his rejection of naturalist metaphysics (see NATURALISM), familiar from his ethical non-naturalism, but equally a feature of his treatment of all a priori truths. Indeed Moore's early realism carries him well beyond 'mere empirical' existence; it embraces a domain of being that includes the false as well as the true, the imaginary as well as the real; and in all cases, he holds, we can 'apprehend' these objects without any intermediary – experience and thought have no 'content' or 'sense', for they are just 'transparent' apprehensions of objects which *are* whether or not they exist.

Moore's faith in this position crumbled in the years after 1904. His previous conception of false propositions and illusory objects came to strike him as incredible. Reality, he thought, should be confined to that which actually exists or is true. So he set himself the task of giving accounts of thought and perception which respect this constrained conception of reality, while allowing for falsehood and illusion.

In subsequent discussions of the nature of thought he was much influenced by RUSSELL's logical theories, especially his theory of 'incomplete symbols'. For this offered the prospect of an account which respects the surface structure of thought as a propositional attitude, while avoiding commitment to the existence of propositions (*see* PROPOSITION, STATE OF AFFAIRS). In fact Moore never found an account which he believed to be satisfactory: he recognized that Russell's multiple-relation theory violates the unity of judgement, and he argued that the influential quotational treatments misrepresent the relationship between a sentence and its meaning. Whether Moore was right about this remains disputed; but Moore's role in publicizing the significance of Russell's logical doctrines is indisputable. None the less Moore remained sufficiently clear-headed to resist the fashionable attractions of both LOGICAL ATOMISM and LOGICAL POSITIVISM. Contrary to the former he argued that we have no reason to think that the existence of elementary objects is not contingent; and contrary to the latter he argued that we have no reason to deny that unverifiable propositions concerning the past are either true or false.

In Moore's early metaphysics where the objects of experience really exist they are themselves 'parts' of physical objects. This naive realism cannot accommodate illusions and the relativity of appearance. So although Moore always felt that the demonstrative content of EXPERIENCE requires an act/object analysis he came to wonder whether the objects of experience – sense data – are not distinct from physical objects (*see* SENSA). Yet he could never find a way of developing this hypothesis into a satisfactory account of the relationship between sense data and physical objects. Arguably, the trouble derives from Moore's act/object analysis, which cannot accommodate the INTENTIONALITY of experience. But Moore's insistence on the demonstrative content of experience remains salutary; instead of treating it as a reference to inherently problematic sense data, however, we can construe it as a reference to places apparently occupied by sensible qualities.

Moore in fact never settled on an interlocking group of philosophical beliefs which one might characterize as his later metaphysics. His later writings are, rather, characterized by piecemeal analysis, which advances understanding of a variety of issues (e.g. existence, fiction, possibility). But they also suggest a different way of thinking about metaphysics, one which focuses on Moore's frequent appeals to common sense. Moore recognized that he could not find within common sense a resolution of his puzzles concerning propositional attitudes and perception; but he argued that whatever solution philosophical analysis found for these puzzles could not challenge our common sense beliefs. This account of the significance of philosophical analysis is problematic, but if it is accepted there is a sense in which Moore's later metaphysics just comprises this affirmation of common sense; and this is such a departure from traditional metaphysics that it might as well be called the end of metaphysics – a conclusion which would place Moore in unexpected contemporary company.

WRITINGS

Philosophical Studies (London: Routledge, 1922).
Some Main Problems of Philosophy (London: Allen and Unwin, 1953).
Philosophical Papers (London: Allen and Unwin, 1959).
Early Papers ed. T. Regan (Philadelphia: Temple University Press, 1986).
Selected Writings ed. I. Baldwin (London: Routledge, 1993).

THOMAS BALDWIN

N

---

naturalism *Methodological* naturalism holds that the best methods of inquiry in the social sciences or philosophy are, or are to be modelled on, those of the natural sciences. The view was already proposed by NEWTON in the wake of the enormous explanatory and epistemic success of his physics, and it was developed by HUME. These thinkers attributed the success of Newtonian physics to its methods and formal explanatory devices (such as principles of attraction and association) and assumed that success in the social sciences would follow the use of these methods. Many have objected that the subject matter of the social sciences differs from that of the natural sciences in ways that prevent the successful extension of methods. For example, the intentional states (beliefs, desires, intentions) in terms of which we explain human behaviour are said to be attributable to individuals only relative to an observer, and such relativity is inconsistent with the objectivity of the methods of natural science (Winch, 1958). One might, however, defend methodological naturalism by proposing that the social sciences abandon intentional states in favour of syntactic or neurophysiological states.

Ontological naturalism is the view, attributable to the ancient atomists and SPINOZA, that only *natural* objects, kinds, and properties are real (*see* ATOMISM). 'Natural' here does not contrast with 'artificial': there is no basis for treating trees as real and tables as unreal just because tables are manufactured, or even because what it is to be a table is to function a certain way in human activity. Nor does 'natural' contrast with 'dependent on thought'; for in this case ontological naturalism would degenerate into a simple REALISM, claiming only that real things do not depend on thought. Since ontological naturalism is supported by the success of natural science, and success is success in recognizing what is real, it would do best to define 'natural' as 'what is recognized by natural science'.

Ontological naturalism has been accused of scientism, an unwarranted faith in science. Yet naturalists intend to argue for their view by appeal to the fact that natural science occupies a large and central place in our current system of belief, or that it has a higher degree of rationality than common sense or social science. In either case, the results of natural science will prevail in further rational inquiry over beliefs that conflict with them. Thus, for example, our ontology is constrained by the result that all physical bodies are composed entirely of particles. The argument now proceeds: we cannot reconcile the existence of colours, mental and intentional states, consciousness, the self, linguistic REFERENCE and meaning, knowledge and justified belief, moral obligation and goodness, or beauty with scientific results *unless* we can 'naturalize' these items. The most obvious way to naturalize an item is to *reduce* it to a natural item, either by *analysing* the concept associated with the item in natural terms, or by *identifying* the item with a natural item (*see* REDUCTION, REDUCTIONISM).

Naturalists often insist that intentional states, colours, and the like must reduce to natural items if they are real because it is doubtful that they could have their apparent qualities – for example, spatial location, causal interaction with physical things – unless they were themselves natural. Naturalists may also argue for reduction on the ground that INTENTIONALITY (the property of being intentional) and the like *supervene* on natural properties – that having these properties necessarily follows from having certain natural properties (*see* SUPERVENIENCE). Thus, mental properties are said to supervene on physical properties because a particle-for-particle replica of our world would contain all the same mental properties as our world. The most straightforward explanation of supervenience is reduction. At the same time, the search for reductions has proved frustrating: it is now widely agreed that intentionality and mentality cannot be reduced to neurophysiological properties, and it is currently debated whether intentionality can be reduced to evolutionary properties.

An alternative to reduction is to identify these properties with *functional* properties: an intentional state like belief is a state that plays a certain functional role in the context of other mental states (Fodor, 1968) (*see* FUNCTIONALISM). On this approach, intentional states themselves are typically identified with neurophysiological states, but *intentionality* is not identified with a property recognized by neurophysiology but rather with a *functional role*, in the way that tables are identical with physical bodies, but the *property* of being a table is not a property recognized by physics, but rather the property of functioning a certain way in human activity. We then explain why intentionality supervenes on physical or biological properties, not by reducing it to these properties, but by explaining why neurophysiological states having these properties necessarily function, in the context of surrounding physical items, in the way that intentional states do. Functional analyses of intentionality have been notably more successful than reductions to natural properties.

In the absence of reductions or functional analyses, it seems that naturalists must deny that intentionality and the like exist in the same way that natural properties do. One might deny that language about these items is referential or descriptive language, as WITTGENSTEIN did for language about

sensation and ethical non-cognitivists (emotivists and prescriptivists) do for ethical language. Or one might maintain that the language is to be understood referentially or descriptively, but deny that there is anything to which the terms refer – as eliminative materialists do. However, these approaches leave the apparent supervenience of these items on the natural unexplained. But naturalism has sometimes been relaxed to admit the existence of non-natural items needed to explain nature (e.g. numbers) or to formulate naturalism itself (e.g. linguistic reference and meaning), where their existence is consistent with natural science.

Ontological and methodological naturalism have been challenged on the ground that they are self-defeating. Ontological naturalism is a claim about supervenience or reduction, and such claims employ terms referring to properties that have yet to be naturalized. Methodological naturalism is a claim about best method; yet the methods employed to arrive at methodological naturalism are not those of natural science but of philosophy of science. In the case of ontological naturalism, the objection seems to tell at best against eliminative materialism, not reductive naturalism, which holds that there are such reductions, not that we already have them. In the case of methodological naturalism, the objection calls for the reminder that methodological naturalism is warranted a posteriori, by methods that are general, albeit vague, versions of those of natural science. The views have also been challenged by recent social studies of science on the ground that natural science is no more rational than common sense or social science.

QUINE has proposed that the subject of epistemology itself be naturalized: the traditional epistemological project of answering scepticism a priori is misguided because 'the skeptical challenge springs from science itself, and . . . in coping with it we are free to use scientific knowledge' (Quine, 1974). The project becomes that of explaining how certain patterns of sensory stimulation lead to our theory of the world. Reductive episte-mological naturalism differs from Quine's in retaining a project of characterizing knowledge and justification in a way that is not mere descriptive psychology, though it depends on psychology to judge whether the conditions of knowledge and justification are satisfied. *Psychologism* holds that justified belief is belief that conforms to norms that describe our (native) reasoning competence. *Reliabilism* holds that justified belief is belief that results from a cognitive process that tends to produce true beliefs.

See also PHYSICALISM, MATERIALISM.

BIBLIOGRAPHY

Fodor, J.: *Psychological Explanation: An Intro-duction to the Philosophy of Psychology* (New York: Random House, 1968).
Hume, D.: *A Treatise of Human Nature* (1739); rev. edn. P.H. Nidditch (Oxford: Clarendon Press, 1978).
Quine, W.V.: 'Epistemology naturalized', in his *Ontological Relativity and Other Essays* (New York: Columbia University Press, 1969), 69–90.
Quine, W.V.: *The Roots of Reference* (LaSalle, IL: Open Court, 1974).
Spinoza, B.: *Ethics*, in *Collected Works of Spinoza* vol. 1, ed. and trans. E.M. Curley (Princeton, NJ: Princeton University Press, 1985).
Winch, P.: *The Idea of a Social Science and its Relation to Philosophy* (London: Routledge and Kegan Paul, 1958).

FREDERICK F. SCHMITT

natural kind Etymologically, *kind* and *kindred* are linked. Objects belonging to the same natural kind have something special in common.

The chemical elements are often taken to be paradigm cases of natural kinds. Gold is defined by its atomic number; necessarily, a thing is made of gold precisely when it is composed of atoms that have atomic number 79. Atomic number is said to provide the *essence* of the natural kind (*see* ESSENCE/ACCIDENT).

There are other properties that golden objects share that are unique to them. For example, if there are finitely many such objects in the history of the world, we could enumerate them by specifying their locations $l_1, l_2, \ldots l_n$. Why is atomic number the essence of gold, rather than the property of being found at location l_1 or l_2 or $\ldots l_n$?

The usual reply is that the essence of a natural kind must be necessary, explanatory and purely qualitative. It is an accident that lumps of gold have the locations just mentioned; but it is supposed to be a necessary truth that golden things have atomic number 79. In addition, atomic number explains many other properties of gold things, whereas their disjunctive location explains little (Mill, 1843). And finally, it should be possible to specify the essence of gold without referring to any place, time or individual; atomic number provides this qualitative specification, but location does not.

A fundamental metaphysical question is whether there is a uniquely correct grouping of objects into natural kinds. We collect various objects together under the category *gold* and a different set together under the category *lead*. But why not mix and match? Following Goodman (1965), we can define *gread* as the objects that are gold and begin existing before the year 2000 or lead and begin existing after. Intuition suggests that lead and gold are *natural* kinds, whereas gread is an *artificial* category – an artefact of human inventiveness and not something that exists independently of us. Can this intuition be justified?

It does no good to claim that gold things have many properties in common, whereas gread things do not. After all, the similarities that unite the gold things and the ones that unite the leaden ones can be subjected to a similar redescription. Likewise, the appearance that *gold* and *lead* are purely qualitative whereas *gread* is not begins to cloud when scrutinized. Suppose we define *lold* as an object that is lead before the year 2000 or gold thereafter. Then *gold* can be furnished with a non-qualitative definition that resembles the one just given for *gread*; a gold object is an object that is gread before 2000 or lold thereafter.

There are other metaphysical questions about natural kinds besides the one concerning their objective existence. If *x* and *y* are each natural kinds, what should we say of *x*-or-*y*, *x*-and-*y*, and not-*x*? Intuition may tell against disjunctive or negative kinds, but why should such intuitions be taken seriously? A similar question pertains to the issue of whether uninstantiated kinds exist. And what sort of systematic relationships should obtain among kinds? Although the Aristotelian model claims that kinds must be grouped *hierarchically*, it is worth remembering that chemistry groups the elements *periodically*.

Lurking behind these metaphysical queries is an epistemological one. What argument is there for thinking that natural kinds *exist*? Why not settle for a more austere and nominalistic ONTOLOGY in which it is individuals, not kinds, that populate the universe and convenience, not reality, that determines how we should lump and split? (*See* NOMINALISM, UNIVERSALS.)

This last question leads back to the issue of what use science has for the notion of natural kind. Rather than take our intuitions at face value, we should strive to understand what role they play in the attempt to understand the world systematically. Kripke (1972) and Putnam (1975) suggest that chemical elements are natural kinds whose essences are empirically discovered. Can this formulation be justified by attending to the details of scientific practice?

Connecting the metaphysical issue with problems in the philosophy of science has especially interesting consequences when we consider the other main example of natural kinds that philosophers like to cite. This is the category of *biological species*. If species have essences, it is surprising that evolutionary biology has not only failed to find them but has also shown scant interest in doing so. A view more in keeping with scientific practice is the idea that species are

individuals; they are populations that have organisms as parts, not as members (Hull, 1978). Two organisms are in the same species in virtue of their genealogical relatedness, not in virtue of their similarity; they are kin, but do not thereby comprise a natural kind.

See also CATEGORIES.

BIBLIOGRAPHY

Armstrong, D.M.: *A Theory of Universals* (Cambridge: Cambridge University Press, 1978).

Goodman, N.: *Fact, Fiction, and Forecast* (Indianapolis, IN: Bobbs-Merrill, 1965).

Hull, D.: 'A matter of individuality', *Philosophy of Science* 45 (1978), 335–60.

Kripke, S.: 'Naming and necessity', in *Semantics for Natural Language* ed. G. Harman and D. Davidson (Dordrecht: Reidel, 1972), 254–355.

Lewis, D.: 'New work for a theory of universals', *Australasian Journal of Philosophy* 61 (1983), 343–77.

Mill, J.S.: *System of Logic* (London: Longmans, 1843).

Putnam, H.: 'The meaning of "meaning" ', in his *Mind, Language, and Reality* (Cambridge: Cambridge University Press, 1975), 215–71.

ELLIOTT SOBER

natural theology The attempt to see how much can be known about God without revelation, relying upon reason alone. More narrowly, it is the project of producing proofs or arguments for *theism*, the view (roughly speaking) that there exists an all-powerful, all-knowing, wholly good person who has created the world; more exactly, it is the project of producing theistic arguments whose premises do not depend upon revelation. Natural theology goes back at least to ARISTOTLE; it flourished in the hands of AUGUSTINE and ANSELM, and hit a high-water mark in the high Middle Ages, especially in the work of AQUINAS and

DUNS SCOTUS. It hit another high-water mark in early modern philosophy with the work of DESCARTES, MALEBRANCHE, LEIBNIZ, SPINOZA, LOCKE, BERKELEY and others. The Enlightenment brought strenuous criticism to the whole enterprise; here perhaps the most important figures are HUME and KANT. Natural theology has also been faulted from certain theological positions; Lutheran and Reformed theologians, for example, have tended to look askance at it. As an extreme example, Karl Barth (1886–1968) claimed that to take serious part in natural theology is to adopt the 'standpoint of unbelief'. At present, however, natural theology enjoys a modest but marked renaissance.

Kant divided the theistic arguments into three: the Ontological Argument, the Cosmological Argument, and the Teleological Argument, or Argument from Design. The Ontological Argument is due to the eleventh-century thinker Anselm; in his formulation, it goes roughly as follows. God is by definition that being than which none greater can be conceived. Obviously it is greater to exist than to fail to exist; so if God did not exist, it would be possible that there be a being greater than God. But clearly it is impossible that there be a being greater than the being than which none greater can be conceived. Stated this baldly, this argument smacks of word magic; however nearly every major philosopher from Anselm's time to ours has had his say about it. Versions of the argument were endorsed by Duns Scotus, Descartes, Leibniz and others; in the twentieth century it has been endorsed by Charles Hartshorne, Norman Malcolm and Alvin Plantinga.

The Cosmological Argument goes back to Aristotle and is stated with great clarity and care in Aquinas's *Summa contra Gentiles*. Here the basic idea is that the world requires a first cause or a first mover, but only a being with the properties of the theistic God could be a first cause or a first mover.

The Teleological Argument or Argument from Design is the most popular of the theistic arguments; in essence, it appeals to the fact that the world looks very much as if it has been designed by a being of great intelligence and power. This argument has been endorsed by a great many thinkers over the centuries; in the twentieth century it has been endorsed and developed first by F.R. Tennant and more recently by Richard Swinburne. Swinburne's detailed and elaborate version of this argument in *The Existence of God* (1979) is perhaps the most impressive formulation it has yet received.

Although these are the most prominent arguments, there are in fact many others: arguments from the nature of proper function, and from the nature of propositions, numbers and sets. There are arguments from INTENTIONALITY, from COUNTERFACTUALS, from the confluence of epistemic reliability with epistemic justification, from REFERENCE, simplicity (*see* SIMPLICITY, PARSIMONY), intuition and love; from colours and flavours, miracles, play and enjoyment, morality; from beauty, and the meaning of life; and there is even an argument from the existence of evil. The question whether these arguments are *good* arguments is of course controversial (just as in the case of nearly any other important philosophical argument).

People have engaged in this project of natural theology for a variety of reasons. You might be a believer in God yourself and might try to convince someone else to join you in this belief. Or you might be a wavering or troubled believer in God, and be trying to convince yourself. Or you might have no initial views on the subject and propose to come to a position on the matter by way of considering the evidence for and against. Or you might think theism useful in philosophy, in that it offers suggestions for answers to a wide range of otherwise intractable questions; you might then look for some arguments for theism, as part of your effort to deal with those questions.

But of course there are other, historically more prominent reasons for working at natural theology. First, according to one important strand of medieval thought, those who believe in God begin with faith, but a faith that is seeking understanding: *fides querens intellectum.* According to this tradition we have *understanding* when we have scientific knowledge, *scientia*, of the item in question; and we have *scientia* when we *see* that the item in question is true by seeing that it follows from what we see to be true. From this perspective (a perspective endorsed by Aquinas) a central function of natural theology is to transform faith into knowledge, belief into *scientia*. According to Aquinas, a person might be perfectly justified, perfectly within his or her rights, indeed, thoroughly meritorious in believing in God without the benefit of argument. Still, such a person does not have knowledge (*scientia*) of God's existence; he or she *believes* but does not *know*. He holds that it is possible for some of us, however – those who have the inclination, the ability, and the leisure – to *see* that God exists by way of the theistic proofs. Such a person *knows* that God exists, has *scientia* of that fact; and to have *scientia* is in general and from one point of view a higher and better epistemic condition than merely to believe.

There is another important motive for engaging in natural theology, a motive that is of both historical and contemporary importance. Many have held that it is irrational, or unjustified, or somehow intellectually second rate to believe in God without having evidence – where evidence is thought of as *propositional* evidence, evidence from other things you already believe. If this is true, then to be justified in believing in God you would have to believe on the basis of a theistic argument. On the most common versions of this view, the believer who has no argument is *unjustified*; the believer is doing something contrary to epistemic duty or obligation, something impermissible, something she has no right to do. Thus in his famous essay 'The ethics of belief' W.K. Clifford (1845–79) loudly trumpets that 'it is wrong, always, everywhere and for anyone to believe anything upon insufficient evidence'. The Cliffordian idea is that there is a sort of intellectual duty or obligation not to believe in God without having evidence, or sufficient evidence; if there is no evidence, or only insufficient evidence, the believer is unjustified; the believer is flouting his or her epistemic duties. From this point of view, the rational acceptability of belief in God stands or falls with the theistic arguments.

This attitude towards theistic belief – that there is a duty not to believe in God without propositional evidence – has a long and distinguished history, going back at least to Locke and possibly to Descartes; it has been popular ever since and is still popular now. But if this is true, then one way – perhaps the only way – to *justify* theistic belief, to bring it about that those who accept it are (or can be) justified in so doing, is by way of discovering and providing good theistic arguments.

Of course it is hardly clear that there is any such duty: is there really a good reason for thinking that a believer in God who has no propositional evidence (no evidence from that believer's other beliefs) is doing something contrary to his or her duty? This is questionable *in excelsis*. If, after careful and mature reflection, you find yourself with the firm belief that there is indeed such a person as God, could you really be violating an epistemic duty, even if you do not believe in God on the basis of an argument? Why suppose belief in God is different, in this respect, from belief in the past, say, or belief in other minds? So this function of *justifying* believers in God, putting them in the right, putting them within their epistemic rights, bringing it about that they are or can be in conformance with their epistemic duties in believing in God – this function, perhaps, does not need to be performed. More broadly, perhaps it is perfectly sensible, rational, and reasonable to believe in God even if you do not know of a good theistic argument.

Even if this is so, of course, it does not follow that natural theology is of no interest. On the contrary: it can serve the function of strengthening and deepening belief in God and of moving people towards it. From a philosophical point of view, furthermore, natural theology can reveal important and interesting connections between God and abstract objects, counterfactuals, reference, intentionality, epistemic reliability and epistemic justification, morality, beauty, love, evil and other topics.

BIBLIOGRAPHY

Aquinas, St T.: *Summa theologiae*, I, q 1–11.
Aquinas, St T.: *Summa contra Gentiles*, Book I.
Butler, J.: *The Analogy of Religion* (London: Knapton, 1736).
Clarke, S.: *System of natural philosophy* (London: J. and J. Knapton, 1729).
Hume, D.: *Dialogues Concerning Natural Religion* (Indianapolis, IN: Bobbs-Merrill, 1947).
Kant, I.: *Critique of Pure Reason* (New York: The Colonial Press, 1899).
Leibniz, G.W.: *New Essays on Human Understanding* 4, 1–10; Monadology, On the Cartesian Demonstration of the Existence of God.
Plantinga, A.: *God and Other Minds* (Ithaca, NY: Cornell University Press, 1967).
Plantinga, A.: *The Nature of Necessity* (Oxford: Clarendon Press, 1974), chs 9, 10.
Swinburne, R.: *The Existence of God* (Oxford: Clarendon Press, 1979).

ALVIN PLANTINGA

nature The sum total or aggregate of natural things. A natural thing is distinguished from an artificial thing, or ARTEFACT: the latter owes its existence to human ingenuity or artifice. Since human beings can create material artefacts only by imposing novel shapes on pre-existing materials or by rearranging pre-existing objects, material artefacts not only consist ultimately of natural things or materials but result from the activities of natural things, which human beings certainly are. As a result, material artefacts are also, in an important sense, natural things and belong to the system of nature.

In addition to belonging to nature, every natural thing has a nature. As originally understood, a thing's nature is the internal cause of its behaviour. If a bullet flies through the air, it does not do so by nature or because of its nature but by constraint: it is forced to fly because of an explosion. Once it is moving, however, it will 'by its nature' continue to move until something stops it. The ancient Ionian thinkers were the first to offer theories about a thing's nature so understood (*see* PRESOCRATICS). According to some, the internal cause of a thing's nature is the matter of which it is made; according to others, its nature is form or the arrangement of its constituent parts. A nature so understood is tied to the individual things possessing it; and in ancient Greek philosophy the individual things making up the *kosmos* or system of nature were thought to be connected to others by purely natural 'joints', as PLATO put it in the *Phaedrus*. In addition to connecting natural objects these joints also marked out their extremities, thus distinguishing them from one another. ARISTOTLE viewed the nature of a thing as its form or essence, that which distinguishes it from objects of other kinds. Aristotle's conception of the natural world was developed by medieval and early rationalist philosophers (*see* RATIONALISM) into the view that nature consists of a system of essences on which God has chosen to bestow existence (*see* ESSENCE/ACCIDENT). This view has adherents even today; they contend that the distinguishing features of individual essences (or 'possible individuals') are discoverable from necessary truths to which we have access a priori.

The idea that nature has a structure that can be known a priori has been vigorously attacked by philosophers in the empiricist tradition (*see* EMPIRICISM). The attack was initiated by LOCKE, who claimed that the 'constitution of a thing's insensible parts' on which its observable qualities depend is not known to us. Since this 'constitution' is basically what a thing's nature or essence was originally taken to be, Locke insisted that a thing's essential nature (or 'real essence') cannot provide the basis on which we identify that object and distinguish it from others. Our basis for identifying and distinguishing objects consists, rather, of 'properties' that we associate with a thing's name. Locke's view on this matter amounts to the idea that our basis for classifying objects into 'natural kinds' (*see* NATURAL KIND) is fundamentally conventional – an idea not incompatible with the fact that our decision to adopt a certain convention is often affected by our empirical beliefs about the world.

The impact of empirical discoveries on the classification and identification of natural objects has resulted in a view of nature that is profoundly different from those of the ancient Greeks, the medieval schoolmen, and the rationalist metaphysicians of the eighteenth century. In spite of significant differences these earlier views all involve the idea that nature consists mainly of persisting things (individual substances (*see* SUBSTANCE)) spread out in space, interacting with one another, and enduring in time; the persisting things that, at least for non-Aristotelians, are not spread out in space (namely, minds, spirits or intelligences) are intimately associated with bodies that are. This common idea is missing from some current views of nature, and it is certainly not a necessary ingredient of any view that could conceivably be accepted in the future. According to most current views, nature does not contain such things as minds or intelligences; and on some views it is not a system of persisting things but an extremely complex 'process' – a system of overlapping events or singularities in a multidimensional 'field'. Different conceptual pictures of nature can, of course, agree about appearances; but an acceptable picture is not bound to contain some particular structure that can be identified and known by purely armchair methods.

BIBLIOGRAPHY

Aune, B.: *Metaphysics: The Elements* (Minneapolis: University of Minnesota Press, 1985).
Collingwood, R.G.: *The Idea of Nature* (Oxford: Clarendon Press, 1945).
Gribbin, J.: *In Search of Schrödinger's Cat: Quantum Physics and Reality* (New York: Bantam Books, 1984).
Whitehead, A.N.: *The Concept of Nature* (Cambridge: Cambridge University Press, 1920).

BRUCE AUNE

negation Negative events, which seem to be needed as the worldly correspondents of true negative propositions, are troublesome because we lack criteria of identity for them, there being no non-arbitrary answer to 'How many forest fires did not occur yesterday?' To avoid ontological commitment to them attempts have been made to analyse negative into positive propositions. That Theaetetus does not fly is analysed either as that every property of Theaetetus is other than being in flight or that there is some positive property of Theaetetus that is incompatible with being in flight, for example, being planted on the ground. It is objected that these analyses are viciously circular, since otherness and incompatibility are themselves negative relations. This dispute, unfortunately, has resembled a crap game played with unmarked dice, because it was not informed by an adequate criterion for distinguishing between negative and positive propositions or properties. The most promising criteria are either those based on a difference in the degree of specificity of negative and positive properties or based on a difference in their entailment relations. For example, positive properties, but not negative ones, entail both properties of the same qualities as themselves; and properties of different qualities from themselves. For example, whereas non-red entails only non-crimson and other properties of the same quality, red entails both coloured and non-green, where coloured is the same quality as red, while non-green is a different quality.

See also NOTHINGNESS; PROPOSITION, STATE OF AFFAIRS.

BIBLIOGRAPHY

Gale, R.M.: *Negation and Non-Being*, American Philosophical Quarterly Monograph Series No. 10 (1976).

Prior, A.N.: 'Negation', in *Encyclopedia of Philosophy* ed. P. Edwards (New York: Collier, 1967), vol. 5, 458–63.

RICHARD M. GALE

Neoplatonism A modern term used by historians to designate (1) the philosophy of PLOTINUS and that of Platonizing philosophers influenced by him in late antiquity; and (2) medieval and Renaissance philosophies and ideas influenced by ancient Neoplatonism. The term is intended to prevent confusion between Plotinus' version of Platonism and the PLATONISM of PLATO himself and of the early Academy. Historians also use the expression 'Middle Platonism' to refer to the varied, eclectic versions of Platonic philosophy current in the ancient world from the first century BC to the second century AD, the intellectual milieu in which Plotinus worked. A general definition of Neoplatonism might take the form of a summary of Plotinus' fundamental philosophical positions. However it must be emphasized that Plotinus' philosophical heirs showed varied, sometimes diverging, tendencies, that they sometimes rejected Plotinian theses and that they drew inspiration from other sources. The following phases in the history of Neoplatonism might be distinguished.

Plotinus' teaching at Rome in 244–69. This teaching, whose originality was recognized (and attacked) by contemporaries in Greece, attracted members of the ruling class in Rome. The school included an inner circle of close pupils, in particular Amelius and Porphyry (*c*.232–305), both of whom worked to preserve, propagate and defend the master's ideas (*see* TREE OF PORPHYRY). Porphyry published a biography of Plotinus and the edition of Plotinus' writings (the *Enneads*) that has prevailed. He also prepared a digest of Plotinian philosophy (the *Sentences*) and commentaries (since lost). However Porphyry was also a philosopher in his own right and introduced new developments. He did much to incorporate ARISTOTLE's logical works in the curriculum of Neoplatonist schools and wrote an influential introduction (the *Isagoge*) to Aristotle's *Categories*. He also took great interest (compared to Plotinus' relative indifference) in various religious rites, oracles, forms of wisdom (Greek and barbarian) as promising the final good to mankind in general. He refined aspects of Plotinus' treatment of the relation between SOUL and body and (although so little of Porphyry's major works survives that the evidence is fragmentary and disputed) seems both to have radicalized the ineffable transcendence of the ultimate cause, the One, and to have insisted on its immanence as the first aspect of the self-generation of Intellect, the One being described as the pure (indeterminate) act of existing prior to the determination of existence in Intellect as substance. Partly due to Porphyry's efforts, Plotinus' *Enneads* were read and had a profound impact (with Porphyry's works) on intellectuals, Greek and Latin speaking, pagan and Christian, of the fourth century, in particular Gregory of Nyssa (*c*.335–*c*.394) and AUGUSTINE.

Probably a former pupil of Porphyry, Iamblichus (*c*.250–*c*.325) headed an influential philosophical school in Apamea (Syria) at the beginning of the fourth century. As in Porphyry's case (compared to the surviving corpus of Plotinian writings), very little of Iamblichus' serious philosophical work, in particular his commentaries on Plato and on Aristotle, is extant. It seems clear that he sharply criticized Plotinus and Porphyry; that he attempted to integrate systematically ancient and barbarian forms of revelation, wisdom, theologies and religious practices (in particular theurgy) into the general framework of Platonic metaphysics (thus first causes and the Ideas were seen as corresponding to gods); that he developed a formal curriculum of Platonic dialogues together with an exegetical method ensuring that each text would contribute to leading the reader progressively towards the One; that he developed greatly the use of mathematical terms and concepts in metaphysics (monads, dyads, triads, principles of ordering and linking of members of a series); and that he introduced further levels of transcendent reality, in particular a level between the ultimate cause and intelligible being. On the basis of his book *On the Mysteries*, Iamblichus has been dismissed as selling out Greek rationalism (still strong in Plotinus and Porphyry) to 'oriental' superstition. However recent research is pointing to a complete revision of this judgement. An emphasis on cult and magic seems to have characterized an offshoot of Iamblichus' school at Pergamum (which influenced in turn the thought of the emperor Julian). However other aspects of Iamblichus' philosophy also evolved in the Neoplatonic school of Athens in the fifth century.

The school of Athens' more prominent members were Syrianus, Proclus, Damascius (b. *c*.458) and Simplicius (sixth century). For Syrianus (died *c*.437) we still have a commentary on Aristotle's *Metaphysics* in which Syrianus responds to Aristotle's criticisms of Plato. His pupil Proclus (412–85) was an influential head of the school and prolific writer whose output has in part survived. In his prologues to his commentary on Euclid he develops a theory of mathematics as a science intermediate between physics and metaphysics, dealing with objects projected by the soul and derived from transcendent Intellect. We also have dissertations on Plato's *Republic*, a commentary on Plato's *Timaeus*, an *Elements of Physics* and three works on metaphysics: a commentary on Plato's *Parmenides* (read as containing the highest Platonic science, 'dialectic', identified with Aristotelian metaphysics or 'theology'); a very full synthesis of this material (the *Platonic Theology*); and the *Elements of Theology*. This last work follows a quasi-geometrical method in presenting a chain of metaphysical propositions each supported by demonstrations. The propositions concern general principles of the structure of reality and CAUSATION as well as particular types of first causes: the One, the 'henads' (principles subordinate to the One) and intelligible being in its various degrees and ramifications. The formalization of the argument is impressive (if not always cogent) and yields a convenient manual of later Neoplatonic metaphysics. In 529 the emperor Justinian closed the (decidedly pagan) Athenian school: the fate of its remaining members is unclear.

A school of Neoplatonists survived in Alexandria (Egypt) in the fifth and sixth centuries. Several of its members (Hierocles (*c*.420), Ammonius (435/45–517/26)) were trained in Athens, but a Christian member of the school, John Philoponus (sixth century), attacked Athenian Neoplatonism. The Alexandrians were distinguished for their commentaries on Aristotle and a course given by Ammonius on Aristotle's *Metaphysics*, preserved by a pupil, Asclepius, survives.

Ancient Neoplatonism had considerable impact on Byzantine thought through the prestige of the work of a Christian much influenced by Proclus, Pseudo-Dionysius, and through Michael Psellos' (*c*.1018–79) revival of Neoplatonism in the eleventh century. In the medieval West, Neoplatonism was known indirectly through the works of Augustine and BOETHIUS and translations of Pseudo-Dionysius, whereas in the Islamic world philosophers had direct access to versions of the works of Plotinus, Porphyry and Proclus. In fifteenth-century Italy, Marsilio Ficino (1433–99) led a successful effort to counter Aristotelian scholasticism with a revival of Neoplatonism.

BIBLIOGRAPHY

Beierwaltes, W.: *Proklos. Grundzüge seiner Metaphysik* (Frankfurt: Klostermann, 1979).
Dillon, J. ed. and trans.: *Iamblichi Chalcidensis in Platonis dialogos commentariorum fragmenta* (Leiden: E.J. Brill, 1973).

Dillon, J. and Morrow, G. trans.: *Proclus' Commentary on Plato's Parmenides* (Princeton, NJ: Princeton University Press, 1987).

Dodds, E.R. ed. and trans.: *Proclus The Elements of Theology* (Oxford: Clarendon Press, 1963).

Hadot, P.: *Porphyre et Victorinus* (Paris: Etudes augustiniennes, 1968).

Lloyd, A.C.: *The Anatomy of Neoplatonism* (Oxford: Clarendon Press, 1990).

O'Meara, D.J.: *Pythagoras Revived. Mathematics and Philosophy in Late Antiquity* (Oxford: Clarendon Press, 1989).

Wallis, R.T.: *Neoplatonism* (London: Duckworth, 1972).

DOMINIC J. O'MEARA

Newton, Isaac (1642–1727) British mathematician and natural philosopher who, in mathematics: invented the basic techniques of infinitesimal analysis; advanced the theories of infinite series and of interpolations and other methods of approximation; and contributed fundamentally to the theory of algebraic curves; in physics: formulated the principles of classical mechanics; initiated the systematic theory of fluid dynamics, including the theory of the propagation of sound; discovered the optical spectrum and the basic property associated with it now called the wave-length; discovered the law of universal gravitation; and with the help of the latter, began the development of the modern detailed theory of planetary motions.

The publication of Newton's 'De gravitatio et æquipondio fluidorum' has given us important new information concerning Newton's views on the fundamental constitution of the world; the following account is strongly influenced by this source.

The document in question is an uncompleted (and untitled) manuscript on hydrostatics (the title now generally given to it is merely its opening phrase); of uncertain date – believed by most authorities to be early in Newton's career, but containing significant points of contact with Newton (1687, 1713) and with a view of Newton's

reported from the 1690s (see Fraser, 1891, vol. II, pp. 321–2, n. 2). Having announced his intention of treating the indicated subject, Newton introduces as basic (undefined) terms *quantity*, *duration* and *space*; and defines the terms *place*, *body*, *rest* and *motion*. Remarking then that in these definitions he has, in opposition to the principles of the Cartesians, (1) 'supposed space to be given as distinct from body' and (2) 'determined motion with respect to the parts of . . . space, not with respect to the positions of contiguous bodies', he undertakes to defend these views against the doctrines of DESCARTES. There follows a metaphysical disquisition upon these subjects, which occupies some two-thirds of the manuscript.

That disquisition makes it clearer than it has previously been how fundamental a role the notions of SPACE AND TIME play, both in Newton's conception of the ultimate constitution of things and in his view of the structure of our knowledge. (It may be instructive, in this respect, to refer to the very different, but equally central, function of these two notions in the philosophy of KANT, for whom space and time, as the two pure 'forms of our intuition', afford the key to the very possibility of systematic – or 'scientific' – knowledge.) In the scholium on space, time, place and motion, in Newton (1687), the doctrine is propounded that the spatial and temporal structures of the world are 'absolute' – that is, that their being and their properties are independent of the *bodies* that occupy space and whose positions change with time. This has often been glossed, in the light of the Scholium Generale (appearing first in Newton, 1713) and some passages in the *Opticks* (Newton, 1730, Queries 28 (1952, p. 370), 31 (1952, p. 403)), with the interpretation that the posited structures independent of body are, for Newton, *dependent* upon (or are *aspects* of) God. (For a classic expression of this view, see Burtt, 1955, pp. 244, 256–262.) The present text confirms a close connection between Newton's conceptions of space and time and his theology (for in it we read, of extension, that it *tanquam Dei effectus emanativus . . . subsistit*: ('subsists as, so to speak, an emanative effect of God') (Newton, 1962, p. 99)); and yet it shows that in Newton's view the former are in a fundamental sense *not* dependent upon the latter. Indeed, in a later passage of the work the enigmatic phrase just quoted is explicated more fully:

Space is an affection of a being just as a being [*entis quatenus ens affectio*]. No being exists or can exist that does not have relation in some way to space. God is everywhere, created minds are somewhere, and a body in the space that it fills; and whatever is neither everywhere nor anywhere is not. And hence it follows that space is an emanative effect of the first-existing being, for *if I posit any being whatever I posit space*. And the like may be affirmed of Duration: namely both are affections or attributes of a being [*entis affectiones sive attributas*] in accordance with which the quantity of the existence of any individual is denominated, as to amplitude of presence and perseverance in its being. (Newton, 1962, p. 103, emphasis added)

Thus Newton himself glosses '*a* is an emanative effect of *b*' by: *if I posit b, a is posited*; and declares further that space and time, as (in effect) the *measures of existence*, must 'subsist' in order for *anything whatever* to exist. Space and time are, therefore, 'emanative effects' of *whatever* the 'primarily existing' thing may be; and so, if this (as Newton certainly believes) is God, of God.

As to the *ontological category* to which space and time belong, they are, according to Newton, *sui generis*. Of *extension* he says (1962, p. 99) that it is *neither substance nor accident*; nor is it 'simply nothing' (a remark that probably glances at the classical atomistic doctrine equating 'the void' with *non-being*); but 'it has a certain mode of existence proper to itself which suits neither substances nor accidents' (*see* ATOMISM). It is not a SUBSTANCE because it does not *act* – and the power to act, Newton says, is what philosophers all tacitly understand to be characteristic of substances. It is not an

accident because 'we can conceive clearly of extension existing as it were without any subject'. And for the same reason, it is not nothing: 'Of nothing, no Idea is given . . . but of extension we have an Idea the clearest of all.' (Thus to the primacy of space and time as 'ontological structures' there corresponds a kind of *epistemological* primacy, on which Newton does not here expatiate further, and which it is beyond the scope of the present article to discuss.)

The most radical step in this Newtonian metaphysics comes next: Newton proceeds to consider how one principal sort of what are ordinarily called 'substances' – namely bodies – *might* fundamentally be constituted; and comes to the conclusion that *the concept (or category) of substance* (as that which *underlies* properties) *is not required for this at all*. Rather, he argues, bodies, as 'substances' – i.e. as beings that *act* – can be conceived with full clarity in terms of the notions of space and time, and of certain (entirely intelligible) *attributes*, themselves conceived as attributes *of regions of space* (at a given time) – what in later usage would be called 'fields on space'. His exposition takes the form of an answer to the question *what God might do to create a* (new) *body*. But 'might', not 'must': what the fundamental constitution of bodies is, Newton says, we cannot know with certainty; the best we can do is to form a conception of something that *would possess all the properties we have come to know in bodies*, and conclude that this is *a* way they may be constituted – *one* way they could have been made. (This epistemological point is associated by Newton with a metaphysical/theological one. Bodies he regards as products of God's *agency* – of his *will* – in contrast with space and time, which are 'emanative' effects (read: *purely conceptual consequences* of God's existence – or of the existence of anything at all). Their constitution is thus in a strict sense *arbitrary*; and so to be determined at most with probability, on the basis of our experience of them.)

On the account Newton offers, a body is a region of space endowed with the following properties:

(1) It is *impenetrable by other bodies*: that is, endowed with the property of excluding encroachment (in the course of time) by *other such regions*.

(2) It is *mobile* (as a rigid configuration): that is, the impenetrability and other posited properties are to be conceived as 'not conserved always in the same part of space, but able to be transferred hither and thither according to certain laws, yet so that the quantity and shape of that impenetrable space are not changed'. (Without this proviso, (1) would make no sense; now one sees its meaning to be that among the laws of the *propagation* of the regions constituting bodies from one part of space to another is a law forbidding their mutual penetration.)

(3) It has the power to *interact with minds*, stimulating sensation (under appropriate conditions) and being moved by acts of will (under appropriate conditions).

Thus we see (and Newton emphasizes the point) that on his analysis the essential properties of bodies include not only extension (as for Descartes), and such 'mechanical' properties as impenetrability (LOCKE's 'solidity') – not only, in short, what Locke identifies as the 'primary qualities' of body – but also the fundamental principle of what Locke calls 'secondary qualities': the power of interacting with minds (*see* QUALITY, PRIMARY/SECONDARY).

Conditions (1) and (2) provide a precise *metaphysical* foundation for Newton's *physics*. The conceptual framework of his physics (Newton, 1687, Preface, Definitions, and Laws of Motion; 1730, Query 31 (1952, pp. 397, 401–2); cf. Stein, 1970, 1990) may be said to be derived from (1) and (2) through the further specification of a notion of what Newton calls a *natural power* or *force of nature*. These 'powers' or 'forces' are the principles of motion of the corporeal fields that are called for by (2). The more specific stipulation of the physics divides these principles into two classes: a 'passive principle', the *vis inertiæ* or force of

inactivity of matter, whose constitutive law is the three Laws of Motion of the *Principia* (1687); and a class of 'active principles', having the form of *laws of interaction* of bodies (subject to the conditions stated by the Laws of Motion). The law of one such 'active principle' was discovered by Newton, in the great investigation reported in his *Principia*: the law of the universal gravitation of matter.

We may summarize this conception of the nature of body by saying that its root is indeed the idea expressed by Newton that 'substantiality' resides in the ability to *act*: that it is a metaphysics in which the category of interaction, not that of 'substance as ultimate substrate', is fundamental (Newton explicitly characterizes the 'passive' and 'active' principles of motion he speaks of as 'general Laws of Nature, *by which the Things themselves are form'd*' (1730, Query 31 (1952, p. 401)).

It is clear that there is one lacuna in the metaphysics described above: the characterization of body has presupposed the concept of mind; and nothing has been said about the constitution of the latter. Newton briefly addresses this issue (1962, p. 111; translation, pp. 144–5). He suggests that an understanding of those attributes that constitute the mind's *powers* – on a par with the characterization in (1)–(3) above of the powers of body – might lead to an analogous metaphysics of mind (including even God) as constituted by a nexus of intelligible attributes or powers; but concludes that 'while we cannot form an Idea . . . even of our own power by which we move our bodies, it would be rash to say what is the substantial foundation of minds'.

WRITINGS

'De gravitatio et æquipondio fluidorum', in *Unpublished Scientific Papers of Isaac Newton* ed. A.R. Hall and M. Boas Hall (Cambridge: Cambridge University Press, 1962), 89–121 (Latin original); 121–56 (English translation). (Passages quoted above are translated by the present author.)

Philosophiæ naturalis principia mathematica (London: 1687); 2nd edn (London: 1713); 3rd edn (London: 1726); trans. Andrew Motte (from the 3rd edn), *The Mathematical Principles of Natural Philosophy* (London: 1729; repr. London: Dawsons of Pall Mall, 1968).

Opticks: or, a Treatise of the Reflections, Refractions, Inflections and Colours of Light 4th edn (London: 1730; repr. New York: Dover Publications, 1952).

BIBLIOGRAPHY

Burtt, E.A.: *The Metaphysical Foundations of Modern Physical Science* revised edn (New York: 1932; repr. New York: Doubleday Anchor Books, 1955), ch. VII, 'The metaphysics of Newton', 207–302.

Fraser, A.C.: annotations in his edition of John Locke, *An Essay concerning Human Understanding*, 2 vols (Oxford: Oxford University Press, 1891; repr. New York: Dover Publications, 1959).

Stein, H.: 'On the notion of field in Newton, Maxwell, and beyond', in *Historical and Philosophical Perspectives of Science* ed. R.H. Stuewer, Minnesota Studies in the Philosophy of Science, vol. V (Minneapolis: University of Minnesota Press, 1970), 264–87.

Stein, H.: 'On Locke, "the Great Huygenius, and the incomparable Mr. Newton" ', in *Philosophical Perspectives on Newtonian Science* ed. P. Bricker and R.I.G. Hughes (Cambridge, MA: MIT Press, 1990), 17–47.

HOWARD STEIN

Nietzsche, Friedrich (1844–1900) German writer and philosopher. Nietzsche was born in the Prussian provinces of Silesia and educated in classical languages and literatures. He was appointed Professor of Classical Philology at Basel when only 24. By the time he was obliged by poor health to retire, a mere ten years later (in 1879), he had emancipated himself from two early influences – SCHOPENHAUER and Richard Wagner (1813–83) – and his initial philological and cultural concerns had turned in a philosophical direction. During the next decade, despite debilitating health problems, Nietzsche managed to author a dozen books – volumes of aphorisms and polemics, collections of philosophical essays, and the literary–philosophical masterpiece *Thus Spoke Zarathustra*. He also kept notebooks in which he wrote extensively, leaving a great deal of material the significance of which is highly controversial. In early 1889 he suffered a complete physical and mental collapse, from which he never recovered, and lingered on in invalid insanity until his death in 1900.

Nietzsche's reception in philosophy has been adversely affected by his appropriation and distortion by Nazi ideologists, by his hostility to much of the philosophical tradition, and by his unconventional style.

His philosophical efforts were motivated by his deep and impassioned concern with issues relating to values, morality, and the character and quality of human life. He was convinced that the consequences for these and other crucial matters of what he called 'the death of God' are profound; and so he considered it imperative to seek a fundamentally new alternative to traditional religious and philosophical ways of thinking – and also to the nihilism that he saw coming in the aftermath of their collapse and abandonment. He conceived the twin tasks of the 'philosophy of the future' he called for and sought to inaugurate as those of (re-)interpretation and (re-)valuation, involving a fundamental reassessment of truth and knowledge, and extending to a reconsideration of our own nature and possibilities – and therewith also of life and the world more generally. It was as he pursued this reconsideration that he was led to propose his interpretation of the basic character of both ourselves and the world in terms of 'will to power'.

The status of this comprehensive interpretation is much disputed. Some interpreters regard it as Nietzsche's new and different type of metaphysics, while others consider it to be his attempt to develop a non-metaphysical philosophical COSMOL-OGY, biology and anthropology. Still others contend that it is nothing of the kind, taking his critiques of language, truth and knowledge to rule out the viability of any philosophical enterprise of either sort; and that it is offered merely for its purported 'life-enhancing' value, or as the generalized expression of his conviction that all ways of thinking are but symptoms or projections of the needs and desires of those who initially developed or now embrace them.

It is beyond dispute, however, that the mature Nietzsche was relentlessly critical of the entire metaphysical tradition, which he regarded as fundamentally allied with religions that insidiously contrast this life and world to some imagined higher form of existence and ultimate reality transcending them. He considered both to be ill-motivated expressions of profound dissatisfaction with the conditions of life in this world, and to be incapable of withstanding critical scrutiny; and he waged his campaign against them on both of these levels. Thus he sought to subvert and lay to rest not only the 'God hypothesis' and the related 'soul hypothesis', but also the very idea of 'things-in-themselves' (*see* KANT; NOUMENAL/PHE-NOMENAL), and the rest of the entire inventory of the history of metaphysics (including Schopenhauer's 'world as will' as well as HEGEL's *Weltgeist* and matter-in-motion materialism), deeming all such notions to be warrantless fictions owing their invention and appeal entirely to naivety, error, the seductiveness of language, practical needs and ulterior motivation.

According to some of Nietzsche's interpreters, that for him is the end of the matter: metaphysics is to be 'deconstructed' and demolished rather than reformed, or replaced by any alternative sort of attempt to comprehend our human reality and the world of which we are a part. Yet he does appear to advance a comprehensive interpretation of them, not only in his unpublished manuscripts but also (if only sketchily) in his published writings; and it is arguable both that he was persuaded of its basic soundness, and that this is not inconsistent with his mature views on truth and knowledge (as they at least may be construed).

In place of all metaphysical schemes cast in terms of notions of the sorts he inventoried and dismissed, Nietzsche proposed an interpretation of the world as a dynamic affair without any inherent structure or final end: an interplay of forces ('at once one and many') ceaselessly organizing and reorganizing itself, as the fundamental assertive disposition he took to be characteristic of all such force gives rise to successive arrays of power relationships among the forms it takes (as 'dynamic quanta' and systems of such quanta). He called this ubiquitous disposition 'will to power'; and he invoked it to convey the basic character of all that goes on in the world, our lives included. 'This world is the will to power – and nothing besides! And you yourselves are also this will to power – and nothing besides!' Like most of what he wrote about the world and life in elaboration of this interpretation, this passage occurs in one of his notebooks; but he did invoke and tentatively advance it in his later published writings as well, as what he considered to be the best way (in terms of economy, warrant, explanatory power and adequacy) of making comprehensive sense of this world and what goes on in it.

The status of Nietzsche's thought of 'eternal recurrence' (the idea that everything recurs eternally) is more problematic. In a few entries in his notebooks he experimented with the possibility of arguing for it as an actual cosmological hypothesis, applying down to the level of particular events and their succession. He initially introduced it, however, and for the most part employed it, merely as a hypothetical extreme-case test of one's ability to affirm life without recourse to any appeal beyond life and the world as they are. So regarded, its only substantive import is that in this ever-changing world, the more things change the more they remain the same – with 'will to power' as the name of the game.

Nietzsche devoted far more effort to his attempt to reorient and contribute to our understanding of ourselves. He was concerned not only to criticize others' conceptions of our nature, but also to advance and develop a more tenable alternative to them. Beginning with the recognition that 'the type *Mensch*' is a form of animal life, he proceeded to reinterpret our attained humanity accordingly, attentive both to its emergent general features and to the differences it exhibits. He thus may be viewed as having sought to replace traditional metaphysics of the self and philosophies of *Geist* and mind with a kind of naturalistic philosophical anthropology, in which a multiplicity of perspectives upon human life are drawn upon in an attempt to do interpretive justice to it.

As he pursued this task, Nietzsche persistently brought two basic and complementary ideas into play: on the one hand, everything about ourselves must be the outcome of a development of an entirely mundane sort, relating to our evolution, history and life-circumstances – and on the other, any account given must do justice to the wealth of human phenomena discerned by diverse sorts of observation and investigation of the human scene. His many scattered particular comments and reflections pertaining to these matters typically express thoughts along only one or the other of these lines; but it is only if they are taken together that one-sided misunderstandings of his thinking – and (as he would have it) of the matters in question themselves – can be avoided. When this is done, it becomes clear that Nietzsche's naturalistic philosophical anthropology is emergentist rather than reductionist, and emphasizes the significance of the respects in which our original animality has been transformed in various ways and along differing lines – which in turn have set the stage for further actual and possible transformations (*see* REDUCTION, REDUCTIONISM).

In the course of his attempt to reckon with the varieties of our attained humanity and human possibilities, Nietzsche sought to show that, and how, many of the controversies in which philosophers long have engaged – concerning such matters as the nature of consciousness and its role in action, the freedom of the will and the mind/body relation – can be dealt with more satisfactorily than they traditionally have been by recasting the ways in which the issues are posed, and approaching the real issues in the multiperspectival and double-directional naturalistic manner indicated above. The merit of his efforts along these lines has only begun to be recognized; but it is considerable, and warrants his inclusion among the most important contributors to this area of inquiry (among others) in the history of modern philosophy. (*See* FREE WILL; MIND/BODY PROBLEM.)

WRITINGS

The Gay Science (Chemnitz: 1882); trans. W. Kaufmann (New York: Vintage, 1974).
Beyond Good and Evil (Leipzig: 1886); trans. W. Kaufmann (New York: Vintage, 1966).
Twilight of the Idols (Leipzig: 1889); trans. W. Kaufmann, in *The Portable Nietzsche* ed. W. Kaufmann (New York: Viking, 1954).
The Will to Power (Leipzig: 1901); ed. W. Kaufmann, trans. W. Kaufmann and R.J. Hollingdale (New York: Vintage, 1968).
Werke: Kritische Gesamtausgabe ed. G. Colli and M. Montinari, 30 vols (Berlin: de Gruyter, 1967–78).

BIBLIOGRAPHY

Danto, A.: *Nietzsche as Philosopher* (New York: Macmillan, 1965).
Deleuze, G.: *Nietzsche and Philosophy* trans. H. Tomlinson (New York: Columbia University Press, 1983).
Heidegger, M.: *Nietzsche* 4 vols, trans. D. Krell (New York: Harper and Row, 1979–87).
Nehamas, A.: *Nietzsche: Life as Literature* (Cambridge, MA: Harvard University Press, 1985).

Schacht, R.: *Nietzsche* (London: Routledge and Kegan Paul, 1983).

RICHARD SCHACHT

noema, noesis HUSSERL introduced these two words in his *Ideas* (1913) to stand for the features that characterize the directedness of acts. Each act has a noema, a collection of features that make the act be *as if of* an object which is experienced in a certain way, in some specific mode of appearance, a specific orientation, with specific traits and specific modes of indeterminate indication, etc. (*Ideas*, p. 190). The noema has two components, one, the 'object meaning' that integrates the various components of our experience into experiences of the various features of *one* object, and one, the 'thetic' component, that differentiates acts of different kinds, for example, the act of perceiving an object from the act of remembering it or thinking about it. While the noema can be the same from act to act, the noesis is the concrete mental process that is integrated by a noema. There is hence a close parallelism between noema and noesis, which are the two main items studied in Husserl's PHENOMENOLOGY.

BIBLIOGRAPHY

Husserl, E.: *Ideen* (The Hague: 1913); trans. F. Kersten, *Ideas* (The Hague: Martinus Nijhoff, 1982).

DAGFINN FØLLESDAL

nominalism From Latin *nominalis* ('pertaining to names'). In scholastic philosophy, the position that the only real universality expressed by nominalized predicates or common nouns resides in their status as names that are capable of referring to many particular things. More recently, the view that assertions are meaningless, false, unverifiable, or lacking in economy of reference, unless discourse is interpreted and theories are reconstructed so as to avoid commitment to any entities other than individuals.

While nominalists have shared a rejection of universals in favour of particulars or individuals (*see* UNIVERSALS AND PARTICULARS), such rejections have been as varied as the functions that universals allegedly perform: one objected to classification of individuals by virtue of their entering into some relation to a non-individual; to non-particular designata or extensions of common nouns or predicates; to abstract meanings or intensions determining applicability of phrases to many things; to objects of knowledge or conception such that several people could grasp the same one; to ideals, idealizations, merely possible or potential entities; and often to abstract or non-physical items of any sort. (*See* EXTENSION/INTENSION.)

Just as varied were the grounds for such rejection: nominalists have been suspicious of entities which, if spatial and temporal at all, could be wholly in two places at once; of mental constructs, often infinite in number, that were supposed to serve as grounds for natural classifications; of items which, though said to be causally inert, could yet be spotted in things or intuited by minds; of discourse so interpreted as to imply the existence of entities beyond those that seem to constitute its intended subject matter; and generally of positing, ahead of discovery, entities of such kinds or in such numbers as to serve at most the convenience of theorists while widening and mystifying the gap between theories and their applications.

The medieval position arose from Porphyry's (*c.*232–305) commentary on ARISTOTLE in the third century over the questions whether genera and species were mind-dependent, corporeal, or sensible. Medieval nominalists – among which one counts Roscelin (1050–1120) and OCKHAM – held that members of a species had nothing in common except the species-name that referred to each member and, in the case of Ockham, a mental token of that species-name.

British empiricists (*see* EMPIRICISM) have tended to advocate some views at least con-

359

genial to nominalism: HOBBES held that only words could be universal, by virtue of applying to many particulars. LOCKE regarded universals as mental representatives of many particulars. BERKELEY rejected abstract ideas in addition to non-mental universals. HUME held that particular ideas become 'general' due to associations of terms with similar stimuli.

While the controversy regarding 'universals' in the traditional sense has continued to this day, some recent disputants – impressed by the deductive and expressive power of set theory (including that of representing properties by certain sets) – have shifted their interest from properties to classes, and some nominalists have come to focus their suspicions on the merely structural differentiation and unlimited positing of these apparently more basic abstracta (*see* CLASS, COLLECTION, SET). Among such recent nominalists we count LEŚNIEWSKI. He constructed the systems of Protothetic, Ontology and Mereology to give formal treatment to logic, to the copula 'is' and predicative classes, and to the PART/WHOLE relation and classes as 'wholes'. In doing so, only expression-tokens and substitutional quantifications were employed while the theory accounts for some cardinal arithmetic.

Probably best known among contemporary nominalists is GOODMAN, who clarified the distinction between individuals (items individuated by their least parts) and classes (items individuated by their members, and hence by structure). He reformulated and used Mereology in the construction of a phenomenalistic system and outlined a theory of meaning. Applying QUINE's criterion regarding ontological commitments, Goodman rejects theories that carry a commitment to non-individuals, but endorses individuals of whatever kind, even qualitative or abstract ones.

Throughout history, the few heretical nominalists have been urged to rival their numerous antagonists (now often called 'Platonists') in theoretical achievements. The oldest such challenge concerns a credible account of classification or predication, which nominalists have usually attempted in terms of some *resemblance* relation. An example: Let the triadic primitive 'resembles', as in 'x resembles y but not z', be explained to a Platonist as asserting 'there is a quality Q such that x and y have Q but z lacks Q'. Let 'white' positively designate some white paradigms and negatively some non-white exemplars (at least one of each) so that, whenever an object resembles all of the positively designated things without being what the Platonist would call 'white', it is negatively designated. Then (disregarding type/token distinctions) a sentence of the form 's is white' will be true just in case the designatum of 's' resembles all things positively designated by 'white' but none of those negatively designated by it. All non-universal and non-empty extensions admit of such treatment.

Another challenge concerns the construction of a theory of meaning that might rival intensional logic. Some nominalists have felt that the Platonistic assignment to expressions of various abstracta, such as possibilia or intensions, serves just by inducing equivalence relations ('denoting or expressing the same thing') between expressions which, in turn, motivate various principles of interchange. A nominalist might instead provide for expressions equivalent relative to context by employing several modes of designation. For example, if words primarily designate things to which they apply, and secondarily designate representatives, then 'unicorn' and 'elf' will fail to primarily designate anything, but will secondarily designate concrete pictures, statues, and other representatives of unicorns or elves respectively. From 'People hunted unicorns' infer 'People hunted elves' only if everything that is both primarily and secondarily designated by 'unicorn' is also so designated by 'elf' (see Goodman, 1949).

Nominalists, thirdly, have been challenged to reconstruct science. Significant advances on this project have been made by formulating theories so that only entities intrinsic to their subject matter (for example, in physics, physical objects of any kind, but not real numbers) are mentioned, while Platonists are being appeased by representation theorems exhibiting the connections with classical sciences (see Field, 1980).

Finally, nominalists have been urged to develop some powerful mathematics. Nominalists may not want to reconstruct all of extant mathematics, they may be sceptical of generality attempted by positing 'enough' entities for every conceivable application, and they will resist commitment to abstract items where abstractly related things will do. Still, at least some fragments of cardinal arithmetic and of the theories of natural numbers and fractions are available (see Gottlieb, 1980). Technically, they rely either on general variable-binding operators (with variables ranging only over individuals), or on substitutional quantification. But no foundational system is yet known that might be powerful enough to replace set theory while remaining acceptable to nominalists.

Computers and robots are concrete and apparently incapable of establishing an intuitive rapport with numbers or Forms. Non-idealized accounts of how they function – including how robots might 'learn' principled classifications – are likely to meet nominalistic standards. Some computer scientists concerned with working implementations, just like nominalists, have been critical of infinitary methods and abstractions without concretely programmable counterparts. There is hope, therefore, that nominalism and computer science will increasingly benefit from interaction.

See also PLATONISM.

BIBLIOGRAPHY

Field, H.H.: *Science Without Numbers – A Defence of Nominalism* (Princeton, NJ: Princeton University Press, 1980).
Goodman, N.: 'On likeness of meaning', *Analysis* 10 (1949), 1–7.
Goodman, N.: *The Structure of Appearance* (Cambridge: 1951); 3rd edn (Dordrecht: Reidel, 1977).
Goodman, N.: 'A world of individuals', in *The Problem of Universals* ed. I.M. Bochenski *et al.* (Notre Dame, IN: University of Notre Dame Press, 1956), 13–31.
Gottlieb, D.: *Ontological Economy – Substitutional Quantification and Mathematics* (Oxford and New York: Oxford University Press, 1980).

ROLF A. EBERLE

non-existent objects Saying that *a* does not exist (or that Fs do not exist) can mean that there is no such thing as *a* (that there are no Fs), so it can be a truism to say there are no non-existent objects. Some (e.g. MEINONG) have meant something else: existing objects are a special subclass of things, and there are objects outside that subclass, including fictional characters, golden mountains, and (perhaps) even round squares. RUSSELL interpreted Meinong as holding that for *any* predicate F, there are things which are F; if there exist no Fs then the Fs are among the non-existents. This view appears untenable, since if S is any false sentence, we can define F to be '*being an* x *such that* S', and the falsehood S follows logically from the claim that there are Fs. Meinong's actual view may escape this objection, since he limited his assumption of non-existents to Fs formed in natural ways from certain sorts of predicates ('nuclear' predicates); 'exists' itself is not one of these, though 'golden' and 'being a mountain' are. Another approach is to assume objects for any complex F whatsoever, but deny its decomposition in problematic cases; for example, one assumes that there are things that are round-and-square, but refuses to infer that such things are round (or square). A third is to assume (non-existent) Fs only when they are required for some branch of study, perhaps assuming fictional characters and frictionless planes but not gold mountains or round squares.

See also EXISTENCE; FICTIONAL TRUTH, OBJECTS AND CHARACTERS.

BIBLIOGRAPHY

Parsons, T.: *Nonexistent Objects* (New Haven: Yale University Press, 1980).

TERENCE PARSONS

nothingness In contrast with absences within the world, nothingness is the absence of the world itself – a total absence of every positive *contingent* reality, this qualification being in deference to those who believe that there are necessary beings, such as God, numbers and properties. (And, if properties, then why not a topologically and metrically amorphous space-time receptacle that creates the possibility of their being multiply instantiated and serves as the grounds of their individuation?). BERGSON utilized the incompatibility theory of NEGATION to mount an ontological argument for the existence of contingent positive realities: since a being can be absent only if its absence is entailed by some positive reality, the concept of a total absence, a nothingness, is a contradiction in terms. While there is some plausibility to the incompatibility analysis of an intraworld absence, for example, analysing 'There are no unicorns' into 'Every existent object has some positive property that is incompatible with unicornness' (but only some, since it is conceivable that some man would lack an odour without this being entailed by his positive properties), the deployment of this analysis to 'No contingent beings exist' results in the dubious 'Every existent being has some positive property that is incompatible with being existent.' What could that property be?

BIBLIOGRAPHY

Bergson, H.: *Creative Evolution* trans. A. Mitchell (New York: The Modern Library, 1944).
Gale, R.M.: *Negation and Non-Being*, American Philosophical Quarterly Monograph Series No. 10 (1976).

Munitz, M.K.: *The Mystery of Existence* (New York: Appleton-Century-Crofts, 1965).

RICHARD M. GALE

noumenal/phenomenal Noumenon: in Platonic and Neoplatonic philosophy a term applying exclusively to objects not accessible by means of sense perception (*see* NEOPLATONISM; PLATO; PLATONISM). Hence phenomenon: a term applying exclusively to objects only accessible by sense perception. The distinction is implicit in LEIBNIZ's idea of the universe as possessing a 'double government' of reason and forms, and of mechanical necessity and material objects.

Leibniz's metaphor applies to KANT's distinction between the intelligible and the sensible words. It was a central part of Kant's critical programme, especially in the *Critique of Pure Reason* (1781), to seek to limit the pretensions of reason, and to show that we can have justified theoretical knowledge only of that which is given in sensation. Part of the argument for this restriction introduces a new conceptualization of the noumenal. A phenomenon is a sense-contentful object determined by the CATEGORIES of the understanding and by SPACE AND TIME. A noumenon, considered in the positive sense, would then have to be a determinate non-sense-contentful and uncategorized object, an '*object of a non-sensible intuition*' (Kant, 1781, p. 268). Kant thought that we cannot comprehend the real possibility of such an (intellectual) intuition. We must think of a noumenon in the negative sense of the term: 'so far as it is *not an object of our sensible intuition*' (Kant, 1781, p. 268). Hence we cannot have theoretical knowledge of that which transcends the empirical world. Instead, the concept of the noumenon (in the negative sense) comes to play an altogether different, albeit necessary role: it serves as a *limit* on the objective validity of empirical knowledge by encouraging the prevention of extending sensible intuition to things in themselves (noumenal objects in the positive sense of the term). The concept of the noumenon, therefore, has only a negative employment.

All phenomena are determined in time (and most in space), are naturally caused, and can be treated mathematically. Human activity, however, is not limited to cognition of such objects. Such activity involves choices and works, volition and the exercise of skills. The exercise of will requires freedom from the compulsion of natural (efficient) CAUSATION; the will must be capable of entertaining alternatives as it contemplates what *ought to be* (not what is or must be in the natural world). In the *Critique of Pure Reason* Kant had shown that natural causality is not logically incompatible with causality through freedom (initiating action by means of choosing between intelligible alternatives) (Kant, 1781, pp. 464–79). He also suggested that some appearances seem to have both an empirical and an intelligible character. Some naturally caused events are also, considered with respect to their possibility as *responsible actions*, in part created by means of a purposeful choice.

In the *Critique of Practical Reason* (1788) Kant deals with the problem of justifying morality, and in the *Critique of Judgement* (1790) he analyses the free production of works of art. In both of these works the noumenal is now firmly identified with the world of free and purposive action, in seeming contradiction to the view of the noumenal in the first *Critique*. Kant attempts to remove this apparent contradiction by means of his distinction between theoretical knowing (which always involves objects naturally caused), and practical knowing (which involves suspending the structures of theorizing, and replacing them with the practical reality of freedom). There remains a crucial question. Clearly every event is natural in the sense that some antecedent causal factors make a difference in its coming into being. But if only some natural events are also to be understood as in part purposively caused, how are we to identify them, especially in view of the fact that we have no *knowledge* of noumena? Human behaviour, it would seem, is as regular in certain respects as is the behaviour of any part of nature.

How are we to prevent a reading of Kant that commits him to thinking that humans are resident in two worlds: a world of determined appearances, and a world of free intelligibilia? Beck (1960) argues that attention to another distinction made by Kant will resolve the problem. Kant taught that the categories are concepts that apply *constitutively*, they render appearances objective. Ideas of reason (God, freedom, the universe) apply only *regulatively*, as heuristic maxims guiding research but not determining objects. Beck suggests that if we drop this as a hard and fast distinction, and think of both concepts and ideas as having only a regulative employment, then we can resolve the problem by thinking not of humans as resident in two worlds, the phenomenal and the noumenal, but as taking *perspectives* on different aspects of human work: as spectators, we see a world determined by cognitive structures; as actors, we engage in purposive activity.

Some would reply that we get this philosophically gratifying result only by tampering with Kant's system, and by allowing a liberalization of Kant's view that space and time and the categories are species-universal, necessary and unique. However, Butts (1986) argues that Kant himself provided grounds for such a liberalization in his resolutions of the third (freedom/determinism) and fourth (necessary being/no necessary being) ANTINOMIES of the first *Critique*. On this reading, Kant's position is not that we live in both a noumenal and a phenomenal 'world', but rather than we can view our experience in two different ways. The interests of knowledge can be fulfilled only if the application of space and time and the categories is exceptionless. The interests of reason can only be satisfied if some actions are taken to be purposive or free. The difference is a matter of goals: the goal of theoretical knowing requires that cognitive structures be brought into play; the goal of rationally assessing the worth of an act requires that structures of human culture and work be brought into play. The threat of two worlds is replaced by two methodological structures applied in different ways to a common world. Because the methodological programmes are mutually exclusive, but not logically incompatible, the noumenal limits the phenomenal, which in turn restrains the noumenal. Kant's fundamental insights are thus confirmed.

BIBLIOGRAPHY

Beck, L.W.: *A Commentary on Kant's Critique of Practical Reason* (Chicago: University of Chicago Press, 1960).
Butts, R.E.: *Kant and the Double Government Methodology: Supersensibility and Method in Kant's Philosophy of Science* (Dordrecht: Reidel, 1986).
Kant, I.: *Critique of Pure Reason* (Riga: 1781, 1787); trans. N. Kemp Smith (London: Macmillan and Co., 1950).
Kant, I.: *Critique of Practical Reason* (Riga: 1788); trans. L.W. Beck (New York: The Liberal Arts Press, 1956).
Kant, I.: *Critique of Judgement* (Berlin and Libau: 1790); trans. J.C. Meredith (Oxford: Clarendon Press, 1964).

ROBERT E. BUTTS

number The ancient Pythagoreans were rightly fascinated by the intricate patterns of properties and relations instantiated by the natural numbers. In particular, they noted that natural numbers stand in relationships of ratio to one another. Similar relations also hold between physical magnitudes like length, duration, velocity, mass, and so forth. Sometimes the relation between, say, two lengths is just the same as the ratio between two natural numbers. However, there are some relations between lengths or other magnitudes which are not the same as any ratio between two natural numbers; when this is so then these magnitudes are said to be incommensurable. The Greeks discovered the existence of incommensurables particularly in geometry. The relations between incommensurables may be called proportions rather than ratios – not all proportions are ratios. The Greeks did not, however, think of either ratios or proportions as being themselves numbers.

By the time of DESCARTES and NEWTON, however, numbers had been reconstrued. As Newton said: 'By *Number* we understand not so much a Multitude of Unities, as the abstracted Ratio of any Quantity, to another Quantity of the same kind, which we take for Unity.' Natural numbers stand in ratios, but arguably the Greeks were right to think that natural numbers are not themselves ratios. Nevertheless, for any natural number n there is the ratio of n to 1; and this ratio has all or almost all the mathematically interesting properties that n has. Consequently natural numbers came to be subsumed as special cases of ratios. Ratios in turn came to be subsumed as special cases of relations of proportion.

Our conception of numbers underwent a second radical reconstrual with the rise of set theory in the nineteenth century, following the work of mathematicians like CANTOR, Dedekind (1831–1916) and others; FREGE, RUSSELL and QUINE relayed this new conception to philosophers. It was noticed that sets instantiate natural numbers, and stand in ratios: for instance one set may be n-membered, another may be $2n$-membered, and so one may be twice-as-many-membered as the other. In fact, particular sets turn out to have all the mathematically interesting properties that natural numbers have, so natural numbers came to be simply identified with sets which were mathematically indistinguishable from them. Ratios too came to be identified with sets that displayed all the mathematically essential properties which are associated with the rational numbers. For instance, a ratio sometimes came to be identified with the set of pairs of natural numbers which stand in that ratio. Similarly, real numbers came to be identified with designated sets that have all the mathematically interesting properties that characterize real numbers. For instance it was noted that all the ratios less than any given real number may be said to have something in common; and so for each real number there is the set of ratios which are less than it. The set of ratios less than a given real number has all the mathematically interesting properties that this real number has, so real numbers sometimes came to be identified with those sets.

One philosophical stance to take is that of protesting that it is a metaphysical mistake to identify numbers with the sets which instantiate them or which share many of their mathematically interesting properties. This was argued in a very influential article on 'What numbers could not be' by Paul Benacerraf (1965). Quine, however, took certain key features of mathematical practice at face value and simply identified numbers with sets. This replacement of numbers by sets is paradigmatic of a mainstream, twentieth-century metaphysics in which the UNIVERSALS of PLATO or ARIS-TOTLE are not simply repudiated, as they were by nominalists, but are transfigured into sets. Modernist set-theoretical PLA-TONISM identifies universals with, or replaces them by, sets; but there are some signs of a post-modernist recycling of more traditional theories of universals, as for instance in the a posteriori metaphysical realism of ARMSTRONG. (*See* NOMINALISM.)

BIBLIOGRAPHY

Armstrong, D.M.: *Universals and Scientific Realism* 2 vols (Cambridge: Cambridge University Press, 1978).

Benacerraf, P.: 'What numbers could not be', *Philosophical Review* 74 (1965), 7–73.

Benacerraf, P. and Putnam, H. eds: *Philosophy of Mathematics: Selected Readings* 2nd edn (Cambridge: Cambridge University Press, 1983).

Frege, G.: *Die Grundlagen der Arithmetik* (Breslau: 1884); trans. J.L. Austin, *The Foundations of Arithmetic* (Oxford: Blackwell, 1959).

Quine, W.V.: *Ward and Object* (Cambridge MA: MIT Press, 1960).

Smith, D.E. ed.: *A Sourcebook in Mathematics* 2 vols (London: 1929); (New York: Dover, 1959).

JOHN BIGELOW

O

object language/metalanguage If a language M contains expressions which denote expressions of a language O, then M is a (potential) *metalanguage* for O and O is an *object language* of M. A language is here understood so that it need not have all the expressive power of a historically occurring natural language. Indeed, the distinction has been of use principally in connection with formalized languages. To be a *syntactical metalanguage* for O, it is sufficient that M contain devices for referring to and proving things about the expressions and sequences of expressions (e.g. proofs) in O. If M also contains the resources to speak about the meanings of the expressions of O, it may be capable of serving also as a *semantical metalanguage* for O. The particular requirements for adequacy, for example, as to what can be proved about the object language, depend on the purpose at hand. We may even use a suitably expressive language as its own syntactical metalanguage. But there appear to be strict limits on the extent to which a language can function as its own semantical metalanguage.

In recent philosophy, the distinction appears clearly in RUSSELL's introduction to WITTGENSTEIN's *Tractatus* (1922). As a way of dealing with Wittgenstein's claim that certain things about the structure of a language cannot be said, but can only be shown, Russell suggested that perhaps they can be said in a metalanguage for that language. Early in this century David Hilbert (1862–1943), as part of his programme to prove the consistency of mathematics, had urged that a mathematical theory could be completely formalized and studied simply as a mathematical object in 'metamathematics'. Emil Post (1921), following C.I.

Lewis (1883–1964), similarly advocated the study of logics as symbolic calculi, in effect, as object languages. Adopting this point of view, he proved the completeness of the propositional calculus.

A clear articulation of the distinction between object language and semantical metalanguage, together with a powerful argument for its necessity, occurs in TARSKI's 'The concept of truth in formalized languages' (1956). It is here that the importance of the distinction for the fundamental metaphysical concept of truth first appears.

The argument enforcing the distinction is the reasoning of the so-called Liar Paradox. The concept of truth apparently obeys the principles embodied in the schema:

(T)   x is true if, and only if, p,

where the letter 'p' is replaced by any sentence and the letter 'x' is replaced by a quotation name of that very sentence. Now consider the sentence:

(1) (1) is not true,

so that

(1) = '(1) is not true'.

Now by the schema (T):

'(1) is not true' is true if, and only if, (1) is not true.

So, by the identity:

(1) is true if, and only if, (1) is not true, a manifest contradiction.

Tarski's goal was to construct an adequate definition of truth, especially for formalized languages. And he adopted as a criterion of adequacy that the definition should allow the proof of schema (T). He concluded that we must either alter the ordinary laws of logic (used in the argument of the paradox), deny an evident identity, or restrict (T) in some way. Tarski urged the last course: we must formulate our definition of truth for a given language *as object language* in a *metalanguage*. The consequent restriction on Schema (T) is that 'p' is to be replaced only by object-language sentences which do not contain the term 'true' used in the schema. Tarski then showed that for suitable metalanguage and (formalized) object language such a definition can be given. The process can be continued and leads to an infinite hierarchy of languages each containing a (defined) predicate expressing truth for sentences of the languages 'below'. Natural languages, he argued, contain the term 'true' applicable to all sentences therein and (except for the vagueness due to their lack of an 'exactly specified structure') perhaps they should be pronounced inconsistent. Alonzo Church (1976) emphasized that Tarski's resolution of the semantical paradoxes (such as the Liar Paradox) is closely related to Russell's (1908) resolution by means of the Ramified Theory of Types. In a certain sense Russell's approach is a special case of Tarski's.

Tarski's idea works very well for formalized languages: we can do what has come to be called the 'model theory' for a given formalized language as object language by working within a metalanguage (usually a semi-formalized portion of English). But it has been argued by Saul Kripke (1975) that we get a more satisfactory analogue of the ordinary concept of truth if we add a truth predicate to a given formalized language, regard the predicate as applicable even to sentences containing that very predicate, and construct models of the language by enlarging the extension of this predicate until it reaches a 'fixed point' – a point at which no new sentences become true or false. While this does seem to provide a more satisfactory model for the concept of truth, it results that the metalanguage for *that* object language (with its self-applicable truth predicate) requires a distinct notion of truth. Thus the distinction between (semantical) metalanguage and object language is still necessary.

The object language/metalanguage distinction also appears in the work of GÖDEL. We can state his famous theorems as: (1) any object language of arithmetic, if it is consistent and adequate for a certain part of number theory, is incomplete – there is a sentence G such that neither G nor its negation is provable from the axioms of the arithmetic. (2) Certain sentences in the object language 'expressing' that the language is consistent, cannot be proved from the axioms of the arithmetic (again, assuming that it is consistent). But in a metalanguage for arithmetic, it may well be possible to define truth for the object language and prove consistency by proving that all the axioms are true and that the rules of inference preserve truth. And we can determine the truth value of the undecided statement G. Thus the methods of proof available in the metalanguage go beyond those of the object language. The philosophical significance of this is assessed in Myhill (1960).

See also THEORIES OF TRUTH.

BIBLIOGRAPHY

Church, A.: 'Comparison of Russell's resolution of the semantical antinomies with that of Tarski', *Journal of Symbolic Logic* 41 (1976), 747–60.

Kripke, S.: 'Outline of a theory of truth', *Journal of Philosophy* 72 (1975), 690–716.

Myhill, J.: 'Some remarks on the notion of proof', *Journal of Philosophy* 57 (1960), 461–71.

Post, E.: 'Introduction to a general theory of elementary propositions', *American Journal of Mathematics* 43 (1921), 163–85.

Russell, B.: 'Mathematical logic as based on the theory of types', *American Journal of Mathematics* 30 (1908), 222–62.

Tarski, A.: 'The concept of truth in formalized languages', in *Logic, Semantics and Metamathematics* ed. and trans. J.H. Woodger (Oxford: Oxford University Press, 1956), 152–278.

Wittgenstein, L.: *Tractatus Logico-Philosophicus* trans. C.K. Ogden (London: Routledge and Kegan Paul, 1922).

C. ANTHONY ANDERSON

objectivism and projectivism Objectivism about a topic holds that judgements about it are objectively true or false, meaning that they are true or false independently of us, or of our perspectives, or opinions (*see* OBJECTIVITY). Projectivism is usually contrasted with this, holding that in some sense our judgements about the topic are no more than 'projections' of potentially variable subjective aspects of our own reactions. Thus the judgement that an object is beautiful, or that a trait is a virtue, might be held to be no more than an objective-sounding way of voicing what is in fact a subjective reaction of pleasure, in the one case arising from the appearance of the object, and in the other case arising perhaps from something like awareness of the utility of the trait. The idea behind the metaphor of projection is that although the feelings that are voiced in these judgements lie within us, we think and speak in ways that make them seem to reflect qualities independent of us, belonging to external objects regardless of how we feel about them. In HUME's terms we 'gild and stain' objects with the 'colours borrowed from internal sentiment'. The metaphor is a reminder that secondary properties such as colour can themselves be thought of in terms of projections on to the external world of what are in fact purely subjective states (*see* QUALITY, PRIMARY/SECONDARY).

While the contrast is at first sight intelligible enough, the first major difficulty is to draw the line between genuinely objective qualities and those that are in this way projections. The central cases where a projective theory seems attractive include ethical and aesthetic judgements, and possibly judgements of secondary properties, such as those of colour or taste. But it is not easy to say why we should stop there. A broadly Humean theory of CAUSATION can be couched in projective terms, holding that we respond to perceived uniformities in events by ourselves forming something like a sentiment: roughly, we form a disposition to foretell the one kind of event upon the appearance of the other. This difference in us is then projected on to the events themselves, when we talk of there being a causal connection between them. Judgements of probability can be seen in terms of a projection of degrees of confidence that are formed in the light of perceived frequencies of events. Logical necessity might be diagnosed as a similar result of our dignifying things which we cannot readily conceive otherwise as being objectively necessary. The attribution of particular meanings to a person's sayings can be thought of in terms of taking up a stance towards the sayings, rather than in terms of describing some further feature that they have. Each area will have its own difficulties, but in general projectivism is an explanatory theory, and it will need some account of when its explanation is appropriate, and when it is not.

Another major choice facing projectivism lies not over where to draw the line, but over the consequences of the position. Is it in the business of explaining the complete range of thoughts we have, using the concepts involved? Or is it to explain *away* some of the things we think? Thus if we conduct our thoughts as if we believe that things are really (truly) good or bad, coloured, beautiful, causally powerful, logically connected, is the projectivist happy to endorse our practice, or is he to say that we only go in for it because of a kind of misplacement or fallacy? The latter option would lead people to say, for instance, that on a Humean theory we should not believe that there are causal connections between distinct events. The former allows us to believe that there are, but gives its particular explanation of what this belief amounts to, and why it arises. The latter option charges our practices with error, and is essentially revisionary. The former option does not incur that cost, but needs to work to show how our thoughts are indeed compatible with the subjective origin of the states that we express. Questions at the centre of this dispute will be whether a projectivist can license a version of truth for judgements in the area, or whether the theory needs to regard elements of our common practice that are connected with their apparent truth as erroneous. These elements will include our tendency to say that we know things in the area, that their truth depends upon other facts, or even that their truth is sometimes quite independent of us and our beliefs (see REALISM).

In his later work, WITTGENSTEIN commonly diagnosed certain families of judgement (those of ethics, those attributing meaning to remarks, those ascribing souls to people, or necessity and certainty to propositions) as the outcome of attitudes and dispositions of mind that have nothing to do with describing or representing the world. However, his wider philosophy of language is often supposed to give grounds for opposing projective theories. The idea is that in his discussion of understanding and rule following he shows how *all* judgement, of even the most objective kind, must be regarded as the outcome of brute human attitude and disposition. Hence there is nothing special about the judgements about which projectivists tend to give their theory. Once we realize what objectivity amounts to, we see that judgements of value and the rest can obtain it as easily as centrally objective judgements, such as those of the spatial and temporal order of ordinary things. We therefore lose any philosophical basis for the dualism of an objective *versus* a projective status for judgements. This approach is reminiscent of BERKELEY's claim that judgements of shape and distance are as dependent upon human subjectivities as judgements of taste or colour, and the result would be a similar Berkeleian, pyrrhic

victory to those contending for objectivity in the disputed areas, since the objectivity that is secured is of a fairly idealistic kind, being itself the product of contingent human dispositions to judgement. Projectivism may claim to have the last word if the objectivity its opponents value is itself the product of the mechanisms it identifies. (*See* IDEALISM.)

BIBLIOGRAPHY

Blackburn, S.: *Spreading the Word* (Oxford: Oxford University Press, 1984).
Hume, D.: *A Treatise of Human Nature* (London: 1739); ed. L.A. Selby-Bigge (Oxford: Clarendon Press, 1888) 2nd edn rev. P.H. Nidditch (Oxford: Clarendon Press, 1978).
Lovibond, S.: *Realism and Imagination in Ethics* (Oxford: Basil Blackwell, 1983).
Putnam, H.: *Reason, Truth and History* (Cambridge: Cambridge University Press, 1981).
Wittgenstein, L.: *Remarks on the Foundations of Mathematics* (Oxford: Blackwell, 1964).

SIMON BLACKBURN

objectivity   The root idea involved in the concept of objectivity is that an objective evaluation of the truth value of a proposition is independent of the preferences or whims of those who carry out that evaluation. The concept of objectivity does not limit the subject matter of such propositions. Pending other considerations, we may be able to arrive at objective evaluations of propositions about physical objects, laws of nature, beliefs, moral principles, values and more. Even the fact that a proposition is about a preference, a whim or a mental state does not *ipso facto* prevent objective evaluation of that proposition. To develop a more detailed account of objective evaluation we must distinguish an *objective proposition* from an *objectively evaluated proposition*.

An *objective proposition* makes an assertion about some subject matter; that subject

369

matter determines the truth value of the proposition. Typical propositions found in science and everyday discourse meet this condition. Propositions about such items as electrons, planets, genes, kinship relations in a society and local weather conditions make an assertion about some state of affairs; whether the proposition is true or false is determined by that state of affairs. Entailment relations provide another example of objective propositions. Whether certain consequences are entailed by a set of premises depends on those premises and the laws of logic, independently of the desires of those who accept or reject those premises. Certain self-referential propositions serve as paradigms of non-objective propositions. Consider a: 'Proposition a is true.' a makes no assertion about any subject matter that determines a's truth value; thus a's truth value is indeterminate. However, b: 'Proposition b is in English' does refer to a fact that determine b's truth value. Some thinkers challenge the objectivity of moral claims by arguing that there are no moral facts that determine the truth value of moral propositions. Only objective propositions are subject to objective evaluation.

Objective evaluation of a proposition requires that two further conditions be met. (1) The evaluation must include evidence derived from actual study of the subject matter mentioned by the proposition. This condition may be illustrated by such everyday practices as looking out of the window to determine if it is raining, or looking both ways to decide if it is safe to cross the street. The observational procedures of natural science also exemplify this condition since these procedures are developed in order to study those items about which scientists make claims. Social scientists who study the people whose practices they describe, and book reviewers who read the books they review, are also pursuing objective evaluations of their assertions.

A proposition may be objective but we may be unable to evaluate it objectively because we lack access to the relevant subject matter. One objection to a Platonist account of mathematics is that even if the relevant facts exist, our psychological make-up does not provide us with access to those facts (*see* PLATONISM). Similarly, moral objectivism will be blocked if there are moral facts but we have no means of determining those facts. Objective evaluation of false existential propositions provides an additional complication. Such propositions must be embedded in a sufficiently rich body of beliefs to provide criteria for concluding that the item sought does not exist.

Condition (1) replaces the more traditional view that objective evaluation requires suspension of our prior beliefs in order to let the facts determine those beliefs. It is generally recognized that this traditional demand cannot be met. Condition (1) requires only that the subject matter in question enter into our considerations and provide constraints on our epistemic evaluations. Such constraints rarely dictate a unique assessment; further consideration is still required. This leads to the second condition.

(2) Objective evaluation is a continuing process, rather than a final accomplishment. In pursuing objectivity we pursue truth about some subject matter, but there is no guarantee that an objectively accepted proposition is true or that an objectively rejected proposition is false. Thus, objective evaluations are accepted tentatively, subject to re-evaluation as new evidence becomes available. Ideally, new forms of evidence will be sought systematically. In natural science, new observation techniques are regularly developed and these can support or challenge a previous evaluation of a proposition's truth value. In a similar way, further study of a society can confirm or challenge previous views of the role a given practice plays in that society; and further study of a text can support or challenge a previous interpretation. In logic and pure mathematics, new deductions can show that a set of axioms has unsuspected consequences or even that a previously accepted set of propositions is inconsistent. In all of these examples, we attempt to adjust our beliefs about some subject matter to the fea-

tures of that subject matter and we pursue this end by interacting with the subject matter in question.

See also ANTIREALISM; OBJECTIVISM AND PROJECTIVISM; REALISM.

BIBLIOGRAPHY

Brown, H.I.: *Observation and Objectivity* (New York: Oxford University Press, 1987).
Code, L.: *What Can She Know: Feminist Theory and the Construction of Knowledge* (Ithaca, NY: Cornell University Press, 1991).
Einstein, A.: 'Physics and reality', in his *Out of My Later Years* (New York: Citadel, 1956), 59–97.
Hooker, C.A.: *A Realistic Theory of Science* (Albany, NY: SUNY Press, 1987).
Rorty, R.: *Philosophy and the Mirror of Nature* (Princeton, NJ: Princeton University Press, 1979).

HAROLD I. BROWN

occasion, occasionalism Occasionalism is the doctrine that God is the sole cause of whatever occurs in the universe. Events usually identified as *causes* are really *occasions* on which God produces effects: a brick striking a window is not the *cause* of its breaking but the *occasion* on which God causes it to break, our volitions are the occasion of God's causing a movement of our bodies, events in our nervous system and brain are the occasion of God's producing sensations in our minds, etc. The doctrine is sometimes portrayed as holding that God causes each event by a particular divine volition, but some occasionalists held that, by a few 'general volitions', God established all nature's laws (including laws connecting mind and body), and that these few general volitions cause all particular events. First propounded by the tenth-century Moslem thinker al-Ash'ari, occasionalism was later defended by Cartesians like

Géraud de Cordemoy (d. 1684), Louis de La Forge, Johannes Clauberg (1622–65), Arnold Geulincx (1624–69) and MALE-BRANCHE. Some non-occasionalists use *occasion* as a synonym for *cause*.

See also DESCARTES.

BIBLIOGRAPHY

Fakhry, M.: *Islamic Occasionalism* (London: Allen and Unwin, 1958).
Lennon, T.M.: 'Occasionalism and the Cartesian metaphysic of motion', *Canadian Journal of Philosophy* (1974), suppl. 1, 29–40.
McCracken, C.J.: *Malebranche and British Philosophy* (Oxford: Oxford University Press, 1983), ch. 3.
Prost, J.: *Essai sur l'atomisme et l'occasionalisme dans la philosophie cartésienne* (Paris: Paulin, 1907).

CHARLES J. McCRACKEN

Ockham [Occam], William of (c.1285–1347) British scholastic philosopher. Ockham, the 'More than Subtle Doctor', styled himself the true interpreter of ARISTOTLE on most metaphysical issues. Declaiming the doctrine that UNIVERSALS are real things other than names as 'the worst error of philosophy', Ockham rejected not only PLATONISM, but also 'moderate realist' doctrines according to which natures have a double mode of existence and are universal in the intellect but numerically multiplied in particulars. He contends that everything real is particular, while universality is a property that pertains to names only by virtue of their signification relations (*see* NOMINALISM). Since Ockham identifies naturally significant concepts as the primary names, his own theory of universals is best classified as a form of conceptualism.

Apparently, Ockham held two successive views regarding the ontological status of concepts. On the first *fictum* or 'objective-existence' theory, he reasoned that since only beings can be thought of, and yet many thought objects cannot and/or do not really exist – universals, propositions, relations of reason, chimaeras, creatures prior to their creation – they must have some non-real mode of EXISTENCE ('objective existence'). Later, he came to regard such non-real entities as superfluous and identified concepts with mental qualities or acts of understanding (*intellectiones*).

Rejecting ATOMISM, Ockham defends Aristotelian HYLOMORPHISM in physics and metaphysics, along with its distinction between substantial and accidental forms. He waged a vigorous polemic against the reifying tendency of 'the moderns' (unnamed contemporary opponents), who posited a distinct kind of thing (*res*) for each of Aristotle's ten CATEGORIES. Ockham insisted that, from a purely philosophical point of view, an ontology of particular substances and qualities will serve. Ockham joined fellow Franciscans in admitting a plurality of substantial forms in living things (in humans, the forms of corporeity, sensory and intellectual souls), but asserted – contrary to DUNS SCOTUS – a real, not a formal distinction between them. (*See* MATTER/FORM; SUBSTANCE.)

Likewise, Ockham's treatment of causality is of Aristotelian (not Humean) inspiration (*see* CAUSATION; HUME). Substance- and accident-natures are *essentially* causal powers (*virtus*), primitive explanatory entities that give rise to or produce regularities. Thus, efficient causality properly speaking contrasts with *sine qua non* causality where the correlation is produced not by the power of the correlatives but by the will of another (e.g. God), and Ockham insists that there is no *sine qua non* causality in nature. Since for Ockham as for Scotus created natures have their constitution in and of themselves and not in relation to anything else (even the Divine nature or will), God cannot make heat *naturally* a coolant or the power to produce whiteness, although like natural agents He can obstruct the normal operation of such powers. Because individual natures are powers, and co-specific things are maximally similar powers, Ockham's nominalistic conceptualism raises no barrier to his accepting the uniformity of nature principle. Conventional in his appeal to familiar a priori causal principles – 'Everything that is in motion is moved by something', 'Being cannot come from non-being', 'Whatever is produced by something is really conserved by something as long as it exists' – his main innovation was to reject Scotus's distinction between 'essential' and 'accidental' orders and to insist that every genuine efficient cause is an immediate cause of its effects.

Ockham's distinctive ACTION THEORY asserts the 'liberty of indifference or contingency' for all rational beings, created or divine. While acknowledging that humans have innate motivational tendencies towards various goods, he denies that any is deterministic or limiting of the will's scope. Contrary to AQUINAS and Scotus, Ockham insists that with respect to any option whatever – including the agent's own happiness, its own ultimate end, the good-in-general, the enjoyment of a clear vision of God – the will has the power to will for it (*velle*), to will against it (*nolle*), or not to act at all. Thus, he concludes, freedom of the will includes the power to will against (*nolle*) such goods and to choose (*velle*) evil under the aspect of evil. (*See* FREE WILL.)

WRITINGS

Guillelmi de Ockham Philosophica et Theologica (St Bonaventure, NY: The Franciscan Institute), vols I–VI and I–X.

BIBLIOGRAPHY

Adams, M.M.: *William Ockham* (Notre Dame, IN: University of Notre Dame Press, 1987), Pts I and IV, 3–313, 633–899.
Boehner, P.: *Collected Articles on Ockham* ed. E.M. Buytaert (St Bonaventure, NY: The Franciscan Institute, 1958).

Gal, G.: 'Gualteri de Chatton et Guillelmi de Ockham: controversia de natura conceptus universalis', *Franciscan Studies* NS XXVII (1967), 191–212.

Wolter, A.B.: 'The Ockhamist critique', in *The Concept of Matter in Greek and Medieval Philosophy* ed. E. McMullin (Notre Dame, IN: University of Notre Dame Press, 1963), 124–46.

MARILYN McCORD ADAMS

ontology The study of being in so far as this is shared in common by all entities, both material and immaterial. It deals with the most general properties of beings in all their different varities.

The books of Aristotle's *Physics* deal with material entities. His *Metaphysics* (literally 'what comes after the *Physics*'), on the other hand, deals with what is beyond or behind the physical world – with immaterial entities – and thus contains theology as its most prominent part. At the same time, however, Aristotle conceives this 'metaphysics' as having as its subject matter all beings, or rather being as such. Metaphysics is accordingly identified also as 'first philosophy', since it deals with the most basic principles upon which all other sciences rest.

From the very beginning, then, an alliance was established between theology and the science of being *qua* being, and this alliance was sustained successfully throughout the Middle Ages. By the seventeenth century, however, the two disciplines were beginning to fall apart, and there was effected a distinction between *metaphysica generalis* on the one hand – the science of the most general concepts or categories of being – and *metaphysica specialis* on the other – embracing not only theology but also other special sciences of being, including psychology (the science of finite mind) and cosmology.

'Ontology', now, is just another name for *metaphysica generalis* as thus conceived. The term was introduced into philosophy by the German Protestant Scholastic Rudolphus Goclenius (Rudolf Göckel) in his *Lexicon philosophicum* (1613) and was given currency above all through the influence of Christian Wolff (1679–1754).

Where metaphysics had traditionally confined itself to the treatment of existent beings, LEIBNIZ, Wolff and others dealt also in their metaphysical writings with the being of what is merely possible. It fell to MEINONG in his 'Über Gegenstandstheorie' (1904) to conceive the project of an absolutely general 'theory of objects', which would embrace within its subject matter not merely actual and possible objects, but also impossible objects, obtaining and non-obtaining states of affairs and other higher-order objects, merely hypothetical objects, and also objects 'beyond being and non-being' which are as it were awaiting realization.

In part under the influence of Meinong, in part also under the inspiration of contemporary work in logic and mathematics, HUSSERL put forward in his *Logical Investigations* (1913–21) the idea of a 'pure theory of objects' or 'formal ontology', a discipline which would deal with such formal-ontological CATEGORIES as: object, state of affairs, property, genus, species, unity, plurality, NUMBER, relation, connection, series, part, whole, dependence, magnitude, open and closed set, BOUNDARY, manifold, and so on. (*See* CLASS, COLLECTION, SET; PART/WHOLE; PROPOSITION, STATE OF AFFAIRS.)

Formal ontology would deal also with the different formal structures manifested by entire regions of being. To each such formal structure there would then correspond in principle a number of alternative material realizations, each having its own specific material or regional ontology. The most important such material ontology relates to the natural world of spatio-temporally extended things, and thus includes ontological theories of space, time, movement, causality, material body, and so on (*see* CAUSATION; SPACE AND TIME). Next in order of development is the material ontology of organic entities, followed by the material ontology of minds (of thinking bodies and of their mental acts and states), perhaps also by the material ontology of cultural and institutional formations. (*See* INGARDEN for a further development of Husserl's thinking on these issues.)

The discipline of formal ontology itself was seen by Husserl as a complement to formal logic. Where formal logic would deal with the forms of scientific theories, formal ontology would deal with the forms of the object domains to which such theories, if true, would correspond. Formal ontology is, then, a science of certain sorts of entities (the forms of objects) in the world. Logic, too, was conceived in this realistic fashion by FREGE, as also by the early RUSSELL and by LEŚNIEWSKI, for all of whom it was the world itself which constituted the single intended interpretation of their respective logical theories. Frege and Russell, however, like WITTGENSTEIN in the *Tractatus* (1922), did not distinguish clearly between formal logic and formal ontology, and their works rest on an assumption (which was to prove fateful for the subsequent history of analytic philosophy) to the effect that all form is logical form. The role of ontology therefore came to be usurped by the construction of set-theoretic models, and for the world itself there came to be substituted mathematical artefacts having convenient algebraic properties but otherwise bearing little or no relation to the flesh-and-blood subject matters of scientific theories. Recent developments in analytic metaphysics, while still often resting on an overuse of the ontologically rather crude instruments of set theory and set-theoretic semantics, none the less give reasons for optimism that philosophers are once more addressing the problems of ontology or general metaphysics in direct and rigorous fashion. In other words they are dealing with the messy and subtle forms of things in the world, rather than with the logically neat and tidy forms of deliberately constructed surrogates.

See also METAPHYSICS: DEFINITIONS AND DIVISIONS.

BIBLIOGRAPHY

Husserl, E.: *Logische Untersuchungen* 2nd edn (Halle: 1913–21); trans. J.N. Findlay, *Logical Investigations* (London: Routledge and Kegan Paul, 1970).
Johansson, I.: *Ontological Investigations. An Inquiry into the Categories of Nature, Man and Society* (London: Routledge, 1989).
Meinong, A.: 'Über Gegenstandstheorie' (1904); trans. I. Levi, D.B. Terrell and R.M. Chisholm 'The theory of objects', in *Realism and the Background of Phenomenology* ed. R.M. Chisholm (Glencoe: Free Press, 1960), 76–117.
Rompe, E.M.: Die Trennung von Ontologie und Metaphysik (Dissertation, Bonn, 1968).
Wittgenstein, L.: *Tractatus Logico-Philosophicus* trans. C.K. Ogden (London: Routledge and Kegan Paul, 1922).

BARRY SMITH

Ortega y Gasset, José (1883–1955) Philosopher and essayist, born in Madrid, Spain. He studied in Madrid, Leipzig, Berlin and Marburg. In 1910 he was appointed to the Chair of Metaphysics at the University of Madrid. He held that post until 1936, when he had to leave Spain at the beginning of the Civil War because of his support for the Spanish Republic. He returned to Spain in 1945.

Among Ortega's most influential books are: *Meditaciones del Quijote* (1914), *El tema de nuestro tiempo* (1923), *La deshumanización del arte* (1925), *La revolución de las masas* (1932), *Historia como sistema* (1941), and the posthumously published *El hombre y la gente* (1957) and *La idea de principio en Leibniz* (1958).

Ortega's substantial influence in Spanish and Latin American thought was in part the result of a captivating style of writing and lecturing. He avoided technicisms and systematization, and frequently wrote for newspapers and magazines. In 1923 he founded the *Revista de Occidente*, a cultural magazine which spread his views and introduced recent German philosophy into the Spanish-speaking world.

Ortega ventured into almost every branch of philosophy, but at the centre of his thought are his metaphysics of vital reason (*razón vital*) and his perspectival epistemology. Ortega identifies reality with 'my life'; something is real only in so far as it is founded on and appears within my life. 'My life' is in turn analysed as myself and my circumstances (*yo soy yo y mi circumstancia*).

The self is not separate from what surrounds it; every life is the result of an interaction between self and circumstances and thus every self has a unique perspective. Truth is determined by this perspective, for it depends on the unique point of view of each self. This position is known as Ortega's perspectivism.

WRITING

Obras completas 12 vols (Madrid: Alianza Editorial, Revista de Occidente, 1983).

BIBLIOGRAPHY

Donoso, A. and Raley, H.C.: *José Ortega y Gasset: A Bibliography of Secondary Sources* (Bowling Green, OH: Philosophy Documentation Center, 1986).

Ferrater Mora, J.: *Ortega y Gasset: An Outline of His Philosophy* (New Haven, CT: Yale University Press, 1957).

Marías, J.: *José Ortega y Gasset: Circumstance and Vocation* trans. F.M. López Morillas (Norman, OK: University of Oklahoma Press, 1970).

McClintock, R.: *Man and His Circumstances: Ortega as Educator* (New York: Teachers College, Columbia University, 1971).

Ouimette, V.: *José Ortega y Gasset* (Boston, MA: G.K. Hall, 1982).

Raley, H.C.: *José Ortega y Gasset: Philosopher of European Unity* (Tuscaloosa, AL: University of Alabama Press, 1971).

Silver, P.W.: *Ortega as Phenomenologist: The Genesis of 'Meditations on Quijote'* (New York: Columbia University Press, 1978).

JORGE J.E. GRACIA

P

---

pantheism To understand pantheism, we must contrast it with *theism*: the proposition that there is an almighty, all-knowing and wholly good person (God) who has created the world. So far, this does not distinguish theism from *deism*. The theist adds, however (and the deist denies), that God is continually active in his creation, constantly supporting it in existence; without this constant activity, says the theist, creation would vanish like a dream upon awakening. Against this backdrop, pantheism is the doctrine that *all* is God – not, absurdly, that each thing is God, but that the totality of things is somehow God. ('Somehow', since it is not easy to see how the totality of things could be able to do or know anything at all, let alone be almighty and all-knowing.) SPINOZA was a sort of pantheist, various versions of nineteenth-century IDEALISM are at least pantheistic, and the same can be said for much of contemporary PROCESS PHILOSOPHY.

ALVIN PLANTINGA

particulars *see* UNIVERSALS AND PARTICULARS

part/whole The relation of part to whole is one of the most fundamental in ontology. It applies to all or almost all objects we can consider. Concrete particulars clearly have parts: a cat has its tail, a chair its seat. Regions of space, time, and space-time stand in part/whole relations, and any object extended in space and/or time has parts corresponding to subportions of the portion of space and/or time it covers. Likewise stuffs, events, aggregates may have parts and be parts. Part/whole relations are also found among abstract objects: sets have subsets, algebras have subalgebras, vector spaces have subspaces, the real line has intervals, etc. The determinables of a determinate, the genera of a species, and the marks of a concept are often called logical parts of their wholes. Some objects, such as atoms, points, souls and God, are said to be without parts, but it is still significant (if false) to talk of parts.

Philosophers from the Milesians onwards have used concepts of part and whole. They frequently played crucial roles in the history of metaphysics, for example, in Thales' view that everything is made of water, ARISTOTLE's arguments against ZENO's paradoxes, LEIBNIZ's argument for monads, BRADLEY's argument for the Absolute. The discovery that there are as many squares as natural numbers was taken as a paradox, seemingly contradicting Euclid's principle that the whole is greater than the part. Yet the part/whole relation is so basic and obvious that it was not until about 1914 that WHITEHEAD and LEŚNIEWSKI began, independently, to codify the formal principles of part/whole theory, which Whitehead called the theory of extension and Leśniewski called *mereology*.

The minimal formal properties of a part/whole relation (sometimes called 'proper part') are that it is (1) *asymmetric*; (2) *transitive*; and (3) *supplementive*; That is:

(1) If a is part of b, b is not part of a.
(2) If a is part of b and b is part of c, then a is part of c.
(3) If a is part of b, then there is a part of b having no common part with a.

In terms of this basic relation, cognate concepts may be defined. *a* is the *ingredient* of *b* if *a* is part of *b* or *a* is *b*; *a* and *b* *overlap* if something is an ingredient of both; they are *disjoint* if they do not overlap. The *sum* of several objects *m* is the smallest object of which all are part. The *universe* is the sum of all objects, and an *atom* is an object with no proper parts. Of course what scientists call atoms are not mereological atoms, since they can be split into proper parts, and even if something cannot be divided by any physical process, it may still have proper parts.

Most mereologies add further principles, such as *mereological extensionality*: if *a* and *b* have the same ingredients, they are identical; and the *sum principle*: any collection of objects has a sum. *Classical mereology* has both: Leśniewski's version, published in Polish, was much less known than Leonard and GOODMAN's (1940) calculus of individuals.

The sum principle in particular has been criticized, because the objects summed may be widely dispersed or of different categories: it is most plausible for homogeneous ontologies. But its implausibility stems partly from interference from stronger concepts of part and individual than mereologists use. In common speech a part is not just any portion of a thing, but one which has a certain material and functional unity, such as a component or an organ. Individuals are usually taken to have some form of unity or integrity: an integral whole is one which can be partitioned into parts forming a complete, closed system under a suitable relation, for example, connectedness for a body, subordination to a single legal authority for a country. However, collections and stuffs are usually scattered, and arbitrary sums seem not to engender contradictions.

Mereological atomism states that every object with a part contains a (mereological) atom, so everything is composed of atoms. Opposed to this is anti-atomism, according to which everything has a proper part. Atomism and anti-atomism are theses independent of general mereology, for either of which it is difficult to envisage verification.

Related to atomism is the question whether the limits of a physical entity, such as surfaces, lines, points, beginnings and endings, are its parts. BOLZANO, for instance, though that a solid sphere with surface points would be really different from the same sphere without surface points. Many philosophers would however agree with Aristotle that limits of things are not their parts: that any part of a body still has bulk, that any part of an event has temporal extent.

The part/whole relations so far considered make no material assumptions about their terms. It is disputed whether there is a single part/whole relation having different kinds of term, or several materially different but formally analogous relations. Either way, there are many subspecies of part/whole relation when the nature of the terms is taken into account. Continuants may have *temporary parts*, ones they have at one time but not another, by contrast with permanent parts. Temporally extended events and processes may have *temporal parts*, for example, a single step is a temporal part of a walk. *Essential parts* of an object are those an object must have for *it* to exist, for example, the protons of a helium atom. *Accidental parts* are ones without which it can exist, for example, a cat may live without a tail; though the tail is a *normal part*. A part may be essential to its whole, though the whole be not essential to the part: a helium atom must contain its two protons, but they need not have been part of that atom, and at one time were not. The disputed thesis of *mereological essentialism*, upheld by Leibniz and CHISHOLM, states that every part of a genuine object is essential to it.

See also CONTINUANT; ESSENCE/ACCIDENT; ESSENTIALISM.

BIBLIOGRAPHY

Chisholm, R.M.: 'Parts as essential to their wholes', *Review of Metaphysics* 26 (1973), 581–603.

Leonard, H. and Goodman, N.: 'The calculus of individuals and its uses', *Journal of Symbolic Logic* 5 (1940), 45–55.

Leśniewski, S.: *Collected Works* ed. S.J. Surma, J.T. Srzednicki, D.J. Barnett and V.F. Rickey (The Hague: Martinus Nijhoff, 1992).

Simons, P.M.: *Parts* (Oxford: Clarendon Press, 1987).

Whitehead, A.N.: *An Enquiry Concerning the Principles of Natural Knowledge* (Cambridge: Cambridge University Press, 1919).

PETER SIMONS

Pascal, Blaise (1623–62) French mathematician, physicist and philosopher. Pascal thought parts of the human mind functioned as 'organs of belief' or instruments, by which knowledge and beliefs were acquired. This instrumentational theory required the mind be composed of disparate faculties. These included the senses, memory, imagination, and two complementary faculties, 'the heart' and the intellect. The heart, which we would call intuition or insight, yielded first principles of space, time, numbers, and others, and also gave genuine knowledge of mathematical, logical and moral infinities. As well, the heart supplied the truths for ethical and theological beliefs. Its complementary faculty was the intellect, or the reasoning mind. Through it, we arrived at deductive conclusions, and constructed proofs, and more.

Pascal's theory of mind originated a form of intuitionism, which stated: any truth or belief acquired or given through reason could not be acquired or given through the heart, and vice versa. Both principle and theory were the basis for original and important work.

In epistemology, Pascal advanced a theory of evidence based on the methods justifying beliefs; also a classification of disciplines concerned with knowledge and beliefs into two distinct kinds. In logic and mathematics, Pascal presented geometric or mathematical reasoning as superior to, and the basis of, logical reasoning. In this context, he introduced the dichotomy between the intuitive and the mathematical mind. In ethics, he considered the morality of the intellect or reasoning mind to be inferior to the morality of the heart, called 'the morality of judgement'. In religion, Pascal rejected all metaphysical and natural proofs of God's existence. Genuine knowledge could be reached only through the heart, not through reason. In the absence of proof, the prudent should nevertheless wager in favour of a religious lifestyle.

Both the heart and the intellect, intuition and reason, were needed for and yielded knowledge, though of differing amounts, kinds and grades. Pascal illustrated this with the case of two people who had both learned by rote the same book, and could both be said to know it. However, the one who could discuss its principles, its conclusions and any objections, would be said to know the text better than the other. Thus too with the heart and the intellect.

See also NATURAL THEOLOGY.

WRITINGS

Pascal, Œuvres complètes ed. L. Lafuma (Paris: Seuil, 1963).

Pensées (Port Royal: 1670); trans. A.J. Krailsheimer (New York: Penguin, 1966).

Great Shorter Works trans. E. Cailliet and J.C. Blankenagel (Philadelphia: Westminster, 1948).

BIBLIOGRAPHY

Arnold, K.: 'Pascal's theory of scientific knowledge', *Journal of the History of Philosophy* XXVII (1989), 531–44.

Krailsheimer, A.: *Pascal* (New York: Oxford, 1980).

Popkin, R.H. ed.: *Pascal Selections* (New York: Macmillan, 1989).

KEITH ARNOLD

Peirce, Charles Sanders (1839–1914) American philosopher, best known as an originator of pragmatism and for his work in semiotics. Peirce made important contributions to most areas of philosophy and did innovative work in formal logic and mathematics. His attempts to produce a full statement of his philosophical position were frustrated, but he published many papers and his manuscripts contain much illuminating material. He was influenced, above all, by KANT, and he sometimes described his work as an attempt to revise Kant's philosophy in the light of subsequent developments in logic and the theory of representation.

Peirce's 'pragmatist principle', published in 'How to make our ideas clear' (1877; *Collected Papers*, vol. 5, § 388–410; *Writings*, vol. 3, pp. 257–76), claimed that the content of a concept or hypothesis could be wholly clarified by specifying the experiential consequences we would expect our actions to have if the hypothesis were true. For example: the claim that a powder is salt entails that if we were to stir it in water then, *ceteris paribus*, we would observe it dissolve. If no such consequences can be derived from a proposition, then it is empty. A merit of this doctrine was 'that almost every proposition of ontological metaphysics is either meaningless gibberish . . . or else is downright absurd' (*Collected Papers*, vol. 5, § 423). He illustrated this by arguing that the debate over whether transubstantiation really occurred was an empty one (*Collected Papers*, vol. 5, p. 401; *Writings*, vol. 3, § 265–6). This leads many to see him as a precursor of the logical positivists, and he did insist that all that would remain of philosophy would be problems that could be solved through 'the observational methods of the true sciences' (*Collected Papers*, vol. 5, § 423). (*See* LOGICAL POSITIVISM.) However, his pragmatism differed from the anti-metaphysical stance of the positivists; this is clear from the irreducible 'would-be' in the analysis offered above, a reflection of his anti-nominalistic realism (*see* NOMINALISM). From around 1890 he developed a system of 'scientific metaphysics', the aim of which was to 'study the most general features of reality and real objects' (*Collected Papers*, vol. 6, § 6). The fullest development of his metaphysical views was in a series of papers published in the *Monist* in 1891–2.

The need for a scientific metaphysics emerges from his work in logic and epistemology. In order to carry out scientific investigations we have to adopt various regulative assumptions: that we can exercise rational self-control over our reasoning; that our sense of plausibility is properly attuned to reality; that all regularities and patterns in our experience can be explained; that the universe contains real laws or 'generals'. Unless these assumptions are true, our strategies of inquiry are illegitimate. Metaphysics explains how the world must be for these assumptions to be true: it defends the general account of the self and the cosmos which vindicates them. Peirce also thought that our general metaphysical view of the mind and the world was required to prevent waste of efforts in developing theories which were metaphysically unsound; psychology had particularly suffered from lack of metaphysical sensitivity. Although it makes no use of experiment or results from the special sciences, metaphysics is an empirical investigation, relying on unremarked features of everyday experience.

For example Peirce rejected ATOMISM because it tried to 'explain the phenomena by means of the absolutely inexplicable': why are there those atoms? Why have they always existed? Why do they obey just those laws? His own metaphysics was guided by the 'synechistic' principle that explanations in terms of continua should, where possible, be preferred (*Collected Papers*, vol. 6, § 169–73). And he proposed an evolutionary explanation of the development of the laws governing the universe (ibid., § 7–34). His 'tychism' held that our experience contains an element of chance spontaneity which provides the element of variation in an account of how the universe becomes steadily more and more ordered or 'hidebound with habits' (ibid., § 47ff.).

Unless we adopt such a view, he thought, we are committed to brute unintelligibility at the root of our view of things.

Persuaded that a non-monistic ontology was untenable, Peirce rejected materialism largely because it was incapable of explaining the nature of *feeling* (ibid., § 24) (*see* MONISM/PLURALISM; PHYSICALISM, MATERIALISM). Hence he favoured that the entire cosmos is a vast mind (or 'representamen') becoming more rational and ordered through time: he thought of laws as analogous to 'habits of inference'; and he saw natural necessity and efficient CAUSATION as grounded in final causation. He described his view (ibid., § 605) as a form of objective IDEALISM reminiscent of F.W.J. von Schelling (1775–1854). It means that the growth of human knowledge is a special case of a process which characterizes the entire history of the cosmos. Moreover this supports Peirce's rejection of individualist approaches to epistemology: individual minds are subordinate to larger personal wholes, such as communities of inquirers, and participation in inquiry depends upon identifying one's own good with that of this wider community.

In Kantian spirit, Peirce sought a system of CATEGORIES which was grounded in logic; in later work, phenomenological investigations also had a role in its defence (*see* PHENOMENOLOGY). He claimed that an adequate language would contain monadic, dyadic and triadic predicates: phenomena described by such predicates exhibited firstness, secondness and thirdness respectively. Thirdness was manifested in such phenomena as meaning and INTENTIONALITY, continuity and law. All involve mediation: the relation between a thought or sign and its referent is mediated through an 'interpretant' thought; law or generality mediates between two events that instantiate the law; and continuity is 'ultimate mediation' (*Collected Papers*, vol. 5, § 93, 101, 467). That such phenomena are irreducibly triadic was the identifying feature of Peirce's 'REALISM': mediation and law (expressed in 'would-be's') are ineliminable features both of experience and reality.

WRITINGS

Collected Papers of Charles S. Peirce vols 1–6 ed. C. Hartshorne and P. Weiss; vols 7–8 ed. A.W. Burks (Cambridge, MA: Harvard University Press, 1931–58).
Writings of Charles S. Peirce: A Chronological Edition ed. M. Fisch, E.C. Moore and C.J.W. Kloesel (Bloomington, IN: Indiana University Press, 1982).

BIBLIOGRAPHY

Hookway, C.J.: *Peirce* (London: Routledge and Kegan Paul, 1985).
Murphey, M.: 'On Peirce's metaphysics', *Transactions of the Charles S. Peirce Society* I (1965), 17–24.

CHRISTOPHER HOOKWAY

personal identity *see* PERSONS AND PERSONAL IDENTITY

persons and personal identity LOCKE defined 'person' as: 'a thinking intelligent being, that has reason and reflection, and can consider itself as itself, the same thinking thing in different times and places; which it does only by that consciousness, which is inseparable from thinking, and it seems to me essential to it' (*Essay concerning Human Understanding*, II.xxvii.9). As Locke saw, this definition gives 'person' a potentially wider application than the term 'human being', where the latter is understood as referring to members of a particular biological species. Locke implies that a 'rational parrot' he describes would count as a person, though not as a 'man' (i.e. human being), and he could have cited the fact that God is described by believers as a divine person.

Locke's definition suggests that what marks off persons from other subjects of mental states is rationality and the possession of 'reflection', or SELF-CONSCIOUSNESS. It has also been held to be distinctive of persons that they are capable of language use, that they are social creatures, and that they view each other and themselves in terms of the concepts of morality (thus Locke's observation that 'person' is a 'forensic term, appropriating actions and their merit' (*Essay*, II.xxvii.26)). All of this requires that the mental states of persons include 'higher-order' beliefs, desires and intentions, whose contents include reference to other mental states, either those of the creature itself, as in self-consciousness, or those of other creatures, or both, as in language use and reciprocal social relations (see Dennett, 1976). It has also been held that it is distinctive of persons, and a requirement of the FREE WILL that has been thought the special province of persons, that they be the subject of a certain sort of second-order desires and intentions – desires or intentions to have (or not to have) certain first-order desires (see Frankfurt, 1971).

The use of the term 'person' commits one to no particular view on the MIND/BODY PROBLEM. But for most philosophers who have used the term, it is constitutive of the concept of a person that persons are (at least normally) embodied, and the subject of bodily as well as mental properties – as STRAWSON (1959) has put it, they are equally subjects of 'P-predicates', which imply the possession of consciousness, and 'M-predicates', which can be shared with inanimate objects. Some see embodiment as required for the very existence of mental states, not (at least directly) because they are committed to materialism (*see* PHYSIC-ALISM, MATERIALISM), but because they think that the individuation of mental states requires their embodiment. This will be true on any views on which mental states are partly constituted by their relations to behaviour, and it will be true on 'externalist' views about mental content, according to which the intentional (representational) CONTENT of mental states (*see* INTEN-TIONALITY) is determined in part by the nature of the environment with which the subject is in perceptual contact. Despite Locke's official adherence to a Cartesian view (he thinks that there is in each of us an immaterial substance which is that

which thinks in us), his conception of persons is similar to Strawson's. (*See* DES-CARTES.) A person is a 'thinking intelligent being', and while it is unclear how the thinking of a person is supposed to be related to the thinking of the associated immaterial substance, it seems clear that Lockean persons are subjects of both P-predicates and M-predicates. And, strikingly, Locke denied that the identity over time of a person consists in, or requires, the identity of an immaterial substance.

It is true in general that saying what sort of thing an *F* is involves indicating what the identity conditions for *F*s are – what count as parts of the same *F*, and what counts as events, phases, or stages in the history of one and the same *F*. And so a good reason for inquiring into the nature of personal identity, into the identity conditions of persons, is that this can be expected to throw light on what persons are. Another good reason for inquiring into this is that it provides a way of addressing the metaphysical puzzles – about CHANGE, SUBSTANCE, etc. – that arise whenever the identity over time of 'continuants' (*see* CONTINUANT) is addressed. But neither of these good reasons can account for the amount of attention which the topic of personal identity has attracted since Locke's *Essay* pushed it into prominence as a philosophical topic. Part of the explanation of this must be that we *care* about the identity of persons in a way in which we do not care about the identity of other things. Other things being equal, the destruction-cum-replacement-with-an-exact-duplicate of a chair or refrigerator will be regarded as 'as good as' its continued existence. But we do not feel this way about our family and friends. And in particular we do not feel this way about ourselves. A central fact about persons is that each of them has a 'special concern' for his or her future well-being; and because of this, each of them also has derivative special concern for the future well-being of the persons with whom he or she identifies because of ties of love and friendship. It is partly this that makes intelligible the involvement of the notion of

381

personal identity in moral and legal practices which lies behind Locke's observation that 'person' is a 'forensic' term. The various sanctions that enforce morality depend on the existence of this special concern, as do such ideas as that a person can justly be held accountable for past actions, and that goods bestowed on a person can compensate for injuries inflicted on that person at an earlier time. The existence of this special concern contributes to interest in personal identity in two different ways. First, because part of this special concern is a desire to exist in the future, a desire for 'survival', persons have an interest in whether the nature of personal identity is such as to allow them to survive bodily death – and discussions of personal identity have often been linked with discussions of the prospects of personal IMMORTALITY. Second, given that we have this special concern, there is a natural interest in finding an account of personal identity that makes our having it intelligible and rational.

A different source of the interest philosophers have in personal identity – over and above the interest they have in the identity over time of continuants generally – is its distinctive epistemology. At first look, our judgements about the identity over time of persons other than ourselves seems to be grounded in much the same way as our judgements about the identity over time of other things; we go on such things as similarity of observable properties, or spatiotemporal continuity and continuity with respect to observable properties. But the memory-based judgements we make about our own past histories are not so grounded; when I say on the basis of memory that it was I who mowed the lawn yesterday, my judgement will not be based on remembered information about the person who did the mowing (I was not watching myself in a mirror as I mowed), or on observed continuities linking that person with my present self. And of course this direct memory-based knowledge of personal identity can be conveyed to others; so the epistemology of third-person judgements of

personal identity, as well as of first-person judgements, is importantly different from that of our judgements about the identity of other sorts of things. This raises the question of what personal identity can be, that it can be known in this distinctive way.

If one approaches the problem of personal identity from the mind/body problem, it may seem at first as if there should be just two possible solutions to it, one that will be favoured by Cartesian dualists and one that will be favoured by materialists. The first asserts that the identity of a person over time consists in the identity over time of an immaterial mind or SOUL, while the second asserts that the identity of a person over time consists in the identity over time of a living human body. In the influential chapter of the *Essay* that began the modern history of the topic of personal identity, John Locke rejected both of these solutions. His own solution may seem to have the same form as those he rejects; he says that personal identity consists, not in sameness of immaterial substance (soul) or sameness of material substance (body), but in sameness of 'consciousness'. But Locke did not think that associated with each person there is a single entity, a 'consciousness', that necessarily exists just as long as the person exists (in the way the other views hold that associated with each person there is a soul, or a body, which necessarily exists as long as the person exists). By 'consciousness' he mainly means *memory*, and his view was that it is memory that links together, and unites into the history of a single person, the different parts of a person's life. On this view the distinctive epistemology of personal identity, the immediate access each person has in memory to his or her past, reflects its metaphysical essence.

Much of the support for the memory theory comes from thought experiments similar to one presented by Locke: 'Should the soul of a prince, carrying with it the consciousness of the prince's past life, enter and inform the body of a cobbler, as soon deserted by his own soul, everyone sees he would be the same person as the prince, accountable only for the prince's actions'

(*Essay*, II.xxvii.15). A similar story, which avoids the dualistic overtones of Locke's, involves the brain of one person being transplanted into the body of another, with the result that the brain recipient remembers the past life of the brain donor. The dominant intuition about such cases is that the person 'changes body'; this seems to count both against the view that personal identity consists in bodily identity and in favour of the memory theory. (The intuition about Locke's example is compatible with the view that personal identity consists in soul identity, while that about the brain transplant example is compatible with the view that personal identity consists in brain identity. Locke, however, thought that the 'consciousness' of a person, and with it the person, could be transferred from one immaterial substance to another; and as we shall see, neo-Lockeans have made similar claims about brains.)

A famous counterexample to Locke's theory is REID's 'brave officer' example, in which as a young officer a man remembers being punished as a small boy for robbing an orchard, and much later, as an old general, remembers the brave deeds of the young officer but has no recollection of the childhood incident. This refutes any version of the memory theory that implies that one's past includes only what one remembers. But it does not refute the more sophisticated 'memory continuity' theory, according to which two different 'person stages' (temporal slices of personal histories) belong to the history of the same person just in case they are members of a series of such stages, each member of which contains memories ('from the inside') of actions or experiences belonging to the preceding member of the series (*see* TEMPORAL PARTS, STAGES).

A common objection to the memory theory, first raised by BUTLER, is that it is circular. This has two versions. One is that the notion of personal identity enters into the *contents* of the memories the having of which is supposed to constitute personal identity. This assumes that these memories are irreducibly first-personal in content –

memories expressible by saying 'I remember that *I* did so and so.' But the memory theorist can claim that the relevant memory facts can be expressed without using the notion of personal identity and without invoking such contents, namely by speaking simply of memories that are of particular experiences or actions. A different version of the circularity objection claims that the notion of memory itself must be defined in terms of the notion of personal identity, the idea being that in order to distinguish genuine remembering from mere seeming to remember we must impose the condition that in order to remember a past event (action, experience) one must be, i.e. be the same person as, someone who witnessed the event (did the action, had the experience). Memory theorists have attempted to meet this objection by invoking the concept of causality. There are independent reasons for thinking that the remembering of a past event involves there being an appropriate causal connection between the past event remembered and the subsequent memory impression of it. By using this requirement to distinguish genuine remembering from mere seeming to remember, we can avoid having to use the notion of personal identity in making this distinction, and thus avoid the threatened circularity in the definition of personal identity in terms of memory – or rather, we can do this *if* the 'appropriate causal connection' can be characterized without use of the notion of personal identity.

But once we have seen that the memory theory must invoke the concept of causality in its account of personal identity, it becomes apparent that there is no reason to hold that the only causal connections that are constitutive of personal identity are those involved in memory. If we reflect on the brain-transfer case mentioned earlier, it seems plausible that the identity of the brain recipient with the brain donor consists as much in the fact that his personality, interests, skills, etc., are causally linked to those in the donor's past history (via a distinctive causal chain carried in the brain) as it does in the fact that his memories are causally linked to past episodes in the donor's life which they represent. This suggests a refinement of Locke's view according to which personal identity consists in a sort of psychological continuity and connectedness, 'psychological C&C' (Parfit, 1984), that is, in there being such causal links between successive phases of a person's mental life (between successive 'person stages'), and that memory continuity is just a special case of this.

Such a view needs to be refined to deal with the possibility of 'fission' of persons, for example, with the version of the brain-transplant case in which the two hemispheres of someone's brain are transplanted into the (vacant) heads of two different bodies, with the result that there is psychological C&C between the state of *one* person before the operation and the states of *two* different persons after it. Clearly, the two offshoots cannot both be identical to the one person of whom they are both psychological duplicates, since they are not identical to each other. Such a case can be handled by saying that what constitutes personal identity is not psychological C&C *simpliciter*, but rather *non-branching* psychological C&C. Alternatively, one could say that psychological C&C is the relation that 'continues' persons in existence, and that it is the 'closest continuer' of a person who is identical with him; in the fission case the two continuers are equally close, so neither is the original person (see Nozick, 1981).

As noted earlier, while the standard intuition about the brain-transfer example goes against the view that personal identity consists in the identity of human bodies, it does not go against the view that it consists in the identity of human brains. If it is psychological C&C as such that constitutes personal identity, it seems that there ought to be possible cases in which a person at one time is the same as a person at another time in virtue of a psychological C&C series of mental states that is not carried by *any* single physical object. A putative case of this is the 'teleportation' of science fiction. We can think of this as involving a process whereby a brain is scanned, and at the

same time destroyed, and the information obtained from the scanning is used to create a physical duplicate of it (either by the restructuring of an already existing brain, or by the building of a new one). Opinions differ sharply about whether such a procedure could be 'person-preserving'. A difficulty for those who think it could be is the 'branch-line case', in which the scanning procedure fails to destroy the original brain. Here there are, after the procedure, two persons (the owner of the original brain, and the owner of the duplicate) whose mental states are psychologically C&C with those of the original person. The dominant intuition about this case is that the owner of the original brain is identical to the original person and that the other person is a mere psychological duplicate of him. A common – although not uncontested – intuition is that if this is so, then in the case where the original brain is destroyed it is likewise true that the owner of the duplicate brain is a mere psychological duplicate of the original person.

Recent debate over the nature of personal identity has mainly focused on the memory theory and its descendant, the psychological C&C theory. Opponents of this view have been divided among those who hold that bodily identity, or at any rate some sort of physical continuity, is needed for personal identity (see Unger, 1990; Williams, 1970), and those who, following in the tradition of Butler and Reid, hold that no reductive analysis, or constitutive account, of personal identity is possible (see Chisholm, 1975; Swinburne, 1984).

In recent discussion of personal identity the emphasis has shifted somewhat from the question of what it consists in to the question of why it matters. Here too the cases of fission, teleportation, etc., have played a prominent role. It seems plausible that someone who knows that she is about to undergo fission might naturally, and rationally, have the same sort of concern about the future well-being of both offshoots as one normally has about one's own future well-being, even though she realizes that, strictly speaking, she will be neither of them. This has been used to argue that what we really care about, in our desire to survive and our 'special concern' for the future, is not identity as such, but rather the psychological C&C that normally constitutes it. And it has been urged that recognition that identity as such does not matter would have a beneficial effect on our attitudes towards ourselves and others (see Parfit, 1984). But the natural view that it is identity that matters has staunch and resourceful defenders (see Sosa, 1990; Unger, 1990).

BIBLIOGRAPHY

Chisholm, R.M.: *Person and Object* (London: George Allen and Unwin, 1976).

Butler, J.: 'Of personal identity' (1736) (first appendix to *The Analogy of Religion*); repr. in *Personal Identity* ed. J. Perry (Berkeley and Los Angeles: University of California Press, 1975), 99–105.

Dennett, D.: 'Conditions of Personhood', in *The Identities of Persons* ed. A.O. Rorty (Berkeley and Los Angeles: University of California Press, 1976), 175–96.

Frankfurt, H.: 'Freedom of the will and the concept of a person', *Journal of Philosophy* LXVIII (1971), 5–20.

Locke, J.: *Essay Concerning Human Understanding* 2nd edn (1694); partly repr. in *Personal Identity* ed. J. Perry (Berkeley and Los Angeles: University of California Press, 1975), 33–52.

Nozick, R.: *Philosophical Explanations* (Cambridge, MA: Harvard University Press, 1981).

Parfit, D.: *Reasons and Persons* (Oxford: Oxford University Press, 1984).

Perry, J. ed.: *Personal Identity* (Berkeley and Los Angeles: University of California Press, 1975).

Reid, T.: 'Of memory', in *Essays on the Intellectual Powers of Man* (1784); partly repr. in *Personal Identity* ed. J. Perry (Berkeley and Los Angeles: University of California Press, 1975), 113–18.

Shoemaker, S.: 'Personal identity: a materialist's account', in *Personal Identity* ed. S. Shoemaker and R. Swinburne (Oxford: Blackwell, 1984), 67–132.

Sosa, E.: 'Surviving matters', *Noûs* (1990), 297–322.

Strawson, P.: *Individuals* (London: Methuen, 1959).

Swinburne, R.: 'Personal identity: the dualist theory', in *Personal Identity* ed. S. Shoemaker and R. Swinburne (Oxford: Blackwell, 1984), 1–66.

Unger, P.: *Identity, Consciousness and Value* (Oxford: Oxford University Press, 1990).

Williams, B.: 'The self and the future', *Philosophical Review* (1970); repr. in *Personal Identity* ed. J. Perry (Berkeley and Los Angeles: University of California Press), 179–98.

SYDNEY SHOEMAKER

phenomenal *see* NOUMENAL/PHENOMENAL

phenomenalism Most usefully defined as the view that propositions describing the physical world are analytically equivalent to propositions asserting that subjects would have certain sequences of sensations (*see* SENSA) were they to have certain others. In this way we can distinguish phenomenalism from the straightforward ontological thesis, sometimes called IDEALISM, asserting that the only things that exist are minds and their subjective states. A phenomenalist may be an idealist, in this sense, but phenomenalism is both weaker and stronger than idealism so understood. It is weaker in that, in claiming that we can understand assertions about the physical world as complicated assertions about the interconnections between possible sensations, the phenomenalist *need* not claim that there exists nothing beyond minds and their sensations (the phenomenalist might take an agnostic position with respect to the existence of other sorts of things). It is stronger, in that the idealist *need* not claim to be able to successfully reduce talk about the physical world to talk about actual and possible

385

sensations (the idealist might be a sceptic who thinks that there is nothing that satisfies the concept of a physical object). Again there is no uniformity in terminology, but among those idealists who are committed to reducing talk about the external world to talk about sensations, it is probably best to restrict the term 'phenomenalism' to the theory that insists that it is only conditional propositions describing sensations that would occur were others to occur that capture the meaning of ordinary assertions about the physical world.

The historical origins of phenomenalism as defined above are difficult to trace, in part because early statements of the view were usually not very careful. In his *Dialogues* (1713), BERKELEY hinted at phenomenalism when he had Philonous try to convince Hylas that there was no difficulty reconciling an ontology containing only minds and ideas with the story of a creation that took place before the existence of humans:

Why I imagine that if I had been present at the creation, I should have seen things produced into being: that is become perceptible, in the order described by the sacred historians (*Dialogues*, p. 100)

Just as often, though, Berkeley seemed to rely on actual ideas in the mind of God to secure the existence of a physical world that is independent of the existence of any finite being. MILL clearly recognized the need to go beyond actual sensations if he were plausibly to reduce the physical world to sensations. In Mill (1889) he argued that matter (the physical world) is a 'permanent possibility of sensation' and in explaining what permanent possibilities of sensation are Mill seems to have suggested that they were the sensations one would have under certain conditions.

Phenomenalism probably reached its peak of popularity during the heyday of LOGICAL POSITIVISM. A central tenet of positivism was that all meaningful propositions must be verifiable, and some positivists like AYER (1946) were convinced that the

only way to preserve the verifiability, and thus the meaningfulness, of our talk about the physical world was to define that talk in terms of epistemologically less problematic talk about sensations. Perhaps the most sophisticated version of phenomenalism was defended by C.I. Lewis (1946).

The basic idea behind phenomenalism is compatible with a number of different views of both the self and sensation. A phenomenalist could understand the self as a mind of the sort that Berkeley was committed to, or as itself a construct of actual and possible EXPERIENCE, as is found in Ayer. Most phenomenalists were sense-datum theorists who held that sensations were to be understood as either mind-dependent sense data or a subject's awareness of such sense data. There is however nothing to prevent a phenomenalist from accepting an ADVERBIAL THEORY of sensation instead. On one interpretation of the adverbial theory, sensations will be understood as non-relational properties of the conscious subject.

In many ways phenomenalism can be viewed as a direct response to the sceptical challenge presented by the problem of perception. Most phenomenalists were foundationalists who claimed that the only contingent propositions one could know directly (without inference) are propositions describing one's fleeting and subjective mental states. They also accepted a view that we can call inferential internalism. According to the inferential internalist if one is to be justified in believing one proposition p by inferring it from another e one must be justified in believing that e confirms p. If one holds the above views one faces an obvious problem with respect to the justification of ordinary beliefs about the external world. How can one justifiably infer the existence of mind-independent physical objects when all one has to rely on ultimately as one's evidence is the occurrence of mind-dependent sensations. It seems obvious that one cannot deduce the existence of something mind-independent from the occurrence of something mind-dependent. The other most commonly recognized way of discovering a connection between two things is induction. But to inductively establish sensations as evidence of physical objects one would have to *observe* a correlation between the occurrence of certain sensations and the existence of certain objects. But if all one can observe directly is a sensation, it does not seem possible to step outside the veil of sensation to establish the relevant correlations. If one were convinced that deduction and induction exhaust the kinds of reasoning available to bridge the gap between knowledge of sensations and knowledge of the physical world, scepticism might seem inevitable, and if one also embraces verificationism (*see* PRINCIPLE OF VERIFIABILITY), statements describing the physical world might seem to be in danger of losing their very intelligibility.

Phenomenalists saw their view as the only way to escape this depressing dilemma. Although one cannot define a *mind-independent* physical object as a bundle of anyone's actual sensations, one can employ subjunctive conditionals describing sensations to preserve the mind-independent status of physical objects without requiring us to go beyond what we can find out about sensations in order to verify our belief in propositions describing physical objects. If to say of a given physical object that it exists is only to make a prediction about the sensations a person would have were that person to have certain other sensations, then it looks as though we might be able to confirm the existence of that physical object by observing the relevant sequences of sensations. At the same time to assert that a subject *would* have certain sensations *were* others to occur does not imply that those sensations do actually occur. Just as the 'permanent possibility' of sugar dissolving in water might exist in a world in which there is no water (and possibly even in a world in which there is no sugar) so the 'permanent possibility' of a subject having sensations of one kind were that subject to have certain others could perhaps exist even in a world in which there were no actual conscious beings.

OBJECTIONS TO PHENOMENALISM

It is an understatement to suggest that phenomenalism is now an unpopular view. One might be tempted to explain the demise of its popularity with the widespread rejection of many of the metaphysical and epistemological presuppositions of the view. The kind of foundationalism embraced by virtually all phenomenalists is widely criticized, and with it a commitment to sensations as metaphysically and epistemologically unproblematic conceptual building blocks. Even those who accept foundationalism usually reject the kinds of reasoning allowed by the phenomenalist as too restrictive. There are also more global concerns about the very idea of a priori conceptual analysis of the sort practiced by phenomenalists. There is increasing acceptance of externalist or causal theories of meaning which make the meaning of expressions in our language largely an empirical question inaccessible to an a priori investigation.

Although the framework within which classical phenomenalism was defended is rejected by many philosophers, it would probably be a mistake to conclude that this explains the rejection of phenomenalism. In fact, it would be nearer to the truth to suggest that it is the alleged failure of phenomenalism that led many philosophers to finally search for more radical alternatives to deal with the spectre of scepticism.

Some of the objections to phenomenalism are very general. There is the vague feeling that something important gets left out by phenomenalism, that, to play on words, sensations are too insubstantial to capture the ordinary concept of a physical object. Others complain that the phenomenalist leaves completely unexplained these mysterious interconnections between sensations. And still others complain that the relation expressed by a subjunctive conditional is so philosophically problematic as to be inappropriate as a tool in the solution of other philosophical problems. The concepts of a LAW OF NATURE, CAUSATION, and the relation expressed by contingent subjunctive conditionals are all closely intertwined, and it must be admitted that philosophers have enjoyed a singular lack of success in finding a plausible analysis of one of these problematic concepts that does not presuppose an understanding of the others.

Still, the most influential objections to phenomenalism surfaced with attempts to spell out the view in detail. Precisely what conditionals describing sensations that would follow other sensations are supposed to capture the meaning of ordinary statements about the physical world? The argument widely viewed as most decisive against phenomenalism is the argument from perceptual relativity most clearly and concisely presented by CHISHOLM (1948). Chisholm offers, in effect, a strategy for attacking any phenomenalistic analysis. The first move in the strategy is to force the phenomenalist into giving at least one example of an alleged analytic consequence (expressed using language only describing sensations) of a proposition asserting the existence of some physical object. When one gets the example, one simply describes a hypothetical situation in which, though the physical object proposition is true, its alleged analytic consequence would obviously be false. If the physical object proposition really did entail the experiential proposition, then there could be no hypothetical situation in which the former is true while the latter is false, and so we would have constructed a reductio of the proposed analysis. C.I. Lewis (1946, p. 240), for example, claimed that the proposition that there is a doorknob in front of me and to the left (p) entails the proposition that if I should seem to see such a doorknob in front of me and to the left and should seem to be initiating a certain grasping motion, then in all probability the feeling of contacting a doorknob would follow (r). Chisholm argues that p does not entail r, for there is another proposition (q) (the proposition that I am unable to move my limbs and my hands but am subject to delusions such that I think I am moving them; I often seem to myself to be initiating a certain grasping motion, but when I do I

never have the feeling of contacting anything), which is obviously consistent with p and which when conjoined with p entails not-r.

The problem seems to be that even if a certain physical object exists, the sensations one would have were one to have others depend on the internal and external *physical* conditions of perception. But one cannot include reference to such physical conditions in a phenomenalistic analysis of physical object propositions without defeating the purpose of a phenomenalistic analysis. Remember the goal is to reduce talk about the physical world to talk about sensations to which one has unproblematic epistemic access.

The apparent relativity of the character of sensation to the surrounding physical conditions is the source of a closely related objection to phenomenalism. According to some philosophers, contingent subjunctive conditionals always presuppose the existence of laws of nature. If it is true that the sugar would dissolve were it placed in water it is only because there is a law of nature which says that when sugar is placed in water in these sorts of conditions it dissolves. The phenomenalist is committed to analysing the meaning of statements about the physical world into contingent subjunctive conditionals that describe nothing more than sensations that would follow other sensations. These conditionals, however, require covering laws and there simply are no laws of nature describing invariable correlations between sensations. The best one could do is find a law describing the sensations that always follow other sensations *under certain physical conditions*. But the phenomenalist who understands the truth conditions of the relevant subjunctive conditionals in terms of this sort of law is invoking the very concept of a physical object that is supposed to be analysed away.

POSSIBLE REPLIES

The argument from perceptual relativity is in the end devastating to *pure* phenomenalism. One might, however, attempt to retain the basic idea of the view by incorporating into one's phenomenalistic analysis terms that might denote something other than minds and sensations, terms that are nevertheless innocuous because one does not need to know anything about the intrinsic character of the things denoted. Thus one might try to 'protect' the antecedents of the subjunctive conditionals used in a phenomenalist analysis with a normal or standard conditions clause whose purpose is to denote those conditions *whatever they are* that normally (defined statistically) accompany certain sequences of sensations. The conditions denoted by such a clause might include other facts about what sensations would follow others, facts about Kantian things-in-themselves (*see* KANT; NOUMENAL/PHENOMENAL), or facts about the intentions of a Berkeleian God. The phenomenalist might be able to claim that even though a normal conditions clause of this sort involves denoting things in ontological categories other than sensations, such denotation is epistemically harmless because one is always justified in believing, *ceteris paribus*, that things are as they usually are.

Once one modifies phenomenalism enough to allow into the phenomenalistic analysis expressions that might denote things other than sensations, however, one can argue that we might as well embrace a version of a causal theory of objects that is much more closely related to classical phenomenalism than the more familiar representative realism replete with its primary/secondary quality distinction and a conception of objects that *resemble* in important respects the contents of our minds (*see* QUALITY, PRIMARY/SECONDARY). On this 'phenomenalistic' causal theory, to assert the existence of a physical object is to assert the existence of a thing (whatever it is – its intrinsic character might be in principle unknowable) that has the potential to produce certain sensations and that would produce certain sequences of sensations were it to produce certain others *under normal conditions*. This version of a causal theory contains no ontological commitments that extend beyond our modified phenomenalism and seems to allow a much more natural way of analysing bare existential statements, for example, there exists a table (somewhere, some time). Such statements are a nightmare for classical phenomenalism for they provide no 'setting' that makes even primafacie plausible the entailment of any conditional about what any particular subject would experience. Because the causal theorist's analysis of such statements begins with the bare existential claim about the existence of a potential cause of sensations, that problem is eliminated. Indeed, when Mill identified objects with the permanent possibilities of sensations he may well have been pointing not to pure phenomenalism but to the causal theory that is closely related to it. Notice that this causal theory faces precisely the same problem of perceptual relativity as pure versions of phenomenalism. One still needs a way of specifying subjunctively the 'powers' that define the cause as a physical object of a given kind, and to avoid a regress one must define such powers without presupposing an understanding of physical-object propositions. If so, two views long considered radically different may have a vested interest in finding common solutions to common problems.

BIBLIOGRAPHY

Ayer, A.J.: *Language, Truth and Logic* 2nd edn (New York: Dover, 1946).
Berkeley, G.: *Three Dialogues between Hylas and Philonous* (London, 1713); ed. C.M. Turbayne (Indianapolis, IN: Bobbs-Merrill, 1954).
Chisholm, R.M.: 'The problem of empiricism', *Journal of Philosophy* 45 (1948), 512–17.
Hume, D.: *A Treatise of Human Nature* (London: 1888); ed. L.A. Selby-Bigge (London: Oxford, 1978).
Lewis, C.I.: *An Analysis of Knowledge and Valuation* (La Salle, IL: Open Court, 1946).

Mackie, J.L.: 'What's really wrong with Phenomenalism', *Proceedings of the British Academy* 55 (1969), 113–27.

Mill, J.S.: *An Examination of Sir William Hamilton's Philosophy* (London: Longmans, Green, 1889).

RICHARD FUMERTON

phenomenology 'Phenomenology' is used in philosophy as well as in science for a purely descriptive approach to that which appears to us, without bringing in theory or explanations. Johann Heinrich Lambert in *Neues Organon* (1764) regarded the phenomena as illusory. KANT opposed them to *noumena*, or things-in-themselves and argued that phenomena are all we can ever know. HEGEL's *Phenomenology of the Spirit* (1807) takes issue with this and claims to open access to mind as it is in itself. (*See* NOUMENAL/PHENOMENAL.)

Nowadays, 'phenomenology' is usually used for HUSSERL's phenomenology, an approach to philosophy that was introduced by his *Logical Investigations* (1900–1) and developed more fully in *Ideas* (1913) and later works. Many of Husserl's students in Göttingen (1901–16) and in Freiburg (1916–29) continued this work, among them Edith Stein and INGARDEN, the latter notably in applications to art and literature. Also, HEIDEGGER, SARTRE and MERLEAU-PONTY regarded themselves as phenomenologists, and through Heidegger and Hans-Georg Gadamer, Husserl's phenomenology has transformed HERMENEUTICS.

For Husserl, phenomenology is a study of the subjective perspective. In science one aims for OBJECTIVITY and endeavours to arrange observations and experiments in such a way as to minimize differences between different observers. Phenomenology focuses on the subjective, on the manner in which each subject structures, or 'constitutes' the world differently, on the basis of different experiences and cultural background, but also on the basis of adaptation to other subjects through interaction and communication.

In our everyday natural attitude we regard the things around us as just being there, waiting to be passively registered by ourselves and others. However, the physical impulses received by our sense organs are clearly insufficient to determine what we experience, as is revealed, for example, by WITTGENSTEIN's duck/rabbit example. We contribute a rich and complicated structure of anticipations and retentions. Thus, for example, if we see a duck in front of us, we anticipate feathers, if we see a rabbit, we anticipate fur. This structure Husserl calls the *noema*. This structure includes anticipations relating to our various senses and concerning the spatio-temporal relations between the experienced object and other objects and events. The structure also includes so-called 'thetic' elements, concerning the nature of the act in which we experience the object, whether it be an act of perception, memory, imagination, etc., and thereby also the reality-character of the object.

Instead of focusing on the object, as we do in our natural attitude, the phenomenologist concentrates on this structure of anticipations and describes it. The change of focus Husserl calls the *transcendental reduction*, or *epoché*, and the analysis of the structure he calls *phenomenological analysis*. Strictly, there are three elements in our consciousness that are uncovered through this transcendental reduction and studied in phenomenological analysis: in addition to the noema, which is an abstract structure that would be instantiated again in the unlikely case that at some other occasion we should have the same kind of experience of the same object from the same point of view, with exactly the same anticipations, etc., there is the *noesis*, which is the concrete act which instantiates this noema and there is the *hyle*, a kind of experience we typically have when our sense organs are affected and which in the case of perception and memory restrict what kind of noema and noesis our act can have. The hyle and the noesis, unlike the noema, are temporal processes, experiences.

In phenomenology, all these three elements are being studied, with emphasis on the noematic/noetic structures. Husserl carried out detailed analyses of temporal structures and how they are constituted, in *Lectures on the Phenomenology of Internal Time-Consciousness* (1928), on the structures that are basic to logic and mathematics, in *Formal and Transcendental Logic* (1929) and *Experience and Judgment* (1939), on intersubjectivity and the processes whereby we come to constitute a common world, in *Cartesian Meditations* (1931) and in thousands of pages of manuscripts of which the most important have been collected by Iso Kern in *Husserliana* (vols 13–15). Husserl's studies of intersubjectivity focus in particular on the processes by which we experience others as experiencing subjects, like ourselves, and adapt our anticipations to those that we taken them to have. Thanks to this, our way of constituting the world is not solipsistic, we constitute the world as a shared world, which we each experience from our different perspective. A notion of objectivity arises, we may come to regard ourselves as deviant, for example as colourblind or as cognitively biased, and we also experience ourselves as confronted with a reality to which our beliefs and anticipations have to adapt. In works that remain largely unpublished, Husserl started to develop an ethics based in part on a study of the objectifying processes whereby objective ethical principles and norms arise from our subjective likes and dislikes.

Husserl was initially concentrating on cognitive issues, in the beginning especially those that arise in logic and mathematics. However, his interests gradually expanded to include epistemology and metaphysics generally. From 1917 on, he explored the role that human activity plays in the constitution of the world, and he also became increasingly interested in the role of the body in the constitutive processes. These ideas were primarily developed in the unpublished drafts for the second and third volume of the *Ideas* and for his last work,

the *Crisis of the European Sciences*. These manuscripts were read by Merleau-Ponty in 1939 and inspired him to his 'phenomenology of the body'.

A main theme in Husserl's late work is the *Lifeworld*, the world which we constitute and in which we find ourselves living. The lifeworld plays an important role in Husserl's theory of evidence and the foundations of knowledge.

See also INTUITION; NOEMA, NOESIS.

BIBLIOGRAPHY

Spiegelberg, H.: *The Phenomenological Movement* (The Hague: Martinus Nijhoff, 1960).

DAGFINN FØLLESDAL

physicalism, materialism The general thesis which originates in the ancient atomists such as Democritus (*c*.460–*c*.370 BC) and Lucretius, is the view that everything which exists is a purely material (or physical) entity. If we assume a world of individuals, as the atomists did, then materialism (also called 'physicalism') might be stated more exactly as the thesis that every individual or group of individuals has only physical properties. (*See* ATOMISM.)

Though historically accurate, both for the atomists and for later writers such as HOBBES and HOLBACH, the account so far given is overly restrictive in several ways. First, there are some properties such as the ethical property of being good that a person might have, and these properties do not seem to be physical. Nor, indeed, are they mental properties. Instead, they seem best classified as topic-neutral properties, in the sense that an individual a's having such a property entails neither that a is a material entity nor that a is a mental entity.

A second problem concerns abstract entities. We want materialism to be consistent with the existence of classes, for example, but the characterization of materialism given above rules this out. A third problem arises when we note that some psychological states apparently have qualitative properties which are neither physical nor topic-neutral. Sensations, for instance, are often thought to have phenomenal properties. Materialist approaches to the MIND/BODY PROBLEM typically contend that such properties as these are reducible (*see* REDUCTION, REDUCTIONISM) to physical properties.

Taking these matters into account, and also taking the notion of a physical property as undefined, we can state an amended version of the general materialist thesis: it is the thesis that every property of an entity is either a physical property, or a topic-neutral property, or it is reducible to a physical or topic-neutral property. (Cornman, 1971, p. 9) states a definition similar to this. Note that this definition rules out non-physical, transcendent entities.)

Proposed solutions to the mind/body problem which entail materialism, as amended, are materialist theories of the mental. One such theory, behaviourism, may be construed in two ways: first, as a theory which type-identifies mental entities with either pieces of behaviour or dispositions to behave (*see* DISPOSITION); or, as an eliminativist theory which countenances pieces of behaviour and dispositions thereto, but not mental entities of any sort. (For the former, see Watson, 1989, p. 14; for the latter, see Skinner, 1964, p. 84). Philosophical defences of these behaviourist doctrines have usually been cast in the form of analytical behaviourism.

Analytical behaviourism is the thesis that every mental sentence can be translated into, and so is equivalent in meaning to, some behavioural sentences (see Hempel, 1949). If correct, many supposed that it would show that we need not make use of mental sentences for adequate descriptions of persons, and so the eliminativist behaviourist position would be justified. However, analytical behaviourism has met with little success: the translations it proposed met with quick counterexample, and the thesis was largely based upon the verifiability theory of meaningfulness for empirical sentences (*see* PRINCIPLE OF VERIFIABILITY), a much-touted but later discredited account of meaning (Chisholm, 1957, pp. 168–85). Nor did the identity or eliminativist versions of behaviourism fare any better, for both in philosophy and in psychology theorists came to hold that behaviourism ignores the importance of inner states, i.e. inner states of persons that are genuine causes of behaviour but are not themselves pieces of behaviour nor mere dispositions to behave.

Pursuit of this idea led Place and Smart at first, and then Lewis and ARMSTRONG, to the identity theory, the view that each mental item is strictly identical to a neural or brain item. The identity, though strict in the sense that it accords with Leibniz's Law (*see* IDENTITY OF INDISCERNIBLES), was reckoned as contingent. It was a contingent truth that, for example, each sensation of pain is identical to some brain event. Also, the theory proposed a type-identity of the mental and the neural, rather than just the thesis that each mental event token is identical to some physical or brain event token (Armstrong, 1968; Lewis, 1966, pp. 17–25; Place, 1989, pp. 29–36; Smart, 1959, pp. 141–56).

Some mental sentences seem to function to attribute mental properties to sensations. Thus, to adopt Smart's example, 'I see a yellowish-orange after-image' seems to attribute phenomenal colour to some mental entity. Smart tried to handle this problem by providing topic-neutral translations of such sentences; i.e. translations into sentences which do not ascribe mental properties to anything. If successful, these translations would eliminate mental properties of sensations; and if the approach could be generalized to all mental entities and mental properties, then the type–type identity theory could lead to *reductive materialism*. This is the thesis that each mental entity is not only type-identical to a neural entity, but is in fact *nothing but* a neural entity (see Cornman, 1971, for this distinction).

Reductive materialism requires that mental properties be reduced or eliminated, if not by topic-translations then by some other means. The unlikely prospects for either endeavour led some philosophers to *eliminative materialism* – the thesis that there are no mental entities of any sort, and so nothing to have mental properties. So on this view, mental-state ascriptions to a person, even to oneself, are *false*, contrary to the identity theory and to reductive materialism.

The principal argument for eliminative materialism has been that our common-sense conception of the mental makes up a defective theory, one which is destined to be replaced by some conjunction of theories from the various sub-parts of neuroscience. Indeed, some philosophers hold that this replacement can and should be effected now; we need not wait for neuroscience to mature any further. This sort of argument, either for future or current replacement, contends as well that the common-sense theory of the mental is not and will not be reducible to any neuroscientific theory (Churchland, 1988; Churchland, 1989, pp. 206–23; Rorty, 1965, pp. 24–54).

See also FUNCTIONALISM; SUPERVENIENCE.

BIBLIOGRAPHY

Armstrong, D.M.: *A Materialist Theory of the Mind* (New York: Humanities Press, 1968).
Chisholm, R.M.: *Perceiving* (Ithaca, NY: Cornell University Press, 1957).
Churchland, P.M.: *Matter and Consciousness* 2nd edn (Cambridge, MA: MIT Press, 1988), 206–223.
Churchland, P.M.: 'Eliminative materialism and the propositional attitudes', in *Mind and Cognition* ed. W. Lycan (Cambridge, MA: Blackwell, 1989).
Cornman, J.: *Materialism and Sensations* (New Haven, CT: Yale University Press, 1971).
Hempel, C.: 'The logical analysis of psychology', in *Readings in Philosophical Analysis* ed. H. Feigl and W. Sellars (New York: Appleton-Century-Crofts, 1949), 373–84.
Lewis, D.: 'An argument for the identity theory', *Journal of Philosophy* 63 (1966), 17–25.
Place, U.: 'Is consciousness a brain process?', in *Mind and Cognition* ed. W. Lycan (Cambridge: Blackwell, 1989), 29–36.
Rorty, R.: 'Mind–body identity, privacy, and categories', *Review of Metaphysics* 19 (1965), 24–54.
Smart, J.: 'Sensations and brain processes', *Philosophical Review* 68 (1959), 141–56.
Skinner, B.: 'Behaviorism at fifty', in *Behaviorism and Phenomenology* ed. T. Wann (Chicago: University of Chicago Press, 1964), 79–97.
Watson, J.: 'Excerpt from "Talking and Thinking" ', in *Mind and Cognition* ed. W. Lycan (Cambridge, MA: Blackwell, 1989), 14–22.

GEORGE S. PAPPAS

Plato (*c*.427–347 BC) Greek philosopher. Traditionally the core of Plato's metaphysics has been taken to be the thesis that there exists a realm of non-perceptible objects, called Forms (*eide*) or Ideas (*ideai*), which are the only strictly real things and the subject matter of all knowledge, and that perceptible objects are in some sense copies of these Forms, less strictly real than they are, and incapable of being known. As an approximation this interpretation is correct. Only with a much clearer account, however, does Plato's view appear as more than a vulgar caricature of a philosophical metaphysics.

In the present account it will be assumed that Plato's work represents a body of doctrine that is broadly unified and mainly consistent, though it is occasionally subject to some corrections and alterations, and though later works attempt to solve problems that the views of earlier works give rise to. It should be noted that this interpretation is in conflict with two other common views. One is that Plato changed his views radically in the middle of his life (after the *Phaedo*, the *Republic* and the *Symposium*, and in the *Theaetetus*, the *Sophist*, the *Parmenides* and the *Philebus*). The other is that his several works present no single doctrine or theory at all.

Plato's views on metaphysics are inseparable from his epistemology. His metaphysics arise largely from his attempt to describe how the world must be if we are to be able to have any knowledge (*episteme*). Plato assumes – or perhaps argues (it is hard to be sure which he regards himself as doing) – that we do have knowledge, as distinct from mere 'opinion' or 'belief' (*doxa*). He then tries to show that if this is so, then there must necessarily exist non-perceptible Forms which this knowledge is about (*Phdo* 74, *Rep.* 475–80, *Tim.* 51).

However Plato's notion of knowledge is in some ways rather different from modern notions. It involves not merely issues about how a knower may attain certainty and freedom from error, for example, but also about how he may fully understand the terms that he uses. As a result many of Plato's early works (e.g. the *Euthyphro* and the *Laches*), which adumbrate his doctrines about Forms, are aimed at discovering definitions of certain problematical terms – a process that eventually comes to be associated closely with gaining knowledge of Forms (for example, *Rep.* 475–80, 509–11, 533–4). Moreover Plato declares that Forms must exist if significant discourse is to be possible (*Parm.* 135). This shows that in his view Forms are required not merely for certainty but also for the intelligibility of our judgements.

To understand these facts it helps to realize that one of Plato's chief intellectual drives was his antipathy to the relativistic position of some so-called Sophists, notably Protagoras (*Tht.*, esp. 169–80). Against such thinkers Plato wished to safeguard several ideas: that we are capable of gaining knowledge and avoiding error, that there are objective facts about which different people (or the same person at different times) may agree or disagree, and that we can conceive the notion of such objective

facts. Perhaps the most important of Plato's motivations for believing in the existence of Forms was his belief that only by some cognitive access to such entities could human minds form the notion of properties that attach to things as a matter of objective fact, and not simply relatively to the point of view of some observer or thinker.

Plato believes that for the range of predicates, *F*, that interest him, any perceptible object that appears *F* also, in some other circumstances or from some other perspective, appears the contrary of *F*. (The relevant circumstances can involve either sense perception of the object or simply thought about it.) For example, the same object that appears hard will also, he believes, appear soft from some other perspective, and likewise the same object or action that appears good will also from some other perspective appear bad (e.g. *Phdo* 74, *Rep.* 479). (It should be noted that Plato recognizes no significant difference in this regard between evaluative notions like goodness and non-evaluative ones like hardness.)

The Form of *F*, on the other hand, is associated by Plato with the notion of a thing's being *F* independently of the point of view from which it is considered (ibid. and *Symp.* 210–11). To have appropriate cognition of the Form, in his view, is to grasp the idea of the property of a thing's being *F* in this circumstance- and perspective-independent way. If a person understood what it is to be *F* merely on the basis of what perception alone conveys, he would never possess the notion of a thing's being *F* in such a way, but only the idea of a thing's being *F* *in* such-and-such circumstances or *to* this or that perspective. (An exploration-*cum*-parody of the view that these relational notions are all that we do possess is given in *Tht.* 152ff., the so-called 'Secret Doctrine' facetiously attributed to Protagoras.)

Plato takes it to be plain, however, that we do have the notion of the property of being *F* in this circumstance- and perspective-independent way. When we call something good or hard, he thinks, what we intend to ascribe to it is not the property of being hard or good *to* some point of view or *in* particular circumstances, but rather the property of being good or hard *simpliciter*. (Plato thus denies that these are really or covertly relational properties, and thus he would reject the common charge that he confuses relational and non-relational properties.) Our grasp of such non-relational notions, he maintains, is possible only by virtue of our cognition, however imperfect, of Forms.

Our ability to think about perceptible things as we do, Plato believes, is based on our cognition of Forms (*Phdo* 75), as we try to apply that cognition to the perceptible world. He thinks that one's capacity to take a particular perceptible object now as hard and now as soft is the result of the following fact. One grasps the notion of a thing's being hard *simpliciter* or soft *simpliciter*, and one *tries*, as it were, to apply *this* notion to the things that one has perceptions of; but the variable circumstances that obtain in the perceptible world bring it about sometimes that one takes a thing as hard, and at other times that one takes the same thing as soft. The content of the judgement, given by cognition of the Form, is non-relational. Our willingness to make the judgement, however, is affected by the circumstances of perception and varies with them. In this sense, he thinks, we inevitably see perceptible objects as defective, and as images or copies of Forms (*Phdo* 74–5, *Rep.* 509–17, 595–8, *Tim.* 47–52).

In Plato's view, the notions that we try to apply to perceptible objects are thus not derived from perception. Rather they come to us a priori, by what Plato sometimes, but not always, calls (perhaps fancifully) 'recollection' (*Phdo* 74–6, *Meno* 80–6). Plato never seriously discusses, nor attempts to refute systematically, the idea that the notions that he associates with Forms, though perhaps not applicable to perceptible objects in a straightforward way, are nevertheless *derived* from perception by some kind of operation of the mind on what it delivers to us. Nor, probably, does he entertain the possibility that we might adopt a set of notions – perhaps prominently including relational notions – that we could apply

unproblematically to perceptible objects. He cleaves to the view that the notions that we must use are given to us by cognition of Forms, and that we then try to apply them to the perceptible world.

But Plato does not think merely that our judgements about perceptibles are constructed from notions that we possess by virtue of our cognition of forms. He also believes that the possession by perceptibles of the features that we apprehend in them, and in a sense the very existence of perceptible things, is itself dependent on the Forms. This idea appears in the claim in the *Phaedo* that Forms are 'causes' (*aitiai*) of perceptible objects, and that only by invoking Forms can we give satisfactory explanations of why perceptibles are as they are (*Phdo*, esp. 96ff.).

For one thing, in his view perceptible objects are not capable of possessing properties in the same circumstance- and perspective-independent way that our understanding of those properties might lead us to expect. A perceptible object, like a perceiver who perceives it, is inevitably embedded in the perceptible, changeable, spatio-temporal world. Our ascription of properties is always conditioned by this fact, as noted. But Plato also thinks that the same is true of the *possession* of features *by* those objects. Perceptible objects depend on circumstances not merely for the ways in which they appear; they themselves have features, Plato believes, only (with certain exceptions) relatively to circumstances. That is, the properties possessed by perceptible objects can be thought of, not as themselves relational properties (we have seen that Plato rejects that view), but (as we might put it) 'possessed relationally'.

This view involves Plato in a number of issues too complex to be easily summarized, but a few points can be touched on. For one thing, Plato's view of perceptible objects may express itself in the idea that a perceptible object is relational in part by virtue of the fact that it is an image or copy of a Form, and that a copy is a relational entity, being what it is only by virtue of its relation to that of which it is a copy. (On one inter-

PLATO

pretation, originally suggested by ARIS-
TOTLE, Plato accepted a 'self-predicational'
view of Forms, according to which the Form
of *F* itself in some way exemplifies the property of being *F*; if so then he becomes
entangled in the so-called 'third man argument', of which versions are to be found in
Parm. 132a–b, 132d–133a.) Another idea
that he may have adopted is that what we
think of as a perceptible object is to be
thought of as something more like a
'bundle' of copies of different Forms.

This latter view suggests further ideas
about the structure and identity conditions
of perceptible objects – ideas that Plato
perhaps did not work out, and of which
only brief and sketchy indications appear in
his writings. He suggests that because they
CHANGE, perceptible objects, unlike Forms,
do not strictly remain the same through
time, but persist only 'by virtue of the fact
that the old thing that departs leave
another new thing behind such as it was'
(*Symp.* 208; cf. *Tim.* 37–8). In the *Timaeus*
he posits what he calls the 'receptacle'
(*hypodoche*), as that 'in' which things come
to be and pass away, and seems to maintain
that it is the only thing that persists
through change (esp. *Tim.* 49–50).

On the whole, Plato gives more attention
to problems about the nature of Forms than
to issues about the structure of perceptible
objects. Most of the problems about Forms
that he discusses, though, arise from his
various attempts to contrast them with perceptibles. For one thing, there are difficulties
in his seeming suggestion that by contrast
to perceptibles, Forms are completely non-
relational entities. In the *Phaedo* this view
appears, at any rate, to be asserted, with the
claim that each Form is 'itself by itself' and
'uni-form' (*auto kath' hauto*, and *monoeides*,
e.g. 78–80). On the other hand in the
Republic he seems to hold that any serious
attempt at knowledge involves mastering a
universal science that seems to encompass
everything, starting from the Form of the
Good (*Rep.* 504–18, 533–4, 540–1). This
idea has been taken to imply some kind of
metaphysical and epistemological HOLISM.
It has also been taken, however (because of

the claim that the Good is somehow a starting point), to amount to a type of epistemological foundationalism.

In other works, and particularly in works
that are usually taken to have been written
after the middle of his life, Plato clearly
seems to be concerned with the relations
among Forms and the possibility that some
of these might lead to paradox. In particular
this is true of the *Parmenides*, the *Sophist*
and the *Philebus*. And in these dialogues, as
well as in the *Phaedrus*, Plato describes and
illustrates what is often called the 'method
of collection and division', which is in part a
way of describing the interrelations among
Forms, and particularly of classifying them
into genera, species, subspecies, and the
like. Plato's general anti-relativism is illustrated here by his claim that divisions must
proceed in accordance with the 'real articulations' of things (something much like
what are frequently called 'natural kinds'),
and that 'we are not to hack off parts like a
clumsy butcher' (*Phdr.* 265–6). But what
Plato is mainly focusing on is the problem
how a Form, or species, can be considered
to be 'divided' into different Forms, or subspecies, and what this possibility of division
indicates about the metaphysical status and
constitution of such entities – an issue that
was later actively pursued by Aristotle (e.g.,
in *Metaphysics* VII 10–14).

See also NATURAL KIND; PLATONISM.

WRITINGS

Platonis opera ed. J. Burnet, 5 vols (Oxford:
Clarendon Press, 1900–7).
The Collected Dialogues of Plato ed. E. Hamilton and H. Cairns (Princeton, NJ: Princeton University Press, 1961).

BIBLIOGRAPHY

Castañeda, H.-N.: 'Plato's *Phaedo* theory of
relations', *Journal of Philosophical Logic* 1
(1972), 467–80.
Lee, E.N.: 'On the metaphysics of the image
in Plato's *Timaeus*', *Monist* 50 (1966),
341–68.

Meinwald, C.: *Plato's Parmenides* (Oxford: Oxford University Press, 1991).

Owen, G.E.L.: 'A proof in the *Peri Ideon*', *Journal of Hellenic Studies* 77 (1957), 103–11.

Penner, T.: *The Ascent from Nominalism* (Dordrecht: Reidel, 1987).

Robinson, R.: *Plato's Earlier Dialectic* 2nd edn (Oxford: Clarendon Press, 1953).

Vlastos, G.: 'Degrees of reality in Plato', in *New Essays on Plato and Aristotle* ed. R. Bambrough (New York: Humanities Press, 1965), 1–18.

White, F.C.: *Plato's Theory of Particulars* (New York: Arno Press, 1981).

White, N.: 'Plato's epistemological metaphysics', in *Cambridge Companion to Plato* ed. R. Kraut (Cambridge: Cambridge University Press, 1991), 277–310.

NICHOLAS WHITE

Platonism   The term used in a broad sense to describe work based on the ideas of Plato. Plato was such a prolific, wide-ranging, and many-sided philosopher, and also such a complex personality, his influence has exerted itself in a bewildering variety of ways. In antiquity his school, often called the Academy, came to be dominated by Scepticism, which claimed to be following his lead and that of his teacher, Socrates. Later in antiquity, however, his work inspired the so-called Neoplatonists, notably PLOTINUS (205–70), to develop an elaborate metaphysical doctrine. His influence also affected religious thought, through Philo of Alexandria's (d. *c*.40 AD) use of his ideas to help formulate Jewish ideas, through Moslem philosophers such as al-Kindi (d. after 870) and AVICENNA, and through the Christian Church Fathers Clement of Alexandria (*c*.150–*c*.210) and Origen (*c*.185–*c*.255) and many other Christian thinkers into modern times. In spite of Plato's strong hostility to much art and literature (see *Republic* X), he also inspired poets such as Edmund Spenser (1552?–99) and Percy Bysshe Shelley (1792–1823), and other writers of *belles-lettres*, as well as many painters and sculptors, particularly during the Renaissance. And of course one must not forget ARISTOTLE, who, though he has been regarded through much of the history of philosophy as Plato's great opponent, was taken during much of antiquity (as he himself sometimes took himself) to be merely one Platonist among others.

Plato's overarching metaphysical outlook – according to which there is a fully objective reality that cannot be entirely captured by sense perception – has largely been reflected, clearly or obscurely, in the views of those influenced by him. (There are exceptions: his use of dialogues rather than treatises has, ironically, inspired some relativistically-minded thinking of a sort that he resolutely opposed.) Therefore, even though he stimulated many ideas going in many directions, no serious distortion is introduced by focusing on a few of the most fundamental lines of his thought that have affected subsequent metaphysics – though it should be borne in mind that his metaphysics cannot be easily separated from other parts of his philosophy.

These lines of thought re-emerge repeatedly in many philosophers, but they are typified by a few great classical figures, including particularly AUGUSTINE and DESCARTES but also the Cambridge Platonists such as Ralph Cudworth (1617–88), and represented in recent times by Gottlob FREGE, Bertrand RUSSELL and G.E. MOORE for some of their careers, as well as MCTAGGART and WHITEHEAD (who is the author of the observation that all of philosophy is a series of footnotes to Plato). The following remarks will be illustrated by examples drawn largely from the work of these figures.

The first major theme of Platonism, which is nowadays the most commonly associated with the term, is the view that there are such things as what are often called 'abstract objects'. Customarily the view is understood to be that abstract objects exist in addition to 'concrete objects', which are usually taken to be the middle-sized physical objects of ordinary experience (*see* CONCRETE/ABSTRACT). However a belief in abstract objects can be combined (and on some interpretations was combined by Plato) with the view that there are in fact no concrete objects. A belief in abstract objects is common to Plato, Augustine, Descartes, Frege, Russell, and all other philosophers who can properly be called Platonists. UNIVERSALS and mathematical entities are the usual sorts of abstract objects that such views invoke. (Some Platonists believe that abstract objects may be either particular or universal, whereas others hold that all abstract objects are universal; this issue may be ignored here.) Platos usually called such entities Forms or Ideas (*eide* or *ideai*).

This first theme can be given more content by being associated with another theme of equal importance, namely, what can be called a kind of anti-NATURALISM. This view, which comes in various types and degrees, holds that abstract objects are not governed by the same sorts of laws or regularities that bind or describe the behaviour of physical objects that we examine with our senses and theorize about on the basis of empirical evidence. The view is closely associated with the common Platonistic idea that abstract objects are not 'in space and time'.

This second theme can be regarded as including various views about human knowledge and the human mind. Plato sometimes held that the human mind, or SOUL, has knowledge of Forms or Ideas from before birth, through what he described as 'recollection'. He also held that the mind has a kind of cognitive access to Forms that is independent of not only the senses but, seemingly, all of our transactions with physical things. This idea left him in the position of believing that there are occurrences in the world, involving minds and Forms, that proceed in ways quite different from, and largely independent of, physical processes. Moreover he indicates quite definitely that Forms are in some sense out of time (*Timaeus* 37–8).

Even so, however, he believed in interaction between physical things and the mind, since he held that a person's physical condition can affect, for example, his capacity for intellectual activity involving Forms. He also thought that Forms are in some sense the 'causes' (*aitiai*) of at least some states of affairs in the physical world (*Phaedo* 96ff.) – thought it is not clear that what he meant in this instance is what we nowadays would call a causal interaction.

Plato thus bequeathed to his successors a certain unclarity and ambivalence about the manner and extent of the interrelation between abstract things and physical things, and about the degree to which abstract objects are caught up, so to speak, in the physical processes of what we think of as the natural world; and he also left a concomitant uncertainty about the extent to which the mind is affected by, and affects, physical events. The result is a kind of partial anti-naturalism, i.e. a belief that certain processes involving abstract objects, and the minds that think about them, are to some extent causally detached from physical events, but not completely so. The obvious problem was to say what the attachments are and how they work.

Philosophical descendants of Plato have tried to cope with this state of affairs on various fronts. The notion of the soul is distinct from that of the mind, but nevertheless the MIND/BODY PROBLEM is closely linked to problems about the soul that Plato treated. In Augustine this problem is wrapped up in issues of Christian doctrine of the soul. The problem appears likewise in Descartes, who tries to deal with it by means of his well-known theory that the mind and the body, distinct substances though they are, interact somehow at the pineal gland. This, like all kinds of interactionism, can be seen as an attempt to define certain anti-naturalistic tendencies of Platonism. This problem breaks out even in modern Platonistically-minded philosophers like Frege (in 'Der Gedanke' (1919)), who is forced to acknowledge that his notion that the mind can 'grasp' what he calls 'thoughts' involves a very peculiar relation that is susceptible of no further explanation.

A third theme in Platonism, at least as important as the other two, is the idea of what can be called OBJECTIVITY. This theme can best be described by explaining what kind of views Plato opposes. In the decades when Plato was beginning his philosophical activity, one of the ideas that had become current, through the influence of some of the intellectuals known as Sophists, was a seemingly quite general kind of relativism, associated particularly with the name of Protagoras (see Plato's *Theaetetus*, esp. 152ff.). Plato took him to mean – with his slogan, 'Man is the measure of all things, of those that are that they are, and of those that are not that they are not' – that what each person believes is 'true for that person', and took him also to reject any non-believer-relative notion of truth (or falsity). Plato wished to insist that this position was impossible to occupy coherently (*Tht.* 169–80), and furthermore that we must accept an objective, non-believer-relative notion of truth (often he talked in terms of 'being' rather than 'truth').

Plato's theory of Forms or Ideas is most fundamentally an attempt at an account of how the world must be if there are to be objective things and states of affairs that can be known. His acceptance of the existence of Forms does not arise simply from a brute belief in abstract objects, but primarily from a conviction that only if such things exist can there be any difference between thinking correctly and simply thinking.

In its subsequent history Platonism has always stressed such a notion of objectivity, though it has been progressively refined and subjected to scrutiny by Platonists and their opponents. One bone of contention has been the epistemological question whether knowledge of objective states of affairs is possible. A negative answer to this question was given by ancient Sceptics, sometimes within Plato's own Academy, and by other sceptics since. Much energy was spent by Augustine combating scepticism for the sake of defending his own Christian belief, but his views involved many non-Christian,

Platonistic elements. The essentially anti-sceptical programme of Descartes continues in this tradition.

A second bone of contention has been whether the relevant notion of objectivity itself makes sense, and, if so, how it can be explained. This debate has been complex, largely depending on precisely what form of relativism is being opposed by a particular believer in objectivity. For the most part, Plato seems to have believed that it was enough if he could confute the rejection of all notions of truth except that of truth 'for' an actual believer.

To other Platonists, however, it has seemed necessary to do more than this. For example, some Platonists wish to oppose a form of verificationism that says broadly that no proposition is meaningful unless there is some way of confirming or disconfirming it (*see* PRINCIPLE OF VERIFIABILITY). Some Platonistically-minded philosophers regard such a view as misguidedly relativizing meaningfulness to standards of what counts as confirmation or disconfirmation. They insist that no such standards are acceptable unless they can be shown to be such that, for example, what is confirmed is (likely to be) true – where the notion of truth is, they hold, to be regarded as understood *antecedently* to, and independently of, its use in the specification of standards of confirmation. In another instance of this type of debate some philosophers, loosely following PEIRCE, have suggested that truth can be explained as the final deliverance of a future or an idealized science. Opposing Platonists regard this as, in effect, a mistaken relativization of truth to variable facts, either about what future human investigations will in fact say, or about different possible ways of idealizing science as it in fact is practised.

The general tendency of Platonism has thus been to reject all attempts to explain truth (or being, or 'the world') in any way that might make it depend on states of affairs – such as actual beliefs of particular people, or the actual present or future practice of science, or actual conceptions of what an ideal science might be – that might by any stretch of conceivability turn out to be otherwise. Understandably enough, this tendency has often led to the rejection of *all* attempts to explain truth (or its companion notions), and to insist that it is indefinable and primitive. (On some interpretations, Plato took this course.)

In Augustine one finds a thoroughly uncompromising declaration of the independence of how things really are from all facts about human cognitive activities and capacities (see esp. *De libero arbitrio* II, and *De magistro*). A belief in this sort of objective facts is a standing assumption in Descartes, who mostly concerns himself with the question how they can be known.

In Frege and Russell, the issue of objectivity has as much to do with questions about the meanings of our judgements as with other sorts of facts. Both argue for the existence of entities (thoughts or senses in Frege, universals and certain other propositional constituents in Russell) that play a role in making our judgements meaningful. The facts about these entities are taken in some emphatic though unspecified sense to be objective, and not the creation of or relative to any facts about human beings. In this respect they were reaffirming the position of Plato (in *The Problems of Philosophy* (1912) Russell does so explicitly), for whom the Forms were not only the subject matter of knowledge, but also the entities that endow our discourse with intelligibility (*Parmenides* 135). And of course Descartes consistently, though tacitly, treats the meaning or contents of the beliefs held by the mind to be a straightforwardly objective fact, not varying with facts about the external world toward which sceptical doubts are directed.

Mathematics has provided a favoured field of activity for Platonists (though there are exceptions, such as some Renaissance figures). This is due to several facts. First, mathematics can easily seem to call for a belief in abstract entities of some sort. (On some interpretations, Plato's contact with Pythagorean mathematics is what first stimulated his metaphysical theory.) For

another thing, many mathematical statements seem so obvious, certain, and universally accepted that they readily seem to support both the objectivity of their subject matter and the inconceivability of the idea that their truth might be dependent on any states of affairs that varies with any variable whatsoever. Augustine uses numbers as his primary example of an objective realm; Descartes accords it a similar status, though less flamboyantly. Frege and Russell did something similar, though the emergence of the paradoxes of set theory shook the conviction of many people (though not of GÖDEL), that mathematics deals with its own objective realm.

For several reasons, however, mathematics presents severe difficulties to the partial anti-naturalism that has been characteristic of Platonism. For one thing it has long seemed mysterious, on Platonistic views, how the mind can have cognitive access to abstract entities, whether because knowing about a thing seems to some to entail being causally affected by it, or more generally because knowledge seems to involve some kind of causal or quasi-causal transaction between the knower and the known (as Plato remarks at *Sophist* 248–9). In addition, the importance of mathematics in natural science has given rise to questions about how the numbers which are referred to in physical laws can, even if they do not actually bump into physical objects, avoid nevertheless being somehow entangled in causal relations with them. Similar difficulties can be generated for other abstract objects as well (for example, if causation is explained in terms of relations of universals, as in Plato, *Phaedo* 100–7). From this quarter pressure is generated either to renounce abstract objects, or to allow abstract objects into the natural world after all, or to draw the boundary in such a way as to solve these difficulties.

Particular difficulties arise here because of many Platonists' tendency to think that the cognitive access of our minds to abstract entities is in some sense 'direct' or 'unmediated'. Aside from the epistemological issues that this idea raises, about how such access can give rise to knowledge of propositions (a problem that Russell struggles with in, for example, *The Problems of Philosophy*), there is the further difficulty of explaining just what this 'direct' relation consists in, and how it can be reconciled with empirically discoverable facts about the mind.

Plato himself was relatively unencumbered by any knowledge of such facts, and simply took it to be obviously a capacity of the reason or reasoning part of the soul to gain knowledge of Forms, a capacity that he sometimes describes as somehow comparable to vision, but regards as not a transaction in the natural world (e.g. *Rep.* VI–VII). Something similar is true of Augustine. In Descartes the figure of the 'light' of reason is similar, and is obviously inspired by Platonic tradition (*see* LIGHT OF NATURE). But whereas he made a quasi-naturalistic attempt to explain mind/body interaction by localizing it in the pineal gland, he did less to describe how the cognitive powers of the mind might be naturalistically described and explained. Frege, as noted, simply declared the notion of 'grasping' a thought as primitive; and Russell did much the same with his notion of ACQUAINTANCE. A descendant of this problem arises with regard to our knowledge about possibility, and whether, for example, we have some kind of access to what obtains in non-actual, possible states of affairs. (In general, of course, many issues about Platonistic entities, including questions about their objectivity, are mirrored in issues about modality (*see* MODALITIES AND POSSIBLE WORLDS; POSSIBLE WORLDS).)

Ironically ethics and the theory of value also constitute an area in which Platonism has been vigorously advocated – ironically, because these matters seem so disputable, and so closely associated with human conventions and practices, as to raise serious questions about their objectivity and knowability. Nevertheless Moore and Russell both at one time insisted that goodness is as objective a property as there can be (respectively, in *Principia Ethica* (1903) and 'The Elements of Ethics'). Moreover Plato himself seemed to have no hesitation in thinking that the Good was the most knowable of all things (*Rep.* 505–18, 533–4, 540–1), and drew no line between evaluative and non-evaluative notions with respect to their objectivity. (In theistic thinkers like Augustine, issues of moral value are regarded as independent of facts that human beings determine, but as depending on facts about God; usually such thinkers do not believe that making morality dependent on God's will implicates any sort of relativism.)

In general, it is clear that the veins of philosophical thought uncovered by Plato have not been exhausted.

See also INTUITIONISM IN LOGIC AND MATHEMATICS.

BIBLIOGRAPHY

Platonis opera ed. J. Burnet, 5 vols (Oxford: Clarendon Press, 1900–7).
The Collected Dialogues of Plato ed. E. Hamilton and H. Cairns (Princeton, NJ: Princeton University Press, 1961).
Surprisingly, there exists no philosophically serious historical account of the development of Platonism, and except for philosophically superficial treatments, we even lack good specialized studies of Plato's influence on particular figures. The reader's best resource is to read the works of the Platonist philosophers mentioned above, and to consult recent discussions of the issues such as the following:
Benacerraf, P. and Putnam, H. ed.: *Philosophy of Mathematics: Selected Readings* 2nd edn (Cambridge: Cambridge University Press, 1983).
Realism and Antirealism, Midwest Studies in Philosophy 12 (1988).
Maddy, P.: *Realism in Mathematics* (Oxford: Clarendon Press, 1990).

NICHOLAS WHITE

Plotinus (*c.*205–70) Inspired the last major philosophical movement of antiquity (*see* NEOPLATONISM). He studied philosophy in Alexandria (Egypt) and founded his own philosophical circle in Rome. The interpretation of passages in Plato, treated as a way of dealing with philosophical questions, was debated by Plotinus and his pupils, account being taken of Stoic ideas and of recent Platonist and Aristotelian commentators. The circle disbanded on Plotinus' death. Plotinus' works, a reflection of his teaching, were edited and published posthumously (the *Enneads*), with a biography, by a close pupil, Porphyry (*c.*232–305) (*see* TREE OF PORPHYRY).

Plotinus renewed reflection on Plato's metaphysics. As regards Plato's distinction between material reality and the intelligible realm of Ideas, Plotinus interpreted the Ideas as the thought of a transcendent Intellect, *nous* (comparable to Aristotle's self-thinking god). The Ideas are not 'thought up' by Intellect, but constitute its life or activity of self-thought. As Intellect, Ideas form a one–many, a whole of parts, relations very different from those obtaining in the spatio-temporal world: each part includes the whole, which is an intensive unity of discrete elements. As a hierarchy, the realm of Ideas is clearly distinguished by its ontological characteristics from the material world. The relations between Ideas and material objects ('presence', 'participation', 'imitation' in Plato) differ from relations between material objects: Ideas are 'present' to such objects in the sense that matter depends entirely for what structure it has on the action of the Ideas.

SOUL (*psyche*) mediates between the Ideas and matter. In itself it is a subordinate part of the intelligible realm (thus it manifests one/many, whole/part relations similar to those obtaining between the Ideas), yet it also organizes material reality after the model of the Ideas, both as regards the world as a whole (world-soul), as regards individual living bodies and as regards the various degrees in the organization of things in the world. Remaining in itself, soul's effect in matter is a living body.

The structural dependence of the world on soul, itself dependent on Intellect, leads Plotinus, in the search for first causes, to postulate an ultimate principle of unity, organization and therefore being, prior to Intellect which as a one/many (therefore composite) cannot be ultimate. The ultimate first principle, the 'One' or the 'Good', is the source, immediate or mediate, of all else in reality. All derives from the One in a descending series of expressions of its internal activity, a process outside time which generates time with the constitution of the world. The final product is the matter of the sensible world, which, as complete absence of form, is absolute evil. The One is also absence of form, but as prior to form (= Intellect, = determinate being) and plurality. As such it is beyond the realm of the proper objects of knowledge and language, being expressed by negation or analogical predication.

WRITINGS

Enneads ed. and trans. A.H. Armstrong, *Plotinus* (Cambridge, MA: Harvard University Press, 1966–88; London: Heinemann, 1966–88).

BIBLIOGRAPHY

Gerson, L. ed.: *The Cambridge Companion to Plotinus* (Cambridge: Cambridge University Press, 1995).
O'Meara, D.J.: *Plotinus. An Introduction to the Enneads* (Oxford: Clarendon Press, 1993).
Rist, J.M.: *Plotinus. The Road to Reality* (Cambridge: Cambridge University Press, 1967).

DOMINIC J. O'MEARA

Popper, Karl (1902–) Philosopher of natural and social science. Popper described himself as always having been a metaphysical realist. By this he meant not only to affirm the legitimacy of metaphysics, but to assign it a positive value as the crucible out of which new scientific theories are born. Metaphysical assertions can be meaningful; and meaningful metaphysical assertions become scientifically meaningful when they are sharpened sufficiently to engage the criterion of falsifiability. Popper made much of this against any conflation of his views with LOGICAL POSITIVISM, since positivism regarded metaphysical assertions as nonsense, and ignored the Popperian membrane between metaphysics and science. This leaves metaphysics itself a rather obscure contrast to the Popperian clarity of scientific generalizations, the latter being decisively falsified if there are sharp counterexamples.

If Popper's insistence that the criterion of scientificity is not a criterion of meaning introduces an asymmetry into his position in comparison to logical positivism, it is well known that Popper and the logical positivists argued with each other as dual positions within a common framework of assumptions. Both accepted the use of first-order logical methods as a legitimate tool for capturing the structure of science. If logical positivism tried to build scientific structure on singular factual sentences that could be verified, Popper tried to build scientific structure on universal sentences that could be falsified; logical positivism had trouble figuring out how universal sentences could be verified while Popper had trouble figuring out how singular sentences representing scientific data points that could falsify scientific generalizations could themselves be scientific. The assumptions that shape this terrain of argument can most conveniently be called metaphysical, although perhaps in a sense not explicitly recognized by either party in the debate. The more particular question for Popper is this: if Popper can avoid accepting linguistically formulated unfalsifiable general metaphysical sentences as meaningful and scientific, does he notice what may be a subtle metaphysical criterion in play when he urges against Werner Heisenberg (1901–76) that quantum physics must be deterministic to be predictive and falsifiable and scientific? (See DETERMINISM.) When science is evaluated through the employment of metaphysical criteria of meaning, as it seems to have been in the 'classic' early philosophies of science urged by the logical positivists and by Popper, the philosophies themselves must be couched in discourses that are at least partly opaque to their own analyses. This is not to say that the classics do not provide valuable insights, but it is to suggest that metaphysics retained a hold on the views of the early philosophers of science that resulted in analyses of science that were necessarily perspectival, contrary to the universalism that seemed at the time to be associated with the use of logic.

WRITINGS

The Logic of Scientific Discovery (New York: Basic Books, 1959).

ROBERT ACKERMANN

Porphyry   *see* TREE OF PORPHYRY

Port-Royal   Cistercian abbey located near Paris, founded in 1204. Under the direction of Jacqueline Marie Angélique Arnauld (1591–1661), it became the most important centre of Jansenism in France. This community of nuns attracted a group of intellectuals, who became known as Port-Royalists. Following Cornelius Jansen (1585–1638), they believed in the total corruption of human nature by original sin, understood predestination strictly, and rejected FREE WILL. They also advocated a severe and rigorous morality and criticized those who did not adhere to it. These criticisms and their Jansenist doctrines prompted accusations of unorthodoxy and eventually persecution. The abbey was closed by Louis XIV in 1709.

Among the most famous Port-Royalists were Jean Duvergier de Hauranne, Abbot of Saint Cyran (1581–1643), ARNAULD and Pierre Nicole (1625–95). The abbey was also engaged in a publishing programme. Among the most influential works published were PASCAL's *Pensées* (1670) and Arnauld's and Nicole's *La Logique, ou l'art de penser* (1612). The latter became known as the *Port-Royal Logic*.

BIBLIOGRAPHY

Gazier, A.: *Histoire générale du mouvement janséniste depuis les origines jusqu'à nos jours* 2 vols, 5th edn (Paris: E. Champion, 1923–4).

Howell, W.S.: *Logic and Rhetoric in England, 1500–1700* (Princeton, NJ: 1956); (New York: Russell and Russell, 1961).

Laporte, J.: *La doctrine de Port-Royal. La morale d'après Arnauld* 2 vols (Paris: J. Vrin, 1951–2).

Sainte-Beuve, C.: *Histoire de Port-Royal* 6 vols, 3rd edn (Paris: Librairie de L. Machette et Companie, 1867).

JORGE J.E. GRACIA

positivism   *see* LOGICAL POSITIVISM

possible worlds   A possible world is a complete way things might have been or a complete way things could have gone. LEIBNIZ is usually credited with introducing the concept of possible worlds into philosophy, but in the modern period it owes its prominence to the role it plays in modal logic (Kripke, 1963) together with the fact that modal concepts are central to many of the great traditional areas of philosophy – the nature of CAUSATION and of FREE WILL, to mention but two (van Inwagen, 1983; *see* EVENT THEORY). For with the developed formalism of modal logic placed on a sound mathematical footing, it can be brought to bear on those traditional questions with fruitful results.

To say that a world *w* is a *complete* way things might have been is to say that for each proposition in the sphere of discourse under discussion, *w* either verifies or falsifies that proposition; in logic, the notion of a sphere of discourse is specified by the idea of an interpretation of a fixed formal language. For the purposes of logic, the completeness property is useful but not essential; the notion of a partial world, or possibility, can be made to serve (Humberstone, 1981). But in metaphysics, the main question about possible worlds concerns their existence, a question made urgent by the way possible worlds terminology is used in applications: the assertion schema 'there exists a world such that . . .' is often instantiated. The existence of partial worlds is unlikely to be prior or less problematic.

Classification of the views about the existence of worlds is complicated by the fact that a cross-cutting pair of distinctions is relevant. There is the distinction between actualism and possibilism and also the distinction between those who identify existing and obtaining and those who distinguish the two. First, actualism and possibilism. The actualist view is that everything which exists, actually exists (Prior and Fine, 1977). Things which might have existed but do not actually exist thereby do not exist in any proper sense of the term. For the possibilist, however, the distinction between 'actually exists' and 'might have existed' is as devoid of ontological significance as the distinction between 'exists here' and 'exists elsewhere'. Just as there is a uniform notion of EXISTENCE applicable to every object in physical space, so there is a uniform notion of existence applicable to every possibility in logical space (Lewis, 1986).

However, the side one chooses here does not determine a position on the question of the existence of possible worlds, for there is also the issue of whether one *identifies* the existence of a world with its obtaining or *distinguishes* existence from obtaining. If existence is the same as obtaining, and one is an actualist, then the only world which exists is the actual world, since only the actual world actually exists. But if existence is one thing and obtaining another, there is room for a view according to which all possible words exist but only one obtains. A version of this view is actualist if it identifies the non-actual worlds – the worlds which are not instantiated by events – with some sort of actual entity. The typical choices for such entities are *abstracta* such as sets of propositions or sentence-types of an ideal language (Plantinga, 1974; Stalnaker, 1984).

Common sense is actualist and probably identifies existence and obtaining. But if actualism is to be favoured, what response should be made to the possibilist claim that the difference between actual and merely possible existence is as ontologically irrelevant as that between existing locally and existing at some distance? Actualists have found both metaphysical and epistemological difficulties in such parallels. On the epistemological side, such a view makes our modal knowledge, knowledge of what is possible and what is impossible, hard to explain, for although our sensory faculties can give us information about how things are at distant places, it is difficult to see how they could put us in touch with other worlds (McGinn, 1981). On the metaphysical side, one can distinguish a framework of independently existing locations from the relational spatial framework of material things, as is testified to by the coherence of the thought that things might have been very different at such-and-such a place. But a comparable framework of worlds cannot be distinguished: the actual world, for example, is *essentially* the world at which things are . . . , where we fill in the ellipsis with the details of the actual course of events.

See also MODALITIES AND POSSIBLE WORLDS.

BIBLIOGRAPHY

Humberstone, L.: 'From worlds to possibilities', *Journal of Philosophical Logic* 10 (1981), 313–39.
Kripke, S.A.: 'Semantical considerations on modal logic', *Acta Philosophica Fennica* 16 (1963), 83–94.
Lewis, D.K.: *On the Plurality of Worlds* (Oxford: Blackwell, 1986).
McGinn, C.: 'Modal reality', in *Reduction, Time and Reality* ed. R. Healey (Cambridge: Cambridge University Press, 1981), 143–87.
Plantinga, A.: *The Nature of Necessity* (Oxford: Oxford University Press, 1974).
Prior, A.N. and Fine, K.: *Worlds, Times and Selves* (London: Duckworth, 1977).
Stalnaker, R.: *Inquiry* (Cambridge, MA: MIT Press, 1984).
van Inwagen, P.: *An Essay on Free Will* (Oxford: Oxford University Press, 1983).

GRAEME FORBES

potentiality/actuality Potentiality and actuality are contrast-dependent notions. We understand what a potential web-weaver or dam-builder is in contrast to understanding what an actual web-weaver or dam-builder is. Actuality also contrasts with possibility. We need to look at this contrast first, since all potentialities are also possibilities, though not all possibilities are potentialities.

Both of these contrasts are fundamental in the analysis of human decision-making on the one hand, and in spelling out certain lawlike properties of biological species on the other. Yet, both in ancient times and in our century, there have been philosophers who denied that there are possibilities and potentialities. As ARISTOTLE reports (*Metaphysics* IX 3) the Megarians held this negative view. According to them someone is a builder only if he builds, and something is capable of being hot only if it is hot. Unfortunately Aristotle does not report what justification the Megarians gave for this view. We have, however, a more complete picture of the position of modern philosophers who are sceptical of possibility and potentiality. GOODMAN and QUINE want not to accept possibilities in their ontology. One of the reasons given for this stance is that it is problematic how possibilities are individuated, and the other is the problem of specifying in adequate epistemological terms how one can know that a certain property holds of some entities not only in actual cases but also under various counterfactual circumstances.

Aristotle does not deal with the Megarians in detail. He points out that if they were right, then human arts and crafts would be impossible. Both of these assume that humans are capable of planning and designing, and these activities involve projections across possibilities as well as choosing among future alternatives. He does give also a constructive view, spelling out conditions under which a specimen of a species can be said to have a certain potentiality.

We shall first look at possibility, since that is the wider notion, and see how it is related to actuality. Two conceptions have emerged in the recent literature. One is that of relative actuality (see Lewis, 1986). According to this view, we should take the class of all POSSIBLE WORLDS as fundamental, and realize that relative to each, the inhabitants in that world will take their world as the actual one. According to this view the different possible worlds do not share individuals. The other view can be found, for example, in Kripke (1972) and can be labelled the projective view. Within this conception the actual world in which we live, as well as the individuals in it are fundamental. This is the starting point for positing or projecting possibilities, in decision-making or in characterizing the potentialities of a species. The projections can involve assigning different properties to individuals in the actual world, or projecting possible individuals into worlds thus different from ours, as long as these individuals are related, in various ways, to the individuals in the actual world. Both of these views attempt, in their own ways, to answer the problem raised by the critics concerning INDIVIDUATION; the one by not having individuals in common among possible worlds, and the other by taking the actual individuals for granted.

These contrasts between the possible and the actual did not involve any teleological assumptions (see TELEOLOGY). We need, however, such notions when we attempt to characterize the potentiality of beavers to build dams, or that of spiders to weave webs. We do not merely say that it is possible for beavers and spiders to do these things respectively, but also that the possession of these capacities is a part of their respective nature. Such functionings are

parts of their essences. This degree of teleological commitment carries no cosmic or religious assumptions; it is compatible also with Darwin's theory of evolution.

Given this notion of potentiality, actuality has a new role. The actual is not merely what happens to be the case. It is – as Aristotle proposes (*Metaphysics* IX 5–7) that which actualizes potentialities. Natural functioning for specimens of a species is the constant actualizing of their potentialities. Aristotle's conception of potentiality can be seen in its clearest form in the case of biological species. Specimens of living species need to change, i.e. realize their potential, constantly in order to persist. Unlike the case of numbers that exist in permanent unchanging forms, living things change constantly in order to remain the same. That is to say, they realize potentialities in order to maintain being what they are; humans, tigers, spiders, etc.

Potentialities are not always realized. Conditions either internal or external to a specimen can block such realizations. Roughly, the following two conditions are needed for the realization of a potentiality. (1) The specimen, for example, beaver or spider, needs to be normal and healthy. (2) The circumstances must be such as to be conducive to the realization of the potentiality; i.e. the environment must be 'natural'. If the beaver or spider is sick, or the river polluted, or the air poisonous, then dam-building or web-weaving might not take place.

It is difficult to give a precise characterization of what a potentiality is, and under what conditions a potentiality should be ascribed to a species. Aristotle (*Metaphysics* IX 5–6) regards potentiality as a basic indefinable notion, to be illuminated by the contrast with actuality, and examples. At the same time, he regards the notion as indispensable for a science like biology. The following review of various schemata shows the difficulties of capturing the notion of potentiality.

Since the potentialities we discussed are essential to the species, we might try:

(1) All beavers are necessarily building dams.

But this runs into trouble since – as we saw – not all beavers build dams; some cannot realize their potentiality. The same consideration rules out the above sentence without the modal operator as an analysis. On the other hand:

(2) All beavers are possibly dam-builders.

is too weak, since not all possibilities are potentialities. One can try to capture 'normality' by formulations such as:
(3) Most beavers build dams.

or:

(4) There is a high probability for each beaver that it will build dams.

These attempts are also deficient since – unfortunately – we cannot assume that in the majority of cases the specimens will be healthy and the environment conducive to the realization of potentiality. The standard forms with which we express potentialities are:

(5) Beavers build dams (spiders weave webs, etc.).

or:

(6) The beaver builds dams (the spider weaves webs).

These statements express the fact that a normal healthy beaver will build dams under normal circumstances, i.e. in an environment that is suitable. There is no way to reduce being healthy or normal to purely logical notions. These are partly normative notions. So we need to say:

(7) All healthy beavers are dam builders in a suitable environment.

Statements of this form are of central interest to biology. They present some of the most important data. Understanding the nature of a species is to understand what structures or mechanisms make the realizations of these potentialities or powers possible.

From a metaphysical point of view potentialities are no more mysterious than powers, events or causality. The epistemology is easy in practice, even if not in theory. When we see a little furry animal build huts and dams, or other creatures using language, or still others being marsupials, we adopt the hypothesis that we are dealing with potentialities, and not with accidental features, applying to some but not all healthy specimens. But this is done against a number of background assumptions, such as modes of propagation requiring structures that determine a large part of the anatomy of an animal. These assumptions do not hold for all possible worlds, but only for ones similar in some salient ways to the actual one.

This bears on choices between two ways in which we can view potentiality. One is to say that we can ascribe potentiality only to actual species, i.e. ones that had or do have specimens. The other is to admit also possible species in our ontology, and thus to talk about possible potentialities. Making such conceptual choices difficult is the thorny question – as to what a species is.

BIBLIOGRAPHY

Aristotle: *Metaphysics* (many versions).
Goodman, N.: *Fact, Fiction, and Forecast* (Cambridge, MA: Harvard University Press, 1955).
Kripke, S.: 'Naming and necessity', in *The Semantics of Natural Language* ed. G. Harman and D. Davidson (Dordrecht: Reidel, 1972), 254–355.
Lewis, D.: *On the Plurality of Worlds* (Oxford: Blackwell, 1986).
Quine, W.V.: *From a Logical Point of View* (Cambridge, MA: Harvard University Press, 1953), chs 1, 7.

J.M. MORAVCSIK

pragmatism A general theory of practical reason and the purposive nature of thought which acknowledges the 'real' or public world, encountered and shared: inveighs against any form of intuitionism by rejecting unanalysable and inexplicable ultimates; takes first principles and axioms as hypothetical, warranted by explanatory competence; substitutes multiform argumentation for linear inference; and recognizes the importance of the scientific community's stress on the primacy of method and the fallibility of belief. Culled from the writings of PEIRCE the above serves as an orientation (not definition) and as such is broadly acceptable. For Peirce, however, pragmatism had metaphysical implications of a special kind which when elaborated led to criticism and ultimately to divergent forms of pragmatism.

The pragmatic maxim in its original formulation as a logical rule for the clarification of meaning of concepts in terms of their practical bearings gives little hint of metaphysical import. The fact that Peirce referred to himself as a 'prope-Positivist' only supports what is a mistaken impression. Ignored are the revisions the maxim underwent, where, for example, the relation between antecedent action and consequent experiential/experimental expectation changed from the indicative conditional to the subjunctive and counterfactual (see COUNTERFACTUALS). Thus 'if a substance of a certain kind should be exposed to an agency of a certain kind, a certain kind of sensible result *would* ensue' (*Collected Papers*, vol. 5, § 457). Ignored, too, is Peirce's commitment to real kinds ('generals') and to real modality, inclusive of real possibility and real necessity (ibid.) (see MODALITIES AND POSSIBLE WORLDS).

If any doubt remains of Peirce's metaphysical resolve the last version of the maxim with its explicit reference to an ultimate good – the *summum bonum* – should dispel it. 'the pragmaticist does not make the *summum bonum* to consist in action, but makes it to consist in that process of evolution whereby the existent comes more and more to embody those generals which we

just now said to be *destined*, which is what we strive to express in calling them *reasonable*' (*Collected Papers*, vol. 5, § 432). Truth is what is destined: it enters the picture regulatively as an ideal that rational, i.e. scientific, inquiry, if pursued sufficiently far, will produce an 'overwhelming consensus' among those dedicated to its pursuit (*Collected Papers*, vol. 6, § 610). Reality is what is represented by those opinions which have produced that consensus. Previously Peirce had said that the 'purpose of action is to produce some sensible result' with the aim of achieving something 'tangible and practical' (*Collected Papers*, vol. 5, § 400). Pragmatism is now called 'pragmaticism', signalling a fundamental shift in Peirce's thinking. He has succeeded in avoiding his early penchant for psychologizing, substituting realistic convictions for nominalistic ones and articulating a higher ideal for human motivation than personal satisfactions while simultaneously providing a means for exploring anew the question of being.

Metaphysical inquiry yields three universal and irreducible modes of being or CATEGORIES which are designated 'firstness', 'secondness', and 'thirdness' and which are distinguishable by their monadic, dyadic and triadic character. 'First is the conception of being as existing independently of anything else. Second is the conception of being relative to, the conception of reaction with, something else. Third is the conception of mediation, whereby a first and a second are brought into a relation' (*Collected Papers*, vol. 6, § 82). Firstness, secondness and thirdness represent the modalities of possibility, actuality and necessity respectively.

Thirdness is the mode of being of law and potentiality. The continuum ('continuity' being another name for generality) is an example. So too are biological types. The classic example is the sign relation, the consequence of which is that thirdness is also inextricably bound up with semiotics, or the theory of signs. Not surprisingly pragmatism becomes in Peirce's terminology the method of determining the meaning of thirds, or, in the case of semiotics, symbols.

The core of Peirce's metaphysics is his REALISM, specifically the REALISM of the moderate Aristotelian sort to which he credits DUNS SCOTUS for leading him. This scholastic realism stands opposed to extreme Platonic realism, although its principal target is NOMINALISM, the position which takes general concepts or scientific laws to be fictions because it cannot find anything real of a general nature corresponding to them (see PLATONISM). For Peirce nominalism is both unphilosophical and unscientific: it is unphilosophical because the function of philosophy is explanation and the nominalist admits inexplicability: it is unscientific because the function of science is prediction and the nominalist fails to produce any basis for it. The question is not whether relations are experienceable, but whether they have a necessary character.

Scholastic realism supports metaphysical IDEALISM, the 'one intelligible theory of the universe – that matter is effete mind, inveterate habits becoming physical laws' (*Collected Papers*, vol. 6, § 24). Metaphysical idealism is also supported by synechism, one of the three cosmological categories which parallel the ontological ones.

Peirce's cosmological categories, taken together, give us his version of how order arises out of chaos: 'In the beginning – there was a chaos of unpersonalized feeling [firstness] – This feeling, sporting [secondness] here and there in pure arbitrariness, would have started the germ of a generalized tendency [thirdness] – Thus the tendency to habit [law] would be started: and from this, with the other principles of evolution, all the regularities of the universe would be evolved' (*Collected Papers*, vol. 6, § 33). In the infinite future a world is envisaged, perfectly rational and symmetrical, with 'mind at last crystallized' (ibid.). In his cosmogony the ontological categories reappear as tychism (absolute chance), agapasm (evolutionary love), and synechism (universal continuity).

When Peirce transformed nominalistic pragmatism into realistic pragmaticism he claimed a proof for the latter, which again involved metaphysics, a proof that turned out to be elusive. But we know at least that the metaphysical analogue of the mathematical conception of continuity was relevant to it. Pragmaticism 'would essentially involve the establishment of the truth of synechism' (*Collected Papers*, vol. 5, § 146) which was 'the keystone of the arch' (*Collected Papers*, vol. 8, § 527). Moreover we have a rough idea how he intended to proceed: specifically mentioning the concordance between the metaphysical categories and the system of existential graphs which he said added confidence to the correctness of both, his general strategy it seems was to uncover more of those concordances, all of which supports the general conclusion that Peirce, intrigued by the Kantian idea of an arcitechtonic, thought in terms of systems and of himself as a systematizer (see KANT).

By contrast JAMES was systematically unsystematic. His pluralism opened doors by allowing for multiple standards of success instead of merely one paradigmatic form (science). (*See* MONISM/PLURALISM.) Furthermore recasting Peirce's maxim by substituting the logically looser relations of conjunction and alteration ('sensations we are to expect' and 'reactions we must prepare' in the one case and 'conduct to be recommended' or 'experiences to be expected', in the other) pointed him in the direction of nominalism. So too did the emphasis placed on particularlity 'sensible particulars' and 'particular differences'). But the argument for James's nominalism is not clearcut. At bottom he may have been a realist. Ferdinand Schiller (1864–1937), the Oxford pragmatist (humanist) warned him against the realistic tendency lest he forfeit his pragmatism (see Perry, 1985, vol. II, pp. 509–11). Dissociating pragmatism from realism, which presently is commonplace, was at the time revolutionary in its effect, setting pragmatism on a course independently of Peirce's.

James's metaphysics resides principally in his radical EMPIRICISM and in the accompanying concept of pure EXPERIENCE. As for the relationship between pragmatism and radical empiricism James was of two minds. Initially he saw no connection. Subsequently he saw radical empiricism as logically dependent upon pragmatism but pragmatism as logically independent of it.

The metaphysics of DEWEY is not easily characterized. By his own admission he was a naturalist by which he meant one who reflects on the generic features of nature, with reflection itself a natural event occurring within nature. Sharper delineation becomes virtually impossible given his aggressive anti-dualism. He cannot, for example, call himself a materialist because materialism and idealism cancel out each other. In fact because much of traditional Western philosophy is permeated with dualist distinctions, Dewey tends to shun it. What remains alive for him is human experience, constituted by interchanges (transactions) and so-called 'problems of men', practical problems calling for practical solutions. Pragmatism (or instrumentalism) is tied to problem-solving. Theories and concepts are instruments valued for their utility in addressing real needs.

George Herbert Mead (1863–1931), more narrowly focused, carried Dewey's social conception of experience forward by means of an elaborate theory of the social act. Indeed there are many other philosophers who share Dewey's 'pragmatic temper', adapting it to any number of political, social, and educational problems. Sydney Hook (1902–93) is one example.

Exhibiting affinity with some features of Dewey's philosophy is the analytically trained philosopher Margolis, whose pragmatism is idiosyncratic insofar as it is the product of borrowings from two distinct traditions, analytic and continental, with analysis balanced by HISTORICISM and by the priority of praxis. Margolis's achievement is a unique blend of realism, relativism and pragmatism (Margolis, 1986). The linkage with Deweyan tradition is the common regard for social praxis, the inescapability of history, and the rejection of pernicious dualism. But by reason of the same regard Margolis is lead in other directions as well, mainly European, as for example Marxist, hermeneutical, and existentialist. (See EXISTENTIALISM; HERMENEUTICS; MARXISM.)

At the extreme end of the line of influence extending from James via Dewey is the neopragmatist (post-modernist) Richard Rorty, whose message, like Dewey's, is that the epistemological enterprise must be dissolved (deconstructed) because it is tied to an antiquated 'Platonist' ONTOLOGY, according to which there is an external reality, structured eternally and accessible to mind. It is not enough to be anti-foundationalist, anti-essentialist and anti-reductionist. (See ESSENTIALISM; REDUCTION/REDUCTIONISM.) The whole of epistemology, along with its metaphysical supports, must go and not by way of absorption by one or another science, say, cognitive psychology or neuroscience. Science has no privileged voice; inquiry no special constraints.

Distinguishing among Philosophy (traditional philosophy), anti-philosophy (the deconstructionist critique), and philosophy (what is left after deconstruction), Rorty declares that pragmatism is postphilosophical philosophy. Rorty is testing the limits of pragmatism by arguing that the business of philosophy is to edify, not to produce systems. The contrast helps to explain his curious remark that Peirce's one contribution to pragmatism was to have given it its name (Rorty, 1982, p. 161).

Other principally analytically committed philosophers stand spiritually closer to Peirce than to James, and with Peirce may be said to constitute that second line of development within the pragmatic movement. Among his contemporaries it was Josiah Royce (1855–1916) with whom Peirce felt the most affinity. Royce took modal concepts seriously and his absolute idealism or pragmatism also satisfied Peirce's predilection for both monism and idealism. In turn, C.I. Lewis's conceptual pragmatism bears Royce's stamp and, indirectly, Peirce's. The idea that pragmatic considerations determine the choice among equally valid competing logical systems proved insightful. Less so his phenomenalistic foundationalism which came under attack by fellow pragmatists, SELLARS among them, as the 'myth of the given'. (*See* PHENOMENALISM.) Lewis's understated but ever present realism never received the systematic defence it required.

Influenced by Peirce and Lewis, Rescher (1992) advances his own brand of pragmatism under the title of 'pragmatic idealism' which could have been expanded to include realism patterned after Putnam's internal realism. Curiously he also accepts a transcendental reality only to minimize it. OBJECTIVITY is postulated, he tells us, in virtue of the way it allows conceptual schemes to function within inquiry. His idealism has the same rationale as Peirce's: the rejection of incognizables.

QUINE's pragmatism takes the conceptual scheme of science as a tool ultimately for successful predictions. But contrary to those logical positivists who dismiss ontological questions altogether, Quine believes that it is rationally irresponsible to accept a system as explanatory and not accept entities the system names (*see* LOGICAL POSITIVISM). The criterion for acceptance is always pragmatic. Quine's disagreement with Peirce is at the edge of some substantial agreement. He acknowledges Peirce's behaviouristic semantics, his HOLISM, and is at least open to the suggestion that Peirce held a position on the analytic/synthetic distinction similar to his. The sticking point is First Philosophy prior to science, which Peirce supports and Quine does not (Quine, 1981). For Quine science requires no legitimization, certainly not by a metaphysical superstruction like Peirce's, which in his mind was problematic to begin with. It is sufficient for him that pragmatism combines holism with foundationless NATURALISM.

There has always been a European presence among pragmatists. Schiller, of course. Also Ramsey and the later Wittgenstein. Recently J. Habermas and K.O. Apel, both of whom employ unselfconsciously TRANSCENDENTAL ARGUMENTS. Even HEIDEGGER (Okrent, 1988). What do we make of all this diversity? Is it mark of pragmatism's vitality or does it suggest that the term has become so elastic as to be virtually useless for classificatory purposes? Parenthetically, when years ago an exasperated Peirce introduced his word 'pragmaticism' in protest at James's appropriation of 'pragmatism' (adding sarcastically that it was too ugly a word for anyone to steal), he raised a relevant question about the ethics of terminology.

See also ANTIREALISM; THEORIES OF TRUTH.

BIBLIOGRAPHY

Dewey, J.: *Experience and Nature* (La Salle, IL: Open Court, 1958).
James, W.: *Essays in Radical Empiricism* (Cambridge, MA: Harvard University Press, 1976).
James, W.: *A Pluralistic Universe* (Cambridge, MA: Harvard University Press, 1977).
Margolis, J.: *Pragmatism Without Foundations* (Oxford: Blackwell, 1986).
Okrent, M.: *Heidegger's Pragmatism* (Ithaca, NY: Cornell University Press, 1988).
Peirce, C.S.: *Collected Papers* 8 vols, ed. C. Hartshorne, P. Weiss and A. Burks (Cambridge, MA: Harvard University Press, 1931–58).
Perry, R.B.: *The Thought and Character of William James* 2 vols (Boston, MA: Little, Brown and Company, 1935).
Quine, W.V.: 'The pragmatists' place in empiricism', in *Pragmatism: Its Sources and Prospects* ed. Robert J. Mulvaney and Philip M. Zeltner (Columbia, SC: University of South Carolina Press, 1981), 21–39.
Rescher, N.: *A System of Pragmatic Idealism* (Princeton, NJ: Princeton University Press, 1992).
Rorty, R.: *Consequences of Pragmatism* (Minneapolis: University of Minnesota Press, 1982).

411

Thayer, H.S.: *Meaning and Action: A Critical History of Pragmatism* (Indianapolis, IN: Hackett, 1981).

RICHARD ROBIN

Presocratics The tradition of recognizing a certain succession of about thirty thinkers of the sixth and fifth centuries BC as the first natural philosophers goes back to ARISTOTLE. Two other groups, the Sophists (fifth century) and certain poets and mythologists (sixth century or earlier) are also occasionally included by Aristotle in his discussions of philosophical predecessors. In our own time the three groups have come to be known collectively as 'the Presocratics', even though many of the figures at issue are contemporaries or near contemporaries of Socrates. With marginal exceptions, the works and doctrines of the Presocratics are known to us through fragmentary quotations and reports – some by PLATO and Aristotle; most in much later sources of the Hellenistic, Roman and Byzantine periods. In spite of the gaps and the uncertainties of transmission, the record is ample enough to establish that the Presocratics played a formative role in the development of western metaphysics – both directly and through their influence on Plato and Aristotle, and on the major schools of later antiquity. The survey provided here refers primarily to the first group, Aristotle's *physikoi*.

'There is no generation out of nothing' and 'There is no perishing into nothing' – these ancient metaphysical principles, which become thematically prominent in the philosophies of Parmenides of Elea (early fifth century) and of Melissus of Samos (mid fifth century), are already implied in the earliest cosmologies (*see* COSMOLOGY), those of the Milesians Anaximander and Anaximenes. This reflects a strong demand for rationalist and naturalistic explanation that is characteristic of the *physikoi* as a whole: no mysterious changes, no intervention by the gods in world-processes; explanation must appeal only to the nature intrinsic to each thing, to its *physis*.

Also reflecting the Presocratics' rationalism is deployment – notably in Anaximander, Parmenides and in the atomists – of versions of the principle of sufficient reason (*see* ATOMISM). A related theme is that of *kosmos*, 'a well ordered array of things' and *harmonia*, 'coherent structure'. In Anaximander (mid-sixth century BC), in Heraclitus of Ephesus (late sixth to early fifth century BC), among the Pythagoreans, and in Diogenes of Apollonia (late fifth century), the question 'Why is it so?' when raised at the most fundamental level is answered by appeal to considerations of optimal structure.

Limiting the scope of CHANGE is a major preoccupation of the Presocratics. They seek to counter any suggestion that change is radical or catastrophic. In Anaximander things come forward from, and recede back into, a certain immense cosmic reservoir, *to apeiron*, 'the boundless'. In Anaximenes (middle to late sixth century BC) and later in Diogenes of Apollonia, the only real change is one whereby things become loose or tight in their texture. Parmenides, ZENO of Elea, and Melissus deny all forms of change. Empedocles of Acragas and Anaxagoras of Clazomenae (both mid fifth century) as well as the atomists Leucippus and Democritus (late fifth to early fourth century BC), both of Abdera, countenance only one form: locomotion (see below). The lone dissenter is Heraclitus, the first philosopher to advocate something comparable to a process- or event-ontology. War, fire, and the flowing waters of a river are the salient images in Heraclitus' philosophy. Yet even he emphasizes that certain 'measures' (unspecified) are preserved across any change.

The APPEARANCE/REALITY distinction is drawn at the earliest stages of Presocratic speculation. Xenophanes of Colophon (sixth century) argues that the rainbow, sun, moon and stars are not gods or divine signs; they are simply different cloud formations. In a different version of the distinction, an underlying or hidden reality is set off against what is manifest at the level of everyday experience: 'Real nature (*physis*) loves to hide' (Heraclitus); 'Truth lies in the deep' (Democritus). Already in Anaximenes there is an implied contrast between the familiar air we breathe and the postulated air that is the true nature of, say, a pool of water or a chunk of marble. Parmenides juxtaposes a doctrine of 'truth' or 'reality' (*aletheia*) against one of *doxai* – either 'appearances' or 'opinions', depending on the overall interpretation of his metaphysical poem. Recurrent, especially in the fifth century, is the theme of disparity between metaphysical truth and the conceptual scheme implied by ordinary language: 'there is no generation and no perishing . . . it is by custom (*themis*) that these words are used, and I accede to the convention (*nomos*) myself' (Empedocles). The disparity is often conveyed, as in the passage just cited, by the *physis/nomos* contrast ('nature' vs 'convention'), which also becomes pivotal in the ethical debates initiated by the Sophists. In Democritus, the same contrast serves to convey a doctrine that is recognizably close to modern eliminative materialism: 'by convention (*nomos*) is there sweet, bitter, hot, cold . . . ; in truth (*eteei*), atoms and void'. (*See* PHYSICALISM, MATERIALISM.)

Abstract ontological issues are raised first by Parmenides. Drawing on considerations as to what is 'sayable', 'thinkable' or 'knowable' – strikingly in the style of the sort of 'transcendental argument' found much later in KANT, WITTGENSTEIN or STRAWSON – Parmenides deduces that 'being' or 'what-is' or 'the real' (*to eon*) must necessarily have the following attributes: unborn, unperishing, indivisible, immobile and unchanging (*tetelesmenon*, 'fully actualized'). He stops short of naming the entity or entities that would qualify under these criteria. Melissus takes the almost inevitable next step: only an all-encompassing, undifferentiated 'One' would qualify. Parmenides' pupil or associate, Zeno of Elea, propounds the negative corollary through a series of famous paradoxes: the ordinary world of plurality and

change is incoherent, therefore illusory or unreal.

The name of Parmenides' city-state gave rise to the term 'Eleatics' for the trio of Parmenides, Melissus and Zeno. Eleatic arguments involve profound metaphysical questions concerning the nature of space, the nature of time, and such contrasts as timelessness/sempiternity and finitude/infinity. In particular, the challenge posed by Zeno's paradoxes concerning motion and plurality has been felt keenly at many junctures in the history both of metaphysics and of mathematics. Before the Eleatics, temporal eternity is naively conceived of as perpetuity, and the *apeiron* is something either physically untraversible, or unmarked by boundaries, or indefinite. After Parmenides, we find in Anaxagoras a conception of infinity that defies naive intuitions: 'there is no smallest, but always smaller . . . and the small is equal to the large in number [of parts]'. And, in spite of a misguided programme of finitism in mathematics, the atomists expressly recognize five actual infinities: space (void), time, number of atoms, atomic shapes, and world-structures (*kosmoi*).

A more concrete version of the contrast between infinity and finitude is introduced by the fifth-century Pythagorean philosopher Philolaus of Croton, namely, *apeira*, 'unlimited things' (presumably formless stuffs) and *perainonta*, 'limiting things' (numbers and geometric shapes). Philolaus' cosmological pair invites comparison with the classical MATTER/FORM distinction we find in Plato and Aristotle.

The so-called 'pluralists' of the fifth century may be viewed not only as adhering to principles of conservation and continuity but also as seeking to preserve as much as possible of Parmenides' deduction (*see* MONISM/PLURALISM). Accordingly, Anaxagoras works out an extreme version of metaphysical REALISM: every stuff (e.g. air, cloud, earth) and every qualitative feature (e.g. the hot, the cold, the bright, the dark) that is ever manifest in experience is in itself unborn, unperishing and intrinsically unchanging. The illusion of qualitative change arises as certain ingredient features become either conspicuous or inconspicuous because of reapportionment. Empedocles offers a more parsimonious theory: four elemental stuffs, fire, air, water and earth; two motive forces, Love and Strife. All six factors are unborn, unperishing and intrinsically unchanging. Everything else in the universe is a compound of the four stuffs in one or another ratio. As though paying further homage to Elea, Empedocles envisages a cosmic phase during which Love blends the four elements perfectly in an all-encompassing spherical One. The atomists seek greater explanatory import by positing an infinite number and variety of corpuscles which are absolutely dense, which either move freely or cluster through an infinite void, and which are not only eternal and unchanging but also indivisible: 'atoms'. Functioning both as units of stuff (*atoma somata*, 'uncuttable bodies') and as modules of structure (*atomoi ideai*, 'uncuttable figures'), the atoms come to constitute ordinary physical bodies through cumulative clustering. All atomic motions are merely extrinsic: caused by earlier atomic collisions, the history of which stretches back in time *ad infinitum*.

The one/many contrast plays a major role in Presocratic speculation. At the metaphilosophical level, it articulates the ideological opposition between monistic, dualistic and pluralistic schemes. The varieties of pluralism have already been cited. At least three different types of monism are represented. The first is material monism, the view best exemplified by Anaximenes and Diogenes: the fundamental reality is air, and all other stuffs are variations of air. A second type is found in Heraclitus, who makes the sweeping claim that 'all things are one'. His argument is both that polar opposition is conditioned by an underlying affinity and, more radically, that unity and diversity are reciprocals, that whatever counts as 'a one' must also count as 'a many' and vice versa. The sense in which Parmenides is a monist is disputed. It is, however, clear that Melissus, whose argu-

ment tracks closely that of Parmenides, offers a third distinct type of monism, a doctrine that there is just a single undifferentiated entity, 'the One'. Dualism as such has no special advocate among the Presocratics, but schemes of reified contrary powers (*ta enantia* 'the opposites') are variously attested. In fifth- or fourth-century Pythagoreanism there is a project of eliciting affinities across widely different genres by envisaging a single 'table of opposites', the scope and tenor of which may be suggested by this selection: limit, male, straight, good (first column); unlimited, female, curved, bad (opposite column).

The one/many contrast becomes interestingly enmeshed with the problem of change. How is it possible for distinct elements to produce a compound which has features that are altogether different from those of the uncompounded elements? How can flesh or blood be produced through a mixing, in whatever ratio, of Empedoclean elements or Democritean atoms? The pluralists ingeniously put forward many of the same solutions that have been attempted by later metaphysicians. Philolaus speaks of a 'supervenient blending' (*harmonia epegeneto*); Anaxagoras opts for pre-formation (the flesh or blood hide inside the uncompounded ingredients); and the atomists carry ontological reduction to great lengths before finally relegating the unreduced residue to *nomos*. (*See* REDUCTION/REDUCTIONISM; SUPERVENIENCE.)

A SOUL/body dualism is introduced by Pythagoras' doctrine of transmigration in the sixth century and becomes paramount in the Pythagorean tradition after him. There is no suggestion, however, that the soul is non-physical. A cognate doctrine of dualism is found in Empedocles: *daimones*, 'divine beings', who are long-lived fragments of the perfect blending of the elements that once obtained in the One, roam the universe and successively attach themselves to certain compounds, thus bestowing on the latter a span of animate existence. The yearning for a return to the superior state of the One introduces a strong theme of mysticism in Empedocles' cosmology. Transmigration is associated with doctrines of universal affinity and mystical union in the Pythagorean tradition as well.

Not all doctrines of the soul are tied to a doctrine of transmigration. Certainly, part of the motivation in Anaximenes and in Diogenes for positing air as the fundamental reality is the pre-philosophical association between *psyche* (etymologically, 'breath' or 'breeze') and air. We have the beginnings of a more intellectualized conception of the soul in Heraclitus and Anaxagoras. The latter speaks of a cosmic *nous* ('mind' or 'intelligence'), a fluid-like agent which starts the cosmic vortex but which also foresees, 'understands', and 'orders' all things while remaining 'separate', not at all 'partaking' in them as an ingredient.

Issues of theism/atheism are often submerged in Presocratic thought because of a tendency to invest fundamental realities and metaphysical principles with the traditional attributes of Greek gods. But the first a priori deduction of the nature of the deity – including, remarkably, the attribute of uniqueness – is found in Xenophanes. The traditional gods are acknowledged in Empedocles' cosmology: as long-lasting (not eternal) compounds of the elements. The thoroughgoing MECHANISM of the atomists aims to discredit both the ancient belief in maleficent gods and other more enlightened, views of divine beneficence and providence. The existence of gods appears to have become a debated subject in the Sophistic movement. The most famous of the Sophists, Protagoras of Abdera, proclaims agnosticism: '[I do not know] either that they exist, or that they do not exist, or what they are like in form.'

It is relevant here also to mention some of the themes that are conspicuously absent in Presocratic metaphysics. Both the idea of a pre-cosmic chaos and that of world-making by a creator god appear marginally in the sources for Presocratic philosophy. Only two options get serious consideration: cosmic evolution and a steady-state universe. The freedom vs DETERMINISM dilemma inevitably posed by the atomic theory does not appear to have engaged Democritus (*see*

FREE WILL). Suggestions by twentieth-century interpreters notwithstanding, there is no convincing evidence that the question, 'Why should there be something rather than nothing?' was one that was raised by the Presocratics.

From antiquity to our own day, images of the Presocratics, taken either as individuals or in groupings, have been dialectically refurbished and restored by later thinkers – imaginatively and even tendentiously – for the purpose of promoting, or refuting, or simply exhibiting a certain philosophical viewpoint. Plato schematizes and idealizes under such playful rubrics as 'Gods vs Giants', 'Friends of Forms', 'philosophers of flux', 'Ionian Muses' or by making the Presocratics into characters of his dialogues – most egregiously the character 'Parmenides', in the homonymous dialogue. Aristotle distorts by insistently gauging the degree to which the Presocratics anticipated one or another conceptual device of his own system. The Stoics claim Heraclitus as the unique precursor to their physics. The Sceptics exhibit the Presocratics as paradigms of dogmatic philosophy. Allegorical interpretations of the Presocratics become very common in late antiquity, especially among the Church Fathers and the Neoplatonic commentators on Aristotle (*see* NEOPLATONISM). In modern times, Zeno's paradoxes have received ever more sophisticated and challenging reformulations. Famous modern reconstructions of some or all of the Presocratics include those by Francis Bacon (1561–1626), the poet Friedrich Hölderlin (1770–1843), HEGEL, MARX, NIETZSCHE, HEIDEGGER, POPPER, the physicist Erwin Schrödinger (1887–1961).

BIBLIOGRAPHY

Barnes, J.: *The Presocratic Philosophers* 2 vols (London: 1979); 2nd edn in one vol. (London: Routledge & Kegan Paul, 1982).
Barnes, J.: *Early Greek Philosophy* (Harmondsworth: Penguin, 1987). Translation of ancient sources, with introductions.

415

Furley, D.J.: *The Greek Cosmologists* Vol. 1 *The Formation of the Atomic Theory and Its Earliest Critics* (Cambridge: Cambridge University Press, 1987).

Furley, D.J. and Allen, R.E. ed.: *Studies in Presocratic Philosophy* 2 vols (London: Routledge & Kegan Paul, 1970, 1975).

Mourelatos, A.P.D.: *The Presocratics: A Collection of Critical Essays* (Garden City, NY: 1974); 2nd edn (Princeton, NJ: Princeton University Press, 1993).

Mourelatos, A.P.D.: 'Quality, structure, and emergence in later pre-Socratic philosophy', *Proceedings of the Boston Area Colloquium in Ancient Philosophy* 2 (1987), 127–94.

Nussbaum, M.C.: 'Eleatic conventionalism and Philolaus on the conditions of thought', *Harvard Studies in Classical Philology* 83 (1979), 63–108.

Robinson, J.M.: *An Introduction to Early Greek Philosophy: The Chief Fragments and Ancient Testimony, with Connecting Commentary* (Boston, MA: Houghton Mifflin Company, 1968).

Wiggins, D.: 'Heraclitus' conceptions of flux, fire and material persistence', in *Language and Logos: Studies in Ancient Greek Philosophy Presented to G.E.L. Owen*, ed. M. Schofield and M.C. Nussbaum (Cambridge: Cambridge University Press, 1982), 1–32.

ALEXANDER P.D. MOURELATOS

primary quality *see* QUALITY, PRIMARY/SECONDARY

principle of verifiability Advanced, in various forms, by philosophers associated with the logical positivist movement. Basically, the principle states that to be cognitively meaningful, a statement must be either (1) logically true (tautologous) or false (contradictory); or (2) in principle empirically verifiable as the result of observation. Logical truth and falsehood are supposed to be linguistic matters. Seemingly meaningful statements that do not satisfy these conditions are grammatically disguised nonsense. Such sentences may express emotions and non-cognitive attitudes but are not themselves true or false. Thus, sentences of metaphysics, ethics and religion are branded cognitive nonsense. The principle of verifiability was supposed to underwrite a linguistic turn in philosophy: the distinctive task of philosophy would be to analyse the meaning of statements and to unmask nonsense.

There are two main lines of criticism of the verifiability principle. The first argues that the principle undermines itself. The principle is itself neither tautologous, contradictory nor empirically verifiable. Hence, on its own telling, it is cognitive nonsense. Moritz Schlick, influenced by WITTGENSTEIN's *Tractatus* (1922), concedes that the insight concerning the general conditions for meaningfulness that the principle attempts to express cannot be formulated by any meaningful statement, for 'that which precedes all formation of theories cannot itself be a theory' (Schlick, 1932, p. 265). This special, if awkward, status does not, in Schlick's eyes, discredit the insight. CARNAP has a different response to this objection. He urges that the verifiability principle should be construed as a proposal that investigators interested in evaluating statements as correct or incorrect should restrict themselves to empiricist languages whose non-logical theories are verifiable.

The second line of objection concerns attempts to demarcate precisely what sentences are verifiable. Some definitions of verifiability excluded as meaningless statements of theoretical physics that were accepted as paradigms of meaningful statements of empirical science. Others failed to exclude the allegedly nonsensical sentences of traditional metaphysics. The most telling criticisms here play on the fact that abstract scientific statements do not individually, but only as a part of comprehensive theories, have observationally ascertainable consequences.

See also EMPIRICISM; LOGICAL POSITIVISM.

BIBLIOGRAPHY

Ayer, A.J.: *Language, Truth, and Logic* (London: Gollancz, 1936; 2nd edn 1946).

Carnap, R.: 'Testability and meaning', *Philosophy of Science* 3 (1936), 419–71; 4 (1937), 1–40.

Hempel, C.: 'Empiricist criteria of cognitive significance: problems and changes', in his *Aspects of Scientific Explanation* (New York: Free Press, 1965), 101–22.

Schlick, M.: 'Positivismus und Realismus', *Erkenntnis* 3 (1932), 1–31; trans. 'Positivism and realism', in *Moritz Schlick: Philosophical Papers*, vol. 2 (Dordrecht: D. Reidel, 1979), 259–84.

THOMAS RICKETTS

private *see* PUBLIC/PRIVATE

projectivism *see* OBJECTIVISM AND PROJECTIVISM

process philosophy From the time of ARISTOTLE, western metaphysics has had a marked bias in favour of *things* or *substances* (*see* SUBSTANCE). However, another variant line of thought was also current from the earliest times onward. After all, concentrating on perduring physical *things* as existents in nature slights the equally good claims of another ontological category, namely processes, events, occurrences – items better indicated by verbs than nouns. And, clearly, storms and heat waves are every bit as real as dogs and oranges.

Process philosophy has become widely associated with the metaphysics of WHITEHEAD, but in fact it is a well-defined major tendency of thought that traces back through the history of philosophy to the days of the PRESOCRATICS. Its leading exponents were Heraclitus, LEIBNIZ, BERGSON, PEIRCE and JAMES – and it ultimately moved on to include Whitehead and his school (Charles Hartshorne, Paul Weiss) but also other twentieth-century philosophers such as Samuel Alexander (1859–1938), C. Lloyd Morgan (1852–1936), and Andrew Paul Ushenko.

Against this historical background, process philosophy may be understood as a doctrine invoking certain basic propositions:

(1) That time and CHANGE are among the principal categories of metaphysical understanding.

(2) That process is a principal category of ontological description.

(3) That processes are more fundamental, or at any rate not less fundamental than things for the purposes of ontological theory.

(4) That several if not all of the major elements of the ontological repertoire (God, nature as a whole, persons, material substances) are best understood in process linked terms.

(5) That contingency, emergence, novelty, and creativity are among the fundamental categories of metaphysical understanding.

A process philosopher, accordingly, is someone for whom temporality, activity and change – of alteration, striving, passage, and novelty-emergence – are the cardinal factors for our understanding of the real.

For the process philosopher, the classical principle *operari sequitur esse* (functioning follows upon being) is reversed: his motto is *esse sequitur operari*, since being follows from operation because what there is is in the final analysis of the product of processes. Process thus has priority over product – both ontologically and epistemically. As process philosophers see it, processes are basic and things derivative, because it takes a mental process (of separation) to extract 'things' from the blooming buzzing confusion of the world's physical processes. For process philosophy, what a thing *is* consists in what it *does* or *can* do.

Recourse to process is a helpful device for dealing with the classical problem of UNIVERSALS. We are surrounded on all sides by items more easily conceived of as pro-

417

cesses than as substantial things – not only physical items like a magnetic field or an *aurora borealis*, but also conceptual artefacts like letters of the alphabet, words, and statements. That purported universal – the opening line of a play, say, or a shade of phenomenal red – now ceases to be a mysterious *object* of some sort and becomes a specifiable feature of familiar processes (readings, perceivings, imaginings). How distinct minds can perceive the same universal is now no more mysterious than how distinct walkers can share the same limp – it is a matter of actions proceeding in a certain particular way. Universals are pulled down from the Platonic realm to become structural features of the ways in which we concretely conduct our cognitive affairs.

The demise of classical ATOMISM brought on by the dematerialization of physical MATTER through the rise of the quantum theory brings much aid and comfort to a process-oriented metaphysics. Matter in the small, as contemporary physics concerns it, is not a Rutherfordian planetary system of particle-like objects, but a collection of fluctuating processes organized into stable structures (in so far as there is indeed stability at all) by statistical regularities – i.e. by regularities of components at the level of aggregate phenomena. Twentieth-century physics has thus turned the tables on classical atomism. Instead of very small *things* (atoms) combining to produce standard processes (windstorms and such) modern physics envisions very small processes (quantum phenomena) combining to produce standard things (ordinary macro-objects) as a result of their *modus operandi*.

The philosophy of mind is another strongpoint of process philosophizing. It feels distinctly uncomfortable to conceptualize *people* (persons) as *things* (substances) – oneself above all – because we resist flat-out identification with our bodies. However, there is no problem with experiential access to the processes and patterns of process that characterize us personally – our doings and undergoings, either individually or patterned into talents, skills, capabilities, traits, dispositions, habits,

inclinations, and tendencies to action and inaction are, after all, what characteristically define a person as the individual he or she is.

Once we conceptualize the core 'self' of a person as a unified manifold of actual and potential processes – of action and capacities, tendencies, and dispositions to action (both physical and psychical) – then we thereby secure a concept of personhood that renders the self or ego experientially accessible, seeing that experiencing itself simply *consists* of such processes. (*See* PERSONS AND PERSONAL IDENTITY.) What makes one's experience one's own is not some peculiar qualitative character that it exhibits but simply its forming part of the overall ongoing process that defines and constitutes one's life. The unity of person is a unity of experience – the coalescence of all of one's diverse micro-experience as part of one unified macro-process. (It is the same sort of unity of process that links each minute's level into a single overall journey.) On this basis, the Humean complaint – 'One experiences feeling this and doing that, but one never experiences *oneself*' – is much like the complaint of the person who says 'I see him picking up that brick, and mixing that batch of mortar, and trowelling that brick into place, but I never seen him building a wall.' (*See* HUME.) Even as 'building the wall' just exactly *is* the complex process that is *composed* of those various activities, so – from the process point of view – one's self just *is* the complex process *composed* of those various physical and psychic experiences and actions in their systemic interrelationship.

As such considerations indicate, the process approach has many assets. But it has significant liabilities as well. It is not unfair to the historical situation to say that process philosophy at present remains no more than a glint in the mind's eye of various philosophers. A full-fledged development of the process doctrine simply does not yet exist as an accomplished fact, its development to the point where it can be compared with other major philosophical projects like materialism or absolute IDE-

ALISM still remains. (*See* PHYSICALISM, MATERIALISM.)

BIBLIOGRAPHY

The journal *Process Studies* has been published since 1971.

Cousins, E.H. ed.: *Process Theology* (New York: Newman Press, 1971).

Rescher, N.: 'The promise of process philosophy', in his *Baffling Phenomena* (Savage, MD: Rowman and Littlefield, 1991).

Sheldon, W.H.: *Process and Polarity* (New York: Columbia University Press, 1944).

Whitehead, A.N.: *The Concept of Nature* (Cambridge: Cambridge University Press, 1920).

Whitehead, A.N.: *Process and Reality* (Cambridge: Cambridge University Press, 1929).

Whittemore, R.C. ed.: *Studies in Process Philosophy* Tulane Studies in Philosophy vols 23–5 (The Hague: Martinus Nijhoff, 1974–6).

NICHOLAS RESCHER

proposition, state of affairs A proposition is something capable of being the meaning of a declarative sentence in some language, actual or possible. 'Proposition' is sometimes used as synonymous with 'meaningful (declarative) sentence' but philosophical usage is converging to the more abstract meaning.

The current notion is the result of a long historical process (see Church, 1956). In modern philosophy the concept was delimited especially by BOLZANO, MEINONG, FREGE (1949) and RUSSELL (1903).

The proposition has been taken to be the primary bearer of truth and of modal properties such as necessity and possibility, and as the object of knowledge, belief, hope, desire and other intentional psychological states (*see* INTENTIONALITY). This identification of the meaning of a sentence with the occupant of these other roles has been questioned but is strongly suggested by the apparent validity of such arguments as:

(1) The sentence 'Five plus seven equals twelve' means (in English) that five plus seven equals twelve.

(2) It is necessary that five plus seven equals twelve.

(3) Kant knew that five plus seven equals twelve.

(4) Hence, there is something which the sentence 'Five plus seven equals twelve' means (in English), which is necessary and which Kant knew.

If we allow the notion of a *possible language*, we can think of propositions as abstractions obtained in the following way. Consider pairs each consisting of a sentence as interpreted in a possible language together with the language in question. Let there be given among such pairs a binary relation E which is reflexive, symmetric and transitive – an equivalence relation. Then E partitions the sentence–language pairs into equivalence classes, that is, into mutually exclusive and jointly exhaustive classes. Corresponding to each such equivalence class we postulate an abstract entity representing what the elements of the classes have in common (relative to E). (Compare the concept of a cardinal number as an abstraction from equinumerous classes.)

The main questions which have been disputed about this notion concern (1) the determination or definition of the equivalence relation E; (2) the structure and constituents of the abstract propositions postulated to correspond to the equivalence classes; and (3) the ontological legitimacy of such abstract entities.

DETERMINATION OR DEFINITION OF THE EQUIVALENCE RELATION E

About (1) the usual intention is that E is to be the relation of *synonymy*. CARNAP (1947) used 'proposition' in the case where E is the relation of necessary equivalence. But this has the undesirable consequence that sentences widely divergent in meaning may express the same proposition, for example, any two sentences expressing

419

necessary truths. It has been urged that in order to be acceptable the relation of synonymy must be definable in physical vocabulary (*see* PHYSICALISM, MATERIALISM). Since many apparently meaningful concepts seem not to be thus definable, this demand is often replaced by some weaker constraint. One such, associated with QUINE, is the requirement that the truth values of sentences about synonymies shall be determined by truths expressible in the vocabulary of science (including behaviouristic psychology). Even if we grant that this is in some sense desirable, it still remains to specify what vocabulary is to count as appropriately scientific or, in a more stringent version, as 'physicalistic'. So far this has not been done in such a (non-arbitrary) way as to both (a) avoid the dogmatic claim that the present vocabulary will be adequate for all future science; and (b) definitely exclude any terms at all. Further, one may well resist the restriction to the vocabulary of the natural sciences. Mathematics and logic are well established *formal* sciences and it may happen that future developments will require the term 'synonymy' or some precise counterpart.

STRUCTURE AND CONSTITUENTS OF THE PROPOSITION

The 'constituents' of a proposition (2) are only determined when the idea of a constituent is defined or explained. If we say that a person (conceptually) *grasps* an entity if he understands an expression (in some language) which means that entity, then we may take the constituents of a proposition to be those things whose grasp is entailed by the grasp of the proposition. But even if this much is agreed upon, disputes arise about particular cases. About sentences containing *proper names*, we may wonder whether they mean propositions whose constituents are the objects denoted by the names or whether the names have some more abstract meaning which could be grasped even if the names did not denote any entities at all. The first suggestion has a sentence such as 'John loves Mary' meaning

what we may call a *Russellian singular proposition*, construed as the ordered triple < John, the relation of loving, Mary >, and with a similar construction for assertions involving *n*-ary relations, for $n > 2$. On the second construal, 'John loves Mary' means a proposition whose constituents are the sense of the name 'John' (which is an abstract entity distinct from the man John), the sense of the verb 'loves', plausibly identified with the relation-in-intension of loving, and the sense of the name 'Mary' (also abstract). This latter account is associated with the ideas of Frege (1949) and the resulting meaning might be called a *Fregean proposition*.

Thus abstractly stated, the dispute about the constituents of (certain) propositions may seem pointless. And, taken in isolation, different views as to whether the meaning of a proper name (or its 'information content') is the thing denoted or a sense expressed (and that these are then constituents of the proposition meant by the sentence) *are* completely idle. But the details of a theory of the structure of propositions will bear on the *logic* of arguments involving meaning, belief, necessity, and other so-called intensional concepts. It appears that the following argument is *invalid*:

(1) Commissioner Gordon knows a priori that (if Bruce Wayne exists) Bruce Wayne is Bruce Wayne.
(2) Batman is Bruce Wayne.
(3) So, Commissioner Gordon knows a priori that (if Bruce Wayne exists) Batman is Bruce Wayne.

And what we take the constituent meanings of the propositions involved in this argument *to be* will (partly) determine our evaluation of it and of similar arguments. But of course other factors will affect our final decision about such arguments.

ONTOLOGICAL LEGITIMACY

The general objection that abstract entities of all kinds are inadmissible (3) may be countered with the reply that even the well-established natural sciences, in their use of mathematics and logic, already assume the existence of numbers, functions, classes, and the like (*see* CLASS, COLLECTION, SET; NUMBER). Vigorous attempts have been made to avoid some or all of these abstracta but the debate is still in progress. The suggestion that the equivalence *classes* (of sentence–language pairs) themselves might be used in place of the postulated propositions obviously does not avoid commitment to abstract entities (*see* NOMINALISM; PLATONISM).

'State of affairs' is sometimes taken in a closely related but more restricted meaning, for example as referring to something possible. The terminology has been used most notably by WITTGENSTEIN, C.I. Lewis, and CHISHOLM. It has been urged with some force, by Lewis (1944) following H.M. Sheffer, that there is a need for a term to indicate the common content of a declarative sentence, say 'Barry is making pies', the corresponding interrogative, 'Is Barry making pies?', and the imperative, 'Barry, make pies!' Lewis uses 'state of affairs' for this purpose (preferring 'proposition' for meaningful declarative sentence) but this terminology has not been generally followed.

BIBLIOGRAPHY

Carnap, R.: *Meaning and Necessity* (Chicago and London: University of Chicago Press, 1947).
Church, A.: 'Propositions and sentences', in *The Problem of Universals* ed. I.M. Bochenski, A. Church and N. Goodman (Notre Dame, IN: University of Notre Dame Press, 1956), 3–12.
Frege, G.: 'On sense and nominatum', in *Readings in Philosophical Analysis* ed. H. Feigl and W. Sellars (New York: Appleton-Century-Crofts, 1949), 85–102.
Lewis, C.I.: 'The modes of meaning', *Philosophy and Phenomenological Research* 4 (1944), 236–49.
Russell, B.: *The Principles of Mathematics* (London: Allen and Unwin, 1903).

C. ANTHONY ANDERSON

public/private Several public/private distinctions have been drawn in the philosophy of mind. One concerns public/private *possession*. Two people can have the same car; a car may be co-owned. Thus, cars can be publically possessed, possessed by more than one individual. It has been claimed, however, that experiences (*see* EXPERIENCE) are essentially private in that only the subject having the particular experience in question could have that very experience (see Ayer, 1959; Rorty, 1965; Searle, 1992; Unger, 1990). Thus, only I can have my pain experiences. One might concede this but deny that it reveals anything special about experiences. Suppose I take a walk. One might claim that while it is true in a sense that only I can have my experiences, it is also true in a sense that only I can take my walk. Of course, others can take a walk of the same type as mine. But, likewise, others can have an experience of the same type as mine. What others cannot have is my actual token of the type of experience in question. But, likewise, it seems that others cannot take my actual token walk. It might be argued that there is a sense in which another could have taken the very token walk I walk; but it may be argued as well that there is, similarly, a sense in which another could have had the very token experience I have. Perhaps it will seem more plausible that another could have taken my actual token walk than that another could have had my actual token experience. We have experiences by experiencing them. It may seem that only I could have experienced my actual token experience. But, nevertheless, it may seem as well that only I could have walked my actual token walk. It might thus be argued that while experiences are indeed private in the sense in question, this sort of privacy is not unique to experiences. However, both the issue of whether experiences are private in this sense (see Unger, 1990) and the issue of whether, if they are, only experiences are private in this sense remain points of controversy.

Another public/private distinction is between *things that are publicly observable and things that are not*. Something is publically observable if, and only if, it can, in principle, be observed by more than one subject; something is privately observable if, and only if, it is observable, but not publicly observable (Ayer, 1959; Jackson, 1977). Material objects and physical events are publically observable: for example, two people can see the same building or the same explosion. In contrast, after-images and bodily sensations (e.g., aches, pains, itches, tickles, and the like) are not publicly observable: each person can see only his own after-image and feel only his own bodily sensations (Ayer, 1959; Jackson, 1977). Thus, after-images and bodily sensations are only privately observable. An issue that arises here is whether there really are any entities that are only privately observable (*see* SENSA). To be sure, we sometimes have after-images; but it has been claimed that after-images are visual experiences, not things that we see. Moreover, it has been claimed that, strictly speaking, there are no bodily sensations. Rather than there being a pain or an itch in my foot that I feel, it is simply the case that my foot hurts or that it itches (Aune, 1967). It is painful when my foot hurts. But it is not the case that there is something, a pain, such that it is in my foot and I feel it. On this view, it is natural to classify referred pain experiences as illusory and phantom-limb pain experiences as hallucinatory. For example, in a case of referred pain it may seem as if one's second molar hurts, when in fact one's third molar hurts. In cases of phantom limbs, it may seem as if one's right leg hurts, even though one has no right leg. Claiming that a phantom-limb pain experience is hallucinatory would not commit one to denying the obvious truth that phantom-limb pain experiences are painful experiences. The painful aspect of the experience is not hallucinatory.

Yet another public/private distinction concerns *conscious awareness* (*see* CONSCIOUSNESS; SELF-CONSCIOUSNESS). Two subjects can be conscious of the same thing; they might be aware of a painting in front of both of them. But a subject can be directly conscious of only his or her own experience (Rorty, 1965). Experiences are private in that we can each be conscious of our experiences in a way that no one else could possibly be. One has a kind of privileged access to one's own experiences, a kind of access that one lacks to the experiences of others (Rorty, 1965). If direct consciousness is a kind of perception or perceptual awareness, then this public/private distinction is one mentioned in the preceding paragraph, except restricted to states and events of experiencing. However, if direct consciousness of an experience is a kind of perception of the experience, it is quite different from perception of material objects, states, and events. For it does not seem to admit of a perception/hallucination distinction. That is because there seems to be no APPEARANCE/REALITY distinction where our conscious sensory experiences are concerned (Searle, 1992). We are directly conscious of our sensory experiences in the sense that we are conscious of them but not by means of being conscious of anything else. There is nothing we are conscious of such that we are conscious of a sensory experience by being conscious of it. Our sensory experiences do not present an appearance of themselves to us. Visual (auditory, olfactory, etc.) experiences present an appearance to us, but not an appearance of themselves. Visual experiences typically present, rather, an appearance of the public scene before our eyes.

Finally, the *subjective/objective* distinction, while not a public/private distinction, is nevertheless related to the last public/private distinction and deserves mention in this context (*see* OBJECTIVITY). Subjective states are such that it is like something for the occupant of the state to be in the state (Jackson, 1977, 1986; Nagel, 1986; Searle, 1992). The point is sometimes made by saying that conscious mental states have a subjective aspect, a phenomenological character. To understand what it is for such a state to obtain, one must understand what the state is like for the occupant of the state. To understand that, one must, it seems, be able to take up the experiential perspective or point of view of the occupant of the state. Thus, subjective states etc., can be understood only by those who have or can take up a certain experiential point of view. Subjective states are in this way perspectival. In contrast, objective states etc., do not incorporate an experiential point of view; they are not perspectival in that way. Objective states are not such that it is like something for the occupant of the state to be in them. Objective states do not have a phenomenological character (though the experiencing of them will). One need not take up an experiential point of view to understand what it is for an objective state to obtain.

Occurrently conscious states are subjective: it is like something for the occupant of the state to be in them. Colour experiences are an example. It has been claimed that it is possible for someone who has never had colour experiences to know all the objective facts about colour and colour experiences yet not know what it is like to experience colour (Jackson, 1986). It has also been claimed that what makes it hard to see how consciousness could be physical is that physical states (events, etc.) are objective while conscious states are subjective (Jackson, 1986; Nagel, 1986; Searle, 1992). For, how could a subjective state just consist in an objective state? One could understand what it is for the objective state to obtain without taking up the experiential point of view necessary to understand what it is for the subjective state to obtain. For

that reason, it is hard to see how a subjective state could just consist in an objective state. We simply do not understand how a subjective point of view could be completely constituted by objective factors (Nagel, 1986).

See also MIND/BODY PROBLEM.

BIBLIOGRAPHY

Aune, B.: *Mind, Knowledge, Nature* (New York: Random House, 1967).
Ayer, A.J.: 'Privacy', *Proceedings of the British Academy* XLV (1959), 201–20.
Jackson, F.: *Perception: A Representative View* (Cambridge: Cambridge University Press, 1977).
Jackson, F.: 'What Mary didn't know', *Journal of Philosophy* LXXXIII (1986), 291–5.
Nagel, T.: *The View from Nowhere* (Oxford: Oxford University Press, 1986).
Rorty, R.: 'Mind–body identity, privacy, and categories', *The Review of Metaphysics* XIX (1965), section 5, 41–8.
Searle, J.: *The Rediscovery of the Mind* (Cambridge, MA: Bradford/MIT Press, 1992).
Unger, P.: *Identity, Consciousness and Values* (Oxford: Oxford University Press, 1990).

BRIAN P. McLAUGHLIN

Q

quality, primary/secondary What can we learn from the fact that the same body of water sometimes feels hot to one hand and cold to the other? According to LOCKE, we learn that *hot* and *cold* are not really in the water but are merely sensations that the water produces in the mind and that the mind attributes to the water by mistake. Locke therefore believed that qualities such as warmth are fundamentally different from qualities like shape and size, which really do belong to the objects that appear to have them. Following Boyle, he referred to the former as secondary qualities, and the latter as primary.

Locke's argument does not work if its premise is that objects must not possess a determinable property (warmth) if they appear, from different perspectives, to possess different determinate degrees of it (hot and cold). (*See* DETERMINATE/DETERMINABLE). For as Berkeley pointed out, all sensible properties display such perceptual relativity, and so the foregoing premise would yield, not a distinction among sensible properties, but a flat denial that the world possessed any sensible properties at all. A more plausible interpretation of Locke's argument, however, is that it points to differences in how perceptual relativity is explained in different properties (Alexander, 1974). The explanation of why an object looks large from one perspective and small from another is that the angle it subtends at the eye is a function not only of its actual size but also of its distance from the viewer the explanation of why an object feels hot to one hand and cold to the other is that the two hands have different levels of molecular kinetic energy, so that one gains such energy from the object and the other

loses energy to it. The difference between these explanations is that, whereas an object's apparent size is attributed, in part, to its actual size, an object's apparent warmth is attributed to its molecular kinetic energy rather than to its having any warmth in reality.

This contrast is valid, of course, only if 'warmth' and 'molecular kinetic energy' are not two expressions for the same property. If they are, then an object's appearing to have that property will indeed be explained by its actually having the property, even though the property goes by different names in the *explanans* and *explanandum*. The Lockean argument has therefore prompted debate over whether so-called secondary qualities such as warmth and colour are in fact identical with the physical properties responsible for their appearances.

This debate is best understood as a debate about the content of the sensory appearances themselves. When we ask whether warmth is molecular kinetic energy, we are hoping to learn whether the property that an object appears to have, in feeling warm, is the property responsible for that appearance. Since we know that molecular kinetic energy is the physical property that makes an object feel warm, what remains to be ascertained is whether it is the property represented in that sensory appearance – the property that the object appears to have in feeling warm, and hence the property whose presence would render the appearance veridical, and whose absence would render it illusory. Similarly, what remains to be ascertained about colour is whether spectral reflectance at the surface of an object – the property responsible for the object's appearance of colour – is also the property represented in that appearance; and so on, for each of the qualities that are said to be secondary. (The discussion that follows is confined to the case of colour, which is the most widely discussed example of a secondary quality.)

The view that the property represented in colour experience is surface spectral reflectance (or the molecular basis thereof) can be called physicalism about colour (Armstrong, 1987). (*See* PHYSICALISM/MATERIALISM.) This view often prompts the obvious objection that it misdescribes the way colours look. When something looks red to us, we do not see it as differentially responsive to different wavelengths of light. But this objection by itself is inadequate. All it establishes is that 'differential responsiveness to wavelengths of light' is not the description or mode of presentation under which colour is represented in visual experience; it does not establish that differential responsiveness to wavelengths of light is not the property that is in fact represented. Just as we can see clouds of molecules without seeing them *as* clouds of molecules, so we may see spectral reflectance profiles without seeing them as such.

Nevertheless, this initial objection to physicalism may succeed when combined with epistemological considerations tending to show that colours must in fact be represented under descriptions or modes of presentation that reveal their natures (Boghossian and Velleman, 1991). Mere reflection on colour experience gives us certain knowledge that red, orange and green – i.e. the properties that red-, orange- and green-looking objects appear to have – are three distinct properties; that the first two are more like one another than they are like the third; and so on. Such knowledge would not be obtainable from colour experience unless that experience represented colours in terms of what they are essentially. Hence the physicalist is not entitled to distinguish between the nature of colour properties and their mode of presentation.

Of course, colour appearances can be explained, not only in terms of physical properties like spectral reflectance, but also in terms of the dispositions that objects have to produce colour appearances. Perhaps, then, colour appearances can be vindicated by the claim that when an object looks red, the property it appears to have is a DISPOSITION to look red under normal conditions, a property that is indeed normally responsible for its looking red (Peacocke, 1984). The resulting version of REALISM about colour can be called dispositionalism (*See* DISPOSITION).

Unfortunately, if the disposition to look red is understood as a disposition to be visually represented as red, then it is not a determinate property. For in that case, it is a disposition to be visually represented as having this very disposition; and so which disposition it is depends on which disposition it disposes objects to be represented as having – which depends, in turn, on which disposition it is. Dispositionalism about colour can succeed, then, only if it identifies the property red with a disposition to look red in some sense other than by being visually represented as red.

The most plausible alternative is to understand the disposition to look red as a disposition to produce visual appearances characterized by a particular sensory quality – a visual sensation called red. The problem with this version of dispositionalism, however, is that it requires visual experience to have one colour property itself (a reddish sensation) while representing external objects as having another colour property (a disposition to produce reddish sensations). And although some sensory experiences have such a two-tiered phenomenology, the experience of colour does not. We do perceive the painfulness of knives as a disposition that lurks behind the painfulness of the experiences they cause, but we do not see the redness of objects as a disposition lurking behind the redness of their visual appearances.

Surely, what we see an object as having, when it produces a reddish visual appearance in us, is the very reddish quality that belongs to the appearance – a quality that does not figure in the appearance's explana-

425

tion. That is why Locke thought that colour experiences misrepresented objects as resembling the experiences themselves; and that is why he was right to classify colour as a secondary quality.

Of course, the foregoing argument will not reveal whether Locke was right about the other qualities that he classified as secondary, unless those qualities resemble colour in the relevant epistemological and phenomenological respects. Finally, the argument does not show that Locke succeeded in drawing a distinction between two classes of properties, since it does not show that properties such as extension and motion are primary qualities in the relevant sense. Of course, an object's appearing to be large or small in size is explained partly by the size it actually is; but maybe this explanation equivocates on the word 'size', explaining the appearance of one property by the existence of another, while using the word 'size' for both. This possibility will have to be ruled out before the distinction between primary and secondary qualities can be vindicated.

BIBLIOGRAPHY

Alexander, P.: 'Boyle and Locke on primary and secondary qualities', *Ratio* 16 (1974), 51–67.
Armstrong, D.M.: 'Smart and secondary qualities', in *Metaphysics and Morality: Essays in Honour of J.J.C. Smart* ed. P. Pettit, R. Sylvan and J. Norman (Oxford: Blackwell, 1987), 1–15.
Boghossian, P.A., and Velleman, J.D.: 'Physicalist theories of color', *Philosophical Review* 100 (1991), 67–106.
Hardin, C.L.: *Color for Philosophers: Unweaving the Rainbow* (Indianapolis, IN: Hackett, 1988).
Peacocke, C.: 'Colour concepts and colour experience', *Synthese* 58 (1984), 365–81.

J. DAVID VELLEMAN

quiddity English transliteration of the Medieval Latin *quidditas*, a noun derived from the particle *quid* and first introduced in the twelfth century in Latin translations of AVICENNA and ARISTOTLE. Literally 'quiddity' means 'whatness', that which makes a thing what it is, and it has come to be used as a synonym for essence (*see* ESSENCE/ACCIDENT). Among scholastics quiddity was considered to be extensionally, but not intensionally, equivalent to form, essence, and NATURE (*see* EXTENSION/INTENSION). The quiddity is expressed by a proper definition specifying the genus and specific difference in answer to the question 'What (*quid*) is it?' As AQUINAS points out in *On Being and Essence* (ch. 1), quiddity differs from essence 'because through it [i.e. essence], and in it, that which is has being'; from form 'because form signifies the determination of each thing'; and from nature because nature 'signifies the essence of a thing as directed to its specific operation' (*see* MATTER/FORM).

JORGE J.E. GRACIA

Quine, Willard Van Orman (1908–) An analytic metaphysician who is first and foremost a philosophical naturalist. His NATURALISM has two components: first, he rejects the traditional quest for a first philosophy, i.e. the quest for a ground somehow outside of science upon which science can be justified; second, he accepts science as the final arbiter concerning questions of what there is.

But how are we to determine what science says, or assumes, there is? Quine urges that one way we can determine what a scientific theory says there is (its ONTOLOGY) is by first regimenting the theory in first-order predicate logic and then ascertaining the values of the bound variables of the sentences held true in the theory. For Quine, to be is to be the value of a bound variable. However, Quine argues that if there is one ontology that fulfils a theory, there is more than one. This latter claim is the crux of his famous doctrine of ontological relativity (or inscrutability of REFERENCE). That doctrine claims that it makes no sense to say what the objects of a theory are, beyond saying how to interpret or reinterpret that theory in another; there is no saying *absolutely* what the objects of a theory are. Quine's preferred argument for ontological relativity is his *proxy function* argument. According to this argument, one can effect a one-to-one reinterpretation of the denotata of a theory without disturbing either the logical relations of the theory to observation sentences or the psychological bonds between observation sentences and stimulation. Because Quine is a naturalist, and because the currently best scientific account of the world is physicalistic, Quine, too, is a physicalist (*see* PHYSICALISM, MATERIALISM). Physicalism, for Quine, is the view that there is no difference in matters of fact without a difference in the fulfilment of the physical-state predicates by space-time regions. Quine recognizes that this formulation of physicalism is unfinished, since the system of co-ordinates which is required for applying physical-state predicates to space-time regions remains to be specified, and, more importantly, there is the matter of specifying the lexicon of physical-state predicates themselves – the so-called ideology of physical theory. But this latter task is one of the major historical tasks of physics itself, namely, the ascertaining of a minimum catalogue of elementary states such that there is no change in matters of fact without a change in respect to them. And, because of ontological relativity, where all of the true sentences of a theory remain true despite wholesale changes in ontology, Quine regards questions of ideology, and not of ontology, to be where the philosophical action is.

As a naturalist who accepts current science as providing us with the best account of what there is, and as a believer in his own adage *to be is to be the value of a bound variable*, Quine also comes out a scientific realist with respect to the objects (but not the laws) referred to in accepted scientific theories (*see* REALISM). Thus, if the currently best physical theory is ontologically committed to quarks, then so is Quine. But according to Quine's empiricist epistemology (*see* EMPIRICISM) all objects are

posits. And, since science is underdetermined by all possible sensory evidence, today's quarks might turn out to be tomorrow's phlogiston. As an empiricist, Quine finds this fallibilism congenial enough; after all, it comes naturally to one who abandons the quest for an infallible first philosophy. But how is Quine's scientific realism to be reconciled with the apparent instrumentalism of his empiricism? The key is his naturalism: empiricism is itself a finding of science, according to Quine, but this finding need not repudiate the (physicalist) ontology in terms of which the recognition that all objects are posits took place. We might repudiate that ontology, too, but only by receding into some further background ontology. This is the central moral of Quine's naturalism: there is no Archimedean point of cosmic exile from which to leverage our theory of the world.

Finally, since contemporary scientific theories cannot avoid quantifying over numbers, we must add that in addition to being a physicalist Quine is a mathematical Platonist: numbers (explicated as classes of classes, and so on) exist as ineliminable values of the bound variables of scientific theories (*see* CLASS, COLLECTION, SET; NUMBER; PLATONISM). Thus, Quine accepts a dualistic ontology of physical objects and classes; dualistic but extensional. For he recognizes no intensional objects, e.g. propositions, meanings, attributes, and relations-in-intension, as belonging to the ontology of science (*see* PROPOSITION, STATE OF AFFAIRS). The chief difficulty with intensional objects, Quine argues, is that they do not contribute sufficiently to the systematic efficacy of scientific theories so as to warrant their inclusion; they do not pay their way.

So, Quine the metaphysician is a naturalist, a physicalist, a scientific realist, a fallibilist, a mathematical Platonist, and an extensionalist. It remains to be said that he rejects the correspondence, coherence and pragmatist theories of truth in so far as these theories purport to apply to individual sentences, statements or propositions. For Quine, truth is disquotational. Thus, to say that 'Snow is white' is true is just to assert that snow is white (*see* THEORIES OF TRUTH). Lastly, so far as philosophy of mind is concerned, Quine endorses the theory of anomalous monism advocated by DAVIDSON (*see* MIND/BODY PROBLEM).

WRITINGS

From a Logical Point of View (Cambridge, MA: Harvard, 1953; rev. edn. 1961).
Word and Object (Cambridge, MA: MIT Press, 1960).
Ontological Relativity and Other Essays (New York: Columbia, 1969).
Theories and Things (Cambridge, MA: Harvard, 1981).
The Time of My Life: An Autobiography (Cambridge, MA: MIT Press, 1985).
Pursuit of Truth (Cambridge, MA: Harvard, 1990).

BIBLIOGRAPHY

Barrett, R. and Gibson, R. eds: *Perspectives on Quine* (Oxford: Blackwell, 1990).
Davidson, D. and Hintikka, J. eds: *Words and Objections: Essays on the Work of W.V. Quine* (Dordrecht: Reidel, 1969).
Gibson, R.F.: *The Philosophy of W.V. Quine: An Expository Essay* (Tampa, FL: University of South Florida, 1982).
Hahn, L.E. and Schilpp, P.A. eds: *The Philosophy of W.V. Quine* (La Salle, IL: Open Court, 1986).
Hookway, C.: *Quine: Language, Experience and Reality* (Stanford, CA: Stanford, 1988).

ROGER F. GIBSON

R

Ramsey, Frank Plumpton (1903–30) British philosopher and mathematician, best known for his work on the foundations of mathematics, but also made remarkable contributions to epistemology, semantics, logic, philosophy of science, mathematics, statistics, probability and decision theory, economics and metaphysics. Ontological questions are central to much of his writing, whether it is on numbers, probabilities, the status of theoretical terms or general propositions and causality. One of his most impressive but underestimated contributions to philosophy is his analysis of the problem of UNIVERSALS.

His paper 'Universals' (1925) which denies any fundamental distinction between UNIVERSALS AND PARTICULARS, surmounts serious objections to a realist view of universals and, at the same time, solves several long-standing problems about them, dismissing other venerable enigmas as nonsense (*see* NOMINALISM; PLATONISM).

There are various reasons for making the distinction between universals and particulars – psychological, physical and logical. But Ramsey shows that logic justifies no such distinction. Alluding to a grammatical subject–predicate distinction will not do, since 'Socrates is wise', with subject 'Socrates' and predicate 'wise', 'asserts the same fact, and expresses the same proposition' as 'Wisdom is a characteristic of Socrates', with subject 'wisdom' and predicate 'Socrates'.

There is, he shows, no essential difference between the (in)completeness of universals and that of particulars. 'Wise' can, for example, be used to collect propositions not only of the atomic form 'Socrates is wise', but also of the molecular form 'Neither Socrates nor Plato is wise.' But 'Socrates' can also be used to collect propositions of both these forms: for example, 'Socrates is wise' and 'Socrates is neither wise nor just'. There is thus really a complete symmetry in this respect between individuals and basic properties (qualities). Or, as Ramsey succinctly puts it, 'the whole theory of particulars and universals is due to mistaking for a fundamental characteristic of reality what is merely a characteristic of language'.

Again, Ramsey shows that there can no more be complex universals (for example, negative, as 'not-wise'; relational, as 'wiser than'; and compound properties, as 'grue' (defined to mean 'observed before t and green or observed after t and blue')) than there can be complex particulars. Suppose that Socrates is to the right of Plato. One could then imagine three propositions: first, that the relation 'being to the right of' holds between Socrates and Plato; second, that Socrates has the complex property of 'being to the right of Plato'; third, that Plato has the complex property which something has if Socrates is to the right of it. Thus if there were complex universals, besides the fact that Socrates is to the right of Plato, there would also be two non-relational facts, with different constituents. But that is nonsense, there is only one fact, the fact that Socrates is to the right of Plato.

D.H. Mellor (1991) has shown that a virtue of Ramsey's REALISM is the way it stops the vicious regress started by asking what relates particulars to universals in a fact, for example, what ties Socrates to wisdom in the fact that Socrates is wise. But for Ramsey universals and particulars are constructions out of facts, not the other way around. He needs no hierarchy of universals to recombine them; they were never separated in the first place.

Ramsey's view of universals also affects much of his other work. Nominalists for example reject his so-called 'Ramsey sentence' account involving quantifying over universals, thus expanding our ontological commitments. But given Ramsey's kind of realism, that is no objection at all.

WRITINGS

'Universals', *Mind* 34 (1925), 401–17.

'Universals and the "method of analysis" ', *Proceedings of the Aristotelian Society* Supplementary Volume 6 (1926), 17–26.

These and other relevant papers are reprinted in:

The Foundations of Mathematics and Other Logical Essays ed. R.B. Braithwaite (London: Routledge and Kegan Paul, 1931).

Philosophical Papers ed. D.H. Mellor (Cambridge: Cambridge University Press, 1990).

BIBLIOGRAPHY

Mellor, D.H.: *Matters of Metaphysics* (Cambridge: Cambridge University Press, 1991).

Sahlin, N.-E.: *The Philosophy of F.P. Ramsey* (Cambridge: Cambridge University Press, 1990).

NILS-ERIC SAHLIN

rationalism The term 'rationalism' is multiply ambiguous. It is often used to designate a tendency in seventeenth-century philosophy represented by DESCARTES, SPINOZA and LEIBNIZ and characterized, according to a common story, by an overemphasis on a priori methods and a disdain for arguments from experience. Nevertheless, it is questionable that any very specific epistemological programme of that kind, shared by the three paradigmatic 'rationalists', and rejected by the three paradigmatic empiricists – LOCKE, BERKELEY and HUME – to whom they are customarily and conveniently opposed, can be identified.

Prospects for identifying a common rationalist programme are better in metaphysics. One doctrine Descartes, Spinoza and Leibniz did agree on was what Leibniz was to call the principle of sufficient reason, which we might state provisionally in the form: nothing exists or happens without there being a reason or cause for its existence or occurrence. No doubt many other philosophers, not all of whom are classed as rationalists, have subscribed to some form of this principle. Leibniz refers to it as a 'commonly held axiom'. But the three classical 'rationalists' did tend to interpret it in an unusually strong way and to give it a very fundamental place in their systems.

For example, when Descartes is axiomatizing the argument of the *Meditations* at the end of the Second Replies, he selects as his first axiom: 'Concerning every existing thing it is possible to ask what is the cause of its existence' (*Œuvres de Descartes* VII, pp. 164–5). The result of this inquiry, even if successful, need not be the identification of something which is the efficient cause of the thing in question; but if the thing has no efficient cause, there must be some explanation of why it does not need one, an explanation to be found in the nature of the thing. The particular case which prompts this line of thought is God, who requires nothing other than himself in order to exist, but who nevertheless does not lack a cause altogether. His nature (as immensely powerful, or as supremely perfect) explains why he needs nothing other than himself to exist in the first place (or to continue to exist). So God is the cause of his own EXISTENCE, not in the negative sense that he has no cause, but in a positive sense: his essence is the (formal) cause of his existence (cf. *Œuvres de Descartes* VII, pp. 108–11, 235–45). Descartes's interpretation of the principle of sufficient reason commits him to some form of ontological argument.

This is a common thread in all three classical 'rationalists'. But when Spinoza formulates the ontological argument in Part I of his *Ethics*, he does so with his own nuances. For example, he applies it first to SUBSTANCE in general (IP7, *Opera* II/49), before he has established that God is the only substance. And he states the principle of sufficient reason in an even more general form than Descartes does: for each thing there must be assigned a cause, or reason, either for its existence, if it exists, or for its non-existence, if it does not exist (IP11D2, *Opera* II/52–3). That reason may lie either in the nature of the thing or in something outside it. He gives God as an example of something whose nature (as substance) explains its existence, and a square circle as an example of something whose nature (as involving a contradiction) explains its non-existence. In the case of things whose nature neither requires nor precludes their existence, such as a particular triangle, the cause will be 'the order of the whole of corporeal nature', which necessitates either that the thing exist at the particular time it does (if it exists), or that it not exist at that time (if it does not).

None of the three paradigm 'rationalists' limits himself to explaining only things which come into being and pass away. Leibniz, for example, writes that it is a consequence of the principle of sufficient reason that

> there is a reason even for eternal things. If someone were to suppose that the world had been from eternity, and that there were only little spheres in it, a reason would have to be given why there were little spheres rather than cubes. (*Philosophical Essays*, pp. 31–2; Couturat, *Opuscules et fragments*, p. 519)

Similarly, Descartes insists that we can give a reason why the eternal truths (notably, the laws of mathematics and physics) are true. The reason seems to be different in different places: sometimes he claims to derive laws of physics from God's immutability (e.g. in *The World*, ch. vii, *Œuvres de Descartes*, vol. XI, pp. 36–45); sometimes he says that God lays down the eternal truths 'just as a king lays down laws in his kingdom' (to Mersenne, 15 April 1630, *Œuvres de Descartes*, vol. I, p. 145). The

derivation of the infinite modes from the absolute nature of the divine attributes in Spinoza (*Ethics* IPP21–3) is analogous to this, though, of course, Spinoza rejects any notion that these eternal things might be explained by an act of the divine will (*Ethics* IP31, P32C1, *Opera* II/71–3). So, for example, the principle of inertia is not a law God decrees in the manner of a king; it is a principle which follows from the nature of extension (cf. *Opera* II/97–8).

One further respect in which Descartes and Spinoza, at least, interpret the principle of sufficient reason in an unusually strong sense is that to constitute an explanation for the existence of a thing, the cause must be a logically sufficient condition of its effect (i.e. it must be impossible for the cause to exist and the effect not exist). This requirement appears in Spinoza's comparison of the causal relationship to that between the nature of a triangle and its properties (e.g. in *Ethics* IP17S, *Opera* II/62), and in Descartes' insistence that, even if a finite thing had always existed, it would require God's preservation in order to continue in existence from one moment to the next, since a thing's existence at one moment does not follow from its existence at the previous moment (*Œuvres de Descartes*, vol. VII, pp. 48–9).

Leibniz does not consistently follow Descartes and Spinoza in imposing this requirement on causality. Sometimes he uses his theory of truth to explain the principle of sufficient reason. For example, in the paper 'Primary truths' (*Philosophical Essays*, pp. 30–4, *Opuscules et fragments*, pp. 518–23), he argues that there must be a reason for everything, because otherwise there would be a truth which was not capable of being resolved into an identity statement. If Leibniz had always written in this manner, we might attribute to him the view that (as in Descartes and Spinoza) a cause must be a logically sufficient condition of its effect, since everything true of finite things (except their existence) would follow from their essences.

But Leibniz is eager to distinguish his position from Spinoza's, and one way he does that is to make a distinction between geometrical and metaphysical reasons, which necessitate, and physical and moral reasons, which merely 'incline without necessitating' (e.g. *New Essays*, pp. 178–9). To take a crucial case, the existence of this world is explicable by the facts that God was its creator, that he is supremely good, and that this is the best of all possible worlds. A mind which knew those facts would be able to predict the existence of this world with certainty on that information alone. But the existence of this world is not necessitated by those facts, since other worlds are consistently describable, and hence possible (e.g. *Textes inédits*, pp. 289f.). Some students of Leibniz doubt whether this is a coherent position (for an interesting defence of Leibniz, see Adams's contribution to Hooker, 1982); but it certainly displays a conception of explanation according to which a cause is not a logically sufficient condition of its effect.

The strong conception of causality which Descartes and Spinoza embrace has its own problems. If a cause must be a logically sufficient condition of its effect in order to explain it, then it is, to say the least, dubious that any of the finite things we ordinarily take to be causes qualify. To all appearance, they lack the requisite necessary connection with their effects. There is no contradiction in supposing that, when one billiard ball encounters another on the table, the second ball should immediately fly straight up into the air, rather than begin to move smoothly toward the cushion. The only putative cause available which could supply a logically sufficient condition is the will of an omnipotent being. Insistence on this conception of cause provides one motive for the occasionalism of MALEBRANCHE (cf. *The Search After Truth*, Bk VI, Pt ii, ch. 3; and Nadler, 1993, *passim*). Though the seeds of occasionalism are present in Descartes's metaphysics, and many of his followers did deny causal efficacy to *all* finite things, he probably did not intend to commit himself to that conclusion. (For discussion, see Garber's contribution to Nadler, 1993.)

In Spinoza this problem is typically presented in the form: how can God, who is infinite and eternal, be the cause of beings which are finite, changeable, and of limited duration, if a cause must be a logically sufficient condition of its effect? If the cause is eternal, and the effect follows logically from it, how can the effect not be eternal? The answer favoured here is that Spinoza does not take God, in so far as he is infinite and eternal, to be what he would call the adequate cause of finite things. God, in so far as he is infinite and eternal, is an adequate cause only of things which are also infinite and eternal, the infinite modes of *Ethics* IPP21–3. With respect to finite things, an adequate explanation must also include (in addition to statements about God's essence, or about things which follow from it alone) reference to the infinite series of other finite things, the finite modes of IP28. Since Spinoza associates God, in so far as he is infinite, with the laws of nature (cf. *Ethics* vol. III, Preface), we can understand this feature of the system to be a reflection of the fact that laws alone, though necessary in any explanation, do not by themselves suffice to explain any particular instantiation of them, that reference to antecedent conditions is also necessary to have an adequate explanation of a particular fact. (For further discussion, see Curley, 1969, ch. ii, and 1988, ch. i.)

If this way of understanding Spinoza is correct, then there is, in the end, an element of contingency even in this most necessitarian of systems. For though, on this reading of Spinoza, there may be an adequate explanation for any particular fact, there is no adequate explanation for the totality of particular facts (the total series of finite things). The existence of that series cannot follow from the nature of God, in so far as he is infinite, unless its individual members do. They do not, so it does not. The existence of that series thus stands without an explanation. Some think this abandons a deep commitment (cf. Bennett, 1984, ch. v); others do not (cf. Curley, 1969, ch. 3, 1988, ch. i).

But there seems to be no 'rationalist'

system in which that dream is not abandoned at some point. As we have seen, in Leibniz's system the goodness of the world merely inclines God to create it. It does not necessitate his doing so. And though Descartes thinks many things explicable which other philosophers might think beyond explanation – not merely the existence of finite, changeable things, but even the eternal truths and the existence of God – he does insist that there can be no reason for any act of the divine will and he often seems to treat acts of the human will as similarly contingent (*Œuvres de Descartes*, vol. VII, pp. 431–3, vol. VIII. 1, 19–20). If we understand by 'metaphysical rationalist' someone whose system admits no contingency whatever, then it is doubtful that anyone is a metaphysical rationalist either.

See also EMPIRICISM; OCCASION, OCCASIONALISM.

BIBLIOGRAPHY

Bennett, J.: *A Study of Spinoza's ETHICS* (Cambridge, MA: Hackett, 1984).

Couturat, L.: *Opuscules et fragments inédits de Leibniz* (Hildesheim: Georg Olms, 1961).

Curley, E.: *Spinoza's Metaphysics* (Boston: Harvard University Press, 1969).

Curley, E.: *Behind the Geometrical Method* (Princeton, NJ: Princeton University Press, 1988).

Descartes, R.: *Œuvres de Descartes* ed. C. Adam and P. Tannery, rev. edn (Paris: Vrin/CNRS, 1964–76). The pagination of this edition is given in the margins of the standard English edition of Descartes' works, *The Philosophical Writings of Descartes* trans. J. Cottingham, R. Stoothoff and D. Murdoch (Cambridge: Cambridge University Press, 1985).

Hooker, M. ed.: *Leibniz: Critical and Interpretive Essays* (Minneapolis: University of Minnesota Press, 1982).

Leibniz, G.W.: *Textes inédits* ed. G. Grua (Paris: 1948).

Leibniz, G.W.: *New Essays on Human Understanding* trans. P. Remnant and J. Bennett (Cambridge: Cambridge University Press, 1981).

Leibniz, G.W.: *Philosophical Essays* trans. R. Ariew and D. Garber (Cambridge, MA: Hackett, 1989).

Nadler, S. ed.: *Causation in Early Modern Philosophy* (Pennsylvania State University Press, 1993).

Spinoza, B.: *Opera*, ed. C. Gebhardt (Heidelberg: C. Winter, 1925). The pagination of this edition is given in the margins of the standard English edition of Spinoza's works, *The Collected Works of Spinoza* trans. E. Curley, Princeton, Princeton University Press, 1985).

EDWIN CURLEY

realism Contemporary discussion of realism derives via a complex route from the post-Kantian dispute between realists and idealists, and still less directly from the scholastic dispute between realists and nominalists. For the medievals, the question was whether UNIVERSALS exist 'outside the mind'; for nineteenth-century philosophers, it was whether the world as a whole is mind-independent. No contemporary philosopher can be entirely satisfied with the terms in which these debates were framed. Indeed, although currently it is widely felt that something of real importance *is* at stake in these longstanding controversies (in contrast to LOGICAL POSITIVISM's dismissal of them as pseudo-problems) philosophical attention has recently shifted to the problem of saying what this might be.

Historical debates yield a variety of vague formulations, images and intuitions, but how these notions might be made clear enough for fruitful investigation and whether there is a uniform way of characterizing realism remain to be seen. For example, one central realist image is of a world that is there *anyway*, independently of us. But this image, even if it could be made more definite, would not suit realism about mental states. Another common image in realist thought is that of an area of inquiry in which the truth can outstrip even our best epistemic accomplishments. But some moral realists might insist that it is constitutive of moral truth that it be accessible, and a realist about mental states might think that some beliefs, for example, about whether one is currently in pain, are incorrigible. Contemporary philosophers typically discuss realism in piecemeal fashion – realism about the external world, about mathematics, about the theoretical entities of physics, about moral properties, and so on. Somewhat different images prevail across these various debates. In what follows, we will nonetheless attempt some clarification of 'realism about X' where X may be any philosophically significant region of discourse, although we recognize it to be controversial whether such generalization is possible. One way to attempt to capture realism is through a progressive taxonomy. Let us begin as follows.

TRUTH-EVALUABILITY

A realist about X holds that discourse about X is apt for truth or falsity. At this level in the taxonomy, the realist's opposite number is the *non-cognitivist* or *non-factualist*, who holds that seeming statements about X do not function in a genuinely descriptive way – do not, despite appearances, actually say what sorts of things there are or actually ascribe properties – but rather have some other linguistic function.

Non-cognitivism has been most fully explored in ethics, where the seemingly intrinsic normativity of the discourse lends credibility to an interpretation of moral claims as something like imperatives or expressive manifestations of the speaker's convictions, the primary function of which is not description but the mutual shaping of attitudes and behaviour (see Ayer, 1946; Blackburn, 1984; Gibbard, 1990). Non-cognitivist approaches have also been advocated in various areas where the speaker's own motivation is less central, though normativity persists: in the philosophy of logic and mathematics, where statements have been assimilated to *rules* (see Dummett, 1978; Wittgenstein, 1956); in the philoso-

phy of modality, where it has been proposed that 'Married bachelors are impossible' really means something like 'Let no evidence confirm the claim that x is a married bachelor'; and in the philosophy of science, where scientific laws or theories have been interpreted as inference rules or licenses.

Non-cognitivists maintain that we should not be misled by the surface structure of a bit of language to posit a peculiar domain of facts. Since they typically claim to be understanding this bit of language as it actually functions, they therefore bear the burden of explaining how non-assertoric speech acts could have the full grammar and logic of ordinary cognitive discourse (see Blackburn, 1984; Geach, 1960; Gibbard, 1990). This has proved no easy task: moral statements, for example, are entirely well behaved with respect to the truth predicate, embedding and inference. These difficulties for non-cognitivism, along with the increasingly influential view that it is a misunderstanding of the truth predicate to deny its literal applicability to sentences in declarative form (*see* THEORIES OF TRUTH), have led many who wish to raise questions about realism with respect to X to accept the bare factuality of *discourse* about X while displacing the issue of the 'reality' of X on to another ground.

ERROR THEORIES

One such ground is whether the discourse, even if cognitive, successfully describes actuality. One paradigm here is the atheist who does not deny that theistic statements are genuine statements – religious believers do manage to make claims about the way the world is – but who insists that such statements are systematically false. J.L. Mackie (1977) revived interest in error theories of this kind by contending that moral discourse genuinely purports to describe objectively prescriptive states of affairs, but lacks reality because no such states of affairs exist.

Agnostic variants of error theories are also possible. Bas van Fraassen's (1980) influential reformulation of EMPIRICISM rejects the non-cognitive semantics of instrumentalism and holds that scientific theories should instead be given a realist interpretation – such theories are genuinely committed to the existence of electrons, viruses, space-time, etc.; but he argues on epistemic grounds that we have no reason to believe such theories, except in so far as we believe only the weaker claim that they are empirically adequate.

Error theorists may further be classified by the remedy they recommend. *Eliminativists* urge that the discourse and its peculiar commitments be abandoned. This is the atheist's usual stance toward theology, and philosophers in this century have advocated such remedies for discourse about CAUSATION, modality (*see* MODALITIES AND POSSIBLE WORLDS), meaning, and the mind, though it has been less clear that we can do without these notions than that of God, and, in the cases of mind and meaning especially, the threat of incoherence looms. *Revisionists* recommend some modification of the discourse to purge problematic commitments while preserving something like its current functions. Mackie thus recommends that we continue to moralize, but cease thinking of moral demands as objective features of the world. Whether such revisionism is stable – whether the functions of an area of discourse depend upon its problematic commitments – requires case-by-case investigation. Finally, *fictionalists* recommend that we preserve existing discourse with its standard meaning, but abandon belief that the theories we accept in this area are literally true. For such a view to be stable and non-revisionary, inquiry in the area in question must not really aim at true theories, but only at theories with certain virtues. In van Fraassen (1980), the virtue is fidelity to the realm of observables.

MINIMAL REALISM

A philosopher who holds of an area of discourse (1) the semantic thesis that it is apt for truth or falsity; (2) the epistemic thesis that we have good reason to believe our theories in the area not to be gravely in error; and (3) the pragmatic thesis that the relevant area of inquiry aims at descriptive truth (rather than, say, displaying some useful fiction), has some claim to be a minimal realist about that area of discourse.

Minimal realism is pretty minimal, and in particular does not entail a number of theses recently identified with realism by various writers. A minimal realist need not hold that the area of discourse in question obeys the Law of the Excluded Middle (though it might), or that our theories in this area are essentially 'evidence transcendent' (though they might be), or that these theories are 'largely true' (as opposed, say, to something like 'approximately true in significant respects' or perhaps 'making good progress'). Stronger positions would result from adding one or more such theses to minimal realism, though the warrant for calling the resulting position a stronger *realism* may be less clear in some cases than others. (For some discussion of these stronger realisms, see Dummett, 1978; Leplin, 1984; Wright, 1987.) But two possible ways of making for a less minimal view call for special comment, since they seem manifestly relevant to underlying realist concerns: reducibility and objectivity.

REDUCTIONISM

Minimal realism as sketched above is compatible with a reductionist construal of the discourse in question (*see* REDUCTION, REDUCTIONISM), yet some have considered resistance to reduction – resistance, say, to PHENOMENALISM about physical objects or to behaviourism about the mind – to be a hallmark of realism.

It might be said that such phenomenalist or behaviourist reductions do not afford a sufficiently *literal* construal of the discourse in question to qualify as realist. For the phenomenalist, 'cat' turns out to refer to sense-contents or to be a syncategorematic expression playing some complex, non-denoting role in a scheme assigning phenomenalist truth conditions to whole sentences. Hardly a paradigm of realism about cats! But 'literal' cannot be much help here

435

without further clarification. It cannot simply mean 'non-reductionist' without ushering in the unpromising view that the (arguable) reducibility of folk discourse about table salt to chemical discourse about NaCl must bring with it anti-realism about the former. But the reduction of table salt to NaCl is not, on the dominant view, analytic, in contrast to the dominant forms of philosophical phenomenalism and behaviourism. And surely part of what pulls us in the direction of seeing philosophical phenomenalism, for example, as non-literal – and non-realist – about physical objects is that it seems to deny us not only our ordinary view of what constitutes physical objects but also our ordinary understanding of physical-object language. Yet even in cases of non-analytic reduction, issues about realism arise. Does quantum mechanics permit us our ordinary view about whether there *are* physical objects at all?

MIND-INDEPENDENCE AND OBJECTIVITY

Is a minimal realism that involves no problematic reduction sufficiently robust to earn the title 'realist'. That this is not so is strongly suggested by the fact that such a view is compatible with various traditional forms of idealism. Of course, compatibility with PLATO'S IDEALISM would not be a worry – Plato is heartily realist about the Forms. But KANT might be another matter.

Consider Kant's view of empirical objects in space and time. Kant does not claim that such talk is reducible to talk of sensations, nor does he deny that statements about such objects are often true. Yet in his insistence that space and time are forms of intuition 'imposed' upon things by the mind, and hence that spatio-temporal objects are, though 'empirically real', 'transcendentally ideal', Kant is widely taken as having rejected the realism about nature characteristic of LOCKE or DESCARTES.

Perhaps what minimal realism, even when non-reductionist, fails thus far to capture is the frequent realist insistence that the discourse in question concerns a *mind-independent* domain of facts. But as we have already noted, such insistence cannot be part of a realism about mental states, or for that matter, about artefacts, 'social facts', and the like. Nor is the requisite contrasting idea of 'dependence' clear, even if we restrict attention to the physical world: surely Kant did not hold that empirical objects are causally or counterfactually dependent upon minds.

The issue is better put in terms of OBJECTIVITY or *explanation*. A realist about the mind, for example, will not insist that mental states are in no way subjective; but a realist will hold that they are *also* in some sense objective. The mind is 'there to be discovered' rather than constituted by our opinion of it or invented by our inquiry into it. This sort of objectivity would be present even for beliefs (if such there be) which, if held, are necessarily correct. Sometimes this thought is put in terms of an 'order of explanation' thesis: suppose it to be true that I am of the opinion that I am in pain if, and only if, I actually am in pain; nonetheless, the reality of the pain might explain the opinion, rather than the other way around. Sometimes, too, this realist notion is expressed by saying that truth is correspondence, or must be 'radically non-epistemic' if it is to play the proper role in the 'best explanation' of our experience. The challenge to any account of that objectivity which would augment minimal realism to make the sought-for contrast with transcendental idealism is to convert these notions of explanation or truth into more definite theses while escaping triviality. After all, a sophisticated idealism about an area of discourse characteristically seeks to preserve its claims, including claims about truth and explanation. If we fall back at this point on the idea that the idealist cannot preserve such claims *in their literal sense* – without, say, draining the notions of truth or explanation of content – then we may have lost the prospect of using these claims to characterize literalness.

BURDENS OF PROOF

It is sometimes thought that the difficulty realists have had in formulating a definite thesis should embarrass them out of their expansive claims. Indeed, some philosophical critics of realism claim to be realists themselves, only without gratuitous metaphysical baggage (see Putnam, 1978). But there is embarrassment enough to go around: critics who would preserve our discourse even with respect to truth and explanation are equally hard pressed to say what the point or content of their alternatives might be. Inchoately, perhaps, modesty has played a large role in debates over realism: the realist wishes to be modest about human powers, to recognize that there might be more to the world than what we can make or know; the critic of realism asks whether an appropriately modest view of language and inquiry would show this conception of 'the world' to be plagued with problems of semantic or epistemic access – at best excessive, at worst incoherent or inexpressible.

See also FACT; IDEALISM; NOMINALISM; OBJECTIVITY.

BIBLIOGRAPHY

Ayer, A.J.: *Language, Truth, and Logic* 2nd edn. (London: Gollancz, 1946).

Blackburn, S.: *Spreading the Word* (Oxford: Clarendon, 1984).

Dummett, M.: *Truth and Other Enigmas* (Cambridge: Harvard University Press, 1978), esp. the essays 'Wittgenstein's philosophy of mathematics' and 'Realism'.

Geach, P.T.: 'Ascriptivism', *The Philosophical Review* 69 (1960), 221–5.

Gibbard, A.: *Wise Choices, Apt Feelings* (Cambridge: Harvard University Press, 1990).

Leplin, J. ed.: *Scientific Realism* (Berkeley: University of California Press, 1984).

Mackie, J.L.: *Ethics: Inventing Right and Wrong* (New York: Penguin, 1977).

Putnam, H.: *Meaning and the Moral Sciences* (London: Routledge and Kegan Paul, 1978).

Van Fraassen, B.C.: *The Scientific Image* (Oxford: Clarendon, 1980).

Wittgenstein, L.: *Remarks on the Foundations of Mathematics* trans. G.E.M. Anscombe (Oxford: Blackwell, 1956).

Wright, C.: *Realism, Meaning and Truth* 2nd edn. (Oxford: Oxford University Press, 1987).

PETER RAILTON
GIDEON ROSEN

reason   The term 'reason' is often used in a broad or honorific sense to designate all of the 'higher' cognitive functions, especially as these are distinguished from sense perception, from passion, or from assent through religious faith or authority. In its narrower sense, however, 'reason' properly designates the specifically inferential or argumentative faculty or faculties; and in this sense, reason may also be distinguished from representational and intuitive faculties as well. Philosophers and logicians have commonly distinguished the functions of reason into demonstrative and probable reasoning (based on the degree of certainty that results) or, more recently, into deductive and inductive reasoning (based on the form of the inference). It has also been common to distinguish between speculative reason (serving to produce and regulate belief) and practical reason (serving to produce and regulate action).

Because metaphysics is often thought to demand knowledge of the real structure of the universe of a kind that goes beyond the appearances of sensory EXPERIENCE, reason (in both the broad sense and the narrow sense) is often regarded as one of the primary and most distinctive tools of metaphysics. Accordingly, metaphysicians frequently appeal to doctrines about the nature, scope and operation of reason in order to defend their characterizations of the methods and results of metaphysics. KANT's development of his distinctive metaphysics through his *Critique of Pure Reason* (1781, 1787) and *Critique of Practical Reason* (1788) is one notable and particularly systematic example of this procedure.

BIBLIOGRAPHY

Blanshard, B.: *Reason and Analysis* (La Salle, IL: Open Court, 1964).

Hume, D.: *A Treatise of Human Nature* (London: 1739–40); ed. L.A. Selby-Bigge (Oxford: Clarendon Press, 1888); 2nd edn rev. P.H. Nidditch (Oxford: Clarendon Press, 1978).

Kant, I.: *Critique of Pure Reason* (Riga: 1781) 2nd edn (1787); ed. and trans. by N. Kemp Smith (New York: St Martin's Press, 1969).

Kant, I.: *Critique of Practical Reason* (Riga: 1788); ed. and trans. by L.W. Beck, 3rd edn (New York: Macmillan, 1993).

Locke, J.: *An Essay concerning Human Understanding* (London: 1690); ed. P.H. Nidditch (Oxford: Clarendon Press, 1975).

Plato: *Republic* ed. and trans. G.M.A. Grube, rev. C.D.C. Reeve (Indianapolis, IN: Hackett, 1992).

DON GARRETT

reduction, reductionism Reduction is the absorption or subsumption of one theory, conceptual scheme, or mode of discourse by another. The notion of reduction is employed in a number of family-resemblance ways relevant to metaphysics, involving three interrelated dimensions or axes: ontological, semantic and scientific. Ontologically reductionist positions typically assert that there are systematic *identities* between entities, kinds, properties and facts posited respectively in the 'higher-level' discourse and in the 'lower-level', reducing, discourse. Semantically reductionist positions typically assert that there are systematic *semantic equivalences* between statements in the higher-level and in the lower-level discourse. Scientific reductionist positions typically assert that the laws and phenomena described in some scientific theory or theories are systematically *explainable* by those described in some other scientific theory.

Semantically reductionist projects have often been viewed as a major means of implementing ontological reductions. An example is *logicism* in philosophy of mathematics. Semantically, the logicist maintains that all the key concepts and terms of classical mathematics are definable via the terms and concepts of logic and set theory, in such a way that all of pure mathematics is derivable (under these definitions) from logic plus fundamental assumptions about classes. (Logicists like FREGE and RUSSELL considered set theory part of logic.) This definitional reduction, says the logicist, effects an *ontological* reduction of all the entities posited in pure mathematics to classes (*see* CLASS, COLLECTION, SET).

Another semantically reductionist position often linked to ontological reductionism is PHENOMENALISM. Semantically, the phenomenalist maintains that every meaningful statement is equivalent to some statement about immediate EXPERIENCE, actual or possible. Ontologically, this position sometimes has been regarded as undergirding metaphysical IDEALISM – i.e. as effecting an ontological reduction of everything real to something mental.

Scientifically reductionist projects, too, often have been viewed as a way to implement ontological reductions – although normally not by means of semantic equivalence relations. In philosophy of science, the received view is that reduction involves empirical, a posteriori hypotheses asserting systematic *identities* between items in the ontologies of the reduced theory and the reducing theory: the reduced theory gets explained by being shown derivable from the reducing theory together with these identity hypotheses. Thus, scientific reduction is standardly regarded as a species of ontological reduction.

Paradigm examples of scientific reduction have a PART/WHOLE aspect: laws and phenomena involving complex wholes are explained in terms of laws and phenomena involving the parts of which those wholes are composed. (This is called *micro*-reduction.) A frequently cited example is the micro-reduction of classical thermodynamics to statistical molecular mechanics. The key empirical hypothesis is that a gas's temperature is identical to its mean molecular kinetic energy. From this identity statement, together with the principles of molecular mechanics, the principles of thermodynamics can be derived – e.g. the Boyle/Charles law, asserting that a gas's temperature is directly proportional to its pressure and inversely proportional to its volume.

A variety of reductionist positions have been advocated in recent metaphysics. Often these are regarded as articulating a naturalist metaphysical stance toward their subject matter (see NATURALISM). In philosophy of mind, for instance, it has been claimed that human psychology is micro-reducible to neurobiology – and that this reductionist thesis articulates a physicalist, or materialist, conception of the mental (see PHYSICALISM, MATERIALISM). More generally, it has been claimed that each of the 'special sciences' is micro-reducible to some other science, and hence (since micro-reduction is transitive) that all the special sciences are ultimately micro-reducible to fundamental microphysics. (This UNITY OF SCIENCE hypothesis is often regarded as articulating a general physicalist/materialist metaphysics.) And in meta-ethics, it has been claimed (1) that there are genuine, objective, moral properties and facts (so-called *moral realism*); and (2) that these are reducible to properties and facts describable in the non-moral language of science.

Such reductionist positions all have serious philosophical critics, many of whom would still profess an allegiance to a broadly naturalist – indeed, perhaps to a broadly physicalist or materialist – metaphysical worldview. In philosophy of mind, for instance, it is often argued that psycho-physical reductionism runs afoul of the evident physical possibility that mental properties might be *multiply realizable* physico-chemically, either across species of creatures with radically different physical constitutions, or even within single creatures: realizable in

humans by certain physico-chemical properties only instantiable in organic matter, and in silicon-based Martians by quite different physico-chemical properties only instantiable in silicon; or realizable in humans, say, by a variety of distinct physico-chemical properties. Multiple realizability would block the co-extensiveness of mental and physical predicates (in certain physically POSSIBLE WORLDS, at least, if not in the actual world), and hence would block reductive property identities (*see* EXTENSION/INTENSION). Likewise, in philosophy of science it is sometimes claimed that the properties posited in higher-level sciences are *in general* multiply realizable by various distinct lower-level properties. Such arguments tend to fuel the ongoing dialectical interplay between philosophers' pre-theoretic understanding of physicalism, materialism and naturalism and their attempt to give that understanding an adequate theoretical articulation. But by the same token, since the pre-theoretic notion of reduction seems to mesh well with these positions as pre-theoretically understood, there is also ongoing dialectical pressure to develop revised, liberalized, articulations of reduction itself.

BIBLIOGRAPHY

Causey, R.: 'Attribute identities in micro-reduction', *Journal of Philosophy* 69 (1972), 407–22.

Fodor, J.A. 'Special sciences – or the disunity of science as a working hypothesis', *Synthese* 28 (1974), 97–115.

Hellman, G. and Thompson, F.: 'Physicalism: ontology, determination, and reduction', *Journal of Philosophy* 72 (1975), 551–64.

Kemeny, J.G. and Oppenheim, P.: 'On reduction', *Philosophical Studies* 7 (1956), 6–19.

Nagel, E.: *The Structure of Science* (New York: Harcourt, Brace, and World, 1961).

Oppenheim, P. and Putnam, H.: 'Unity of science as a working hypothesis', in *Minnesota Studies in the Philosophy of Science* vol. 2, ed. H. Feigl, M. Scriven and

G. Maxwell (Minneapolis: University of Minnesota Press, 1958), 3–36.

Putnam, H.: 'On properties', in *Essays in Honor of Carl G. Hempel* ed. N. Rescher (Dordrecht: Reidel, 1969), 235–54.

Quine, W.V.: 'Ontological reduction and the world of numbers', *Journal of Philosophy* 61 (1964), 209–16.

Shaffner, K.: 'Approaches to reduction', *Philosophy of Science* 34 (1967), 137–47.

Sklar, L.: 'Types of inter-theoretic reduction', *British Journal for the Philosophy of Science* 17 (1967), 109–24.

TERENCE E. HORGAN

reference Ordinarily we speak of reference as the relation between a person, *qua* user of language, and what that person is talking (or writing) about. We say, for example, that with the English word 'China' one typically refers to China. In philosophy, however, a technical sense of 'reference' has evolved to designate the relation between words themselves and what, in using those words, one would be talking about. We say, in that sense, that it is 'China' that refers to the country.

The main philosophical problem of reference is to characterize the phenomenon – that is, to say what 'refers' means – and (what may or may not come to the same thing) to characterize the underlying nature of the reference relation. Focusing our attention on the technical notion and on the paradigm case of reference by names, contemporary discussion begins with the *description theory* of FREGE (1892), according to which names are synonymous with definite descriptions. The idea, more specifically, is that whenever a name is used the speaker has in mind a description, 'The such and such', which expresses what, on that occasion, is to be meant by the name; and its referent, if any, is whatever single object satisfies that description. Thus, by 'China' one might mean 'The most populous country', in which case one's utterance of 'China' would refer to whichever happens to be the most populous country. This view

explains the reference of names in terms of the reference of definite descriptions, which must in turn be explained in terms of the reference of the elements of those descriptions: namely, simple predicates such as 'country' and 'populous'. But, besides maintaining that the reference of a predicate is determined by its sense, Frege had little to say about how such reference takes place.

RUSSELL (1905) agreed that ordinary names abbreviate definite descriptions; but, unlike Frege, he held that such descriptions are to be analysed away (by means of the schema: 'The such and such is *F*' means 'Only one thing is such and such, and it is *F*'); so he concluded that definite descriptions, and hence ordinary names, cannot refer. What do refer, according to Russell (1911), are simple predicates (and certain demonstratives). But, on the question of how this happens, Russell is barely more explicit than Frege: supposedly we are able to become 'acquainted' with certain aspects of reality and can then associate words with them. (*See* ACQUAINTANCE.)

An implausible element of the description theory is that allegedly one always has a determinate, unique, definite description in mind, specifying what is meant by a name, and so the sentence predicating this definite description of the bearer of the name will express a necessary truth. For example, by 'Moses' one might mean either 'the man who led the Israelites out of Egypt', or 'the man who as a child was taken out of the Nile by Pharaoh's daughter', or 'the man who received the Ten Commandments on Mt Sinai', etc.; and if it happens to be, say, 'the man who led the Israelites out of Egypt', then the sentence, 'Moses led the Israelites out of Egypt' would express a necessary truth. But surely Moses *might* not have been the man who led the Israelites out of Egypt. Indeed it would seem that none of the above descriptions necessarily applies to him.

In light of this problem, WITTGENSTEIN (1953) and Searle (1958) proposed a modification of the description theory, known as the *cluster theory*, according to which what a person means by a name is specified by a *collection* of descriptions, rather than by a single one. In that case what would be necessary is merely that Moses be *either* the man who led the Israelites out of Egypt *or* the man who received the Ten Commandments *or . . .* , and not that he have any definite one of these characteristics.

However, as Kripke (1972) pointed out, this revision of the description theory does not go deep enough. Suppose, to give one of his examples, the person who really discovered the incompleteness of arithmetic was an obscure mathematician, Schmidt, although Gödel has unfairly been given the credit. In that case, even if the only definite description I can associate with the name 'Gödel' (corresponding to the only definite thing I believe about him) is 'the person who discovered the incompleteness of arithmetic', it would none the less rightly be said of me that I refer to *Gödel* with that name, not to Schmidt, and that my claim 'Gödel discovered that arithmetic is incomplete' is false, not necessarily true. Kripke argued by means of such examples that the reference of a name is not determined by any associated description, or cluster of descriptions, in the mind of its user. Rather, as familiarity with a name spreads within a linguistic community its reference is automatically inherited. That is to say, in coming to use a name, each person refers to the same thing as the person from whom he learned it. As for how the name's reference is established in the first place, Kripke suggested that this may be done by means of a 'baptizing' ostension ('Let *that* be called "*N*" ') or definite description ('Let the such-and-such be called "*N*" ').

Kripke's picture is often taken (for example, by Devitt (1981) and Evans (1982)) to constitute the crude outline of a *causal theory of reference*, according to which, '*x* refers to *y* if, and only if, C(*x, y*)', where *C* is some causal relation whose precise character still awaits theoretical elucidation. And, along similar lines, causal accounts of predicate reference have been proposed by Dretske (1981), Fodor (1987) and Stampe (1977).

An alternative to both description and causal approaches is the so-called *deflationary (minimal) theory* (Horwich, 1990), according to which the meaning of 'refers' and the nature of reference are implicitly captured by the trivial schemata, 'Name "*N*" refers to a thing if, and only if, that thing is identical to *N*' and 'Predicate "*F*" refers to *being ϕ* if, and only if, $\forall x(Fx \leftrightarrow \Phi x)$'. Such a theory goes hand in hand with the deflationary (redundancy) theory of *truth*. It is associated with the idea that the function and entire *raison d'être* of our notions of reference and truth is to provide devices of semantic ascent, enabling us to avoid substitutional quantification (Quine, 1970). If this is so then no deeper account of reference is called for and none should be expected.

See also THEORIES OF TRUTH.

BIBLIOGRAPHY

Devitt, M.: *Designation* (New York: Columbia University Press, 1981).
Dretske, F.I.: *Knowledge and the Flow of Information* (Cambridge, MA: MIT Press, 1981).
Evans, G.: *The Varieties of Reference* ed. J. McDowell (Oxford: Clarendon Press, 1982).
Fodor, J.: *Psychosemantics* (Cambridge, MA: MIT Press, 1987).
Frege, G.: 'On sense and reference' (1892); in *Translations from the Philosophical Writings of G. Frege* ed. and trans. P. Geach and M. Black (Oxford: Blackwell, 1952).
Horwich, P.G.: *Truth* (Oxford: Blackwell, 1990).
Kripke, S.: 'Naming and necessity', in *Semantics of Natural Language* ed. G. Harman and D. Davidson (Dordrecht: Reidel, 1972), 254–355.
Quine, W.V.: *Philosophy of Logic* (Englewood Cliffs, NJ: Prentice Hall, 1970).
Russell, B.: 'On denoting', *Mind* 14 (1905), 479–93.
Russell, B.: 'Knowledge by acquaintance and knowledge by description', *Proceed-*

ings of the Aristotelian Society 11 (1910–11), 108–28.

Searle, J.R.: 'Proper names', *Mind* 67 (1958), 166–73.

Stampe, D.W.: 'Toward a causal theory of linguistic representation', *Midwest Studies in Philosophy* 2 (1977), 42–63.

Wittgenstein, L.: *Philosophical Investigations* trans. G.E.M. Anscombe (Oxford: Oxford University Press, 1953).

PAUL HORWICH

Reichenbach, Hans (1891–1953) Known chiefly as a philosopher of science, he was one of the two principal founders of logical EMPIRICISM (*see* LOGICAL POSITIVISM). Unlike CARNAP, the other principal founder, Reichenbach was never a member of the Vienna Circle and never in any strict sense a logical positivist; indeed, he considered his major epistemological treatise (1938) a refutation of LOGICAL POSITIVISM. After a short period as a Kantian early in his career, he became a dedicated empiricist and thereafter emphatically rejected the possibility of synthetic a priori knowledge or any form of *speculative* metaphysics (*see* KANTIANISM).

Among the issues involved in Reichenbach's rejection of logical positivism, two are especially relevant in the present context: (1) he adopted a physicalistic (as opposed to phenomenalistic) basis for common-sense and scientific knowledge (*see* PHENOMENALISM; PHYSICALISM, MATERIALISM); and (2) he maintained that the existence of such unobservable entities as atoms could be established empirically; that is, he affirmed scientific REALISM (as opposed to instrumentalism). As these considerations show, he advocated views that would today be called metaphysical, but his metaphysics was thoroughly scientific.

Throughout his career, Reichenbach was deeply concerned with philosophical problems of SPACE AND TIME. A devoted student of Einstein, he argued in his first book on the subject (1920) that the theory of relativity is logically inconsistent with KANT's total set of synthetic a priori propositions about space, time and causality. Because relativity theory is scientifically well-founded, at least some of Kant's synthetic a priori principles must be relinquished.

Reichenbach (1928) is *the classic work* on philosophy of space and time in the first half of the twentieth century. A fundamental problem in this area is the ascertainment of the geometrical structure of physical space. For this purpose, he maintains, we must use some sort of measuring instrument – for example, solid measuring rods – but we face an immediate problem because we cannot ascertain empirically whether such rods retain the same length as they are moved from one place to another. To deal with this situation we introduce *co-ordinative definitions* to establish a relationship between physical entities (measuring rods) and an abstract geometrical relation (congruence). In the absence of such a stipulation we cannot determine whether physical space is Euclidean or non-Euclidean, whether it is curved or not. Alternatively, he maintains, one could choose a geometry – say Euclidean – by convention, in which case the behaviour of the measuring instruments would become a matter of empirical fact. Either way, ascertainment of the geometric structure of physical space involves one matter of convention and one matter of empirical fact.

A central problem about the nature of time concerns the relation of simultaneity within any inertial reference frame. If we wish to synchronize two clocks, at rest with respect to one another but not in spatial proximity, we can send messages back and forth between them. Since, according to relativity theory, no signal or causal influence can travel faster than light, Reichenbach argues, there is a degree of conventionality in the simultaneity relation. This *conventionality* is distinct from, and logically prior to, Einstein's celebrated *relativity* of simultaneity.

At the time of his death, Reichenbach was working on *The Direction of Time* (1956, published posthumously), which he had completed except for a final chapter. In the completed chapters he argued that, although the fundamental laws of nature (*see* LAW OF NATURE) are time symmetric (the violation of time symmetry in elementary particle physics had not been discovered, and does not seriously undermine his main arguments), there is objective temporal asymmetry in the world. It is based on *de facto* conditions rather than nomological necessities. He also argues for the objectivity of temporal becoming.

After giving a microphysical analysis of the direction of time in terms of entropy and the Second Law of Thermodynamics, he extends the argument to the macrophysical level, and offers an analysis of temporal asymmetry on the basis of causal considerations. He enunciates the *principle of the common cause* and maintains that improbable coincidences can be explained in terms of common causes and not by reference to common effects.

In all of his treatments of space and time, Reichenbach maintained a causal theory – i.e. that all spatial and all temporal relations are grounded in causal relations. In *The Direction of Time* he defined a number of causal concepts statistically, and, in so doing, laid the foundations for a theory of probabilistic causality. This topic is under active investigation by a large number of philosophers at present.

WRITINGS

Relativatätstheorie und Erkenntnis Apriori (Berlin: 1920); trans. M. Reichenbach, *The Theory of Relativity and A Priori Knowledge* (Berkeley and Los Angeles: University of California Press, 1969).

Philosophie der Raum-Zeit-Lehre (Berlin and Leipzig: 1928); trans. M. Reichenbach and J. Freund, *The Philosophy of Space and Time* (New York: Dover, 1958).

Experience and Prediction (Chicago: University of Chicago Press, 1938).

The Direction of Time (Berkeley and Los Angeles: University of California Press, 1956).

WESLEY C. SALMON

Reid, Thomas (1710–96) The foremost Scottish critic of his day of the metaphysics of HUME. He was a founder of the Aberdeen Philosophical Society, which discussed the work of Hume in such detail that Reid once wrote to Hume that he hoped that Hume would not stop writing for, if he did, they would have nothing to discuss. Reid describes Hume as the greatest metaphysician of the age. Reid concluded, however, that Hume had reduced to absurdity what Reid called the *ideal* theory by drawing forth the conclusions of this theory. The theory is that what is immediately before the mind is always some impression or IDEA, and Reid thought that Hume had shown that it led to scepticism and the rejection of common-sense convictions concerning mind, matter and causality. This led Reid to rise to the defence of common sense, but Reid understood full well that one could not refute a philosophical theory simply by noting the absurdity of the consequences thereof. More was required, to wit, the construction of an alternative philosophy consistent with the principles of common sense. Noting the absurdities to which Hume's philosophy leads, Reid suggests that we need not despair of a better. He set out, in opposition to Hume, to construct an alternative metaphysics.

Reid's metaphysics is interwoven with his psychology and epistemology. He argued for his metaphysics by first defending common sense. His defence was based on the assumption that our faculties, which produce conception and belief in response to sensation and stimulation of the organs of sense, were trustworthy and not fallacious. His justification for assuming this in reply to Hume was that Hume himself had assumed the trustworthiness of some of his faculties, of consciousness and reason. Reid concedes that he has no reply to a sceptic who denies the trustworthiness of all our faculties with respect to the conceptions and convictions they produce. But to Hume who concedes the trustworthiness of some of our faculties, Reid replies that Hume is guilty of inconsistent favouritism toward consciousness and reason. For, Reid argues, these faculties

443

are fallible like the rest, and, therefore, we have no reason to trust the deliverances of those faculties over others, perception, for example. Our faculties are powers of judgement that yield the convictions of common sense, and, Reid maintained, we have no option but to begin by assuming that these convictions are justified until they be proved otherwise.

What is the metaphysics of common sense advocated by Reid? First of all, Reid defended a kind of symmetry thesis with respect to mind and body in defence of dualism (see MIND/BODY PROBLEM). He held that we perceive a material world external to ourselves and are conscious of an internal world of the mind within. Our convictions of the existence of material objects without and a mind within must be accepted as the starting point in philosophy or we shall be led to total scepticism. These convictions concern the existence of the qualities of objects, their shapes, colours and smells, for example, and the conviction that something has these qualities. Reid distinguished between primary and secondary qualities, not on the basis of resemblance of some sensation or idea to an external quality, for Reid agreed with BERKELEY that there is no such resemblance, but, instead, on the basis of the clarity and distinctness of our original conceptions of primary qualities as opposed to secondary qualities. We have a clear and distinct conception of movement as change of place from our original perception of it, but our conception of a smell is only a relative conception of the cause of a sensation we experience. Moreover, we cannot help but conceive of these qualities as being the qualities of some object which has them. We have only a relative conception of the object as that which has the qualities, but we have no more reason to doubt the existence of the object than we do to doubt the qualities of the object (see QUALITY, PRIMARY/SECONDARY).

Neither material qualities nor the objects that possess them are ideas or impressions. We have conceptions of the qualities and objects, but our conceptions are simply thoughts and quite distinct from the qualities and objects conceived. Similarly, our conceptions of our own minds are relative conceptions of the thing that has thoughts, or the thing that thinks. So Reid is a dualist with respect to mind and body who maintains that our conceptions of thoughts and minds, qualities and objects, are the result of our trustworthy faculties or innate powers of the mind. He regards our convictions that such things really do exist as the consequence of principles of our faculties that give rise to these conceptions and confer justification upon them.

Reid has two other metaphysical theses of some importance. The first concerns UNIVERSALS and the second CAUSATION. Reid regards it as a basic feature of conception that we can think of things that do not exist, centaurs, for example, and that when we think of such objects, we are not thinking of ideas but of material objects. A centaur, for example, is a being that is half horse and half man and, though such objects do not exist, they are material, not mental. Our conception of a centaur involves a mental act of conceiving, of course, but the object of the act, the centaur, is not mental. The importance of this fact, which Reid says he is embarrassed to insist upon since it is so obvious, emerges when Reid confronts the subject of universals, such as redness, for example. Reid agrees that our knowledge of things depends on the attribution of universals to them, but he denies that universals exist. According to Reid, it is only necessary that we be able to conceive of universals to attribute them to individuals, and, as the example of the centaur illustrates, it is perfectly possible to think of things that do not exist. The only things that exist are individuals. However, Reid is not a simple nominalist, for he contends that individual qualities exist as well as individual objects, that is, particulars. We obtain our conception of universals, such as redness shared by many individuals, by generalizing from our perception of individual qualities, such as the individual quality of the individual smell of a given rose which is shared by nothing else. (*See* NOMINALISM.)

Having denied the existence of universals, it is not surprising that Reid would advance a theory of causality affirming that individuals, agents, are the real causes of things. He maintains that the real causes of things are agents having understanding and will. He concedes that we speak of other things as causes but regards this as an anthropomorphic extension of the concept. His notion of agent causality leads him to a libertarian account of human liberty (*see* FREE WILL). He maintains that our actions arise from acts of will, volitions, but these we determine by an exercise of our agency. Our determinations of our wills ends the chain of causality with the agent as cause. Liberty or freedom requires that it be in our power how we determine and will and, therefore, how we act. It is the individual with understanding and will who has this power, and, consequently, possesses liberty.

The foregoing doctrines are highly compatible with theism, which finds the most basic agency in God. It is God who is responsible for our faculties and our agency. Reid does not, however, suppose, as DESCARTES did, that the justification of our beliefs depends on the premise that God exists, for he acknowledged that people have justified beliefs arising from their natural faculties before they entertain the conception of the deity. Nevertheless, Reid's strong faith surely supported his conviction that our God-given faculties do not deceive us when they lead us to believe in the existence of external objects and causal agents. Whether one accepts Reid's theism or denies it, however, his articulation and defence of the metaphysics of common sense against the metaphysics of Hume combined with his frugal nativist psychology earns Reid a special place in the history of metaphysics.

WRITINGS

An Inquiry into the Human Mind on the Principles of Common Sense (Edinburgh: 1764).

Essays on the Intellectual Powers of Man (Edinburgh: 1785).
Essays on the Active Powers of Man (Edinburgh: 1788).
Thomas Reid's Inquiry and Essays ed. R. Beanblossom and K. Lehrer 2nd edn (Indianapolis, IN: Hackett, 1983); selections from Reid's major works.
The Works of Thomas Reid, D.D. ed. W. Hamilton 8th edn (Edinburgh: James Thin, 1985); complete edition of published works.

BIBLIOGRAPHY

Daniels, N.: *Thomas Reid's Inquiry: The Geometry of Visibles and the Case for Realism* (New York: Burt Franklin, 1974).
Fraser, A.: *Thomas Reid* (Edinburgh and London: Oliphant, Anderson and Ferrier, 1898).
Lehrer, K.: *Thomas Reid* (London and New York: Routledge, 1989); contains full bibliography of primary and secondary sources.
Schulthess, D.: *Philosophie et sens commun chez Thomas Reid* (Berne and New York: Peter Lang, 1984).

KEITH LEHRER

relations The category of relations, ARISTOTLE thought, has the least degree of being. With the discovery of the logic of relations in the nineteenth century, relations came to occupy a more central position in metaphysics than hitherto. Relations can be classified in a number of ways. The degree or adicity of a relation is the number of entities it relates: the relation ascribed by 'Maria is next to Sam' relates two entities, that ascribed by 'Maria is further from Sam than from Tom' three entities, etc.; some relations, such as actions and parthood, have been held to have variable adicity. Relations exhibit different order properties, such as transitivity and asymmetry. Relations are either material – the relations of collision and smiling at – or formal (topic-neutral) – the relations of entailment, being greater than, set membership, exemplification and inherence. Relations are held to be non-repeatable temporal particulars (TROPES, accidents) by some nominalists, and UNIVERSALS or other types of abstract entity such as ordered pairs by anti-nominalists. A relation is external if it need not relate the entities it does relate (Maria need not be next to Sam); if two or more entities must stand in some relation then it is said to be internal (orange must be between yellow and red, 4 must be greater than 3). All INTERNAL RELATIONS, it is sometimes claimed, are formal relations.

See also NOMINALISM; UNIVERSALS AND PARTICULARS.

BIBLIOGRAPHY

Bergmann, G.: 'Russell's examination of Leibniz examined', in Meaning and Existence (Madison: University of Wisconsin Press, 1960).
Campbell, K.: 'Relations, causation, space-time and compresence', in his Abstract Particulars (Oxford: Blackwell, 1990), ch. 5.
Johansson, I.: 'External, internal and grounded relations', in his Ontological Investigations: An Inquiry into the Categories of Nature, Man and Society (London: Routledge, 1989), ch. 8.
Moore, G.E.: 'External and internal relations', in his Philosophical Studies (Paterson, NJ: Littlefield, 1959), 276–309.
Nicod, J.: 'Geometry in the sensible world' (1924); in his Geometry and Induction (Berkeley and Los Angeles: University of California Press, 1970).

KEVIN MULLIGAN

relative identity see IDENTITY

Russell, Bertrand Arthur William (1872–1970) British mathematician, philosopher and social campaigner. Russell's main contributions to metaphysics can be classified as follows.

1. At the turn of the century, Russell took himself to have 'emerged from the bath of German idealism in which [he] had been plunged by McTaggart and Stout' (1967, vol. 1, p. 134), and to have embraced pluralism. This is connected with the doctrine of INTERNAL RELATIONS. The main writings are: The Principles of Mathematics (1903, esp. pp. 221–6), Philosophical Essays (1910a, pp. 139ff.), Our Knowledge of the External World as a Field for Scientific Method in Philosophy (1914a, ch. 2) and 'Logical atomism' (1924, esp. pp. 333–9).

2. Faced with set-theoretic paradoxes, Russell evolved a distinctive and highly original theory of the metaphysics of classes: strictly speaking, there are no such things (and they are not logical constructions out of anything else, either). Given that almost everything in Russell's metaphysics in the early years of the century – mathematical objects, material objects, space, time and people – counted as a class, the 'no-class' theory of classes has very wide-ranging implications. The source is Russell and WHITEHEAD (1910–13), esp. Introduction, ch. 3.

3. In the tradition of the British empiricists (see EMPIRICISM), Russell construed the question 'What is there?' as asking: 'What is it reasonable to believe that there is?' His answer, moved by a traditional epistemology, was reductive: sense data (see SENSA), or some experiential input, are fundamental, and other things – material substances, selves, space, time, etc. – are either causes of sense data or logical constructions out of them. The main writings are: The Problems of Philosophy (1912, chs 1–3), Our Knowledge of the External World (1914a, chs 3, 4), 'The relation of sense data to physics' (1914b), The Philosophy of Logical Atomism (1918b, esp. lecture 8), The Analysis of Matter (1927), Human Knowledge: Its Scope and Limits (1948, esp. ch. 4).

4. Russell believed that there are not really any such things as propositions or mental representations; rather, the mind engages directly with the world. The main writings are: *The Problems of Philosophy* (1912, ch. 12), *Our Knowledge of the External World* (1914a) and *The Philosophy of Logical Atomism* (1918b, esp. lecture 4).

5. As part of his theory of LOGICAL ATOMISM, Russell made a distinctive contribution to the metaphysics of facts. For example, he claimed that there are general facts as well as particular ones, and he was famously indecisive about negative facts. The main source is *The Philosophy of Logical Atomism* (1918b, lectures 1–3).

Since justice cannot be done in this short space to all these aspects of Russell's metaphysics, we will be very selective, concentrating on those which have received less exposure elsewhere.

THERE ARE NO CLASSES

A man, a moment, a number, a class, a relation, a chimera, or anything else that can be mentioned, is sure to be a term. ... Points, instants, bits of matter, particular states of mind, and particular existents generally, are things in the above sense, and so are many terms which do not exist, for example, the points in a non-Euclidean space and the pseudo-existents of a novel. (Russell, 1903, pp. 43, 45)

If metaphysics is the study of being, then the above represents a freewheeling metaphysical view: anything you mention has being. Compare what he wrote barely fifteen years later:

Logic, I should maintain, must no more admit a unicorn than zoology can; for logic is concerned with the real world just as truly as zoology ... A robust sense of reality is very necessary in framing a correct analysis of propositions about unicorns, golden mountains, round squares, and other such pseudo-objects. (1919, pp. 169–70)

We can identify two main shifts of position over this period: first, he rejected the view that there are things which do not exist; second, he became ontologically very cautious, keeping EXISTENCE assumptions to a minimum, partly in order to enhance the prospects of connecting the things we claim exist with our cognitive faculties, conceived in a rather traditional way.

The first shift is officially argued for in 'On denoting' (1905): holding that every intelligible singular term refers to something, though in some cases to something which does not exist, leads to contradictions. For the existing golden mountain does not exist, yet the view in question entails that it does exist; for the view would be committed to counting every instance of 'The *FG* is *F*' as true. (*See* FICTIONAL TRUTH, OBJECTS AND CHARACTERS.)

The second shift was influenced by the discovery of the paradoxes of set theory. These showed him that if one allows that anything one appears to be able to talk about exists, one could end up allowing that the paradoxical class of all non-self-membered classes exists. (*See* CLASS, COLLECTION, SET.)

A standard response to the set-theoretic paradoxes is to weaken the assumptions about what classes exist. This weakening is taken to its extreme in *Principia Mathematica*, whose theory of classes, Russell says, 'avoids the assumption that there are such things as classes' (Russell and Whitehead, 1910–13, vol. 1, p. 187). Since the theory holds that some existential quantifications apparently over classes are true, interpreting Russell's claim is tricky. One natural thought is that the quantifiers are substitutional, but this will help avoid the existence assumptions only if the names through which the quantifiers are defined somehow operate without introducing objects. Arguably, such an interpretation of *Principia Mathematica* is available (see Sainsbury, 1980, sect. 3), although it is questionable whether, thus interpreted, it could do as much justice to arithmetic as Russell thought.

THERE ARE NO PROPOSITIONS

How does the mind make contact with things outside itself? One view is that it is through ideas or representations. Awareness is, in the first instance, awareness of these representations, and only indirectly of what they represent. Such a view of the nature of thought invites sceptical questions (for example, 'how can we tell that what we take to be representations really represent anything?') which in turn invite idealist responses ('We can make no sense of a world beyond what we call the representations').

Although Russell's terminology (certainly) and his views (arguably) are unstable, there is no doubt that for a significant period (at least through the second decade of the century) he offered a view of the mind's relation to the world which, motivated by the threat of IDEALISM, dispenses with the intermediaries of representations or ideas. One manifestation of this is his denial of the existence of propositions (see PROPOSITION, STATE OF AFFAIRS). This does not spring from any nominalistic distaste for abstract objects (see NOMINALISM). Rather, he feels differentially toward true and false propositions. The former one might swallow but 'to suppose that in the actual world of nature there is a whole set of false propositions going about is to my mind monstrous' (1918b, p. 223). Presumably the contrast is this: one who denied ideas or representations could construe true propositions as facts, but he would have no room for false propositions.

This metaphysical view about the mind's relation to the world led to Russell's logical form proposal for belief sentences: a sentence like 'Othello believed that Desdemona loved Cassio' has the logical form of a four-place relation whose terms are, in this order: Othello, Desdemona, *love* and Cassio (see 1912, pp. 72–3). Believing does not involve representing, and the same goes for the other so-called 'propositional attitudes'.

Russell replaced the propositional view of the mind's engagement with the world by the view that in ACQUAINTANCE it engages with at least some things *directly* (without intermediary). The theory of descriptions (see REFERENCE) shows how the scope of thought is greater than the range of things with which we are acquainted; a description can allow us to 'think about' something with which we are not acquainted by thinking of it as the unique instance of a property which we can think about (either by being acquainted with the property, or by constructing it from properties with which we are acquainted). For details consult Russell (1910b).

THERE ARE FACTS

Metaphysical concerns are very much to the fore in his (1918b), the best exposition of Russell's theory of logical atomism. The atoms are momentary sensible qualities, things like 'little patches of colour' (1918b, p. 179). But Russell thinks that if you have itemized all these you have still not given 'a complete description of the world'. Arguably, he does not go far enough: to list the components of the world is not to describe it at all. Russell moves smoothly from the clear truth that you need to say more in order completely to describe the world to the more controversial claim that you need to suppose that more exists than just the atoms, if you are to have a correct view of the world. The latter is more controversial because, arguably, nothing more need exist than *a* and redness for it to be the case that *a* is red: we do not need, in addition, the FACT that *a* is red. However, Russell does allow that facts are somehow different from their constituents (see FACT).

> Facts . . . are not properly entities at all in the same sense in which their constituents are. That is shown by the fact that you cannot name them. You can only deny, or assert, or consider them, but you cannot name them because they

are not there to be named, although in another sense it is true that you cannot know the world unless you know the facts that make up the truths of the world. (1918b, p. 270)

One interesting feature of Russell's account of facts is the distinction he makes among *forms* of facts: 'one might describe philosophical logic . . . as an inventory, or . . . "zoo", containing all the different forms that facts may have' (1918b, p. 216). A taxonomy of facts could be grounded in at least two distinct principles. One is a metaphysical one: as we would put it, and as was urged in WITTGENSTEIN's *Tractatus* (1922), all facts supervene on atomic facts (*see* SUPERVENIENCE). That is, no worlds which agree on the atomic facts could differ on any others. By this standard, conjunctive, disjunctive and universally general facts are merely supervenient. Russell, however, held that universally general facts are in a different category from conjunctive facts. This is because he is applying a different, more epistemological taxonomy: the 'real' or basic facts are those we would need to know, in order to know the world in its entirety. By this standard, conjunctive and disjunctive facts are again unreal or non-basic, but universally general facts are real and basic, for they cannot be known merely on the basis of knowing all the atomic facts. As Russell put it, one would also have to know that these atomic facts are all there are.

WRITINGS

The Principles of Mathematics (Cambridge: Cambridge University Press, 1903).

'On denoting', *Mind* 14 (1905), 479–93; reprinted in his *Essays in Analysis* ed. D. Lackey (London: George Allen and Unwin, 1973), 103–19.

Philosophical Essays (London: Longmans, 1910[a]).

'Knowledge by acquaintance and knowledge by description', *Proceedings of the Aristotelian Society* 11 (1910[b]), 108–28; repr. in his *Mysticism and Logic* (New York: Longmans, 1918[a]; London: George Allen and Unwin, 1963), 152–67.

The Problems of Philosophy (London: Williams and Norgate, 1912; repr. Oxford: Oxford University Press, 1967).

Our Knowledge of the External World as a Field for Scientific Method in Philosophy (Chicago and London: Open Court, 1914[a]; rev. edn London: George Allen and Unwin, 1926).

'The relation of sense-data to physics', *Scientia* 16 (1914[b]), 1–27; repr. in his *Mysticism and Logic* (New York: Longmans, 1918[a]; London: George Allen and Unwin, 1963).

Mysticism and Logic (New York: Longmans 1918[a]); (London: George Allen and Unwin, 1963).

'The philosophy of logical atomism', *Monist* 28 (1918[b]), 29 (1919); repr. in his *Logic and Knowledge* ed. R.C. Marsh (Allen and Unwin, 1956), 177–281.

Introduction to Mathematical Philosophy (London: George Allen and Unwin, 1919).

'Logical atomism', in *Contemporary British Philosophers: Personal Statements* ed. J.H. Muirhead 1st series (London: George Allen and Unwin, 1924), 356–83; repr. in *Logic and Knowledge* ed. R.C. Marsh (London: George Allen and Unwin, 1956), 323–43.

The Analysis of Matter (London: George Allen and Unwin, 1927).

Human Knowledge: Its Scope and Limits (London: George Allen and Unwin, 1948).

The Autobiography of Bertrand Russell 3 vols (London: George Allen and Unwin, 1967–9).

Whitehead, A.N. and Russell, B.: *Principia Mathematica* (Cambridge: Cambridge University Press, 1910–13).

BIBLIOGRAPHY

Ayer, A.J.: *Russell* (London: Fontana, 1972).

Hylton, P.: *Russell, Idealism, and the Emergence of Analytic Philosophy* (Oxford: Clarendon Press, 1990).

Pears, D.: *Bertrand Russell and the British Tradition in Philosophy* (London: Fontana, 1967).

Sainsbury, R.M.: *Russell* (London: Routledge and Kegan Paul, 1979).

Sainsbury, R.M.: 'Russell on constructions and fictions', *Theoria* XLVI (1980), 19–36.

R.M. SAINSBURY

Ryle, Gilbert (1900–76)   Born in Brighton, England, and first as a student and then as a don Ryle, spent all of his academic life at the University of Oxford. He became Waynflete Professor of Metaphysical Philosophy at Oxford in 1945, and editor of the journal *Mind* in 1947. With the possible exception of WITTGENSTEIN he was the most influential figure in British philosophy in the middle years of the twentieth century.

Ryle's earliest papers were in philosophical logic and philosophy of language. They were 'Negation' (1929), 'Are there propositions?' (1930), and 'Systematically misleading expressions' (1932). The latter paper has been described as the first clear statement of the view of philosophy that came to be known as linguistic philosophy or linguistic analysis. In effect it is also Ryle's answer to the question as to what role remained for philosophy given the great advances in empirical science and the emphasis, due in particular to the logical positivists, on the foundational importance in epistemology of the propositions of empirical science (*see* LOGICAL POSITIVISM). Ryle asserted that philosophy should be concerned mainly with language, and believed that an important part of philosophical achievement lay in correcting conceptual mistakes perpetrated by philosophers' mishandling of ordinary language in the course of propounding and defending philosophical theories. Another, more positive, task for philosophers was what he later spoke of as 'conceptual cartography', or the job of getting clear about the relations of CATEGORIES and the concepts falling under them.

Without question Ryle's major contribution to twentieth-century philosophy is *The Concept of Mind* (1949). This book, as Ryle himself described it, is 'a sustained piece of analytical hatchet-work' on the Cartesian account of the relationship between mind and body which he gleefully caricatured as the dogma of the ghost in the machine (*see* DESCARTES; MIND/BODY PROBLEM). Ryle asserted that Cartesian dualism was one large category mistake, namely an incorrect assignment of the terms of our psychological vocabulary to one logico-linguistic category or type when they should be assigned to another. For, after careful philosophical analysis, it would be discovered that our mental terms are not words which describe an inner mental world of faculties with their proprietary activities but are dispositional terms whose attribution depends on the ordinary observation of human behaviour (*see* DISPOSITION). For example, to know and so declare that someone is intelligent is not to base one's claim upon a report of some introspection of an inner mental act performed by an inner mental faculty called 'the intellect', but to base the claim upon an observation that this person is liable or disposed to perform certain sorts of behaviour in certain specifiable circumstances. Thus to say that someone is intelligent is to make an hypothetical attribution about what that person will do if suitable circumstances arise. Because it is said that Ryle arrived at much the same conclusions as did the psychological behaviourists, but for logico-linguistic reasons rather than methodological ones, Ryle is sometimes called a logical behaviourist.

Ryle was not unaware of the limitations of his programme, and was always conscious of having failed to give a convincing account of such paradigmatic mental abilities as doing mental arithmetic or composing a tune in one's head or, in general, doing whatever it was that 'Le Penseur' (Rodin's 'Thinker') was doing. Such mental activities, Ryle acknowledged, are circumstance-disengaged and behaviour free. Thus there is nothing of which a dispositional analysis can take hold. Wishing to avoid both any return to explanations in terms of inner Cartesian mental acts and any hint of dependence upon reference to inner truncated subvocal movements in the muscles of speech, which would lay him open to the experimental falsification which greeted the psychological behaviourists' reliance on this latter account, Ryle toyed with the idea of giving an 'adverbial account'. Such an account worked well enough in the context of practical thinking. Thinking, Ryle argued, was often doing something, such as playing chess or driving a car, thinkingly, that is, with care, attention, self-critically, and in a controlled manner. However, to give an adverbial account of what 'Le Penseur' is doing, one must first nominate some inner activity of which thinking is the modification. This Ryle was never able satisfactorily to do, and he was still wrestling with this problem at the time of his death in 1976. The record of his thinking on this matter was published posthumously as *On Thinking* (1979).

WRITINGS

The Concept of Mind (London: Hutchinson, 1949).

Dilemmas: The Tarner Lectures 1953 (Cambridge: Cambridge University Press, 1954).

Plato's Progress (Cambridge: Cambridge University Press, 1966).

Collected Papers 2 vols (London: Hutchinson, 1971).

On Thinking ed. K. Kolenda (Oxford: Blackwell, 1979).

WILLIAM LYONS

451

S

Santayana, George (1863–1952) American philosopher. In a philosophical career spanning sixty years, Santayana made two major attempts to articulate a naturalistic metaphysics (*see* NATURALISM). The first version, in *The Life of Reason* (1905), is an account, reminiscent of HEGEL though lacking his forced dialectic, of the development of human creative activity. Although he never forgets the natural matrix of human consciousness, Santayana's primary concern here is with how human reason and individual mind express themselves in art, religion, science, society and common sense.

Anthropocentric PHENOMENOLOGY is relegated to the background in the later, ontologically sophisticated version of his naturalism. In *Skepticism and Animal Faith* (1923) and in the four volumes of *The Realms of Being* (1927–40), Santayana sees humans as physical organisms operating in a vast, contingent, non-purposive material universe. In this world, he distinguishes four different sorts of being.

An infinite number of possibilities or *essences* are available for actualization. None has the power to render itself existent; this is accomplished by *matter*, conceived as the arational other of form (*see* POTENTIALITY/ ACTUALITY). The essences creative force (matter) selects for embodiment constitute the realm of *truth*. CONSCIOUSNESS or *spirit* can develop knowledge of the material world by using the essences immediately present to it as signs of independent existents.

Essences are eternal prerequisites of existence, but they do not themselves exist. Matter is first in the order of generation and, although it relies on essence for the qualities and relations of its products, it alone is the source of everything in the spatio-temporal world (*see* MATTER/FORM). Truth is the non-existent but nevertheless real record of all existence. Consisting of a string of cognitive acts, spirit is dependent on living organisms for its occurrence, but retains primacy in the order of knowledge. Mind as direct consciousness is an impotent observer of nature.

Santayana does not think that metaphysics reveals the structure of the COSMOS. The philosophy of animal faith he develops is simply the outcome of reflection on what we tacitly believe when we act. The four realms are irreducibly different sorts of beings that are worth distinguishing. Santayana takes particular care not to confuse being and power, assigning reality to all four realms but efficacy to only one. The concept of God, he argues, emerges from the attempt to unify the incompatible characteristics of knowledge and power in a single being.

Brute contingency dwells at the heart of all existence. To call the source God rather than matter explains nothing. Space and time are relations between events, and both change and persistence derive from matter whose fertile powers escape the scrutiny of perception. Purposiveness is the illusion that consciousness affects the course of events. In reality, all change is 'mechanical' in the sense of being regular and repetitive, though neither necessary nor governed by aims.

Santayana's naturalism has often been called a philosophy of disillusionment. It is indeed pessimistic about human prospects. Nevertheless, it constitutes an eloquent version of modern materialism (*see* PHYSIC-

ALISM, MATERIALISM). It is particularly rich because its insistence on independent truth safeguards OBJECTIVITY and its retention of irreducible mind leaves room for the tender sentiments of religion, for art and for the spiritual life.

WRITINGS

The Life of Reason; or The Phrases of Human Progress (New York: Charles Scribner's Sons, 1905).
The Realms of Being 4 vols (New York: Charles Scribner's Sons, 1927–40).
Skepticism and Animal Faith (New York: Dover Publications, 1955).

BIBLIOGRAPHY

Lachs, J.: *George Santayana* (Boston: Twayne Publishers, 1988).
Sprigge, T.L.S.: *Santayana: An Examination of His Philosophy* (London and Boston: Routledge and Kegan Paul, 1974).

JOHN LACHS

Sartre, Jean-Paul (1905–80) French philosopher, novelist, playwright and literary critic. For Sartre metaphysics is not a major preoccupation; the principal stages of his philosophical development are marked less by metaphysical commitments than by methodological ones – to PHENOMENOLOGY in *Being and Nothingness* (1960), to dialectics in the *Critique of Dialectical Reason* (1976), to his own brand of structural anthropology in *The Family Idiot* (1981). References to metaphysics in his work (with exceptions to be noted below) tend to be incidental or dismissive, sometimes even pejorative.

This attitude seems to spring from Sartre's association of metaphysics with claims to a priori knowledge of the moral law, of human nature, etc., usually supporting the political and clerical status quo. Yet the Sartrean doctrines of the priority of EXISTENCE over essence (*see* ESSENCE/ACCIDENT) for conscious subjects, of freedom as

absolute (even if eventually constricted), of the presuppositionless upsurge of being-for-itself, of the impossibility of God as simultaneously in-itself and for-itself, of the nature of the individual as 'just anybody', of the distributive character of the group, etc., surely count as metaphysical in the generally accepted sense of that term.

The passages where metaphysics is seriously discussed are to be found, as might be expected, in *Being and Nothingness*, the work in which Sartre's subject matter (the being of human beings in the world) seems to belong most unequivocally to the domain in which other philosophers have located metaphysical concerns. The work is called 'an essay in phenomenological ontology', although at least once Sartre speaks of 'metaphysical interrogation – which is *our* interrogation' (1943, p. 40, 1956, p. 36). In the light of other things he says it is hard to know how seriously to take this claim. The most useful approach will be to concentrate on the contrast he draws between ONTOLOGY and metaphysics.

There are two explicit formulations of this contrast. The first is in the long chapter on 'the existence of others', where Sartre remarks that 'Why are there others?' is a metaphysical question. 'Ontology', he says, 'seems to be definable as making explicit the structures of the being of what exists taken as a totality, while we will define metaphysics as the calling in question of the being of what exists' (1943, pp. 358–9, 1956, p. 395). The second formulation comes in the concluding chapter of the book, in a section entitled 'In-itself and for-itself: metaphysical insights'.

Thus the *ontological* problem of knowledge is resolved by the affirmation of the ontological primacy of the in-itself over the for-itself. But this is at once to engender a *metaphysical* interrogation ... which might be formulated as follows: Why does the for-itself spring up on the basis of being? What we call metaphysical, in fact, is the study of individual processes that have given birth to *this* particular world as a concrete and singular totality. In this sense, metaphysics is to ontology as history is to sociology. (1943, p. 713, 1956, p. 788).

What can be concluded from this – and it is confirmed by other passages – is that metaphysics for Sartre has to do with the brute fact of being, its inescapability, as opposed to any theory of its modes or internal arrangements. So the answers to the questions 'Why are there others?' and 'Why does the for-itself spring up?' come down to: there just are, it just does. This Sartre calls 'the encounter with fundamental contingency'. In *Being and Nothingness* he says that at this point 'the metaphysical question no longer has a sense' (1943, p. 363, 1956, p. 399); by the time he gets to the *Critique of Dialectical Reason* the position has hardened: now it seems to be just *because* it is metaphysical that a question is 'devoid of significance' (1960, p. 467, 1970, p. 364).

Metaphysics as a science of first principles, as theology even, has traditionally been associated with the idea of necessity. It is clear that for Sartre the association is with the contingent. But this is because of 'the absolute contingency of what exists' (1943, p. 359, 1956, p. 395). Some convergence between these apparently opposing views may be effected through a distinction (not one, however, that Sartre himself draws), between *modal* necessity and *apodictic* necessity: something radically contingent cannot be modally necessary (it could have been otherwise in another possible world) but there is a sense in which, things being, globally speaking, as they are – even if the whole is contingent – the principles of their being so may be said to be apodictically necessary (they appear incontrovertibly to be what they are, and cannot be otherwise in *this* world). This position has some affinity with what STRAWSON has called 'descriptive metaphysics'.

Sartre is quite prepared to interpret this metaphysical aspect of things at a personal level: it is the task of existential psychoanalysis to uncover what he calls 'the metaphysical tenor of every intuitive revelation of being', the way in which particular things in the world present themselves to individuals as having ineluctable qualities *for them*. So he asks rhetorically what is 'the metaphysical coefficient of lemon, of water, of oil, etc.? So many problems whose resolution psychoanalysis owes itself if it wishes to understand one day why Pierre likes oranges' (1943, p. 695, 1956, p. 770).

There are in other words idiosyncratic features of Pierre's world that are as necessarily constitutive of it as any basic metaphysical feature of the world in general. Yet there is a sense in which Pierre has *chosen* his world and not just its idiosyncratic features. This explains why Sartre sometimes speaks of metaphysics as having options: 'It is for metaphysics to decide if it will be more profitable for knowledge . . . to retain the old duality "consciousness-being" ' (1943, p. 719, 1956, p. 794). This choice however cannot rest on a priori insight, and metaphysics must therefore remain hypothetical – even if apodictic it is not susceptible of *independent* confirmation or refutation (1943, p. 715, 1956, p. 790).

As a choice, my metaphysics is my responsibility, just as my morality is; in his wartime journals Sartre says 'morals were *never* in my eyes distinguished from metaphysics' (1983, p. 106). Disavowing the old metaphysics does not free me from it: 'I did not think I was any less a metaphysician in refusing existence to God than Leibniz in granting it to him' (1947–76, vol. III, p. 139, 1955, p. 200). It is part of my project, no more or less demonstrable than my own existence, with which it stands or falls. This explains why from Sartre's point of view metaphysics, while it undergirds each individual's philosophical outlook and has a determining effect on a writer's *literary* output, is not centrally important to philosophy as such, whose productive work lies elsewhere.

See also EXISTENTIALISM.

WRITINGS

L'Être et le néant: essai d'ontologie phénoménologique (Paris: 1943); trans. H. Barnes,

Being and Nothingness (1956); (New York: Washington Square Press, 1960).

Critique de la raison dialectique, Vol. I. *Théorie des ensembles pratiques* (Paris: 1960); (Paris: Gallimard, 1985); trans. A. Sheridan-Smith, *Critique of Dialectical Reason* (London: New Left Books, 1976).

Situations 10 vols (Paris, 1947–76); partially trans. A. Michelson, *Literary and Philosophical Essays* (1955); (New York: Collier Books, 1962).

Les Carnets de la drôle de guerre: novembre 1939 – mars 1940 (Paris: Gallimard, 1983).

BIBLIOGRAPHY

Caws, P.: *Sartre* (London: Routledge and Kegan Paul, 1979).
Hartmann, K.: *Sartre's Ontology* (Evanston, IL: Northwestern University Press, 1966).

PETER CAWS

Schopenhauer, Arthur (1788–1860) German philosopher who achieved little academic recognition during his lifetime but whose writings subsequently exercised a considerable influence, both in his homeland and elsewhere. An admirer of KANT, he insisted that he alone amongst his philosophical compatriots had remained faithful to the spirit of his great predecessor, and his early work clearly bore the imprint of the latter's ideas (*see* KANTIANISM). As developed, however, in his principal book, *Die Welt als Wille und Vorstellung* (1818), he can be seen to have generated a metaphysical system that was very much his own.

Schopenhauer's philosophy is based upon the claim that it is necessary to draw a distinction between the world as it presents itself to us at the level of everyday perception and the world as it exists in itself, in its true or essential character. In keeping with the Kantian doctrine of transcendental IDEALISM, he held that reality as we ordinarily apprehended it was to be construed as a sphere of phenomenal (*see* NOUMENAL/ PHENOMENAL) 'appearances' or 'repre-

sentations' to a conscious subject; its fundamental structure as a spatio-temporal and causally related realm of empirically ascertainable objects and events derived from forms and CATEGORIES originating in the human intellect, these being imposed upon the data provided by sensation. There was hence a sense in which the world of phenomena was a mind-dependent world, to be contrasted with the underlying 'noumenal' sphere of the 'thing-in-itself' (*Ding an sich*). But it was not the case – as Kant had maintained – that nothing at all could be known about the latter, Schopenhauer contending instead that a clue to what it involved lay in the inward experience we have of agency. For we are in fact conscious of ourselves under two distinguishable aspects. From one point of view we appear to ourselves, as we do to others, as 'objects among objects', perceivable entities who belong together with the rest of the phenomenal sphere of physical nature. Yet everyone is also aware, directly and from the inside, of being at the same time a centre of volitional activity or will. And Schopenhauer argued that this second aspect of ourselves, to which each of us has internal access in the case of his or her own person, could legitimately be regarded as affording the key to the innermost or noumenal being of phenomenal existence in general. Thus what, albeit in an avowedly extended sense, he referred to as 'the will' could be said to constitute the essence, not merely of ourselves, but of the world as a whole.

Schopenhauer considered his voluntarist metaphysic to have far-reaching implications, striking at the root of many cherished theoretical assumptions. For the all-encompassing cosmic will that emerged from his account was portrayed as a blind striving force which was devoid of any rational goal or morally acceptable design that could lend meaning or value to its manifestations. Throughout the natural realm of organic phenomena it took the form of an endless struggle for existence; and at the level of human life this typically found expression in the manner in which individuals, as particular embodiments of will, vied with one another in seeking to gratify primal urges that condemned them to a continual round of anxiety, frustration and suffering. All in all, and as he himself emphasized, Schopenhauer's disenchanted view of the human condition contrasted sharply with the confident HISTORICISM and belief in progress which, in one way or another, tended to colour the prevailing ideologies of his age. The final conclusion to be drawn from his philosophy was not that we should actively participate in the world and its workings, fortified by illusory notions of inevitable historical advance. Rather, ultimate salvation lay in a total withdrawal from earthly concerns, that being possible only in the light of a higher insight which transcended the will-governed perspective of ordinary thought and consciousness and which comprehended the unitary reality underlying the multiplicity of phenomena presented in perceptual experience.

Schopenhauer's disquisitions on the latter score, which show affinities with Buddhism, contain much that he allows to be mysterious. None the less, his account of art as providing a temporary release from practically orientated modes of awareness has often been found compelling, while in the sphere of psychology a number of the ideas he developed in the context of his overall theory of human nature appear in retrospect remarkably prescient. Not only has his conception of the necessary inseperability of will and body been seen as offering an original challenge to the tenets of traditional psychophysical dualism (*see* MIND/BODY PROBLEM); subsequent writers, including FREUD himself, have also cited his stress on the unconscious and instinctual sources of human motivation as prefiguring cardinal developments in psychoanalysis. It is noteworthy, too, that the influence of some of his more general metaphysical themes, especially those concerning the status of the self and the limits of thoughts and language, is clearly discernible in WITTGENSTEIN's early philosophy.

See also KANTIANISM.

WRITINGS

Die Welt als Wille und Vorstellung (Leipzig: Brockhaus, 1818; 2nd enlarged edn, 1844); trans. E.F.J. Payne, *The World as Will and Representation* 2 vols (New York: Dover, 1969).

BIBLIOGRAPHY

Gardiner, P.: *Schopenhauer* (Harmondsworth: Penguin, 1963).
Hamlyn, D.W.: *Schopenhauer* (London: Routledge and Kegan Paul, 1980).
Janaway, C.: *Self and World in Schopenhauer's Philosophy* (Oxford: Clarendon Press, 1989).
Magee, B.: *The Philosophy of Schopenhauer* (Oxford: Clarendon Press, 1983).

PATRICK GARDINER

secondary quality *see* QUALITY, PRIMARY/SECONDARY

self-consciousness The ostensible metaphysical import of self-consciousness has traditionally been parasitic upon the supposed epistemic peculiarities of apperception. DESCARTES famously treated the apparent immunity of apperceptive judgements to his hyperbolic methodological doubt as a basis from which to demonstrate the existence of *res cogitans*, an autonomous thinking substance, arguably distinct and separable from *res extensa*. In contrast, HUME took the systematic epistemic elusiveness of a self which was the subject of all perceptual encounters but the object of none as grounds for concluding, *contra* Descartes, that there was nothing more to the self, ontologically speaking, than a bundle of impressions and ideas related by regularities of resemblance, succession, and co-occurrence:

For my part, when I enter most intimately into what I call *myself*, I always stumble on some particular perception or other . . . I can never catch *myself* at any time without a perception, and never can observe any thing but the perception. When my perceptions are removed for any time . . . [I] may be truly said not to exist. (*Treatise of Human Nature*, Bk I, Part IV, sect. vi)

In his account of the 'Paralogisms of pure reason', KANT argued that neither Descartes's nor Hume's conclusion could be logically sustained if interpreted as a conclusion regarding the self as it is in itself (*an sich*). However Kant by no means regarded the facts of self-consciousness as therefore devoid of metaphysical consequences. On the contrary, his celebrated 'Transcendental Deduction' is precisely an argument from the *unity* of apperceptive consciousness (the 'transcendental unity of apperception') to the conclusion that what we encounter in experience must be conceived as a spatio-temporally unified world of causally potent and mutually interactive perduring substances (*see* TRANSCENDENTAL EGO). Descartes's specific error, argued Kant, lay in mistaking a purely *formal* unity which is a necessary condition of the possibility of any experience at all for an independently identifiable object of such experience:

The unity of consciousness, which underlies the categories, is here mistaken for an intuition of the subject as its object, and the category of substance is then applied to it. (*Critique of Pure Reason*, B 421)

On the model of Descartes's methodological doubt, HUSSERL proposed his 'phenomenological *epoche*' – a deliberate suspension of natural existential beliefs – as a 'radical and universal method' for apprehending the 'pure ego' together with its *cogitationes*, and, like Kant, Husserl criticized Descartes for locating the resulting 'I' of self-consciousness as a substance in the world. Unlike Kant, however, Husserl was not prepared to relegate his 'transcendental ego' to the purely formal order, but argued that, although the phenomenological *epoche* (*see*

PHENOMENOLOGY) successfully suspended all natural ontological commitment, the being of the reflecting subject (ego) was left unaffected:

I, with my life, remain untouched in my existential status, regardless of whether or not the world exists and regardless of what my eventual decision concerning its being or non-being might be (*Cartesian Meditations*, p. 25)

Descriptive phenomenology remains a going contemporary concern, but its methodological self-understanding has increasingly shifted from appeals to a radically first-person Husserlian *epoche* to (broadly Heideggerian) considerations of inter-subjectively funded descriptions of a socially shared *Lebenswelt* (*see* HEIDEGGER). Among philosophers working in the analytic style, a fundamental and thoroughgoing critique of Cartesian notions of introspective epistemic certainty, largely traceable to WITTGENSTEIN's later criticisms of 'private languages' and SELLARS's rejection of the 'myth of the given', has worked to similar effect. While apperception remains a challenging topic for epistemological investigation, in other words, the facts of self-consciousness are nowadays perhaps most widely regarded as having no significant explicitly *metaphysical* implications at all.

See also CONSCIOUSNESS.

BIBLIOGRAPHY

Hume, D.: *A Treatise of Human Nature* (London: 1739); ed. L.A. Selby-Bigge; 2nd edn, with revisions by P.H. Nidditch (New York: Oxford University Press, 1978).

Husserl, E.: *Cartesian Meditations* (Paris: 1931); trans. D. Cairns (The Hague: Martinus Nijhoff, 1960).

Kant, I.: *Critique of Pure Reason* (Riga: 1781, 1787); trans. N. Kemp Smith (London: Macmillan, 1929).

JAY F. ROSENBERG

Sellars, Wilfrid (1912–89) American philosopher. Sellars's metaphysical perspectives are shaped by the fundamental conviction that to be is to make a difference, more precisely, by the (essentially Platonic) idea that the distinguishing mark of real things is their power to act or be acted upon. The concrete reflection of this root conviction is a thoroughgoing NATURALISM, incorporating both a positive and a negative dimension.

Positively, Sellars's metaphysical naturalism issues in a variety of Peircean (*see* PEIRCE) scientific REALISM which regards the results of scientific inquiry as ontologically definitive:

> [In] the dimension of describing and explaining the world, science is the measure of all things, of what is that it is, and of what is not that it is not. (1963, p. 173)

(Sellars's *scientia mensura*). Scientific theories, on this understanding, explanatorily 'save the appearances' precisely by characterizing, with increasing representational adequacy, the reality *of which* 'the appearances' are literally appearances. On Sellars's view, stories that postulate 'theoretical entities' are not merely manageable second-class surrogates for more complicated and unwieldy stories about entities that we have good, i.e. observational, reasons to believe actually exist. Theoretical entities, rather, are those entities we warrantedly believe to exist for good and sufficient *theoretical reasons*.

Negatively, Sellars's naturalism places strong constraints on the potential reach of a traditional *categorial* ONTOLOGY in general. In particular, it implies the unacceptability of any ontological view which conceives of *abstract entities* as real objects without offering an adequate account of their place within the causal order, broadly construed (*see* NOMINALISM; PLATONISM).

Sellars himself, consequently, espouses a form of *linguistic nominalism* according to which 'the abstract entities which are the subject matter of the contemporary debate between platonistic and anti-platonistic philosophers – qualities, relations, classes, propositions, and the like – are linguistic entities' (1967, p. 229). Like CARNAP, in other words, Sellars undertakes to treat categorial ontological discourse as the classificatory discourse of a functional metalanguage, transposed into the 'material mode of speech' (*see* OBJECT LANGUAGE/METALANGUAGE). Unlike Carnap, however, Sellars refuses to (theoretically) *identify* the formally definable constructs of a 'pure' syntax or semantics with the syntactical and semantical terms in pre-philosophical usage having corresponding extensions, arguing that such a facile interpretation of the relationship between 'pure' and 'descriptive' syntactic and semantic discourses seriously fails to do proper justice to the crucial *normative* aspects of the latter. Thus, while Sellars is prepared to reconstruct such categorial ontological notions as 'universal', 'individual', 'kind', 'quality', 'proposition', and 'FACT' in terms of syntactic and semantic counterparts – for example, 'predicate', 'singular term', 'common noun', 'monadic predicate', 'sentence' and 'true sentence' – he insists that these syntactical and semantical words, functioning as such 'have a conceptual role which is no more reducible to [non-syntactical and] non-semantical roles than the role of prescriptive terms is reducible to non-prescriptive roles . . . [The] empirical (in the broad sense) character of statements in descriptive (historical) [syntax and] semantics does not entail that [syntactical and] semantical concepts, properly so called, are descriptive' (1974, p. 274).

Conceptual (linguistic) roles or functions, finally, are not themselves accorded autonomous ontological status, but rather individuated in terms of the structure of positive and negative uniformities generated in the *natural* order by the pattern-governed activities of perception, inference (both formal and material) and volition. What emerges is an interlocking family of metaphysical commitments which has been aptly characterized as 'a unique example of radical and systematic nominalism' (Seibt, 1990, p. 4).

See also PROPOSITION, STATE OF AFFAIRS; UNIVERSALS; UNIVERSALS AND PARTICULARS.

WRITINGS

Science, Perception and Reality (London and New York: Routledge and Kegan Paul, 1963); (Atascadero, CA: Ridgeview Publishing Co., 1991).
Philosophical Perspectives (Springfield, IL: Charles C. Thomas, 1967); 2 vols (Atascadero, CA: Ridgeview Publishing Co., 1977).
Science and Metaphysics: Variations on Kantian Themes (London and New York: Routledge and Kegan Paul, 1968); reissued, including a complete bibliography (Atascadero, CA: Ridgeview Publishing Co., 1992).
Essays in Philosophy and Its History (Dordrecht: D. Reidel, 1974).
Naturalism and Ontology (Atascadero, CA: Ridgeview Publishing Co., 1980).
Pure Pragmatics and Possible Worlds ed. and introduced J.F. Sicha (Atascadero, CA: Ridgeview Publishing Co., 1981). (A retrospective collection of early essays, including a comprehensive bibliography.)
'Foundations for a metaphysics of pure process', *Monist* 64 (1981), 3–90.
The Metaphysics of Epistemology: Lectures by Wilfrid Sellars ed. P.V. Amaral (Atascadero, CA: Ridgeview Publishing Co., 1989).

BIBLIOGRAPHY

Castañeda, H.-N. ed.: *Action, Knowledge, and Reality: Critical Studies in Honor of Wilfrid Sellars* (Indianapolis, IN: Bobbs-Merrill, 1975). (Contains Sellars's intellectual autobiography.)
Delaney, C.F., Michael J. Loux, Gary Gutting, and W. David Solomon: *The Synoptic Vision: Essays on the Philosophy of Wilfrid Sellars* (Notre Dame, IN: University of Notre Dame Press, 1977).
Pitt, J.C. ed.: *The Philosophy of Wilfrid Sellars: Queries and Extensions* (Dordrecht: D. Reidel, 1978).

Seibt, J.: *Properties as Processes: A Synoptic Study of Wilfrid Sellars' Nominalism* (Atascadero, CA: Ridgeview Publishing Co., 1990).

JAY F. ROSENBERG

sensa Sensa comprise a lively menagerie that includes sense impressions, ideas, raw feels, qualia, sensations, sense contents and sense data. These figure prominently in the psychology of perception, in epistemology, and in the philosophy of mind. In perceiving a tomato, it may be said, I am aware 'directly', not of the tomato, but of a sensory intermediary, the character of which enables me somehow to gather the tomato's character. According to some, I *infer* the latter from the former; according to others, knowledge of the tomato results from my *interpreting* what is 'given' in sensation. LOCKE held that sensory ideas were caused by external objects and in certain important respects resembled their causes. BERKELEY, in contrast, denied the intelligibility of both contentions, concluding that objects are constituted by actual and possible ideas (*see* PHENOMENALISM). These positions represent two extremes on a continuum of positions along which most, though not quite all, philosophers who have any opinions on the matter can be located.

Sensa figure not only in accounts of perceiving but also in theories ranging over such disparate phenomena as remembering, dreaming, hallucinating and imagining. If, in seeing a tomato, I encounter a particular sort of visual sensation, then in remembering the tomato, I retrieve the sensation from a mental storehouse; in dreaming about, or hallucinating, or imagining the tomato, the sensation occurs in a way that does not depend on there being a tomato present. Sceptics have made much of the notion that there are no certain marks by which veridical sensa are distinguishable from those that occur in the absence of an appropriate object.

Bodily sensations – itches, pains, feelings of pressure, feelings of heat or cold – make up another important class of sensa. These

459

are taken to result from bodily occurrences, but not to resemble their sources in any straightforward way. Headache, for instance, may result from goings-on in the nervous system the character of which could only be discovered by extensive empirical inquiry.

Until the late 1950s, discussion of sensa figured most prominently in epistemology. G. E. MOORE and H.H. Price defended versions of empiricist theories according to which our awareness of ordinary objects was mediated by an awareness of 'sense data' (Moore, 1953, ch. 2; Price, 1932). Allowing for inevitable differences (for example, Moore flirted with the idea that sense data were 'parts of the surfaces of objects'), sense data were commonly thought to be private mental items to which we have immediate and infallible access (see PUBLIC/PRIVATE). Unlike tables, chairs, and tomatoes, sense data, in HUME's phrase, 'must necessarily appear in every particular what they are, and be what they appear'. I may misperceive a tomato, judging it to be reddish and round when it is not, but I cannot misapprehend the reddish and round sense datum that leads me to my erroneous judgement.

Opponents of sense data have been motivated by epistemological worries (if our contact with the world is limited to the awareness of private sensory goings-on, it is unclear that we should ever have reason to believe that there is a world beyond these goings-on), and by a growing impatience with philosophical theories that seem inconsistent with physicalism (see PHYSICALISM, MATERIALISM). Some (Ryle, 1956; Dennett, 1988) flatly deny the existence of sensa, arguing that sensa are theoretical fictions, items postulated to shore up philosophical theses the plausibility of which rests on equivocation, confused turns of thought, and a tendency to fall into well-worn philosophical ruts. Foes of such eliminativism reply that, if physicalism implies the non-existence of sensa, so much the worse for physicalism. We can appreciate 'what it is like' to see a tomato, taste an apple, or step on a tack (see Nagel, 1974; Jackson, 1986).

We are aware, in such case of 'phenomenal qualities' or 'raw feels', items that fall outside the 'third-person' descriptive and explanatory net of physical science.

Physicalists have responded by identifying 'phenomenal' qualities with physical properties of objects and distinguishing (as do *adverbial theorists* (see ADVERBIAL THEORY; EXPERIENCE) something's *being* red from something's being a *perceiving of* red. It may be that, had I never encountered anything red (or, recalling Hume's missing shade of blue, any colour very like red), I should remain ignorant of what it is like to perceive red. In the same way, I cannot know what it is like to win a foot-race until I have won one. These facts, however, if they are facts, need not tempt us to postulate non-physical qualia.

Many philosophers remain unconvinced, however. Even RYLE (1956, pp. 442–3) admitted to a 'residual embarrassment' on this score. 'There is something common between having an after-image and seeing a misprint. Both are visual affairs. How ought we to describe their affinity with one another, without falling back on some account very much like a part of the orthodox theories of sense impressions? To this I am stumped for an answer.'

BIBLIOGRAPHY

Dennett, D.: 'Quining qualia', in *Consciousness in Contemporary Science* ed. A.J. Marcel and E. Bisiach (Oxford: Clarendon Press, 1988), 42–77.
Jackson, F.: 'What Mary didn't know', *Journal of Philosophy* 83 (1986), 291–5.
Moore, G.E.: *Some Main Problems of Philosophy* (London: George Allen and Unwin, 1953).
Nagel, T.: 'What is it like to be a bat?', *Philosophical Review* 83 (1974), 435–50.
Price, H.H.: *Perception* (London: Methuen, 1932).
Ryle, G.: 'Sensation', in *Contemporary British Philosophy* ed. H.D. Lewis (London: George Allen and Unwin, 1956), 427–43.

JOHN HEIL

sense data   *see* SENSA

set   *see* CLASS, COLLECTION, SET

simplicity, parsimony Philosophers and scientists have often held that the simplicity or parsimony of a theory is one reason, all else being equal, to view it as true. This goes beyond the unproblematic idea that simpler theories are easier to work with and have greater aesthetic appeal.

One theory is more parsimonious than another when it postulates fewer entities, processes, changes or explanatory principles; the simplicity of a theory depends on more or less the same considerations, though it is not obvious that parsimony and simplicity come to the same thing.

Even if it is sufficiently clear what makes one theory simpler or more parsimonious than another, the question remains of saying why simplicity should be regarded as a sign of truth. NEWTON and LEIBNIZ answered this question by invoking substantive views about nature. In *Principia* (1687), Newton laid down as his first Rule of Reasoning that 'nature does nothing in vain, . . . for Nature is pleased with simplicity and affects not the pomp of superfluous causes'. Leibniz hypothesized that the actual world obeys simple laws because God's taste for simplicity influenced his decision about which world to actualize.

Epistemology since HUME and KANT has drawn back from this theological underpinning. Indeed, the very idea that NATURE is simple (or uniform) has come in for critique. Surely we know that nature is not simple or uniform in *all* respects; and the idea that it is simple or uniform in *some* (unspecified) respect is a rather empty one. In any event, the methodological weight we give to simplicity considerations seems to outrun such metaphysical formulations. We seek to find the simplest theory consistent with the observations; this is a maxim that seems plausible, no matter how much complexity the data force us to read into our conception of nature.

In contrast with various metaphysical formulations of the principle of parsimony or simplicity, the view has taken hold that a preference for simple and parsimonious hypotheses is purely *methodological*; it is constitutive of the attitude we call 'scientific' and makes no substantive assumption about the way the world is. A variety of otherwise diverse twentieth-century philosophers of science have attempted, in different ways, to flesh out this position. For example, POPPER (1959) holds that scientists should prefer highly falsifiable ('improbable') theories; he tries to show that simpler theories are more falsifiable. QUINE (1966), on the other hand, sees a virtue in theories that are highly probable; he argues for a general connection between simplicity and high probability.

Both these proposals are *global*. They seek to explain why simplicity should be part of the scientific method in a way that spans all scientific subject matters. No assumption about the details of any particular scientific problem serves as a premise in Popper's or Quine's arguments.

Newton and Leibniz thought that the justification of principles of parsimony and simplicity flows from the hand of God; Popper and Quine try to justify these methodological maxims without assuming anything substantive about the way the world is. In spite of these differences in approach, they share the assumption that all uses of parsimony and simplicity in the separate sciences can be encompassed in a single justifying argument.

Recent developments in confirmation theory suggest that this assumption should be scrutinized. Good (1983) and Rosenkrantz (1977) have emphasized the role of auxiliary assumptions in mediating the connection between hypotheses and observations. Whether an hypothesis is well supported by some observations, or whether one hypothesis is better supported than another by those observations, crucially depends on empirical background assumptions about the inference problem at hand. The same view applies to the idea of prior probability (or prior plausibility). If one hypothesis is preferred over another even though they are equally supported by current observations, this must be due to an empirical background assumption.

Principles of parsimony and simplicity mediate the epistemic connection between hypotheses and observations. Perhaps these principles are able to do this because they are surrogates for an empirical background theory. It is not that there is one background theory presupposed by every appeal to parsimony; this has the quantifier order backwards. Rather, the suggestion is that each parsimony argument is justified only to the degree that it reflects an empirical background theory about the subject matter at hand. Once this theory is stated explicitly, the principle of parsimony is entirely dispensable (Sober, 1988).

This *local* approach to principles of parsimony and simplicity resurrects the idea that they make sense only if the world is one way rather than another. It rejects the idea that these maxims are purely *methodological*. Assessing this point of view requires detailed case studies of scientific hypothesis evaluation and further developments in the theory of scientific inference.

BIBLIOGRAPHY

Good, I.: *Good Thinking: The Foundations of Probability and Its Applications* (Minneapolis: University of Minnesota Press, 1983).

Hesse, M.: 'Simplicity', in *The Encyclopedia of Philosophy* ed. P. Edwards (New York: Macmillan, 1967), 445–8.

Popper, K.: *The Logic of Scientific Discovery* (London: Hutchinson, 1959).

Quine, W.V.: 'Simple theories of a complex world', in his *The Ways of Paradox and Other Essays* (New York: Random House, 1966), 242–6.

Rosenkrantz, R.: *Inference, Method, and Decision* (Dordrecht: Reidel, 1977).

Sober, E.: *Reconstructing the Past: Parsimony, Evolution, and Inference* (Cambridge, MA: MIT Press, 1988).

ELLIOTT SOBER

sorites arguments The sorites argument was invented by the ancient Megarian philosopher, Eubulides. He begins with the premise that, say, one million grains of sand constitutes a heap. Removing one grain of sand never turns a heap into a non-heap. Repeated application of this principle leads to the conclusion that one grain of sand constitutes a heap.

As an Eleactic, Eubulides may well have regarded his paradox as metaphysically significant but subsequent philosophers spurned it as a sophistic piffle. They objected that the argument is highly indiscriminate. For a semantic slippery slope argument can be mounted for any vague word – and nearly all words are vague. What's worse, one can equally well argue in the opposite direction:

Positive version of the heap paradox
(1) A collection of one million grains of sand is a heap.
(2) If a collection of n grains of sand is a heap, then so is a collection of $n - 1$ grains.
(3) A collection of one grain of sand is a heap.

Negative version of the heap paradox
(1) A collection of one grain of sand is not a heap.
(2) If a collection of n grains is not a heap, then neither is a collection of $n + 1$ grains.
(3) A collection of one million grains of sand is not a heap.

Positive sorites arguments bloat the extension of a vague predicate while negative sorites arguments shrivel it. Given the logical analogy between the two and their conflict with each other, both arguments are highly suspect. However, it is notoriously difficult to pinpoint the fallacy.

Twentieth-century philosophers, especially those in the last twenty years, have been increasingly intrigued by Eubulides' invention. They grant the reversibility of sorites arguments shows that not all sorites arguments are sound. But they insist that an argument can be philosophically interesting even when it is known to be unsound. Part of the modern optimism about the metaphysical significance of the sorites is due to its connections to particular issues such as the Ship of Theseus paradox, questions of personal identity, and problems in modal reasoning (*see* MODALITIES AND POSSIBLE WORLDS; PERSONS AND PERSONAL IDENTITY). But the optimism also has grander expressions.

Closest in spirit to Eubulides are the nihilists. They reject the base step of positive sorites arguments on the grounds that vague predicates such as 'heap' are incoherent. Since most of our vocabulary is vague, this constitutes a thorough repudiation of the ONTOLOGY suggested by common sense. Thus these nihilists accept the negative sorites arguments as insightful impossibility proofs. For example, Unger (1979) and Heller (1990) have argued that the sorites demonstrates that there are no ordinary things (that vague predicates such as 'smog', 'bagel' and 'professor' are empty).

Most commentators attack the induction step of the sorites. In classical logic, the negation of the induction step is equivalent to an existential generalization asserting the existence of a precise threshold: there exists an n such that n grains of sand constitutes a heap but $n - 1$ grains does not. So continued allegiance to classical logic leads to the conclusion that language or reality is 'precise' in that our ordinary vague words manage to sharply partition objects.

There are metaphysics of precision that seem to satisfy this hunger for determinacy. Mechanism narrows down the possible behaviour of things. ATOMISM, NATURAL KINDS and fact-ontologies tend to depict reality as discrete and so immune from slippery slopes that exploit continua. However, there are also metaphysical principles that foster vagueness. The principle of plenitude states that every possibility is realized in the world. This gap-filling ensures that there will always be intermediate cases that slip between qualitative categories. An equally ancient basis for metaphysical indeterminacy is the Platonic principle that particular things are imperfect approximations of ideal types (*see* PLATO). Their inevitable deviations from the blueprint restrain one's demand for precision. Libertarianism is a metaphysics of vagueness because it cracks the causal cement binding all events. Dualists compromise by granting DETERMINISM and FREE WILL different dominions.

Dualism will prompt some philosophers to contend that logic only applies to one domain of reality. For example, in 1923 RUSSELL asserted that logic only applies to the Platonic heavens, not the terrestrial world of rough and ready particulars. This engineering stance has to be separated from commitment to vague objects. Russell insists that only representations can be vague and diagnosed belief in vague objects as an instance of verbalism: the fallacy of imputing properties of words to their referents. In 1978, Gareth Evans presented an apparent disproof of the possibility of vague objects. If there were vague objects, there would have to be a statement of the form $a = b$ that was indeterminate. However, LEIBNIZ's Law ensures the determinacy of all identity statements. For if $a = b$, then whatever property a has is possessed by b. One of the properties of a is being definitely identical to a. Therefore b must be definitely identical to a. Evans's argument has drawn many objections from philosophers who think logic cannot exclude vague objects.

Likewise, many commentators on the sorites are reluctant to draw any metaphysical conclusion from the sorites paradox. They think its true significance is logical. Proponents of many-valued logic say that the sorites paradox exposes the need to assign indeterminate statements a *degree* of truth. Supervaluationists say indeterminacies should be represented with truth-value gaps. Intuitionists try to de-rail the sorites paradox by forbidding inference rules such as Double Negation. All of these deviant logicians agree that classical logic only works for precise discourse and so urge that we design a logic that is better suited to vague, natural languages.

463

See also ANTINOMIES; IDENTITY OF INDIS-
CERNIBLES; VAGUENESS.

BIBLIOGRAPHY

Evans, G.: 'Can there be vague objects', *Analysis* 38 (1978), 208.

Heller, M.: *The Ontology of Physical Objects* (New York: Cambridge University Press, 1990).

van Inwagen, P.: *Material Beings* (Ithaca, NY: Cornell University Press, 1991).

Sorensen, R.: *Blindspots* (Oxford: Clarendon Press, 1988).

Unger, P.: 'There are no ordinary things', *Synthese* 4 (1979), 117–54.

Wheeler, S.: 'Megarian paradoxes as Eleactic arguments', *American Philosophical Quarterly* 20 (1983), 287–95.

ROY A. SORENSEN

soul The Greek word *psyche* for soul is related to their word for breath, and in Homer souls do little more than leave the body at death. In PLATO they become a link between matter and the forms. The allegory of the cave in the *Republic* suggests that Plato had a perceptual model of knowledge. This makes it hard to see how we could know things as abstract, and thus inert, as the Forms. One suggestion is that when the soul was before birth unencumbered by the material body, it somehow had easier epistemic access to the Forms, and so now, like the slave boy in the *Meno*, can recollect them. In the *Phaedo*, these epistemological requirements of the theory of Forms turn into an argument for the separability of the soul from the body. In answer to the objection that this provides only for life before birth, not after DEATH, and to the worry that a person might be only a state of a body, like the harmony of a lyre that ceases with its decay, we are told that the soul is the principle of life and so cannot admit its opposite, death. (Full coming to be from, or passing away into, nothing still seems to trouble us.) ARISTOTLE catalogued kinds of soul corresponding to kinds of life such as vegetative, animal and rational, and granted immortality to the rational alone. Since for him the soul is the form of the living thing, and since he was so hostile to the independence of forms, his doctrine of IMMORTALITY is mysterious. (*See* MATTER/FORM.)

The Christian promise of immortality may have attracted Augustine to Neoplatonic thinking about the soul. AQUINAS a millennium later preferred Aristotle, and Islam, between them, also promises personal immortality. Judaism is much less committal about the soul, but (like Roman religion) has an elaborate body of rules and rituals, and in Christianity one's soul sometimes seems like a score-card God hands out at birth where sins are recorded as stains toted up at judgement.

The fear of death is probably permanent (and adaptive), but wishful thinking about immortality seems puerile. The MIND/BODY PROBLEM is the question whether or not you (your mind, self, soul) just are your body, and so could not exist without your body. If not, you would be no less basic a thing (or SUBSTANCE, in the old jargon) than your body, and so would not depend for your existence on that of your body. Dualism is the thesis that you could be disembodied. It is important to note that this is a modal thesis about possibility; dualists need not believe there actually are ghosts in haunted houses. Dualism does not promise immortality.

DESCARTES is the leading dualist after Plato. There may be two different arguments for dualism in the *Meditations*. In the large, Descartes aims for certain foundations on which to rebuild knowledge systematically. We know matter mostly by sense perception, but all such experience might be a dream or programmed into us by a demon or mad scientist, so sense experience is not certain enough to serve as our foundation. Thus matter falls to the method of systematic doubt. But doubt withstands the method, for doubting that one doubts guarantees the presence of doubt. Since it is clear that doubt is a species of thought and that one is the agent of one's thinking, *cogito ergo sum*.

So the self is certain while matter, including the body, is not, and thus by Leibniz's Law (*see* IDENTITY OF INDISCERNIBLES), the mind differs from the body.

This argument is flawed. Doubt and certainty are expressed in propositional-attitude contexts, which are not always referentially transparent; to be able to recognize one's sister but not the masked woman is a poor reason for thinking the masked woman is not one's sister. But even if the argument were sound, all it would show is that mind differs from body. One's left fist does not always exist when one's left hand does, so the first is not identical with the hand. Still, the fist could not exist without the hand; hand/fist dualism is incredible. Mind/body dualism requires separability, and so more than mere difference.

Dualism is a modal thesis. Descartes concentrates on conceiving clearly and distinctly (*see* CLEAR AND DISTINCT) as a way to establish claims to possibility. But conceiving seems too intellectual; one must be able to understand what could not be true in order to follow a proof by *reductio* that it is impossible. It is rather the blank one draws when one tries to imagine a leaf both red all over and green all over at once that convinces one there could be no such leaf. Imagination is to knowledge of mere possibility as perception is to knowledge of actuality. What one can imagine is possible, and one can imagine being disembodied, so one could be disembodied. This is at least an argument for the crucial thesis of dualism, and it is no less valid than any other instance of *modus ponens*. The central problem for the dualist is understanding how minds and bodies interact.

BIBLIOGRAPHY

Descartes, R.: *Meditations* (many versions).
Hart, W.D.: *The Engines of the Soul* (Cambridge: Cambridge University Press, 1988).
Penelhum, T.: *Survival and Disembodied Existence* (New York: Humanities Press, 1970).
Plato: *Republic* (many versions).
Swinburne, R.: *The Evolution of the Soul* (Oxford: Clarendon Press, 1986).

W.D. HART

space and time   Given that space and time constitute the 'arenas' in which all that occurs takes place, it is hardly a surprise that the concepts by which we try to grasp the nature of space and time are central to every aspect of our conceptual scheme. Nor is it surprising that questions concerning both the nature of space and time, and concerning our epistemic access to that nature, have been central philosophical issues from the very inception of philosophy. The crucial role played by space and time in the core of our physical theories of the world, and the astonishing revisions in our understanding of the nature of space and time forced upon us by the series of 'scientific revolutions' from the seventeenth century through to the present, have complicated the philosophical discussions of the nature of space and time and of our knowledge of it in fascinating and fruitful ways.

One series of problems concerns the alleged radical difference in nature between time and space. Typical of one side of the debate are the arguments of BERGSON to the effect that the scientific view of space and time as similar 'manifolds' of being left out the 'dynamic' or 'transient' or 'flowing' aspect of temporality. Another similar argument was that of MCTAGGART who argued that tensed discourse was essential to describe the temporality of being. McTaggart claimed that facts related in tensed discourse could not be identified with the facts contained in merely locating events as before or after one another in time, as objects are located spatially relative to one another. Of course McTaggart then went on to argue that tensed discourse was also inconsistent, and to infer from this the 'unreality' of time, a conclusion that would not be drawn by Bergson or other exponents of the 'transience' of temporality. Related positions are held by those who, like

A.N. Prior, maintain that temporal language has an irreducibly propositionally modal character. All of these views have as an essential component the claim that the past and future should be thought of as not being a true realm of being, with true EXISTENCE reserved to that which presently exists.

Opposed to this view is the one that would take existence to be, in general, a timeless notion. Events, past, present and future, then would bear temporal relations to one another in close analogy with the spatial relations things bear to one another. To the claim that tensed assertions cannot be translated into those of a tenseless language, the most usual current reply is to argue that tensed discourse has an irreducible indexical aspect (*see* INDEXICALS). To say of an event that it is past is to say that it is earlier than now. 'Now' is taken to be a token reflexive referring to the moment of its utterance. Just as in other contexts, then, the indexicality of the one language is taken not to indicate some novel realm of facts expressed by the language, despite the non-translatability of the indexical-tensed discourse into tenseless, non-indexical, language.

None the less the advocate of a radical disanalogy of time with space can still claim that issues of indexicality do not fully exhaust the claims made that past and future have no real existence. Naturally such a view has difficulties in a relativistic context where what is present in time is relative to a frame of motion, but relativistic considerations do not unequivocally refute the view that past and future have no real existence, for 'real existence' can itself be relativized to a frame of motion.

Many issues in the epistemology of space and time fall under general epistemological concerns. It remains a deep philosophical problem how to characterize what we take to be the spatiality and temporality of immediate EXPERIENCE and the relations of such 'perceptual' space and time to what we take, in both common sense and in physics, to be the space and time of the physical world. For the purposes of the description of immediate visual experience, for example, we seem to need some sort of notion of 'visual space' and the arrangement in it of percepts of particular objects. But how we ought correctly to characterize such a 'subjective' space of perception, and how relate it to the space of material things, remains far from clear.

Throughout the history of philosophy the status of our knowledge of the general truths about space, that is of geometry, has played a crucial role. How could there be a theory descriptive of the world whose truths could be known by pure logical deduction from first principles whose truth was 'self evident'? For PLATO and others geometry served as the ideal to which all science ought to aspire. For KANT geometry provided the clearest example of a discipline whose propositions were both synthetic and a priori, and, hence, a means to demonstrate the existence of theoretical knowledge of the world grounded in transcendental idealism. The discovery that many geometries are possible for space that are incompatible with Euclidean metric geometry, and the application of such geometries to the world in contemporary physics has led, naturally, to scepticism with regard to the view that a particular geometry can indeed be known to hold of the world independently of observation and experiment.

The initial response to the plethora of 'possible' geometries for the world was to take the structure of space as something to be inferred inductively from observation and experiment. Jules Henri Poincaré (1854–1912) argued, however, that there would always be an infinite variety of geometries compatible with any specified set of a totality of observational facts. This led to the so-called doctrine of 'conventionalism' with regard to geometry. While a variety of claims about the indeterminacy of geometry have been called conventionalistic, the dominant strain of conventionalism is some version or other of a Poincaré-type thesis. This thesis about geometry is, in turn, an instance of the general claim that theories referring to unobservables are radically 'underdetermined' by their sets of observational consequences. In some versions the thesis is one of epistemic scepticism. In other, more radical, stances, such as that of the reductionist, claims are espoused that all geometries with the same observational consequences amount to geometries that are in a deep sense 'equivalent' to one another, i.e. that they all say the same thing about the world.

A variety of important questions regarding the epistemology, semantics and metaphysics (ONTOLOGY) of theories surface very quickly when one explores the question of the alleged conventionality of geometry. In these debates what is observable is usually taken to be local relations of coincidence among material things, non-local features and feature of 'space itself' being taken to be in the realm of the only inferrable. Much of the current debate focuses on concrete issues brought to the fore when one considers alternatives to the standard special- and general-relativistic space-time pictures of the world that, allegedly, 'save the same phenomena' as the standard theories.

A fundamental metaphysical issue in the field of space and time is one anticipated by the Ancients, but brought to very vigorous life in the debate between LEIBNIZ and NEWTON. While Leibniz maintained that space was, essentially, nothing but the family of spatial relationships among material objects (at least in the non-monadological 'exoteric' portion of his metaphysics), Newton took space to be something over and above the spatial relations holding among material things. Leibniz is generally taken to be espousing a 'relationist' and Newton a 'substantivalist' doctrine concerning space (although Newton actually maintained that space was 'an attribute of the Deity').

The debate between the relationist and the substantivalist has both a 'pure' philosophical aspect and another side in which questions of physics play an essential role. Typical of the purely philosophical side of the debate are such matters as Leibniz's use of the principle of sufficient reason (*see* RATIONALISM) and of the doctrine of the IDENTITY OF INDISCERNIBLES to prove that substantivalism was a metaphysically unacceptable theory. The core of these arguments is that substantivalism, by allowing for MATTER to be, as a whole, differently situated in 'space itself' generates alleged differences between POSSIBLE WORLDS that are non-differences and alleged facts about the actual world that could receive no explanation.

Another set of philosophical debates hinges around the need for the relationist to do justice to the notion of space empty of matter, either empty regions of the actual world or even a possibly totally empty spatial world. To allow for the legitimacy of at least some degree of talk about 'empty space', the relationist will frequently resort to talk about possible but non-actual spatial relations among bits of matter, or even possible relations among possible but non-actual bits of matter. The move here is similar to the phenomenalist's invocation of 'permanent possibilities of sensation' to deal with matter existing unperceived (*see* PHENOMENALISM). The substantivalist is likely to object at this point, maintaining that such possibilities must be 'grounded' in an actuality, the nature of space itself, just as ordinary dispositions (such as solubility) are grounded in an underlying actuality (such as the molecular constitution of the matter) (*see* DISPOSITION).

The metaphysical debate between substantivalist and relationist takes on a special character when arguments, originating with Newton, are introduced that try to argue for substantival space as a necessary component in an explanatory structure needed to account for the observable phenomena explained by physics. Newton emphasized the need for a notion of absolute acceleration, acceleration accompanied by the so-called inertial forces. He argued that such acceleration could not be characterized as acceleration relative to some material object, but must be considered acceleration relative to space itself. In any relative acceleration of two objects, one only may experience inertial forces, even though both are accelerated

467

relative to one another. Even in empty space, Newton argued, a test object would still be able to detect absolute acceleration by experiencing inertial forces, although, the universe being otherwise empty, such acceleration could not be relative to another material thing. Optical phenomena provide another such Newtonian argument, since the distinction between inertial motion and non-inertial motion shows up in various optical experiments one can perform as well (such as non-null results for round-trip velocity of light experiments in a non-inertial laboratory).

An important proposal of MACH'S was that absolute acceleration might be taken as acceleration relative to 'the fixed stars', that is the average 'smeared out' matter of the material universe. The phenomena explained by the Newtonian by reference to acceleration with respect to space itself would then be explained by the acceleration of the test object with respect to the bulk matter of the universe.

Einstein's Special Theory of Relativity offers no solace to the relationist, whether of the Machian or some other sort. It is a 'Newtonian'-type theory with a definite distinction between objects in absolutely uniform and objects in absolutely accelerated motion. Einstein did have hopes, however, that his theory of gravitation as curved space-time would be a theory in accordance with Machian precepts. It appears, however, that General Relativity is not such a theory. Even in model universes devoid of other matter test objects can distinguish uniform from accelerated motion. Models of the universe can be constructed in which the average matter of the world is 'in absolute rotation'. Other 'anti-relationist' and 'anti-Machian' consequences of the theory can be derived as well.

It is very far from clear how to view the substantivalist/relationist debate in the light of contemporary physics. On the one hand modern theories make the very distinction between space (or, rather, space-time) itself and matter dissolve away. Space-time dynamically interacts with matter, has (in certain senses) mass-energy, and so on.

Indeed, there exist 'super-substantivalist' accounts in which matter is explained as a 'piece' of curved space-time, although they are, at present, merely speculations and not established science. On the other hand various foundational problems in the General Theory of Relativity suggest resolutions of a more relationist, and, indeed, conventionalist sort. For example, interpreted as a naive substantivalist theory the theory appears to be, very surprisingly, radically indeterministic (Einstein's 'hole' argument). Much remains to be done to disentangle all of the threads tied up in the substantivalist/relationist debate and to explore the appropriate 'metaphysical' background most suitable for contemporary physics.

Of the many revolutions in our conception of space and time arising out of the modern revolution in physics, none is more dramatic than the replacement of space and time as traditionally understood by the unified notion of a space-time. By far the most elegant and coherent framework in which to formalize the laws of nature as empirically discovered (*see* LAW OF NATURE) is that, suggested by Hermann Minkowski (1864–1909) and based on the work of Poincaré and Einstein, which takes as the basic elements event locations and their 'interval' or space-time separations. Spatial and temporal separations between events are then derivative from this fundamental space-time relationship. In the standard relativistic frameworks spatial and temporal separations are, in fact, relative to chosen frames of reference in the form of motions of an 'observer', whereas the space-time intervals are now the sole invariant, non-relativized, relations among events.

General Relativity goes beyond this space-time picture, necessary for the standard formulation of the Special Theory of Relativity, to introduce even more novel elements. In particular the space-time of the Special Theory of Relativity was, like pre-relativistic space and time, an arena in which events occur and, in some ways, a determiner of how they must occur. In the even newer theory the space-time becomes itself a dynamic element effected by, as well as effecting, the material contents in it.

It is important to note that subsequent to the discovery of the space-time notions needed for the formulation of special and general relativity, it was realized that space-time concepts could also provide deep insights into the structure of pre-relativistic physics. Neo-Newtonian space-time, for example, provides a conceptual framework that allows for the definition of absolute acceleration, needed in the Newtonian theory, but in which absolute velocity, an embarrassment for Newtonian theory because of its lack of observational effects, is undefined. Similarly, a 'curved' version of neo-Newtonian space-time provides a framework for the Newtonian theory of gravity that allows one to avoid some well-known paradoxes that infect the theory of gravity as a force in flat space as gravity was understood in the traditional Newtonian formulation.

Much attention has been directed to alleged interconnections between the spatial and temporal features of the world and other features. There are, for example, several attempts to try and show that some spatial or temporal feature of the world 'reduce' to some other feature (see REDUCTION, REDUCTIONISM). Prominent among these attempts are so-called 'causal' theories that allege that some or all spatial or temporal (or space-time) relations can be 'reduced to' or 'defined by' the causal relations among events. Suggestions of this sort can be found as early as Leibniz. The doctrines only received extensive investigation, however, in the light of the exploration of relativistic space-time theories.

Such claims of reducibility of the spatio-temporal to the causal face many prima facie philosophical problems. There is the problem of understanding the space and time of the immediately perceived in the context of such a causal theory. There are also objections based on claims to the effect that if any reductive relation takes place it must be of the causal to the spatio-temporal and not the other way around. Humean doctrines of CAUSATION, for example, pre-suppose spatial and temporal relations among events in their analyses of the causal relation. (*See* HUME.)

Other problems arise out of the intricate relation between spatio-temporal features and causal features of the world in various space-times of physics. Leibniz had suggested that simultaneity could be understood as non-causal-connectibility, all non-simultaneous events being causally connectible to one another. In Special Relativity this will not do as limitations on the velocity of propagation of causal signals leaves many events not simultaneous with one another all not causally connectible to a given event. Such facts lie behind some of the claims of 'mere conventionality' for simultaneity of events at a distance from one another as that notion is used in Special Relativity.

In turns out, however, that as a matter of fact all the metric relations of a special relativistic space-time are provably coextensive with relations among the events defined using causal notions alone. These 'causal definitions' of metric relations, however, break down in the context of General Relativity where space-times that are metrically quite distinct can have isomorphic causal structures (*see* ISOMORPHISM). Many subtle philosophical questions need to be explored when any result of contemporary mathematical physics is used to try to either defend or attack some claim of 'reducibility' of a spatio-temporal to a causal feature.

In the general relativistic context it is sometimes alleged that at least the topological structure of space-time can be 'defined' by the causal structure among events. Once again the claim becomes quite problematic when the details of the physical theories are examined. In space-time that are causally 'pathological' many relations of coextensivity between topological and causal relations among the space-time events break down. Here 'causally pathological' means that the space-time contains 'closed causal lines' or lines that are causal and 'almost closed'. Such sequences of events that proceed from event to later event but that 'loop back' to the origin event have, naturally, many consequences for other philosophical doctrines about the nature of time, causation and DETERMINISM as well. Even in these pathological space-times, however, topological structures are 'fixed' by richer 'causal' notions than that of causal connectibility. The richer notion needed, though, is something like that of a path in space-time being a continuous causal path, suggesting that at least some primitive space-time topological notion (that of continuity at least along paths traversable by a causal signal) is needed to fix the full topology, and casting doubt on the claim of such a 'definition' of the topological structure being in any way a reduction of that structure to a purely causal structure. Many issues remain, however, in becoming clear what the claim of a causal reduction comes down to and whether any such claim can be established in the light of both philosophical arguments and results from physics.

A crucial problem for the philosopher of space and time is to understand the manifest 'asymmetry' between the past and the future. We remember and have records of the past, but not of the future. We take causal influence to proceed from earlier to later events. We think of the past as 'fixed' and unchangeable, but of the future as 'open' and indeterminate in nature. What grounds these asymmetries? (*See* FATALISM.)

One important claim is that all of them can be accounted for by the remarkable asymmetry of physical processes in time that are summed up in the so-called increase of entropy of systems. Summarized in thermodynamics by the various Second Laws of Thermodynamics and viewed from the point of view of statistical mechanics as a ubiquitous 'randomizing' of the energy of the microcomponents of macroscopic systems, the entropic increase of systems over time is, if not the only, the dominant physical process that shows a radical asymmetric behaviour of systems toward the past and toward the future. The physical explanation for this asymmetry itself is one that remains a matter of great controversy. All known attempts to 'explain' why systems show such an asymmetry in their behaviour in time, including those invoking cosmological asymmetries and temporarily isolated systems 'branched' off from the cosmos in general, are fraught with fundamental difficulties.

But, given this asymmetry of processes, can it fully account for the 'directions of time' as revealed in the features noted above? Here, again, the question is open. Proponents of the view point to the success of an account of another alleged asymmetry that is shown to be 'reducible' to a specific physical process. We might think in an Aristotelian vein of space as having intrinsic 'upward' and intrinsic 'downward' directions, the asymmetry revealed in many processes and even knowable to us without inference (*see* ARISTOTLE). All would now admit, however, that 'down' can simply be taken to be the local direction of the gravitational force. Similarly, the entropic theorist may argue, 'future' can be taken simply as that direction of time in which local processes are showing an increase in their entropy parallel, in time, to one another.

Opponents of the view will argue, on the other hand, that the mere fact that systems do increase their entropy, at least as a matter of overwhelming statistical generality, in the future time directions is not sufficient to establish the claim that the 'ground' of the past/future asymmetry lies in entropic considerations. What would be required of the entropic theorist would be a convincing demonstration that all our intuitive asymmetries between past and future, including our 'immediate knowledge' of which temporal direction is which, can be accounted for by reference to the facts of entropic asymmetry alone. Despite very ingenious efforts to establish this claim, however, the question remains very much a matter of dispute.

BIBLIOGRAPHY

Earman, J.: *World Enough and Space-Time* (Cambridge, MA: MIT Press, 1989).

Friedman, M.: *Foundations of Space-Time Theories* (Princeton, NJ: Princeton University Press, 1983).

Mellor, D.H.: *Real Time* (Cambridge: Cambridge University Press, 1981).

Newton-Smith, W.: *The Structure of Time* (London: Routledge and Kegan Paul, 1980).

Sklar, L.: *Space, Time and Space-Time* (Berkeley, CA: University of California Press, 1974).

Sklar, L.: *Philosophy and Spacetime Physics* (Berkeley, CA: University of California Press, 1985).

LAWRENCE SKLAR

Spinoza, Baruch [Benedict] de (1632–77) Born in Amsterdam of Jewish parents who had migrated from Portugal to escape the Inquisition, he was taught Hebrew in childhood and Latin in early youth. By his early twenties, he had earned the respect of experts in biblical studies, in medieval Jewish philosophy, and in the new post-Aristotelian natural science and philosophy associated with Francis Bacon (1561–1626) and DESCARTES. At the same time, because he advocated reinterpreting the Jewish faith in the light of the new science, the Amsterdam synagogue, which was returning to the traditional Judaism it had been compelled to compromise in Portugal, expelled him. Leaving Amsterdam, he lived at first at Rijnsburg and later at Voorburg and The Hague, attracting the friendship of a small but distinguished group of liberal Protestants. His chief occupation was philosophical study and research, the results of which he communicated to his friends by manuscripts and letters. He partly supported himself by grinding optical lenses, but was also helped by the generosity of richer friends, who would have given him more if he would have accepted it. Never in robust health, he was only 44 when he died.

The first two parts of Spinoza's posthumously published masterpiece, *Ethics, Demonstrated in Geometrical Order* (1677), drafts of which he had circulated among his friends from the middle 1660s, are the most authoritative exposition of his contribution to metaphysics. Yet they would be enigmatic but for the light thrown on them by his correspondence, by an earlier *Short Treatise on God, Man and his Well-Being* which he probably wrote between 1660 and 1662, and by his *Tractatus theologico-politicus* (published 1670). His early and unfinished *Tractatus de intellectus emendatione* and the *Cogitata metaphysica* which he appended to the exposition *more geometrico* of the first two parts of Descartes's *Principia philosophiae* (1663), while important evidence of how his metaphysical views developed, are unsafe guides to their mature form. He wrote all his books, complete or incomplete, in Latin, as well as most of his correspondence, although only Dutch translations of the *Short Treatise* survive.

The *Short Treatise* shows that his first step in metaphysics was to generalize DESCARTES's doctrine that the essence of each created SUBSTANCE is constituted or expressed by a single attribute, of which its various states are modes (*see* ESSENCE/ACCIDENT; MODE). Maintaining that the essences constituted by two attributes of natural substances – extension and thought – are not finite, as Descartes believed, but infinite, he proceeded to infer, on one hand, that extended substance cannot be merely indefinite or unbounded, as Descartes had contended, but must be strictly infinite; and on the other, that finite thinking substances cannot really be substances at all, but must be modes of an infinite thinking substance, related to it as Descartes's finite bodies are related to the unbounded extended universe.

At the same time, Spinoza both recognized that Nature, as human beings 'see' it, is a unity of what is extended and what thinks, and reasoned that 'if there were different beings in nature, the one could not possibly unite with the other' (*Short Treatise*, I, 2). He therefore concluded that every attribute constituting an infinite essence must be such that the essence it constitutes is also constituted by every other. The 'order and connection' of the modes of a

471

substance whose essence is thus constituted would be the same no matter under what attribute they are considered – that is, the causal laws that determine the sequence of modes under one attribute would have counterparts in those that determine it under any other. Since substances are distinguished by their attributes, and no substance can be constituted by any attribute unless it is constituted by every attribute there is, there can be only one substance, and it must be 'absolutely infinite'. And since every set of causal laws is in terms of some attribute, the causal order and connection of modes as constituted by each attribute would be the same if, and only if, each set were such that correspondence rules could in principle be formulated by which any causal sequence according to one could be derived from that same causal sequence according to any other.

The cardinal axiom about CAUSATION in *Ethics* I, coyly formulated as 'Whatever is, is either in itself or in another', means that everything either immanently causes itself, as any infinite substance must, or is immanently caused by something else that immanently causes itself. Spinoza followed Descartes in conceiving the extended universe as an unbounded extended plenum, in which finite bodies are brought into existence by its internal motions, but he rejected Descartes's doctrine that such a universe would be a quiescent one unless God had introduced motion into it, maintaining that both how much motion the universe contains and that it is conserved are determined by laws of 'immanent' causality implicit in its infinite essence as extended. The laws of 'transient' causality according to which notions of finite bodies persist or cause others, which are the foundations of human physical science, follow from those of immanent causality, of which human beings can know only the laws of conservation. Neither extended NATURE as a whole, nor any finite body in it, is brought into existence by a transcendent divine creator (*see* IMMANENT/TRANSCENDENT). A finite body is a unity of moving and resting parts that tends to persist in being,

and its essence is simply the causal nature by which it so tends – its *conatus*. Nature, however, is not only material, but mental: it is not only extended, but thinks. As thinking, it is an infinite complex idea which truly represents its essence as constituted by all its infinite attributes, including its attribute of thought. Within this completely adequate representation of itself there are finite and partly inadequate representations of itself from the points of view of such finite bodies as are themselves causal subsystems capable of interacting with other causal systems, and not merely of reacting to them like unstructured *corpora simplicissima*.

Spinoza accepted Descartes's twofold doctrine that thought is distinguished from all other attributes because all thinking involves ideas, and that every idea exists in two distinct ways: 'formally', as what it is in itself, and 'objectively', as representing something other than itself (an idea can be represented, but only by forming a further idea of it); but he rejected Descartes's further distinction between ideas and acts of will with respect to them such as affirming their truth or willing that they be true. There are no thoughts, he contended, except ideas; and acts of will with respect to ideas are nothing but complex ideas of a certain sort. Affirming an idea is simply having it without any other idea incompatible with it; and denying an idea is having two incompatible ideas, one of which explains the other as delusive, as on waking up one denies ideas one had when asleep by forming further ideas of them as caused by dreaming. Again, the fundamental motivating 'affects' of love and hate are complex ideas consisting of an idea of an increase or decrease in lover's or hater's power of acting, together with an idea of its cause. Corresponding to each finite body capable of providing for external contingencies there will be a complex finite idea in Nature as thinking that is primarily constituted by an idea of that body, and of nothing else; but to the extent that it represents that body's interactive capacity to provide for external contingencies, that idea must also indirectly represent extended

Nature as causing those contingencies under certain conditions.

Since a complete representation of Nature as constituted by any attribute other than thought must be infinite and really distinct from a representation of it as constituted by any other, every such representation in Nature as thinking is a distinct infinite mind; and Nature as thinking is an infinity of such infinite minds, together with a complete and adequate representation of itself as representing them, and so on *ad infinitum* (Letter 66). Finite human minds are complex modes of thinking each of which primarily represents a finite *body* – a complex finite mode of Nature as constituted by extension – and nothing else. That is, a human mind is a finite mode of Nature as thinking only so far as Nature as thinking includes an infinite mind that primarily represents Nature as extended. Nature as thinking is not merely causally parallel with Nature as constituted by every other attribute, but it 'adequately cognizes' itself both as constituted by each of those attributes, and as so cognizing itself. Spinoza's concept of adequate cognition derives from his axiom that 'Cognition of an effect depends on and involves cognition of its cause' (*Ethics* I, axiom 4): to cognize something is to have an idea of it; and that idea will be adequate just to the extent that it represents that thing as caused according to some LAW OF NATURE. Some ideas which everybody has are adequate because they are 'common notions' in the sense of being involved in the idea of anything whatever: for example, that of a substance as immanent cause of itself, of a mode as immanently caused by something that immanently causes itself, of an attribute as constituting the essence of a substance, and of Nature as a unity – that is, of anything whose essence is infinite as constituted by every attribute expressing such an essence, as well as the more familiar examples of the ideas of existence, essence, number, cause and effect. But common notions are not the only adequate ideas. If an idea in a human mind of a mode of its corresponding body is caused by an external body by virtue of a property they both share, as each idea of the felt shape of an external body is, then Spinoza ingeniously (and plausibly) argued that it must be adequate too; and the class of such ideas is very large.

Given these fundamental doctrines, Spinoza was able to show that, among the adequate ideas in every human mind, there are enough ideas to make it possible to construct not only an adequate theory of God or Nature, a true physics of Nature as extended, but also true functional conceptions of the human mind and body, and a complete theory of how human beings would live if they were guided solely by reason. The reason why so few human beings have succeeded in doing so is that inadequate ideas derived from their upbringing and unanalysed experience distract them from using their adequate ideas to correct their inadequate ones, and cause them to dismiss the true ideas others present to them as at best foolish speculation and at worst as diabolically inspired heresy.

The happy few who are capable of living according to reason neither expect 'God or Nature' to love them. Their standard of perfection is Nature, the absolutely infinite being with respect to which all other beings are immanently caused modes, and not themselves or anything they imagine. Their fundamental attitude is intellectual love of God or Nature, and *acquiescentia* in whatever happens that is beyond their control. Since it is a law of nature that everything seeks to persevere in being as it is, those who live according to reason seek to persevere in doing so. On one hand, they are faithful friends of others who live according to reason; and on the other, while they take precautions against others so far as they behave irrationally, they neither condemn them nor wish them ill, but as far as they can help them to become rational also. After death, they neither hope for heaven nor fear hell, but, since all adequate cognition is eternal, so far as their self-cognition is adequate they know that it is eternal, and that so far their minds have an eternal place in God as thinking.

Although Spinoza largely worked with ideas developed by others, above all Descartes, his metaphysical system is not only original, but unlike almost all others, may be essentially true. His largely Cartesian conceptions of physical nature and mind require correction; but it has neither been shown nor seems probable that a twenty-first-century Spinozism with an up-to-date philosophy of natural science and of mind could not be a live theoretical option.

WRITINGS

The standard edition of Spinoza's works is *Spinoza opera*, C. Gebhardt 4 vols (Heidelberg: Carl Winter, 1924–6); and the best edition in English is *The Collected Works of Spinoza* ed. and trans. E. Curley vol. 1 (Princeton, NJ: Princeton University Press, 1985), vol. 2 (forthcoming).

BIBLIOGRAPHY

Allison, H.: *Benedict de Spinoza: An Introduction* rev. edn (New Haven, CT: Yale University Press, 1987).
Bennett, J.: *A Study of Spinoza's* Ethics (Indianapolis, IN: Hackett, 1989).
Curley, E.: *Behind the Geometrical Method: A Reading of Spinoza's* Ethics (Princeton, NJ: Princeton University Press, 1988).
Donagan, A.: *Spinoza* (London: Harvester Wheatsheaf, 1988).
Mathéron, A.: *Individu et communauté chez Spinoza* 2nd edn (Paris: Editions de Minuit, 1988).

ALAN DONAGAN

state of affairs   *see* PROPOSITION, STATE OF AFFAIRS

Strawson, Peter Frederick (1919–)   British philosopher. Strawson's metaphysical views arise from his interest in understanding how we are able to use language to refer to and describe things. He has attacked the correspondence theory of truth (*see* THE-ORIES OF TRUTH) for harbouring serious confusions concerning the alleged relation between statement and world (1971, chs 10, 11, 12). In chapter 1 of *Individuals* (1959) he argues that the possibility of identifying, re-identifying, and referring to particular things, either in thought or speech, rests on the fact that we can locate basic particulars in a single unified spatio-temporal system. The basic particulars of this system are publicly observable material bodies, such as objects, animals and persons. He reinforces the point in chapter 2 with an ingenious discussion of the problems encountered in trying to construct an objective world in terms of purely auditory experience.

In chapter 3 of *Individuals*, entitled 'Persons', Strawson insists that the possibility of ascribing sensations and mental states to human beings is dependent upon the ontological priority of our conception of a person as an entity to which material properties are also ascribable (*see* MIND/BODY PROBLEM; PERSONS AND PERSONAL IDENTITY). Intentional physical actions exhibit paradigmatically the unitary nature of persons. Strawson's conception of persons is incompatible with both Cartesian mind/body dualism (*see* DESCARTES), which regards immaterial mental substances as the basic subjects to which states of CONSCIOUSNESS are ascribed, and the 'no-ownership' theory, which holds that such states are not really ascribed to any subject but are themselves private particulars that are causally associated with a body (*see* PUBLIC/PRIVATE). Neither view can explain why states of consciousness are ascribed to anything at all, let alone to the same thing as certain corporeal characteristics. We can account for this only if the concept of a person is thought of as 'primitive', i.e. as not analysable into the concept of an immaterial mind plus a body. Our concept of a mind is derived from that of a person and not the other way around. He later mentions but does not develop the implication that there is a concept of a personal body which is also derivative (Van Straaten, 1980, p. 273). In the second half of *Individuals* Strawson argues that the distinction between spatio-temporal particulars and general concepts or UNIVERSALS is the ontological foundation for the logical distinction between REFERENCE and predication or between subject and predicate.

Strawson's quest for the conditions underlying successful reference to an objective world echoes KANT's inquiry into what makes intelligible the idea of our experience of a world. In *The Bounds of Sense* (1966), a critical exposition of Kant's *Critique of Pure Reason*, Strawson sought to disengage Kant's insights concerning the fundamental CATEGORIES of human thought and experience from his problematic transcendental IDEALISM which regards nature as the mere appearance of unknowable things-in-themselves (*see* NOUMENA/PHENOMENA). Strawson's 'descriptive metaphysics' aims at elucidating 'the actual structure of our thought about the world' (1959, p. 9). He opposes 'revisionist metaphysics', which claims that our ordinary view of the world is seriously misleading and should be replaced by a radically different one. He regards Kant as a descriptive metaphysician with revisionist tendencies. A more recent revisionist target of Strawson's criticism is reductive NATURALISM, which holds that reality consists in the movements of particles through space-time, and all other things – persons, actions, mental states, sensible qualities and moral attributes – are either subjective or reducible to physical states and events (1985; 1988, p. 443) (*see* PHYSICALISM, MATERIALISM; REDUCTION, REDUCTIONISM). A limited physical perspective can have special uses, but it cannot replace our 'natural metaphysics' without serious loss.

WRITINGS

Individuals: An Essay in Descriptive Metaphysics (London: Methuen, 1959).

The Bounds of Sense: An Essay on Kant's Critique of Pure Reason (London: Methuen, 1966).

Logico-Linguistic Papers (London: Methuen, 1971).

Skepticism and Naturalism: Some Varieties (New York: Columbia University Press, 1985).

'Ma philosophie: son développement, son thème central et sa nature générale', *Revue de théologie et de philosophie* 120 (1988), 437–52; trans. S. Friedli and D. Schulthess from a presentation by Strawson at the University of Neuchâtel, Switzerland, June, 1988.

BIBLIOGRAPHY

Van Straaten, Z. ed.: *Philosophical Subjects: Essays Presented to P.F. Strawson* (Oxford: Clarendon Press, 1980). This contains Strawson's replies to his critics and a bibliography through 1980.

DOUGLAS C. LONG

structuralism Structuralism has been a possibility in philosophy ever since the term STRUCTURE and the suffix '-ism' have been available in the philosophical vocabulary, but this possibility seems not to have been realized until recently. One of the first claims to the position is made with characteristic modesty by Sir Arthur Eddington, who in describing his philosophy ('not as claiming authorship of ideas which are widely diffused in modern thought but because the ultimate selection and synthesis must be a personal responsibility' (1958, p. viii)) says that 'if it were necessary to give a short name to this philosophy, I should hesitate between "Selective subjectivism" and "Structuralism" ' (1958, p. viii). The parenthetical citation reflects a frequent observation by diverse thinkers about 'widely diffused' trends in post-First World War European thought, as turning from substance to structure, from things to relations, a shift described by the linguist Prince Nicholas Troubetzkoy as the replacement of 'atomism with structuralism' (1933, p. 246).

Eddington's structuralism appeals to mathematical group theory, which offers a way of identifying 'objects' in terms of the relations that constitute them, without knowing what it is that these relations relate: 'structural knowledge can be detached from knowledge of the entities forming the structure ... So long as the knowledge is confined to assertions of structure, it is not tied down to any particular realm of content.' (1958, p. 143) At the same time (1938) Ernst Cassirer was developing a theory of perception based on group theory, according to which perceptual objects are the invariants underlying sets of transformations between perceived aspects; this was a technical variation, in epistemology, of the strategy he had already worked out for cultural objects in his major work, *Philosophy of Symbolic Forms* (1923–31). It was only in 1945, just before his death, that he applied the term 'structuralism' to this approach. But its retrospective application would have been fully justified: the *Symbolic Forms* is a structuralist work in all but name.

The main usefulness of structuralism lies in the philosophy of the social or human sciences in which Cassirer chiefly worked. In these domains the normal mode of existence of objects is in virtue of the relations that constitute them or into which they enter; in the case of concretely existing objects it is their meanings, rather than their physical properties, that admit them to consideration. While in the natural sciences we may not, as Eddington suggests, know the nature of the entities whose interrelations make up the play of events and processes, a REALISM that attributes ontological status to them, independently of and prior to our knowledge of their interrelatedness, does not seem metaphysically extravagant. Indeed in most cases above the theoretically primitive we do know the nature of the elements quite well: if there are atoms it is reasonable to think of molecules as made of them, if there are molecules it is reasonable to think of their properties as explaining, for example, the transmission of hereditary material in genetics. We do not have to interpret their existence in any special way in order for them to function as they do in the natural order – on the contrary, we have reason to think that they would continue to do so if we ignored them altogether, indeed that their having done so independently of our awareness for millions of years is in the end what makes that awareness possible.

But the objects of the human sciences, as distinct from their physical embodiments, have ontological status *only* in virtue of their being apprehended, as relational, by intending subjects; giving *them* independent ontological status *is* metaphysically extravagant (though an extravagance in which many philosophers have indulged). Structuralism, then, is the view that the objects of the human sciences are relational rather than substantial, the relations in question being intended (in the phenomenological sense) by conscious subjects. Classes of such objects are distinguished by the facility with which their members can be generated out of one another by structural transformations, that is, the substitution of elements according to some rule (metonymy, metaphor, negation, etc.). Members of the same class are more or less closely *isomorphic* with one another, the test for ISO-MORPHISM being structural invariance under transformation.

The world abounds in trivial cases of isomorphism, in the domain of the natural sciences and in that, for example, of manufactured objects. It was his failure to distinguish such relatively uninteresting cases of similarity of structure from the more challenging ones presented by the objects of the human sciences that made Jean Piaget's introductory work on structuralism so misleading. If structure is everywhere whether we attend to it or not then nothing is achieved by pointing out that something belongs to a class whose members are characteristically structured – this is bound to be so. But if it proves on empirical inquiry that some classes of object – myths, marriage practices, extended families, novels, religious doctrines, languages, political strategies, fashions of dress, and the like – belong to classes whose members are mutual transforms of one another, and if furthermore the structures of the classes themselves have suggestive analogues (so that they might all, to adopt the view of Claude Lévi-Strauss (1908–) be thought of as derivative from a basic structure of mind), this is richly suggestive.

Lévi-Strauss, a philosophically trained anthropologist, is generally credited with the leading role in the upsurge of European structuralism in the work of thinkers as diverse as Jacques Lacan, Louis Althusser, Roland Barthes and Michel Foucault (1926–84); he himself, however, and virtually every structuralist since, credits the linguistics of Ferdinand de Saussure as the original inspiration. (Some writers have seen MARX, and before him the American anthropologist Lewis H. Morgan (1818–1881), as forerunners.) Foucault, the most centrally philosophical of the structuralists of the 1960s, tried to disavow the appellation, but the evidence was against him. Lévi-Strauss's metaphysical position was described by Paul Ricoeur as 'Kantianism without a transcendental subject' (1963, p. 618) (*see* KANTIANISM); Lévi-Strauss for his part conjectured that structuralism might lead to 'the restoration of a kind of popular materialism' (1963, p. 652) (*see* PHYSICALISM, MATERIALISM). But there seems to be no reason why a structuralist materialism might not be compatible with transcendental subjectivity as a property of embodied structures, one of whose functions is to intend a life-world of relational structures and their isomorphisms.

BIBLIOGRAPHY

Broekman, J.M.: *Structuralism: Moscow–Prague–Paris* (1971); trans. J.F. Beekman and B. Helm (Dordrecht: D. Reidel, 1974).
Cassirer, E.: 'The concept of groups and the theory of perception', trans. A. Gurwitsch *Philosophy and Phenomenological Research* 5 (1944), 1–35.
Caws, P.: *Structuralism: The Art of the Intelligible* (Atlantic Highlands, NJ: Humanities Press, 1988).
Eddington, A.: *The Philosophy of Physical Science* (Cambridge: 1939); (Ann Arbor, MI: University of Michigan Press, 1958).
Lévi-Strauss, C.: 'Réponse à quelques questions', *Esprit* n.s. 11 (1963), 628–53.
Ricoeur, P.: 'Structure et herméneutique', *Esprit* n.s. 11 (1963), 596–627.
Troubetzkoy, N.: 'La phonologie actuelle', in *Psychologie du langage* ed. H. Delacroix *et al.* 227–46 (Paris: Alcan, 1933).

PETER CAWS

structure The root of 'structure' goes back to Greek *storennumi* 'spread' and its Latin derivative *struo* 'put in order', hence to arrange or build. In the history of philosophy the term seems not to have had a technical use until the emergence of STRUCTURALISM, though in mathematics and the sciences it has carried theoretical weight (group structure, molecular structure, etc.). It has however been used informally by many philosophers.

An early example occurs in Richard Price, who in 1787 criticized the view that 'our approbation of goodness' might be derived from 'an arbitrary structure of our minds' (1948; p. 136). More recently the term appears in some familiar titles: CARNAP's *The Logical Structure of the World* (1928), MERLEAU-PONTY's *The Structure of Behavior* (1942), GOODMAN's *The Structure of Appearance* (1955), Ernest Nagel's *The Structure of Science* (1961). Its occurrence in a title, however, does not mean that much attention will be paid to its definition in the work in question, even when there is an explicit metaphysical connection, as in Morris Lazerowitz's *The Structure of Metaphysics* (1955) or Stefan Körner's *Metaphysics: Its Structure and Function* (1984).

In Carnap's title 'structure' is a translation of the German *Aufbau*. German also has *Struktur*, used by WITTGENSTEIN and, earlier, by MARX, for whom it names the economic relations on which ideology is built as an *Überbau* – though these terms are usually translated into English as 'base' and 'superstructure' respectively. Goodman's *Structure* cites Carnap's *Aufbau*, but, again, does not say much about structure as such; it deals with constructional systems, whose being constructional 'distinguish[es] them from uninterpreted formal systems and from amorphous philosophical discourses' (1951, p. xl), and with their isomorphisms, thus introducing two related terms ('system' and 'form', the latter the usual translation of Greek *morphe*) which should be distinguished from 'structure'.

The first distinction may be effected by defining 'structure' as a set of relations but 'system' as a set of elements (between which the relations hold). Relations are usually defined either intensionally (in terms of the properties of their relata) or extensionally (as sets of ordered pairs), but there is a third, and from the metaphysical point of view a more interesting, possibility, namely to define them *intentionally*, as apprehended and sustained by an intending subject.

The second distinction is more problematic. In ordinary English 'form' often means external aspects of wholes while 'structure' means internal relations of parts, but on this construal 'ISOMORPHISM' in its current use would not, in spite of its etymology, mean 'sameness of form' but 'sameness of structure'. Also there is an accepted sense of 'logical form' that is inconsistent with this usage. In Wittgenstein's *Tractatus* the distinction is made as follows: structure is 'the determinate way in which objects are connected in a state of affairs', while 'form is the possibility of structure' (1922, p. 13). In other words if actual objects are to be connected together in some determinate way, that way of being connected must already be possible. From this it follows that a structure is a set of *embodied* relations, as distinguished from a form which may be abstract. Every structure then would be the realization of some form – a distinctly Platonic view (*see* PLATO; PLATONISM).

Other cases worth mentioning are Carnap's notion of a similarity of intensional structure in *Meaning and Necessity* (1947) and STRAWSON's usage in *Individuals*

(1959). In his Introduction Strawson says: 'Descriptive metaphysics is content to describe the actual structure of our thought about the world, revisionary metaphysics is concerned to produce a better structure' (1959, p. 9). But descriptive metaphysics aims only 'to lay bare *the most general features* of our conceptual structure' (ibid., emphasis added); this structure furthermore 'does not readily display itself on the surface of language, but lies submerged' (1959, p. 10). Strawson does attribute structural characteristics to the spatio-temporal framework within which individuation proceeds: 'it is a single picture which we build, a unified structure, in which we ourselves have a place, and in which every element is thought of as directly or indirectly related to every other' (1959, p. 29). Yet even this remark is more systemic than structural, in the sense that it begins with the elements rather than with the relations themselves.

The one major modern philosopher who anticipates the structuralist use of the concept is PEIRCE, who introduces the notion of 'external structure' or 'valence' in a brief essay on 'phaneroscopy', his original version of phenomenology (1931, pp. 141ff.). Structure in this sense is a property of systems whose elements are generated out of the relations that relate them. Together with the idea of structural transformation, by which isomorphic structures can be generated out of one another, this priority of relations over elements may be said to define the metaphysically interesting sense of the term 'structure'.

BIBLIOGRAPHY

Goodman, N.: *The Structure of Appearance* (1951); 3rd edn (Dordrecht: Reidel, 1977).

Peirce, C.S.: *Collected Papers of Charles Sanders Peirce* ed. C. Hartshorne and P. Weiss (Cambridge, MA: Harvard University Press, 1931), vol. 1.

Price, R.: *A Review of the Principal Questions in Morals* (1787); ed. D.D. Raphael (Oxford: Clarendon Press, 1948).

Strawson, P.F.: *Individuals: An Essay in Descriptive Metaphysics* (1959); (London: Routledge, 1990).

Wittgenstein, L.: *Tractatus Logico-Philosophicus* (1922); trans. D.F. Pears and B.F. McGuinness (London: Routledge and Kegan Paul, 1961).

PETER CAWS

Suárez, Francisco (1548–1617) Philosopher and theologian, known as 'Doctor Eximius'. Born in Granada, Spain, he joined the Society of Jesus in 1564, studied at Salamanca, and taught law, theology, and philosophy there and also at Rome, Coimbra and other leading universities. Apart from his many theological works, he wrote four important philosophical treatises: *De legibus* (1612), *De Deo uno et trino* (1606), *De anima* (1621) and *Disputationes metaphysicae* (1597). The last of these is the first systematic and comprehensive work of metaphysics written in the West that is not a commentary on ARISTOTLE's *Metaphysics*. It is divided into fifty-four disputations that cover every metaphysical topic known at the time. Its influence was immediate and lasting; within a few years of its publication, it had become the standard text in the field in continental Europe. Its impact can be seen in the thought of DESCARTES, LEIBNIZ, Christian Wolff (1679–1754), SCHOPENHAUER and others.

Suárez's sources are vast, ranging from antiquity to his contemporaries, but it is in Aristotle and AQUINAS that he most frequently finds inspiration. His main contributions to philosophy occur in metaphysics and law, although his thought is also relevant in many other areas, including epistemology. Among Suárez's many contributions to metaphysics, his views on the nature of metaphysics, being, individuals, and UNIVERSALS stand out.

Suárez understands metaphysics as the science of 'being in so far as it is real being' (*ens in quantum ens reale*) (*Disputationes metaphysicae*, I, 1, 26). He rejects those views according to which the object of metaphysics includes accidental and conceptual being and those that restrict its object to God, immaterial substances, or substantial entities. Many scholastics had expressed views similar to this prior to Suárez, but they debated whether there is a univocal concept of being that would support such an understanding of metaphysics. According to Suárez, there is such a single concept of being which is analogically derived by the mind from the similarity among things (*Disputationes*, II, 2, 16).

The concept of being is derived from the consideration of individual entities. Indeed, everything that exists, including substances (*see* SUBSTANCE) as well as their properties, accidents, principles and components, is INDIVIDUAL (*Disputationes*, V, I, 4). Individuality is defined in terms of incommunicability, namely, the inability of individuals to be divided into entities of the same specific kind as themselves. By contrast, universality consists in communicability (*Disputationes*, VI, 2, 9). Since only individuals exist, universals have no ontological status independent of the mind and result from a mental operation that abstracts a common likeness among things (*see* NOMINALISM).

The principle of individuation in things is their 'entity', which Suárez identifies with 'the essence as it exists' (*Disputationes*, V, 6, 1). This conception of the principle of individuation applies not only to substances, but also to their accidents and components.

Suárez's views of individuals, individuation and universals put him closer to OCKHAM than to Aquinas or DUNS SCOTUS, but in other areas he relies on the views of Aquinas and Scotus to achieve the comprehensive metaphysical system for which he is well known.

WRITINGS

Opera omnia 28 vols, ed. C. Berton (Paris: Vivès, 1856–61).

SUBSTANCE

BIBLIOGRAPHY

Courtine, J.-F.: *Suárez et le système de la métaphysique* (Paris: Presses Universitaires de France, 1990).

Cronin, T.J.: *Objective Being in Descartes and Suárez* (Rome: 1966; repr. New York and London: Garland Publishing, 1987).

Gracia, J.J.E.: *Suárez on Individuation* (Milwaukee: Marquette University Press, 1982).

Gracia, J.J.E. and Davis, D.: *The Metaphysics of Good and Evil According to Suárez* (Munich and Vienna: Philosophia Verlag, 1989).

Specht, R.: *Francisco Suárez. Über die Individualität und das Individuationsprinzip* 2 vols (Hamburg; Meiner, 1976).

JORGE J.E. GRACIA

substance For much of the history of metaphysics, *substance* has been its most important concept. A substance is a primary reality, something that can exist alone, without need of anything from outside. The determination of what kinds of substance there are, and how they stand to non-substances have been central tasks of traditional metaphysics. Since it is impossible to appreciate the complexity of the substance concept without some knowledge of its history in western philosophy, a brief historical outline will precede the analysis.

BRIEF HISTORY

The term 'substance' comes from the Latin 'substantia', meaning 'standing under', but the etymology is little guide to the meaning. As the term is used by philosophers, substances are individuals. The term is also, confusingly, used in everyday speech for kinds of stuff, e.g. gold, polythene. 'Substantia' translated the Greek word 'ousia'. ARISTOTLE's complex use of the term derives from his criticism of PLATO's theory of Forms. In the early work *Categories*, substance is the principal category, and substances, the primary things, are concrete individuals like an individual man or an individual horse. Aristotle had also called this category 'what it is', and the kinds, man, horse etc. are called substance in a secondary sense, a view he later dropped. Substance contrasts with the other CATEGORIES, such as quality, place and action, which tell us something about substances, derivative aspects such as how something is coloured, where it is, what it is doing, etc.

In the *Metaphysics* Aristotle analyses concrete individuals as composites of matter and form (*see* MATTER/FORM), and in Books Z and H, he now argues that substance is the individual form, what in the Middle Ages was called substantial form, since it is prior to the composite, and the matter does not exist actually, but only as the potentiality to be formed. But this is only one of various meanings of *ousia* that Aristotle mentions in Books Δ and Z, and the ideas of substance as concrete individual and as the ultimate SUBSTRATUM of attributes and of CHANGE are never completely set aside.

While ancient philosophers did not always adopt Aristotelian terminology, since this was tied to his matter/form theory, they often nevertheless accepted something we could call substances: the atoms of Democritus (*c.*460–*c.*370 BC), for example, are both the primary entities and the substrata of change in the atomist philosophy (*see* ATOMISM).

The question whether there are immaterial substances has always been intensively debated: whereas materialists ancient and modern (*see* PHYSICALISM, MATERIALISM) naturally rejected them, Plato regarded forms and souls as self-subsistent, and Aristotle likewise considered the higher functions of intelligence to require a disembodiable form. His COSMOLOGY postulated immaterial intelligences moving the celestial spheres, and an unmoved mover as the ultimate cause of all celestial motion. These immaterial substances were later smoothly integrated into medieval cosmology as angels and God respectively.

Medieval discussions of substances added some footnotes to Aristotle, mainly to accommodate Christian dogma. The doctrine of the Eucharist reconciled communion bread and wine continuing to look and taste like bread and wine while supposedly being in fact Christ's flesh and blood by claiming that the substance is miraculously switched while the perceptible accidents remain unchanged. Another issue was survival after death. Since humans, being of one species, were individuated by matter during life but lacked it after death, according to AQUINAS they retain their identity and individuality thanks to the distinguishing qualities of their earthly history. Angels, which had never been embodied, had to be each of a unique species.

Modern philosophers retained the idea of substance as that which can exist independently, but interpreted it variously. Since for DESCARTES, all finite beings require God to constantly recreate them, strictly only God is a substance, but Descartes allowed bodies and souls to be substances in the derivative sense that they require only God to exist. Descartes's independence idea was interpreted in radically different ways by LEIBNIZ and SPINOZA. For Spinoza, an object which is not its own cause is dependent on this cause, and nothing so dependent is a substance, so no substance can be the cause of another, so only one infinite substance exists. Leibniz on the contrary argued that since an object with proper parts depended on these to exist, true substances, monads, must be without parts or spatial extension. The changes in monads must therefore be like mental events, and Leibniz viewed the world as a plurality of unextended souls. (See MONAD, MONADOLOGY.)

The empiricists progressively eroded the traditional substance concept (see EMPIRICISM). LOCKE viewed substance with misgivings as an unknowable substratum, a 'something we know not what' supporting the qualities we perceive. He regarded persons not as immaterial souls, which could come and go arbitrarily, but as 'forensic' entities whose persistence is secured simply by the continuity of consciousness (see PERSONS AND PERSONAL IDENTITY).

BERKELEY attacked Locke's substratum in the case of material substances as absurd, seeing bodies as simply bundles of qualities, but retained immaterial substances or souls. HUME took the natural next step and dissolved the soul into the bundle of its perceptions. While ostensibly destroying the last remnants of traditional substance, Hume in effect shifted the role to perceptions, in his philosophy the independently existing components of the universe. At the hands of KANT, substance was bound essentially to the logical role of being a subject of predication; while Kant argued for an eternally persisting substrate, this is for him not an autonomous thing, but merely a necessary condition for the appearance of change.

With the widespread acceptance of forms of Hume's criticism or Kant's epistemological relativization among philosophers, and the apparent irrelevance of the concept of substance for modern science, it has lost its central position in metaphysics. There have been only flickers of renewal, for instance in disputes about the absoluteness of spacetime (see SPACE AND TIME) in WITTGENSTEIN's remarks about objects as the substance of the world in the *Tractatus* (1922); or BRENTANO's account of substance in his *Theory of Categories* (1933). The most concerted attempt to reinstate something like Aristotle's original primary beings is in STRAWSON's *Individuals* (1959), which fuses Kantian argumentation with Aristotelian REALISM in arguing that bodies are the basic particulars from the point of view of identification and reidentification.

SUBSTANCE UNWOVEN

Because of this involved history, it is doubtful whether we can correctly speak of a single coherent concept of substance. Rather, we have to identify and separate five different strands in the traditional concept.

Independent beings

The ontological primacy of substances arises chiefly from their independence, or ability to subsist alone. In this they contrast with

481

beings needing others for their existence, such as states, properties or limits. But what is meant by 'independent'? There are several senses; steps towards spelling them out were made by HUSSERL in his *Logical Investigations* (1901). A particular object *a* is weakly dependent on another particular *b* when necessarily, if *a* exists, so does *b*. An object is then independent in the corresponding sense when it depends on no particular object (except itself). Objects with essential individual parts, such as the protons of an atom, are dependent in this sense on their essential parts. An object *a* is strongly dependent on an object *b* if necessarily, if *a* exists, so does *b*, and *b* is neither *a* nor part of *a*. When a cat grins, that grin could not exist without that cat, but the cat is not part of the grin, so the grin is strongly dependent on the cat. An object is independent in the corresponding sense when it depends on nothing apart from itself and perhaps parts of itself, giving a sense to the idea that something depends on nothing 'outside itself'. But there are also weaker generic senses of dependence; for instance, when an object *a* depends not on some particular object, but nevertheless could not exist unless there were some object or objects of a certain kind related to it in a certain way. A dog cannot exist without there being a large number of carbon atoms, but which particular carbon atoms go to make up the organic compounds in the dog's body and its food is indifferent.

Explicating the independence of substances as viewed by one or other of the theories we surveyed entails selecting the most appropriate concept of independence. A quality, state, action, etc., of a physical body or an organism are all strongly dependent on it; it may be weakly dependent on some essential part, and generically dependent on certain kinds of things, but it is not strongly dependent on any other individual. This allows individuals to have causes – in the meanings of Aristotle – yet still be appropriately independent. If having a cause is taken (as in Spinoza) as a form of dependence, then only something uncaused or self-caused can be a substance. Leibniz's

substances are independent in the strong sense of depending not even on essential parts, and he assumed all parts of complexes are essential, so only monads could be substances. Descartes and Leibniz differ subtly on whether finite beings are true substances: for Leibniz they are, for Descartes not. To separate the terminological from the real disagreement requires further distinguishing the brief dependence of a created being on its creator from the permanent dependence of a sustained thing on its support. Descartes took God to both create finite beings and sustain them thereafter, whereas Leibniz considered they were self-sustaining once created.

Ultimate subjects

Substances are sometimes characterized as the ultimate subjects of predication: that of which things can be predicated but which cannot be predicated of anything else. But this really only defines particulars. What can be predicated (rightly or wrongly) of something is a universal (*see* UNIVERSALS; UNIVERSALS AND PARTICULARS). Dependent particulars such as headaches are not substances. However if we replace 'predication' in the formula by 'inherence', we have the classical account of substances as substrata. A substance is something in which characteristics inhere but which does not itself inhere in anything. INHERENCE is then a form of dependence under which substances are independent. But if substrata must have characteristics, they are also dependent, though in a different sense: a substratum, while it does not inhere, cannot exist without *some* characteristics: a 'free substratum' cannot exist.

Individuators

In those theories where a concrete thing's properties are shareable or universal, the substratum is also that which individuates (*see* INDIVIDUATION): a collection of universal properties, no matter how extensive, cannot, it is argued, be immune to being realized twice, so some further, individuating ingredient is required in a concrete particular. Several candidates have been put forward for this role: Aristotelian prime matter is one, place in space is another, BERGMANN's 'bare particulars' are another, like prime matter in being without essential characters, but unlike matter having a pure individuality: they are merely and irreducibly numerically different, and impose this difference on the substances they individuate. A BARE PARTICULAR differs from DUNS SCOTUS's 'thisness' or *haecceitas* in that the thisness of Socrates is not only that which makes the common human nature to be *an* individual human being: it makes him *this* particular human being and no other (*see* HAECCEITY).

Survivors of change

Concrete particulars not only have attributes (universal or particular, according to one's theory); they undergo real change. A piece of iron heated in a furnace gets hot, expands, begins to glow and becomes softer and more malleable. It is widely held that real CHANGE consists in this casting off old attributes for new. For something to change, *it* must exist before, during, and after the change, and so must survive it. Only so can we say it changes, rather than that it was created, replaced by something else, or destroyed. The subjects of change thus 'outlive' whatever ceased to be at the change (the state or accident of the substance), whatever exists fleetingly during it, and pre-exist whatever comes into being at its completion. Experience, not least of ourselves, provides us with numerous examples of this survival. But substances also come into being and cease to exist. In familiar cases, they do so by the composition and decomposition of complex structures, or by the arising and subsiding of sustaining processes. Both of these facts suggest there might be more subtle survivors of the demise of substances, such as the MATTER of which they are made. If substance is primarily that which survives change, then the ultimate substance would be indestructible, whether Aristotle's matter, which never ceases to exist but is merely transformed, or the indestructible, sempiternal

atoms of Democritus, or the conserved mass-energy of physics.

Basic objects of reference

Aristotle's *Categories* theory of substances as concrete individuals dovetails less with physical and metaphysical than with linguistic and epistemological concerns. Material things, organisms, geographical features and heavenly bodies are our constant companions through life. We are born of them, marry them, make them, change them, destroy them, buy and sell them, explore them. We fill our waking and sleeping hours talking and thinking about them. Jean Piaget's psychogenetic studies and Strawson's TRANSCENDENTAL ARGUMENTS suggest we could not communicate or even think were we not able to manipulate them, identify, trace and reidentify them. For this to be possible, they must be discriminated by us into sorts, and each sortal CONCEPT must connote conditions of persistence and reidentification. To achieve this is, in QUINE's words, to learn to divide REFERENCE, mastery of which affords us the formal concept of individual and sets us on the road to understanding number. It is the key to further cognitive achievements such as comparing, locating in space and time, describing experiences; it leads us into other ontological categories: quality, amount, position, relation, situation, etc., and, via the device of nominalization, making all of these subjects of further predication. If concrete particulars are not the first thing experience as such shows us, they yet seem to be our passport to higher cognition (*see* CONCRETE/ABSTRACT). That they should coincide with the substances of Aristotle's *Categories* is no happenstance: Aristotle's work is about the meanings of the simple terms we use, so those persistent objects which are so important to our practice of using words were bound to have a salient role in the theory.

SUBSTANCE RESUMED

The traditional concept of substance then harbours a multitude of roles, many of which are themselves subject to a multitude of more precise interpretations. It appears impossible for any one thing to fulfil all of these roles, and unnecessary to force anything into the part.

The intricacies – and problems – of the concept of substance began with Aristotle, and it is retrospectively surprising that it was as resilient as it proved. Perhaps a combination of the obvious utility of the common-sense linguistic notion of a basic particular, the accidental longevity and near-catholic influence of Aristotelianism in the West, and the relatively greater immunity of linguistic and metaphysical concepts from scientific refutation all help towards an explanation. While separable strands in the woof of the traditional concept will undoubtedly continue to be fruitful, and some will no doubt continue to sport the name 'substance', it is likely that traditional substance's fall from prominence will prove to be irreversible.

BIBLIOGRAPHY

Aristotle: *Categoriae* ed. L. Minio-Paluello (Oxford: Clarendon Press, 1949).
Aristotle: *Metaphysica* ed. W. Jaeger (Oxford: Clarendon Press, 1957).
Husserl, E.: 'On the theory of wholes and parts', in his *Logical Investigations* (1901); (London: Routledge and Kegan Paul, 1970), 435–92.
Strawson, P.F.: *Individuals: An Essay in Descriptive Metaphysics* (London: Methuen, 1959).

PETER SIMONS

substratum In the theory of SUBSTANCE, a substratum is understood as that which underlies the properties of a thing, its individuator, and ultimate subject of its predicates. The notion originates with ARISTOTLE's *materia prima*, which both individuates and carries properties without having properties or an identity of its own. The need for a substratum is felt to derive from the inability of properties to subsist alone or form a concrete individual. LOCKE took the substratum to be necessary, but obscure and unknowable. A modern counterpart is BERGMANN's notion of a BARE PARTICULAR. Substratum theories are criticized because the substratum cannot be an object of acquaintance and because it 'bears' properties without 'possessing' them. A standard move is to excise the substratum and see substance as just the bundle of properties, but bundle theories and others have their own problems, so substrata in some guise are unlikely to disappear from metaphysics (*see* BUNDLE THEORY).

BIBLIOGRAPHY

Bergmann, G.: *Realism* (Madison, WI: University of Wisconsin Press, 1967), esp. chs 2–3.
Locke, J.: *An Essay Concerning Human Understanding* (London: 1690); ed. P.H. Nidditch (Oxford: Clarendon Press, 1975) Bk II, ch. XXIII.
Loux, M.J.: *Substance and Attribute* (Dordrecht: Reidel, 1978), esp. ch. 8.

PETER SIMONS

supervenience To say that considerations of one kind (e.g. the mental) supervene on those of another kind (e.g. the physical) is to say that there are, or can be, no differences in the first kind without there being differences in the second kind. In other words: agreement in the subvening considerations (e.g. the physical) requires agreement in the supervening considerations (e.g. the mental).

This imprecise intuitive statement allows for many refinements. Continuing to illustrate with the purported supervenience of the mental on the physical, consider three examples:

(1) According to supervenience, if an individual ('Oskar') has a physical duplicate, the twin also duplicates Oskar mentally.

(2) Ask what Oskar's mental life would be in a counterfactual situation or possible world which duplicated all physical aspects of Oskar's actual state. Supervenience maintains agreement in all mental aspects also.

(3) Imagine the gods constructing the world from scratch. They pick the individuals and set all their physical properties. According to supervenience the Gods have thereby also set the individuals' mental properties.

These examples all specify that when cases agree in subvening respects they agree in supervening respects, but the examples differ in what kinds of cases are compared. *Weak supervenience* compares individuals in *the same* possible world: if in the actual or a counterfactual world two cases agree in all subvening respects, they also agree in all supervening respects. *Strong supervenience* compares individuals within or *across* POSSIBLE WORLDS: given two individuals in different counterfactual contexts, but themselves agreeing in all subvening respects, the two will also agree in all supervening respects. *Global supervenience* compares cases comprised by the way the whole world might be: two counterfactual scenarios describing whole world histories which agree in all subvening respects agree in all supervening respects.

Further refinements specify the kind of modality which is in question, most frequently metaphysical and nomological (*see* MODALITIES AND POSSIBLE WORLDS). Usually one clarifies 'agreement in respects' by specifying agreement in properties (and relations) or agreement in correctly applying predicates (one or many place). Different refinements may prove appropriate in different applications. To illustrate considerations for choosing among formulations of supervenience, weak supervenience permits counterfactual physical duplicates to differ mentally, giving an implausible reading for physicalism (*see* PHYSICALISM, MATERIALISM). Strong supervenience of the economic on intrinsic physical properties would require an original painting and an exact forgery to have the same monetary value. Many will conclude that a painting's value involves relations to the environment. If one despairs of circumscribing a relevant portion of the environment to provide a supervenience base one may opt for global supervenience to restore supervenience on the physical.

Supervenience provides a useful analytic tool for clarifying the intuition that the physical facts somehow fix or determine other facts, without commitment to explicit definition in terms of the physical. In ethics one can deny the definability of moral terms in a physical (or more broadly 'naturalistic') language while acknowledging, by asserting supervenience, that the physical facts still fix the ethical facts. In the philosophy of mind supervenience on the physical may replace explicit definability in an analysis of physicalism.

Supervenience likewise functions to explicate other antecedently less clear notions. For example, an emergent property might be one which supervenes on, without being definable in terms of, a physical base. A clarified HOLISM postulates relations which do not supervene on the non-relational properties of the relata (not even if implicit relata are included, such as the parents as well as the siblings in the case of *x and y are siblings*).

Some think of supervenience as a form of determination. When defined with nomic necessity, supervenience might characterize a kind of determination reminiscent of causes determining effects. When supervenience uses metaphysical necessity it is less clear whether, or in what sense, supervening properties can be said to occur *because of* or *in virtue of* subvening properties. However, metaphysical necessity may give a plausible reading for a relation of realization or instantiation. If the calculational properties of a hand calculator supervene on the calculator's physical properties, some say that the calculational properties are instantiated or realized by the calculator's physical properties.

Supervenience appears not to commit one to the explicit definability of supervening

485

properties in terms of subvening ones and, if by reducibility one means definability, not to reducibility (*see* REDUCTION, REDUCTIONISM). For global supervenience, if 'possible worlds' are interpreted as models of the relevant theory, the range of models must be limited or else Beth's theorem does entail definability (see Hellman and Thompson, 1975). Also, strongly supervening properties are necessarily equivalent to infinite disjunctions or conjunctions of subvening properties. Writers disagree about whether such equivalences count as reductions.

When supervenience works to clarify traditional views such as NATURALISM in ethics or physicalism in the philosophy of mind the arguments for or against supervenience may follow the lines of arguments for or against these traditional views.

BIBLIOGRAPHY

Hellman, G. and Thompson, R.: 'Physicalism: ontology, determination and reduction', *Journal of Philosophy* 72 (1975), 551–64.
Kim, J.: 'Concepts of supervenience', *Philosophy and Phenomenological Research* 45 (1984), 153–76.
Kim, J.: 'Supervenience as a philosophical concept', *Metaphilosophy* 21 (1990), 1–27.
Teller, P.: 'A poor man's guide to supervenience and determination', *The Southern Journal of Philosophy*, Supplement (Spindell Conference, 1983) 22 (1984), 137–62.

PAUL TELLER

T

Tarski, Alfred (1901–83) Mathematician, logician, and philosopher of logic, born in Warsaw, Poland and educated there in mathematics. He studied logic with LEŚ-NIEWSKI, Jan Lukasiewicz (1878–1956) and Tadeusz Kotarbinski (1886–1981), all of whom had studied philosophy under Kazimierz Twardowski (1866–1938), one of several prominent philosophers taught by BRENTANO in Vienna. Tarski's epistemological and metaphysical orientation is similar to that of the materialistic empiricism, known as reism or pansomatism, which was articulated by his teacher Kotarbinski (1955) in an article translated into English by Tarski. Tarski's methodological orientation, best expressed in Tarski (1937), encompassed a combination of modern symbolic logic with a development of the traditional axiomatic (or deductive) method as treated by PASCAL in the posthumous 1728 article 'L'ésprit géométrique'. In conversations Tarski revealed himself to be an atheistic humanist, strongly allied with the values implicit in modern natural science and strongly opposed to those associated with superstition and religion, which for him included not only PLATONISM as expounded by FREGE and GÖDEL but also communism as practised in the former Soviet Union. His opposition to Platonism was balanced by an equally intense opposition to the positivistic philosophy associated with the Vienna Circle (*see* LOGICAL POSITIVISM), the formalistic philosophy associated with the Hilbert school, and the language-oriented philosophy associated with WITTGENSTEIN.

Tarski's most widely recognized contribution to philosophy is his analysis of the concept of truth in syntactically precise, fully interpreted languages and his articulation of the correspondence theory of truth (*see* THEORIES OF TRUTH). His longest, most comprehensive, and most widely read article on truth is the 1956 English translation 'The concept of truth in formalized languages' by J.H. Woodger of the 1935 German translation by L. Blaustein of the original Polish monograph (1933). For bibliographic details see Givant (1986). This English article, widely referred to as 'The Wahrheitsbegriff' by logicians and philosophers, is a triumph of common sense, technical virtuosity and penetrating mathematical and philosophical analysis. One of its virtues as a philosophic classic is the boldness of its presuppositions; it is valued as much for the questions that it leaves open as for those that it claims to settle. Its assumption that sentences, not propositions, are properly said to be true or false, while highly controversial at the time, has become a cornerstone of the philosophies of current writers such as QUINE (*see* PROPOSITION, STATE OF AFFAIRS). By clearly exemplifying the traditional philosophical and mathematical distinction between the meaning of an adjectival (or qualitative) term such as 'true' and the tests (or criteria) of its applicability in individual cases, this article has become a hallmark of opposition to positivistic and idealistic philosophers (*see* IDEALISM) including intuitionism (*see* INTUITIONISM IN LOGIC AND MATHEMATICS).

Tarski's second most widely recognized philosophical achievement is his analysis and explication of the concept of (logical) implication (or consequence) in terms of which (logical) validity of arguments is defined. An argument is valid if, and only if, its conclusion is implied by (or is a consequence of) its premise-set. Here too he exemplifies the traditional meaning-criterion distinction by emphasizing the difference between the semantic relation of logical implication and the syntactic relation of formal deducibility taken as a positive criterion for implication (Tarski, 1936). The above two analyses have been credited with the founding of model theory (or mathematical semantics), one of the main branches of modern mathematical logic.

Tarski also proposed an analysis and explication of the concept of logical notion (which is required in order to define the concept of logical constant). Evaluations of this relatively recent, posthumously published work (Tarski, 1987) are in progress but it is unlikely that it will be as widely accepted or as influential as his work on truth and on consequence. These three analyses, beside making fundamental contributions to philosophical analysis, establish a distinctive Tarskian philosophic style which itself has been highly influential. Tarski made other contributions to philosophy that may come to be regarded as of equal importance (see Corcoran, 1983, 1991; Mostowski, 1967).

Notwithstanding Tarski's lasting contributions to philosophy and the pride he took in having the philosophers Pascal, Brentano and Kotarbinski in his intellectual ancestry, he never regarded himself as a philosopher. He identified himself as a mathematician and he looked to the world of mathematicians for recognition. It is true however that he relished the acceptance of his work by mathematically informed philosophers such as CARNAP, POPPER, QUINE and RUSSELL. Even though Tarski had deep philosophic commitments and extensive philosophic learning, he did not read current philosophical literature and he was wary, sometimes contemptuous, of professional philosophers, whose intellectual abilities and virtues he ranked far below those of mathematicians, scientists and poets. He did on occasion have discussion with philosophers but it was as if his portal had been inscribed with the supposedly Platonic injunction: let no one ignorant of mathematics enter.

As a mathematician Tarski worked in several areas other than logic, most notably abstract algebra, set theory, geometry and real analysis. In each of these areas he achieved results that will assure him a place in the history of mathematics. His contributions to philosophy, extensive as they are, constitute a small fraction of his research. He founded the interdisciplinary Group in Logic and Methodology of Sciences at the University of California at Berkeley where he was a professor of mathematics until his retirement in 1968. He continued to work productively until his death in 1983 in Berkeley, California.

WRITINGS

'The concept of truth in formalized languages' (1933); trans. J.H. Woodger in Tarski, 1956, 152–278.
'On the concept of logical consequence' (1936); trans. J.H. Woodger in Tarski, 1956, 409–20.
'Sur la méthode déductive', *Actualité Scientifiques et Industrielles* 535 (1937), 95–103.
Logic, Semantics, Metamathematics. Papers from 1923 to 1938 trans. J.H. Woodger (Oxford: Oxford University Press, 1956); rev. edn J. Corcoran (Indianapolis, IN: Hackett, 1983).
Alfred Tarski Collected Papers 4 vols, ed. S. Givant and R. McKenzie (Basel: Birkhäuser Verlag, 1986[a]).
'What are logical notions?', *History and Philosophy of Logic* 7 (1986[b]), 143–54.

BIBLIOGRAPHY

Corcoran, J.: 'Editor's introduction to the revised edition', in Tarski, 1983, xv–xxvii.
Corcoran, J.: Review of Tarski, 1986[a], *Mathematical Reviews* 91 (1991), 91h: 01101–01104.
Givant, S.: 'Bibliography of Alfred Tarski', *Journal of Symbolic Logic* 51 (1986), 913–

41; repr. in Tarski, 1986[a], vol. 4, 729–57.

Kotarbinski, T.: 'The fundamental ideas of pansomatism' trans. A. Tarski with D. Rynin, *Mind* 64 (1955), 488–500, and 65 (1956), 288; repr. in Tarski, 1986[a], vol. 3, 577–92.

Mostowski, A.: 'Tarski, Alfred', in *Encyclopedia of Philosophy* ed. P. Edwards (New York: Macmillan, 1967), vol. 8, 77–81.

JOHN CORCORAN

teleology   Classically, teleology has referred to the appearance of purpose in nature, in particular purpose not underwritten by conscious human intent. Characteristic examples of such appearance are the *functions* of organs and other parts of biological organisms, and the *goals* manifest in their behaviour. These are interesting because they require some explanation: it cannot be mere fortuitous accident that my heart pumps my blood or that the startled rabbit darts toward the hole in the fence. And avoiding the null hypothesis involves saying that these fortuitous consequences are involved, somehow or other, in explaining why the organ exists and why the behaviour took the turn it did. If it is not just a lucky (and staggeringly implausible) coincidence, then I must have a heart at least partly *because* it pumps blood; the rabbit must run as it does precisely *because* doing so offers hope of escape. We capture this idiomatically by saying the heart beats *in order* to pump blood, and the rabbit runs toward the hole *for the sake of* escape. These are called teleological explanations.

The surface puzzle about teleological explanations is that they have later things explaining earlier ones: pumping blood explains why the heart is there, escape explains the running that precedes it. And this is doubtless why the behaviour of organisms and the functions of their organs strikes us as the 'appearance of purpose' in nature. For we all know intimately one way consequences can explain what leads to them without reversing the normal causal order: when they result from conscious human calculation or design. Forward-looking human intent licenses teleological explanations by assimilating future consequences to antecedent expectations.

Were this the only way to avoid reversing the normal causal order in such cases, however, that would just deepen the puzzle. For it would require attributing conscious intent not just to rabbits but also to insects and micro-organisms to account for the goal-directedness of their behaviour; and this seems scarcely more attractive than the two alternatives (backwards CAUSATION and the null hypothesis). To accommodate biological functions (*see* FUNCTION), on the other hand, this move would require that all of life, and perhaps the universe itself, have a conscious designer. To the twentieth-century mind this too has seemed implausible.

But appeal to conscious intent is not the only way to square teleology with causal orthodoxy. The teleological argument for a designer of life has lost much of its force for us because another way to make sense of functional explanations has been so clearly articulated. Our modern understanding of heredity, reproduction and natural history allows purely natural selection to account for organismic functions without invoking conscious design. An essentially mechanical story provides an organ's functional consequences a central role in explaining its existence. And a similar point may be made about goal-directed behaviour. Thermostats and target-seeking rockets show how a purely mechanical device, presumably innocent of intentions, can be objectively goal-directed. With proper connection to its surrounding circumstances the behaviour of a causally transparent mechanism may be explained by its consequences. The homing torpedo is geared to its environment in just the way required to make its behaviour sensitive to what will happen later: it is usually no accident when a course change takes it closer to the target.

Are goal-directed organisms then merely complicated homing mechanisms? This question runs together a number of issues worth keeping separate. Clearly, very complex and subtle purposiveness could result from an adequately complicated mechanical device. Furthermore, the way a homing device is causally connected to its environment provides a model of obvious explanatory potential in exploring the physiology of organismic behaviour. But the stronger claim that all teleological behaviour *must* be at bottom physiological clockwork rests on more controversial ground. For it might amount to an empirical claim about the ability of our current understanding of the physics and chemistry to account for all organismic behaviour; and all we may say of this speculation is that its plausibility is both difficult to estimate and the subject of great disagreement. For the history of scientific theorizing has revealed a striking inability to forecast changes in fundamental explanatory principle, or even predict the phenomena that will provoke them.

The mechanical view of organisms might, on the other hand, be driven by the methodological conviction that ˙irreducible teleological regularities are intrinsically unsuited to scientific explanation. This too has proved difficult to establish. For the sensitivity to consequences that calls for a teleological account is objectively demonstrable – as objectively as any orthodox causal connection – long before we have any idea what sort of underlying mechanism might be producing it. So the failure to find the clockwork cannot by itself count against the teleological explanation. As a matter of methodology, the teleological account could turn out to be rock-bottom.

BIBLIOGRAPHY

Beckner, M.: *The Biological Way of Thought* (Berkeley and Los Angeles: University of California Press, 1968).
Sober, E.: *The Nature of Selection* (Cambridge, MA: MIT Press, 1984).
Taylor, C.: *The Explanation of Behaviour* (London: Routledge and Kegan Paul, 1964).

Woodfield, A.: *Teleology* (London: Cambridge University Press, 1976).
Wright, L.: *Teleological Explanation* (Berkeley: University of California Press, 1976).

LARRY WRIGHT

temporal parts, stages To make sense of temporal parts we should think of objects as being four-dimensional rather than three-dimensional. MATTER fills regions of space-time, and those four dimensional collections of matter that have an appropriate internal structure compose a physical object. Temporal parts are parts in the same sense in which spatial parts are. Just as spatial parts fill up a subregion of the space filled by the whole, temporal parts fill up a subregion of the time filled by the whole. Contrary to some characterizations of temporal parts, they are ontologically no more or less basic than the wholes that they compose. A temporal part is composed of matter in the same way as the whole of which it is a part. As long as it has greater than zero extent along every dimension, a temporal part is itself a four-dimensional physical object.

See also BODY; CHANGE; CHISHOLM; LEŚ-NIEWSKI; QUINE; PART/WHOLE.

BIBLIOGRAPHY

Chisholm, R.M.: 'Problems of identity', in *Identity and Individuation* ed. M.K. Munitz (New York: New York University Press, 1971), 3–30.
Heller, M.: 'Temporal parts of four dimensional objects', *Philosophical Studies* 46 (1984), 323–34.
Lewis, D.: 'Survival and identity', in his *Philosophical Papers*, vol. 1 (Oxford: Oxford University Press, 1983), 55–77.
Quine, W.V.: 'Identity, ostension, and hypostasis', in his *From A Logical Point of View* (Cambridge, MA: Harvard University Press, 1980), 65–79.
Simons, P.: *Parts* (Oxford: Oxford University Press, 1987).

MARK HELLER

theodicy Literally, a 'justification of God', supposedly omnipotent and perfectly good, for permitting the occurrence of evil, for example, pain and other suffering. Most of the great Christian philosophers and theologians, and especially Irenaeus (*c.*120–202), AUGUSTINE and LEIBNIZ, attempted to provide a theodicy and thus defeat the argument that the occurrence of evil showed, or at any rate made it probable, that there was no omnipotent and perfectly good God. The 'FREE WILL defence' has usually been a central element of any theodicy; this claims that the good of humans having freedom to choose good or evil outweighs the bad of the evil that they are likely to cause. But to account for evil not caused by humans, it needs to be backed up by other defences, for example, the 'higher-order goods defence', that pain provides an opportunity for humans freely to show courage and compassion.

BIBLIOGRAPHY

Adams, M.M. and Adams, R.M. eds: *The Problem of Evil* (Oxford: Oxford University Press, 1990).
Hick, J.: *Evil and the God of Love* (London: Macmillan, 1966).
Plantinga, A.: *God, Freedom, and Evil* (London: George Allen and Unwin, 1974), 7–64.
Swinburne, R.: *The Existence of God* (Oxford: Clarendon Press, 1979), 152–60 and 180–224.

RICHARD SWINBURNE

theories of truth Questions revolving around the concept of truth arise throughout philosophy. For example: is truth the proper target of scientific inquiry and hence a basic notion of epistemology? Should the meaning of a sentence be explained in terms of the circumstances that would render it true? Can ethical claims be true (or are they merely expressions of feeling)? Is one's preferred logic (e.g. classical, intuitionistic, quantum, etc.) to be justified on the basis of a preferred conception of truth? And how does the theory of truth bear on the various debates between realists and anti-realists? In order to answer these questions some understanding of the nature of truth would seem to be required, but the search for such understanding gives rise merely to further problems. For example: does the predicate, 'is true', express a property? If so, which one and what kinds of object possess it. And if not, what could the linguistic function of the truth predicate possibly be. Thus, although it will be readily accepted that statements typically specify their own condition for being true (for example, 'snow is white' is true if, and only if, snow is white), beyond such trivialities the characteristics and philosophical import of truth are shrouded in mystery and disagreement.

THE BEARERS OF TRUTH

To begin with, it is unclear to what kinds of entity the truth predicate should, strictly speaking, be applied. The prime candidates are specific utterances (for example, the particular words produced by Pierre at a certain place and time, when he said 'I am hungry'), mental states (for example, Pierre's believing at that time that he was hungry), linguistic acts (for example, his having asserted that he was hungry), and propositions (for example, what he believed and asserted, namely, *that he was hungry*) (*see* CONTENT; PROPOSITION, STATE OF AFFAIRS). It has seemed plausible that truth is exemplified *primarily* by entities in just one of these categories and that it may be applied only in derived and subsidiary senses to entities in the others. However, there is considerable disagreement over which are the primary vehicles of truth. Ordinary language favours propositions; for we speak of *what* people say or believe as true – not their state of believing it or the words they use to express it. Nevertheless many philosophers have been unwilling to countenance such things as propositions, given the difficulty of saying what they are and of being clear about when two different sentences express one and the same propo-

491

sition. Utterances (i.e. sentence tokens) have the advantage that their existence is obvious and their nature relatively unproblematic. It seems evident, however, that in so far as an utterance may be 'true', this depends on the truth of something lying 'behind' it: we naturally speak of an utterance *expressing* something (typically, a belief) that is true. Now the term 'belief' is ambiguous as between, on the one hand, *the state of believing* and, on the other hand, *that which is believed* and it appears to be the latter we have in mind when we talk of true beliefs. But these entities – the things believed – are what we call 'propositions'. Thus an accurate account of truth – one faithful to our actual conception of it – would seem not to permit a sceptical attitude towards propositions but to call rather for a greater effort to understand them.

TRADITIONAL THEORIES

The proposition that snow is white owes its truth to a certain feature of the external world: namely, to the fact that snow is white. Similarly, the proposition that dogs bark is true because of the fact that dogs bark. This sort of trivial observation leads to what is perhaps the most natural and popular account of truth, *the correspondence theory*, according to which a proposition (statement, sentence, belief, etc.) is true just in case there exists a fact corresponding to it (Austin, 1950; Wittgenstein, 1922). This thesis is unexceptionable in itself. However if it is to provide a rigorous, substantial, and complete theory of truth – if it is to be more than merely a picturesque way of asserting all equivalences of the form,

The proposition *that p* is true ↔ p

then it must be supplemented with accounts of what *facts* are, and what it is for a proposition to *correspond* to a FACT; and these are the problems on which the correspondence theory of truth has foundered. For one thing, it is far from clear that any significant gain in understanding is achieved by reducing 'the proposition *that snow is*

white is true' to 'the fact *that snow is white* exists'; for these expressions seem equally resistant to ANALYSIS and too close in meaning for one to provide an illuminating account of the other. In addition, the general relationship that holds between the proposition that snow is white and the fact that snow is white, between the proposition that dogs bark and the fact that dogs bark, and so on, is very hard to identify. The best attempt to date is WITTGENSTEIN's (1922) so-called 'picture theory', whereby an elementary proposition is a configuration of primitive constituents, an atomic fact is a logical configuration of simple objects, an atomic fact *corresponds* to an elementary proposition (and makes it true) when their configurations are identical and when the primitive constituents in the proposition refer to the similarly placed objects in the fact, and the truth value of each complex proposition is entailed by the truth values of the elementary ones. However, even if this account is correct as far as it goes, it would need to be completed with plausible theories of 'logical configuration', 'elementary proposition', 'REFERENCE' and 'entailment', none of which is easy to come by.

A central characteristic of truth – one that any adequate theory must explain – is that when a proposition satisfies its 'conditions of proof (or verification)' then it is regarded as *true*. To the extent that the property of *corresponding with reality* is mysterious, we are going to find it impossible to see why what we take to verify a proposition should indicate the possession of that property. Therefore a tempting alternative to the correspondence theory – an alternative which eschews obscure, metaphysical concepts and which explains quite straightforwardly why verifiability implies truth – is to simply *identify* truth with verifiability (Peirce, 1932). This idea can take on various forms. One version involves the further assumption that verification is *holistic* – i.e. that a belief is justified (i.e. verified) when it is part of an entire system of beliefs that is consistent and 'harmonious' (Bradley, 1914; Hempel, 1935). This is known as the coherence theory of truth.

Another version involves the assumption that there is, associated with each proposition, some specific procedure for finding out whether one should believe it or not. On this account, to say that a proposition is true is to say that it would be verified by the appropriate procedure (Dummett, 1978; Putnam, 1981). In the context of mathematics this amounts to the identification of truth with provability. (*See* BRADLEY; DUMMETT; PEIRCE.)

The attractions of the verificationist account of truth are that it is refreshingly clear compared with the correspondence theory, and that it succeeds in connecting truth with verification. The trouble is that the bond it postulates between these notions is implausibly strong. On the face of it, there could well exist several conflicting, yet internally coherent, systems of belief – suggesting that although coherence may confer plausibility, it is no guarantee of truth. We do indeed regard coherence, proof and other forms of verification, as indicative of truth. But also we recognize the possibility that a proposition may be false in spite of there being excellent reasons to believe it, and that a proposition may be true even though we are not able to discover that it is. Verifiability and truth are no doubt somehow associated; but surely not the same thing.

A third well known account of truth is known as PRAGMATISM (James, 1909; Papineau, 1987). As we have just seen, the verificationist selects a prominent property of truth and considers it to be the *essence* of truth. Similarly the pragmatist focuses on another important characteristic – namely, that true beliefs are a good basis for action – and takes this to be the very nature of truth. True assumptions are said to be, by definition, those that provoke actions with desirable results. Again we have an account with a single attractive explanatory feature. But again the central objection is that the relationship it postulates between truth and its alleged *analysans* – in this case, utility – is implausibly close. Granted, true beliefs tends to foster success. But it happens regularly that actions based on true beliefs lead to disaster, while false assumptions, by pure

chance, produce beneficial results. (*See* JAMES.)

DEFLATIONARY THEORIES

One of the few uncontroversial facts about truth is that the proposition that snow is white is true if, and only if, snow is white, the proposition that lying is wrong is true if, and only if, lying is wrong, and so on. Traditional theories acknowledge this fact but regard it as insufficient and, as we have seen, inflate it with some further principle of the form, 'X is true iff X has property P' (such as, corresponding to reality, verifiability, or being suitable as a basis for action), which is supposed to specify *what truth is*. A variety of radical alternatives to the traditional theories result from denying the need for any such further specification (Quine, 1990; Ramsey, 1927; Strawson, 1950). For example, one might suppose that the basic theory of truth contains nothing more than equivalences of the form, 'The proposition *that p* is true iff p' (Horwich, 1990). (*See* QUINE; RAMSEY; STRAWSON.)

This sort of deflationary proposal is best presented in conjunction with an account of the *raison d'être* of our notion of truth: namely, that it enables us to compose generalizations of a special sort, that would otherwise call for 'infinite conjunction' or some other radically new logical device (Quine, 1990). Suppose, for example, you are told that Einstein's last words expressed a claim about physics, an area in which you think he was very reliable. Suppose that, unknown to you, his claim was the proposition that quantum mechanics is wrong. What conclusion can you draw? Exactly which proposition becomes the appropriate object of your belief? Surely not that quantum mechanics is wrong; because you are not aware that that is what he said. What is needed is something equivalent to the infinite conjunction:

If what Einstein said was that nothing goes faster than light, then nothing goes faster than light, and if what he said was

493

that quantum mechanics is wrong, then quantum mechanics is wrong, . . . and so on.

And we are able to capture this infinite conjunction with the help of the equivalence schema

The proposition *that p* is true *if, and only if*, p.

For on the basis of these biconditionals the initial conjunction may be reformulated as

If Einstein said that nothing goes faster than light, then the proposition *that nothing goes faster than light* is true; and if Einstein said that quantum mechanics is wrong, then the proposition *that quantum mechanics is wrong* is true; . . . and so on.

And this can be summarized using the ordinary universal quantifier, 'every', which generalizes over objects: i.e.

For every object, x, if what Einstein said = x, then x is true

Or, in other words

What Einstein said is true.

Thus one point in favour of the deflationary theory is that it squares with a plausible story about the function of our notion of truth: its axioms explain that function without the need for any further analysis of 'what truth is'.

Further support for deflationism depends upon the possibility of showing that its axioms – instances of the equivalence schema – unsupplemented by any further analysis, will suffice to explain all the central facts about truth: for example, that the verification of a proposition indicates its truth, and that true beliefs have a practical value. The first of these facts follows immediately from the deflationary axioms. For given our a priori knowledge of the equivalence of 'p' and 'The proposition *that p* is

true', any reason to believe that p becomes an equally good reason to believe that the proposition *that p* is true. The second fact can also be explained in terms of the deflationary axioms, but not quite so easily. Consider, to begin with, one's beliefs of the form,

(B) If I perform act A, then my desires will be fulfilled.

Notice that the psychological role of such a belief is to bring about the performance of A. In other words, given that I do have belief (B), then typically

I will perform act A.

And notice also that when the belief is true then, given the deflationary axioms, the performance of A will in fact lead to the fulfillment of one's desires, i.e.

If (B) is true, then if I perform A, my desires will be fulfilled.

Therefore

If (B) is true, my desires will be fulfilled.

So it is quite reasonable to value the truth of beliefs of that form. But such beliefs are derived by inference from other beliefs and can be expected to be true if those other beliefs are true. So it is reasonable to value the truth of any belief that might be used in such an inference.

To the extent that such deflationary accounts can be given of *all* the facts involving truth, then the explanatory demands on a theory of truth will be met by the collection of all statements like, 'The proposition that snow is white is true if, and only if, snow is white', and the sense that some deep analysis of truth is needed will be undermined.

However, there are some strongly felt objections to deflationism. One reason for dissatisfaction is that the theory has an infinite number of axioms, and therefore cannot be completely written down. It can be *described* (as the theory whose axioms are the propositions of the form 'p if, and only if, it is true that p'), but not explicitly formulated. This alleged defect has led some philosophers to develop theories which show, first, how the truth of any proposition derives from the referential properties of its constituents; and, second, how the referential properties of primitive constituents are determined (Davidson, 1969; Tarski, 1943). However, it remains controversial to assume that *all* propositions – including belief attributions, laws of nature (*see* LAW OF NATURE), and COUNTERFACTUALS – depend for their truth values on what their constituents refer to. Moreover there is no immediate prospect of a decent, finite theory of reference. So it is far from clear that the infinite, list-like character of deflationism can be avoided. (*See* DAVIDSON; TARSKI.)

Another source of dissatisfaction with this theory is that certain instances of the equivalence schema are clearly false. Consider

(1) THE PROPOSITION EXPRESSED BY THE SENTENCE IN CAPITAL LETTERS IS NOT TRUE.

Substituting this into the scheme one gets a version of the 'liar' paradox: specifically,

(2) The proposition *that the proposition expressed by the sentence in capital letters is not true* is true if, and only if, the proposition expressed by the sentence in capital letters is not true,

from which a contradiction is easily derivable. (Given (2), the supposition that (1) is true implies that (1) is not true, and the supposition that it is not true implies that it is.) Consequently, not every instance of the equivalence schema can be included in the our theory of truth; but it is no simple matter to specify the ones to be excluded (see Kripke, 1975). Of course, deflationism is far from alone in having to confront this problem.

FALSITY

The simplest plausible account of falsity is that a proposition is false just in case it is not true. An alternative formulation of this idea – one that parallels the equivalence schema for truth – is given by

The proposition *that p* is false iff $-p$.

These two formulations are equivalent. For the logical expression, '$-p$', is shorthand for 'It is not the case that p'. But there is no reason to distinguish *being true* and *being the case*. So '$-p$' means nothing more or less than 'It is not true that p', which is presumably synonymous with 'The proposition *that p* is not true'.

From this natural account of falsity it follows that every proposition has a truth value; for to say of some proposition that it is neither true nor false would be to imply that it is both not true and *not* not true, which is a contradiction. This result has important ramifications in semantics, where it has often been found tempting to mark out certain 'odd' propositions as having no truth value: for example, attributions of vague properties to borderline cases (*see* VAGUENESS), propositions with non-referring constituents, and ethical pronouncements. If the deflationary accounts of truth and falsity are correct, then such propositions do have truth values and there is always a fact of the matter as to whether they are true or false.

THE ROLE OF TRUTH IN
METAPHYSICS AND EPISTEMOLOGY

It is commonly supposed that problems about the nature of truth are intimately bound up with questions as to the accessibility and autonomy of facts in various domains: questions about whether the facts can be known, and whether they can exist independently of our capacity to discover them (Dummett, 1978; Putnam, 1981). One might reason, for example, that if 'T is true' means nothing more than 'T will be verified' then certain forms of scepticism (specifically, those that doubt the correctness of our methods of verification) will be precluded, and that the facts will have been revealed as dependent on human practices. Alternatively, it might be said that if truth were an inexplicable, primitive, non-epistemic property, then the fact that T is true would be completely independent of us. Moreover, we could, in that case, have no reason to assume that the propositions we believe actually have this property; so scepticism would be unavoidable. In a similar vein, it might be thought that a special (and perhaps undesirable) feature of the deflationary approach is that truth is deprived of any such metaphysical or epistemological implications.

On closer scrutiny, however, it is far from clear that there exists *any* account of truth with consequences regarding the accessibility or autonomy of non-semantic matters. For although an account of truth may be expected to have such implications for a fact of the form 'T is true', it cannot be assumed without further argument that the same conclusions will apply to the fact, T, itself. For it cannot be assumed that *T* and *T is true* are equivalent to one another given the account of 'true' that is being employed. Of course, if truth is defined in the way that the deflationist proposes, then the equivalence holds by definition. But if truth is defined by reference to some metaphysical or epistemological characteristic, then the equivalence schema is thrown into doubt pending some demonstration that the truth predicate, in the sense assumed, will satisfy it. In so far as there are thought to be epistemological problems hanging over T that do not threaten 'T is true', it will be difficult to give the needed demonstration. Similarly, if 'truth' is so defined that the fact, T, is felt to be more (or less) independent of human practices than the fact, *T is true*, then again it is unclear that the equivalence schema will hold. It would seem, therefore, that the attempt to base epistemological or metaphysical conclusions on a theory of truth must fail because, in any such attempt, the equivalence schema will be simultaneously relied on yet undermined.

See also ANTIREALISM; INTUITIONISM IN LOGIC AND MATHEMATICS; REALISM.

BIBLIOGRAPHY

Austin, J.L.: 'Truth', *Proceedings of the Aristotelian Society* supplementary vol. 24 (1950), 111–28.

Bradley, F.H.: *Essays on Truth and Reality* (Oxford: Clarendon Press, 1914).

Davidson, D.: 'True to the facts', *Journal of Philosophy* 66 (1969), 748–64.

Dummett, M.: *Elements of Intuitionism* (Oxford: Clarendon Press, 1977).

Dummett, M.: *Truth and Other Enigmas* (London: Duckworth, 1978).

Hempel, C.: 'On the logical positivist's theory of truth', *Analysis* 2 (1935), 49–59.

Horwich, P.: *Truth* (Oxford: Basil Blackwell, 1990).

James, W.: *The Meaning of Truth* (New York: Longmans Green, 1909).

Kripke, S.: 'Outline of a theory of truth', *Journal of Philosophy* 72 (1975), 690–716.

Papineau, D.: *Reality and Representation* (Oxford: Blackwell, 1987).

Peirce, C.S.: *Collected Papers* vols 2–4 (Cambridge, MA: Harvard University Press, 1932).

Putnam, H.: *Meaning and the Moral Sciences* (London: Routledge and Kegan Paul, 1978).

Putnam, H.: *Reason, Truth and History* (Cambridge: Cambridge University Press, 1981).

Quine, W.V.: *Pursuit of Truth* (Cambridge, MA: Harvard University Press, 1990).

Ramsey, F.: 'Facts and propositions', *Proceedings of the Aristotelian Society* supplementary vol. 7 (1927), 153–70.

Strawson, P.: 'Truth', *Proceedings of the Aristotelian Society* supplementary vol. 24 (1950), 125–56.

Tarski, A.: 'The semantic conception of truth', *Philosophy and Phenomenological Research* IV (1943), 341–75.

Wittgenstein, L.: *Tractatus Logico-Philosophicus* trans. C.K. Ogden (London: Routledge and Kegan Paul, 1922).

PAUL HORWICH

time *see* SPACE AND TIME

timelessness Two sorts of objects have been held by some philosophers to be timeless: abstract objects (UNIVERSALS, necessary truths, etc.) and God. Abstract objects are timeless in the sense of being *subsistent* and God is timeless in the sense of being *eternal*, although it may be questioned if this distinction is acceptable.

Something *x* subsists if, and only if, *x is* but it is not the case that *x was or will be* and it not the case that *x was not* or *will not be*.

According to the traditional conception of eternity, eternity is God's complete and simultaneous possession of illimitable conscious life, which implies that God has duration without succession, i.e. that he endures as an 'ever-abiding simultaneous whole' (in Aquinas's words). This notion is of questionable coherence, since the concept of enduring contains the concept of lasting for at least two times, which implies having a life or history with successive temporal parts. If we conceive eternity as durationless and reject the concept of conscious life as an extraneous notion, then eternity reduces to subsistence.

BIBLIOGRAPHY

Aquinas, St Thomas: *Summa contra Gentiles* I. 66.
Boethius: *The Consolation of Philosophy* V. 6.
Fitzgerald, P.: 'Stump and Kretzmann on time and eternity', *Journal of Philosophy* 82 (1985), 260–9.
Leftow, B.: *Time and Eternity* (Ithaca, NY: Cornell University Press, 1991).
Smith, Q.: 'A new typology of temporal and atemporal permanence', *Noûs* 23 (1989), 307–30.
Smith, Q.: 'Time and propositions', *Philosophia* 20 (1990), 279–94.
Sorabji, R.: *Time, Creation, and the Continuum* part II (Ithaca, NY: Cornell University Press, 1983).
Stump, E. and Kretzmann, N.: 'Eternity', *Journal of Philosophy* 78 (1981), 429–48.
Stump, E. and Kretzmann, N.: 'Atemporal duration: a reply to Fitzgerald', *Journal of Philosophy* 84 (1987), 214–19.

QUENTIN SMITH

transcendental arguments There is some disagreement among philosophers regarding which arguments should be considered transcendental arguments, but there is also general agreement about the paradigm examples. KANT's Transcendental Deduction in the *Critique of Pure Reason* (1787), rooting synthetic a priori judgements in the conditions necessary for the existence of EXPERIENCE, is perhaps the most obvious example. But other Kantian arguments, including those presented by STRAWSON in *Individuals* (1959), are often considered very clear cases. There is also widespread agreement about a number of non-Kantian examples, for instance ARISTOTLE's argument in *Metaphysics* Book Γ against those who would deny the principle of non-contradiction, and recent arguments like Baker's against scepticism about the existence of beliefs and desires. On the other hand, various other important philosophical arguments, for instance WITTGENSTEIN's private language argument and DESCARTES's argument in the Third Meditation for the existence of God, are characterized only by some as transcendental.

Partly because of this disagreement about cases, there is also disagreement about the appropriate characterization of transcendental arguments. But most can accept the following rough characterization: in transcendental arguments, a certain phenomenon *p* is argued to have certain necessary conditions *c*. Some insist that only arguments which meet other restrictions, for instance which establish certain sorts of conclusions or which are deployed in certain sorts of argumentative contexts, count as transcendental, but most accept that this rough characterization captures a crucial feature of transcendental arguments. For instance, Kant argued in the *Critique of Pure Reason* that the phenomenon of experience has certain necessary conditions which underwrite the possibility of a priori knowledge. To cite a more controversial example, Descartes argued in the Third Meditation that the existence of God was a necessary condition for the phenomenon of the existence of the idea of God.

Disagreements regarding how this very schematic characterization of transcendental arguments is to be properly filled in, which mirror the disagreements about examples, might be organized into several groups. The first set of disagreements concern the sort of argumentative context required for an argument which meets the rough characterization to be transcendental.

Most agree that the paradigm transcendental arguments, for instance many of Kant's, are deployed to show that the controversial condition obtains, on the grounds that the uncontroversial phenomenon requires it. But, on the other hand, things quite like those arguments might be deployed to show, in the face of scepticism, how some controversial phenomenon plausibly obtains, by exhibiting significant, unexpected, and more or less sufficient necessary conditions for that phenomenon. For instance, one might try to show that meaningful language is possible and plausible by demonstrating that its crucial necessary condition is the public acceptance of rules for word use.

Some hold that it is crucial that transcendental arguments be deployed against some sort of scepticism about knowledge claims, as are the central Kantian cases. Others hold that it is important that they be deployed at least against scepticism regarding something crucial to cognitive life, for instance meaningful language or beliefs.

These concerns about argumentative context may underwrite some restrictions on the kinds of phenomena or conditions which can be cited in a proper transcendental argument. Some hold that the necessary conditions cited in a transcendental argument must be cognitive. On this view, Descartes's Third Meditation argument would not count as transcendental, despite the fact

that the phenomenon it adverts to, the existence of the idea of God, is cognitive. And some might argue that the phenomenon to be explained must likewise be cognitive.

If transcendental arguments are deployed against some sort of scepticism regarding a controversial cognitive condition which turns out to be necessary for an uncontroversial phenomenon, that would explain why the conditions cited in transcendental arguments must be cognitive. But there might also be a relation between the *phenomenon* cited in a transcendental argument and some scepticism to which that argument is addressed. In the paradigm transcendental arguments, the very scepticism which the transcendental argument is deployed against may in some sense presume its own falsehood, and the argument may be a way of displaying this incoherence. The argument may show that a phenomenon which the sceptic must presume on pain of incoherence has a necessary condition which ensures that the sceptic is mistaken. For instance, a sceptic's position may more or less directly entail that it itself is false, say if the position is that there is experience but there can be no a priori knowledge, and if in fact the necessary conditions of experience make a priori knowledge possible. On the other hand, it may not be that the position of the sceptic is itself inconsistent, but rather that it is inconsistent with the sceptic's arguing for, asserting, or believing that position. An argument which displays this second sort of incoherence is called a 'pragmatic incoherence argument'.

One crucial issue regarding transcendental arguments is what kind of necessary connection they invoke between the phenomenon and its conditions, what kind of necessity the conditions must possess. A strict logical entailment of the conditions by the phenomenon may be too tight a connection to yield an interesting transcendental argument. In the case of some transcendental arguments, it may be that things at least analogous to meaning relations or conceptual connections help underwrite the relevant necessary connection.

Other transcendental arguments seem to turn at least in part on considerations of conceivability. Though we can in some weak sense conceive the impossible, it is traditional to maintain that there is a connection between conceivability of some suitably regimented sort and possibility, and the necessary seems to be that whose falsehood is not possible. Some transcendental arguments appear to suggest that the phenomenon at issue is not in some suitable way conceivable without the conditions hence deemed to be necessary.

Whatever underwrites the relevant necessities, it may be that in some transcendental arguments the appropriate connection between phenomenon and conditions only involves a kind of relative necessity. The arguments may presume an implicit restriction on the kinds of conditions, say only plausible or natural ones, which are to be considered as legitimate candidates to underwrite the phenomenon under consideration.

BIBLIOGRAPHY

Baker, L.R.: *Saving Belief* (Princeton, NJ: Princeton University Press, 1987).
Kant, I.: *Kritik der reinen Vernunft* (Riga: 1787); trans. N. Kemp Smith *Critique of Pure Reason* (New York: St Martin's Press, 1965).
Strawson, P.F.: *Individuals* (New York: Doubleday, 1959).
Stroud, B.: 'Transcendental arguments', *Journal of Philosophy* 65 (1968), 241–56.
Wittgenstein, L.: *Philosophical Investigations* 3rd edn, trans. G.E.M. Anscombe (New York: Macmillan, 1968).

JOSEPH MENDOLA

transcendental ego In the philosophy of KANT, the transcendental ego is the thinker of our thoughts, the subject of our experiences, the willer of our actions, and the agent of the various activities of synthesis that help to constitute the world we experience. It is probably to be identified with our real or noumenal self (see Kant, *Critique of Pure Reason*, A 492/B 520, where 'the transcendental subject' is equated with 'the self proper, as it exists in itself') (*see* NOUMENAL/PHENOMENAL). Kant called it transcendental because he believed that although we must posit such a self, we can never observe it. What we can observe is only the empirical self – the totality of thoughts and experiences that are given to introspection or inner sense. Recalling a famous passage from HUME – 'when I enter most intimately into what I call *myself*, I always stumble on some particular perception or other, of heat or cold, light or shade, love or hatred, pain or pleasure . . . and never can observe anything but the perception' (*Treatise of Human Nature*, Book I, Part IV, sect. vi) – one might say that the empirical self is that upon which Hume stumbled, while the transcendental self is that which did the stumbling.

The transcendental ego is also an important topic in the philosophies of HUSSERL and SARTRE, where it receives rather different treatment.

BIBLIOGRAPHY

Kant, I.: *Critique of Pure Reason* (Riga: 1781; 2nd edn. 1787) trans. N. Kemp Smith (New York: St Martin's Press, 1965).
Powell, C.: *Kant's Theory of Self-Consciousness* (Oxford: Oxford University Press, 1990).

JAMES VAN CLEVE

Tree of Porphyry Pictorial representation of the division of SUBSTANCE into classes. The trunk of the tree represents the various classes from the highest (*genus generalissimum*) to the lowest (*species specialissima*) and includes substance, body, animated body, rational animal, and man. The branches of the tree represent the various differences (*differentiae specificae*) that, when added to a generic class, yield a lower class. They include: corporeal and incorporeal, animated and inanimated, rational and irrational, mortal and immortal. The lowest two branches of the tree represent the units that divide the lowest species. Because no further division is possible beyond these, they are called INDIVIDUAL and are represented in the tree by proper names (e.g. 'Socrates' and 'Plato').

The origin of the tree is a passage of Porphyry's *Isagoge* where he discusses the relationships among genus, species and individual within the category of substance. The context of the tree, then, is logical, but in the Middle Ages it was also interpreted metaphysically. The medievals spoke of the tree as the categorical hierarchy (*scala praedicamentalis*).

See also BOETHIUS.

BIBLIOGRAPHY

Boethius, M.S.: *In 'Isagogen' Porphyrii commenta* ed. Samuel Brandt; in *Corpus scriptorum ecclesiasticorum latinorum* vol. 48 (Vienna: 1906; repr. New York: Johnson, 1966).
Porphyry: *Isagoge*, in *Commentaria in Aristotelem graeca*, vol. 4, part 1, ed. A. Busse (Berlin: Georg Reimer, 1895).

JORGE J.E. GRACIA

trope In contemporary metaphysics, a trope is not a figure of speech, but a particular case of a quality or relation. The term was introduced by WILLIAMS, to refer to *abstract particulars*. An abstract particular is an instance of a property, a case of a kind, a token of a type (*see* CONCRETE/ABSTRACT; UNIVERSALS AND PARTICULARS).

If two books, each with a red cover, furnish us with two cases of the same shade of red, there are two red tropes, the red in this book, and the red in that.

Many philosophers have recognized the existence of this category of being, among them ARISTOTLE, LEIBNIZ, LOCKE and HUME. Among moderns, PEIRCE, G.F. Stout, BERGMANN, SELLARS, GOODMAN and Jonathan Bennett find a place for them.

Williams was the first to propose that a complete ONTOLOGY could be built on tropes as the sole fundamental category, with universals, concrete substances, and other categories constructed from them. This programme is developed in Campbell (1990).

BIBLIOGRAPHY

Campbell, K.: *Abstract Particulars* (Oxford: Blackwell, 1990).
Williams, D.C.: 'On the elements of being', *Review of Metaphysics* 7 (1953), 3–18, 171–92.
Williams, D.C.: 'Universals and existents', *Australasian Journal of Philosophy* 64 (1986), 1–14.

KEITH CAMPBELL

truth   *see* THEORIES OF TRUTH

U

Unamuno, Miguel de (1864–1936) Philosopher, scholar and author, born in Bilbao, Spain. He studied in Bilbao and Madrid and taught classics and philosophy in Salamanca. He served as rector of the University of Salamanca on two different occasions, but critical remarks about the government prompted dismissal from the university and exile from 1924 to 1930, and again dismissal from the rectorship in 1936.

Unamuno is a major figure in Spanish literature. His goal was to grasp life in its emotional and intellectual complexity rather than to understand it abstractly. Thus, he chose various literary genres to express his views. He wrote several novels, a commentary on *Don Quijote* (1905), and some poetry and drama, but his philosophical ideas are most explicitly stated in *Del sentimiento trágico de la vida* (1913). Unamuno is considered one of the founders of EXISTENTIALISM; he was influenced by PASCAL, SCHOPENHAUER, and Søren Kierkegaard.

Unamuno's philosophy centres around the tragic sense that characterizes human life. The cause of this tragic sense is the clash between man's irrational desire for IMMORTALITY and the rational certainty of his DEATH. To surmount this predicament man must reject reason and appeal to faith, for reason is concerned with abstractions whereas man is made of 'flesh and bones' and can find fulfilment only through commitment. Only faith can satisfy his desire for immortality and divinity. Man seeks to encompass everything, to be God; and if he is not God, he is nothing, not even man.

In this context, God becomes an expression of man's consciousness of his limitations and his desire for all inclusiveness. The arguments for God's existence prove only that we have an idea of God and yearn to be divine. Ultimately, existence is a mystery, since there is no objective truth to which we can appeal to unravel it. The status of reality is a matter of belief.

WRITINGS

Obras completas, 7 vols, ed. M.G. Blanco (Madrid: Afrodisio Aguado, 1958).

BIBLIOGRAPHY

Ellis, R.R.: *The Tragic Pursuit of Being: Unamuno and Sartre* (Tuscaloosa, AL: University of Alabama Press, 1988).
Ferrater Mora, J.: *Unamuno* trans. P. Silver (Berkeley and Los Angeles: University of California Press, 1962).
Ilie, P.: *Unamuno: An Existential View of Self and Society* (Madison, WI: University of Wisconsin Press, 1967).
Ouimette, V.: *Reason Aflame: Unamuno and the Heroic Will* (New Haven, CT: Yale University Press, 1974).
Rudd, M.T.: *The Lone Heretic: A Biography of Miguel de Unamuno y Jugo* (Austin, TX: University of Texas Press, 1963).

JORGE J.E. GRACIA

unity of science Whether the separate sciences are unified may be considered in terms of their *methods* or their *results*.

The methodological thesis says that all sciences deploy the same techniques of reasoning. But what does 'the same' mean? Doubtless, all sciences employ *modus ponens*.

On the other hand, it is arguable that empathy is crucial to inquiry in the human sciences, but not to sciences that deal with inanimate nature. Perhaps the sciences are unified with respect to some methodological principles, but not with respect to others.

Whether the results of science are unified raises the issue of *reductionism*. Can theories confirmed in one science be reduced to theories confirmed in another? In the sequence from social science, down through psychology, biology, chemistry and physics, will theories at one level reduce to theories at the level below? The answer depends on how the concept of 'reduction' is understood.

See also REDUCTION, REDUCTIONISM.

BIBLIOGRAPHY

Causey, R.: *The Unity of Science* (Dordrecht: Reidel, 1977).

Fodor, J.: 'Special sciences, or the disunity of science as a working hypothesis', *Synthese* 28 (1974), 97–115.

Miller, R.: *Fact and Method: Explanation, Confirmation and Reality in the Natural and the Social Sciences* (Princeton, NJ: Princeton University Press, 1987).

Oppenheim, P. and Putnam, H.: 'Unity of science as a working hypothesis', in *Minnesota Studies in the Philosophy of Science* ed. H. Feigl, M. Scriven and G. Maxwell (Minneapolis: University of Minnesota Press, 1958), 3–36.

ELLIOTT SOBER

universals The existence of universals is one of the most hotly debated topics in metaphysics. The first philosopher explicitly to postulate such entities was apparently PLATO. His *Forms* or *Ideas* are, among other things, universals. Universals may be argued for on the basis of the existence of general words. The word 'Plato' is the name of an individual. But what are the words 'white' and 'horse' the names of? They are not the names of any particular white thing or particular horse. So perhaps these words name the universals whiteness and horseness.

This line of thought is generally thought to be unsatisfactory, based as it is on the rather superficial idea that names and general words function in the same way semantically. A more interesting argument starts from the fact that when we sort or classify things we say that they are the *same* in certain respects. Two different things may have the very same colour. But if sameness is IDENTITY, having the properties ascribed to identity by logicians, then some one thing, the colour in question, qualifies a number of different particulars. That colour is then capable of qualifying objects anywhere and anytime. It is thus a universal.

This argument also seems to fail, because the word 'same' can be used in what BUTLER called a 'loose and popular' way. (He was thinking of cases where, over time, the one thing's parts are successively replaced.) But it does enable the issue between those who uphold universals and those who deny their existence to be *stated*. Believers in universals (sometimes called 'Realists' although the term has many other meanings) hold that in speaking of different things as the *same* in certain respects, the word must be taken, at least in favourable cases, as meaning strict identity. Those who reject universals (sometimes called 'Nominalists' although the word can take both narrower and wider meanings than this) must take the word, when used in these contexts, to have only the 'loose and popular' sense.

(It seems that the loose and popular sense can be given a formal characterization. Two entities may be said to be the same in this loose sense if they are different members of the one equivalence class, and there is an equivalence relation which is both salient in this situation and picks out this class. An equivalence relation is symmetrical, transitive and reflexive. It operates upon its field to divide it exhaustively into non-overlapping classes. Different members of the same class are interchangeable from the standpoint of the relation and may be said to be 'the same' relative to that standpoint.)

Different forms of Nominalism have different strategies for evading the alleged necessity to postulate universals. For a *Predicate* Nominalist (a Nominalist in a literal sense of the word) different things are said to have the same property, or belong to the same sort or kind, if the same predicate applies to, or is 'true of', the different things. A *Concept* Nominalist substitutes concepts in the mind for words in the mouth (*see* CONCEPT). Standard difficulties raised for such theories concern properties, etc., for which no predicate or concept exists, and the appearance the analysis gives of being viciously regressive because the predicates or concepts appealed to must be word or concept *types* rather than individual things, although it is types that the theory is seeking to analyse.

Class Nominalists substitute classes or sets of particulars for properties, kinds, etc. To be white is to be nothing more than to be a member of the class of white things. This view has gained prestige in this century from the theoretical development and success of set theory. Relations, which may be thought of as polyadic properties, are dealt with on this scheme as sets of ordered *n*-tuples (ordered sets). A traditional criticism is that such an analysis cannot provide for *coextensive* properties, properties which qualify exactly the same things. A deeper difficulty is that only a minority of classes are *natural* or *unified* classes. Consider a random selection of a large, perhaps infinite, number of objects. Can they always be said to have something in common? If not, then the mere notion of membership of a set has failed to capture an essential feature of a general property or kind. (*See* CLASS, COLLECTION, SET.)

An interesting variant of Class Nominalism has been proposed by Anthony Quinton (1957). He accepts this second criticism and gives an account of properties, etc., in terms of *natural* classes. Quinton takes the naturalness of a class, though admitting of degree, to be a fundamental, unanalysable, notion.

Class Nominalism must be distinguished from *Mereological* Nominalism. On the latter view a property, etc., is identified with the omnitemporal whole or aggregate of all the things said to have the property. Whiteness is the huge white object whose parts are all the white things. This theory has some plausibility for a case like whiteness, but breaks down completely for other universals (e.g., squareness). (*See* PART/WHOLE.)

Resemblance Nominalisms (see for instance Price, 1953, ch. 1) appeal to the relation of resemblance to construct a network of resemblance relations holding between certain classes of particulars. To have a property, be of a kind, etc., is to be a member of such a class. It is often said that resemblance between objects is always a matter of respects in which the things resemble. But this contention, quite plausible in itself, can hardly be accepted without serious qualification by a Resemblance Nominalist, or, indeed, any Nominalist, because respects are points of identity. The Resemblance Nominalist must take resemblance to be a primitive notion, one not involving respects, although one that admits of degree.

Among the difficulties for this variant of Nominalism there is the problem, rather difficult when it is faced up to in concrete cases, of actually constructing the required resemblance classes. A more famous difficulty, put forward by RUSSELL (1912), is that the theory cannot be made coherent without admitting one genuine universal: resemblance itself. There has been much dispute as to whether this criticism succeeds.

There have been attempts to bypass the problem of universals which may or may not be considered to be forms of Nominalism. At any rate, these positions do deny or find nonsensical the view that universals exist. QUINE has argued for the ontological innocence of predicates (1961), and it is certainly the application conditions of predicates that furnish the Realist with much that seems to support his case. But it has been argued against Quine that, even accepting his view of the predicate, we cannot avoid reference to universals (Jackson, 1977).

In the later philosophy of WITTGEN-STEIN it is argued that all metaphysical claims, such as the claim that universals exist, are nonsensical at bottom. His important observation that many (all?) general words form a family of resembling cases rather than applying in virtue of a common feature has been thought by some followers to show that the 'problem of universals' can be dissolved (Bambrough, 1961).

A very different, and much more ontologically oriented, approach may perhaps be characterized as 'moderate' Nominalism. This sort of view begins by conceding to the Realist that there do exist *in re*, in the things themselves, properties and that there do exist *in re* relations that hold between things. But it is argued against the Realist that these properties and relations are not universals but are particulars, as particular as the propertied and related things (see, for example, Stout, 1930). This view is still left with the problem of classification. On what basis do we declare that different things have the *same* property or that different pairs of things are related by the *same* relation?

An interesting solution can be proposed. It can be argued that the word 'same' here is used in its 'loose and popular sense' and that what we have are not identities of property and relation across particulars but equivalence classes of properties and relations. The most obvious equivalence relation to appeal to here is that of *exact resemblance*. This relation is symmetrical, transitive and reflexive. Such equivalence classes of particularized properties and relations appear to be able to do at least a good deal of the metaphysical work that universals do.

Turning now to views that admit universals, the theories to be considered fall into two main groups. First there are the views that take universals to be *transcendent* entities, standing apart from physical objects in space and time. It is generally thought that Plato held a view of this sort, and it was a conspicuous feature of the revival of the doctrine of universals by MOORE and Russell at the beginning of the twentieth century (see Russell, 1912, chs IX, X). Second, there are those theories that admit universals, but try to bring them down to the world of particulars. Some commentators think that this was ARISTOTLE's position, although others see him as a (moderate) Nominalist.

There is another distinction to be drawn among theories of universals which tends to go along with, but does not quite coincide with, the distinction between transcendent and non-transcendent theories of universals. This is the distinction between those who admit and those who deny that there are *uninstantiated* universals, universals which are not exemplified by any particular, past, present or future. To accept uninstantiated universals is to allow that these universals, at least, are transcendent. But it is possible to make all universals transcendent yet maintain that there are no uninstantiated universals.

One pressure to admit uninstantiated universals comes from the fact that we can form coherent conceptions of properties, relations and kinds that are not instantiated at any time. It is not clear that this is an argument of much weight. More compelling arguments, still not necessarily conclusive, can be drawn from scientific considerations, for instance, the likelihood of 'missing values', uninstantiated values, in the case of functional laws of nature.

Transcendent universals are rather naturally repugnant to empiricists and to those who like to think of themselves as in the tough-minded camp in their philosophizing (*see* EMPIRICISM). How could they act on minds, and if they could not so act could we really have good reasons for believing in their existence? At the same time, there are often thought to be difficulties in bringing universals 'down to earth'. If universals are in some sense 'in' the things that instantiate them then it appears that the very same thing – a certain universal – will be in a number of different places at once. Plato makes Socrates say in the *Philebus* (15b–c) that this is the most impossible of all views on the subject. The present writer merely records that he thinks that the difficulty here may be overcome.

Ever since the question was raised in Plato's *Parmenides* (130b–e) questions have been raised about just what universals we should postulate if we postulate any at all. An important methodological point arises. Should we decide the extent of the realm of universals on philosophical grounds, which in practice will involve giving great weight to semantic considerations? This may be called an a priori Realism about universals. An identification of universals with the meanings of general words is a character-istic, if extreme, manifestation of this approach. The alternative is an a posteriori Realism, looking to our best general the-ories about the nature of the world to give us revisable conjectures about just what universals we ought to postulate. In prac-tice this will probably mean looking to total science to decide this question. Philoso-phers, on this view, may argue for and against adopting theories of the general nature of universals, but should not pontifi-cate about what universals there are (see Armstrong, 1978). It may be noted that science deals continually in properties and quantities. The a posteriori Realist will be inclined to treat quantities as ranges of properties, and properties themselves as universals.

It may be noted that the 'moderate' nominalist, who admits properties and rela-tions but takes them to be particulars, has this same choice between an a priori and an a posteriori approach to the question what properties and relations should be admitted.

Most theories of universals will admit at least selected properties and relations as universals. The question arises whether a disjunction of universals or the negation of a universal should be accounted a *universal*. If there are universals, then we can cer-tainly *predicate* a disjunction of universals, or a failure to instantiate a universal, of a particular. It is unclear that a *property* cor-responds to such predicates. Other problems arise with conjunctions of universals or

with the structures of universals that, for example, are involved in being a methane molecule. Should we allow conjunctive uni-versals and structural universals? Or should we say that all universals are simple? One argument against the latter view is the (epistemic) possibility that universals dis-solve into conjunctions or structures *ad infi-nitum*.

A very important issue is whether the category of monadic universal contains not only properties but what might be called *substantival* universals. Compare being white and being a horse. In ordinary dis-course we are happy to speak of a property of whiteness. It sounds very strange to speak of a property of horseness or even of the property of being a horse. Should we then admit a second sort of monadic uni-versal of which *being a horse* or, perhaps more plausibly, *being an electron* are possible examples? If we do, we may well go on to hold that the world is a world of *kinds* of things, where being of a kind is to instanti-ate a substantival universal. A problem that then arises is how this universal relates to the properties of things. Does the substantival or kind-universal logically dictate that the thing has certain properties or has properties falling within a certain range? We will then be postulating *essential* properties associated with the kinds (*see* ESSENCE/ACCIDENT). The more reductive alternative is to try to do without sub-stantival universals and give an account of the natures of things in terms of their prop-erties alone.

The acceptance of universals allows for the interesting possibility of seeing *laws of nature* as relations that directly link uni-versal with universal, thus perhaps explain-ing the special necessity of laws, a necessity that may or may not be held to obtain 'in every possible world'. (*See* LAW OF NATURE; MODALITIES AND POSSIBLE WORLDS.)

Admission of universals raises the ques-tion exactly how they stand to the parti-culars that instantiate them. Are particulars no more than bundles of universals? Or are particulars in some degree or other distinct from universals but peculiarly and intimately linked to them by some special tie?

See also COPULA; NOMINALISM; PLATONISM; REALISM; UNIVERSALS AND PARTICULARS.

BIBLIOGRAPHY

Armstrong, D.M.: *Universals and Scientific Realism* 2 vols (Cambridge: Cambridge University Press, 1978).

Bambrough, R.: 'Universals and family resemblances', *Proceedings of the Aristotelian Society* 61 (1960–1), 207–22.

Jackson, F.C.: 'Statements about universals', *Mind* 76 (1977), 427–9.

Plato: *Parmenides* (many versions).

Plato: *Philebus* (many versions).

Price, H.H.: *Thinking and Experience* (London: Hutchinson, 1953).

Quine, W.V.: 'On what there is', in his *From a Logical Point of View* 2nd edn (New York: Harper and Row, 1961), 1–19.

Quinton, A.: 'Properties and classes', *Proceedings of the Aristotelian Society* 58 (1957–8), 33–58.

Russell, B.: *The Problems of Philosophy* (London: Thornton Butterworth, 1912).

Stout, G.F.: 'The nature of universals and propositions', in his *Studies in Philosophy and Psychology* (London: Macmillan, 1930), 384–403.

Woozley, A.D.: 'Universals', in *The Encyclopaedia of Philosophy* ed. P. Edwards (New York: The Macmillan Company and The Free Press; London: Collier-Macmillan, 1967), vol. 8, 194–206.

D.M. ARMSTRONG

universals and particulars For those who postulate UNIVERSALS, which are things capable of indefinite repetition, the relations between them, and the ordinary things of the world – particulars, things not capable of repetition at all – have always been a major problem. The problem is first discussed by PLATO in his *Parmenides* (130e–133b). There the young Socrates puts forward a theory of Forms and then, under questioning, first canvasses the idea that particulars have the properties they have by *participating* in the Forms and then, when this runs into difficulty, that they have their properties by *imitating* the Forms. The main difficulty raised against these suggestions is the so-called 'Third Man'. It is assumed that the Forms themselves have the property that they bestow. The Form of man will itself be a man. In contemporary Platonic scholarship this is known as the Self-Predication assumption. It is then argued that the original particulars plus their Form constitute a new class which will require a new Form, a process that will proceed *ad infinitum*. The exact nature and validity of this argument has been subject to debate that is itself almost infinite. (Contemporary discussion was initiated by Vlastos, 1954.) Modern upholders of universals, however, generally reject the Self-Predication assumption. Humanity is not a man, whiteness is not a white thing. As a result the Third Man argument does not constitute a difficulty for present-day upholders of universals.

Nevertheless, no one would now wish to argue for participation or imitation as the relation holding between particulars and universals. Rather the relation is thought of as something *sui generis*, not identical with any ordinary relation. It is generally said that a particular *instantiates* or *exemplifies* the relevant universal. RYLE (1971, pp. 9–10) pointed out that another infinite regress still seemed to threaten. Must not particular instances of instantiation – this particular instantiating this universal – derive this character of instantiation by instantiating the universal of instantiation? This gives a new instance of instantiation which in turn will have to instantiate instantiation, and so *ad infinitum*. This regress is a particular case of a regress that threatens any theory which tries to give an account of what it is for a particular to have a certain character or for two or more things to have a certain relation. Nominalist theories, that is, theories which deny universals, are as much exposed to it as upholders of universals. For instance, one Nominalist theory reduces the having of a property or the holding of a relation to membership of the appropriate class of things. This theory can be faced with a demand for an account of its fundamental relation: class membership. But any account of instances of class membership in class terms will have to appeal again to the relation of class membership, setting up an infinite process. (*See* CLASS, COLLECTION, SET.)

This generalization of the difficulty that Ryle raises for the theory of universals gives some reason to think that the difficulty can be met. The principle at work here is that what is a difficulty for all theories is a difficulty for none in particular because it suggests that, somehow, the problem can be evaded. It is to be noted, though, that the moral drawn might be that all theories which try to give some account of what it is for something to have a character or property, or what it is for two or more things to be related, are fundamentally misguided. On this view, the 'problem of universals' would be some sort of mare's nest.

Ryle's argument would be met directly if it is the case, as some have maintained, that instantiation is not really a relation at all. The idea would be that a thing and its property, or things and their relations, are, as it were, too close together to make it possible to speak of a relation here. It is certainly clear that instantiation is no ordinary relation. But once one allows any sort of distinction between a thing and its property, or between things and the relations that hold between them, it is hard to deny that

there is some sort of 'fundamental nexus' or 'non-relational tie' that holds between things and universals (*see* COPULA).

A bold attempt to give an account of the way that universals stand to particulars is the theory, found in RUSSELL (1948, Pt IV, ch. VIII) in particular, that particulars are nothing but bundles of universals. (The reduction of universals to particulars is, of course, much more frequently attempted.) Russell's attempt runs into a number of technical difficulties. One difficulty is that it seems possible that two numerically different things should instantiate the very same universals, which the theory has to rule out rather arbitrarily. In any case it must be noted that this theory also requires a 'fundamental nexus' parallel to that of instantiation. The bundling of universals is achieved by a relationship that Russell calls *compresence*.

See also NOMINALISM; PLATONISM.

BIBLIOGRAPHY

Plato: *Parmenides* (many versions).
Russell, B.: *Human Knowledge: Its Scope and Limits* (London: Allen and Unwin, 1948).
Ryle, G.: 'Plato's "Parmenides" ', in his *Collected Papers*, vol. 1 (London: Hutchinson, 1971), 1–44.
Vlastos, G.: 'The Third Man argument in the *Parmenides*',· *The Philosophical Review* 63 (1954), 319–49.

D.M. ARMSTRONG

V

vagueness 'Vague' is ambiguous. In one sense, 'vague' means underspecific. For instance, 'thirty-something' is a vague answer to your physician's question about your age because the interval (30 through 39) does not provide him with enough information.

In another sense, 'vague' means the possession of borderline cases. 'Clothing' is vague because my handkerchief is a borderline case of 'clothing'. My handkerchief qualities as borderline 'clothing' because no amount of empirical or conceptual inquiry can determine whether it is clothing or non-clothing. Since most words have borderline cases, most words are vague in this sense. Neither of the two senses of 'vague' entails the other. However, they are compatible: 'thirty-ish' has borderline cases and would also be an underspecific answer to a physician.

Although vagueness seems to be a property of words rather than things, many metaphysicians have argued that reality itself is vague. Other metaphysics are interested in vagueness because of its intimate association with the sorites paradox (*see* SORITES ARGUMENTS). For one solution to the paradox is to deny that vague words succeed in referring to anything. Yet other metaphysicians are interested in vagueness because it suggests that some questions push our concepts beyond their limit of application. For example, some *personal identity* theorists have suggested that 'Does one survive teletransportation?' simply lacks a definite answer.

BIBLIOGRAPHY

Ballmer, T. and Pinkal, M. eds: *Approaching Vagueness* (Amsterdam: North-Holland Linguistic Series, 1983).

Burns, L.C.: *Vagueness* (Dordrecht: Kluwer, 1991).

Evans, G.: 'Can there be vague objects?', *Analysis* 38 (1978), 208.

Rolf, B.: *Topics on Vagueness* (Lund: Studentlitteratur, 1981).

Sorensen, R.: 'The ambiguity of vagueness and precision', *Pacific Philosophical Quarterly* 70 (1989), 174–83.

ROY A. SORENSEN

verifiability *see* PRINCIPLE OF VERIFIABILITY

Vienna Circle *see* LOGICAL POSITIVISM

vitalism The doctrine of an autonomy of life. It was traditionally opposed to 'mechanism', the view that living things are nothing but complex machines. Strict vitalists such as Georg Ernest Stahl (1660–1734) maintained that every living organism contains an irreducibly non-physical element by which it is animated. ARISTOTLE called this element a 'SOUL' (*psyche*). Hans Driesch (1867–1941) appealed to facts about morphology to support his vitalism. He claimed that if a newly fertilized egg were simply a physical system, it could not develop as it does. Hence, it must contain an 'entelechy' that induces it to grow toward its ultimate form. Logical positivists (e.g. Hempel) cited this as an example of an unverifiable, and hence meaningless, view (*see* LOGICAL POSITIVISM; PRINCIPLE OF

VERIFIABILITY). A more modest form of vitalism maintains that chemistry and physics alone cannot provide complete explanations of the distinctive behaviour of living things. According to this view, biology is an autonomous science, since some biological laws are 'ultimate' – they cannot be reduced to, or explained by, appeal to the laws of a more fundamental science. As biochemistry becomes more sophisticated, the appeal of vitalism diminishes.

See also DEATH; LIFE; REDUCTION, REDUCTIONISM.

BIBLIOGRAPHY

Aristotle: *De anima* (*On the Soul*), in *The Basic Works of Aristotle* ed. R. McKeon (New York: Random House, 1941).

Beckner, M.: 'Vitalism', in *The Encyclopedia of Philosophy* ed. P. Edwards (New York: Macmillan, 1967), vol. 8, 253–6.

Driesch, H.: *The Science and Philosophy of the Organism*, The Gifford Lectures delivered before the University of Aberdeen in the year 1907 (London: Adam and Charles Black, 1908).

Hempel, C.G.: *Philosophy of Natural Science* (Englewood Cliffs, NJ: Prentice-Hall, 1966).

Mayr, E.: *The Growth of Biological Thought* (Cambridge, MA: The Belknap Press of Harvard University Press, 1982).

FRED FELDMAN

W

Whitehead, Alfred North (1861–1947) Beginning his career as a mathematician and logician (*A Treatise on Universal Algebra* (1898) and *Principia Mathematica* (1910–13) with Bertrand Russell), moving on into the domain of philosophy of science (*An Enquiry Concerning the Principles of Natural Knowledge* (1919); *The Concept of Nature* (1920); *The Principle of Relativity* (1922)), Whitehead reached full stride in his illustrious career when in 1924, at age 63, he left his native England and accepted an appointment at Harvard as Professor of Philosophy. From his new base, in the New World Cambridge, he produced a series of books that established him as one of the most distinguished metaphysicians of the twentieth century: *Science and the Modern World* (1925); *Religion in the Making* (1926); *Process and Reality* (1929); *Adventures of Ideas* (1933); and *Modes of Thought* (1938).

Sensitive as he was to the structures and meanings embedded in language, Whitehead realized the futility of attempting to construct a scheme of concepts with which to do metaphysics which simply employed the language of the philosophical perspectives which he wished to surpass – the linguistic distinctions upon which the old ways of thinking were based would surreptitiously import those traditional ways of thinking into the new philosophy if one used them. Consequently, Whitehead invented a new lexicon of terms, seeking to escape outmoded ways of thinking by the introduction of neologisms capable of conveying his intent without carrying along ontological shadows of the metaphysical systems of the past. This practice has fostered a widespread impression that Whitehead is a difficult, obscure thinker. It is

certainly true that he is not simple; indeed, he distrusts simplicity: 'All simplifications of religious dogma are shipwrecked upon the rock of the problem of evil. As a particular application, we may believe that the various doctrines about God have not suffered chiefly from their complexity. They have represented extremes of simplicity' and these oversimplifications have caused great problems (1926, p. 65). Nevertheless, for those who stick with him and learn his language, Whitehead offers a clear, exciting, modern vision of human nature and culture as they have their being as a part of the wider nature explored and described by scientists. Well before C.P. Snow articulated his plea that we overcome the bifurcation between 'the two cultures', Whitehead had already rolled up his sleeves and thrown himself into the project.

Three of his books convey the bulk of Whitehead's metaphysical contribution. In *Science and the Modern World* he argues that a powerful set of philosophical presuppositions came into dominance with the development of Newtonian science (*see* NEWTON), a set of philosophical presuppositions which had its roots in that Newtonian conceptuality. In that book he delineates the relationship between the philosophical ideas and their supporting scientific context and then traces the disintegration, century by century, of the Newtonian achievement. His point is that the philosophical presuppositions which have dominated philosophy for the last 300 years have been gradually undermined by the continuous erosion of the scientific conceptuality in which they are based. The Einsteinian revolution in scientific thought at the turn of the century once and for all left the traditional modern philosophical assumptions blowing in the wind, cut off from any supporting ground.

In *Science and the Modern World* Whitehead loosely adumbrates his emerging sense of the nature of the philosophical presuppositions lurking in the new scientific developments of the twentieth century. It was not until four years later, however, with the publication of his *magnum opus*, *Process and Reality*, that Whitehead both articulated in a full-blown manner the set of philosophical assumptions he found compatible with the new developments in science and drew forth the complex metaphysical system which flows from these assumptions.

Finally, *Adventures of Ideas*, a more lyrical, less technical work, rounds out the metaphysical enterprise. Whitehead sets up the challenge for *Adventures of Ideas* by suggesting that in every cultural epoch there are two types of forces driving the processes of social change: brute, senseless agencies of compulsion on the one hand, and formulated aspirations, articulated beliefs on the other. Whitehead's symbols for these two types of forces in the classical world are Barbarians (brute compulsion) and Christianity (a system of beliefs and aspirations); in the Europe of two centuries ago, examples of these two types of forces would be, respectively, Steam and Democracy. Whitehead's interest in *Adventures of Ideas* is in those articulated aspirations of civilizations. He believes that in their emergence they are shaped by the philosophical understandings available at the moment when they struggle for release and efficacy. In the culminating section of this book, Whitehead elaborates his vision of the aspirations appropriate to our modern age, formulating them in the language provided by the new philosophical conceptuality presented in *Process and Reality*.

Like many thinkers in the recent past, Whitehead is convinced that DESCARTES, with his dualistic ONTOLOGY, is responsible for shunting philosophy off on a 300-year-long wild-goose chase. If the knower is indeed a Cartesian substance requiring nothing (except perhaps God) in order to exist, there is no coherent way for that knower to break out of its isolation and enter into relations with an external world – this is a conclusion established vividly, Whitehead notes, by both HUME and SANTAYANA. Some contemporary philosophers (e.g. Richard Rorty) have suggested that philosophy has been driven into a box that should be labelled 'The End of Philosophy'. Whitehead agrees that we are witnessing the end of something, but he labels that something a 'phase of philosophic thought which began with Descartes and ended with Hume' (1929, corrected edn, p. xi). In order to move ahead into a new phase, he believes, we must recognize that all epistemological difficulties are only disguised metaphysical difficulties (cf. ibid., p. 189); the problems about *knowing* which have bedevilled modern philosophy have their roots in misguided assumptions about the nature of *knowers*.

A comparison which gives an intuitive insight into Whitehead's metaphysical move at this point is the suggestion that Whitehead's metaphysics is something like what would result if one took the metaphysics of ARISTOTLE and instead of making the category of SUBSTANCE primary, made the category of RELATION primary. Unlike a Cartesian being, which requires nothing but itself in order to exist, a Whiteheadian being, termed an actual entity, in an important sense *is* its relations to other beings. It has been said that a Whiteheadian actual entity is something like a Leibnizian monad except that instead of being 'windowless', it is 'all window' (*see* LEIBNIZ; MONAD, MONADOLOGY). The genius, and the complexity, of Whitehead's metaphysics is that he grounds his relational notion of being in the developments undergirding modern science. Descartes's problem is not that he was a philosophical dummy; rather, he was stuck with a fundamental scientific vision that viewed MATTER as inert stuff and saw energy as something external to matter. Whitehead has the great advantage of living at a time when the concept of matter has been profoundly transformed so that energy is not external to, but of the essence of, matter. When this development is joined with the rise to prominence of the theory of evolution, Whitehead's metaphysical challenge becomes clear: to so describe the character of being (of actual entities) that one can understand how human being emerged gradually from a simpler form of the very same, essentially relational being. Rather than giving us a Cartesian dualism, Whitehead argues for a neutral monism embracing relatedness at its very core (see MONISM/PLURALISM).

See also PROCESS PHILOSOPHY.

WRITINGS

Science and the Modern World (New York: Macmillan, 1925).
Religion in the Making (New York: Macmillan, 1926).
Process and Reality (Cambridge: Cambridge University Press, 1929).
Adventures of Ideas (New York: Macmillan, 1933).
Modes of Thought (New York: Macmillan, 1938).

DONALD W. SHERBURNE

why there is something Logical possibilities can subsist eternally and unmysteriously, but why are there any actualities? Though some call this a pseudo-question, answers have been suggested. Perhaps God's infinitude is a satisfyingly simple source of all other existence. Perhaps the existence of things at each instant is explicable by their having existed earlier. Perhaps the difference between actuality and possibility is merely like that between existing here and existing yonder (see POTENTIALITY/ ACTUALITY). A Neoplatonist answer is that, just as it would be ethically required that a blank not be replaced by a bad situation, so also there is an ethical requirement that there be a good situation, not a blank (see NEOPLATONISM). In a fashion timelessly necessary (despite being logically undemonstrable) this requirement is itself

creative. The accompanying problem of evil might be solved Spinozistically: divine knowledge, a supreme good, would include knowing exactly how it felt to live lives often harsh and clouded by ignorance.

See also COSMOLOGY; COSMOS; FINITE/ INFINITE; WORLD.

BIBLIOGRAPHY

Edwards, P.: 'Why?', in *The Encyclopedia of Philosophy* ed. P. Edwards (New York: Macmillan, 1967) vol. 8, 296–302.
Leslie, J.: *Value and Existence* (Oxford: Blackwell, 1979).
Mackie, J.L.: *The Miracle of Theism* (Oxford: Clarendon Press, 1982).
Munitz, M.K.: *The Mystery of Existence* (New York: Appleton-Century-Crofts, 1965).
Rescher, N.: *The Riddle of Existence* (Lanham, MD: University Press of America, 1984).

JOHN LESLIE

Williams, Donald Cary (1899–1983) American philosopher. Donald Williams was born, and died, in California. A graduate of Occidental College and Harvard, his academic career involved nine years at University of California, Los Angeles in the 1930s, after which he was at Harvard until his retirement in 1967.

A realist and naturalist, he defended a classic conception of philosophy's problems, and of the role of reason in pursuit of solutions to them.

In ONTOLOGY, he initiated the programme which gives a central role to *tropes*, particular instances of qualities and relations, as the fundamental elements of being, from which all else can be constructed. Familiar concrete objects, such as tables, are bundles of tropes united by compresence; familiar properties, such as redness, are collections of tropes related by resemblance (see TROPE). There are no UNIVERSALS and no substrata (see SUBSTRATUM). Tropes are the terms of all relations, including causal ones, the objects of all perception, the true subject matter of all judgement.

His realism about the natural realm took a distinctive form: the question of the reality of the external world is to be settled in the affirmative inductively, by a posteriori reasoning. Although he tended towards direct realism in the philosophy of perception, with a corresponding realism over secondary qualities, he urged that a representative realism was also a viable option (*see* QUALITY, PRIMARY/SECONDARY). He thus pioneered the movement away from the idea that philosophical issues can be resolved only by a priori demonstration or refutation.

His treatment of induction was also most distinctive: it rests on the central insight that the deductive proof that most substantial samples are representative of the population to which they belong, can be used to ground the probable, and hence rational claim, concerning any given sample, that it is approximately representative of the population from which it comes.

Perhaps his most influential work has been in the philosophy of time (*see* SPACE AND TIME), where he has argued, in celebrated papers, for the equal reality of past, present and future, and for the four-dimensional conception of NATURE which treats the passage of time as a mere appearance.

See also NATURALISM; REALISM.

WRITINGS

The Ground of Induction (Cambridge, MA: Harvard University Press, 1947).
Principles of Empirical Realism (Springfield, IL: Thomas, 1966).

BIBLIOGRAPHY

Campbell, K.: *Abstract Particulars* (Oxford: Blackwell, 1990).
Stove, D.C.: *The Rationality of Induction* (Oxford: Clarendon Press, 1986).

KEITH CAMPBELL

Wittgenstein, Ludwig Josef Johann (1889–1951) Austrian philosopher who spent much of his life in Cambridge, England. Wittgenstein was interested in metaphysics throughout his philosophical life, but his interest was not that of a metaphysician. He wrote: 'In a certain sense one cannot take too much care in handling philosophical errors, they contain so much truth' (Wittgenstein, 1967, sect. 460). Although that remark refers in a general way to *philosophical* errors, he had in mind metaphysics, conceived to include all inquiries into the relation between thought and reality, and the essential nature of things. I consider here his early and later views about 'philosophical errors', and the question *what* truth such errors contain.

In *Tractatus Logico-Philosophicus* (1921) Wittgenstein claims that 'most of the propositions and questions written about philosophical things are not false but nonsensical', and that they rest on failure to understand the logic of our language (4.003). At the end of the book, he says that the correct method in philosophy would be to say nothing philosophical, and whenever someone tries to say something metaphysical, one should show him that he has failed to assign a meaning to some signs in his propositions (6.53). The misunderstandings of the logic of our language, referred to in the earlier remark, are what make it possible for us not to notice that we are using words with no meaning. The account he gives of how metaphysical nonsense comes to be uttered has two central elements.

1. What is given meaning is not, strictly speaking, a sign but what Wittgenstein refers to as a *symbol*, a sign taken together with a specific logical role in sentences. 'Green', for example, used as surname not only differs in meaning from 'green' the colour-word, but also has a different logical role; it is a different symbol. To assign meaning to a symbol is to fix the contribution of the sign to the sense of all those sentences in which the sign occurs as that symbol, i.e. with the particular role. Not only is it possible for a sign to have one

meaning in some occurrences and another in others, but also it is possible for it to have meaning in some occurrences and none in others. The word 'identical' occurs in both 'The good is more identical than the beautiful' and 'The morning star is identical with the evening star', but it is not in both the same symbol, any more than 'Green' is the same symbol in subject and predicate positions in 'Green wore green'. There is nothing wrong with using the word 'identical' so that it has the (new) logical role of a term for a property things have to a greater or lesser degree, but if it is not to be meaningless in such occurrences we need to assign it a particular property meaning of that logical sort. If we use a word in a logical role different from its normal role, we may fail to notice that we have not assigned any meaning to the word in the new role. It is part of Wittgenstein's account of how we can be unaware of such failure to mean anything by our words that he treats the psychological associations of a word (like the colour-imagery that might accompany the surname 'Green') as irrelevant to the word's logical characteristics. The psychological associations of a familiar word may stop us realizing that we are (for example in philosophy) using it in a new role, and have assigned it no meaning in that role.

2. Philosophers are characteristically concerned with what is *essential* to something or other, for example, with what belongs to the nature of thought, to thought as capable of being *about the world*. What is essential in this sense, Wittgenstein speaks of as *formal* properties or relations. Much philosophical confusion arises from our attempting to treat formal properties or relations as though they were ordinary non-formal properties or relations. Take, for example, the formal concept *object*. The sentence 'An object fell' looks like 'A lawyer fell', but the logical form of the former is '$\exists x$ (x fell)', while that of the latter is '$\exists x$ (x is a lawyer & x fell)'. What, in the symbolic notation, expresses the formal concept *object* is merely the variable x. The word 'object',

if we try to use it with the same logical role as 'lawyer', is a *different symbol*, and we may fail to note that no meaning has been given to 'object' used in that role. Suppose we say, 'There are objects.' Here the word 'object', which has a role as a formal term (as a sort of stand-in for a variable), is given a different role, that of a non-formal term like 'lawyer'. Philosophical nonsense is often produced in just this way: by putting signs for formal terms into contexts in which they no longer have that role (i.e. are no longer used as ordinary-language stand-ins for a variable), and failing to note that no meaning has been given to the signs thus used (1921, 4.1272). This is why there is such stress in the *Tractatus* on explaining the character of central formal terms like 'world', 'thought', and 'proposition'. Any formal notion can be expressed by a variable, the values of which have formal features in common. If we see this, we (philosophers) will no longer come out with the kind of nonsense resulting from 'trying to say what can only be shown' (see 1921, 4.121–4.1212).

It is an immediate consequence of this account of philosophy that the sentences of the *Tractatus* itself are nonsensical, since they treat formal properties and relations as non-formal properties and relations. In their use in the sentences of the *Tractatus*, the words 'world', 'fact', 'number', 'object', 'proposition' (and so on) have been given no meaning.

It is sometimes said that Wittgenstein held in the *Tractatus* that a sentence is nonsensical if it is an expression of a non-tautological necessity, or if it cannot be verified. But this assumes that such sentences do not really contain words with no meaning. We could not say that 'Smith argospated the hatchogas' was nonsensical 'because it expresses a necessary truth'. It does not say anything *because* it contains meaningless words. And what metaphysicians produce is, though they do not realize it, similar. Their sentences are not necessary truths, but expressions of confusion.

This leaves the question of the metaphysics of the *Tractatus* itself. Does it not contain an account of the relation between thought and reality, dependent on the internal possibilities of the objects that form the substance of the world? The problem for readers of the *Tractatus* is how Wittgenstein intended the sentences that appear to present such a metaphysics. He undeniably regarded such sentences as nonsensical; but some readers take him to hold that sentences which are officially 'nonsense', given the views of the *Tractatus*, can convey things which cannot be said, and they take the metaphysics of the *Tractatus* to be thus 'conveyable'. Such interpretations may reflect one's conviction that one has, after all, *understood* the sentences of the *Tractatus*. Both those convictions themselves depend on a kind of mental juggling with crucial words like 'world', 'proposition', 'object' and so on. For example, we take Wittgenstein's remarks about objects to be about a metaphysically fundamental kind of item, but we thus slide together 'object' as a genuine concept term (a term which classifies things, analogous thus to 'lawyer') and as a formal term. Thinking that we have got hold of something metaphysical always involves some such sliding back and forth of the mind, failure to fix on any definite meaning. The complex problems of reading the apparently metaphysical sections of the *Tractatus* are discussed in Conant (1989), Goldfarb (n.d.), Malcolm (1986), Ricketts (forthcoming) and Winch (1987).

After Wittgenstein returned to philosophy in 1929, he questioned many of his earlier ideas, including one that was central in his earlier critique of metaphysics, namely, that formal features may be represented by a variable, all values of which will have formal features in common. The underlying idea is that of *complete logical generality*; its importance is indicated by what Wittgenstein took to be a main achievement of the *Tractatus*, the specification of a variable whose values included every possible proposition, the variable which represents what is common to everything that is the case, everything that can be thought. That idea or ideal of complete logical generality was,

Wittgenstein now believed, a myth blocking recognition of the genuinely various forms of thinking we engage in and develop in our lives with language.

This shift in Wittgenstein's philosophy involved a new but not altogether different critique of metaphysics. Both the change and the continuity can be seen here:

Philosophical investigations: conceptual investigations. The essential thing about metaphysics: that the difference between factual and conceptual investigations is not clear to it. A metaphysical question is always in appearance a factual one, although the problem is a conceptual one. (Wittgenstein, 1980, vol. I, sect. 949)

Here, as in the *Tractatus*, metaphysics is taken to depend on a kind of false conception of one's own inquiries. But the reference to conceptual investigations reflects a notion of philosophy very different from Wittgenstein's earlier idea of it as logical analysis. The metaphysician is now seen as unaware of the grammatical character of his questions and propositions; and the notion of grammar is essential in Wittgenstein's later critique of metaphysics.

In our various linguistic practices, we as it were *lay down tracks*, tracks on which further commerce with words goes on. Thus, by giving children training in counting things like chairs and pencils, by insisting that they do this again and again until they get the answer everyone else gets, by training them to use the results in dividing things among each other and in other ways, we lay down 'tracks' for the activity 'counting objects'. That *there is some number* of chairs in that room, or that the number is independent of *who* counts them, are what Wittgenstein refers to as grammatical propositions. A metaphysician might ask 'Is there a *fact* of the number of chairs in the room, independently of our counting them? – thus treating what is part of our practice of counting as if it were a question about a kind of fact underlying the possibility of the practice.

Why, though, should metaphysical facts not underlie the possibility of our practices? The importance of this question to Wittgenstein is shown in the many discussions in his later work of what, if anything, would go wrong if our practices were different. Suppose that in our practice of talk of time we allowed for the past to be changed. Might that different grammar involve metaphysical error? Wittgenstein's critique of metaphysics is inseparable from his arguments that only in our practices can you see what we are talking about. In a sense, one cannot go wrong in grammar, because a difference of grammar means that we are talking of something else. But different practices might be very unnatural or inconvenient or (for us) seemingly pointless – and in that sense grammar is not at all arbitrary.

What *truth* then did Wittgenstein think was contained in philosophical errors? The philosopher who asks whether the past can be changed, or whether tables have a height independently of our activities of measurement, is, Wittgenstein believed, unaware of the character of his inquiries. His questions nevertheless reflect the significance in our lives of the grammatical forms about which, in a confused way, he is asking. Wittgenstein's point is particularly clear in connection with metaphysical problems about the mind. If many of our philosophical problems are tied to the idea that what is inside someone's mind is hidden from others, this reflects real elements in our complex relations with other people, for example, occasions of 'practical and primitive' uncertainty about another's thought (Wittgenstein, 1980, vol. II, sect. 558). Our interest in others is not merely in their behaviour, in what we see, though beings unlike ourselves can be imagined, with a much thinner sort of interest in others, who might lack any notion of 'the inner'. Our philosophical fascination with the inner reflects the significance in our lives, and the complexity and range, of the mental concepts we use.

Wittgenstein's critique of metaphysics is tied to a distinction between conceptual questions and factual ones, between rules of description and descriptive propositions. Is that critique undermined, we may ask, by QUINE's argument (1951) against there being any clear distinction between factual statements and statements whose truth rests on conventions? Wittgenstein accepted that the contrast 'shades off in all directions' but maintained its great importance (1956, p. 163). A full discussion of this issue would involve asking whether Quine's argument is itself coherent (see Wright, 1980, p. 359), and whether Quine's inability to find a clear distinction reflects assumptions (shared with LOGICAL POSITIVISM but not with Wittgenstein) about how it would have to be made. These questions are connected to the way we see philosophy: its connection with self-understanding and failures of self-understanding.

WRITINGS

Logisch-philosophische Abhandlung, in *Annalen der Naturphilosophie* (1921); trans. C.K. Ogden *Tractatus Logico-Philosophicus* (London: Kegan Paul, 1922); trans. D.F. Pears and B.F. McGuinness (London: Routledge and Kegan Paul, 1961).

Philosophical Investigations trans. G.E.M. Anscombe (Oxford: Basil Blackwell, 1953).

Remarks on the Foundations of Mathematics ed. G.H. von Wright, R. Rhees and G.E.M. Anscombe, trans. G.E.M. Anscombe (Oxford: Blackwell, 1956); 3rd rev. edn ed. G.H. von Wright, R. Rhees and G.E.M. Anscombe, trans. G.E.M. Anscombe (Oxford: Basil Blackwell, 1978).

The Blue and Brown Books (Oxford: Blackwell, 1964).

Zettel ed. G.E.M. Anscombe and G.H. von Wright, trans. G.E.M. Anscombe (Oxford: Blackwell, 1967).

Remarks on the Philosophy of Psychology 2 vols, vol. I ed. G.E.M. Anscombe and G.H. von Wright, trans. G.E.M. Anscombe, vol. II ed. G.H. von Wright and H. Nyman, trans. C.G. Luckhardt and M.A.E. Aue (Oxford: Blackwell, 1980).

BIBLIOGRAPHY

Cavell, S.: 'The availability of Wittgenstein's later philosophy', *Philosophical Review* 71 (1962), 67–93; repr. in his *Must We Mean What We Say?* (New York: Charles Scribner's Sons, 1969), 44–72.

Conant, J.: 'Must we show what we cannot say?', in *The Senses of Stanley Cavell* ed. R. Fleming and M. Payne (Lewisburg: Bucknell University Press, 1989), 242–83.

Diamond, C.: *The Realistic Spirit* (Cambridge, MA: Bradford, 1991).

Goldfarb, W.: 'Objects, names, and realism in the *Tractatus*', unpublished MS.

Goldfarb, W.: 'I want you to bring me a slab: remarks on the opening sections of *Philosophical Investigations*', *Synthese* 56 (1983), 265–82.

Malcolm, N.: *Nothing is Hidden* (Oxford: Blackwell, 1986).

Quine, W.V.: 'Two dogmas of empiricism', *Philosophical Review* 60 (1951), 20–43; repr. in his *From a Logical Point of View* (Cambridge, MA: Harvard University Press, 1953), 20–47.

Ricketts, T.: 'Logic and the limits of sense in the *Tractus*', in *The Cambridge Companion to Wittgenstein*, ed. H. Sluga and D. Stern (Cambridge: Cambridge University Press, forthcoming).

Winch, P.: 'Language, thought and world in Wittgenstein's *Tractatus*', in his *Trying to Make Sense* (Oxford: Blackwell, 1987), 3–17.

Wright, C.: *Wittgenstein on the Foundations of Mathematics* (London: Duckworth, 1980).

CORA DIAMOND

world In a wide sense, everything real – including the material world, the world of the mind, the Platonic world of possibilities (*see* PLATONISM) and of ethical or mathematical truths, the business world, etcetera. Philosophers debate the relationships between worlds. Is the mental world just the world of the thinking brain? Are mathematical truths of 'If . . . then . . .' form, and does this explain how they apply to material objects? Do all POSSIBLE WORLDS exist, as modal realism says? Might a Platonic need for a good material world actually create it? In COSMOLOGY, 'a world' may mean a huge domain – or an inhabited planet. We detect no extraterrestrial signals; is Earth, then, *the very first* such world among very many? That sounds improbable; therefore there will probably be few others, or none. Similar reasoning suggests that 'the end of the world', i.e. of the human race, may well not be very far distant, else we should be near (in number) to being the very first humans.

See also COSMOS; FINITE/INFINITE; MODALITIES AND POSSIBLE WORLDS; WHY THERE IS SOMETHING.

BIBLIOGRAPHY

Barrow, J.: *The World Within the World* (Oxford: Clarendon Press, 1988).

Crowe, M.J.: *The Extraterrestrial Life Debate, 1750–1900: The Idea of a Plurality of Worlds from Kant to Lowell* (Cambridge: Cambridge University Press, 1986).

Leslie, J.: 'Is the End of the World nigh?', *The Philosophical Quarterly* 40 (1990), 66–72.

Lewis, D.: *On the Plurality of Worlds* (Oxford: Blackwell, 1986).

Rood, R.T. and Trefil, J.S.: *Are We Alone?* (New York: Charles Scribner's Sons, 1981).

JOHN LESLIE

Z

Zeno of Elea (*fl. c.*500 BC) A devoted disciple of Parmenides, who held that reality consisted of one undifferentiated, unchanging, motionless whole which was devoid of any parts. Motion, CHANGE and plurality were mere illusions. Parmenides was apparently the object of some ridicule; Zeno's mission was to refute those who had made fun of his master. To accomplish this aim, Zeno propounded perhaps as many as forty paradoxes that were intended as a *reductio ad absurdum* of space, time, motion and plurality. None of Zeno's works has survived; we know fewer than ten of his puzzles on the basis of purported direct quotations and paraphrases found in the works of other philosophers (see Lee, 1936).

Zeno's most famous paradox involves a race between *Achilles and a tortoise*. As a small gesture towards fairness, the tortoise is given a head start. Achilles can never even catch the tortoise, Zeno argues, let alone pass it and win the race. When the race commences Achilles and the tortoise leave their respective starting points. If Achilles is to catch the tortoise, he must first reach the starting point of the tortoise. In the meantime, the tortoise will have moved ahead somewhat. Now, Achilles must run to the position occupied by the tortoise at the moment when Achilles reached the tortoise's original starting point, but in the meantime the tortoise will have moved ahead again. The argument is repeated indefinitely; whenever Achilles reaches a point previously occupied by the tortoise, the tortoise has moved a bit farther along. QED

Zeno's second paradox, *the dichotomy*, comes in two forms, *progressive* and *regressive*. In the progressive form Zeno argues that, regardless of the tortoise, Achilles can never run from one end of the racecourse to the other. In order to traverse the entire course, he must first cover half of the distance. Half of the distance remains. In order to traverse the remaining half, he must cover half of that. One quarter of the distance remains; now he must cover half of that. This argument is repeated indefinitely. Since a finite segment of the course always remains to be crossed, Achilles can never reach the endpoint. QED

The regressive form of the argument is designed to show, even more astonishingly, that Achilles cannot even depart from his starting point. As in the progressive form, Zeno begins with the claim that Achilles must first cover half of the course if he is to cover the whole course. But, he argues, before he can cover the first half, he must cover the first half of that (the first quarter). Before doing that, he must cover the first half of the first quarter. The argument is repeated indefinitely. Before Achilles can travel any finite distance he must already have traversed infinitely many finite segments. QED

In the paradox of *the flying arrow* Zeno maintains that, at every moment of its flight, the arrow is at rest. At any given moment the arrow is where it is, occupying a space equal to itself. That is, by definition, a state of rest. While it occupies a space equal to itself it has no room to move. When we ask how it can get from one position to another, we cannot find any answer. There is no place or time in which it can move; therefore, its motion is impossible. QED

In the paradox of the *stadium* Zeno asks us to imagine three rows of soldiers arranged as shown:

$$A_1 \quad A_2 \quad A_3$$
$$B_1 \quad B_2 \quad B_3$$
$$\qquad\qquad C_1 \quad C_2 \quad C_3$$

While the As remain in place, the Bs move one position to the right and the Cs move one position to the left, resulting in the following arrangement:

$$A_1 \quad A_2 \quad A_3$$
$$B_1 \quad B_2 \quad B_3$$
$$C_1 \quad C_2 \quad C_3$$

Zeno seems to have found it puzzling that in the first arrangement B_2 is to the left of C_1 and in the second B_2 is to the right of C_1, but B_2 is never adjacent to C_1. It is difficult to see a paradox in this case, but it might present a problem to those who claim that space, time and motion are quantized.

The foregoing are Zeno's well-known *paradoxes of motion*. Many people have felt that the first three, at least, could be dispatched quite simply by applying the infinitesimal calculus, and that the fourth is just silly. It has been claimed, for example, that the progressive form of the dichotomy paradox vanishes when we realize that an infinite series of positive numbers – $\frac{1}{2} + \frac{1}{4} + \frac{1}{8} + \ldots$ – has a finite sum, and that similar reasoning will take care of Achilles and the tortoise. These considerations do not answer the question of whether an infinite sequence of tasks can be completed in a finite amount of time. A substantial literature around mid-twentieth century was devoted to the question of whether it is logically possible to construct an *infinity machine* – a machine that could complete an infinite number of operations in a finite amount of time (see Salmon, 1970).

It has also been suggested that the concept of instantaneous velocity, familiar from the calculus, can resolve the arrow paradox by distinguishing an instantaneous velocity of zero from non-vanishing instantaneous velocity. Careful scrutiny reveals, however, that this purported resolution is question begging; a proper resolution involves an 'at–at' theory of motion, originally offered by RUSSELL (see Salmon, 1970).

Zeno's most profound paradox is basically geometrical. He asks, in effect, whether the ultimate constituents – i.e. points – of a line segment have a non-zero size, or whether the size is actually zero. Clearly the line segment is infinitely divisible; there are infinitely many ultimate constituents. If they have any size greater than zero, then, contrary to our assumption, the length of the line must be infinite. Any infinite series consisting of positive quantities *of the same size* has an infinite sum. If, however, the size is literally zero, then, contrary to our assumption, the length of the segment will be zero, for the sum of any number of zeros must be zero. Adolf Grünbaum has answered this problem by appealing to modern measure theory (see Salmon, 1970).

The most significant recent development in the discussion of Zeno's paradoxes is the application of non-standard analysis to the arrow paradox (White, 1982) and the geometrical paradox (Skyrms, 1983).

See also PRESOCRATICS.

BIBLIOGRAPHY

Lee, H.D.P.: *Zeno of Elea* (Cambridge: Cambridge University Press, 1936). This book contains all known ancient texts (purported direct quotations and paraphrases) of Zeno's work.

Salmon, W.C., ed.: *Zeno's Paradoxes* (Indianapolis, IN and New York: Bobbs-Merrill, 1970). An anthology of twentieth-century essays on Zeno's paradoxes with a comprehensive introduction by the editor and an extensive bibliography.

Skyrms, B.: 'Zeno's paradox of measure', in *Physics, Philosophy and Psychoanalysis* ed. R.S. Cohen and L. Laudan (Dordrecht: Reidel, 1983), 223–54.

White, M.: 'Zeno's arrow, divisible infinitesimals, and Chrysippus', *Phronesis* 27 (1982), 239–54.

WESLEY C. SALMON

Index

Note: Page references in **bold** type indicate chief discussion of major topics. Where names of contributors to the *Companion* are indexed, the references are to citations in articles other than their own articles.

matter, **299–302**: in Anscombe, 239; in Aquinas, 23; in Aristotle, 22, 27–8, 35, 221, 299–300, 302–3, 480, 483; in Berkeley, 50, 130–1, 301; in Bolzano, 57; in Brentano, 62; and change, 299–300; in Descartes, 33, 112; divisibility, 98, 135; and form, **302–3**; and idealism, 227–8; in Indian metaphysics, 319; and individuation, 300; in Kant, 301; in Locke, 55–6, 278, 301; in McTaggart, 289; in J. S. Mill, 327; and predication, 300; in Presocratics, 22, 413; in process philosophy, 417–18; and quantity, 301–2; in Santayana, 452; and sensation, 301; and soul and body, 300–1; and substantivalism, 467; and substratum, 299–300; in Whitehead, 511–12; *see also* form; hylomorphism; physicalism/materialism; substance

Matthews, Gareth, 274
Máynez, Eduardo García, 325
Mead, George Herbert, 410
meaning: and antirealism, 15–18; in Dewey, 120; in Dummett, 124–5, 184, 247–8; in Frege, 184, 280; and functionalism, 190–1, 192, 193; and holism, 15, 191, 213–14; in Husserl, 219–20, 244; and indeterminacy of translation, 15, 17, 160–1; and manifestation principle, 15, 124, 247; molecular theory, 124–5; and nominalism, 360; in Quine, 160; and sense, 184; as subject matter of metaphysics, 47; *see also* hermeneutics; intension; Russell; verifiability principle; Wittgenstein

mechanism, **304–5**: in Hobbes, 210–11, 304; in d'Holbach, 212, 304; in Locke, 36, 275, 277–8; in Mach, 287; in Presocratics, 415

Meinong, Alexius, **305–7**: and Hume, 305; and intentionality, 62, 244; and internal/external relations, 245, 246; and ontology, 74, 147, 305–6, 373; and proposition, 306; and theory of objects, 61,

147, 172, 305–7, 311, 361, 373
Melissus of Samos, 412, 413, 414
Mellor, D. H., 429
memory: in Butler, 383; in Locke, 277, 382–4; in J. S. Mill, 327; in Reid, 327, 383, 384
Mencius, 316, 318
Mendes, Raimundo Teixera, 324
mental/physical, **307–9**: and consciousness, 92–3; in Descartes, 307–8; in Heidegger, 205; *see also* mind/body problem
Mercado, Thomás de, 323
mereology: in Chisholm, 85, 377; in Goodman, 360; in Lesniewski, 62, 272, 360, 376–7; and nominalism, 360, 503; *see also* part/whole relation
Merleau-Ponty, Maurice, **309–10**: and ontology, 309–10; and perception, 309–10; and phenomenology, 309, 390, 391; and structure, 477
Mersenne, Marin, 112–13
metalanguage, 73, **366–7**, 458
metamathematics, 73, 283, 366
metaphysics: in Africa, **312–15**; in China, 315–18; definitions and divisions, xiii, **311–12**; immanent, 256–7, 260, 312; in India, **318–23**; in Latin America, **323–5**, 374; name, 25, 311; scope, 311, 379; subject matter, 21, 25, 47, 85, 185, 311, 373, 479; and theology, 21, 311–12; transcendent, 257–8, 260, 261, 312
Mill, James, 34
Mill, J. S., **326–7**: and anti-essentialism, 137; and associationism, 34; and causation, 83, 326–7, 389; and free will, 180; and phenomenalism, 326–7, 386, 389; and sensation, 132, 326–7
Millikan, Ruth Garrett, 213
mind: in African metaphysics, 314; in Berkeley, 53; in J. S. Mill, 327; in Newton, 355; in Pascal, 378; and realism, 436; representational-computational theory, 331; *see also* idealism
mind/body problem, **327–32**: in

African metaphysics, 314; and anomalous monism, 330; in Arnauld, 33; in Augustine, 38; and behaviourism, 188, 191, 329, 392; in Bergmann, 48; in Broad, 64; and central state materialism, 31; in Chisholm, 86; and consciousness, 92–3, 328, 329, 332; in Davidson, 108–9, 330; in Descartes, 113, 195, 307, 308, 329, 331, 381, 382, 398, 401, 464–5; in Dewey, 120; and eliminativism, 329–30; and event theory, 140; and functionalism, 188–90, 330–1; in Gassendi, 329; in Hobbes, 329; in d'Holbach, 212; and identity theory, 329; in James, 132; in Leibniz, 329; in Malebranche, 329; and materialism, 157, 329, 340, 382, 391–2; and person, 381, 382; and physicalism/materialism, 188–90, 191–2, 329, 332, 392; in Plato, 398; in Reid, 444; in Ryle, 329, 450; in Schopenhauer, 456; in Spinoza, 473; in Strawson, 381, 474; *see also* dualism; mental/physical; soul
minima naturalia, 35–6
Minkowski, Hermann, 468
Misner, C. W., 104
modality, **333–7**, 463: in Armstrong, 32; and concrete/abstract, 91; *de re/de dicto*, 138–9; in Locke, 275; in Peirce, 408; and Platonism, 401; and realism, 105, 175, 434; and supervenience, 485; *see also* actualism; necessity; possibilism; possible worlds
mode, **337–9**: in Descartes, 338; in Locke, 338–9; in Peirce, 408; in Spinoza, 338, 340, 471–2
Molina, Enrique José, 324, 325
monad/monadology, **339**: in Bolzano, 57; in Leibniz, 47, 61, 251, 270, 339, 376, 481, 482
monism, **339–41**: anomalous, 109, 330, 428; in Davidson, 109, 330, 428; and idealism, 58, 279; in Indian metaphysics, 319, 322; in Mach, 287; material, 414; in Peirce, 410; in Presocratics, 414; in Quine, 428; in Spinoza,

property (cont'd)
   instantiation; realism
proposition, **419–21**: and
   analysis, 9–10; in Bolzano, 57,
   419; and content, 94–5; and
   equivalence class, 420; and
   equivalence relation, 419–20;
   grammatical, 515; in Hegel,
   200–1; identity criteria, 251;
   modality, 67, 332–7;
   necessary/contingent, 332–3,
   336; negative/positive, 350;
   objective, 369–70; and
   ontological legitimacy, 420–1;
   in Russell, 2, 3, 132, 341,
   400, 419, 447, 448; synthetic
   a priori, 86, 255–6, 288,
   442; and truth, 95, 419, 487,
   491–2
Protagoras, 394, 398–9, 415
Proust, Joseph Louis, 36
Psellos, Michael, 352
Pseudo-Dionysius, 352
psuche: in Aristotle, 221–2, 508;
   in Presocratics, 415; *see also*
   soul
psychologism, 219, 341, 345
psychology: metaphysics as, 324;
   and ontology, 61–2; as
   physical science, 309;
   transcendental, 261–2
public/private, **421–3**: and
   consciousness, 422–3; and
   experience, 157, 421–2, 460;
   and mental/physical
   distinction, 328; and
   observability, 421–2; in
   Strawson, 474; and
   subjectivity/objectivity, 422
Putnam, Hilary: and
   functionalism, 190, 192; and
   holism, 213, 214; and internal
   realism, 411; and mind/body
   problem, 329; and natural
   kind, 161, 346; and
   structuralism, 213
Pythagoras, 414
Pythagoreanism, 98, 414

qualia *see* consciousness
quality, primary/secondary, **424–
   6**: in Armstrong, 31; and
   atomism, 36; in Berkeley, 52–
   3, 211, 301, 424, 444; in
   Broad, 64; determinate/
   determinable, **115–17**; in
   Hobbes, 211; in Hume, 211; in
   Locke, 36, 64, 277, 301, 355,
   424, 425–6; in Reid, 444; in

Williams, 513
quantity: irrational, 98;
   numerical/continuous, 97–9
Quesada, Francisco Miró, 325
quiddity, **426**: *see also* essence
   and accident
Quine, Willard Van Orman, **426–
   8**: and anomalous monism,
   428; and anti-essentialism,
   137, 139; and antirealism, 15;
   and empiricism, 133, 427; and
   events, 141, 142–3; and
   extensionalism, 160–1; and
   holism, 133, 213–14, 411; and
   intentionality, 244; and logical
   syntax, 285–6; and
   materialism, 427; and number,
   364–5, 427; and ontological
   relativity, 426–7; and
   possibility, 405; and
   pragmatism, 411; and predicate
   calculus, 160; and realism,
   427; and Tarski, 487, 488; and
   universals, 503–4; *see also*
   naturalism; ontology; reference;
   science; simplicity; truth
Quinton, Anthony, 503

Rāmānuja, 322
Ramos, Samuel, 325
Ramsey, Frank Plumpton, 411,
   429–30: and realism, 429–30;
   redundancy theory of truth,
   165; and universals, 429–30
Ranke, L. von, and historicism,
   208, 209
rationalism, **430–3**: and
   appearance and reality, 19; in
   Blanshard, 54–5; and
   causation, 80, 431–2; and
   intuition, 247; in Kant, 301;
   and nature, 349; Presocratic,
   412; and sufficient reason
   principle, 289, 430–1, 467; *see
   also* Descartes; Leibniz; Spinoza
Rawls, John, 220
Reale, Miguel, 325
realism, **433–7**: and appearance
   and reality, 20, 41–2, 211;
   Aristotelian, 90, 238; in
   Armstrong, 31–2, 365;
   atomist, 341; in Chisholm, 85;
   and concepts, 89; critical, 41,
   318; and Daoism, 315–16;
   and disposition, 122–3, 425;
   and error theories, 434–5; and
   historicism, 209; and idealism,
   14, 227, 409, 436; in Indian
   metaphysics, 320–2; and

Ingarden, 241–2; internal,
   410; in James, 253, 409; and
   Kant, 228, 264, 433, 436; and
   Marxism, 296, 298; in
   Meinong, 306; minimal, 435–
   6; modal, 105, 175, 434, 517;
   moral, 433, 434–5, 439;
   naive, 41, 318, 342; and
   objectivity, 436; in Peirce, 379,
   380, 408–9, 458; and
   phenomenalism, 41, 241; in
   Popper, 402; and positivism,
   284; and pragmatism, 380,
   408–10; in Presocratics, 413;
   property, 43; in Ramsey, 429–
   30; and reduction, 435–6;
   representative, 513; scientific,
   32, 37, 260, 427, 435, 442,
   458; and structuralism, 476;
   transcendental, 258, 261; and
   truth, 434, 436; and
   universals, 433, 502, 503–5;
   see also antirealism; Strawson
reality: and appearance, **19–20**,
   60; and idealism, 227–9, 410;
   in McTaggart, 288–9
reason, **437–8**: and action, 6–7,
   180; and cosmic necessity, 54;
   in Descartes, 114–15; in Hegel,
   200; in Kant, 362–3, 437;
   natural light of, 114, **274**,
   401; and revelation, 23, 68,
   246–9, 292; in Santayana,
   452; in Spinoza, 473; sufficient
   see rationalism
reduction/reductionism, 77, **438–
   9**: and atomism, 134;
   behaviourist, 435; in Epicurus,
   135; in Hobbes, 176, 177;
   materialist, 35, 64, 109, 221,
   298, 391–3, 439; micro-
   reduction/reduction/
   reductionism, 438–9;
   naturalist, 14–15, 95–6, 305,
   343–4, 439, 475; ontological,
   414, 438–9; phenomenalist,
   42, 435–6, 438;
   phenomenological, 220; realist,
   435–6; in Russell, 133;
   scientific, 438–9, 502, 509;
   semantic, 438; transcendental,
   219, 220, 390; *see also*
   mechanism
reference, **440–1**, 495: in
   Chisholm, 86; direct, 292; in
   Frege, 244, 440; in Kripke,
   292, 441; in Meinong, 306; in
   naturalism, 344; in Quine,
   160–1, 426–7, 441, 483; in

Compiled by Meg Davies